BROWN AT 10

Praise for *Brown at 10*

'A truly gripping and important book of contemporary history.' Robert Skidelsky

'Anyone seriously interested in modern British political history will want *Brown at 10* around for reference. The authors have read everything and interviewed almost everyone, and tell the story in remorseless detail.' Francis Beckett, *The Guardian*

'A riveting and authoritative account of Brown's premiership.' Benedict Brogan, *Daily Telegraph*

'Given unprecedented access to Gordon Brown's close friends and Cabinet colleagues, two of our most distinguished political historians have written the authoritative book on his time as Prime Minister.' *Daily Mail*

'A crackerjack of a book. Anthony Seldon and Guy Lodge chased down and interviewed just about every relevant major and minor actor involved. The result is a book written in the finest tradition of empiricist history.' Frank Carrigan, *The Australian*

'Seldon and Lodge's book is the product of deep historic research and sheds fresh light on both Gordon Brown and his extraordinarily problematic premiership. It is the definitive history and will be read for years to come.' Dennis Kavanagh

Brown's Downing Street
ker side.' Peter Riddell

BROWN AT 10

Anthony Seldon and Guy Lodge

Biteback Publishing

First published in Great Britain in 2010.

This paperback edition published in 2011 by
Biteback Publishing Ltd
Westminster Tower
3 Albert Embankment
London
SE1 7SP

ISBN 978-184954-122-0

10 9 8 7 6 5 4 3 2 1

A CIP catalogue record for this book is available from the British Library

Set in Adobe Caslon Pro

Printed and bound in Great Britain by
CPI Group (UK) Ltd, Croydon, CR0 4YY

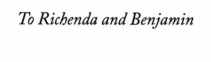

To Richenda and Benjamin

Contents

Acknowledgements

We would like to thank above all the extraordinary team of young researchers who worked with us on this book, and who put in quite exceptionally long hours. Special thanks go to Tristan Stubbs and James Plunkett for organising the team at critical periods – to the former for overseeing the production of the briefs, and to the latter for drafting key domestic policy sections. The team began working in late June and finished in early November. We would like to express our deep gratitude to, in order of length spent attached to the project, Stephen Carolin, Mike Coombes, Rachel McCulloch, Jonathan Meakin, Tom Lowe, Sam Sims, Georgina Hood, Daisy Picking, Illias Thoms, Adam Seldon, Conor Turley, Jessica Seldon and Emma Plunkett. We'd also like to thank Daniel Chandler who helped get the project off the ground earlier in 2010. We are also very grateful to Mike Coombes for compiling the polling data that appears at the end of the book. We used to say that we had to work at least as hard as they do in Number 10 if we were going to produce the book. The team all rose to this challenge and more. We are sure that they will all go on to remarkable careers and we wish them every success.

The team often met together and worked from Wellington College, and we would like to thank Sandra Hughes-Coppins and Jean Lovell for looking after everyone. A vital member of the team who worked from the alternative base in Brighton was Julia Molony, who typed every single word of the typescript, and most of the corrections and the interviews. To say she was a saint would fail to do her justice.

We are deeply grateful to all those we interviewed. Many of these would prefer not to be mentioned by name and we have decided thus to make this a general acknowledgement of our appreciation. The names of all those who are happy to be mentioned can be found in the endnotes. Many of the readers, too, would prefer to remain anonymous, but we would like to thank the following for reading either the whole book or specific sections of it and for offering invaluable comments: Vernon Bogdanor, Patrick Diamond, Richenda

Gambles, Anthony Goodenough, Dennis Kavanagh, Michael Kenny, Rick Muir, Will Paxton, Peter Riddell and Joanna Seldon. We would like to thank those in the offices of those who we interviewed, who showed exceptional patience in fitting us in to busy diaries. Most were very helpful, but at the apex comes Joyce Llewellyn from Douglas Alexander's office.

We were very fortunate to have this book published by Biteback Publishing. They were an excellent publisher to work with. Our thanks above all to Iain Dale for backing the project, and for his generous support and patience throughout. James Stephens was wonderful to work with, as was Jonathan Wadman before his departure. Our thanks also to Hollie Teague at Biteback, Cormac Bakewell, Rachel Bray and John Schwartz at SoapBox, and Georgina Kyriacou, Mayerlene Engineer and Chris Parker for their work producing the final script, under great time and pressure. We would like to thank many who have helped in a whole variety of ways: Nick Bouras, Asa Briggs, Sir Martin Gilbert, Louise Hayman, Peter Hennessy, David Owen, Andrew Roberts, Robert Skidelsky and Rory Stewart MP.

Guy Lodge in particular would like to thank the following: Robert Brandon is the reason why I was ever in a position to be able to write about a Prime Minister and I am especially grateful to him. At IPPR I would like to thank my former co-directors Lisa Harker and Carey Oppenheim for giving me a four-month sabbatical to work on the book, and Nick Pearce, my new director, for being so patient while I finished it. I would also like to thank Will Paxton, Michael Kenny and Rick Muir, close friends, who have done so much to shape my thinking about British politics, and who have been a constant source of encouragement throughout. My parents deserve special praise for all the opportunities they have given me over the years. I am immensely grateful to them. Thanks also to Robin and Ro Gambles for all their help while the book was being written. My deepest and most profound thanks, however, are to Richenda, my wife and best friend, and to our wonderful son, Benjamin. Without their support and inspiration this book would never have been written. Dedicating it to both of them is the very least we could do to show our immense gratitude for the endless sacrifices they have made.

Anthony Seldon in particular would like to express his gratitude to the following: Daniel Collings, for conducting the US interviews for the book, and to him and my other long-established writing colleague over several books, Peter Snowdon, for their constant encouragement, inspiration and support, as well as for reading drafts. From the *Blair Unbound* team I would also like to thank Kunal Khatri in particular for reading some chapters, Rob McNamara and Susanna Sharpe for their pioneering work on that book which made such a difference to *Brown at 10*. I would like to thank Ion Trewin for his formative work on my writing and Andrew Gordon, who was my editor at Simon &

Schuster, for the two Blair volumes, and who proved such an outstanding encouragement and support, and who has shaped my writing and thinking so much. Ian Drury at Sheil Land has proved a patient agent. I would like to offer my thanks to Li Jing and her husband at RDFZ School in China for sending through countless audio files during a summer holiday conference in Beijing. I would like to thank equally the staff at the Anchor Inn in Walberswick, the Quayside Hotel in Brixham, the Dar Said hotel in Sidi Bou Said, near Tunis.

At Wellington College I would like to thank all my colleagues, governors and students. In particular, I would like to thank my sensational chairman, Anthony Goodenough, and my colleagues on senior management, above all Robin Dyer, Roger Auger, Delyth Draper, Justin Garrick, Jane Lunnon, Lucy Pearson, Ed Schneider, Jamie Walker and Liz Worthington. Paul Fairclough, Nick Maloney and Nick Gallop have been particularly stimulating colleagues. I have been fortunate all my life to have had a succession of remarkable PAs, but none surpass Angela Reed, who was a massively intelligent support throughout, as was Paula Maynard.

Guy Lodge was a stunning partner, whose subtlety of mind and depth of understanding, as well as quality of writing, far outstripped my own powers. In five months, we spoke ten times a day, but never exchanged a cross word. Nick Pearce was a guide from the very first to the very last on this project, and my thanks go to him as well as to the IPPR and all its staff. Many of the Brown team were quite exceptionally helpful, considerate, and, to my surprise and delight, objective. Most would not want to be mentioned by name, but I hope David Muir will not mind if I single him out for thanks.

Finally, I would like to thank my family, not least for losing me again throughout a summer holiday, including during our five-day annual mystery holiday to Tunisia. My three children, Jessica, Susannah and Adam, all helped the book greatly, and encouraged me throughout. My greatest debt is due to Joanna, who again, despite her reservations, helped the book from beginning to end, not least by reading it, adding many helpful suggestions, and being uncomplaining for five months when I did not take a day off. I promised her after *Blair Unbound* that I would never write another biography about a Prime Minister. I have now undertaken never to write another *book* about a Prime Minister. Working 18/7 for the last six months has finally convinced me that she is right. She always is.

We have been granted many interviews for this new edition. The subjects would prefer to remain anonymous, though the interview references have been catalogued and will be available, together with the interviews, in thirty years at the Bodleian library. We would like to thank Christopher Everett for his corrections to the first edition, Larry Culliford for advice on psychology, and Philip Davis and Adam Seldon for their research and typing.

Brown at 10, its sources and methodology

I took the decision in principle to write a book on Gordon Brown, concentrating only on the premiership, back in 2008, but decided that it would only make sense if I had the same level of access into Number 10 as I had with the previous three volumes in this series on British Prime Ministers. The messages from the Brown camp, however, were constantly changing and difficult to interpret. As a result, the research and the writing did not begin in earnest until June 2010. The delay meant this project was constantly under pressure. Guy Lodge joined the team in early 2010, but we spent half a year drumming our fingers, waiting for the right smoke signals to emerge from the chimneys of Downing Street. If it was Everest we were climbing – an analogy we frequently used – the delay meant missing the most clement season. The pressure was never less than intense. Of the four books, it was far and away the most difficult, and the most precarious. We hope the final text does not reveal the frequent agonies required to produce it.

The principal source material for the book lies in more than 250 original interviews. This bank of contemporary reflections forms the biggest single source of research. The interview transcripts approach a million words. Where possible, endnotes refer to interviewees by name. However, serving officials and others often insisted on anonymity in return for speaking candidly, hence the ubiquity of the phrase 'Private interview' in the endnotes. Sometimes, for stylistic reasons, we have used quotations without indicating their origin in the text. In each case these quotations have come from one of those interviewed.

Some three-quarters of the book came from interviews, of which half were with aides or ministers, and half with civil servants. Another significant source, accounting for one-fifth of the book, came from unpublished contemporary diaries, kept by a variety of different figures, mostly from within Downing Street. For reasons of confidentiality these rarely have the author's name attached to them. The remaining material in the book comes from newspaper accounts and published diaries and memoirs. We accept that readers must take much on trust. The 250 interviews and all other documentation from the book are being placed in the Bodleian Library, to be stored alongside the material from the earlier three books. A full record has been made for the source for every single endnote in the text, which those consulting the library in thirty years' time will be able to consult.

Another major source of information was derived from sending passages of the book out to those who took part in the events described. This immensely time-consuming exercise produced considerable quantities of extra material. These, too, are referred to in the endnotes as 'private interviews', and the sources of these will again be made known in the Bodleian Library in thirty years.

This is the fourth book produced using more or less the same method. The interviews for this volume were conducted solely by Guy Lodge and myself. Jointly, we debated the architecture for the book, with much of the detail being supplied by Guy, who then oversaw the production of the 'briefs' covering the 10 chapters. The briefs contained the raw material for each sub-section within the chapters, blending interviews with diary material and other sources. My comparatively simple job was to compose the text of the first draft, which I did speaking into a dictaphone that was then emailed to Julia Molony, who transcribed it and then corrected the one or two reworkings of each chapter that I subsequently made. Guy then revised the text, which improved it immeasurably. The team then checked the facts, oversaw the permissions and reader comments, and produced a final brief from which Guy and I both worked to produce the final draft. The remaining errors are entirely my own and will be corrected in a second edition.

Preface

Four Books on British Prime Ministers, 1990–2010

Brown at 10 is the fourth and final volume on British Prime Ministers that I have written in a series spanning twenty years of premiership, from John Major moving into Number 10 in November 1990 to Gordon Brown leaving it in May 2010. These books were written with a small army of researchers, and with four intellectually brilliant co-authors – Lewis Baston, Daniel Collings, Peter Snowdon, and, in this case, Guy Lodge.

All four volumes share the same analytical approach: one can only judge a Prime Minister against the circumstances, the ideas, the interests and the individuals that they encountered.

Major: A Political Life (1997) argued that, once the deafening and highly personal scorn about him and his premiership died away, one would be left with his decisions on policy, notably on the economy, Europe and Northern Ireland, that were credible and, in the last case, inspired. Major's circumstances were profoundly adverse. Any leader taking over the Conservative Party from Margaret Thatcher in November 1990 would have had a difficult ride: the party was deeply divided, and there was no clear direction for it to travel. Major performed well, given his context, and left the country and economy in a fundamentally strong state in May 1997.

Blair (2004) broke away from the conventional chronological approach to the writing of biographies. The core question it tried to answer was how did a man with no early interest in, or ideas about, politics, become one of the most effective and ambitious party leaders of the modern age? The answer the book provides is the influence of twenty powerful individuals and twenty life-changing events. This meant that he came to Number 10 with only the loosest idea about what he wanted to do with power, and how to use it. The result was that his first term (1997–2001), with the notable exceptions of the Good Friday Agreement and NATO intervention in Kosovo, was largely barren of personal achievement: the undoubted successes of the Labour government during this period were principally achieved by his nemesis, Gordon Brown. Blair's greatest weaknesses, the book says, were his lack of deep thinking, his vanity, and his unwillingness to stand up to powerful men, including Brown, Bill Clinton, George W. Bush, and Rupert Murdoch, and pursue his own agenda despite them.

Blair Unbound (2007) picks up that story from 2001. It argues that, in contrast to the pattern for most political leaders, who see their influence diminish the longer they remain in office, Blair became increasingly effective, not the least because he succeeded in freeing himself of the influence of Brown. Not until 2002/03 did his personal agenda cohere – choice and diversity in public services. Only in his final four or five years did he thus become 'unbound'. The price of his slow start was that he had squandered his most promising years in power. As a result, his domestic agenda was only partially completed. His desire to make a mark on the national and world stage meanwhile, which began so promisingly in his second term with his response to 9/11, later was responsible in part for his largely uncritical support for the US in the war in Iraq, which he failed, and still fails, to read correctly. His record as Prime Minister conflicts starkly with his success as Labour leader, in which role he won three general elections and changed the culture of the party. Overall, though Blair fell short of achieving his goal of leading one of Britain's 'great radical reforming governments' of modern times.

Brown at 10 describes a Prime Minister whom many, including members of his own Cabinet, wrote off before he even entered office, but who turned out to have one of the most eventful and surprising premierships of the recent period – one that will surely be among the most studied by modern historians. To underline the proximity between when the book was written and the events it describes, it opens and ends in the present tense.

These three Prime Ministers, John Major, Tony Blair and Gordon Brown, in power from 1990 to 2010, all had 'troubled' premierships. While they had very different personalities, they all saw their leadership coloured by some remarkably similar factors. All three tried to govern from the centre ground, and had more difficulty with their own disaffected party members than with the official Opposition. Each faced an overwhelming crisis that dominated the perception of their period in power: the ejection of Britain from the European Exchange Rate Mechanism in September 1992 with Major, the Iraq War with Blair, and the banking and economic crises with Brown. Thatcher cast a long shadow over her three successors, establishing in the mind of the public, as well as the leaders themselves, the notion that a premiership, to be successful, has to have an intellectually coherent and distinctive personal agenda. None of them rose to this exacting standard.

All three premierships were diminished by the demands of 24-hour media, and by the slavish way they chose to respond to it. All three were essentially reactive. Major had no time to prepare, given the suddenness of his predecessor's departure and the uncertainty of the succession; Blair had three years, and Brown had thirteen. Yet none of them was ever sufficiently clear in what they wanted to do with power. It took Blair five years to discover his domestic agenda, Brown until almost the end of his premiership, and Major arguably never defined it, his premiership becoming essentially a postscript to Thatcher's. Blair came to power under extraordinarily favourable conditions, on which he failed to capitalise fully; Major and Brown faced unusually unfavourable circumstances, but achieved more than might have been expected. None can be considered a wholly successful premiership. All were troubled. The books set out to examine why.

All four aspire to be works, not of journalism or memoir, but of contemporary history, in traditions championed by the Institute of Contemporary British History (now the Centre for Contemporary British History), which Peter Hennessy and I founded in 1986. The distinctive aim of this approach is to write about the recent past using the tools and rigour of the historian, and to do so in an impartial and contextualised way. The source material for all four books is substantially made up of interviews; some 1,200 were conducted, producing three million words in transcript, all of which are secreted away in the Bodleian Library in Oxford. Interviewees often read out or handed over contemporary documents, adding to the record. Passages from the books were shown extensively to the participants to verify accounts, add fresh material, and ensure that different points of view were accurately represented.

Over the twenty-year period covered by the four books, less and less came to be written down in formal minutes, memos and letters. Cabinet under Blair and then Brown (after initial protestations to the contrary) rapidly became a talking shop, rather than a significant decision-taking body. Threat of leaks and personal chemistry mostly denuded both Cabinets of meaningful deliberation. Brown was Britain's first 'email' Prime Minister: he was an inveterate sender and receiver of electronic messages. Moreover, much of the business of his premiership was conducted in meetings without third parties present, or by mobile phone calls and text messages, records of which often do not survive. Historians acting on the belief that the 'document is king' might find the cupboard surprisingly bare. Interviews help fill the gaps.

Another difference between contemporary history and journalism is that the former attempts to answer longer-term questions. In the case of this book, there have been ten overarching lines of enquiry:

> ›   What was Brown's thinking on policy on coming to office? Why did he find it so hard to develop a clear and distinctive domestic agenda, and to convince his Cabinet that he had one?

> Was his premiership doomed from the outset, and might another leader have dealt better with the events and context he encountered?
> How far did his ramshackle and tribal leadership style undermine the effectiveness of his premiership, and did his methods improve over time?
> What was the impact of Blair and the Blairites on his premiership: to what extent did they fatally handicap it?
> How effective were his political team and his Cabinet, and how much did they help him achieve his objectives?
> Why did he face so much turbulence from within his own party, and how effectively did he deal with it, including three attempted 'coups'?
> What were his major foreign policy and defence opportunities and challenges, and how well did he handle them?
> How well did he manage the financial crisis and its impact on the real economy? Was Britain's economic position by May 2010 better or worse thanks to his leadership?
> Why did he not achieve more on constitutional reform, and why did he find it harder to respond to the MPs' expenses crisis than the financial crisis?
> What did he achieve as Prime Minister and what will history say of the Brown premiership? Did he become Prime Minister too late?

Guy Lodge and I have tried to write this book from the perspective of 2040, when the passions and the ambitions we record will be long spent. While it is unlikely that official documents or memoirs will reveal many significant facts not known today, biographers and historians in that distant future will have the benefit of knowing how the key stories, in particular the Afghan conflict, the economic downturn and the unity of the Labour Party, were ultimately resolved. The early playing out of events does not reflect too badly on Brown. Neither the Obama nor the Cameron administrations found a way forward on Afghanistan in the summer and autumn of 2010 that suggested Brown had overlooked any blindingly obvious solution. His embattled response to the recession has not yet ended in the economic disaster many predicted (even if his intransigence over addressing the deficit has created serious *political* problems for his successor). The Labour leadership election and relatively smooth accession of Ed Miliband in late September 2010 suggests he bequeathed a reasonably cohesive party. Our aim is that the consensus on the Brown premiership in thirty years' time will be fundamentally the same as the views we express here.

Anthony Seldon
October 2010

Introduction to the paperback edition

In the year since the first edition of *Brown at 10* was published, greater clarity has become possible on the tempestuous three years of the Brown premiership, and the period that led up to it. Memoirs and books by Tony Blair, Gordon Brown, Peter Mandelson, and Jonathan Powell, diaries from Alastair Campbell, in-depth accounts from authors Andrew Rawnsley and Steve Richards, and more particularly the greater willingness of witnesses to speak to us, have revealed more about the unique dysfunctionality of Brown's years at Number 10, and the harm done to Blair's premiership by their relationship. Brown was the most damaged personality to have been Chancellor and Prime Minister since the Second World War. This extended introduction expands on the period leading up to Brown's entry to Number 10, when the seeds of his later problems as Prime Minister were all sown.

1. The argument of Brown at 10

It is fashionable to denigrate Brown's premiership; there is no mileage nor money in anyone from left or right defending it, and plenty in doing precisely the opposite. Explanations for his failure focus on his personal deficiencies as leader, the damaging influence of his acolytes and the lack of a clear path for Labour post-Blair. The book sees truth in these, and other theses, but differs from the prevailing *zeitgeist* in arguing that Brown achieved more as Prime Minister than is widely acknowledged (his accomplishments are discussed below in the section '*Brown at 10*: assessing his premiership'), and in stressing that it was weaknesses in his character that prevented him achieving more. The achievement not only of his government, but of the ten years of Blair's premiership before it, was significantly damaged by his personality problems, which he never adequately addressed in office, nor has he in his retirement.

Brown's ministerial life falls into three periods. A broadly successful six years as Chancellor from 1997–2003, beginning with independence for the Bank of England days after the general election and concluding with his success in overruling Blair's second attempt to take Britain into the European single currency in the spring of 2003. During these years, Brown ran the nation's finances prudently and was responsible for driving many of the economic and social successes of the government. All this changed in 2003–8, when he became a pale imitation of his former self. His dominant mode shifted, without him acknowledging it, from being constructive to being destructive, and from an obsession with policy to a preoccupation with *politics*. He became obsessed with machine politics and scheming with short term tactics taking precedence over strategy and policy, and his creativity all but dried up. His strict rules on financial discipline were sacrificed. Beginning with the 7 per cent hike in NHS funding at the start of this period, he became addicted to spending money, often on projects that failed to deliver commensurate benefits, as a way of emboldening his own position in the party. The Treasury came under pressure from his office to massage forecasts to convey an optimistic picture that Brown wanted the world to see. The longer his delay before becoming Prime Minister, the more money he spent to pave his way with gold flagstones into Number 10. An over-dependence on revenue from the banks and housing market, his failure to regulate financial markets better, or to tackle pensions, were among other failings of this period as Chancellor.

During this second phase, his hostility and negativity to Blair's policy reached new heights, while at the same time he conveyed a clear impression that he had his own distinctive agenda which he would unveil when at Number 10, whilst fatally underestimating the difficulty of achieving this. Rather than reaching out beyond his narrow clique to others in the party, to academics and think tanks, he became ever more insular. He began plotting systematically against Blair in a manner and style that was inappropriate for one who held such high office. When he came into Number 10 in June 2007, his first fifteen months, after a brief honeymoon, were a fiasco, and he reversed key aspects of Blair's legacy out of spite not strategy. Only in his final eighteen months did he begin to assert leadership in reaction to the financial crisis. Brown was at his best as Prime Minister when reacting to events. Had he been more positive in his second period from 2003, he would have been a much more constructive and strategic Prime Minister.

The result of his deliberate policy of attacking Blairites and damaging any rivals with claims to lead the party meant that, when the leadership election was held to succeed him in September 2010, there was only one Blairite in the race (David Miliband standing against Ed Miliband, Diane Abbot, Ed Balls and Andy Burnham). Blair is thus wrong when he wrote in his memoirs, *A Journey*, that New Labour's period of power can be divided into '10+3'. The effectiveness of Blair's own ten years was severely blunted by Brown, for personal far more than for policy reasons, while Brown's final eighteen months witnessed a return to some of Blair's New Labour domestic policies. But Brown's rediscovery of some of his New Labour credentials came too late to be fully enacted. Had a Lib-Lab coalition been formed after the 2010 general election, then he might have seen this agenda blossom. As it was, Brown will go down in history as the creator and destroyer of New Labour, and then, at the last minute, its guilty and ineffective reviver.

2. *Brown before 10*

The cold war against Blair: 1992–2005

Brown's suspicion and hostility to Blair first emerged a full two years before the death of Labour leader John Smith in May 1994. Hitherto, for the nine years following their election as MPs in 1983, they had been inseparable. Brown regarded himself as the more senior, the more intelligent, the more capable and the more Labour. He convinced himself that he would become Labour's leader first and then Blair possibly after him. Labour's defeat in the 1992 general election, followed by the departure of Neil Kinnock and Roy Hattersley as leader and deputy, brought the first crisis in their relationship. Blair wanted to seize the opportunity of the vacuum at the top, and for Brown to stand as leader and he as deputy. But Brown's caution on such major decisions, which was seen so often later on, prevailed. Brown refused to stand himself and dissuaded Blair from doing so also. The experience made Brown immensely suspicious of Blair and his ambitions, and he was never to fully trust him again. Cherie Blair emerged now as a key figure in the deterioration of her husband's relationship with Brown.

From 1992 onwards, Brown's character began to change. In place of the jovial and companionable figure he once was, he began to become dark, brooding and profoundly suspicious of Blair, resenting the success he was enjoying as shadow Home Secretary in contrast to the torrid time he was having as shadow Chancellor. At this vulnerable point, two pivotal figures entered Brown's life. One was Ed Balls. Then a 25-year-old leader writer at the *Financial Times*, he went on to become not only the most dominant force on Brown's work as Chancellor and Prime Minister, but the most powerful *eminence gris* in modern British political history. The other figure was Charlie Whelan, brought in at the suggestion of Peter Mandelson, ironically given their later disliking, to boost Brown's media image. Neither Balls nor Whelan had worked for Brown when his relations with Blair had been flourishing: both rapidly concluded that Blair was a popinjay, strutting vacuously on the stage, a figure of little substance, and the sooner they established their own principal in his place, and themselves in pole positions by his side, the better. The fact that Blair was so slow in developing his own domestic policy agenda, the argument of *Blair*, played neatly into their hands. The change that came over Brown at this time was similar to that of an earlier Prime Minister, Edward Heath (1970–74). Philip Zeigler, his official biographer, describes his transition from a popular and urbane politician to one who was deeply suspicious and tribal.

But nothing before 1994 anticipated Brown's and Blair's terrible rowing following the death of Smith. Brown thought that Blair cheated his way into the leadership, a ghastly usurpation that put murderous thoughts into his mind. Thereafter, war between both was the norm and harmony existed only when Brown thought that their interests coincided.

Labour's first term from 1997-2001, as further evidenced by Campbell's diaries, was one of constant battles between both men and their camps. Brown was determined to show that he, not Blair, was effectively in charge of the government. If he did not win every new battle against Blair, he descended into a terrible rage. The Treasury was effectively run by a small cabal from the Chancellor's office, consisting of Brown, Balls and a tight group of officials and aides, including Whelan, and Ed Miliband. As the 2001 general election approached, Brown and Balls looked back at the previous four years and saw that the achievements, above all economic stability, prosperity and welfare reform, were due to their efforts, not Blair's, and they were angry that they had received insufficient credit. Hostilities were stilled in the run up to the general election, bar the odd scene such as when Balls shouted at Blair in Number 10 over election timing. Brown considered the election result, a Labour majority of 167, to be a personal triumph. The campaign was chaired by him and fought on his agenda, Mandelson being out of the picture following his second resignation in January 2001. Now, Brown felt, his moment had arrived and Blair should rapidly leave the stage in line with understandings hammered out in the summer of 1994 after Smith's death.

Brown was in for a rude shock. Blair did not accept his reading of the general election and he sought to put his Chancellor in his place. Brown was incandescent when Blair refused to give a date for his departure, dismissing talk of any 'deal' as delusional. Brown had to watch from the wings in deep frustration as the 9/11 crisis placed the spotlight firmly on Blair, powerfully boosting his international profile and domestic ratings. Buoyed by his new found confidence, Blair was bracing himself for a confrontation with Brown in the New Year.

But in January 2002, Brown's new born baby, Jennifer, died. Brown had married Sarah Macaulay in 2000, and the loss was a profound tragedy for both of them. It did not make Brown himself more outgoing and open to others, as grief can, but the opposite. Brown retreated into his tent, while he and Balls became suspicious that Blair's team were grooming a younger successor to take the crown, a suspicion which reached a highpoint when an article in *The Times* in April 2002 discussed the merits of 'skipping a generation'. 'We seized on any attempt to destabilise the PM. The whole game was about positioning Gordon against Tony. The policy was very much second to the politics', said a member of Brown's inner circle who has broken its rule of *omerta*. During the remainder of 2002–03, Blair's emerging 'choice' agenda including 'foundation hospitals' became the focus of a deeper and rawer hatred. In early 2003, the battleground shifted to Blair's second attempt to take Britain into the Euro. Brown and particularly Balls rejoiced in outsmarting Blair and his Number 10 team and Blair's pet scheme was dead in the water. Treasury officials, like their counterparts elsewhere in Whitehall, liked their minister to win battles, especially against Number 10, and Brown had proved very good at it.

Iraq became another source of tension. Number 10 was deeply antagonised that Brown would not do more to argue in public the case for the war. Brown was conflicted over it, and his inner court debated the merits. They were worried that Robin Cook would steal a march on them opposing the war, perhaps even costing Brown the leadership. But they decided that it would be far safer for him to succeed Blair after the Iraq war rather than precipitating a crisis by challenging Blair over it, as Cook and Clare Short had done. Brown initially thought the war would be a success, as did his team, though Ed Miliband had reservations: he also realised there'd be heavy costs to pay in his relationship with Washington as well as with the Murdoch press if he did not support Blair.

Some observers look back at the build up to the Iraq war as the best opportunity Brown had to oust Blair. Brown's innate caution played a part in his stepping back from the brink, but far more decisive was his and Balls's cold calculation of political advantage. Brown and Balls did not judge this to be the moment for a full frontal assault on Blair. A new low followed in the autumn of 2003 with Blair's and Brown's speeches to the party conference when they sparred dangerously with each other, followed by Blair keeping Brown off the NEC in November. When it became clear that he was not going to quit during 2004, Brown was pushed beyond the brink. Withdrawal was one of his ploys. So initially in the 2005 general election, he refused to campaign with Blair and only changed his mind when it was made clear to him that he would damage his own chances of succeeding if his aloofness was blamed for loss of seats in the election.

The hot war against Blair: 2005–2007

The 2005 general election had not been easy for Blair. On polling day, Thursday 5 May, Blair was at home in his Sedgefield constituency. At one point in the early evening, he went upstairs to his bedroom and was seen rocking himself back and forth, repeating the words 'Iraq', which he blamed for costing the party so many votes. He had been bolstered by Brown's late support during the campaign, but on the day of the results, he slammed the door firmly back in his face, making it clear that the reshuffle and the new agenda was going to be his own. 'You fucking bastards', was Brown's reaction. Brown was beside himself, his sense of betrayal at an all time high. Together with Ed Balls, as well as Damian McBride, who had become Head of Communications at the Treasury in 2003, they decided that they would have to embark on open warfare and plot if they were ever to get Blair out. Emails between Brown's inner circle, which were published in the *Daily Telegraph* in June 2011, document their thinking, though the facts were already known.

No plot was hatched in 2005 because of the 7/7 attack on London whilst Blair was chairing the G20 at Gleneagles. Blair's commanding response to events gave him an authority, and a palpable reason for remaining, which lasted well into the autumn. The conspirators would have to bide their time.

The first actual 'plot' to get Blair out of Number 10 came in early 2006 over the 'cash for honours' episode. Blair had been vulnerable on the question of party funding ever since the Ecclestone affair in November 1997, exacerbated by question marks over the activities of his friend and Labour fundraiser, Lord Levy. A spotlight focused on the link between the giving of funds to Labour and the granting of honours. Brown sensed the opportunity and phoned Cabinet colleague Harriet Harman, wife to Jack Dromey, the Labour Party treasurer. He instructed her to tell her husband to make a speech advocating 'cleaning up' Labour's funding, knowing it would profoundly embarrass Blair. Immediately after, on 15 March, Dromey announced an inquiry into secret loans given to the Labour Party. The speech came in the midst of a knife-edge vote in the Commons on education. Blair was described as being 'clinically angry' about Dromey's intervention and particularly his implication that Number 10 must have known about the funding arrangements but kept them secret from the Labour Party. Number 10 blamed Harman and Brown for stirring up the issue, though they knew nothing at the time of the phone call. Brown's response to Number 10 was 'nothing to do with me', to which Number 10's response was 'it's never anything to do with him, is it?' Brown shrugged his shoulders. 'When are you going to fuck off out of here?' he shouted at Blair. The first coup failed to unseat Blair, but had the vote on the Education Bill been lost, it's unlikely that he would have survived beyond the May local elections. Shortly after Dromey's intervention, and to Blair's disgust, the Metropolitan Police launched an inquiry into Labour funding which dragged the issue on to the end of his premiership.

Blair was losing authority at home, while abroad the Iraq war was dragging on without any sight of finishing. Despite four committees investigating aspects of it, questions over Blair's conduct of the war were refusing to go away.

A second coup was planned for the immediate aftermath of the May 2006 local elections. For weeks, Number 10 had been anticipating disastrous results and were debating intently how Brown might respond. Election day, Thursday 4 May, saw Labour achieve just 26 per cent of the national vote, behind the Lib Dems on 27 per cent and the Conservatives on 40 per cent. Brown sensed his opportunity. Number 10 knew he would strike, but didn't know how and when. Brown spoke to several close Parliamentary friends including Nick Brown and Andrew Smith, who had been deposed as Work and Pensions Secretary. Smith promptly told the *Guardian* that there needed to be a proper timetable for Blair to go and that the uncertainty was going on too long. Brown himself was due to speak just after 8 am on the Radio 4 *Today* programme that Friday morning: 'we have got to renew ourselves ... it must start now', he intoned. But he pulled back from giving a much stronger call for Blair to go. Balls was enraged: 'you fucking tosser, you bottled it', he screamed down the phone at his boss. When Anthony Seldon published a much milder version of Balls's statement in *Blair Unbound* in 2007, Balls went onto Radio 4 to deny he had ever said it. Brown and Balls were very cautious in ensuring that records of the conversations between their tight group were not recorded, though Balls himself is believed by some colleagues to be keeping a diary. Balls was right in realising that, if Blair was to go prematurely, it would require a much bigger lead than Brown had given. Number 10 knew at once that they had survived and that Brown had missed another opportunity: 'had Gordon talked about Margaret Thatcher staying on too long on the *Today* programme, it would have been fatal', said one of Blair's close circle.

No further opportunity presented itself before the recess. Over the summer, Balls concluded that Brown was too weak to push Blair and that 'he would back off at the sound of gunfire and refuse to put the knife in himself', in the words of one of Brown's inner team: 'Ed concluded that Gordon had left it too late. If he didn't press the button himself, nothing was going to happen'. Blair's position was now much weaker in the party following his refusal to criticise Israel for its actions against Palestinian militants in Lebanon that summer. Balls spoke to Tom Watson, the Brownite MP, and the plan was hatched for a series of letters from the 1997, 2001 and 2005 intakes of Labour MPs calling on Blair to stand down. Brown knew fully about the plan, though not the extent of the pace. When Balls walked into his room, holding the Tom Watson letter to Blair from the 2001 intake declaring 'we ask you to stand aside', Brown was shocked: 'fucking hell, are you sure that is not going too far?' 'It's too late', was Balls's cold reply. For some hours Blair's team thought that the game was up. He survived, but only after he had given a public assurance that he would go within the year. Brown's camp claimed victory, Blair's camp that he had merely said in public what he had already said in private. The irony was that, for all the plotting against Blair in 2005-07, these years were to prove the most fruitful in domestic policy terms for Blair personally, the argument of *Blair Unbound*.

Brown's character weaknesses

The evidence of Brown's problem personality were all amply on display before 2007. We will never know for sure *why* Brown became such a difficult man. What can be described is the impact that character had. By the time he became Chancellor, he was profoundly tribal to the point of exhibiting paranoid tendencies. He would see enemies where there were none and would create them gratuitously. He was unable to take criticism objectively and would attack the personal motives of anyone who criticised him. His mistrust of others made him seek to control everything in sight, including his public image as seen in two generous books by Paul Routledge (1998) and Robert Peston (2005). He was driven by powerful and unconscious forces to be the top figure, without the self-knowledge to realise that he lacked the skills required for it, or the empathy to credit the skills of his rivals. His greatest weakness was his lack of self-knowledge and the ability to learn. He was oblivious to his own failings and to the impact of his actions on others. He blinded himself to the methods of those around him and to their actions. In a democracy, it would be wrong to deny the chance of office to anyone on the grounds of an unsuitable personality. Nevertheless, the damage he did, and the trail of misery he left in his wake, which are still insufficiently acknowledged, would suggest that fellow politicians and officials could have done more to stand up to him. The constitutional failures of the Brown years extend far beyond his personal deficiencies.

Brown's weakness made him far too dependent on the emotional and intellectual support of others. If these voices were positive, as they were in his latter days in Downing Street, it mattered far less than when the voices were negative as they were overwhelmingly in his second period, from 2003-08. During this time, he lacked the psychological and intellectual strength to be a positive force, with inevitable consequences. His inability to inspire trust and loyalty further meant that, once he was in Number 10, the Brownites splintered, while the Blairites within just a few months were conspiring to oust him. The tragedy is that without these character flaws, Brown's compassion for his fellow citizens at home and for the underprivileged abroad, combined with his intellect and unique energy, could have made him a politician of the very first order.

The unique significance of Ed Balls

Ed Balls has one of the most brilliant minds of his generation. His profound grasp of economics easily outstripped Brown's own, which helps explain Brown's complete dependence upon him. Balls's great intellectual strength was tenacity and self belief if not originality; nevertheless it was he who was responsible for many of the most successful innovations at the Treasury in Brown's first phase, 1997-2003. There is another side to this story. While Brown himself must remain responsible for all his decisions, Balls's influence on him as Prime Minister was often far from positive, and the pattern of their umbilical relationship was evident long before 2007.

Balls has staunchly defended himself against any charge of plotting against Blair. It is 'nonsense', he has said, that he had contempt for Blair, while it was 'total nonsense' that he helped plan the third coup in September 2006. Others around Brown, principally Ed Miliband and Alexander, must share responsibility for the pressure on, and the undermining of, Blair: but their influence pales into insignificance beside that of Balls. His defence is that he was merely involved in negotiations about the transfer of power between Blair and Brown. The response of the Labour leadership to the emails published in the *Daily Telegraph* in June 2011, is that they were raking up 'ancient history'. This is dishonest, as the devisers of the response will know.

The charge sheet against Balls has further questions to be answered. He has to defend himself against allegations that he was a bully, 'the most unpleasant bully I have ever come across' in the words of a former colleague. Brown, Balls and McBride employed "divide and rule" tactics in the Treasury, favouring those who fell in with them, and marginalising those who did not. Balls was considered by some a calculating and threatening force while Brown was more overt if less effective. In contrast, neither Alexander nor Ed Miliband were considered bullies. The criticisms of Balls up to 2007 include his role in massaging the forecasts and hiking up spending beyond sensible levels which sometimes resulted in substantial waste. 'The Treasury was saying we had to increase taxes or reduce spending. But Ed put pressure on officials to produce forecasts that Brown wanted to hear', said an official. 'Balls's mastery meant neither Brown himself nor officials, some of whom were "smitten" by him, dared challenge him.' Treasury officials now accept that they failed in key areas to assert themselves effectively against the Chancellor's office in these years. Balls further has to answer the case that, in Brown's final budget as Chancellor in the spring of 2007, he reversed his initial scepticism to become a staunch supporter of Brown's proposal to abolish the 10p tax band, which hit the most vulnerable in society, a stance which he has since adamantly denied.

Balls's traits before June 2007 were all in evidence after it. As the pages that follow reveal, which are based on testimonies from several members of Brown's own inner circle, Cabinet ministers, civil servants and Labour political advisers, Balls has to answer a number of charges about his actions after Brown became Prime Minister. Against the wishes of Gus O'Donnell, who moved from the Treasury to become Cabinet Secretary, he insisted on McBride going with Brown into Number 10 as his own 'eyes and ears'. Once there Balls urged Brown against removing him despite a succession of people, including Douglas Alexander, Stephen Carter and Peter Mandelson, advising that McBride was not suitable. Balls was primarily responsible for creating an emasculated Number 10 in June 2007, which he himself could dominate. His policy instincts were often wrong, as on anti-social behaviour and education reform, and he did not prove an impressive Schools Secretary. He was responsible for putting immense and underhand pressure on Darling as Chancellor in an attempt to destabilise him, hoping for the job himself. With Brown, he also undermined Labour's economic credibility by appearing to be in denial about Britain's spiralling deficit from 2008 onwards. Balls has avoided serious examination of his modus operandi for the last fifteen years through a mixture of brilliance, charm, fear and the offering of privileged information to selected journalists. In a House of Commons not conspicuous for brilliant minds or flair, Balls stands out. But one day there will be a reckoning.

The elimination of the Blairites and the triumph of the Brownites
Brown was clear that he was not going to countenance anyone else succeeding Blair but him. A series of possible successors from the Blairite wing of the party – David Blunkett, Charles Clarke and John Reid, quit politics deciding they had had enough, while Alan Milburn's life was made such a misery by Brown and his team that he decided to fall on his sword. Others like James Purnell and John Hutton quit after 2007 because they no longer felt comfortable in Brown's Cabinet. David Miliband, the major Blairite survivor, was knocked out, if not indefinitely, in the September 2010 leadership contest. The result is a whitewash for the Brownites, with Ed Miliband, Balls and Alexander in the three most powerful positions in the shadow Cabinet (and Balls's wife, Yvette Cooper, shadow Home Secretary). Any friendship between the three had disappeared long before 2007; Alexander and Balls had fallen out in Blair's first term, while both Eds became far too rivalrous soon after to be close, a rivalry which continued after 2010 with Balls's ambition for the top job remaining undimmed.

The party will never fully move on until it comes to terms with the history of these fifteen years. Despite all Blair's doubts about Brown, he neither domesticated him nor successfully schooled him for leadership; nor did he adopt the course of grooming another for the succession, failing to promote David Miliband to Foreign Secretary in 2006 or to push him more against Brown in early 2007. If the Blairite succession imploded, it is partly their own fault. The Brownite rump now in control of the party have a duty to be honest about their role in pressurising Blair to leave, in undermining others, in holding back Blair's public service reform agenda, and indulging in a form of machine politics in which political positioning triumphed over strategy. If they are to succeed they will have to free themselves from the mindset that led to Brown's own failure. They need, unlike the clique around Brown, to reach out far wider in search of fresh ideas to renew the party. It will not be easy for them as they have known little beyond the world of Brownite politics, but having to reach out is *sine qua non*. The lack of strategy and cohesion in the shadow Cabinet in the last year has been the inevitable consequence. Indicatively, the greatest success Ed Miliband has enjoyed to date as party leader with his performance in the News International phone hacking scandal has been not in advocating fresh policies, but in reacting to events.

3. Brown at 10: *assessing his premiership*

Our book, while critical, does not damn Gordon Brown as a Prime Minister, nor does it dismiss his premiership as an unequivocal failure. History ultimately judges Prime Ministers on how they handle the major decisions with which they are confronted and, on this measure, Brown compares quite favourably with other postwar premiers. Like James Callaghan, Prime Minister from 1976 to 1979, Brown faced an overwhelming economic crisis, but he handled it with far more dexterity and confidence than his Labour predecessor. He managed the major decision of his premiership better than immediate predecessors – John Major, with Britain's ejection from the Exchange Rate Mechanism in 1992, and Tony Blair, whose judgements regarding the invasion and occupation of the Iraq are still the cause of much anger and resentment. Brown's decisive leadership during the banking crisis in late 2008 and early 2009, the details of which are examined later in the book, was admired and emulated by many overseas governments. At the London G20 summit in early April 2009, he was acknowledged by other world leaders as the man of the hour. His subsequent handling of the recession, while more controversial, focused on ensuring Britain came through the downturn with the minimum possible economic suffering, particularly among the most vulnerable. His actions helped prevent unemployment, repossessions and business closures from soaring in the way they had in some earlier recessions, which was all the more remarkable given that between 2008 and 2009, economic output in Britain fell more dramatically than at any time since the Great Depression. The accusation that he was a fair-weather Keynesian – spending in the downturn but not building up a surplus in the good times – has some force, however, particularly when combined with his hubristic claim to have ended 'boom and bust'.

However, there is more to Brown's premiership than his response to the economic crisis. In Northern Ireland, he showed skill and tenacity in bringing to a conclusion the long process of devolution that had begun twelve years earlier with the Good Friday agreement and that many felt, wrongly as it turned out, had been resolved once and for all by Blair. As Labour Party leader, he survived a series of attempted coups against him, as much by luck as by judgement, which revealed either considerable resilience or, as his many enemies around the Cabinet table put it, sheer obstinacy. Labour performed very badly in the May 2010 general election, registering its second worst result since 1918, but Brown brought the party back from the brink in 2008 and 2009 to deny the Conservatives an overall majority. During his final hours in Number 10, he conducted himself in a way that won him respect across the political spectrum. Unlike Harold Wilson in 1976, with his 'Lavender' resignation honours list that hinted at unsavoury contacts, or Callaghan in 1979, with bitter recriminations over his election timing and the 'Winter of Discontent', and even Blair in 2007, with outstanding questions over Iraq and suspicions over party funding, Brown left with his personal integrity and honour intact. The manner of his departure from Number 10 enhanced his standing, whereas that of his Labour predecessors often diminished theirs.

Brown's principal passion as Prime Minister was not at home, but, to the surprise of many, on the global stage, where he achieved a level of respect unknown in Britain. Building on his ten years as Chancellor, he developed a distinctive 'Brownite' international agenda that had the clarity and coherence so conspicuously lacking in his domestic policy. For a Prime Minister battling to find his path, the making of Brown was to be the economic tsunami that swept the world in 2008. He saw this as representing the 'first crisis of globalisation', and believed it could only be tackled through strengthened global institutions and greater international cooperation. By definition, this was not a mission he could execute alone, but he was one of its most articulate proponents. Climate change was another issue that clearly needed a coordinated global response, but here, despite investing prodigious energy and personal capital, he failed to make the impact he sought at the Copenhagen summit in December 2009. For him, this issue was one of social justice as well as environmental protection: rich nations are the biggest emitters of greenhouse gases but the effects of climate change hit the least well-off countries hardest. He proved a significant multilateralist, helping to make the G20 into the forum for taking decisions on the world economy. For all his initial antipathy to the EU, he could also be impressive at bilateral relationships, above all with Merkel and Sarkozy.

The world's poor were never far from Brown's mind. As Prime Minister, he continued to champion the cause of development, ensuring it did not disappear from view during the economic crisis. Untold numbers of the world's most deprived people had their lives enhanced because of actions he took. That the Conservative Party undertook to protect the international development budget in the 2010 general election is testament in part to the way he transformed the profile of this issue. He dreamt great dreams, and his hopes – of pushing Israel towards a lasting peace with the Palestinians, of an end to landmines, and even a nuclear-free world – were to be dashed, though not for want of trying. As a war leader, he handled Britain's withdrawal from Iraq sensitively. Afghanistan proved much the harder challenge. Mortified personally by the escalation in troop casualties, he was unable to reassure the nation about the reasons for this sacrifice or build support behind a clear strategy. Only in his final months did he manage to reassert civilian control from the military and oversee a coherent policy.

It is a Prime Minister's performance in the domestic arena, however, which most shapes the public's view. Here, with the exception of his handling of the recession, Brown's achievements are much more limited. His biggest domestic failing was his reluctance to talk about cutting the deficit, which made him appear hopelessly out of touch and badly damaged his own economic reputation, and that of the Labour Party. He deserves limited credit for his health policy, especially where he was inspired by the surgeon-cum-minister Ara Darzi to roll out imaginative initiatives in the realms of preventative and community health. But overall, tough decisions in health were sidelined, and no clear lead was given. In education, he bequeathed control of policy to his principal lieutenant Ed Balls and, to the surprise of many, innovation and the drive on school improvement stalled. On law and order, he began by reversing the Blairite agenda and only late in the day, as the election approached, did he seek to make it a priority. Overall, Labour lost significant ground under Brown on public-service reform. On constitutional reform his early promises of change came to nothing. Had he done more initially, he might have been able to turn the MPs' expenses crisis to his advantage: for a man who talked the language of character and morality, and whose lack of personal greed was such a strength, his failure to provide national leadership during this toxic scandal was a conspicuous failure. As a result he received little credit for the solutions he found. Some promising ideas were produced towards the end of his administration, including high-speed rail and a 'national care service', but they came too late to be enacted. Had he got to these earlier, his domestic legacy would be more memorable. Philosophically he oversaw a significant shift toward the notion of the 'entitlements' citizens could expect from public services, but he lacked the patience and the drive to turn this into a coherent agenda. It took Blair five years to identify his defining theme in domestic policy: Brown arrived at his during his final months, under pressure to find an attractive platform for the election. In his final weeks and days at Number 10, his 'progressive governance' agenda for 2010–2015, to be enacted either by Labour alone or in coalition with the Liberal Democrats, was advocated with zeal; but electoral arithmetic was to ensure it never left the drawing board. To the end, his was the 'might have been' premiership.

Apart from a brief spell at the beginning, and in his final twenty-four hours, the British public never warmed to Brown. His sweeping international vision was never likely to resonate with a domestic audience, either in the country at large, or among the opinion formers in the press. His deep difficulty communicating meant that, with some rare exceptions, he consistently failed to connect with the electorate. Unlike Blair, he was no actor. Nor was he a charmer. Indeed, egged on by his coterie, as Chancellor he turned gracelessness and rudeness into a personal style, and he could not altogether rid himself of these traits after 2007. As a result, he became one of the most unpopular Prime Ministers in recent history. Much was made of this by the media, which had fallen out of love with New Labour in general and Brown in particular, especially after his catastrophic handling of decisions over whether to call an election in the autumn of 2007. Thereafter, the press had little interest in reporting his successes.

Overall, however, to dismiss Brown as an unpleasant bully and his premiership as a failure would be unhistorical and two-dimensional. The interesting question is not why did he fail, but rather, why did he not achieve more? Five separate reasons can be given.

Brown's inheritance

One can only judge a premiership historically after weighing the circumstances faced by the Prime Minster. Any Labour leader who succeeded Blair in June 2007 would have encountered difficulties. The party was divided, not just between Blairites and Brownites, but by the still raw wound of the Iraq invasion. On policy it was in conflict over its direction and unsure how to refresh itself as a centre-left party after ten years in power. To make matters worse there was little left in the coffers to fund a revitalised policy programme. Brown's inheritance bears some resemblance to that of James Callaghan, who succeeded Harold Wilson in 1976, with a majority dwindling to zero in the midst of a worsening economic crisis. His situation when entering Number 10 compares, too, to that of John Major in November 1990, taking over from a leader who, while increasingly embattled, was still beloved by many of the party faithful. Major and Brown both became Prime Minister at a time when their party had been in government for around a decade and a resurgent Opposition was able to tap into a widespread desire for change. These were difficult conditions for any leader to prosper in, even before considering the three major external challenges the incumbent of Number 10 would face *after* June 2007: the banking and economic crisis, evident within weeks of taking power, the expenses crisis in summer 2009, and the increasingly problematic war in Afghanistan.

The contrast with Blair's situation in May 1997 is stark. He enjoyed benefits that most incoming Prime Ministers could only dream of: a united party, a landslide victory, an enfeebled Opposition, a strong economy, a benign media and a sympathetic intellectual climate. Historians have yet fully to take stock of how fortunate Blair was, and thus how much more might have been expected of him, or, by comparison, how unfortunate Brown was. When they do, it is likely that the reputation of both men will be re-evaluated.

Expectations of a new beginning in 2007 had, however, been ramped up to almost impossibly high levels, not least by Brown and his acolytes. Moreover, by contributing to the factionalisation of the party by deliberately discouraging a leadership contest in the spring of 2007, but failing to come to power equipped with a clear agenda for renewal, he was in many ways the author of his own misfortune.

Deficient leadership qualities

Brown possessed few of the qualities required of a political leader; in particular he lacked an overarching vision which could command loyalty and respect. He had an *international* vision, which he outlined in the most powerful oratory of his premiership – his address on development to the UN General Assembly on 31 July 2007, his speech to the US Congress on 4 March 2009 and his talk at the 'TED' Global conference in Oxford on 22 July 2009. But these offered a programme for a more just and better-connected world rather than an agenda for improving domestic policy.

He further lacked the skills needed for team-building, and was a poor chairman of the Cabinet and its committees. Oddly for a man who had been a senior government minister for so long, he displayed little sympathy for, or interest in, motivating his Cabinet colleagues. He made it all too clear that he was not interested in the great majority of them, nor did he make them feel that he valued or even liked them. It is unsurprising then that, within a few months, the Cabinet were openly discussing amongst each other how they could get rid of him. He failed to understand that in the Whitehall system, Cabinet ministers drive policy; he failed to trust them, and tried to be effectively a departmental minister from Number 10. After initial moves toward a more collegial approach, Cabinet meetings rapidly became a talking shop. Even at the end, most ministers felt excluded from discussions about forming a coalition with the Liberal Democrats. Within Number 10, Brown was poor at recruiting and utilising his team, and his working practices were chaotic. He continuously bypassed structured decision-making processes, preferring to take advice through informal channels, which was a source for inertia or confusion. He was fortunate to have had some high calibre civil servants and aides to advise him. Without them, his deficiencies would have been still more cruelly exposed.

Brown further lacked the communication skills necessary for effective leadership. He was capable of speaking with brilliance and passion, especially abroad, but was all too frequently wooden and repetitive at home or in forums that required more spontaneity. Rarely did his words inspire, particularly in the House of Commons, where his performances at the despatch box were largely unconvincing. His two most effective domestic speeches, to the Labour conference on 23 September 2008 and to Citizens UK on 3 May just before the 2010 general election, show the extent of his true potential. Yet, he struggled especially to connect with 'middle England' – a part of the country for which he appeared to have little instinctive feel.

He often lacked the judgement and instinct possessed by natural leaders, and was not inclined to take responsibility or acknowledge his own failings. Slow at taking decisions, he preferred to procrastinate until a crisis point was reached: his decision-making was often thus best under pressure, when he had no option but to reach a conclusion. In such circumstances he could be calm and commanding, as he showed with his response to the banking crisis, or during the London G20 summit. He would often though indulge in opportunism and attempt to wrong-foot the Opposition. This almost always rebounded on him badly, as it did over proposals for 42-day detention without trial for terrorist suspects and the 10p tax-rate débâcle in 2008, or, perhaps most devastatingly of all, the aborted election in the autumn of 2007.

Deficiencies of character
We have seen how Brown's psychological difficulties marred his performance as Chancellor. Not that he was lacking altogether in personal qualities. Brown possessed many character strengths – notably, high intelligence, a capacity for relentless hard work, personal integrity and frugality, and even, though few saw it, deep sympathy for those in difficulty. His beliefs were inspired by a genuine compassion for people at home and abroad. His father instilled in him a profound sense of moral duty, which was reinforced by Nelson Mandela, to whom Brown wrote a thank-you letter as his final act as Prime Minister. He was inspired by their example, as he regularly admitted, to do worthy deeds. These positive traits were, however, occluded and often trumped by his negative characteristics, which contrasted so strongly with Blair's optimism. He lacked the emotional stability and self-confidence to be a consistently strong Prime Minister. He was a highly 'defended' leader, with a tendency to go underground when things went wrong, to be cliquey and mistrustful of those outside of his inner circle, to harbour deep resentments against slights both real and perceived, and to find it difficult to control his mood swings. When events turned against him, as they did after the autumn of 2007, he could become deeply depressed and lose focus. When he felt let down – as on a trip to Pakistan in April 2009 – or when he considered that he had been given wrong advice – as on the handling of the Iraq Inquiry in June 2009 – his behaviour became like that of a spoilt child; he would sulk, scream at people and occasionally throw objects. A short time afterwards, he would feel

chastened and contrite, ashamed of losing control and upsetting others. In this, his behaviour mirrors another former Prime Minister, who had also been kept waiting for over ten years to lead his party – the legendary outbursts of Anthony Eden (1955–57) would also be followed by grovelling apologies.

Brown reacted with hurt, shock and anger to the suggestion that he was a 'bully'. The idea conflicted starkly with his own self-image, and with his sense of what his father would have admired in him. When he let himself see the hurt he had caused others through his shouting, aggression and psychological pressure, he could feel remorse. He was certainly not a 'bully' in the calculating and cold-hearted style of his acolytes.

Brown's diffidence meant that he often relied on a cadre of aides whose practices were unbecoming to the dignity of the office of Chancellor of the Exchequer, let alone that of Prime Minister. The principal culprits were Balls, Charlie Whelan (Brown's press secretary until he was forced to resign in 1999, and an unofficial adviser thereafter), and Damian McBride, who took over as press secretary from 2005 and became a powerful member of the inner team until he, too, was forced to resign in 2009. All three were highly intelligent and capable, but they were also impressionable, and Brown must bear a significant measure of responsibility for the actions they carried out on his behalf. Brown also looked to a group of close followers, including MPs Ian Austin, Nick Brown and Tom Watson, to look after his interests in the Parliamentary Labour Party. This way of working heightened his sense of insecurity, and did little or nothing to encourage him to think creatively or deal openly with other party colleagues. Indeed, his dependence on a team that was ready and willing to resort to intimidation damaged Brown's integrity and authority, while reinforcing his insularity.

If Margaret Thatcher had a 'one of us' way of judging individuals, based on their adherence to her free market beliefs, so too did Brown, but his was based less on ideology than on tribalism. He could be very dismissive of large swathes of people because they were viewed as being uninteresting or unsupportive. As Prime Minister, he continued mainly to ignore the Foreign Office, Treasury, Ministry of Defence and Cabinet Office, most of his Cabinet colleagues and fellow EU leaders. He was also contemptuous of most journalists and nearly all policy thinkers. Blair had a tendency to rule with a small clique, but Brown turned it into an art form.

After arriving in Number 10, Brown sought to operate a 'cleaner' and more inclusive administration than Blair's, and one that was unsullied by spin. But his actions and style were to do much to undermine trust in government. He felt bruised by his own experience of life and had come to believe that success in politics required periodic acts of brutality. After all, it was this toughness that had ousted his nemesis, Blair, and propelled him into power. Callaghan and Brown may have both presided over governments that were swamped by events, but Callaghan was meticulous in ensuring Number 10 conformed to the highest moral standards. Many of Brown's political aides were high-minded and laboured hard to bring out the best in him – these included Gavin Kelly, Justin Forsyth, Kirsty McNeill, David Muir, Nick Pearce and Stewart Wood. One key strand of the story of Brown's premiership is how these better people came to drown out the 'bad voices', regardless of what the Prime Minister himself may have wanted.

The corrosive impact of Blair on Brown, 1994–2007

We will never know what Brown would have done if he had succeeded John Smith as Labour leader in July 1994. He would certainly have been a very different figure to the one who finally realised his ultimate ambition in June 2007, a full thirteen years later.[1]

Those thirteen years took a severe toll on Brown, both physically and emotionally. The prolonged battles with Blair exhausted him, while running the Treasury for ten years – the longest unbroken spell of any Chancellor in modern history – further drained his reserves of energy, not least because of his obsessive ways of working. The long wait damaged his prospects of success in other ways, too. According to Douglas Alexander: 'If he had taken over ten or even five years before, he might well have been more mentally agile and more open to new ways of thinking.'[2] Had he become Prime Minister in 2004, he would have had the team at Number 10 he always wanted, with Ed Balls serving as his chief of staff and Ed Miliband his head of policy. When his time finally came, his young lieutenants were pursuing their own political ambitions.

The most damaging period of all was 2004–07. 'Not getting the premiership in 2004 weakened him irreparably,' says one member of his close team. Three years passed when Brown squandered energy and ideas on infighting that he could have devoted to leading the country.[3] It exposed his all-powerful ambition in a way many found distasteful and even repugnant. It made him enemies instead of forging alliances, with the result that when he came to power, his support, especially at Cabinet level, was paper thin.

His attempt in June 2007 to form an inclusive government was built on sand: barely anyone trusted him. 'He was corrupted by his ambition to be Prime Minister and it distorted everything that he did and said,' says Tessa Jowell. 'Whether somebody is with me or not was all he cared about, and the Prime Minister cannot be like that.'[4] A retired Treasury mandarin speaks for many bruised officials: 'As someone who had wrecked somebody else's premiership, he was always going to have problems with his own. His core failure was his inability to be a team player, his inability to share, and his need always to be right – the clever boy in the class.'[5]

Lack of policy clarity

Effective leaders need to have a clear programme of action. Brown only achieved this at an international level, and failed to explain to a domestic audience how his efforts on a global stage were addressing concerns at home. His success as Prime Minister came when he was reacting to events, not when he outlined his own agenda for the future. The lack of clarity was all the more serious because his pressure on Blair to leave had been predicated on the assumption that he himself had a much stronger claim to be Prime Minister based on a distinct policy approach. Expectations ran incredibly high. Yet many of those who worked with Brown in Number 10 from June 2007 were astounded to find that 'the cupboard was virtually bare'. His determination to ascend to the Labour leadership unopposed in 2007 not only denied him a 'mandate', it also meant he had no requirement to set out his stall to his party or the wider electorate. Petrified of losing the support of Blairites on his right, and uncertain what his own centre-left domestic agenda would look like, he lurched from speech to speech, issue to issue, and crisis to crisis. Only in his final year did he begin to outline anything approaching a coherent personal agenda, when he realised that electoral logic meant he had to appeal to the middle ground. That meant embracing the market-based approach to public service reform that he had done so much block when it was proposed by Blair. It meant also flying in the face of Balls, who resisted the move, not the least in his own schools department. That was never going to make for an easy life.

These five factors that marred the premiership provide the background for *Brown at 10*. This is the story of one of the most complex, cerebral and tragic Prime Ministers ever to enter Downing Street, and one who presided over one of the most troubled periods in domestic British politics.

I

Power at Last

(June to September 2007)

Day Zero

Wednesday 27 June 2007 is a day that Gordon Brown has dreamt of for years, just as it has been dreaded for years by Tony Blair. Resigned though Blair is to it, he knows that his work over the previous ten years is far from complete, and that the principal reason for that is the resistance put up by Gordon Brown. For Brown, this is the day to put behind him all the broken promises of power he believes Blair has offered him. On this day, feelings are running high on both sides. Wednesday 27 June 2007 is the day that one of the most troubled political relationships in British history ends, and one of its most turbulent premierships begins.

Brown spends the morning with his advisers in the Chancellor's office in the Treasury, frantically going over last-minute Cabinet appointments, arrangements for the day, and the historic speech he will give on the steps of Downing Street. Blair spends the morning in Number 10, in his office at the end of the Cabinet Room, preparing intently for Prime Minister's Questions (PMQs). His aides will say he worked as hard on them as he had ever done. He is tired following a small party he held the night before for his close team, at which he talked about what he would and would not miss about being Prime Minister. In the latter category he included 'living his life in a constant state of nervous anticipation about what would happen next'. The emotion of the last few days is beginning to get to him.

Shortly before noon, Brown travels with his staff from his office along Whitehall to the House of Commons for Blair's final PMQs, where he sits down on Blair's left. They do not speak. They have little to say to each other. Blair had offered to advise the new Labour leader on how to cope with the pressures of what awaited him, but Brown had shown no interest.

At noon, Blair begins to speak, offering his condolences to the family and friends of three British soldiers killed over the previous seven days. He pays elaborate tribute, very deliberately, to the bravery of the armed forces. Conscious of the occasion, David Cameron asks serious questions about the floods, which will dominate Brown's first month as Prime Minister, and about the Middle East. The Leader of the Opposition pays generous compliments to the man who has been his adversary for the past two years: Cherie Blair, watching with her children in the side gallery facing Cameron, mouths the words: 'Thank you.' Blair is overwhelmed as he speaks his final words in the House of Commons and chokes as he says: 'Some may belittle politics, but we, who are engaged in it, know that it is where people stand tall … it is still the arena which sets the heart rate beating a little faster … I wish everyone, friend or foe, well. And that is that. The end.' After a moment of hesitation, MPs from all parties rise to their feet. It is the first time anyone can remember the whole House giving such a round of applause. Watching him intently on flat-screen TVs in the State Dining Room in Number 10 are all his staff, tears in their eyes.

At 12.30pm, as they rise from the government benches, Brown, sporting a blue tie, pats Blair, with a red tie, on the back. He returns quickly to the Treasury where he speaks individually to the team who have served him so loyally over the years. Gathered in his room are his close staff, including Sue Nye, Shriti Vadera, Gavin Kelly, Spencer Livermore, Stewart Wood, Dan Corry, Michael Ellam and his principal private secretary, James Bowler. He is 'extraordinarily emotional', thanking them for everything they have done in the past to make this day possible.[1] 'Everyone knew how difficult he could be, but we all accepted him as he was. There was an incredibly strong bond between us.'[2] At 1.46pm the longest-serving Chancellor in modern history prepares to leave the Treasury.

At 12.40pm, Blair returns to Downing Street, goes up the stairs for one final time and greets the 200 or so Downing Street staff who are assembled in the three interconnected state drawing rooms where he has brought them all for a glass of champagne. His principal private secretary, Oliver Robbins, taps a glass for silence so Blair can give an impromptu speech. Midway through, his wife and their children arrive. He tells his audience how wonderful they have all been, from 'switch' on the telephones to his senior advisers, and how much his family have enjoyed living in the building. The longer he talks, the more affected he and his audience become. 'Between half and two-thirds had tears running down their cheeks,' says one witness.[3] With no time to bid farewell to them all individually, he slips one final time into the 'den' – the small rectangular room through the double doors at the end of the Cabinet Room – while the staff come down the staircase to line the corridor from the Cabinet Room to the front door. As he walks along with Cherie and the children, he shakes a few hands and says some words of encouragement. On the street outside, still overcome with emotion, he declines to say anything. At 1.07pm the car leaves Downing Street, arriving at Buckingham Palace at 1.12pm, where he tenders his resignation in a private audience with the Queen.

At 1.46pm, Brown walks along the corridor outside the Chancellor's room to the applause of staff. Down in the Treasury's atrium, he says a few final words of thanks and leaves. Outside the Treasury, he and his wife, Sarah, climb into the Chancellor's official red Vauxhall Omega. At 1.51pm, their convoy sweeps through the gates of Buckingham Palace into the Royal Quadrangle and the Browns disappear inside the building, where they spend almost an hour with the Queen. She offers Gordon Brown the job of Prime Minister and they discuss his hopes as well as the challenges he will face. Neither could have guessed what lies in store; he will be tested like no other holder of the post since the Second World War.

At 1.50pm, Blair's staff begin a last, frantic tidy-up of Downing Street, collecting all their papers and clearing their computers; they will not be allowed to return. They are told they cannot leave through the famous black front door, and are shown speedily out through the link to the Cabinet Office at 70 Whitehall, handing over their prized Number 10 passes to the Garden Room secretaries as they leave. 'It is like leaving a fantasy world and re-entering reality,' says one.[4] Several of them disappear into Soho and drink until late. At 2.30pm, the Blairs arrive at London's King's Cross station, where they carry their own bags, boarding a GNR train bound for the North-East.

At 2.47pm, Brown steps out of Buckingham Palace as Prime Minister and gets into his official Jaguar to be driven to Downing Street. His staff joining him from the Treasury had a frantic rush after he left, dashing up Whitehall with their bags and entering Number 10 via the same route by which Blair's team has just departed. They are met by their new secretaries, who take them to offices they have never seen before. They gather to watch Brown leaving the Palace on the television in Spencer Livermore's office by the Cabinet Room. They see him being driven away and pull up in Downing Street outside.

At 2.50pm, Blair's train pulls out of the station. 'That's it. I'm no longer in charge. I'm going to get on with the rest of my life and let Gordon and the government get on with it,' he says as he speeds northwards. On one point he is adamant: 'I'm not going to talk to people about what Gordon is doing or not doing. I don't want anyone to say that I'm carping from the sidelines.'[5]

At 2.52pm, with Sarah at his side, Brown delivers his carefully prepared speech. He chooses to memorise it to avoid the risk of a malfunctioning autocue at such an auspicious moment. 'On this day I remember words that have stayed with me since my childhood, which matter a great deal to me today – my school motto: "I will try my utmost". This is my promise to all of the people of Britain. And now let the work of change begin.'[6]

The Browns enter Number 10 and are greeted by the same staff who applauded Blair an hour before. Theo Bertram – one of the few members of the Blair team to stay on under Brown – recalls: 'When Tony left we had champagne and then clapped him out. When Gordon Brown arrived, we clapped him in and then had coffee upstairs. It set the tone for his premiership.'[7] Outside the Cabinet Room he is greeted by Cabinet Secretary Gus O'Donnell and Oliver Robbins before he disappears into the 'den'. Into the room pile Gavin Kelly, Spencer Livermore, Sue Nye and Michael Ellam. Brown looks 'incredibly overwhelmed and emotional about the fact that he had finally achieved his goal'.[8] They have a few moments of mutual congratulation before they all leave to get on with their work. The task has finally begun.

In his heart, Brown wanted to put the past behind him, a past he knew had too often been unsavoury as his ambition had got the better of him. This was the moment he had yearned for all his adult life. Now he had the crown he craved. Whatever had gone wrong in the past, he was determined that this would be a new start: 'doing his utmost' meant fulfilling his dreams for a fairer Britain and a more equitable world, as well as governing in a way becoming to the dignity of the highest elected office in the land. But would the demons that had bedevilled him since 1994, and before, still come back to haunt him?

Brown knew the public would not give him long before delivering their judgement. He needed to establish himself quickly as a refreshing change from Blair without upsetting the continuity that, in a year's time, would justify him if he went ahead with the plan of asking the British people for a fourth Labour term. It would be a difficult balance: change but continuity, the dichotomy that was to be the leitmotif of his premiership. To add to the urgency, he was taking on the premiership at the end of June, rather than in May, when incoming Prime Ministers often assume power after a general election. That meant July would be absolutely critical.

In the first weeks, Brown knew that three decisions would be key. First, he needed to assemble his own Cabinet. This meant thanking Brownite loyalists who had helped him along the way, but also healing the wounds of the previous thirteen years. His fight for power had left him with a deeply divided Parliamentary Labour Party (PLP). His Cabinet appointments would be critical to soothing those divisions. Second, he needed to make the curious building that is Number 10 his own. Blair's Downing Street machine had closely reflected the nature of his premiership. The terms 'sofa government' and 'denocracy'⁹ had been coined to define Blair's style of ruling with a small clique of advisers – most notably his chief of staff, Jonathan Powell, and director of communications and strategy, Alastair Campbell – riding roughshod over Cabinet and Parliament and widely seen as obsessed with the media – a style that reached its apogee during the Iraq War. Brown needed a new style, and a new machine to execute his agenda. Third, and most importantly, he needed to set out that agenda. What, after all, had he been waiting for? His aides knew well that in the first few weeks, a series of substantive announcements would be needed to establish a clear Gordon Brown agenda – distinct enough to prove refreshing, yet steady enough to reassure. Each area represented a significant challenge, but also an opportunity: used well, each would give him critical tools with which to convince the public to accept him as Prime Minister.

Building the Cabinet: June

Few, if any Cabinets in history have been as long pondered-over, written out, binned and then rewritten, as Brown's first Cabinet. Eventually, only one minister, Des Browne at Defence, remained in the same position he had held in Blair's last Cabinet. No fewer than seven ministers were given Cabinet positions for the first time, while five were under forty, to help convey the impression of a youthful government and a fresh approach. When Brown boasted to Bush at Camp David the following month about the youthfulness of his Cabinet, Bush responded: 'You must be feeling damned old then!'¹⁰

In his final weeks at the Treasury, Brown was endlessly scribbling away on a plain piece of A3 paper, playing around with names of potential ministers: 'He used a pencil so that names could be frequently rubbed out and fresh names put in their place,' said one aide.¹¹ His jottings were too messy to be comprehensible, so his team used a large magnetic board, with potential ministers' names on different labels that could be regularly switched from one post to another. When the day finally came, the famous board was to have a canopy placed over it, and be transported from the Treasury to Number 10, where it was to become a regular feature of reshuffles.¹²

The dominant figure influencing the appointments was Ed Balls, who, as well as being Economic Secretary to the Treasury was one of Brown's most long-standing and loyal lieutenants. Sue Nye, a shrewd assessor of individuals, their talents and loyalties, provided a powerful second opinion.¹³ As if to underline his theme of change, Brown broke with tradition and did not appoint any Cabinet Ministers on his first day as Prime Minister. Day one was to be about Brown himself. 'You cannot underestimate the simple fact that changing Prime Minister is a major event in itself, and the people should be given a chance to appreciate that,' says a former Brown aide.[14] This, at least, was how it was spun. But the delay was, tellingly, because the new Prime Minister still could not make up his mind.[15] 'It was clear on the day he went to the Palace that he still didn't know who his Cabinet would be,' said an official.[16] When the reshuffle did take place, on the morning of 28 June, Brown conducted it, not, as usually occurred, in Number 10, with successful and departing ministers parading themselves before TV cameras, but in the quiet of the Prime Minister's office in the House of Commons, behind the Speaker's chair, with Gus O'Donnell, Gavin Kelly, and Nye in attendance. After their meetings with Brown, the appointees met with deputy chief of staff Kelly and head of the policy unit Dan Corry who gave them each a short paper explaining what the Prime Minister considered to be the key issues in their respective departments.[17]

The position Brown had agonised over most was the Treasury. He regularly toyed with making Balls Chancellor – the job his young protégé craved. At various points over the previous years, and indeed weeks, Balls's name was pencilled in for the chancellorship, and Brown would dearly have loved to appoint him. Balls was the only person the Prime Minister felt had the full range of abilities to do the job effectively, including an unparalleled understanding of the economy and of the Parliamentary Labour Party (PLP). Brown needed him for his judgement and confidence in taking tough decisions. More than that, as one in Number 10 puts it: 'He had thirteen years of intimate friendship with Gordon in which they built up a unique bond of trust.'[18] Two days before the announcement, Nye said to an official: 'I hope he'll be brave,' which was taken to refer to making Balls Chancellor. Balls, however, was disappointed but resigned when Brown told him the post was a step too far, at least for the time being. The younger man knew that such a move would prove deeply divisive in the party, especially with the Blairites, who had demonised him, fairly or unfairly, as the representation of everything that they disliked about Brown himself. A governing consideration for Brown in forming his government was building bridges, and he deemed appointing Balls as his Chancellor was 'too big a risk'.[19] One of his longest-serving advisers comments: 'He wanted to move on from the binary world of Blairites and Brownites.'[20] Balls even planted a story via journalist Alex Brummer in the *Daily Mail* saying that he would not be moving into the Treasury. Brown was apparently cross with Balls, who justifies the action saying: 'I decided to do it to make the decision easier for him.'[21]

'Plan B' for keeping Brown's most trusted colleague close to him was to give Balls a hybrid role as minister for the Cabinet Office (i.e. a de facto Number 10 chief of staff) and Chief Secretary to the Treasury.[22] It was a novel plan that could have meant far closer links between Number 10 and the Treasury than had existed under Blair. In those long final months of waiting, it was a scheme Brown kept returning to. But the plan fell apart because of Balls's unwillingness to enter such an untested ministerial arrangement. Having spent fourteen years in Brown's shadow, seeing the older man take the credit for his thinking, he thought it was important to become a public figure in his own right, particularly if he was to stand a chance of succeeding Brown as party leader. Did his acute antennae also warn him that Brown's premiership would be bumpy, and he would be better off to distance himself? Probably. In addition, he did not think it 'would work having me as Chief Secretary to the Treasury because it would place the Chancellor in an impossible position knowing that I was so close to the Prime Minister'.[23]

During the period of transition, Balls had been chairing 'machinery of government' meetings to examine the new shape of Whitehall under Brown. During these talks, a case was made for placing children's policy in one department, to be called the Department for Children, Schools and Families. Initially the new department was also to include youth justice, but incoming Justice Secretary Jack Straw insisted that responsibility for this be shared with his department. Balls maintains that even on the day before the transition, he still did not know where he was going to go, believing Chief Whip Jacqui Smith would go to Education and that he might himself go into Health. But in the final day or two, because of his midwife role in the creation of the new department, the idea 'emerged' that he would run it himself. Appointing Balls suddenly to the department was, however, to create new problems of its own.

For the Chancellorship, Brown was left with two principal options: his long-term ally Alistair Darling, or Environment Secretary David Miliband. Appointing the latter to the job he wanted would have made 'Balls go quite ballistic', according to one of the inner team. Miliband was, therefore, given the post of Foreign Secretary, meaning the Treasury went to Darling almost by default.[24] No two ministerial relationships with Number 10 were to be so strained over the next three years as those of Darling and Miliband, the former periodically, the latter permanently. Education Secretary Alan Johnson was moved to the Department of Health in the hope that his emollient personality would help rebuild relations with the NHS following a troubled period under Blair's ally Patricia Hewitt. Jack Straw was given the Ministry of Justice, but was not made Deputy Prime Minister, a role he coveted, while Harriet Harman, the newly elected Deputy Leader, was appointed Leader of the House. Together with Geoff Hoon, discussed below, these were the big beasts of the Cabinet. Only with Darling did Brown enjoy a personal friendship. The others were Brown sceptics from the outset; their loyalty was contingent on him providing competent leadership that won the confidence of the party. They would give him the benefit of the doubt for the time being and no more.

Brown knew this, hence his desire to field an inclusive Cabinet. A cynic might be tempted to ask whether Brown's outbreak of affability to Blairites was a Machiavellian device to ensure a united and plot-free party in the run-up to a planned general election a year or so away. Having won his prized mandate, he would then thrust his own supporters into all the key positions, dispatching the Blairites to the outer darkness. None of his inner camp, however, believed that this thought was at the forefront of his mind. That is not to say that the appointments were not political. Brown knew he was widely viewed as a partisan politician of the old school. By courting Blairites, his first reshuffle would send a powerful message. Nonetheless, the lengths that Brown went to are startling. James Purnell, a known sceptic, not to say enemy of Brown, was promoted to the Cabinet as Culture Secretary, while John Hutton, who had earlier confided that he thought Brown would be 'a fucking disaster as Prime Minister',[25] was made Secretary of State at the newly formed Department for Business, Enterprise, and Regulatory Reform.

Most symbolically of all, Andrew Adonis – the Blairite *sans pareil* – was retained as schools minister to oversee the academy programme, the previous administration's key education policy. The peer had barely spoken to Brown in five years and expected to leave office at the same time as Blair. 'I was a litmus test for Gordon. I was called to his office and it was just the two of us,' says Adonis. 'He asked me about education policy and took voluminous notes. "I hope you'll be staying," he said. I replied that, as long as he kept the commitment to academies, the excellence agenda and Teach First, I would.'[26] Brown had already determined who would be schools minister before his last-minute decision to put Balls in charge of the department. The latter had been against retaining Adonis and he was equally against the academies programme. As Secretary of State, Balls set about watering down the independent aspects of the academy model;[27] it did not make for an easy relationship between the two men.

'Before we came to power we worked hard to ensure the Blair/Brown split did not continue to undermine things. We tried hard not to appear too cliquey,' says one adviser.[28] Jacqui Smith was one of the most senior Blairites to be brought into Brown's Cabinet. The appointment of the first female Home Secretary was intended to be eye-catching and the move was described by Fiona Gordon, Brown's political secretary, as 'the key decision of the reshuffle'.[29] 'This will come as a bit of a shock to you,' Brown told Smith at their meeting.[30] He had been impressed by her work as Chief Whip, he said, and saw her grip over the Blairite MPs as vital to his own project. Geoff Hoon, Defence Secretary during the Iraq War, was another key Blairite to make the cut, succeeding Smith as Chief Whip. However, under pressure from Balls, the Prime Minister appointed ultra-loyalist Nick Brown as Hoon's deputy, effectively emasculating the latter from day one. This appointment proved to be the most controversial. 'Geoff was dead against it as he knew that Nick Brown would basically be the real Whip. Nick was seen by some as a very divisive figure and people were shocked that Gordon had appointed him,' says one Blairite.[31]

The list of Blairite ministers continued to grow: Andy Burnham as Chief Secretary to the Treasury and Caroline Flint as minister for employment and welfare reform, while Blair favourite Tessa Jowell was retained as minister for London and the Olympics, albeit without permanent Cabinet status. Jowell's appointment was the only occasion on which Blair directly intervened. He had expressly told Brown in the build-up to the handover that there were key members of the Cabinet whom it would be wise to keep on, but then took a back seat until he learned that she might be dropped. 'Tony fought hard for me to remain in the Cabinet at the time of the transition,' says Jowell, and a compromise was reached – she kept her job, but with a lower status than she had enjoyed under Blair, which did not please her one bit.[32]

The price of all the prizes going to Blairites was that jobs for Brownites were squeezed. Some of the Prime Minister's key supporters were disappointed and angered at the extent to which their leader had gone to placate his rival's followers. Nonetheless, Brown's three closest advisers aside from Balls all received significant posts. Douglas Alexander was made Secretary of State at the Department for International Development – an appointment that underlined the critical importance of the area to Brown – while Ed Miliband picked up one half of the job that Balls had declined – minister overseeing a beefed-up Cabinet Office. 'Ed was not wholly chuffed, but someone needed to be around Gordon, given that Ed Balls and Douglas were going elsewhere,' recalls one in Number 10. Shriti Vadera, the brilliant and fiery City analyst who had been central to Brown's financial and industrial decision-making, was elevated to the Lords and joined Alexander at International Development as a junior minister, and the two soon fell out. What of Brown's parliamentary clique? Few received the rewards for years of loyal service they may have hoped for. Tom Watson, still a controversial figure given his role in the attempt to unseat Blair in September 2006, merely joined the Whips Office, while Ian Austin became Brown's parliamentary private secretary, a role that did not even carry ministerial rank, though one which did keep him close to Brown's side. Nick Brown, meanwhile, sulked in his tent at his 'demotion' to Deputy Chief Whip. Other Brown loyalists on Labour's backbenches – too numerous to mention by name – received even less than that.

Brown's desire to be inclusive went 'beyond narrow party interest', as a senior adviser puts it.[33] 'For two years he had been interested in the idea of working with the Liberals – Brown always called the Liberal Democrats, the "Liberals",'

says a Number 10 official.[34] Brown had a long-standing relationship with
Menzies Campbell and Paddy Ashdown, and even offered to make the latter
Northern Ireland Secretary the week before he became Prime Minister, but was
rebuffed. He had more success with other Lib Dems in the House of Lords
who were offered advisory roles: Shirley Williams agreed to advise on nuclear
proliferation, Anthony Lester on constitutional reform and Julia Neuberger on
the third sector. Brown also tried to enlist the support of Williams's fellow SDP
founder David Owen, calling him into Number 10 on 12 September; Owen
was not entirely clear whether this was to be offered a ministerial or advisory
role, but he declined as he did not believe he had a meaningful contribution to
make.[35] The defection of Quentin Davies, the Europhile Conservative MP, who
castigated David Cameron for his lack of any 'clear convictions', was trumpeted
at the same time. Brown also tried unsuccessfully to secure the defection of
future Speaker John Bercow. The involvement of Liberal Democrats did not go
down well with many of Brown's own supporters in the party, particularly when
coupled with his failure to promote figures like Balls's wife, Yvette Cooper,
as well as John Healey and Rosie Winterton. 'People who thought they had
Gordon's ear didn't like having Liberal Democrats involved. We told him that
if things went wrong, it would come back to haunt him,' says one.[36]

Still more jibbing from Brownites greeted another innovation, described
by constitutional authority Peter Hennessy as 'the greatest import of experts
of a non-political background since World War Two'.[37] Brown's initiative was
termed the 'government of all the talents' and the eminent individuals drafted
in were described as 'GOATs'. 'GOATs were about showing inclusiveness and
desire to appeal to all sections to get the best possible broad-based national
talent for the government,' says one Number 10 official.[38] That was not a
disingenuous claim: Brown had long valued the advice of outside experts, and
was sincere in wanting their contributions to his government. But the GOATs
were also a consciously tactical move, helping to convince a sceptical public that
they should rethink their preconceptions of Brown as a deeply tribal politician.

Brown's appointments included Mark Malloch Brown, a former Deputy
Secretary General of the UN, as minister of state in the Foreign Office, the
business leader Digby Jones as minister of state for trade, and former First
Sea Lord Alan West, who was made security minister. Not all invitees
accepted: the Prime Minister failed to persuade Andrew Lloyd Webber to
join the government as a cultural ambassador.[39] His most successful GOAT
was the celebrated surgeon Ara Darzi: 'This is your opportunity to make your
policy wishes come true. I need a clinician to do this,' Brown told Darzi after
contacting him without warning.[40] The Prime Minister refused to accept
Darzi's protestations and, in the end, the latter gave way. Despite the mixed
record of GOATs, Brown remained attached to the idea, and subsequently

appointed businessman Paul Myners as his City minister, the banker Mervyn Davies as a trade minister, and the high-profile entrepreneur Alan Sugar, who became a non-ministerial business adviser.

The reshuffle was well-received. '[It] was generally regarded as one of the most polished in the modern political era ... the culmination of months of thinking,' according to *The Observer*.[41] Not all the machinery of government changes worked: the Department of Innovation, Universities and Skills under John Denham – a minister whom Brown had brought into the Cabinet following the former's resignation from the front bench over the Iraq War – lasted only until June 2009, when it was merged into the Department for Business, Enterprise and Regulatory Reform. But the *Daily Telegraph* thought the overall initiative was radical and bold in the way it redesigned the departmental geography of Whitehall, attempting to deliver a semblance of 'joined-up' government.[42]

Brown's new government was bold, and it bore the Prime Minister's unmistakable stamp, for all his agonising over it. But would the gamble of filling so many positions with Blairites and others who owed him no political or personal loyalty pay off when the chips were down? And how would Brown warm to his new Cabinet personally? Brown's newfound collegiality lasted into his first Cabinet meeting, held on 28 June, the day the appointments were announced. The meeting lasted three hours, during which he went around the Cabinet table, asking all his new ministers what they thought. 'This was a deliberate contrast to the Blairite style of Cabinet. As a team we were very keen to build bridges at every opportunity,' says an adviser.[43] But early on, the tensions emerged. 'It quickly became apparent that he really didn't rate key members of the Cabinet like Jacqui Smith and David Miliband,' says one senior adviser. 'The only people he initially wanted to spend time with were Ed [Balls], Ed [Miliband] and Douglas [Alexander].'[44] Brown had always worked with a tight-knit tribal group of close political aides and officials. Now he would have to inspire and motivate a large team of Cabinet ministers. He knew a radical change of approach was required from how he ran the Treasury, and he was determined to make that transition and become an acknowledged leader.

Brown's Number 10

For ten years, Brown had eyed Blair's Number 10 with a mixture of envy – at its size and resources – and disgust – at its superficiality and the way he saw it as being driven by the 24-hour news cycle (which was rich given Brown's own obsession with spin). Brown was determined that his own Number 10 would be smaller, cleaner and fitter. He had little interest in how the Blair operation ran: he delegated Nye to talk to Blair's deputy chief of staff, Liz Lloyd, but she thought Nye's questions were perfunctory. 'There seemed little genuine interest in learning how we did things.'[45] Blair had been equally dismissive of any guidance on how to run Number 10 in 1997, thinking, fatally, that he knew how to do it. 'They'll all be gone by Christmas,' Brown told an official of the private office he inherited from Blair.[46] Similarly, little attempt was made to retain Blair's political team. 'I knew a number of people who would have been happy to stay on, but that wasn't on the table,' said one rare adviser who survived the transition.[47] When the day came, as Blair's staff left through the back 'link door' to the Cabinet Office, they passed Brown's coming in like ships in the night. A Brown aide recalls: 'These were people we had known for ages. We barely spoke: it was odd.'[48] One senior Blair adviser offered 'to go through everything', from the running of the famous Number 10 'grid' to other details of the long-established private office, 'but there was no particular appetite'.[49] Having Blairites in Cabinet and across Whitehall was one matter: having those associated with Blair in the holy of holies at Number 10 was quite another.

The 'politicisation' of the civil service, and a cavalier disregard for time-honoured conventions of good government had been key dynamics of Blair's premiership and Brown sought to reverse both. On his first day at Number 10, he revoked the controversial order in council that had given Alastair Campbell and Jonathan Powell authority to give instructions to civil servants. Brown trusted the civil servants he liked, and he wanted to see some of the old Whitehall orthodoxy return. To help show that the days of spin were also over, he decided that Number 12 Downing Street would be handed back to its traditional owner, the Chief Whip, and that it would no longer be occupied by the large media team that had resided there under Blair. He would later reverse this decision.

In place of Jonathan Powell, the Blair appointee who had run Number 10 for ten years, Brown expressly wanted a civil servant. Tom Scholar had been his intellectually brilliant principal private secretary at the Treasury from 1997 to 2001, before going to Washington to work for the IMF. 'It had been axiomatic that Tom would become chief of staff in charge of Number 10 when Gordon became Prime Minister. Gordon loved him. Tom was unstuffy, popular and extraordinarily able,' says an adviser.[50] Balls was responsible for recruiting Scholar, and it took some persuasion to convince him to take up the job. Brown also spoke to him in Washington in April, but Scholar did not finally accept the job until May; even then he only agreed to serve one year, and would not be available until Brown moved in to Number 10. To balance the appointment of an official as chief of staff, Brown made Gavin Kelly 'deputy' chief of staff – a more political role.

Brown entrusted Balls with overseeing plans for revamping the arrangements at the heart of government. An important part of this involved strengthening the Cabinet Office, presided over by Gus O'Donnell, whom Brown had known well at the Treasury. 'We wanted to build up the Cabinet Office to enhance the Prime Minister's reach, and the numbers of civil servants at our disposal,' says Balls.[51] He claims he was particularly concerned about how the Blair administration had marginalised the civil service and held conversations with O'Donnell when planning the transition. O'Donnell told him that if Brown returned power to the Whitehall officials, he would be supported by as effective and capable a civil service machine as that enjoyed by any previous Prime Minister.[52] O'Donnell, a highly political official, who had managed to serve three very different Prime Ministers – Major, Blair and now Brown – was extremely anxious to achieve what his three predecessors as Cabinet Secretary had failed to manage – a traditionally run centre for Whitehall with civil servants in their correct positions of influence.

Balls's plan was to beef up three Cabinet Office directorates to assist Brown in running that centre. The foreign directorate was to be led by Simon McDonald, a bright Foreign Office official considered to be in the Brown 'can-do' mould. Europe and international finance was to be run by Jon Cunliffe, a confidant of Brown's from the Treasury, while responsibility for domestic policy was given to Jeremy Heywood. Heywood had come to Brown's attention at the Treasury and later as Blair's principal private secretary at Number 10, where he had been one of the very few members of Blair's staff whom Brown and his team trusted. He had left Whitehall in December 2003 to join the investment bank, Morgan Stanley, and Brown had personally persuaded him to come back. Collectively, Cunliffe, Heywood and McDonald were known as the 'three amigos'.[53] Heywood was the most gifted civil servant of his generation. No official since Norman Brook, who had been Cabinet Secretary from 1947 to 1962, had been so dominant in Whitehall. 'It was a very popular move to have Jeremy Heywood coming into the Cabinet Office. He was widely respected, and well known to some of us, including Ed Balls,' says Kelly.[54] Ensuring that these three directors would work with strategic purpose was Ed Miliband, minister for the Cabinet Office.

No facet of Blair's Number 10 aroused more consistent criticism than communications, and its director, Alastair Campbell, who was blamed for creating a culture of spin. In another attempt to create a clean break with the past, Brown appointed another Treasury official whom he trusted and respected as his official spokesman. Michael Ellam was a retiring character, in sharp contrast to Campbell's brash, bullish demeanour, and Brown had initially approached him about taking up the position in January 2007.[55] Ellam's role was limited to briefing the lobby – the group of journalists who report on Westminster – and did not include developing a wider media strategy for Brown's government. In charge of political communications was Damian

McBride, a former Treasury civil servant who had become one of Brown's most trusted special advisers. McBride was a controversial figure, known for his aggressive tactics in pursuing his political master's interests; Balls selected him because of their close relationship and similar outlook. The irony of bringing McBride into a 'cleaned-up' Number 10 communications structure seems to have escaped Brown: beholden to Balls, the Prime Minister appeared oblivious to what was being done on his behalf. Also from the Treasury came Sue Nye as gate-keeper, Spencer Livermore as director of political strategy, Dan Corry as head of the policy unit, and Stewart Wood, Matt Cavanagh and Michael Jacobs as senior members of the Downing Street policy unit. Nick Pearce, then director of the Institute for Public Policy Research, was drafted in as an adviser on education and skills and the lead on long-term thinking; he was to succeed Corry as head of the policy unit in the autumn of 2008.

For foreign policy advice within Number 10, the genial Foreign Office official Tom Fletcher was selected in September, which raised eyebrows on account of his comparative youth and inexperience: the job would inevitably involve him in much of the work previously undertaken by Nigel Sheinwald, Blair's heavyweight foreign policy adviser, who had been appointed British ambassador to Washington. Brown wanted a slimmed-down foreign and defence policy operation in Downing Street, intending to rely on the newly empowered Cabinet Office.

Ed Balls says of the set-up: 'The thinking was to establish a structured relationship between the Prime Minister and the civil service machine, with political and ministerial input, which had worked so well for Gordon at the Treasury.'[56] The interface between Number 10 and the Cabinet Office had been crafted with considerable thought; the question was, how well would it work?

Number 10, June 2007

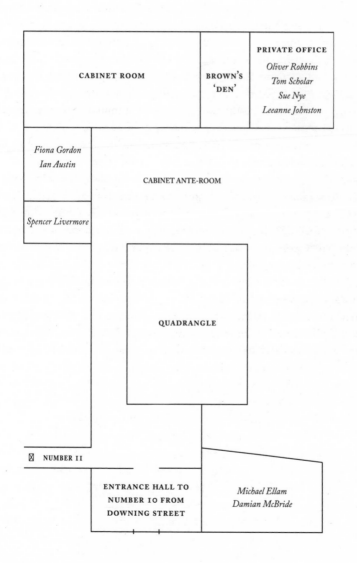

CABINET ROOM

BROWN'S 'DEN'

PRIVATE OFFICE
Oliver Robbins
Tom Scholar
Sue Nye
Leeanne Johnston

Fiona Gordon
Ian Austin

CABINET ANTE-ROOM

Spencer Livermore

QUADRANGLE

⊠ NUMBER 11

ENTRANCE HALL TO NUMBER 10 FROM DOWNING STREET

Michael Ellam
Damian McBride

Brown's Agenda

The question most often asked of Brown at this time was: 'What is his agenda?' It is a question asked of all newcomers to the role of Prime Minister, but now it took on increased significance. Following Blair's resignation, it had taken Brown just six days to secure 313 nominations for the party leadership from Labour MPs. There was no need for a salesman's pitch – he was the only game in town. At the time, the lack of a contest had been greeted by Brown and his team with relief, but some now regretted the missed opportunity to set out his stall. One senior minister spoke for many when he said that the absence of a contest meant 'Gordon had no intellectual reckoning and no chance to clearly say why he wanted to be Prime Minister'.[57] It is one of the great paradoxes of Brown's premiership that, despite having been at the top of British politics longer than any post-war Prime Minister since Anthony Eden, when he arrived at Number 10, it was far from clear what he wanted to do.

That did not mean that expectations were low. Having wrestled the crown from Blair's grasp, it was widely anticipated that Brown's leadership would strike out in a new direction. Brown himself had fuelled that feeling during his first speech as Prime Minister on the steps of Downing Street, in which he undertook to lead a government of 'change'. The question was, what shape would that change take? From the autumn of 2006, intensive work had taken place among Brown's team in the Treasury to prepare for power, building on and refining ideas that had already been readied for the false start in 2004, when Brown had believed that Blair would stand aside for him. His team intended him to hit the ground running once in Number 10 with a series of policy initiatives. 'We discussed at length how to plan it, knowing that July would be the pivotal month when the public would make up their minds about him. We knew we had to get July right,' says one Treasury official who worked on the handover.[58] 'In the event, the public did make up their mind about Gordon Brown by the end of July, and it was very favourable.'

Yet, Brown was also acutely aware that, on domestic policy, he needed to strike a difficult balance, moving away from the unpopular aspects of the Blair regime and thus refreshing Labour in office without compromising the strengths that had won the party three successive elections. Continuity or change? It was a dilemma that would define and, at times, suffocate the development of policy during Brown's time in Number 10. For six months and more, as he and his team at the Treasury prepared for power, the debate had raged within his inner circle. From the start, Balls and Ed Miliband urged him to prioritise the change dimension of the equation, believing there was appetite for a more distinctively social-democratic project. 'All those working closely with him were saying you have to be about change,' says Balls. 'Throughout

2006 to 2007 I was saying to him to look again at his John Smith Memorial Lecture in 1996[59] [in which Brown set out the New Labour case for social justice] and update it.'[60]

Focus groups and surveys conducted by Spencer Livermore and Brown's personal pollster, Deborah Mattinson, suggested that what concerned the public most about Brown was that he was 'too associated with the past, and would not bring about the change they craved'.[61] But Brown was more cautious. His rhetoric may have been big on change – in his leadership acceptance speech in Manchester on 24 June he had used the word twenty-eight times – but when it came to the substance of policy, he worried deeply about being portrayed as 'Old Labour'. This was a favourite attack line of the Tories, who liked to paint Brown as a roadblock to reform. The Prime Minister believed that any too-sudden moves risked losing him more support than they would attract. Advisers could not budge him.

Brown's preferred option was to build consensus as a 'father of the nation' figure. Balls explains that 'he tried to appeal at the same time to the readers of the *Daily Mail* and *The Times*, as well as to readers of *The Guardian* and the liberal intelligentsia' – two constituencies Brown believed had been let down by Blair.[62] For the former, Brown offered a programme of social conservatism with a series of announcements calling into question aspects of Blair's policy that had irritated the *Daily Mail*, such as plans for 'super-casinos' (11 July), the reclassification of cannabis (18 July) and 24-hour drinking laws (22 July). These seemed to hit the spot; in a piece for *The Independent* entitled 'I am a Tory, but I must admit I find myself seduced by the cut of Gordon Brown's jib', journalist Michael Brown wrote: 'Mr Cameron poses as the social liberal but it is the middle-aged, socially conservative puritan, Mr Brown, who captures the sombre mood of the middle class.'[63]

Liberals on the centre left, meanwhile, were to be placated by the promise of constitutional reform, designed to contrast with Blair, who had been famously uninterested in the issue. For his first speech as Prime Minister to the House of Commons, on 3 July, Brown launched the 'Governance of Britain' green paper, which called grandly for a 'new constitutional settlement'. This decision was very much Brown's own. 'It ran against the judgement of some of his team who thought he should begin with more "kitchen-table" issues, like health or education,' says Corry.[64] The green paper promised to consider measures to strengthen the power of Parliament, particularly in relation to the executive, including giving the legislature a direct role in approving declarations of war. Following the controversy over official advice given on the legality of the Iraq War, it also raised the possibility of reforming the office of Attorney General. In its detail, the document reflected a high degree of political caution and indecision, but at the time it was relatively well-received. *The Guardian*'s

Jonathan Freedland spoke for many liberals: 'That Brown had chosen to make his maiden prime ministerial speech on [constitutional reform] was replete with significance. For many long years [it] has been the poor relation in British politics. Yet now Brown has declared that it counts and that he means to spend serious political capital on it.'[65] Little did Freedland know that Brown had written an alternative draft of the speech that was far more forthright than the one he delivered, including a boldly argued case for a written constitution.

Brown received praise from the same quarters for his announcement that Cabinet meetings would be longer and more discursive, and policy announcements would be made first by ministers in the House of Commons rather than on the BBC Radio's *Today* programme. These were exactly the assurances that those concerned with the rising 'democratic deficit' in Britain yearned to hear. They were also a targeted riposte to Blair's 'sofa government' approach, which had been widely criticised, above all during the Iraq War, and which Brown believed to have damaged trust in government. They were changes to style more than substance; one aide explains: 'We were seeking to move away from the spin and the actor Blair towards a genuine straight-talking guy.'[66] But many of these symbolic changes would not last: a media obsessive such as Brown was never going to stick with the pledge to announce policy only in Parliament.

In another bid to be more open, Brown broke with tradition by publishing a draft Queen's Speech on 11 July to facilitate public debate and consultation on the government's legislative programme. Domestic priorities were to be housing, education and health. The pledge to build three million houses by 2020 was a major new commitment. It had been urged by Number 10 advisers and the new housing minister Yvette Cooper on the basis that Labour had not focused sufficiently on this area during its time in office, and had concentrated too much on refurbishment rather than new building. Here was Brown's opportunity to be associated with a landmark reform. On education, the draft Queen's Speech included a bill requiring all young people to stay in education or training until the age of eighteen – a policy agreed under Blair – and an ambitious 'Children's Plan'.

On 30 June, just three days after taking office, Brown visited Kingston Hospital in London. The hospital's management had been praised for reducing the number of MRSA infections, and the Prime Minister used the visit to trial a new drive on infections to be launched the next day. A team of experts would be set up in the Department of Health, and health minister Ara Darzi would be asked to develop a strategy to tackle the problem. Brown's intervention proved effective: having been significantly off-track when he took office, the government later hit its target to halve MRSA infections. Darzi would prove to be one of the most inspired appointments of Brown's premiership, as he delivered wide-ranging reform of the health service, from the roll-out of polyclinics to extended opening hours for GPs' surgeries.

But despite high-profile action on hospitals, public-service reform per se did not feature prominently during the opening weeks of Brown's premiership. He pledged that health and education would be priorities, alongside housing, but the initiatives that had defined the Blair years, from academies to foundation hospitals, were noticeably absent. It was in many ways a conscious decision. Blair's insistence on constantly altering the way in which public services were delivered had drawn increasing irritation from practitioners during his final years as Prime Minister. Brown had deliberately set out at a calmer pace, rebuilding relationships with professionals, especially in health, where Alan Johnson was seen to have 'settled things down' after a period of turbulence.[67]

In other areas, continuity was the order of the day. Brown felt that a national ID card scheme was an expensive waste of money, but decided not to cancel its introduction for fear of looking weak on security.[68] Blair's anti-social behaviour agenda was retained, if not championed, not least because responsibility for the 'respect' taskforce was transferred from the Home Office to Balls's new children's department. Tuition fees were another Blair policy that Brown had long opposed, but advisers disagreed with the Prime Minister's plans for a graduate tax, and the fees stayed, albeit tempered by reforms to alleviate the burden they imposed on low-income families. One aide admits: 'We thought the change on tuition fees was our most significant new policy, but it hardly got any attention at all.'[69] The error of judgement was telling: anxiety about moving away from Blair's policy platform made even small deviations seem significant to Brown's team. One senior minister calls tuition fees 'the perfect illustration' of Brown's inability to decide whether he represented continuity or change.[70]

Nonetheless, it added up to what seemed like a well-crafted strategy: sweeping away unpopular aspects of Blair's agenda, and capitalising on Brown's personal traits. Here was the social conservatism and moral leadership of the son of the Presbyterian minister, in stark contrast with the glamour, and perceived sense of moral decay that had come to taint Blair. Constitutional reform lifted Brown above the politics of spin, to a newfound level of seriousness. Action on the NHS demonstrated an appreciable straightforwardness: hospitals would be deep-cleaned, GPs would be more accessible. The message was clear – this would be a refreshingly different style of premiership, and one that Brown alone was able to deliver.

By the end of July, it appeared that Brown had managed to achieve a successful balancing act on policy. He had avoided unsettling the ever-watchful Blairites while managing to carve out some fresh lines of his own, notably his promises on democratic renewal. Jonathan Freedland's verdict was typical of the views expressed by the commentariat at the time – 'Brown's first month looks like a striking success' – and went down very well in Number 10. Freedland also described Brown as 'solid, reliable and grown-up' and concluded that the new Prime Minister possessed 'gravitas'.[71]

Terror, Floods and Foot-and-Mouth: June to September

Brown's known strengths were dealing with the expected. He had become an expert at orchestrating the grand, periodic Treasury set-pieces of the Budget, and the three-year spending rounds. A question mark hung over how he would deal with crises that emerged out of a blue sky. He did not have long to wait before he was tested. Rarely has any peacetime Prime Minister had to cope with separate challenges of such magnitude in their first weeks. The first emerged on his third day in office – 29 June. In the early hours of that morning, two unexploded bombs were discovered in London. A meeting of the Cabinet's crisis-response committee, COBRA, was convened and chaired by Home Secretary Jacqui Smith. The following day, Kafeel Ahmed and Bilal Abdullah, two Islamist extremists, drove a blazing Jeep into Glasgow Airport. Was this the beginning of a concerted al Qaida-style attack on Britain? Another meeting of COBRA was convened that evening, chaired by Brown himself. 'He showed not a jot of panic, even though he, like me, had absolutely no induction for this job,' recalls Smith. 'He was commanding in laying out what he expected to happen.'[72]

That evening in front of television cameras, Brown addressed the nation from Number 10, promising an instant tightening of security at airports and other public places. Insiders were struck by 'how calm and authoritative he was with the developing events', leaving an adviser with the impression that Brown 'had a very sure touch'.[73] Shami Chakrabarti, director of the human rights pressure group Liberty, praised how he had 'addressed the nation, briefly, calmly, [with] no cracking voice, no emotive statements, no lip quivering'.[74] Brown listened carefully to advice from the Home Office about how to handle the events and what to say about the Islamist threat.[75] A close adviser says: 'He was clear that there was going to be no finger-pointing at the Muslim community. Nor did he want a series of policy measures such as Blair had introduced after 7/7. He spoke about criminality rather than trying to establish a lineage back to 9/11.'[76] Brown had come through his first crisis as Prime Minister with flying colours. It revealed that in time of emergency, he could be decisive – a trait he was to display again during the banking crisis. He had also demonstrated an ability to handle the most sensitive intelligence reports about security threats to Britain, and to digest briefings from the directors of MI5, MI6 and GCHQ. Here was virgin territory for Brown, and one of the loneliest and most burdensome aspects of the job for any Prime Minister.

A second crisis had originated two days before he arrived at Number 10, when torrential rainfall had triggered severe flooding across Britain.[77] Three people had been killed on 25 June alone, and on 19 and 20 July, another period of prolonged and heavy rainfall led to a second wave of severe flooding. On 23 July, reports came into Number 10 that GCHQ at Cheltenham, Gloucester prison and the Waltham power station, which supplies electricity to half a million homes, were all in danger. A senior official recalls: 'If the water had risen just a little further, it could have been immensely serious.'[78] Criticised for not responding quickly to the June floods in the North, Brown was determined not to be wrong-footed again. On 7 July, he promised £14m in aid, a figure increased to £46m on 25 July. Employment minister Caroline Flint, whose Don Valley constituency had been badly affected, took advantage of the Prime Minister's official car and travelled with him from Doncaster to Hull. No ally of Brown, she was struck 'by how well he seemed to be handling it. He was impressively prime ministerial.'[79] In stark contrast, David Cameron flew to Rwanda on a pre-arranged trip after a brief visit to his own flooded constituency, which, however unreasonable, reflected badly on him: the lesson drawn was that Brown had his finger more firmly on the national pulse. Most of the work in handling the floods was undertaken by government agencies, but Brown understood that the public wanted to see the Prime Minister personally involved. The crisis proved he could listen to advice on the appropriate moment to delegate. Newly appointed Environment Secretary Hilary Benn – widely liked but not renowned for his skills as a communicator – asked at one point whether 'Gordon could visit'. Brown responded: 'This is a moment for a minister to be at the front line, not me.'[80]

The third crisis – foot-and-mouth disease – was the most protracted, and potentially most disastrous. 'We all remembered the 2001 outbreak of foot-and-mouth. It had spread in a starburst because we had not contained it. The lesson we learned was that we had to act quickly,' says Benn.[81] That episode had cost the British economy some £3bn. On 3 August, a week into the parliamentary recess, cases of the disease were confirmed at a farm in Surrey. Brown was en route to a family holiday in Dorset when he was told the news but lost no time in deciding to return to London to take charge. 'We called it the classic Gordon holiday – he was away for only four hours,' recalls one in Number 10.[82] His staff wondered whether he had really wanted to take time off, so immediate was his decision to cut the break short: in truth, the prospect had never excited him.[83] 'He was very happy indeed to be in the action,' says one senior adviser.[84] Back in Number 10, he chaired five meetings of COBRA over the following few days; over the next two weeks 'he worked every hour God sent him',[85] even talking on the phone to helicopter pilots, until, on 18 August, the government announced an easing of restrictions imposed when the disease was detected.

On 12 September, another outbreak of foot-and-mouth was reported at a farm near Egham, Surrey, and there followed a further series of meetings of COBRA to discuss the government's response. At one point Brown's team became worried that he was becoming overly involved.[86] 'He loved convening COBRA,' recalls another.[87] By the end of September the crisis was over. His high-profile presence during the crises was mostly cosmetic. The real work was done by public servants. But his hands-on approach provided reassurance and boosted the morale of those in the field. Hitherto, Brown had a reputation of Macavity, T. S. Eliot's disappearing cat. No longer. Cometh the crisis, cometh Brown.

The Prime Minister's personal approval ratings suggested that the public also thought highly of his contribution: 62 per cent of respondents to an opinion poll in August thought that he was doing 'well' in the role.[88] On 12 August, a poll indicated that Labour's lead over the Conservatives was greater than it had been at any time since before the 2003 Iraq invasion. Brown had been enraptured by the new challenges, and was buoyed by the knowledge that he had inspired trust in those working at the heart of Whitehall. 'The way that Gordon Brown reacted to these crises gave him a great deal of confidence and a sense that he could manage the job,' a senior official recalls.[89] In late June the British public had seen him as an unelected premier without a mandate: by the end of August, they were viewing him as a national leader with a sure touch, and he knew it.

Bush and Camp David: July

Before July was over, however, Brown faced a final challenge: how would he handle the all-important relationship with President George Bush? Here again he needed to differentiate his approach from that of Blair, which he viewed as being too submissive to the US administration. It would require a careful balance; Bush had only eighteen months of his term remaining and an overly familiar relationship could prejudice Brown's chances of building a close relationship with the victor of the US presidential election in November 2008. But the Blairites and right-wing press would judge him harshly if he did not make a positive impression on the incumbent. The incoming British ambassador to Washington, Nigel Sheinwald, advised Downing Street: 'You will find it much harder to establish a working relationship with the new administration if you have not already established a very close relationship with the Bush White House. There is a big carry-over.'[90] Brown's team listened, even if, as it turned out, the advice was incorrect. The Prime Minister himself had a deep knowledge of, and regard for, the US, particularly its political history, and had regularly holidayed in Cape Cod, where he enjoyed close personal relationships with the New England Democrat elite, including Senator Ted Kennedy. Brown counted US pollster Bob Shrum as one of his closest transatlantic friends and, as a young Labour MP, he had attended the 1984 Democratic National Convention in San Francisco, and developed a bond with Bill Clinton long before the Arkansas Governor secured the party's nomination for the presidency in 1992.

'The US relationship was a big thing for us. Our worry was: "How do we pull this relationship off and get it right without us doing a Tony?"' says a senior adviser.[91] A change of tone was set by Foreign Office minister Lord Malloch-Brown, an outspoken critic of US foreign policy during his time at the UN, who said on 13 July that the US and Britain would no longer be 'joined at the hip'.[92] Douglas Alexander, the new International Development Secretary, then made a speech in the US championing multilateralism, forcing Number 10 to deny that this was intended to mark a new, post-Blair direction in Britain's relations with its key ally.[93] Brown's first overseas trips were to Europe, not to the US: he visited Angela Merkel in Berlin on 16 July and Nicolas Sarkozy on 20 July: 'We wanted to signal a change from Tony's style: it was deliberate. We were clear that the first trip wasn't going to be to the US,' says an adviser involved.[94]

To the White House, Gordon Brown was 'a largely unknown person', as recalled by David Manning, British ambassador to the US until the autumn of 2007.[95] The administration was not hostile to him, but they were distinctly apprehensive of him. The change was an unwelcome distraction to them, and they would have much preferred it 'had Blair – the guy they knew and who they had been through the rapids with – remained as Prime Minister and seen Bush out'.[96] John Sawers, British ambassador to the UN in New York, noticed some wariness from the US administration towards Brown as a result of his role in precipitating his predecessor's departure from office.[97] This meant Blair's help was needed and he reassured Bush that, in Brown, he would find 'an ally' and 'a man of stature and substance'.[98] During video conversations with Bush in his final weeks as Prime Minister, Blair told the President that Brown shared their evaluation of Iraq.[99] Blair also advised Brown on how he had to present himself to the White House. 'They are worried that you won't be tough enough,' he said, and suggested that News International would become concerned 'if Gordon tried to break the consensus', recalls Balls.[100] Before Brown became Prime Minister, Manning also spoke to the White House to reassure them himself about continuity over Iraq.[101] Their principal worry was that Brown would go the way of Romano Prodi of Italy and José Zapatero of Spain, and distance the UK from the US strategy. The White House was taking no chances. Within ten minutes of his arrival at Number 10 on 27 June, Leeanne Johnston, Brown's diary secretary, told him: 'The President is on the phone.' Bush was the first head of state to congratulate the new Prime Minister, and during the call, Brown sought to reassure the President that he would stand firm on Iraq.[102] The country then forced itself on to Brown's first Cabinet agenda when news came in that three British soldiers had been killed while on duty in Basra.[103]

Bush and Brown had spoken some weeks beforehand when Blair arranged for the then Chancellor to visit the White House before he took over as Prime Minister.[104] As Brown was not yet a head of government, protocol prevented him from having a formal meeting in the Oval Office; according to Simon McDonald, this was circumvented by organising a meeting with National Security Advisor Steve Hadley, with an expectation that the President would 'drop by'.[105] Brown had been talking to Hadley for just a couple of minutes when the latter said: 'Any minute I should warn you the President will enter.' Bush impressed Brown with his preparations for the encounter. 'I admire your passion for Africa,' was one of the President's opening gambits, and they talked about the role of faith on the continent, striking up an immediate rapport. Bush impressed not only Brown, but also his team. 'He remembered little people like us. He remembered our names. He knew about us. He asked us about our families,' says one on the trip.[106]

However, as Brown entered Number 10, no immediate word had come through about the date of a formal meeting in the US, which the Prime Minister hoped would take place later that summer. Out of the blue, about a week in, Hadley called McDonald to say: 'The President wants to invite the new Prime Minister to the United States and he wants to do something special for him, so he's going to invite him to Camp David.'[107] Brown was immediately cast into 'a panic of indecision'.[108] A visit to the President's country retreat was better than he had expected. Top dollar on Bush's menu was a stay on his private ranch in Crawford, Texas – something very personal to him and an honour afforded to Blair, but very few other foreign leaders. The usual offer was thirty minutes in the Oval Office, so this invitation was 'the very best thing he could offer a new leader', according to McDonald.[109] Yet 'Brown dithered for a week whether to accept,' recalls an official.[110] Of course, he knew he had to accept with gratitude, and this was duly communicated to the White House. The date was fixed for 29 to 30 July, and, as the time approached, intensive discussions took place in Downing Street about how to handle what would be Brown's 'first major test on the international stage'.[111] His team were prepared to work with Bush, despite their ideological differences, but they were adamant that this was not to be the 'pally' relationship that Blair had, but was to be solidly 'professional'.[112] On a conference call from McDonald's room in the Cabinet Office with Hadley, the Number 10 team were so insistent that there would be no informal shots of the two leaders together at Camp David that Hadley said, only half-jokingly: 'You do realise that it is your visit to us.'[113] The attitude of the Brown team to the White House at that point was 'schizophrenic'.[114]

As he took to the air, the Prime Minister put out a press release stating: 'The United States is our single most important bilateral relationship.'[115] After arriving at Andrews Air Force Base, he and his team took the President's helicopter to Camp David where Bush collected Brown in a golf buggy. This caught Brown off guard and, according to one present, the Downing Street team joked that this was Bush's 'revenge' for their insistence on the meeting being kept formal.[116] Selecting the right clothes had loomed surprisingly large among Brown's concerns; Camp David is in the woods of Maryland and the outdoors experience that it offers requires guests to dress appropriately, but Brown is not a 'dress-down' kind of person. As one insider comments: 'Gordon's apprehensions about the visit had as much to do with sartorial points as with questions about what he should be saying to the archpriest of American capitalism.'[117] On their first evening Bush and Brown went to a Camp David cabin for a private dinner while their teams dined together. The President deliberately wore a tie and jacket for the first day, in deference to Brown: it was perhaps the only time during his presidency that Bush donned formal wear at the retreat.[118] Brown returned to his team early, tired because of the time difference, but told them that the dinner had gone well. He expressed surprise that Bush had not wanted to talk shop, but made the conversation personal, discussing Scotland, his family and his childhood.[119] Bush was struck by the way Brown had overcome both the devastating blow of the loss of his eye and the still-profounder tragedy of losing his baby daughter, Jennifer. After dinner, the Number 10 team played ten-pin bowling with the Americans, who beat them convincingly.[120]

The substance of the meeting was tabled for discussion on 30 July, with Iraq the main topic on the agenda. Morning discussions, however, were overtaken by the emerging prospect of a war between Israel and Syria. The CIA and MI6 had learned from the Israeli intelligence service that Damascus was working on a covert nuclear project and the Israeli government wanted the White House to take immediate action. Brown was flattered to be included in the debate on how best to respond, and the consensus was that such a course would be precipitous. Instead, they encouraged the Israelis to apply diplomatic pressure on Syria and take the issue to the International Atomic Energy Agency. In the end, the Israelis decided to take matters into their own hands, bombing the Syrian facility later in 2007.[121] The issue of Darfur was also raised, and Brown was surprised to find Bush highly responsive: it was obvious to all present that both leaders shared a genuine and profound commitment to improving conditions on the continent.

On Iraq, the White House knew that the UK's role was set to change as Blair had already said publicly in February 2007 that the British Army had to 'reposition' itself, reducing the number of its troops in the Basra region to 5,500. British forces had effectively withdrawn from three of the four provinces in southern Iraq over which it had a UN peacekeeping mandate, and Brown now reiterated that their role would also steadily diminish in the fourth province. The Prime Minister said that, with the exception of some 500 soldiers who would remain at Basra Palace, the remaining contingent would be relocated to Basra Airbase, where they would focus on training the Iraqi army, who were to take on prime responsibility for security. This phased withdrawal contrasted starkly with the Americans' 'surge' under General Petraeus, in response to the Sunni insurgency in Baghdad. The key point for Bush's team was to avoid Brown saying in public that he wanted to leave Iraq quickly, as this would cause considerable embarrassment.[122] The US administration was reassured by the confirmation that the withdrawal of British troops from southern Iraq would be weighed according to 'factors on the ground' – i.e. on military advice rather than political considerations – and that the White House would be kept informed at every step.

American anxieties had not been imaginary. Brown had been under heavy pressure to accelerate the withdrawal, not only from those in the Labour Party who had been most opposed to Blair's policy, but also from senior figures in the military, who wanted to concentrate their forces on Afghanistan. Chief of the General Staff Richard Dannatt had outlined his thinking on this in a speech in October 2006. Within Brown's own team, ultras like Balls wanted to quit Iraq as quickly as possible: Damian McBride had leaked to the London *Evening Standard* that Simon McDonald's prime job was to get Britain out of Iraq as quickly as possible 'without the US minding overly much'.[123] 'Brown came under huge pressure to get out quickly, with many telling him they wanted a new direction in Iraq,' recalls Matt Cavanagh, Brown's adviser on Iraq in the policy unit. 'Countervailing pressures, not the least from Blair, emphasised the risks of alienating the press and public if it looked like a "scuttle",' he adds.[124] In June and July, Brown spent much time in the lead-up to the US visit reading papers on Iraq and talking to all concerned. In the end, a Number 10 aide explains that the argument carrying most force was that 'if we pulled out too quickly we would run the risk of Iraq imploding after we left'.[125] A powerful second factor was concern that a rapid pull-out would be strongly resisted and resented by the US, who were planning to take over when the British left.[126]

While Chancellor, Brown had been heavily involved in economic regeneration in Palestine. He had become a firm believer that injections of capital could redevelop areas ravaged by conflict and was convinced that the same approach could be applied to Iraq.[127] Brown outlined to the Americans his personal desire to shift the British emphasis from military force to taking a lead on the economic reconstruction of the country, a position he also emphasised in his first call to Iraqi Prime Minster Nouri al-Maliki, on 5 July.[128] Brown believed that showing continued British commitment to helping Iraq, not through counterinsurgency, but economic reconstruction, 'helped heal a very real breach with the Americans'.[129]

The Camp David visit exceeded Brown's expectations on both an official and a personal level. At the concluding lunch on 30 July, US Secretary of State Condoleezza Rice and Foreign Secretary David Miliband flew in from Washington to join the two leaders. Much of the meal was spent discussing the forthcoming presidential election, with Brown and Miliband impressing their American hosts with their interest in, and knowledge of, their country's politics.[130] A short time afterwards, Bush told outgoing British ambassador Manning how pleased he was about his encounter with Brown, and how he now believed they could 'work together fine'.[131]

Brown flew from Camp David to Washington for conversations with Nancy Pelosi and leading Democrats on Capitol Hill, and then stopped off in New York to address the UN. On the return flight to London, he was in good spirits, knowing that he had made the grade, and that the press was positive. The *Washington Post* summed up the spirit with its headline 'More Bulldog Than Poodle'.[132] As the plane sped back through the night, the team talked about their surprise at Bush's ability, his knowledge of the detail of foreign policy and the fact that he could be 'very funny'.[133] McDonald notes: 'Brown was surprised by how much he liked Bush. He found Bush to be much smarter than he had imagined. Bush consulted him and listened to him and that was helpful in building the relationship.'[134] All were struck by Bush being reconciled to his own 'political mortality' without losing any of his commitment to developing fresh relationships. Tom Fletcher, who became the Prime Minister's private secretary shortly after the trip, describes how Brown was drawn in closer and closer to Bush, and his wariness of Blair's relationship with the President soon became a thing of the past. Brown was fascinated by men of power and had not hitherto appreciated what a shrewd operator Bush was in the flesh. He had long speculated on how he would fare up close with the US President. It was a mystery no longer, and Brown chalked him up as an ally – one he was to call on more than he might have imagined.

On his return, Brown hand-wrote a personal letter to Bush: 'I hope you will find that I am straightforward, direct, and will do exactly as I say.'[135] He sent him the book of his father's sermons. To Hadley, gestures like this made a big impact on the President. 'The question that Bush always asked of leaders is: "Is this a person of courage?" That's his test of a leader. That kind of letter said to the President, Brown understands what leadership is,' he recalls.[136] A Number 10 private diary recorded that summer: 'Brown is slowly building atmospherics with Bush but Bush remains the prominent figure.'[137] By the end of the year, insiders felt that Brown had become relaxed with the President, and the balance of power was equalising. They would speak by video link or on the phone roughly once a month (with Blair and Bush it had been approximately every fortnight). Sheinwald says: 'They spoke much more often than [Brown] would later speak to Obama: for Bush, national security was the dominant issue and he invested tremendous personal diplomacy in it.'[138] Their early conversations, though never re-creating the jokey atmosphere of the Blair–Bush relationship, settled into a comfortable rhythm, despite Brown's desire to talk about development and world trade, subjects on which Bush was never entirely at home, least of all with someone whose command of the detail was as precise as the Prime Minister's.[139]

Brown and Foreign Policy

Brown took to foreign policy with an ease that surprised both him and others. In May, the *New Statesman* commented: 'Brown will arrive at Number 10 with only the sketchiest record in foreign affairs.'[140] Yet, during his premiership, international matters came to take almost up to half his time – above all Afghanistan, Iraq, Iran and trade and development. Brown had, perhaps unwisely, shunned Blair's ideas to move him from the Treasury to the Foreign Office to broaden his experience. Before 2005, he had shown little interest in diplomacy beyond attending the spring meetings of the IMF and the World Bank, and the regular 'EcoFin' meetings of EU finance ministers, and showed little sign of liking them, his demeanour frequently verging on the boorish, according to advisers.[141] But Brown was no blank page on international affairs. No other Prime Minister in recent memory had come to office with as strong an instinct for appreciating the challenges and opportunities of globalisation.

Just a month into his premiership, he delivered a wide-ranging speech to the United Nations in which he lambasted his fellow leaders for their collective failure to achieve the Millennium Development Goals and called for the forging of 'a new global alliance for peace and prosperity'.[142] They were themes he would return to again and again throughout his premiership. Over time, he would refine them into an agenda on the international stage that was more powerful, and more coherent, than any he would develop in the domestic arena.

If anything, Brown's aversion to foreign policy had been less the result of a lack of interest than of personal style. He was wary of the Foreign Office and had an inverted snobbery about the public-school background of many of the UK's ambassadors, preferring to stay in hotels rather than British embassies on official trips abroad. When, in November 2005, Brown announced he planned to stay with the British ambassador, Sherard Cowper-Coles, on a trip to Riyadh, Saudi Arabia, the Foreign Office's permanent secretary sent anxious messages about the importance of making a good impression on the man who was highly likely to become the next Prime Minister.[143]

At Number 10 Brown was to develop close relationships with very few ambassadors: Peter Westmacott in Paris, Kim Darroch at the EU, and Dickie Stagg in Delhi being rare exceptions.[144] John Sawers at the UN was a particular favourite: in 2009 Brown sent his foreign policy adviser, Tom Fletcher, on a secret mission to New York to persuade him to become the Prime Minister's National Security Adviser, but Sawers took up an offer to become head of MI6 instead.[145] Brown was often impatient with the advice he received from the Foreign Office, even though he was more assiduous than Blair in reading his briefs. His private office in Number 10 would often edit the advice, knowing it would irritate him. Brown made it clear on his arrival in Number 10 that he did not 'do glad-handing', and often became impatient when the Foreign Office demanded he see an international dignitary. 'Why the fuck are you making me do this?' he would complain to Fletcher before almost every such meeting.[146] Brown saw all foreign leaders, institutions and indeed the Foreign Office purely as a means of furthering his principal aims, which were economic development and ameliorating the world economy. An instinctive Atlanticist, he was also no lover of the EU.

As September rolled around, Brown was busy in Downing Street preparing for his first party conference. His mood was upbeat. His Cabinet composition had gone down well, the Parliamentary Labour Party was happy with him, and the Blairites appeared to have buried the hatchet. The first elements of his domestic agenda had been rolled out, and met with praise both from liberals and those on the right. He had enjoyed a successful first meeting with Bush and found a way forward on Iraq, crises had been dealt with and the Labour Party's poll ratings were high. The one slight cause for concern was his wooden performances at PMQs in the Commons, where he appeared less sure of himself. Nonetheless, the British public were warming to their prosaic new Prime Minister. Yes, he lacked the charm of his predecessor, but the public had become tired of Blair's strutting ways and were in the mood for change. Sensing this, Brown's advisers even sought to turn his perceived weaknesses into assets and the advertising agency Saatchi & Saatchi came up with the slogan 'Not Flash, just Gordon'. No wonder he was happy. In the words of one senior adviser: 'It couldn't have gone better.'[147] At last in the job he had craved for so long, he had used his first weeks to build a powerful base for the year ahead.

Questions Emerge: September

How deep did the foundations go? By mid-September, questions were beginning to be raised on a number of fronts. The answers to them would determine the success of his premiership.

First, was the Brown policy agenda sufficiently meaty? Even before the transition, Brown's advisers at the Treasury were worried that there was not enough substance, especially in the public-service areas where Brown had let Blair take the lead and where he lacked a strong instinctive agenda of his own.[148] As the summer played out, these worries became more pronounced. 'Looking back, it was all pretty naïve,' says one present. 'We had it good for the first forty days with our detailed grid, but after that, it was flat.'[149] Nick Pearce adds: 'Having a policy deliberately designed to contrast with Blair was enough to get us through the first weeks, but it was no agenda for the future.'[150] What Brown had presented to the country was a political strategy not a programme for government; it was all about positioning him as a 'father of the nation' figure. Much of his 'change' agenda was symbolic and presentational, and explicitly intended to address his own critics in the party and country. There were hints of new policy – on constitutional reform and public services – but no firm decisions were taken and, in stark contrast to his early period as Chancellor, there were no major policy announcements to define his first 100 days. 'He didn't want to face up to the difficult choices,' says Balls. In particular, Brown's indecisiveness on how much to distance himself from Blair would become a running theme. 'Gordon simply couldn't make up his mind up whether or not he represented continuity or change, so we ended up with a fudge,' Balls adds.[151]

The seriousness of these concerns first became apparent as advisers gathered to draft Brown's first speech as Prime Minister to the Labour Party conference. 'There didn't seem to be a plan,' one senior adviser recalls. 'It was very strange. The conversation was dominated by throwing slogans around. As I sat there I thought, what is this government actually about?'[152] Some hoped that Brown's undoubted 'values' would provide them with direction, 'but they didn't seem to'.[153] Michael Jacobs, at the policy unit, recalls a meeting of Brown's inner circle in July. He witnessed them 'knocking around alternative narratives of the most fundamental kind' and concluded: 'The stereotype really seemed to be true – they were effectively saying: "Now we've got here, why are we here?" They had no idea what they were going to do.'[154] One former minister says: 'It surprised us all, especially those close to Tony, that there had been so much anger in late 2006 and early 2007 because Gordon had been saying that we were stymieing his mission. But there was nothing. I don't understand it. I can't understand it. I simply cannot explain to you why Gordon had no plan.'[155] Why was the initial agenda not fuller? It was a question that would be returned to again and again.

A second question mark hung over the team at Number 10. By the end of July, although they were patting themselves on the back, several old hands were saying that the operation was not working properly, and there was an almost complete lack of clarity about who was in charge.[156] Douglas Alexander realised the full extent of the problem in August, when he travelled to Afghanistan and was told by a senior Foreign Office official: 'Downing Street is utterly hopeless. You can't get an answer out of them.' Alexander began to get worried once he realised that the concerns had spread as far as Kabul.[157] He immediately reported his concerns back to Number 10, but they went unheeded.

Blair's Downing Street operation, with Powell and Campbell, as well as Anji Hunter and Sally Morgan, had once been derided by Brown's team at the Treasury, but now it began to be spoken about wistfully, almost with awe. The absence of a political chief of staff in Brown's Number 10 was felt particularly keenly.[158] Tom Scholar, who had joined the team in July, was much more comfortable as a principal private secretary than as a political enforcer. He had neither an interest in nor the mandate for the latter role, and had been handicapped both by not being part of the transition team and his absence during Brown's first weeks. 'It would have been crazy for Cameron not to have had his chief of staff by his side from day one,' says one adviser.[159] Worse, Scholar was never given the authority by Brown to get on with the job, so never became properly established.[160] Brown wanted his former praetorians, Balls, Ed Miliband and Alexander, with him at Number 10, and was frustrated that they were now busy with their own careers.

The inexperience of Brown's team, which was mainly made up of old Treasury hands, rapidly became obvious, in particular on the press and strategic communications side. They had coped well with the more limited field of economic policy, but were dangerously stretched by the broad canvas, constant pressure and unpredictability of life in Number 10. One of the handful of figures that worked for both Blair and Brown believes that Balls made a major error in disbanding the Blairite structures and 'de-politicising' Number 10 by placing so many civil servants in the key positions.[161] More alarmingly a number of Brown's inner circle believed that Balls deliberately set out to create a weak and emasculated Number 10, which he could easily dominate. The first few weeks also saw early signs of the factionalism that bedevilled Number 10 in 2008 and early 2009. Whereas some members of Brown's old Treasury team, such as Nye, Kelly and Wood, willingly integrated themselves, and Brown was prompted early on to go around the building meeting the staff, a small clique comprising McBride, Livermore and Ellam set themselves apart. One official who witnessed the transition says: 'Right from the start they were secretive and cliquey, as they had been at the Treasury.'[162]

Difficulties were compounded by Brown himself being unsure of what he needed. 'He would have the team in and berate them for not supporting him, but we'd say: "We don't know what you're trying to do."'[163] A long-standing adviser says: 'It was so striking that he didn't have a plan for his premiership. It was so much in contrast to how he had been in 1994 to 1997.'[164] Under Blair, many of the matters that required decision were handled by Powell, and only the most important went up to the Prime Minister. But within weeks, Brown was acting as his own chief of staff. Every decision was coming to him, and he had neither the space, nor time to focus. It was a mess.[165] Brown soon confided to one of his closest friends: 'Every day I get up with a clear idea of what I want to achieve, and within thirty minutes something comes along which fucks it all up.'[166]

Then, of course, there was the economy. Brown's reputation had been largely built upon his performance as Chancellor over the preceding ten years. Unlike Blair in May 1997, he did not arrive at Downing Street on the crest of the wave of a landslide victory and a personal mandate. He needed the guarantee of continued economic growth all the more if he was to sustain his premiership. But all was not well.

Northern Rock, a large bank based in Newcastle, had issued a profit warning as Brown moved in to Number 10, causing its share price to fall by 10 per cent that day. Although she was constantly travelling for her new job at the Department for International Development, Shriti Vadera was still able to pick up increasing concerns from the market. Before the summer break she told Brown and Darling that the Treasury was being too docile and they needed to find out more about what was going on. As the summer progressed she became increasingly worried and spoke again to Brown, airing her anxieties about the severe turbulence in the commodity markets. Brown began to turn his attention to the US, where the money markets were experiencing increasing difficulties as a result of the unravelling of investments based on 'sub-prime' mortgages. By August, the problems were spreading across the global financial system with the result that credit markets were in dire trouble. On 10 August, the FTSE 100 suffered its biggest drop for more than four years. Brown's initial thinking – or hope – was that his stewardship of the economy had insulated Britain from the upheavals. On 11 August, he said on the BBC that Britain was in 'as good a shape as it could be to weather the storm'.[167]

Two days later, Northern Rock told the Financial Services Authority (FSA) that it was facing potentially serious difficulties. Mervyn King, the Governor of the Bank of England, was informed on 14 August and the Treasury alerted the following day, but it took until 29 August for Darling to be told in writing that the FSA believed Northern Rock was 'running into quite substantial problems'. Emergency discussions between Darling, the Bank of England and the FSA did not provide lasting solutions. Northern Rock was forced on 13 September to ask the Bank for emergency financial assistance to make up the shortfall on its day-to-day operations. When BBC journalist Robert Peston broke the news at 8.30 that evening, panic ensued and, on 14 September, long queues formed outside Northern Rock branches, marking the first run on a UK bank for more than a century. Darling came under attack for not immediately guaranteeing customers' savings, which he finally did on the BBC's *Today* programme on 17 September. However, his words had little effect on the queues or the sense of panic; Northern Rock shares fell promptly by 40 per cent, forcing the Chancellor to announce a new plan to guarantee 100 per cent of deposits in time for the six o'clock news bulletins that evening. This time the queues did disperse and the bank's share price rose by 16 per cent. The problem appeared to go away as quickly as it had arisen. Britain's reputation for financial regulation may have been undermined, but there was no apparent political damage to the government or Brown's own standing. The Prime Minister returned to his preparations for the imminent party conference, unaware that the financial woes would return with a vengeance before the end of the year. The episode had a lasting effect on the Chancellor's relationship with the Bank of England. Darling was very disconcerted by Mervyn King's comments about Northern Rock: their relationship deteriorated and never properly improved.

Brown's record until 2007 showed he possessed many leadership skills, including high intelligence, sophisticated political nous and prodigious energy. But the thirteen years of waiting had left scars. The first two months in power had helped to convince many that those scars were healing. He had created an impression of strength, gravitas and bipartisanship. But serious questions remained, not least of which was how fundamental was the redesign? In the months ahead, Brown would need to answer firmly the growing doubts about his agenda, his newly formed Downing Street operation, and the stability of the economy he had helped build. He would need to show he was harnessing his known strengths in the job, while developing new abilities to take big decisions, communicate effectively and get the best from his team. He would also need to show that he had truly left behind those weaknesses he had displayed in the past. Gus O'Donnell commented that Brown found the transition to Number 10 difficult, but so do most incoming Prime Ministers, taking over a job for which nothing can fully prepare them.[168] Brown possessed some inner qualities vital to the role, but an outer shell scarred by events. The question was, under pressure, which would dominate? He was about to find out.

2

Savage Autumn

(September to November 2007)

Brown badly needed a confident autumn during which he would retain the initiative and keep the pressure on David Cameron's faltering Conservatives. The polls were looking optimistic. If he could carry the strong position into the New Year, it would provide the springboard for him to call a general election in May or June 2008. 'It was somewhere between "implicit and explicit" that the election would come then,' says Ed Balls. 'It was never in his mind to do the full three years.'[1] But instead of an autumn in control, through a series of savage events Brown lost the initiative. His premiership never fully recovered.

The 'Brown Bounce': Summer

When he came to power, no one had foreseen an election as early as the autumn.[2] 'When Gordon Brown spoke on the steps of Downing Street when he became Prime Minister, no one was thinking of an election in just three or four months,' says Douglas Alexander.[3] Blair's record was forever at the forefront of Brown's mind. Blair – albeit with Brown's considerable help – had fought and won three general elections. Brown did not want to fight one and lose it. Even before he became Prime Minister in late June, there had been press speculation that he would try to call an election to win the mandate that he was lacking. His response was an emphatic 'no early election', and that a new Prime Minister does not need a new mandate.

In July, Spencer Livermore, in his capacity of director of political strategy for Brown, had become captivated by the Brown 'bounce' in the polls, and began to wonder whether an election in the autumn of 2007 might not be preferable to the early summer of 2008. 'July was going very well: events we could never have anticipated like the floods had moved polls in our favour. I thought: "Why don't I try out with a few people the idea of an autumn election?"'[4] But Livermore's audacious idea fell on deaf ears in Number 10, with Brown the most reluctant. 'Gordon was not at all keen on going early. In his own mind, he thought early summer 2008, that would be a year since he took over,' recalls Fiona Gordon.[5] Brown, however, did not kill talk of a poll: the idea of destabilising Cameron by the prospect of an early election appealed to him. But on the substance, he was clear. Brown was no ingénu: he knew all new Prime Ministers enjoy a honeymoon and that they never last for long. His fear was less that he would lose, going down as the shortest-serving holder of the office in modern history, and more that he would end up as a lame duck with a smaller majority than the sixty-six that Blair had won in the May 2005 election. Much of his advice within Number 10 disagreed with this verdict: sure, the party's majority might fall, but it would be outweighed by the benefit of Brown gaining his own mandate, which would transform his premiership, and they wondered whether Labour's position would ever be as good again.[6]

Proponents of an autumn election were bolstered by the Ealing Southall by-election on 19 July. Despite five visits from Cameron to the constituency during the campaign, the Labour candidate won with 41 per cent of the vote. Alexander, as Labour's election coordinator, began conducting an audit of the party's election capability with Peter Watt, Labour's general secretary. A few days after the by-election, they presented the findings to Brown in the Cabinet Room, arguing that the longer Labour went without calling an election, the greater the gulf in spending with the Tories, who were being funded by Lord Ashcroft and other rich benefactors.[7]

On 26 July, a political cabinet was held at Chequers: the Cabinet and other senior ministers attended, but not civil servants. This was party politics stuff, not suitable for officials. With the mood very upbeat, Alexander gave a presentation on the state of the party and pollster Deborah Mattinson presented her latest findings, showing Labour on an 8 per cent lead. Her analysis suggested that on every policy area except immigration Labour led the Tories, and that Brown's message of 'change' was well received by the general public. The Prime Minister's personal ratings were high too, and he was felt to trump Cameron in all but 'likeability'.[8] 'I remember the day was very sunny and there was a great sense of optimism which was incredibly infectious. The day had the air of a new beginning. There was a sense that we could really do things,' recalls Northern Ireland Secretary Shaun Woodward.[9] The prospect of an autumn election was not mentioned, but after the meeting was over, as the ministerial cars were arriving at the front door to whisk their masters away, a small group consisting of Brown, Alexander, Livermore and Sue Nye convened in the Chequers front hall. Livermore told them that his confidential opinion was that they should think very seriously about 'going early'. 'You mean next April?' Brown asked. 'No, when I say early, I mean properly early,' Livermore responded.[10] Brown laughed and dismissed the idea.[11] Winding up Cameron was all very well, but he had no intention of giving time to election preparations. His mind was already on the Camp David visit. Ministers present that day, however, clearly got wind of the fact that the autumn might be a possibility, and when back in London began to talk about it. Inevitably it leaked to the press, giving rise to further speculation in Westminster, heightened when, the day after the Chequers meeting, the polls showed Labour on 41 per cent – nine points clear of the Conservatives. 'The politicians were very excited about it,' says one senior adviser. 'They didn't realise quite what a bubble they were creating.'[12] But with Number 10 immersed in the trip to the United States, the subject disappeared off the radar.

Livermore went on holiday to Italy that August. His mind kept returning to the advantages of an autumn election. It became almost an obsession. When he returned mid-month, he went straight into Number 10 and tapped out a two-and-a-half-side, highly secret document in which he laid out the arguments for and against going early. 'It's obviously the right thing to do,' he thought to himself. 'It would be insane not to go for it.'[13] A key factor was his anxiety about a decision in Brown's final Budget as Chancellor, in the spring of 2007, to remove the 10p tax band, which he foresaw would play very badly with Labour's traditional voters when it came into force in the spring of 2008.[14] He was aware of the need for extreme confidentiality with the note, and made just one copy, which he presented to Brown in the 'den' at the end of the Cabinet Room. Balls, Ed Miliband and Alexander were all present, and Brown passed the note around. The attraction of going early was considerable, but the risks were enormous. Nothing was decided at the meeting. Brown barely gave the idea much thought over the next ten days, his mind very much focused on the forthcoming party conference. He would later tell Livermore that he deeply 'regretted' not using those ten crucial days to decide one way or the other.[15] The memo also included two critical pieces of advice. The first was that discussions should be conducted in strictest privacy. The second was that a final decision must be made before Labour conference.[16] Brown was to ignore both.

Livermore's memo divided opinion within the group. Ed Miliband was against going early, in part because he had responsibility for the manifesto, and he doubted that the policy work could be completed in time. Balls took a similar view, albeit not as strongly, and did not rule out continuing discussions. Like Brown, he recognised that talk of an election was making life uncomfortable for the Tory leadership. The most enthusiastic of the three was Alexander, who had been emboldened by his audit of the Labour Party's capability: the party had invested in technology to ensure that in a short campaign it could send centrally produced but localised literature to circumvent the growing funding advantage of the Conservatives.[17] His case was strengthened by a YouGov poll that had appeared on 12 August, putting Labour ten points ahead of the Conservatives on 42 per cent. The Prime Minister was unimpressed. 'It won't last. It means nothing,' he told one adviser.[18]

Speculation Mounts: September

When politicians began to trickle back to London after the August bank holiday, speculation about an early election began to wax. At the end of August, Brown met veteran Labour politician Roy Hattersley in Edinburgh, who asked about the election. Brown was very cool, saying the polls made it hard to justify, and he wanted more time to prove himself. Hattersley left convinced that he did not want to go early.[19] But others were taking no chances. The Conservatives had drawn up an emergency manifesto, as was revealed in a memo leaked to the press on 17 August. Four days later, Labour announced it had received £1.5m in funding. On 24 August, Cameron launched his 'Broken Britain' agenda, claiming he was ready for the election. On 30 August, his party began inviting advertising agencies to pitch for its general election contract, while on 31 August, the *Daily Telegraph* suggested that Brown should go now after a YouGov poll placed Labour on 41 per cent, eight clear points ahead of the Conservatives.[20]

By early September, Cabinet ministers were busy discussing the prospect of an early election with each other, but opinion was divided. Transport Secretary Ruth Kelly was one of the first to form a strong view, believing that the party should go to the country in the autumn.[21] Jacqui Smith, who held a marginal seat, felt ready, too. But others were sceptical, believing that the party was not sufficiently organised.[22] Naturally, the Cabinet looked to Brown for leadership, but his position was studiously noncommittal. 'Gordon didn't sum up his own position. It was classic Gordon Brown: nothing to do with me,' says one Cabinet minister.[23] 'It was an awkward phase when we were all left waiting,' says another.[24] But Brown knew it was risky to express his own views because he worried about his colleagues leaking information to the press. As his Cabinet looked to him for guidance on one of the pivotal decisions of his premiership, Brown left them to draw their own conclusions.

Still the momentum built. Within his inner circle, the balance of opinion had now tilted towards calling an election. Even Ed Miliband, the most sceptical, was beginning to thaw.[25] Alexander became even more of an advocate. 'I became convinced in September, that if we were to win a fourth

term, it would require audacity. I was always aware of the massive risks, but I
felt we could win,' he recalls.[26] Bowing to the pressure, on 7 September, Brown
gave an explicit instruction to 'get the party ready', though falling far short of a
commitment to proceed with an election. Alexander began to prepare the party
in earnest for a campaign, finalising the process of selecting an advertising
agency.[27] David Muir, who had been brought in by Alexander from the
advertising industry, supervised the competition. On 14 September, Saatchi &
Saatchi won the advertising contract with the slogan 'Not Flash, Just Gordon',
thought brilliantly to sum up Brown's serious-minded approach to being Prime
Minister, in contrast to the razzmatazz, not to say superficiality, of Blair. On
16 September, the BBC reported that Brown was set to announce the election
at the Labour Party conference and on 19 September – the day that he met
high-profile former New York mayor, Rudy Giuliani, in London – an ICM
poll in *The Guardian* put Labour still on 40 per cent and the Conservatives on
32 per cent. That day a meeting was held at Number 10, in which Mattinson
presented the latest internal polling, highlighting the benefits of an early
election, but without conclusively pointing to a significant Labour majority.
Three days later, the first poll since the run on Northern Rock, carried out by
YouGov, had Labour still six points ahead, which was seen as a positive sign.

Brown, ever the party politician, understood the advantages of maintaining
pressure on the Conservatives, but in his heart remained cautious, still wary over
whether the benefits of an autumn election outweighed the profound dangers.
Some believed he was set against. 'Brown never intended to hold an election. He
enjoyed taunting the Conservatives about the possibility, but it was not a risk he
was willing to take,' said one minister.[28] Veteran US pollster, Stan Greenberg,
was another who questioned Brown's seriousness. A week before the conference
he thought Brown would not go for it.[29] Livermore, the strongest advocate of
going early, kept in regular touch with the Prime Minister, but was not able to
extract a definite answer from him. 'Gordon's reaction, in effect, was: "I've spent
my life trying to get here. I'm not going to gamble it within three months. It
could all go terribly wrong,"' he recalls.[30] Team Brown, however, were firming
up their conviction almost day by day. As they surveyed the months ahead – the
looming 10p tax issue, the likely deterioration of the economy, and the endemic
problems that all long-serving administrations suffer – they were concluding:
'This wasn't just Gordon's best chance of winning, it was Gordon's only chance.'[31]
Dan Corry adds: 'A number of us also believed that he would not feel his own
man and fulfil his potential as PM until he had his own mandate.'[32]

On 21 September, on the very eve of the conference, Brown convened a
lunch at Chequers with Alexander, Livermore, Balls, Ed Miliband, Damian
McBride and Bob Shrum. At the end of the meal, the election topic was raised.
'Look at the polls. There is a clear case for holding one,' said Livermore. 'If

that's the case, we should be much better-prepared,' Brown retorted, rather gracelessly telling his team that if they had wanted an election, they should have cancelled their holidays. 'We needed a holiday. We were all knackered. We need to look at the current situation. Cameron's doing badly. We have a big poll lead,' Livermore replied. Debate raged, concluding with Brown's agreement to commission detailed polling in marginal seats. 'We need to get the work done to see precisely where we stand with the country,' he said.[33] Despite not having made up his mind, Brown's team went away with one further instruction: talk up the possibility with journalists in order to panic Cameron.[34]

Labour and Conservative Party Conferences

After they left Chequers, Brown returned to working intensively on his first party conference speech as Prime Minister.[35] Selected leaks from McBride and Balls had worked their magic. Labour went off to Bournemouth with sections of the media whipping each other up into a frenzy. 'The problem was that it got out of hand and became public. The media found out that there was a deliberative process going on, and that was bound to create huge problems of its own,' says policy adviser Nick Pearce.[36] But Brown was fuelling the fire, allowing his team to talk up the prospect of a poll. Alexander, as election coordinator, responded to journalists' constant queries by telling them: 'No decision has been taken, but we do have a decision to take.' His comments reflected Brown's uncertainty while also acknowledging implicitly that preparations were being made.[37] Balls says now that 'we went into Bournemouth not thinking that we were going to have an early election.'[38] However, he had briefed that there might well be one.[39] Cabinet were bullish. 'Many of us definitely thought it was going to happen,' says a former minister.[40] Labour's regional officers began phoning the constituencies and saying: 'Get ready to go.'[41] In Jacqui Smith's home constituency of Redditch, her offices were geared up, the letterheads and strap lines ready. 'We were quite a long way down the track,' she says.[42] Balls asked his team to open up a campaign office in his constituency.[43]

Brown, who enjoyed conferences and elections, was not, however, in a good mood on the journey to Bournemouth. He was always unsettled when his key lieutenants held different views, and he spent hours talking to them on the phone or in person. Still no clear message emerged, to his intense frustration. In an interview in *The Guardian* that Saturday Alexander was quoted as saying that the party would be 'ready whenever the Prime Minister fired the starting gun',[44] while Balls recorded an interview on Radio 4's *The World This Weekend* in which he tried to quell speculation and leave options open by stressing that 'it was important that the public were allowed to see the political choice' before any election was held.[45] Gavin Kelly, as deputy chief of staff covering political operations, spoke regularly to the Prime Minister, but later confessed: 'I never knew where Gordon was on the election timing.' Weighing most heavily on Brown's mind, he thought, remained his desire to win well and be able to govern, and the fear of ending up with a smaller majority. 'Gordon was extremely nervous of that happening,' Kelly adds.[46] At a meeting on the Saturday before the conference in Brown's suite in the Highcliff Hotel, McBride advised: 'We don't want to shut this one down.'[47] On the Sunday morning, Brown gave a bland interview to Andrew Marr on BBC1, which did nothing to enlighten anyone on his plans; nor did his interview in the *Sunday Times*, which was described as 'robotic'.[48]

All day on Sunday, while finalising his speech, Brown's mind played over the question of timing, and the impact of that judgement on what he should say. The mood in his camp seemed to firm up on the Sunday; Ed Miliband whispered to Balls: 'My God, we've got to do it.'[49] Balls now agreed; with his highly tuned political radar, he was one of the few members of Brown's team to see that the media frenzy now made it impossible to pull back. He told the Prime Minister that he believed most papers would now endorse him, which they would not do in a year's time.[50] Most of the Cabinet had begun to favour an early election by the time they got to Bournemouth. Hoon as Chief Whip was a key voice, and believed that, if there was to be an autumn poll, it should take place before the end of British Summer Time, on 28 October. The Cabinet's 'greybeards', Darling and Straw, in contrast, remained sceptical.[51] Their worry was that Labour supporters might not bother to vote after work if it was dark, and it was believed that a low turn-out would adversely affect the party's vote.

Brown realised disaster loomed if he did not achieve clarity, so he convened an urgent meeting in his hotel suite of Balls, Livermore and Greenberg whom fellow pollster Bob Shrum had advised Brown to consult. Greenberg's advice was unequivocal: 'You will win and you should run, though you will have a reduced majority of forty to fifty seats.'[52] However, he was stunned by what he heard and saw. Brown's speech was only hours away, but his team were frozen in the headlights about the election timing, and hence what agenda he should set out. They had failed entirely to take the advice in Livermore's memo and make a decision before conference. More problematically, they had deliberately stoked up media speculation. Panic was beginning to set in. Greenberg found himself in an impossible position. 'For me to do serious polling on voting intentions, I needed concrete messages to communicate, but the Brown agenda was totally empty, even though Gordon Brown had been waiting for a decade or more,' he says.[53] Greenberg tried to spur Brown on to take the decision, reminding him that politics 'is full of risks'.[54]

Number 10 continued to give out mixed messages on the Sunday. It briefed the media just after the Balls Radio 4 interview went on air to say he had not, in fact, intended to discount the possibility of an election in the autumn. This only added to the confusion, as did Brown's remarks in a question and answer session chaired by the broadcaster Mariella Frostrup. When asked about the likelihood that he would go to the country, he said: 'Charming as you are, Mariella, I think the first person I will have to speak to is the Queen.'[55]

In the days leading up to the conference, the Prime Minister had put in considerable work at Number 10 on the topic most dear to his heart – international development – concentrating on pressing issues such as trade and Sudan. At the conference itself, he was moved by the words of Ikhlass Mohammed, a refugee from Sudan who spoke emotionally about the plight of Darfur.[56] Many anticipated a deeply personal speech, reverberating with his own journey, and discussing his core values, on development, trade, poverty and social justice. As *The Guardian* reported, since June, '[Brown] has given the impression of change, and used that word often ... but this does not yet amount to anything specific'. The paper compared him to 'a skilled aromatherapist [who] has conjured up a relaxing environment, soothing away many of the stresses left by Tony Blair', but had yet to clarify what action he intended to take.[57]

The tone Brown was to adopt in his speech had been foreshadowed in the period immediately leading up to it. Two weeks earlier, at the TUC conference on 10 September, he had spoken about insisting that migrants learn English. On 13 September, he used Margaret Thatcher's visit to Number 10 to reveal a newfound enthusiasm for her achievements. The trip had been arranged several weeks beforehand, against Balls's express advice,[58] in response to a warm letter that she had written Brown on his appointment, and he sensed an opportunity to discomfit the Conservatives at this volatile time. In addition, the Prime Minister had been batting back and forth to his exasperated policy team 'shopping lists of announcements', which he loved to make in his big set-piece speeches.[59]

However, with the continuing uncertainty over election timing, he decided against delivering a speech driven by his core values, opting instead for one tilted towards populism with an eye on an autumn poll. If he was to increase Labour's majority, he needed to bring back voters who had gone over to the Conservatives. Brown's aides compared the approach to President Reagan's successful bid in the 1980s to woo Democrats disillusioned by their party's record.[60] Brown heaped praise on Liam Byrne, one of the rising stars of the Cabinet, who had come to see him shortly after he became Prime Minister to persuade him of the virtues of an 'Australian-style' points-based system to restrict extra EU immigration to the most skilled workers.[61]

The speech was clearly aimed at appealing to a number of key target groups, such as the 'C2' social class, who were unhappy about immigration and its impact on jobs and wages, and women, many of whom were floating voters, according to Labour's polling. 'Like many parents', Brown said, he was concerned how 'our children can be safe'; he was worried about 'binge drinking', and wanted to promote the virtues of 'hard work and doing your duty'. He reminded delegates of the events of the summer and hailed John Smeaton, who had tackled the Glasgow airport bombers, as a 'hero'. At points he sounded almost Churchillian, with phrases such as 'the small number of people on this small island'. A commitment to British values and history ran deep within Brown. 'Gordon Brown was much more of a patriot than is realised,' confirms one eminent British historian.[62] For example, when he became Prime Minister, he noticed empty flagpoles along Whitehall on his drive from Downing Street to the House of Commons and said: 'Why do we leave the flagpoles bare? They should fly the flag.' Thus did the Union flag begin to blossom in central London. His introduction of 'Armed Forces Day' was another result of this patriotism. The most-repeated part of the speech, however, was the populist line promising Labour would support 'British jobs for British workers', a theme he had previously addressed at length in his speech to the TUC.[63]

Away from the conference hall, one of Brown's most significant acts was to attend the annual late-night party held by the *Daily Telegraph*, a paper that had been much courted by McBride. He spoke to guests about his admiration for the publication and its values, as well as his contempt for what he saw as the vacuity of the Conservatives. After he left, guests also expressed their disdain for Cameron and his failure to articulate a clear vision for his party.[64] The Tory leader had been under intense pressure for several months, most notably over his grammar schools policy, and Brown's speech cleverly added to his woes. Political editor Patrick Wintour wrote in *The Guardian* that Brown had 'completed a daring incursion into Tory heartlands, stealing item after item of Conservative clothing. It was unclear if anything was going to be left at all in David Cameron's wardrobe next week.'[65] The *Daily Mail* concluded that 'nobody should be in any doubt that [Brown's] oration has made the election *more* and not less likely'.[66]

In Brown's hotel suite, the consensus was now strongly in favour of proceeding with an election. A YouGov poll taken immediately after his conference speech gave Labour an eleven-point lead. Within two hours of Brown stepping down from the podium, Kelly, Pearce and Dan Corry started to draft the outline of the manifesto. Over the following week, the Policy Unit worked on it flat out, producing a draft of some 25,000 words, the big theme being 'opportunity' and the main policy area education.[67] On the Tuesday evening Mattinson arrived in Brown's conference suite to present the results of the private polling, commissioned before the conference, which she had conducted with Greenberg. It was a critical meeting, and 'unbelievably tense'.[68] Shrum, Nye, Ed Miliband, Alexander and Livermore were all in attendance. Greenberg explained that Labour's central problem was poor performance in what he termed the 'Southern East Middle Class' demographic, where the Tories enjoyed a 5 per cent lead, much to Brown's chagrin. If Labour were to win important marginal constituencies in the South, this was a group of crucial importance: garnering their support had been an implicit goal in Brown's speech the previous day.[69] The Prime Minister was visibly drained, and further distracted by accusations, made by Daniel Finkelstein in *The Times*, that he had been guilty of plagiarism in his conference speech. 'The Finkelstein plagiarism charge really did piss him off,' says one senior adviser.[70] Brown had a real tendency to be side tracked by media stories such as these. He also lost clarity during the meeting because of the way Greenberg presented his polling material using American terminology, which confused and irritated the Prime Minister.[71] He failed to rise above such trivial matters to keep his eye on the wider picture.

Brown's speech may have gone down well with the media, with whom he was still in his honeymoon period, but it did not please either the left or the right of his own party. To arch-Blairite Purnell: 'The speech was a real low point. Brown had an opportunity to define the purpose of his premiership, but the speech lacked any argument.'[72] The left, meanwhile, were upset by the populism, when they had been looking, after thirteen years of Blair, for some 'Old Labour' red meat. The speech even worried members of Brown's close team, already wary of his desire to throw every conceivable policy initiative into his speeches. 'We ran around collecting stats and small policy announcements that didn't add up to a row of beans,' says one.[73] What concerned them most was that it read like 'a shopping list with no overarching narrative' – a further sign of the absence of a clear plan for government.[74] 'We worried it was a smörgåsbord of policies. It would only make sense if there was going to be an election,' says one.[75]

Brown's mind remained in a state of flux about it for the remainder of the conference. On the final day, Thursday, he convened another meeting in his suite where a new poll was presented to him. These findings suggested further grounds for caution. Brown listened attentively and summed up with the words: 'Let us reflect on it.' He asked his staff to commission further research to allow them to take the best possible decision 'when the time came'.[76] Cabinet ministers, none of whom felt they knew what was happening, had become increasingly frustrated over the course of the week by speculation on the election timing. Some objected that there had been no meeting to discuss it. That Thursday, the *Daily Telegraph* published an article saying that Cabinet was split on the issue. It reported that the two core enthusiasts in the 'go now' camp within Brown's inner circle were Alexander and Balls, who were joined in their enthusiasm by the Cabinet 'young guns', such as David Miliband, Ruth Kelly and Purnell. The cautious camp, in contrast, included Alan Johnson, Straw and Darling.[77]

What of Ed Balls? Brown would have been strongly influenced by his opinion, and the School Secretary had given the question of an early poll careful consideration. As Greenberg notes: 'I was surprised by how much thinking Ed Balls had done on this.' In July and August, he had been a sceptic, but by the time of conference 'he and Livermore were the two principal advocates'. Balls's reputation would be badly damaged by the 'election that never was' because many suspected he was behind vicious briefings against his colleagues, but on the election decision itself, he had called it right: he had shared Brown's doubts at the beginning, knowing that the honeymoon could be temporary. And once momentum had built, at Brown's own instigation, he realised more than anyone that pulling back would be suicide. He swung behind the election not only because he believed it could be won, but also because he realised it was too late to cancel.[78] Brown would have no one to blame but himself.

Thus Cabinet ministers and delegates left Bournemouth with no clear idea what was happening. The day after, the last polls appeared giving Labour a double-digit lead, equating to a Commons majority of more than 100. That weekend, Brown went to Chequers. Eager to give the impression that he was entirely relaxed about events, he let it be known that he was entertaining Alan Greenspan, the 81-year-old former Chairman of the US Federal Reserve, and they planned to play a few sets of tennis. 'Brown is great at serving but awful at rallies,' an aide told the *Sunday Times*.[79]

Brown chose to bide his time and keep his own counsel regarding the election, keeping his cards unusually close to his chest. Ever the historian, he contemplated the choices made by his Labour predecessors. Blair's timing in 2001 and 2005 he considered sound, but he knew that Harold Wilson had gone to the country in June 1970 when riding high in the polls; only for the rise in support to prove to be short-lived when there was a large swing to the Tories. Meanwhile, James Callaghan's decision to postpone a poll from the autumn of 1978 to May 1979 was considered to be an equal error, as it led to Margaret Thatcher's first victory. Brown also recalled that the last time there had been an autumn election was thirty-three years before, and Wilson's early election in October 1974 had won him only a narrow majority.

That Sunday, he convened a lunchtime meeting of his closest aides at Chequers. He told them he had still not reached a decision, but wanted several preparatory steps put in place now, in recognition of how narrow the window would be. He would visit Iraq during the Conservative Party conference, to highlight his status as a national leader and statesman, and deflect attention from their deliberations. Five million leaflets (at a cost of over £1m) should be immediately printed for marginal constituencies, more staff taken on at Labour Party headquarters, and the manifesto finalised.[80]

In contrast to the rising euphoria in the Labour camp, the Conservatives were deeply anxious. The party's high command had been wrong-footed by Brown's success as Prime Minister. 'We constantly told ourselves not to underestimate Brown, but we were surprised when he did even better than expected. He seemed to have reinvented himself. It was demoralising,' Tory frontbencher Francis Maude told the historian Peter Snowdon.[81] Cameron's widely criticised trip to Rwanda in late July coincided with rumours of disquiet and a story in the *Sunday Telegraph* that several Conservative MPs were seeking a vote of no confidence in his leadership.[82] 'Morale in the parliamentary party was very low indeed when MPs left for the summer break,' wrote Snowdon. At a shadow Cabinet 'away day' just after Brown's speech, Cameron told his senior team that they had to 'perform the biggest turnaround in a party's poll fortune in modern political history'.[83] Press reports on the eve of his conference suggested that the Conservative leader was 'very down'.[84] The media was in agreement: this was make-or-break time for Cameron. The pressure was on.

The party was petrified that Brown would call the general election for the autumn – some even speculating he would announce it in the middle of their conference – so its hidden strategy was 'all about spooking Gordon Brown into not calling the election by the end of the week'.[85] Cameron had to call Brown's bluff. On Sunday 30 September, he looked deliberately calm in front of the television cameras and said he would relish an early election – he was ready. Nevertheless, Labour went into that week by far the stronger party, but emerged in shreds. Why?

Out of the blue came a Tory move that left Labour reeling: shadow Chancellor George Osborne's announcement on the Monday that his party planned to raise the threshold for paying inheritance tax to £1m. At a stroke, this would exempt some nine million voters from much-resented 'death taxes'. To pay for it, Osborne devised a new charge of a £25,000 levy on 'non-doms' – wealthy foreign residents of the UK.

Before the 2007 Budget, Brown's own team had debated populist alternatives to please the electorate, including a 2p cut in income tax funded by the removal of the 10p tax band, as well as raising the inheritance-tax threshold. Had the latter option been selected, it would have pulled the rug from under Osborne and avoided the 10p tax revolt in 2008.[86] Brown came 'close' to choosing this option, according to Treasury officials, but was deterred by the £1bn cost.[87] Moreover, Balls strongly opposed the move.[88] It was thus doubly galling for Brown's team to watch Osborne pull off a populist coup that could have been their own. Livermore was watching coverage of Osborne's speech with Alexander at Labour headquarters in London's Victoria. 'That's it, we can't have an election,' he told Brown.[89] Advisers were in no doubt about the significance. 'It was the turning point,' says one.[90]

Osborne's coup de grâce put Labour in a flat spin. How can it have come as a surprise? Inexplicably, Brown's team had failed to foresee that the Conservatives might respond to the pressure of a possible election. They had talked up an early poll to spook them, but had failed to look even one move ahead. Now it was they who were on the defensive. On the Monday and Tuesday, Brown had long phone calls with Balls in which they debated how to react. Suddenly, the whole dynamic had changed, and the possibility of an early election looked in jeopardy. They came up with a plan to raise the inheritance-tax threshold, but not as high as the £1m Osborne had proposed. Ed Miliband was told to include it in the manifesto, and Darling to put it in the imminent Pre-Budget Report.[91]

Brown's opportunistic plan to upstage the Conservatives with a visit to Iraq on the Tuesday of their conference now fell flat on its face. Following his Camp David visit in July, conditions in Basra on the ground had continued to deteriorate. Brown had discussed the position with Nigel Sheinwald when the latter visited Number 10 before flying to Washington to take up his role as British ambassador at the end of the summer. They discussed US sensitivities about a military withdrawal, and the Prime Minister stressed that, despite the strains that the troops were under, they should leave in a way that showed that, despite the loss of so many soldiers' lives, their mission had achieved a positive end.[92] During his surprise trip to Basra, Brown announced that 1,000 troops would be brought home by Christmas, reducing the overall number to 4,500. The fact that the departure of 500 of these troops had already been revealed the previous month heightened scepticism about his motivations. John Major, in a rare sally into front-line politics, told the BBC: 'This is a statement that should probably have been made to Parliament. Brown is marching to the drumbeat of an election.'[93] The trip and announcement were quickly seen as a cheap stunt, especially because of the delicacy of Britain's position in Iraq, and it damaged Brown's standing with the right, which he had worked so painstakingly to build the week before.

Cameron knew that he was fighting not just for his party, but also for his own future, and would have to deliver an even stronger performance on Wednesday 3 October than in Blackpool two years previously. The original plan was to deliver the speech from notes, but as his confidence grew in the days leading up to it, he decided to speak from memory. Sensing Brown was on the run and he was regaining control, he roared out: 'So, Mr Brown, what's it going to be? Why don't you go ahead and call the election? Let the people pass judgment ... call that election.' He left the conference hall as quickly as he could with his wife, Samantha, chief policy aide Steve Hilton and others, speeding from Blackpool towards the main railway line at Preston to catch a train back to London. On the outskirts of the town, they stopped at a pub where Cameron offered the verdict: 'Well, it wasn't great, but I think it's going to be okay.'[94] The polls, however, suggested that his speech and, indeed, the entire Tory conference had been more than just 'okay'. A YouGov poll for the *Daily Telegraph*, compiled on 3 to 4 October, showed Labour on 40 per cent (down four points), the Conservatives on 36 per cent (up three). Labour's lead from the previous week had been cut from eleven points to just four.[95] The heat was now on Brown. It was about to become very intense.

The Climb-Down: October

On Wednesday the mood in Number 10 and the Labour Party headquarters was bleak. Mattinson's mind travelled back almost a quarter of a century. 'The shift that we saw in voter attitudes, reminded me of the shift I'd witnessed during my very first Labour focus groups after Neil Kinnock's famous speech against Labour militants in 1985,' she recalls.[96] Brown's team forensically scanned the data on the marginal seats, concluding that there were just too many uncertainties to make any confident predictions.[97] Mattinson told Brown that she was not sure that Labour could count on automatically winning seats from the Liberal Democrats. Worse still, polls showed Tories were making significant inroads into the centre party's vote. 'We couldn't go many more days before calling the election. We were right up against the timetable,' she said.[98] Brown, fatigued from his Iraq visit, was described as 'very tense' as he witnessed Labour's polls sliding.

Crunch time came on Friday 5 October in Downing Street. Intense conference calls had been taking place from early on that morning. The first private poll results from key marginals were showing a small Tory lead, but Balls believed it was too late to go back. At 6am he spoke to Brown, who indicated his agreement. Tension mounted with the knowledge that Michael Ellam, as the Prime Minister's official spokesman, had to brief the lobby at 11am on the business for the following week. With winter coming up fast, Brown's team knew the window was tiny if there was to be an election. Ellam's announcements would be critical. If there was to be a November election (it was now too late for an October poll), two vital bits of government business had to be got out of the way: a statement by Brown to the House of Commons on his Iraq visit, and the Pre-Budget Report and Comprehensive Spending Review. Downing Street advisers decided the Iraq statement should be first, as it could be seen as cynical if this was Brown's last action before travelling to Buckingham Palace to ask the Queen to dissolve Parliament.[99]

A fraught meeting took place that morning, in the ground-floor, bow-windowed room at the front of Number 10, attended by Brown, Alexander, Ed Miliband and Livermore, as well as pollsters Mattinson, Shrum and Greenberg. Everyone was in a gloomy mood, and Mattinson describes Brown as 'late, tired, and monosyllabic', both impatient to be told the conclusions and frustrated by them.[100] It was a disjointed meeting, constantly interrupted by late entrances and hurried departures. The one major absence was Balls, who was spending the day in his Normanton constituency.[101] A report of the meeting in the *Daily Telegraph* by Patrick Hennessy, one of McBride's favoured journalists, suggested that, against all the evidence, Balls had been 'one of those urging caution' in the face of the upbeat advice of his fellow top aides.[102] Greenberg and Mattinson presented their findings, which offered a less optimistic picture than the week before. Greenberg said that Labour would win a November election, but it would be 'close and risky', leaving Labour with a reduced majority. The principal reason he gave was Tory spending money in the marginal seats. Brown was described as being 'very negative' at the meeting.[103] He had entered the room a cautious advocate of proceeding: now he had the shakes, and he halted it. After thirty minutes, the formal meeting broke up, and Brown left 'without comment' to attend to other business. As he passed him, Shrum prophetically remarked: 'Remember, three years is a long time, you know. That's all JFK had.'[104]

By the end of that meeting, most present were saying that 'they did not believe that it was going to work'.[105] Livermore was almost the only person still arguing for a November election, and Shrum was the biggest sceptic.[106] The evaporation of confidence in the room was principally down to the polls in the marginals, extreme doubt as to whether the sixty-six majority from 2005 could be bettered, and increasing scepticism about any plausible story they could tell about why they were calling a general election after just two and a half years, especially when Brown patently lacked any new personal agenda or case to offer the country.[107] Desultory discussions continued after lunch. By early afternoon, Alexander thought Brown was moving to thinking it would all have to be called off.[108] The Prime Minister worked in the Cabinet Room that afternoon, deep in thought. In late afternoon, he called Balls to say: 'It is all off.' Balls urged him to reconsider, but Brown said: 'It is too late.'[109] Balls was 'distraught' and told Brown he was making a terrible mistake.[110] In the early evening, many of the group reconvened and the decision not to go ahead was finally taken. 'That's it. We can't do it,' Brown said. He realised the enormity of what had happened and he had tears in his eyes when he spoke.[111] Everyone was very quiet.

On Friday evening, Brown was whisked up to Chequers. Local residents had rarely been inside the Buckinghamshire house given to the serving Prime Minister in 1917 as a country retreat, and he persuaded the trustees they should open its doors to the public. Brown was in his element as he escorted them through the rooms and showed them some of the features, including Cromwell's death mask and Lady Jane Grey's portrait. Wilf Stevenson, who helped with the visit, noticed how calm the Prime Minister was, describing him as 'a brilliant host'. To an old friend Brown confided: 'I never believed the figures and now I've decided. I'm not going to go. End of story.'[112]

The question now was: how to let the world know? There was no easy way to do this. Brown was insistent there would be no press conference, which could have been very humiliating. McBride decided he should announce it on Andrew Marr's Sunday-morning programme on BBC1 in an interview pre-recorded at Number 10 on the Saturday. The reason Marr was selected was thought, by some, to have been because Balls had tipped him off a few days before that the election was definitely going to happen, and he and McBride thought it was a way of squaring the veteran journalist – a claim Balls denies.[113] Immediate dissent broke out among his team. 'It was a really crazy decision to announce: "We are not going to be calling a general election." Crazier still to give it to just one outlet,' says one aide.[114] On Saturday 6 October Brown had been scheduled to see some Burmese monks, who had been involved in a protest in support of their country's opposition politician Aung San Suu Kyi. Should the meeting be postponed? A bizarre debate ensued, but Brown insisted it went ahead. His main frustration that morning was that his team had not briefed the media about his seeing the monks and his views on Burma; he had the country high on his agenda throughout his time in Number 10 and was always asking to be briefed on developments.[115] Some of his team admired the way even in the heat of a major political crisis Brown still found time to champion political reform in another part of the world. For others it revealed a serious weakness: a tendency to 'displacement activity'.[116] Part of the morning was spent pacing the garden with Balls discussing what he should say, while kicking a football with Brown's son John, who was celebrating his fourth birthday.[117] That afternoon, Brown and his wife took John and some friends to Whipsnade Zoo in Bedfordshire for a birthday treat. The incongruity and complexity of family life at Number 10 struck them as never before.

The media were, as the team predicted, furious at the manner that Number 10 had chosen to communicate this major news story. 'We were all watching Downing Street very intently that weekend and the notion that they could call someone in and that one person would keep the news quiet was simply absurd,' says Sky News political editor Adam Boulton.[118] Marr himself was embarrassed to have been 'given the nod' and, after the interview in Number 10, he came out and made a point of briefing the reporters in the street about the story that was supposedly embargoed until the next day. The media had tipped each other off about the interview: 'We all knew that a poll for the *News of the World* was showing the marginals were not looking good for Labour, so we all rushed to be outside Number 10, in anticipation of the story,' adds Boulton.[119]

Marr announced on the doorstep that Brown had told him: 'There is not going to be an election this year, and unless there's an extraordinary circumstance, [he] was pretty clear that there will not be an election next year either.'[120] He described Brown as 'remarkably calm', but added: 'He knows the single phrase that is going to be used most often about him is that he "bottled it".'[121] The weekend was appalling for Brown and the government, with almost every media outlet condemning him. The cack-handed manner of the announcement allowed Cameron to appear on television before Brown put his case to the nation on the Sunday morning.

On Monday, as he arrived at the rostrum to start his monthly press conference at Number 10, Brown looked worn and grey. He was accused repeatedly, just as he knew he would be, of 'bottling it' at the last minute. Visibly shaken, his premiership seemed to be collapsing around him, and in the most public of settings. He told journalists that he 'accepted full responsibility for everything that has happened' in the whole saga.[122] Taking responsibility for allowing the story to run, and his joke that the journalists had probably enjoyed 'a better weekend than he' allowed him to leave with some credit. But he made a cardinal error in denying that the polls had influenced his decision. It was the most transparent of lies. By saying so, he fractured the trust between himself and key members of the lobby, and indeed the electorate, which, in turn, generated far more hostility than would have otherwise arisen. The image of a dissembling Prime Minister only served to compound the damage the episode had already caused. Already indecisive, partisan, and opportunist, he now appeared fundamentally dishonest.

Brown's attempt to control the agenda and show he was a leader in control was forlorn. Polly Toynbee led the charge in *The Guardian*, writing about the 'horrible humiliation for the Prime Minister' and asking how he had managed 'to shipwreck himself and his party'.[123] The venom against him was exacerbated by his lack of candour: 'The Prime Minister offered every excuse, apart from the obvious truth,' said a newspaper editorial.[124] Another mantle lost was that of 'father of the nation', or 'plain Gordon', doing the right thing – as Tom Clark put it in *The Guardian*: 'Heady summer notions of Brown as a leader who transcended the party-political fray have been decisively dispelled.'[125]

The heat generated beyond Number 10 was nothing compared to the fury within it. Balls and McBride seized control of the agenda, and decreed that the principal scapegoat was the election coordinator, Douglas Alexander. Alexander himself offers a charitable explanation for this: 'Both were trying to direct attention elsewhere as a way of protecting Gordon Brown, and I was merely the fall guy.'[126] But suspicion rapidly arose within Number 10 about Balls's true motivations. One observer who witnessed the drama unfold says: 'He and McBride were not trying to protect Gordon Brown – they were trying to protect Ed Balls. Balls worried about his credibility, and once the election was called off, he had to protect himself and ensure he was nowhere near the blame.'[127] Paul Sinclair, who was working as a special adviser for Douglas Alexander at the time, was one of the figures to be phoned by the journalists saying that an 'officially sanctioned' briefing from Number 10 blamed the 'inexperienced' Alexander for whipping up the early election fever. 'I couldn't believe they were blaming Douglas. It wasn't just utterly disloyal and scandalous: it was also crazy,' he says.[128] Balls flatly denies he briefed against anyone.

It was a defining episode. For the first time in his premiership, the dark heart of Brown's Treasury operation had shown it was still in business. Those in Number 10 who had hoped that Balls and McBride would operate differently now that Brown was Prime Minister were disillusioned. 'They were the same old paranoid attack dogs,' said Paul Sinclair.[129] Since his earliest days as Chancellor, Brown had shown a weakness for letting his lieutenants exercise excessive influence over him. As early as 1999, Blair had felt it necessary to ask Brown to dismiss his press secretary, Charlie Whelan, because of his poisonous briefings. It was in Whelan's wake that Balls had grown in stature, rising to become unquestionably the greatest influence on Brown as Chancellor, for good and bad. As Alexander had now been reminded, Balls did not flinch from employing the dark arts of politics. Observers describe him as a 'mafia politician' who believed that 'bullying, briefing and aggression were all legitimate tools'.[130] That bred resentment, and must qualify some of the comments made about Balls. As one adviser says: 'The most important thing to remember about Ed is that he never ever – ever – wanted to lose any argument. If threatened, he would attack; that makes enemies.'[131] Again, Balls roundly denies these traits.

Alexander himself was now a victim of that approach. He felt he had been poorly treated, and that 'it made it very difficult to have strategic conversations based on trust in the future'.[132] Brown must have sensed the problem, even if he did not know about the briefing directly. Why did he not respond, and castigate Balls? Undeniably, Balls was a deeply valued adviser. His intellect and grasp of politics and economics were unrivalled among his peers. As one senior official in the Children's Department comments: 'He could focus for twelve hours at a time, with a level of intensity unmatched by anyone else in the government. It was incredible to watch.'[133] But Brown's relationship with his senior lieutenant was far more complex than that. In their time at the Treasury together, as their political journeys had developed, they had become increasingly co-dependent. 'Ed compensated for Gordon's lack of intellectual confidence by being decisive,' says one long-standing colleague. 'His all-encompassing certainty became a crutch for Brown for his own intellectual and psychological insecurities.'[134] In the bitter atmosphere of the Blair years, that had led to a dangerous, spiralling dynamic. Brown 'contracted out to Balls his evaluation of people', says one Treasury official, and Balls thought Blair little better than an imbecile.[135] In those difficult years while Brown waited desperately for power, Balls had protected him from attacks, and Brown remained deeply grateful. An aide who worked with both men at the Treasury says: 'Ed came to personify "Bad Gordon". But he didn't just reflect the bad Gordon: he exaggerated it.'[136] The hope had been that, with Blair gone, Balls would operate differently.

By the time he arrived in Number 10, Brown's relationship with his young adviser had come to diminish them both. 'Gordon became far too reliant on Balls, and often did not trust his own judgement without him. It paralysed him,' says one close colleague.[137] For Balls himself, the legacy would be unhelpful. In those early years at the Treasury, he had the potential to become a major presence in the early twenty-first century political landscape, a figure of almost Disraelian brilliance and effectiveness. In the event, the methods he practised under Brown lost him friends across the party. One can only speculate as to whether Balls would have developed in the same way had his political destiny not been so irrevocably hitched to that of Brown, and whether he would have proven more successful in his 2010 run for the Labour leadership. It was a tragedy that he was so overwhelmingly influenced by just one mentor. By the time he tried to strike out and become his own man, as a Cabinet minister, his personal traits were too deeply engrained.

The briefing episode had a lasting effect on Brown's premiership. Not only had it lifted the lid on Brown's operation, but relations between Balls, Ed Miliband and Alexander, already badly fractured beforehand, now deteriorated so badly that the three would never trust each other again.[138] 'The three pillars of Gordon's chancellorship – the two Eds and Douglas – were gone for ever,' says one.[139] Livermore was the second figure to be blamed in the private press briefings. After eleven years of such treatment, he decided he had 'had enough'. McBride put out that 'he was badly scarred by the experience' and Simon Walters in the *Mail on Sunday* reported, on their word, that Livermore was 'reduced to tears' after Brown had exploded at him over his responsibility for the election fiasco.[140] Livermore says there is no truth in this. He claims Brown never shouted nor even had an angry word with him, and, indeed, appears to have been genuinely sad when Livermore left Downing Street early in 2008. 'Gordon hates losing any member of his team and the way he deals with it is not to say goodbye. An aspect of Brown's denial mechanism is that it dictates that, if you don't say farewell, then someone really might not leave,' adds Livermore.[141] Not for the first time the press had given a wholly misleading account of life in Number 10. The episode pointed the finger in two places: the media, whose reporting of the Brown premiership was poorer than for any recent premiership, not least for being overly influenced by selective leakers whose stories were lazily accepted by some journalists; and at Brown himself. Why did he not assert himself and stop his old political lieutenants from spreading the dirt?

The Pre-Budget Report and the Comprehensive Spending Review: 9 October 2007

If Brown's first major public speech as Prime Minister was to the Labour Party conference, Alistair Darling's as Chancellor was to the House of Commons on the Pre-Budget Report. And it, too, was to be ruined by the aborted election. Number 10's sudden announcement on Friday 5 October that the Pre-Budget Report was going to be delivered at 3.30pm the following Tuesday resulted in a frantic task for Treasury mandarins to complete the statement and print it in time. Osborne's announcement about inheritance tax had convinced Brown and Balls to pressure Darling and the Treasury to come up with their own tax giveaways, but the Chancellor protested, not least because of the limited timescale. He was already nervous as he anticipated having to downgrade the economic growth forecasts made by Brown in his final Budget the previous March.

Brown told Darling straight that he had to include an inheritance-tax giveaway in the report, which the latter accepted, but with what was politely described as 'reluctance' by a senior Treasury official.[142] Brown believed this would enable Labour to claim the Tories were only acting to help the rich, whereas Labour would raise the inheritance tax threshold but still have money left in the kitty to invest in public services. 'That became the dividing line for him,' says one senior adviser.[143] 'Although the [inheritance tax] move rebounded badly at the time, it later worked very well as an attack line on the Tories and featured heavily in late 2009/early 2010.'[144] Whatever the logic, Darling felt his judgements at the Treasury were constantly being second-guessed, not only by Brown, but also by Balls. 'Alistair felt there were two Chancellors. Every time he walked in to the study at Number 10 to see Gordon, there would be Ed. It was like Ed was marking his homework. It was humiliating,' says one witness to these events.[145] In the event, the Pre-Budget Report doubled the inheritance-tax threshold for couples to £600,000. Osborne had also foreshadowed two other eye-catching proposals in Darling's speech the week before – taxes on non-domiciled residents, and on aircraft (which Liberal Democrat Treasury spokesman Vince Cable claimed his party had come up with even earlier). Balls admits: 'That was not a good [Pre-Budget Report]. Why? Because it was written for an election that we didn't call.'[146]

The report caused further controversy with its capital gains tax proposals, which were seen to incentivise short-term speculation over long-term investment, damaging faith in the government's economic competence. Osborne knew he was on to a winner, describing the move as 'a desperate, cynical stunt from a desperate and weak Prime Minister', adding: 'He should have called that election and let us give the Budget. Instead, we had a pre-election Budget without the election.' Sensing the moment, he delivered words that struck home because their truth was entirely obvious to the whole House: 'A week after we put forward our own plans, the Prime Minister and the Chancellor scrabbled around in a panic thinking of something to say … this is not leadership, it is "follow-ship", Prime Minister.'[147] At around this time Number 10 began to become suspicious of how Osborne knew so much about what Darling was thinking. They began suspecting the Tories had a mole in the Treasury, which turned out to be true, although the culprit was never identified.[148]

Press reaction to the report was contemptuous. 'Whose Pre-Budget Report was it anyway?' was the headline in the *Daily Telegraph*, while the paper's Andrew Porter, one of the key outlets for Balls and McBride and hence no supporter of Darling, called it 'larceny'.[149] *The Economist* warned that tax stunts would not help Labour if the public finances continued to deteriorate. 'Seldom have the naked politics of a sober budgetary event been more evident than in Alistair Darling's first big day as Chancellor of the Exchequer,' it said.[150] Simon Jenkins was more succinct in *The Guardian*, calling the statement 'in truth, George Osborne's first Budget'.[151] The City and industrialists were not the only ones disenchanted with the Pre-Budget Report – the left of the Labour Party felt equally betrayed, feeling that the inheritance-tax proposals favoured the well-off, and not enough was being done to champion Brown's beliefs in 'fairness for all', including social programmes on child poverty. The verdict of Polly Toynbee in *The Guardian* was that 'this was the week that social democracy ebbed away in England'.[152]

Financial recklessness was another charge levelled against Brown and Darling. The belief was that their actions to shore up the economy in the event of troubled times ahead were insufficient, and they had been duplicitous in the presentation of growth and debt figures. The financial commentators were unanimous. Hamish McRae wrote in *The Independent*: 'In truth, Alistair Darling's figures only add up if the global economic cycle is dead.'[153] According to Liam Halligan, writing in the *Daily Telegraph*, Brown and Darling 'displayed almost no understanding ... of the long-term economic challenges facing this country. ... Just as Brown has before him, Darling tried hiding much of his extra borrowing by pushing it into the future.'[154] *The Economist* rounded it up: 'Mr Brown may come to rue the day that he did not put [public finances] on a firmer footing when he had the chance as Chancellor.'[155]

Brown displayed little adroitness at PMQs in July, and his plans to return with a newfound confidence in the autumn were now in disarray. At the session on 10 October, flanked by a visibly dismayed Darling and Harriet Harman, he had to endure Cameron's most impressive parliamentary performance to date. Excoriating the Prime Minister for his lack of honesty, the Opposition Leader asked: 'Do you realise what a phoney you now look?' To howls of laughter from his party, he accused Brown of stealing Conservative tax plans and taunted him: 'You are the first Prime Minister in history to flunk an election because you thought you could win it.' Cameron summed up his damning indictment: 'Last week he lost his political authority. This week he is losing his moral authority. ... No conviction, just calculation. No vision, just a vacuum.'[156]

Completing a terrible week for Brown, an ICM poll for the *Sunday Telegraph* put Labour on just 36 per cent and the Conservatives on 43 per cent. Reports circulated of disaffected Blairite Cabinet ministers, including Charles Clarke, Stephen Byers and Alan Milburn, decrying Brown for his 'lack of vision'.[157] The first stirrings against Brown's leadership date to this week. The large ranks of the discontented – those who believed he should never have become Prime Minister – now had their proof.

The Queen's Speech: November 2007

The Queen's Speech on 6 November was Brown's opportunity to regain the initiative, but it was also blighted by the autumn election débâcle. He refused to accept publicly that falling support for Labour in the polls had put him off going to the country and insisted that he had made this decision because he wanted time to set out his own agenda. This put too much pressure on the Prime Minister and his Downing Street team to come up with the distinctive policy programme that had been so lacking before the summer. A Populus poll conducted between 2 and 4 November showed Brown's personal ratings had dropped five points in a month, to 49 per cent – ten points below their mid-summer peak. The proportion of voters who thought he was 'likeable' was down nine points from the summer high to 44 per cent.[158]

Inside Number 10, the atmosphere had changed almost overnight: tension and defeatism were now prevalent. Brown's team felt that whatever their boss said or did would either be ignored or criticised: they thus anticipated the reception of the Queen's Speech with a sense of foreboding. The twenty-nine bills it listed did indeed find few admirers, in part because much of the content had been trailed in a draft version of the speech released for consultation in July. A rare generous verdict came from Steve Richards who said in *The Independent* that it contained some 'genuinely radical' measures, but he also acknowledged that the fact that 'we've known about most of the contents for several months' diminished the impact.[159] This applied to the bill for young people to stay in education or training until the age of eighteen and the impetus given to increasing the availability of affordable social housing.

Number 10 was furious about an allegation made by Nick Robinson that Brown's hand had been trembling during the Queen's Speech debate; it was the first time that the BBC political editor's reports had seriously irritated Downing Street and it would not be the last.[160] However, by railing against the BBC and the press, Number 10 was missing the point. Brown's own Cabinet was not impressed by the speech, with ministers asking what it was supposed to be about. One recalls: 'We were bewildered. Anyone who had thought bad things about Gordon, now started saying them in public, and he had no significant personal achievements to date to counteract that criticism.'[161] The Cabinet increasingly felt that they were drifting without any clear sense of direction. The draft manifesto, prepared hurriedly by Kelly, Pearce and Corry after the party conference, had contained new ideas, but barely any made it into the government's legislative programme. 'It was deemed important to hold them for future election, but we also lacked time for full Whitehall clearance, and we were anxious not to knock out other bills,' says Corry.[162]

During the autumn, it became evident that Brown lacked an interest in the work of many government departments, and he was compared unfavourably to his predecessor. For all Blair's deficiencies as a manager, he could be a good motivator of Cabinet ministers, and monitored their work carefully. In contrast, Brown did not summon colleagues to Number 10 for regular 'stock-takes'. One minister complains: 'In three years under Gordon Brown, I had just twenty-five minutes with him alone on my work.'[163] Nor did Brown even have regular discussions with his Policy Unit in the way Blair did.[164]

As the days shortened, Brown's problems deepened. On 1 November, the date that the election would probably have taken place, Cameron took the opportunity to accuse the Prime Minister of treating the public like fools by denying that he had called it off because of the polls.[165] A YouGov poll in mid-November in the *Sunday Times* showed the Conservatives moving 6 per cent ahead of Labour.[166] Brown was still reeling from the negative response to the election débâcle and the Pre-Budget Report, and he had neither the energy nor the spirit to provide confident leadership, let alone weave his thinking together into a coherent vision for his premiership. While defeatism stalked Brown, Cameron found he could do little wrong. At the end of November, the Conservatives had opened up an 11 per cent lead, while Brown's own popularity rating fell further to a miserable 23 per cent, according to YouGov.[167]

Brown's team concluded that all their woes had one cause: 'After the cancelled election, there was no way back,' says one Number 10 aide.[168] However, attributing all the problems of the next two and a half years to this one source is simplistic; it was more a symptom than cause and Brown still had ample opportunity to turn around his premiership. But there was no avoiding the severity of the blow, and assessments written during the 2010 election campaign identified it as a defining event of Brown's period in Number 10. Mattinson agrees: 'It was the decisive moment of his premiership. Everything changed within just twenty-four hours.'[169] Stephen Carter, who was to join the Downing Street team in January 2008, said the non-election was 'like scar tissue which led to an attitude inside Number 10 that we had just two years to make our mark'.[170]

Why had the episode been so destructive? One aide says: 'Our whole strategy had been built on the idea of strength and conviction. It was totally destroyed by not going for the election.'[171] But it was not just Brown's reputation for strength that lay in tatters. When he had arrived in Number 10 in June, he had been determined to establish a new, clean image – to be a Prime Minister who wanted an honest dialogue with the public, and who would restore trust to politics. He had tangibly warmed to his 'father of the nation' status; now, he had allowed short-term party advantage to cloud his judgement. Having previously risen above politics, he had allowed himself to be painted as a tribal opportunist. And it was not just his image – his election road map also lay in tatters. His plan to go to the country after a year and secure his own mandate now looked fanciful.

The episode had also shattered Brown's team. Alexander and Livermore had been deeply wounded. Balls, despite calling the decision right, had shamed himself by sanctioning briefing against close colleagues in the name of self-preservation. The ripples would be felt well into 2010's Labour Party leadership election, when Brown's three closest lieutenants would be found in opposing camps, with Balls and Ed Miliband running as candidates, while Alexander supported David Miliband's campaign.

But perhaps the deepest impact was on Brown himself. His self-image, and his confidence, were destroyed. He appeared uniquely weak among modern Prime Ministers, lacking both a mandate from his party, following his coronation in June 2007, and the country. In late November, a close Cabinet colleague went to see him at Number 10. Entering the first-floor room that Mrs Thatcher had used as her study, and in which Brown loved at that time to work, the minister was shocked by the shrunken figure he found – a man seemingly so troubled and distant. 'I remember thinking: "I hope no one will see how this is weighing on him." You could almost feel the tension between his incredibly strong sense of public duty and his sense of personal responsibility for what had happened. It was incredibly poignant. He seemed profoundly lonely.'[172]

3

Battles to Regain Control

(November 2007–April 2008)

Brown's premiership had suffered a severe blow in October; in the months that followed he battled to regain control of policy and put Number 10 onto a more stable and purposeful footing. He was nothing if not a fighter, and during these months he drew on reserves of strength he barely knew existed within him. But attempts to re-launch his agenda at home and abroad were to be undermined by a series of domestic events, and a continued lack of definition to his premiership.

Events Take Control: November–December

The non-election débâcle had transformed the way the media and the public viewed the Brown premiership. Its credibility, and his own, were seriously undermined. In November and December, he lurched from one crisis to another and was constantly in fire-fighting mode. 'We were simply reacting to events that were thrown at us one after another,' says one Number 10 aide.[1] The honeymoon was well and truly over, but, at every stage, Brown was handicapped by his inability to impart any clear sense of purpose to his premiership. He was a cork adrift in a hostile sea.

The first event to hit him was cruel luck. On 18 October, two computer discs containing the entire Child Benefit database, including the private details of approximately 25 million people, were sent by HM Revenue & Customs (HMRC) to the National Audit Office (NAO). The package, which, incredibly, was sent neither recorded nor registered post, never reached its destination. On

24 October, a concerned NAO told HMRC the bad news. A second copy was
sent by registered post. This time it did arrive, but what of the first package? It
was not until 8 November that senior HMRC officials were informed of the
loss of the discs. They told Darling, who passed the story up to Brown.[2] 'I just
thought: "This is a disaster. This is terrible,"' says Darling. 'I said: "We have to
search the place from top to bottom." One of them said: "We'll start Monday."
I said: "No, we start today." I phoned Gordon up. I said: "We appear to have
lost two discs containing the personal details of just about every family in the
country." We knew it was bad.'[3] Darling ordered an immediate search of all the
premises where the package might have been. On 14 November, he called in
the Metropolitan Police. Six days later, a profoundly embarrassed Chancellor
made a statement about the loss to a shocked House of Commons, but failed
to reassure them about the discs' whereabouts. To this day, they have not turned
up, though they have apparently not been used for sinister ends.

Public dismay at the loss was heightened because it followed earlier clumsiness
by the government over the security and distribution of data.[4] 'Systemic failure
at HMRC', was the response from the Conservatives. The finger of blame was
pointed squarely, if unfairly, at Brown, who had merged Inland Revenue with
HM Customs & Excise in 2005, creating, the argument went, an unwieldy
monster.[5] Only later did an official report into the loss in June 2008 conclude
that the discs had been lost because of flaws in HMRC's management structure,
poor communication and low morale.[6] But by then the damage had been done.

Brown chose to claim responsibility: 'I profoundly regret and apologise
for the inconvenience and worries that have been caused to millions of
families who receive Child Benefit,' he intoned.[7] By being so forthcoming in
apologising, in part to sidestep one of the criticisms of him that he blamed
others, he weakened his position. Brownite MP Tom Watson is in no doubt:
'He completely overcooked the tax disc issue. It was an own goal.'[8] 'What else
could he have done?' retorted his aides.[9] He was in a trap from which there
was no escape. Brown took the episode incredibly badly and was described
as becoming 'very, very low' over it.[10] The fact that he had needed to take the
blame for a failing over which he had no control infuriated him. Sitting in his
office at the end of the Cabinet Room in a meeting with advisers to discuss the
issue, he erupted in fury and hurled his mobile phone at the wall. Afterwards,
the duty clerk collected the pieces and Number 10's IT staff rebuilt it. Ever
circumspect, when handing back the phone to Brown, the duty clerk said: 'I
think it will work better now.'[11]

One aide reflects: 'It had a terrible impact in destroying our trust with
the British public.'[12] Inside Number 10, it heightened the sense Brown had
that he was no longer in control of the government. The media homed in on
the sense of drift, with *The Independent* saying: 'Governments do not become

accident-prone by accident ... Mr Brown must convey a much clearer sense of purpose or he will remain the victim of bleak events.'[13] How things had changed: only a few months earlier he was hailed as a national leader for his response to floods and foot-and-mouth; now he was the incompetent head of an incompetent government. This sense was further highlighted when on 12 November it was revealed that the Home Office had cleared 5,000 illegal immigrants to work as security staff.[14]

Brown was still reeling when a party-funding scandal broke. The *Mail on Sunday* alleged on 25 November that David Abrahams, a property developer from Tyneside, had illegally donated over £600,000 to Labour between May 2003 and July 2007 through various third parties. Under the law, passed by Labour, third parties had to disclose details of where the money was coming from and political parties themselves were expected to know the source of those pouring money into their coffers. Fiona Gordon, at Number 10, learned of the problem on the morning of Saturday 24 November when the Labour Party press office phoned to say that journalists were sniffing around the question but reassured her that all was in order. They spoke prematurely. 'Oh no, it's not going to be alright,' was the next phone call she received from Labour headquarters that afternoon. She knew she had a problem and the Prime Minister was in Uganda.[15]

Brown was attending the Commonwealth Heads of Government meeting in Kampala, where his mood was already described as 'bleak'. This news was to make matters much worse.[16] Fiona Gordon broke it to him over the phone. Brown always struggled when he found his own propriety being called into question. Attacks on his personal integrity hit him deeply as he had such pride in his own moral lifestyle and financial probity. 'How could I be associated with sleaze?' he would often say at this time. Less admirably, Brown was heard to say: 'This is Tony's fault.'[17]

Brown was desperate to distance himself from any blame and to set the record straight. Acting on advice, he decided that Labour's general secretary, Peter Watt, would have to be sacrificed. The party official duly resigned on Monday 26 November, admitting that he had known about Abrahams's money (he would later argue that he had not realised that the money had been given illegally).[18] In a development reminiscent of the Blair era, the police were called in to investigate. The crisis escalated when it emerged that Harriet Harman had received £5,000 for her deputy leadership campaign from an Abrahams conduit. She insisted that the money had been taken in good faith and that she had no knowledge that it had come from Abrahams. The difficulty, however, was that both Brown and Hilary Benn had refused money from the same third party for their own leadership and deputy leadership campaigns.

Back in London for his monthly press conference on 27 November, Brown told journalists that he had had no knowledge until the Saturday evening, either of the donations or of the way that they had been given. His words were 'the money was not lawfully declared' and he said it would be duly returned. Watt's resignation was 'a necessary first step', with further action following to ensure that Labour acted according to the 'highest standards in the future'. Lord McCluskey, a retired judge, along with Lord Harries, the former Bishop of Oxford, were being appointed to advise on reforms to tighten up donations.

Brown had found himself in another impasse. If he had clung to Watt over such a sensitive issue, the criticism would have become cacophonous. 'He had no choice but to do what he did,' says one Number 10 aide. 'He would never have got through the next PMQs if he had not let Watt go.'[19] Elements of the Brown machine took great pride in the way Watt was ruthlessly dealt with. Just before Jack Straw was about to be interviewed about the affair, Ian Austin turned to him with this chilling advice: 'Just remember that we're not like the last lot. When someone does something wrong we do them over.' But by acting on the advice from Number 10 and dispensing with the Labour general secretary, he created further problems. The remaining party employees were livid. Many were still loyal to Blair and resented Brown's role in pushing his predecessor aside. Watt was also viewed as a Blairite and his colleagues felt that their boss was being hung out to dry unfairly; they believed that Brown should have waited for the inquiry to report on the rights and wrongs of the matter. Watt himself was incensed. He resented in particular Brown's suggestion at the press conference of 'unlawful' behaviour, which Number 10 later claimed had been a slip of the tongue.[20] Subsequently, he felt that, though Brown had treated him kindly when he initially resigned, he had then been dumped. 'Gordon should at least have given Peter a call after a fortnight. That was not the kind of call that Gordon gets up in the morning to make, so those around him should have prompted him,' says an aide.[21]

The damage done to relations was to return to haunt Brown. In May 2009, Watt was cleared by the Crown Prosecution Service of wrongdoing, and his belief that he had been a scapegoat grew. In January 2010, he published a hard-hitting book *Inside Out*, in which he gave his side of the story. The episode was also bad news because of the tension it caused between Brown and Harman. When repeatedly asked whether he supported his deputy at the press conference on 27 November, Brown appeared reluctant to give her his unequivocal backing. Harman felt a 'deep sense of betrayal' not only with the way Brown treated her over the Abrahams affair but also because she felt she was not properly consulted about discussions over the early election.[22] Brown had indeed taken her for granted. He began to regret backing her as deputy leader.[23]

Brown had entered Number 10 promising to rebuild trust in government, with a clear mission to distance himself from the 'cash for honours' funding scandal that had tarnished Blair's final days in office. Yet here he was engulfed in his own funding crisis. Nor would this be the last of it: in January 2008 Peter Hain was forced to resign as the Work and Pensions Secretary after the police were asked to investigate allegations surrounding donations of over £100,000 to his campaign for the deputy leadership. Brown's claim to be guided by a moral compass looked hollow – even hypocritical. A ComRes survey in the wake of the Abrahams scandal put the Tories on 40 per cent, while Labour suffered a six-point slump, down to 27 per cent, assumed to be a reaction to the series of mishaps.

Brown, the Generals and Afghanistan: November–December

Britain's top brass, noticing the Prime Minister was wounded, chose this moment to pay him back for what they considered had been his slights to the military and his parsimony when he had been Chancellor. Brown's patriotism, and his high personal regard for the gallantry of soldiers, were beyond doubt. But, unlike Blair, he did not enjoy the company of generals any more than he did diplomats. Jock Stirrup was Chief of Defence Staff (CDS), a ubiquitous presence who stayed glued to Brown's side on trips to Iraq and Afghanistan, and the military figure with whom he spent most time as Prime Minister. 'Gordon sensed Stirrup did not have the prejudices against him of other top officers, and that he respected the office of Prime Minister,' says one aide.[24] To Brown's three defence secretaries, Des Browne, John Hutton and Bob Ainsworth, his relationship with Stirrup was too intimate: they were at times driven to distraction as Stirrup encouraged Brown to take decisions outside government committees, often leaving them cut out of the loop.[25]

On 11 November, Lord Guthrie (CDS 1997–2001) in an interview in *The Independent* bluntly criticised Brown's approach to the armed services. The Prime Minister, he said, had no grounding in defence policy and, because the military were being starved of funds, 'lives will be lost if we go on doing what we're doing'.[26] Guthrie displayed an intensely visceral hatred of Brown, which grew over the next two years.

Brown barely had time to absorb the broadside before, a week later, the *Sunday Telegraph* carried a story about a leaked 'top-level report' written by General Richard Dannatt, the Chief of General Staff (CGS), who was responsible for running the army. It echoed the criticisms of Guthrie, saying that troops felt 'devalued and angry because of insufficient funding'.[27] The story claimed that Dannatt believed that 'the military covenant is clearly out of kilter' and that British soldiers were being insufficiently looked after. Former holders of the CDS post now joined up to stick the knife into Brown, including Lords Bramall (CDS 1982–85), Inge (CDS 1994–97) and Boyce (CDS 2001–03).

For a Prime Minister trying hard to take the defence aspect of his role seriously these were cruel attacks. They stretched to breaking point the convention that former Chiefs of the Defence Staff do not criticise government policy, not least when they themselves were party to the spending and procurement decisions in question. Whether the accusations of starving the military of funds were justified is a question that Brown was to confront in March 2010 before the Chilcot Inquiry into the Iraq War. His constant refrain – that the real issue was less the lack of funds than how those funds were spent – was strongly attacked by the Conservatives at the time, but it was the line they themselves adopted after they came to power.

Brown can fairly be criticised for not taking personal interest in the military when Chancellor. He cannot, however, be criticised for the same oversight as Prime Minister. Early on in his premiership he convened a series of working breakfasts at Number 10 with the Chiefs of Staff and Defence Secretary, which later fell into abeyance in 2008, as the financial crisis began to dominate his time.[28] During his three-year premiership, he also made some ten trips to see troops in Iraq and Afghanistan. However, he secured little praise for these efforts. He was criticised for going too often and for public relations rather than military reasons, and he was criticised for going through the motions, intoning 'thank you for what you are doing' to all and sundry. On his first trip, Brown was criticised by the media for wearing a suit: on later trips, he was criticised for wearing protective clothing. 'The most preposterous photograph of the year so far stars Gordon Brown sitting in a helicopter gunship, complete with bulletproof vest,' wrote Richard Littlejohn in the *Daily Mail*.[29] Brown repeatedly felt the sharp injustice of not being given a fair hearing.

Brown went to Afghanistan for his first time as Prime Minister on 10 December. His visit to Camp Bastion coincided with a period of intense fighting for British troops who were involved in retaking the town of Musa Qala in Helmand province from the Taliban. Addressing the troops Brown suggested that defeating the insurgents was crucial for securing not only 'a new democracy in Afghanistan' but also for 'defeating terrorism around the world.'[30] Observers noticed he was clearly out of his element, in a combat zone for the first time in his life. He fumbled with his helmet, was uncomfortable putting on his body armour and, with his poor eyesight and in the dark, ill at ease getting into a helicopter. 'Where am I?' he asked at one point apprehensively, as his party was landing. 'Coming down in a Taliban minefield, Prime Minister,' said an official who had already concluded that he was no Blair.[31]

Gordon Brown made his first statement about Afghanistan to the Commons on his return. He promised to commit £450m in aid between 2009 and 2012 and to maintain troop levels in the country at around 7,800. Most significantly, he uttered the important lines: 'I make it clear that we will not enter into any negotiations with [the Taliban].'[32] He delivered his statement well; a contemporary diary records: 'One of my initial tasks is fulfilled, getting GB up to speed on Afghanistan.'[33] An earlier draft of Brown's statement had contained carefully calibrated words about the need to complement the fighting in Afghanistan with keeping open lines of communication to the more acceptable elements of the insurgents. In strict secrecy, Brown had given approval for exploratory work in this area. The Foreign Office was particularly keen to see such a dialogue and Foreign Secretary David Miliband would later become a strong advocate of a political, as opposed to a purely military, way forward in Afghanistan. But enthusiasts within the department were believed by Number 10 to have 'over-briefed' this section to the press, leading to lurid headlines in the *Daily Mail* that made much of the move. A story appeared also in *The Independent*: 'Gordon Brown is ready to talk to the Taliban, in a major shift in strategy which is likely to cause consternation among hardliners in the White House.'[34] Brown thus felt compelled to react by hardening his language and rule out any kind of talks.[35] He was very frustrated about the Foreign Office briefing. Although he was sceptical whether talks would lead anywhere – he was very suspicious about whether 'the Taliban were the kind of people that government could do deals with' – Brown was still prepared to examine the possible effectiveness of dialogue.[36] Now the door was slammed shut.

Brown was always wary of being attacked from the right for being soft on terrorism, or jeopardising relations with Washington. But this retreat from the language of dialogue with moderates in the insurgency was to restrict his possibilities, and would later strain relations with Miliband over how to handle Afghanistan.

The EU and Lisbon Débâcle: December

The autumn woes had taken their toll on Labour's standing. Brown was much dispirited by a ComRes poll for *The Independent* towards the end of the year that gave the Conservatives a commanding thirteen-point lead over Labour, their biggest margin since Margaret Thatcher was in power in 1988. Vince Cable, stand-in leader for the Liberal Democrats after Menzies Campbell's resignation on 15 October, appeared to capture the public's verdict on Brown's performance in this period. At PMQs on 28 November he delivered the killer lines: 'The House has noticed the Prime Minister's remarkable transformation in the last few weeks from Stalin to Mr Bean … creating chaos out of order rather than order out of chaos.'[37] It wounded Brown. He was angry and frustrated by his inability to know how to respond, or to find a way to regain control. His natural instinct in adversity was to try to take some action (not always wisely). No immediate avenues for action were obvious to him, which caused him even greater anguish.[38] He was like a trapped animal impaled on a post.

Hopes of a quiet run-up to Christmas were rudely upset by one final humiliation, and this time it came on the European stage. Brown's first major European Council of his premiership was scheduled for mid-December. Blair had not always been popular with his fellow EU heads of government, but they were distinctly apprehensive when it became clear that Brown would be succeeding him. As Chancellor, he had not enjoyed a good reputation, making his impatience with the institutions of the EU evident to all, conveying the sense that he had little time for the finance ministers personally. Famous for twice thwarting Blair's attempts to join the single currency, he was seen as possessing the Treasury's traditional scepticism about the EU – that Britain should have nothing to do with any attempt to interfere with its freedom of action in the running of the economy. As Chancellor, Brown's style had been to brief the press, principally the *Daily Mail*, the *Daily Telegraph* and *The Times*, the night before the 'EcoFin' meetings with details of the 'lecture' he was going to deliver to his fellow finance ministers, the script usually suggesting that they should be following his economic policies. He would then turn up late at the meeting, deliver his piece, and leave early. 'He had become notorious for this approach and was deeply unpopular,' remarks a Foreign Office official.[39] Speaking rather than listening, and suspicion rather than friendship, were the hallmarks of his attitude as Chancellor towards Europe.[40]

In his Mansion House speech in 2005, Brown had described himself as a 'pro-European realist'.[41] It was far from clear what exactly he meant by this. The truth is he never had an overriding vision or strategy for the EU, and he had a patchy understanding of how its institutions worked. What fired him was policy and his vision for the Union's role in the world economy, and he doubted even whether the European Commission needed to exist.[42] Where he was happiest was dealing with Europe as a confederation of individual states, interacting with whichever country he needed to at the time.[43] Unlike Angela Merkel, Nicolas Sarkozy and European Commission President José Barroso, he saw Europe, not as a united entity, but as a series of floating alliances on different issues.[44]

But, on one level, he wanted to handle the EU differently as Prime Minister: he made a conscious effort to brush up his personal act. Gone were the graceless manners of his chancellorship. This was to be the new Gordon Brown. At his first EU meeting, he made a major effort to go around the room, smiling and shaking everyone's hand while making pleasant comments, an exercise for which he had to be guided because of the difficulties with his eyesight. 'It was clearly something of a trial for him, because it didn't come naturally,' says an official who observed the spectacle.[45] Some of the heads of government were disconcerted by this newfound bonhomie and were not sure what to make of it.[46] It resembled Malvolio from *Twelfth Night*, attempting to discard his customary melancholy and 'smile'.

The two EU leaders Brown bonded with most were Merkel and Sarkozy. He admired Merkel for leading the biggest country in Europe and he realised quickly that she was the key figure to influence in the whole piece. He invested much time in befriending her, including inviting her to Chequers twice, a gesture he afforded no other European leader.[47] His relationship with Sarkozy went back to their time as finance ministers together. As part of his carefully choreographed first month at Number 10, Brown had deliberately flown to see Merkel (16 July) and Sarkozy (20 July) ahead of the Bush visit. He arrived in Paris in a foul mood, worsened when Sarkozy kept him waiting at the Elysée Palace. The British ambassador, Peter Westmacott, was on the receiving end of a classic tantrum. After the meeting was over, however, Brown became all 'sweetness and light'.[48] Brown admired Sarkozy's 'can-do' spirit, but found him often deeply frustrating. The chemistry was based partly on an attraction of opposites: as Sarkozy said to him once: 'Gordon, you like text don't you? I don't like text. I like doing press conferences. We're a great combination, you and me. You do the text. I'll do the media.'[49] Sarkozy is very tactile, and would want to be physically affectionate to Brown, whom he genuinely liked. Brown was emotional and affectionate, but only with those he had known for a long time: he was not given to male hugging, but learned to cope with his effusive Gallic partner.[50]

What of other EU leaders? Brown struggled with Italian Prime Minister Silvio Berlusconi, and was affronted by his indulgent lifestyle, although they bonded over football.[51] He felt some affiliation for José Zapatero of Spain, and towards the end of his premiership, for George Papandreou of Greece.[52] But he saw neither the need, nor had the gift, to maintain his charm offensive on all twenty-six EU leaders. Barroso was one European leader too far: Brown had a 'scratchy relationship' with him and with his European Commission, and never felt him to be particularly supportive of the UK interest.[53]

After the first few months, Brown adopted a dogged and mechanistic approach to the EU. Before Councils, he would write a letter to the EU President, copying in other heads of government, which would arrive the evening before the meeting, setting out Britain's objectives. He would draft it himself, and send it to his officials to check. His aim was to build up an issue in public that others did not care much about and which he thought he could win. When he did, it was always presented as a triumph.[54] He would remorselessly go through the final text, line by line, on the second morning of the meetings, ensuring by sheer force of will that he achieved what he wanted.[55] As a result, he proved a more ruthless and tenacious negotiator than Blair. Indeed, as Prime Minister, Brown would often infuriate fellow leaders by demanding that pre-agreed communiqués be rewritten so as to make them more ambitious. Such unlikely settings would come to see Brown at his most impressive – passionately pushing the causes he cared deeply about, particularly development policy and global justice.

Control and calm judgement were exactly what was lacking, however, in his first major foray into the EU, the meeting in Lisbon on 13 December 2007 to sign the final text of the Treaty of Lisbon. It was the finale to a prolonged and often agonising process: the Treaty emerged from the wreckage of the failed EU Constitution, which had been rejected by French and Dutch voters in 2005. Blair had promised to hold a referendum on the original Constitution but then attracted controversy when he argued that the provisions in the subsequent Treaty were not sufficiently 'constitutional' to warrant a public vote. Brown was thus left to finalise the content of the Treaty and ratify it, then deal with the fallout from the Eurosceptic press, which accused Labour of breaking a manifesto commitment to hold a public vote on the changes.

The Treaty had been debated intensively at Blair's final European Council the previous June, where Jon Cunliffe had acted as Brown's proxy, ensuring that Blair acted in accordance with his successor's wishes. Brown was on the phone to Cunliffe almost every hour raising 'objection after objection', until in the end, an irritated Blair decided he would ignore his Chancellor one last time.[56] Brown never knew quite what he thought about the Lisbon Treaty, other than sensing he did not like its supranational elements, in part because he knew it would also play badly with the press. After he moved into Number 10, his fellow heads of government waited throughout August and September with increasing impatience while Brown mulled over whether or not he would accept the final text. By the early autumn they gave him just one week to decide whether he would agree it or exercise his veto. With so much on his mind in his first weeks, Brown had been reluctant to address an issue for which he felt no instinctive empathy. After long prevarication, Cunliffe eventually managed to see the Prime Minister in Downing Street, where he was told to secure assurances that Britain would not have various measures imposed upon it, particularly in justice and home affairs. Characteristically, Brown drafted personally an elaborate mechanism to ensure the opt-outs could not be overridden. The other EU heads were so desperate to move ahead that they accepted Brown's stipulations, surprised and indeed relieved that he had agreed at last to sign.[57]

EU leaders wanted a big show for the formal adoption of this major Treaty. Late in the day, the Portuguese President hit on the plan for heads of government and their foreign ministers to travel to Lisbon on 13 December for a signing ceremony, before flying on to Brussels for the Council meeting the following day. Brown was the only head of government of the twenty-six member states who did not attend, leaving David Miliband to represent the UK alone. As each delegation signed, the head of government and foreign minister shook hands; Miliband was reduced to shaking hands with the Portuguese official holding the pen. It was 'comic and pathetic' complains one Foreign Office official.[58]

Where was Brown? He was delayed because he decided he needed to attend a meeting earlier that morning of the Parliamentary Liaison Committee, an innovation introduced by Blair that brings together the chairs of House of Commons select committees to grill the Prime Minister. This created a farcical situation in which Brown would end up signing the Treaty on his own after the formal ceremony was over. 'It was an absolute joke,' says one official. 'As the cars of the other leaders were pulling away to the airport, Brown's own car passed them. He was photographed signing the document on his own, too embarrassed to look up into the cameras.'[59] But what really damaged Brown was the way the affair was interpreted. The accusation was that, ever the tactician, he was trying to have it both ways: his critics suggested he contrived the delay in a flawed effort to distance himself from the agreement. He seemed to be giving out the coded message: 'This is Tony Blair's Treaty. Had I been in charge I would never have agreed to it.' The truth, however, is more complicated. Brown's claim that there was a genuine diary clash is valid: his appearance in front of the committee was agreed before the Lisbon date had been confirmed. Moreover, Number 10 were well aware of the stakes involved and therefore asked the chairman of the Liaison Committee whether they would be prepared to change the timing of the session to 8am but they refused. The committee agreed to bring it forward an hour but this still didn't give Brown time to get to Lisbon. One senior official recalls: 'We received a number of messages from them saying how it would not be possible to reschedule without disrespecting Parliament, which is why we ended up with the disastrous attempt to do both.'[60] Respect for Parliament weighed more heavily on Brown's mind than did his concern for European affairs, which were rarely at the top of his agenda.[61] At the outset of his premiership he declared he wanted to strengthen Parliament's ability to hold the government to account and so was determined not to do anything to confuse this message. Moreover, he worried that if he didn't go to the Liaison Committee he would be portrayed as a coward. He said to a senior Foreign Office official: 'The press will have a field day and say: "Brown always ducks out of a fight."'[62]

But this doesn't get Brown off the hook. What really did it for him was his entirely counterproductive media operation. Someone in his team briefed *The Sun* newspaper that the Prime Minister's real reason for delaying his arrival in Lisbon was so he could snub his fellow EU leaders. Instantly this briefing contradicted the official line from Number 10, which accurately explained that Brown would be late because of a diary clash. Several members of the Cabinet were contemptuous. 'He briefed out that he would deliberately snub other EU leaders by arriving late,' says one. 'Then when it played badly, he said it was because of a diary cock-up.'[63] *Sun* editor Rebekah Wade shared the derision, furious that Brown's people had briefed her paper one way only to produce a 'cock-and-bull opposing story'.[64] The Prime Minister was also at fault for not taking the signing ceremony seriously enough. Alex Ellis, British ambassador in Portugal, as well as Kim Darroch, the UK representative to the EU in Brussels, had made it abundantly clear to Number 10 that this was a significant event that Brown should certainly attend but he believed the Foreign Office was worrying too much about protocol.[65] David Miliband came to see Brown and personally persuade him to attend but 'as ever with David, Gordon was suspicious of his real motives'.[66]

Brown knew what lay in store for him as he headed to Lisbon. His instinct told him the press would 'give him a massive kicking and that he had made a huge mistake'.[67] 'There was a lot of gallows humour on the flight. There was a lot of banter about how ridiculous it was that he was going to a meeting that everyone had just left,' recalls one senior official.[68] But it was no laughing matter. Merkel was just one European leader to privately berate him for damaging the EU's reputation.[69] In contrast to his triumphant first trip to the US just five months before, his first major outing to the EU was an unmitigated disaster.

'Some people say Gordon Brown's problem is that he's not decisive and he lacks political courage. He couldn't have done more to confirm that with the most ridiculous fudge,' crowed William Hague, the shadow Foreign Secretary. 'He's dithered for over a week and now he's decided that he'll sign the Treaty, but he doesn't have the guts to do it in public. His excuses fool no one: he must stop treating people like fools.'[70] The leader in the *The Guardian* was fierce: 'Quite simply, his late arrival in Lisbon is an insult to our European partners, and a national embarrassment to Britain. Mr Brown has let himself down. More seriously, he has let the country down too.'[71] The *Daily Telegraph* was more succinct, saying the Prime Minister's maladroit handling of the issue had left him looking 'indecisive and weak'.[72] Brown had made a major error of leadership. He was not helped by a dysfunctional Number 10. As Christmas approached, Brown knew that his Downing Street set-up was not working well enough for him, and that, if his premiership was indeed to take off in the New Year, fundamental change had to come.

Brown Tries to Bring Order to Number 10

That Brown's Number 10 team was not coping with the challenges of supporting the Prime Minister became increasingly obvious from September to December 2007. At the Treasury they had been used to working towards the set pieces of Budgets and Spending Reviews: but this was no preparation for the pressures of overseeing all areas of government.[73] The absence of a political big-hitter like Jonathan Powell had been felt increasingly over the autumn. Brown regularly talked about missing Balls, Ed Miliband and Douglas Alexander, who had been a constant presence at the Treasury. 'They're not interested in me any more,' he would lament morosely.[74] Increasingly, he would turn to a far-from-keen Shriti Vadera, with whom he would have long conversations in his flat.[75] Miliband was meant to be fulfilling some of Powell's role, but he was no good at political fixing, 'so absolutely no one was doing it'.[76] Chief of staff Tom Scholar, Ed Miliband and Gavin Kelly tried to arrange daily planning meetings with Brown at 8.30am, but the Prime Minister would not commit himself to the discipline: they would turn up to the meeting but frequently he would not.[77] An equal problem with Number 10 was Brown himself, and his idiosyncratic, inefficient ways of working; he was the most chaotic Prime Minister in modern British history. 'We have now had an epic Gordon Brown strop,' recorded a contemporary Downing Street diary from the Christmas period of 2007. 'He works in a shambolic and unfocused way. He's endlessly tinkering on speeches, he's sending emails around the clock on topics we don't want to hear about. His mind is all over the place, and he's not responding to things we do want him to respond to.'[78] Another official says: 'He would regularly send emails in the middle of the night, either because he was up late, or because he had just woken up very early in the morning and shuffled over to his keyboard, at which he would tap away noisily using his two fingers.'[79] His personal disorganisation was a serious trial for his team. He carried with him everywhere what they called his 'mad bag', a black holdall into which he had squirreled away scraps of A4 paper containing random drafts of speeches and articles he had composed over the years. 'It was like a comfort blanket to him; he was terrified of losing it.' You never saw it in official photographs, as his daily clerks would carry it for him, but he always felt much happier when reunited with it. Brown's 'mad bag' symbolised his shambolic working practices.

Brown could be effective at responding to immediate crises but he was also incredibly prone to getting bogged down in the day-to-day detail. Strategic leadership was utterly lacking. A daily 7.30am conference call had emerged soon after the transition as a device to bring order to Downing Street: the principal figures involved were Brown, Gavin Kelly, Spencer Livermore, Sue Nye, and Damian McBride from Number 10, as well as Balls, Ed Miliband and Brown's Parliamentary Private Secretary, Ian Austin. Several of them were in despair. 'I had to put the conference call button on mute because I was so frightened that I would blurt out something terrible in dismay,' recalls one, aghast that 'after all the years planning for power, there was so little clarity about what we were doing. There was no big picture. It was all just about day-to-day handling of the media.'[80] Brown had little time for the calls, which bored him, and his involvement rapidly became perfunctory. His staff never knew whether or not he would come on the line. When he did, he was often bad-tempered, and just wanted to sound off about what he had heard that morning on the *Today* programme.[81]

Brown lacked even the rudimentary discipline of taking decisions in meetings with the appropriate people, and then following these up. Instead he preferred to seek views from multiple and conflicting sources in secretive, bilateral conversations. 'A real weakness of Gordon's was that he took advice from a wide range of informal advisers which often cut across what we were doing in Number 10 and which created confusion,' says a senior aide. 'It was a total nightmare as no one ever knew what was going on.'[82] Another adds: 'he regularly allowed himself to be influenced by the last person he spoke to.' Livermore compared Brown to a 'spider at the centre of a web'. The Prime Minister may have liked the analogy, but an organisation can only be run in this way if the spider communicates, and he did not.[83] 'Gordon has no concept of management. He is incapable of it. He was a hopeless team manager,' complains one aide.[84] When his team tried to drag him to planning meetings to allow him to maximise his time, he would complain: 'Why am I in this bloody meeting?'[85] The lack of a clear chain of command meant that 'Gordon would often ask two people to do the same thing, choosing people who often knew nothing about the issue'.[86] Worse, neither would know the other had been asked. As a model of leadership, it defied belief.

Sarah Brown admitted to her friends: 'Gordon is finding it much harder than he thought it would be. It is a big step up, bigger than he realised.'[87] For Brown the major problem was the lack of time to think things through.[88] His response to the difficulties he encountered, like Boxer in *Animal Farm*, was to work harder. This meant he was often sucked into the minutiae. One aide recalls Brown phoning him to ask about progress on a specific cycle lane. 'What is the Prime Minister doing worrying about these things?' he despaired.[89] Jacqui Smith was surprised that when dealing with Number 10 on Home Office issues, she would often have to ring Brown himself.[90] Email made the problems even worse. He was the first British Prime Minister to use email, and he used it incessantly. His team knew the way to get an immediate response from the boss. 'Being able to email him destroyed any hierarchy in Number 10. It put huge pressure on Gordon personally and broke down the sense of order and cohesion in Number 10,' says one adviser.[91] Staff would ingratiate themselves with Brown through email and use it to enlist his support in their policy areas. 'We shouldn't have done it. We knew he should only be intervening on the big things that matter,' said one of his Policy Unit.[92]

A crisis point was reached as Christmas approached. Brown would call in his political team and berate them. 'You're not delivering,' he would accuse them angrily. 'You're not defining what you want,' they would respond.[93] Brown started lashing out in all directions. He brought great opprobrium on himself when reports appeared in the *Financial Times* that he had shouted at the 'Garden Room Girls', the elite cadre of Whitehall secretaries that has served the Prime Minister since the time of Lloyd George from their rooms overlooking the garden at the back of Number 10; being rude to them was considered throughout Whitehall as very bad form indeed.[94]

Cabinet ministers were increasingly annoyed by the anarchy. 'Decisions were not made early enough or quickly enough. Things piled up in red boxes around Number 10,' recalls Peter Hain.[95] Nye started worrying about Brown's distant relations with his Cabinet, and began instituting a series of small parties on Monday evenings for him to chat to them in a relaxed atmosphere.[96] 'It was a struggle to get him there. He wanted to see his Cabinet ministers less and less. He found them boring,' says an official.[97]

Morale hit rock bottom. 'It was a very hard place to work in because we were constantly buffeted by events,' says an aide.[98] For a long time, Brown succumbed. 'The stress and pressure of the job and the exposure at PMQs for a man whose instinct was to be on top of all the details all the time – he found that very difficult,' says Balls.[99] Journalist Steve Richards reports Brown admitting to a friend: 'Every time I walk into a room people think: there is the guy who has made a mess of everything.'[100]

Neither of the top-flight civil servants brought into Number 10 – Oliver Robbins, who left in November 2007, and Scholar – were able to bring order to the chaos. When the chips were down, Brown would turn to Balls, the person he trusted more than anyone. A senior official working for Balls observed: 'In the first phase of his premiership, Ed was in Number 10 every day, and he was on the phone to GB several times a day. Gordon was endlessly reaching out to Ed.'[101] At the Treasury, it was Balls who compensated for Brown's chronic indecisiveness, but now even while Balls was in regular contact with Brown he was still often away in his own department, leaving his master cruelly exposed. And Brown knew it which is why he repeatedly tried to persuade Balls to come and run Number 10 in this period. Balls, however, refused Brown's pleas. He would later say that 'Gordon's big mistake was that he failed to replace me, not that he couldn't convince me to oversee the Downing Street operation.'

No one was surprised when Balls attended the private Number 10 Christmas party for political staff.[102] Brown always took great trouble at Christmas, and would buy his staff presents, usually books from Amazon. At the party that year, he was in high spirits, despite all the problems around him. He joined in a round of 'Jerusalem' and later the Italian socialist anthem 'Bandiera Rossa', with Jonathan Ashworth from the political team providing the song sheets. It was a moment when the tensions in the building could ease, melting, albeit temporarily, the most bitter feuds. 'Damian did a staff quiz, sat in a chair with a Santa Claus hat on, and a bottle of Budvar in his hand,' recalls one senior aide. 'It was really quite amusing.'[103] Brown asked one of the external guests: 'What are people saying about us?' When told that the feeling was that 'Number 10 needs to get some grip', Brown said: 'Don't worry, I'm going to do something about that.'[104]

Brown was an impulsive person when faced with difficulties, and in October, after the problems arising from the Pre-Budget Report, he had started calling Jeremy Heywood into Number 10, to help out on the muddle over capital gains tax.[105] The Prime Minister had long admired Heywood – for good reason – and before long was asking him to replace Scholar, who was clearly unhappy in the role of Downing Street chief of staff. Heywood declined, for the time being: he was content overseeing domestic policy from the Cabinet Office. Brown persisted, and just before Christmas, Heywood finally relented, on the clear understanding that he was not going to return to his former role of principal private secretary and that he could continue to hold a strategic policy brief. 'Yes, yes,' said Brown, only too happy to agree.[106] Heywood was promised the new post of 'permanent secretary' at Number 10, and in that capacity he was to give Brown a grip on the machine he had hitherto lacked. No one understood Whitehall politics and policy as clearly as Heywood, and he possessed both diplomatic skills and the integrity to command respect.[107] Brown could have left it there, but, on the advice of his friend Alan Parker, chief executive of PR firm Brunswick, he had another trick up his sleeve.[108]

On 22 December, Stephen Carter, a senior Brunswick executive, received a call from 'switch' at Number 10 and was told that the Prime Minister wanted to speak to him. Over Christmas an intrigued Carter held a number of discussions with Brown at Chequers and Downing Street, as well as with Cabinet Secretary Gus O'Donnell, and became increasingly enthused about the idea of joining Number 10. In Brown's mind, Carter and Heywood would be the supreme double-act: Carter with his organisational brilliance and knowledge of public relations in the private sector, and Heywood, the civil servant sans pareil.[109] But Brown had overlooked one or two basic details in the appointment process; in particular, to tell Heywood what he was doing. On Christmas Eve, an ebullient Brown called to ask him whether he had heard of Stephen Carter. Heywood told the Prime Minister that he had tried to recruit Carter during his time at Morgan Stanley but was taken aback when informed of plans to appoint him as 'political chief of staff' at Downing Street. 'Why doesn't he come and run Number 10 then, and I will stay in the Cabinet Office?' asked Heywood. Brown flashed back: 'No. I would still need you as the senior civil servant; you would be my chief policy person. He would be my chief political adviser.' Heywood said he would have to think about this, and left it there.[110]

Three days later, on 27 December, Carter called Heywood to say he was coming to Clapham in south London to see O'Donnell and asked whether they could meet up. During the course of their discussion, Heywood established that Carter did not know Brown, had not been a member of the Labour Party for a long time, and by his own admission, was not political. Heywood had heard enough. He told Brown and O'Donnell flatly that Carter would be doing the job that he had been offered, and that he wanted to remain in the Cabinet Office. Again, Brown persisted and persuaded Heywood to join him in Number 10. Heywood was far from happy with the arrangement, and Carter was equally unsure whether it would work. He suggested to Brown the idea of a one-month trial, but Brown made it clear that he wanted him in for a minimum of a year.[111]

Brown had been so carried away with excitement about his new plan, and relief that it would solve his strategic management and communications problems, that he also neglected to tell the Number 10 staff about Carter's arrival. The first they heard about it was when they picked up emails over the Christmas holiday, which Carter sent to Brown, and which contained some fairly direct observations about them and the office. Suspicions were immediately aroused that he would be axing political staff. He began his job thus on the worst possible footing.[112] Difficulties then arose over office space – always at a premium in the cramped Number 10. Carter and Heywood were given the much-prized double office to the left of the Cabinet Room, and existing staff found themselves moved out. Carter's arrival in Downing Street with his own secretary, believed to be on a high salary, further contributed to tension.[113] While Heywood was on holiday in the Canaries, he received a succession of calls and BlackBerry messages from worried colleagues at Number 10, asking: 'Who on earth is Stephen Carter?'[114]

Carter did not begin gradually. Downing Street staff were told by him that he was going to be very managerial, with a new regime of information systems, formal routines of meetings and observance of correct process at every point.[115] Where Heywood brought reassurance, Carter did not. The latter earned respect for his genial personality, but his gung-ho ideas rapidly unsettled most in the building, exacerbated further by Brown's failure to communicate what exactly he had brought him in to do: was he political chief of staff or director of political communications?[116] Worse for Carter, Brown managed to convey very early on the impression that he did not carry his full support, undermining his position.[117] Within days, the talk on the corridors was that Carter was not 'political'. Some staff were furious with Brown for appointing him, and failing to let them know in advance. Few were angrier than Balls. 'Every appointment that Gordon has ever made on his own has been a disaster,' he is reported to have said.[118] Balls sulked for the first few months of the Carter period and became less of a presence in Number 10.[119] Further unrest was caused by the departure of the popular Scholar, in January, and Livermore, in March, whom many felt had been poorly treated by Brown.[120] Nye's precept – 'Gordon treats people like shit, but he looks after his own'[121] – was looking shaky. One bright note at this time was the arrival in March of David Muir from marketing services company WPP. Muir had been recruited to oversee political strategy at the suggestion of Douglas Alexander, who had worked with him the previous autumn, during the selection of advertising and marketing agencies for a potential autumn election. Within six months he was to become a member of the core team around Brown and would act as a formative influence on the Prime Minister during the second half of his premiership.

Brown had identified the right problem – a dysfunctional Number 10 – and had produced an answer, in the form of Heywood, that was half right. Carter brought some benefits, though his hyper-managerialism was never going to coexist happily with the hyper-chaotic Gordon Brown. In January and February, things marginally improved – there was a grid that gave a structure to the week at Number 10, there were proper strategy and diary meetings, and more decisions were taken out of Brown's hands and given to others. 'The mood is more chipper in Number 10,' notes one insider of the atmosphere in the early weeks of the New Year.[122] Such a view was not, however, shared across Whitehall, for which Number 10 remained every bit as chaotic and dysfunctional.[123]

Grand Visions at Home and Abroad: January and February

Blair's apparently limitless ability to bounce back from adversity had been widely admired: this was another gift Brown found it difficult to emulate. But over the Christmas break, Brown defied expectations. On holiday in North Queensferry, in Fife, with his family, he found a second wind, spending much of the time playing with his sons, John and Fraser, or on the telephone and drafting speeches for January.[124] He found time also to follow minutely the emerging crisis in Kenya, and, in the opinion of John Sawers, British ambassador to the UN: 'He was the first international leader on it, phoning other leaders to work towards a peaceful resolution.'[125] The disputed Kenyan presidential election of 27 December had brought the country to the brink of civil war. On 1 January, mobs burned down a church and thirty were killed in rioting. In phone conversations with the opposing candidates, Mwai Kibaki and Raila Odinga, and regional leaders, Brown worked to bring the country back from the brink by internationalising the problem, but with a strong African flavour.[126] Brown became so engrossed in the Kenyan crisis that he abruptly left guests at his own New Year's Eve party held at Chequers to discuss the situation with his advisers. UN Secretary-General Ban Ki-moon was impressed with Brown, and by the genuine concern he showed for peace in a country where Britain had no obvious national advantage. When Ban had encountered Brown the previous July in New York, he felt he had been taken advantage of. But the Prime Minister's handling of the Kenyan crisis established a bond of trust between both men that Brown was subsequently to find much to his advantage. The murder of Benazir Bhutto, also on 27 December, was another international development that took up much of Brown's attention. 'He was on the phone over it for long periods, and was deeply impressive,' recalls Carter.[127]

When Brown returned to Number 10 in early January, staff noticed that he was 'relaxed, confident and ready to fight'.[128] He was determined to begin the New Year seizing the initiative, and not fold as he had in the autumn. Before Christmas, he had asked the Policy Unit for strategic papers to spell out the government's priorities and policies for 2008.[129] His aim was to offer a series of major announcements as his response to the media's accusations of drift. In January, a speech on health was planned, and, in February, a big announcement on immigration. Work was also under way to deliver a major new commitment on education.

Brown wasted no time, setting out his domestic policy plans in a speech on New Year's Day. His speech contained more substance than the Queen's Speech of two months before; the government would be setting out 'important legislation, making long-term changes in energy, climate change, health, pensions, planning, housing, education and transport'.[130] The long-term challenges facing Britain were discussed, from 'globalisation and global warming' to the 'great unfinished business of social reform'. The economy, however, would be his overriding priority. Even though Brown grasped the seriousness of the global credit crunch better than most, he was unaware just how much economic matters would dominate the rest of his premiership. The statement was a deliberate attempt to demonstrate a long-term vision: now that he had ruled out an election in 2008, he could ill-afford perceptions of a long, empty road ahead. He needed a policy programme that was coherent, and that would sustain the government until an election in late 2009, at the earliest. The statement begged the question: would he be able to produce detailed policy proposals in all the areas he had outlined?

On 7 January, he gave a major speech on health at the Florence Nightingale School of Nursing at King's College London. After a long, troubled period at the end of Blair's premiership, when Patricia Hewitt was Health Secretary, the Conservatives had overtaken Labour as the party most trusted on the NHS. Brown deeply resented the loss of Labour's lead on this issue, given his deep personal commitment to the NHS. He worked hard on the speech over Christmas, batting drafts around with Nick Pearce, Gavin Kelly and with Greg Beales, his health adviser in the Policy Unit.[131] On Christmas Eve, Beales was surprised to receive an email from Brown that said: 'Here are Tony's comments on my health speech. We should incorporate all of these.' Blair's input into Brown's premiership was regular and intensive, but it was comparatively rare for him to offer comments so openly and directly on a domestic policy subject.[132]

It revealed the importance Brown was placing on the speech, and his anxiety about pitching the words correctly across the party.[133]

The speech marked a shift in thinking on the NHS by Brown, who had been traditionally statist, and heavily informed by his knowledge of healthcare in Scotland. So it was a departure when he spoke about opening up provision and giving patients more say over their treatment. 'Our ambition must be to give everyone a choice,' he said.[134] Michael White in *The Guardian* alighted at once on the phrase, saying: 'It is always nice to catch [Brown] using the Blairite big "C" word – "choice".'[135] The speech was a blend of New Labour language on patient choice, with Brown's own belief in the need for parity between private provision and the NHS. The speech foreshadowed a new drive on prevention, including extending health screening for a number of major diseases, personalisation, reflected in the promotion of personal health budgets, the establishment of 'minimum standards', and a push to allow high-performing foundation hospitals to take over failing hospitals, a mechanism that, towards the end of his premiership, Brown would seek to extend across the public services more generally.

The *British Medical Journal* welcomed the speech, particularly the strong focus on prevention, and praised Brown for setting out a 'future direction for reform'. The gap in Brown's thinking, it believed, concerned the absence of a clear Brownite delivery model for transforming public services. Much of the creative elements were down to health minister Lord Darzi, whose wide-ranging review into the NHS had been proceeding apace, and gave a strong backbone to Brown's developing agenda. Public confidence in Labour's stewardship of the NHS began to recover. In Alan Johnson, Brown had found an ideal Health Secretary, whose lack of policy ambition was paradoxically proving to be a significant asset, because he was so open to utilising the expertise of Darzi, and the political savvy of Beales in Number 10, without feeling threatened by them. Ideas such as Brown's earlier 'deep clean' of hospitals to tackle MRSA, and measures to extend GP opening hours into evenings and weekends, would often have their genesis with Beales, and be worked up in detail by Darzi, with Johnson promoting the agenda publicly. Health was a rare example of a relative domestic policy success for Brown: as with education early on under Blair, much depended on having the right combination of secretary of state and policy specialist in Number 10. Of Brown and his time in the Department of Health, Johnson says: 'I've been in five government departments, and I've never been in one where the Prime Minister was more committed, or more generous with resources.'[136] It was not a view shared by all Cabinet ministers, most of whom complained about a lack of direction and support from the top.

Brown turned his attention next to immigration as his principal policy concern, with a speech looming to the Institute for Public Policy Research (IPPR) in north London on 20 February. He had long intended a major policy statement.

Immigration for Labour was a boil that needed lancing. Brown had paved the way in announcements in the autumn, but his position remained 'a bit of a mess' in the words of one adviser,[137] so now clarity was needed. When discussing immigration, Brown would instinctively turn to the notion of Britishness and the concept of citizenship – which entailed finding the appropriate balance between rights and responsibilities. Some in Number 10 felt this muddied the issue, and believed he should speak more directly to public concerns about the level of immigration. Immigration minister Liam Byrne had long pushed for the idea of replicating the Australian 'points-based system', under which access to Britain (for non-EU citizens) would be granted on the basis of the economic contribution that immigrants could make. Labour pledged to introduce a points-based system in their 2005 manifesto but it fell to Brown, in this speech, to formally launch the scheme which would begin to come into effect later that month. The fine detail was refined in the run-up to the speech with the criteria for entry becoming progressively tougher. It fitted with Brown's strong personal belief that the public would feel more positively about immigration if they had confidence in the system. That pointed to another idea in the speech: the notion of 'earned citizenship'. This meant ending the automatic path to citizenship for long-term residents, and replacing it with a conditional status, dependent on abiding by the law, and demonstrating a commitment to Britain. Combined, the points-based system and the notion of 'earned citizenship' made for a more restrictive overall approach. Throughout January, Brown held a series of bilateral meetings with Home Secretary Jacqui Smith to discuss the policy challenges, but spoke more regularly to Byrne directly. 'Liam definitely made an impact on Gordon in the run-up to the speech,' says Matt Cavanagh, Brown's immigration adviser.[138] Byrne soon came to be spoken of in Number 10 as one of the few policy 'entrepreneurs' in the government, when most other ministers were seen as having 'gone native' in their departments.

Brown was gloomy when he turned up in Camden to deliver the speech. 'Knowing my luck, I'll trip over my shoelaces in front of everyone,' he said when waiting to be called to the podium.[139] Advisers were disappointed with his speech. It was felt to be 'typical old-style GB – too long, and with too much micro stuff in it'.[140] But on the upside, 'it meant Gordon had put down a marker on immigration', says an adviser.[141] It had been a genuine attempt to intervene in a difficult policy area, on the belief that Labour could move the debate in a reasoned direction. By the time the Prime Minister returned to the immigration question a year later, electoral logic dictated that he returned to the populist 'British jobs for British workers' theme he had expounded to the TUC in September 2007.

Brown's attempt to find an original 'line' on immigration was part of a quest to find a post-Blairite agenda on law and order. Brown and Balls had felt a strong political urge to distance themselves from Blair's much-vaunted crime and anti-social behaviour agenda. Though totemic policies like the Asbo remained, Brown had stopped pushing on anti-social behaviour, and had all but abandoned the 'Respect' agenda that Blair had pursued with such vigour. Instinctively, Brown was never at one with Blair's tough stance on crime, while Balls, according to one senior Number 10 aide, 'always took the side of the youth lobby, and favoured the preventative approach over the punitive'.[142] Civil servants in the Department for Children, Schools and Families had never been enthusiastic about Blair's agenda, so when pressure from above was removed, they breathed a sigh of relief. A senior civil servant explains: 'Officials had always been against this stuff, so when Gordon gave them an inch they took a mile.'[143]

Education was the third domestic policy area on which Brown wanted to make progress in the New Year. With Balls running the relevant department, expectations ran very high, and Brown's chief lieutenant poured enormous energy into developing his flagship policy initiative – the Children's Plan. More than any Cabinet minister, Balls was determined to move decisively away from Blair's legacy, which he saw as a narrow focus on school standards and exam grades in particular. The Children's Plan sought to do just that, by outlining, in a single document, a far broader approach to improving quality of life for children. It was a significant piece of thinking, and drew on input from across the department and beyond: but when it was published in December, it contained few fresh announcements – and more alarmingly it lacked an overarching argument which ensured that it failed to connect with the public. An expansion of free nursery care, and a review of the primary curriculum, sat alongside plans to send parents text messages about their children's behaviour, and the commissioning of a report on the impact of computer games. 'It was full of cosmetic bits and pieces,' complains one former minister.[144] 'To be frank it had very little substance, and has now vanished without a trace.'[145] Another former minister says dismissively: 'Ed's big move at this time was to paint himself as "Mr Children".'[146]

Brown differed from Balls in feeling much less compulsion to depart from Blair's agenda on schools. Both men came to it from different angles: Brown wished to keep in with the Blairites and right-wing press, who wanted the standards agenda, Balls to establish his name in a department and carve out his own territory. Appointing the Blairite minister Andrew Adonis to the schools portfolio, against Balls's advice, committed the government to continue with the academies programme. With concern growing in Number 10 that Balls was taking 'his foot off the gas on school standards',[147] it was all the more important that Brown himself weighed in on education. In October 2007, he had delivered a speech that put down a marker by outlining his plans for schools. It contained one major policy pledge that, though lost temporarily in the howling winds of autumn, would go on to form the heart of what was to be Brown's main education initiative. He promised the elimination of 'failing schools': by 2011, no school would have less than 30 per cent of its pupils receiving five good GCSEs, including English and Maths. Advisers in the Department for Children, Schools and Families spent the start of the year working up a plan to deliver the commitment. 'The National Challenge', as it became known, enabled failing schools to be either taken over by high performing schools, including independent schools, or turned into academies. It marked an implicit move away from Blair's obsessive focus on school choice and freedoms, and hinted at a future and distinctive Brownite reform agenda.

Timetabling speeches was a tactic often used by Brown's advisers to get him to engage in domestic policy. 'We always had to find a way to force a decision, otherwise he would never tell us what he thought about anything,' recalls an official.[148] It was not ideal: his chaotic working methods meant that speeches would, according to several of his staff, often 'be a complete nightmare' to produce, not least because of the Prime Minister's apparent compulsion to fill them with new, and often minor, policy announcements that would often cloud any wider strategic arguments. 'No Gordon speech was complete unless it had twenty announcements in it,' complains one adviser.[149]

Brown cared deeply about education, and had two further priorities. The first was teacher quality. In November 2007, Pearce, at this time Brown's education adviser, had absorbed the lessons of a report about the world's most successful school systems by Blair's head of delivery, Michael Barber. The single most important factor in explaining the quality of a school system, it concluded, was the standard of teachers. Pearce had visited Finland, home to one of the world's leading school systems, and seen the force of Barber's conclusion on the ground, reporting back his findings in a memo to Brown.[150] Improving the standard of teachers was to remain a priority for Brown throughout his premiership: 'You can see it as a major thread in all of his education speeches,' says Pearce.[151] It also explains the Prime Minister's enthusiasm for a Blairite innovation, Teach First, which had been set up to encourage top graduates into the profession.

A deeply personal commitment to one-to-one tuition was Brown's other enthusiasm, stemming from his personal conviction that state-funded public services should seek to emulate the best of the private sector. It was the domestic policy issue he would return to again and again during the course of his premiership. When Chancellor, he had already said he aimed to raise per pupil state-school funding to the level of the independent sector – a bold if almost unrealisable ambition. Now, he wanted to give state-school children access to the private tutoring enjoyed by those who could afford it. 'He kept asking: "What do you get if you have money?"' says Dan Corry, Brown's first head of policy. 'The answer we came up with was one-to-one tuition. So that's what he wanted for state schools.'[152] The Prime Minister repeatedly urged his team to achieve more in this area, and was visibly moved by encounters with children who had benefited from government programmes like Every Child A Reader, which gives individual tuition to children falling behind with their literacy. He often told the story of one young boy from Hackney, who had visited Downing Street for an Every Child A Reader reception. Having previously struggled with his reading, the boy now stood before a crowd in the grand, Pillared Room on the first floor of Number 10, and read with perfect fluency a passage about his ambitions for the future. One-to-one tuition engaged Brown at the same emotional level as international development: his desire to do good and spread opportunity was a powerful driver within him.

The Prime Minister was never the ideological opponent of academies and diversity that Balls was, but his heart beat faster to educational tunes different from Blair's. Before long, Brown's new priorities nudged Blair's from centre stage, a process accelerated by Balls, who was working hard to rein back on the independence previously granted to academies.[153] Balls's motivation went beyond that of an instinctive centraliser – it was blatantly to reject Blair's agenda, something that frustrated Adonis deeply, and would eventually prompt the schools minister to leave the department.

As the spring approached, Brown's New Year 're-launch' was proving a moderate success: the ideas he had now outlined on health, immigration and education helped to steady the ship, and gave commentators some evidence at least that his premiership had purpose. Some optimism again began to permeate Number 10. Staff no longer felt they had to justify themselves. One says: 'We spent the latter part of 2007 trying to work out what the PM wanted to do. Things started to materialise in 2008. He wanted to lead a radical government.'[154] But without a powerful organising theme, even a radical list of new policies would not solve Brown's 'domestic policy problem'. Towards the end of his premiership, Blair's mantra of 'choice and diversity' had come to define his approach to public services. By freeing up schools and hospitals, and giving more choice to their users, the theory went, services would become more responsive, and standards would improve. Though unpopular with many in his party, the clarity of Blair's vision had proven a substantial asset, not just driving work in Whitehall, but also acting as an anchor to steady his premiership against the storm of events. For his successor, the non-election débâcle had revealed with excruciating clarity that he had no such anchor.

Brown had come to realise this, and knew that policy announcements alone would not be enough. With Heywood, he had turned to one of Blair's key people. He now turned to another. Michael Barber had left government to join prestigious management consultancy firm McKinsey, leading its work on public services. Brown looked to him to help piece together what his premiership would be all about. The men had a fruitful conversation on domestic priorities for the coming year and advisers began to feel more confident. 'The fact that

Gordon wanted to listen to [Barber] showed that he understood the importance of having a clear agenda,' says one official.[155]

Brown now asked Barber to work with officials on a new publication, setting out a convincing account of his public-service reform agenda. 'Gordon wanted to put his own stamp on what he felt public-service reform should be. He wanted it to be not Old Labour, but New Labour, but also distinct to what had gone before,' says Barber of Brown's not wholly clear brief.[156] The resulting document, 'Excellence and Fairness', was published in June. It was reasonably well-regarded among policy wonks but its three-pronged model of 'empowering citizens', 'fostering professionalism', and 'strong strategic government' was hardly the stuff to ignite bar-room conversations. 'It was all too technocratic and civil service-inspired. At the end of the day it was all a bit mushy,' says an aide.[157] Significantly, 'Excellence and Fairness' had been developed largely by civil servants, and was not a political brainchild in the way that Adonis's work had been under Blair. Yet, it lacked popular resonance, and policies and a message with appeal were what Brown needed badly. By the summer of 2008, he was no nearer to discovering his overarching theme.

Anxieties began to grow in Number 10 that the attempts to resolve this conundrum could prove as distracting as they were helpful. Brown began to see publishing documents as a substitute. 'We had to edit these kinds of documents repeatedly. It was hugely time-consuming,' remembers one senior adviser.[158] And so, as the year drew on, the big idea remained as elusive as ever, and Brown clutched still more desperately at straws. To the dismay of his advisers, he became fixated on one idea as the theme for his premiership that drove them to despair – 'unlocking talent'. 'In the early days, we would often ask him: "Why are you here as Prime Minister?"' says an aide. 'His answer was always: "To do whatever it takes to help individuals to fulfil their talents."'[159] Incredibly the inspiration for the talent agenda was the popular TV show, the X-Factor, which the Brown family watched religiously. One official explains: 'He's intrigued by these programmes and their suggestion that there's all this latent talent out there waiting to be tapped.' In late 2007, wanting to make the idea more concrete, Brown established the 'talent and enterprise task force'. To chair the body, he invited his friend Alan Parker's sister, Lucy Parker, who had worked in public relations and broadcasting.[160] Her influence over Brown would become a deep source of frustration for his Number 10 team who believed she was totally out of her depth working in government. Departments were asked to weave their work into the 'unlocking talent' agenda, but they completely ignored it, even if they did put the logo on their publications.[161] In the face of implacable resistance from the Policy Unit, which remained adamant that talent was not the big idea he had been looking for, he would return to the theme again and again, often egged on by Parker. It was a curious manifestation for a man of such high intellect who had waited so long for the premiership.

Failure in the first half of 2008 to find his raison d'être left Brown dangerously exposed when, in that summer, he had to contend with the first serious assault on his leadership. His speeches and documents in the first half of the year failed to gain much attention, or to inspire. As James Purnell would say later: 'There was no ideological washing line on which to hang everything.'[164] Brown himself, like a recidivist, would keep returning to the same theme. From anti-social behaviour to schools policy, the Prime Minister asked again and again 'whether a policy constituted change or continuity with Tony', rather than the more fundamental question: 'What am I myself trying to achieve?'[165] Beneath his radar, and despairing of any alternative, his advisers had already begun to develop a reform agenda that would eventually take root, but would not flower until spring 2009. For the time being it was all they could do to stop Brown framing everything in terms of talent.

Brown's Overseas Visions: January

What of his international vision? Brown understood clearly that Britain needed to reach out to the emerging 'BRIC' powers – Brazil, Russia, India and China – if her position in the world was to be optimised in the face of their rise. He was thus far happier spending time with the leaders of these countries, such as India's Manmohan Singh and Brazil's Lula da Silva, than he was with most EU leaders, whom he placed in the same dull camp as most of his Cabinet. Aside from the US, China was Brown's prime focus: he thought it essential to tie it into the international community, while also championing the rise of India as a counterweight to the potentially authoritarian presence that the massive one-party state could become in the world.

Brown was, therefore, excited when he travelled east at the beginning of 2008 for official visits to China and India, taking with him the now-mandatory entourage of captains of industry, including Richard Branson of Virgin, Richard Lambert of the CBI and Willie Walsh of British Airways. They arrived in Beijing on 18 January, where Brown was thought to have handled the discussions well, impressing British officials and the Chinese, and establishing a good relationship with Premier Wen Jiabao.[166] Brown's message was simple: please invest in Britain. He believed that some US and European hostility to Chinese investment presented a major opportunity for the UK. Pushing the slow-moving Doha Development Round of the World Trade Organization was a particular priority for Brown: ever the historian, he saw parallels with the inter-war period and worried that the global economy might 'retreat into a new protectionism'.[167] The only difficulty arose over China's support for the military regime in Burma, a topic on which Brown had deep convictions. Feelings were also running high in the UK: the new Liberal Democrat leader Nick Clegg criticised the Prime Minister for complaining about atrocities in Darfur while failing to confront China over its support for the Sudanese.[168] Brown was anxious not to alienate Wen but also recognised the need to raise concerns about human rights issues and so he proposed that China suspend the death penalty during the Olympic Games and let it be known he had also pushed the Chinese hard on Darfur.[169] The trip was particularly memorable for Brown because he managed to persuade Wen to participate in a town hall meeting, at which both leaders would answer unscripted questions from a crowd of 10,000 people. This was not what Chinese leaders were used to. There were enough party stooges in the audience to ensure that no serious embarrassments would arise for the premier but nevertheless, when it was over, Wen, shaking with excitement, told Brown how pleased he was to have taken part.[170] For Brown's officials, a worrying moment came later on in the trip when they arrived at a venue and, to their horror, discovered a table-tennis table dominating the dais. They feared that Wen was going to challenge the Prime Minister to a game and, as Brown was unable to see anything as small as a table-tennis ball,[171] it would have caused huge embarrassment. But Wen went straight into speeches and a force-ten media storm was avoided.

On 20 January, the delegation flew on to India and within hours of landing Brown was sounding off on another of his favourite themes – that the country be given a permanent seat on the UN Security Council, calling it 'their rightful place'.[172] He handled the softer aspects of the trip with some aplomb, including receiving an honorary doctorate of letters from Delhi University. He also discovered he liked Prime Minister Singh. The main substance of their negotiations was terrorism and globalisation, and agreements were reached to enhance intelligence-sharing between British and Indian security agencies, with particular reference to Pakistan and Afghanistan. Brown made another of his great rallying cries – for an overhaul of global institutions to counter financial crises and to deal more effectively with common issues, including climate change. Singh seemed pleased with the trip, saying it had brought 'a fresh momentum to our strategic partnership'.[173]

After returning home, the Prime Minister had only two days in London before he was off travelling again; this time to Davos for the World Economic Forum. Nothing was going to put him off having a whale of a time – neither domestic political turbulence, nor the bad weather, which delayed his plane's landing.[174] Brown was in his element. Forum founder Klaus Schwab introduced him with high praise: 'You, Mr Brown, are the finest example I know of a prime minister who governs in the global public interest. You have led global initiatives to cure diseases in Africa, to promote education, to end global poverty.' The audience listened intently as Brown warned that the interconnectedness of the global economy was now spreading, not prosperity, but contagion, and only an international response would suffice to put the financial system back on its feet. Joined on another platform by Microsoft's Bill Gates, rock star Bono and Queen Rainia of Jordan, he was, in the words of *Times* journalist Anatole Kaletsky, 'unquestionably the star of the show'.[175] Even Alan Rusbridger, editor of *The Guardian* – a newspaper that was to be such a thorn in the Prime Minister's side – wrote: 'Brown looked as if life was, indeed, beautiful – bubbling with confidence, gravitas and some quite good (if old) jokes.'[176] Brown was the most confident he had been on any public stage since becoming Prime Minister, communicating and connecting with the audience in a way that he rarely managed in Britain. Heads of government and others present struggled to understand why he was receiving such a bad press at home, when he was clearly so commanding and articulate on the world stage. He easily stole the limelight from David Miliband, who was also on good form.

Carter compares Brown's skills with Blair's in commercial terms. 'Gordon is a great wholesaler, whereas Tony Blair was clearly an outstanding retailer. Gordon was much more comfortable when engaged in discussing complicated issues at a high level. He thrived when dealing with knowledgeable people, which is why he was so successful at international summits,' he says.[177] Here, indeed, was one of the great paradoxes of the Brown premiership – he squeezed and shifted like a constipated parakeet to produce anything coherent on domestic policy, but, on the international stage, wise words and ideas rushed out. The verdict of commentators after his China and India trips, and his speech at Davos, was that his international authority was restored after the disaster of Lisbon.

Nationalising the Rock

The striking contrast in Brown's performance and fluency on the international and domestic stages puzzled those close to him. Part of the reason for this is that Brown had spent years immersing himself in international finance; much of domestic policy, oddly, was new to him. After one successful international speech, Douglas Alexander turned to Ed Miliband and asked: 'Why can't he be this good all the time?' Miliband replied: 'Because the *Daily Mail* isn't here.'[178] Abroad Brown could let himself go, but at home he forever worried about how his words would be interpreted. Being painted as an 'Old Labour' dinosaur was something he was most anxious to avoid. This fear was to lead him to act indecisively over the first major test he would face in 2008: the future of Northern Rock.

Following the Bank of England's intervention in September 2007, Northern Rock's short-term liquidity crisis appeared to have been resolved, but the underlying problems did not go away. Confidence in Northern Rock was disappearing and, despite the extension of further credit facilities from the Bank of England and continuing guarantees by the government of customers' savings, depositors continued to transfer their accounts to other institutions, slowly bleeding the bank to death. A collapse in confidence in the British housing market reduced the market value of the bank's mortgages, and turned a liquidity crisis into a solvency crisis for the Rock. House prices had peaked in late summer, but then began to fall at the fastest rate since the 1930s. By December, even if Northern Rock had been able to liquidate all its mortgages, it would still have been unable to raise enough money to repay its depositors and the Bank of England in full.

The signs were ominous. While mortgage lending collapsed, commodity prices, notably oil and food, were also rising alarmingly. The political team in Number 10 became worried about the impact this would have on many swing voters. Brown nevertheless remained upbeat. His 2008 New Year message had tried to show he understood the seriousness of the deteriorating global economic climate, but he argued that his ten-year stewardship of the economy placed Britain in a uniquely strong position. Just as the country had weathered previous crises, including those in Asia and the United States, and the ending of the dot.com bubble, so now, he claimed: 'Britain will meet and master this new challenge by a determination to maintain stability and low inflation.'[179] However, Brown's words no longer inspired the confidence they once did. The 'tripartite' regulatory framework for the financial system, of which he had been principal architect, now came under the spotlight, with the FSA criticised for failing to supervise Northern Rock's fragile business model and the Treasury attacked for being slow to respond. 'The reputation of New Labour was built on their reputation for economic competence and economic stability,' said Nick Robinson on the BBC. 'No one can say it's been stable in recent days.'[180]

With Northern Rock breaking up before his eyes, Brown had to act, and swiftly. He had three options. The first was to sell it, and, desperate as he was to avoid nationalisation, this was his favoured choice. Some believed this was wishful thinking, but a Treasury team, headed by senior official John Kingman, was tasked from September with trying to find buyers for the bank. On 12 October, Richard Branson's Virgin Group announced that it would inject £1bn into the business and retain its stock-market listing, rebranding it as 'Virgin Money'. For a short time, it seemed like being the answer but, as a Treasury official puts it scornfully: 'Branson was only serious in the sense that he is always serious: he puts up very little money himself and expects the rest to come from others.'[181] Lloyds TSB was another possibility. Cameron was later to castigate Brown and Darling for missing the opportunity to have 'rescued Northern Rock the weekend before the run by taking the offer from Lloyds TSB'.[182] But it soon became apparent that none of the potential bidders was willing to shoulder full responsibility, and all demanded what were considered unacceptable financial guarantees from the government.

The Treasury came under 'immense pressure' from Number 10 to settle on a purchaser, but held its ground, irritated by the argument that selling the bank was the easy option. 'There's a great difference between listening to any old investment banker with a plausible "cunning plan", and executing a sustainable deal which is good value for money for the taxpayer,' says one senior Treasury official.[183] By October, Kingman and his team had concluded that there was no likelihood of finding a private purchaser on terms the government could defend.

By the following month, it was clear that Northern Rock would only be sold if the government promised to keep funding it; towards the end of the year, these promises became more and more generous. In December the government had extended its guarantee scheme to cover a third of the bank's liabilities, which amounted to a little over £100bn. In early January, Goldman Sachs produced a deceptively attractive proposal but it came to nothing, and two days later, the Treasury invited new bidders, unveiling a taxpayer-backed £24bn bond issue as a sweetener. Kaletsky in *The Times* was apoplectic, writing: 'Northern Rock is Gordon Brown's "Black Wednesday".'[184] Meanwhile, Vince Cable, back in his role as Liberal Democrat Treasury spokesman, sneered: 'This is not a private-sector solution. The private sector isn't taking any risk. It is the taxpayer that is taking all the risk.'[185]

A second option was bankruptcy, but allowing Northern Rock to fail was never going to be acceptable for political and economic reasons. Darling feared that putting the bank into administration would endanger the taxpayer money already tied up with it – estimated to be between £2bn and £10bn – and that it could have severely exacerbated market turbulence, as he told the House of Commons on 21 January.[186] Moreover, the bank had underpinned the economy in the North-East of England, one of Britain's poorest regions and a key Labour heartland.

That left only the third option – nationalisation. George Osborne was later to castigate Brown and Darling for 'months of dither and delay', and called for the Chancellor to be sacked.[187] However, they were concerned about how the market would respond to a precipitous takeover: would it see Northern Rock as an isolated case rather than as part of a potentially far more serious, systemic problem? Might it not provoke runs on other banks? They also knew they were vulnerable to the accusation that they had 'nationalised prematurely, without giving private buyers a proper chance'.[188]

The Treasury admitted that finding the right solution took more time than it should have done, and pleaded in mitigation that it was the first time a retail bank had got into serious difficulties since the 1980s, and the bank in question – BCCI – was unlike Northern Rock in that it catered only for a niche market, meaning it offered a poor precedent to follow.[189] That said, it was predominantly Brown who was to blame for the leaden response (he was later to apologise on the BBC's *Andrew Marr Show* in September 2009 – the interview in which he was also asked about taking prescription drugs – for being slow to spot the banking crisis).[190] Philosophically, the Treasury had accepted the likelihood of nationalisation as early as the end of October, but still believed they had a duty to look at the other options.[191] Together with permanent secretary Nick Macpherson, Kingman now began a Treasury pincer movement on Darling to persuade him that nationalisation was the only feasible way forward. At Number 10, Heywood and Carter performed a similar lobbying exercise on Brown, but with less success.[192] Brown still held out against the inevitable – he had not become Prime Minister to be a nationaliser.

Balls became closely involved in the crisis from early in the New Year. 'I was worried about contagion. We didn't know whether there were more Northern Rocks to come,' he says.[193] His concern was that spending so long trying to find a market solution, with the impression that government was prepared to play fast and loose, was becoming a significant destabilising force.[194] 'I knew the Treasury wanted to act. I knew that Gordon was trying to avoid it,' says one senior minister.[195] Brown, according to Balls and Number 10 aides, was paralysed by fear of accusations of carrying out an 'Old Labour' nationalisation: 'Gordon was definitely reluctant. He was worried about the signals it might give politically at a time when the Conservatives were so against it.'[196] This interpretation is endorsed by a Treasury official: 'He was very cautious about doing anything which might look like nationalisation. He had a deeply ingrained New Labour fear of stepping back into the past.'[197] At a meeting in Downing Street with Brown, Heywood and Carter late in the week beginning 11 February, Balls told the Prime Minister straight: 'You've just got to get on with it. You've got to give Darling the green light.'[198] When Balls talked, Brown listened.

On 15 February, Brown paved the way for the decision during an interview on ITV's *News at Ten* in which he said he was prepared to 'look at every option' including 'taking the company into public ownership'. Still Brown could not bring himself to utter the dreaded word 'nationalisation'. The formal act was announced by Darling the following Monday. None of the existing private offers on the table represented 'value for money to the taxpayer', he said, and thus he was taking the bank into 'temporary public ownership', but only, he stressed, as a 'temporary measure'. At last Brown had taken the inevitable decision to nationalise, but his procrastination had damaged him.

Even though it was the Conservative leadership that, by opposing nationalisation, ended up on the wrong side of the economic argument, it was Brown who struggled to get a fair hearing for his position. 'It is troubling that the government found it so difficult to make this decision, merely because it was desperate to avoid being labelled "Old Labour",' respected commentator Martin Wolf wrote in the *Financial Times*.[199] Brown and Darling were also lashed for the failings of the banking oversight regime. *The Guardian*'s economics editor Larry Elliot wrote in the paper: 'Darling and Brown … created the tripartite system – a system that … worked well in peacetime but not when war broke out.'[200] Brown's reputation for financial competence and economic judgement had taken a severe blow. Before another month was over, it was to suffer another, still worse setback.

US Highpoint: April

Like many of his predecessors in Downing Street, Brown was beginning to realise that 'foreign' could be a welcome distraction from pressures at home. From the beginning of the year, he and Bush had settled down into a regular rhythm of secure video calls, for which the Prime Minister would disappear into a specially prepared room in the basement of Number 10. According to Steve Hadley, Bush's National Security Advisor, the President found these encounters essential in enabling him to understand Brown's mind.[201] Their first call of the year in January was dominated by Pakistan, following the assassination of Benazir Bhutto. How the country's President, Pervez Musharraf, would cope, and whether Afghanistan might be destabilised, were their main concerns. Brown also pushed Bush hard on trade, development and Burma. 'You don't get much time with the American President, and Gordon made certain he used every minute to press [Bush] on what was important to him,' says an official.[202] A contemporary diary note describes it as 'fantastic', while noting: 'Gordon Brown still too serious.'[203] Blair's was a constant voice in Brown's ear, advising him on how to handle the Americans. During this month, the former Prime Minister also advised Brown to take more time off and 'be less dramatic'. 'The nation wants a leader, not a workaholic,' he said.[204]

In their March video call, Bush turned political pundit, saying: 'I'm the only person in the White House who still thinks Hillary Clinton will win.' The President also joked to Brown that 'even my daughter has Obama-mania'.[205] Iran was the principal subject of this conversation: Hamas had admitted that hundreds of its fighters had been trained in Tehran, and the concern was how Israel might react,[206] with the possibility of an Israeli strike on Tehran's nuclear facilities very much in the air. A proposed two-day visit to the UK by Bush in June was also discussed.[207] Brown, however, was less than enthusiastic about a major visit by the lame-duck President to London, and raised the idea of their meeting in Belfast.[208]

The Republican presidential candidate, John McCain, came to London on 19 March, and had a 45-minute meeting in Downing Street, discussing principally Iraq and Afghanistan. The Arizona Senator was not Brown's favoured choice to take over from Bush and, by then, his prospects were on the wane. McCain also saw Cameron, who had invited him to speak at the Conservative Party conference in 2006. During his visit to Number 10, McCain committed the faux pas of sitting in the Prime Minister's chair in the Cabinet Room – an easy mistake to make, as it is the only chair with armrests and hence the only one that does not fit under the table. He took an interest in the small piece of moon rock that President Nixon had presented to Number 10 after the 1969 lunar landing, prompting the Prime Minister to 'make positive comments about Nixon as President'.[209] Brown had his heroes among US presidents, notably Franklin Roosevelt and John F. Kennedy, but this was the first time anyone heard him praise the discredited President.

A month later, Brown travelled to the US for conversations with Bush and each of the three front-running candidates, and to deliver a speech at the John F. Kennedy Presidential Library in Boston. His trip coincided with a state visit to the US by Pope Benedict XVI, which threatened to overshadow it. Republican commentator Grover Norquist wrote: 'Most Americans are not aware of Mr Brown, and most Republicans in Washington are not aware of any change in the special relationship other than Tony Blair, a pal, has left. There was more buzz about the arrival of the Pope next week.'[210] Brown tried to boost his profile by appearing on the popular television show *American Idol*, and pledging £200m for mosquito nets for Africa.[211] The knowledge that he lacked Blair's cachet was hard for him to swallow, for all his predecessor's advice on how to maximise his appeal to the Americans.

The meeting with Bush was the least interesting on the trip's agenda. Hadley noticed how much more 'confident and relaxed' Brown had become since the Camp David visit ten months before.[212] The two leaders' wives joined them for a private dinner at the White House and at a press conference in the Rose Garden. Bush went out of his way to praise Brown as a 'good friend', singling out his response to the terrorist attack on Glasgow Airport the previous July as 'brilliant'. 'We have a great relationship,' the President insisted.[213] Bush knew that Brown, like all his visitors from overseas, would be looking to the future, and was 'entirely relaxed' about the Prime Minister meeting the people who aimed to replace him in the Oval Office, telling him 'the US people will always choose youth over experience'. Number 10 foreign policy adviser Simon McDonald, who was accompanying Brown, sensed that Bush already knew who was going to succeed him.[214]

Arranging for the three candidates, all of whom were busy on the campaign trail, to come to his Washington residence to meet Brown was a triumph for British ambassador Nigel Sheinwald, and his first secretary, Jonathan Sinclair. Number 10 were delighted: 'No other country pulled off such a coup.' The event was choreographed with clinical precision, with the candidates arriving at 9am, 10am and 11am. Sheinwald greeted them in the hall and walked them up the elegant staircase where they were met by Brown. They then walked along the upstairs corridor where they had their photographs taken with the Prime Minister before the meetings in the drawing room.[215] The McCain visit was something of a formality: it was reasonably clear that the Democratic Party would win, though the candidacy was still balanced between Barack Obama and Hillary Clinton. Downing Street was rooting for the Democrats; when Sheinwald left to go to Washington in October 2007, Clinton was the favourite. However, within months, the ambassador began reporting back the increasingly evident frailties in her campaign.[216] By the time of Brown's visit to Washington, despite losing some primaries, Obama was emerging as the likely winner.

Brown was very pumped up for these meetings. At the end of each session, he debriefed Stewart Wood, McDonald and fellow foreign policy adviser Tom Fletcher. Clinton was the candidate he knew best, and 'in his heart he still hoped that she would win'.[217] The Prime Minister had worked closely with her on development issues and the fact that the Clintons were close friends of the Blairs did nothing to reduce Brown's warmth towards her.[218] She wanted to spend the time talking about economics and foreign policy and had brought her aides, including former Clinton White House aide Sidney Blumenthal, who asked Brown's team: 'Do you know what those Obama bastards are saying?'[219] However, it was Obama who made the biggest impression on Brown. 'He was very struck by how Obama was taking it all in his stride, how comfortable he was in his skin and how self-effacing,' says McDonald. 'He liked the way that Obama kept asking him lots of questions, on Afghanistan and the economy in particular.' [220] While Obama was speaking to the Prime Minister, his aide, Dennis McDonough, chatted to Brown's team. 'He was Mid-Western, no tie, informal, shooting the breeze, and that established the relationship,' says an adviser.[221] The embassy found relations with the Obama staff much easier than with the tighter-knit Clinton team.[222] The warmth of the meeting was enhanced by Obama releasing a statement describing Brown as a 'crucially important partner for the United States . . . we look forward to working with him many years ahead'.[223] At the end of three hours, Brown was tired but elated.[224] After a final debrief with Sheinwald and his team, his attention shifted to his keynote speech, which he tinkered with as he flew north to Boston.

Brown had first started talking about this speech in the autumn of 2007. He saw it as his opportunity to further define his view of the world, encapsulating his themes that the architecture of global relationships needed to change and nations needed to work with greater interdependence.[225] Building on his words in New Delhi and Davos, he wove into the text reform of global institutions, taking climate change more seriously, financial reform and giving development higher priority. It was perfectly attuned for his audience, and he was greeted with great warmth by Teddy Kennedy, who became seriously ill shortly afterwards, and by the New England Democrat fraternity. His language remained wooden, but the power of his thinking shone through. In the spirit of President Kennedy, he challenged his audience to think how they themselves could make interdependence work for the benefit of all: 'I believe a new global deal is possible ... the benefits will flow most widely if instead of trying to pursue beggar-my-neighbour policies ... we cooperate across frontiers to maximise the opportunities.'[226] The event marked one of the personal highpoints of Brown's premiership, and he rarely felt more at home than when he was being wined and dined by his hosts, among friends and in a part of the world which had long meant so much to him. But his good mood on the journey home was shortly to be shattered by domestic events, when decisions he had taken the year before in the Treasury came back to haunt him.

Brown's Worst Blunder - 10p Tax: March–April

Number 10 had still not recovered from the reverberations of Northern Rock when Brown scored an own goal, of far greater damage to him personally. The Kennedy speech had showed him at his best. In a pattern that was to become familiar, a personal success would be followed by an event that saw him descend to the depths. The 10p tax débâcle displayed the Prime Minister at his very worst, with a mind closed to common sense, taking decisions for short-term, tactical reasons (and jeopardising the economy in doing so), and pandering to the next day's headlines. Brown would appear entirely out of touch with both his party and its supporters in the country – leaving him in a terrible place in the run-up to the local and London mayoral elections. For many Labour MPs the 10p episode was the final confirmation that the party had made a monumental error of judgement in anointing him leader.

The 10p tax story went back to 1995, and a paper Brown wrote with Balls about his aspiration of bringing down the basic rate of income tax to 20p. He made some progressive changes in his 1999 Budget, and brought the basic rate down in 2001. Knowing that his final Budget would be in the spring of 2007, and with an eye to history, Brown wanted to go out with a bang as a tax-reforming Chancellor.[227] Gaining plaudits from the right-wing press, whose good opinion he sought even more given his aspirations to move into Number 10, weighed heavily with him, thought Balls.[228] It was this part of the media he had in mind when, at the end of his Budget speech, he announced his surprise decision to cut the basic rate by 2p. However, the only way to afford this daring reduction, he believed, was to abolish the 10p rate of income tax for low earners. Livermore, a senior political adviser, was fiercely opposed, as Balls later claimed himself to be.[229] Balls's claim is strongly contested by those present at the time – indeed, it is wholly implausible that a man with such powerful influence over Brown's economic thinking would not have carried the day had he indeed backed it. Livermore repeatedly told his boss that the 10p move was 'very regressive' – i.e. it would hit the least affluent the hardest, and while they could compensate for its impact on certain groups, such as pensioners, it would hit many Labour voters hard. Brown begged to differ and believed that the poorest would be protected by the complex regime of tax credits he had put in place.

With no resolution achieved, a meeting was convened in the Chancellor's room in the Treasury in February 2007 in the presence of civil servants, where Livermore and Balls again aired their doubts. According to one account, a meeting between Brown and Balls resulted in the latter switching his position and becoming an advocate of abolishing the 10p rate; in return he received a 'rock-solid' commitment that he would be given a department of his own rather than being kept in Number 10 when Brown became Prime Minister.[230] Balls denies this version but Brown did subsequently say to Livermore: 'Ed has agreed to support me now on 10p, will you?'[231] His 2007 Budget, which announced the changes, was greeted with cheers from the Labour backbenchers. The media, too, praised Brown's performance, paying particular attention to the 2p reduction in the basic rate of income tax. But Frank Field, the former minister, was particularly exercised about the consequences of the move on the poor. He duly wrote an amendment to the finance bill to compensate those most affected, but the initiative achieved neither enough support to gain a majority in Parliament, nor indeed the attention of journalists. 'The media were too lazy to have picked up on the issue then,' he says.[232] Brown had achieved his objective, and received the praise from the right-wing press he sought. For the time being there was no pain – the measures would only come into effect in April 2008.

In the months leading up to his 2008 Budget, Darling would question Brown on the wisdom of the decision, but the Prime Minister remained adamant. Another key figure expressing concern was Balls's wife, Yvette Cooper, who had taken over from Andy Burnham as Chief Secretary to the Treasury in January 2008. She kept emphasising her worries about the social impact of the measure, 'in the context of a recession, the distributional table I'm seeing is really worrying'.[233] But Brown, she said, didn't want to know.[234] Fiona Gordon's attempts to encourage discussion about its impact also got nowhere, because 'Gordon [Brown] was so sure of his decision'.[235] Brown clung on to the idea that, taken together with a series of other measures, the abolition of the 10p tax rate would not have a negative impact on the most vulnerable. The problem that he had not fully anticipated was that people would view the 10p decision in isolation.

Darling duly delivered the Budget on 12 March 2008 and, contrary to all his advisers' fears, the 10p tax-rate issue received little attention as most commentators focused on the increases in alcohol and motor taxes. *The Guardian* described it as 'a deliberately low-key Budget',[236] while George Osborne dismissed it as a 'bad news Budget'.[237] It took fully three weeks for the consequences of the tax change to hit home. Labour MPs noticed warning signs principally while campaigning for the May local elections. When the subject came up at a Parliamentary Labour Party (PLP) meeting on 31 March, it turned into a disaster for Brown. The Prime Minister was clearly not in a good mood when he arrived, and was not pleased to hear backbencher Eric Martlew say that a constituent had complained about the forthcoming change at his weekly surgery two days before.[238] The flashpoint came, however, when Nia Griffith, MP for Llanelli, asked Brown how she and other MPs should respond to concerns raised by their constituents about the abolition of the 10p rate. A fairly innocuous and reasonable question, most thought. In a calmer frame of mind, Brown might have thanked Griffith and offered to discuss the details with her, but instead he lost his cool. 'No one is going to lose out from this change,' he said, complaining that people had not understood the policy and telling his parliamentary colleagues that they should work harder to get across to voters the message that 'the government is on their side'.[239]

MPs' jaws dropped – they all knew that this had become a serious problem on the doorsteps, and that it would get worse a week later, on 6 April, when the abolition came into effect. The PLP was left with the impression that their Prime Minister either did not know what he was talking about and was completely out of touch, or was deliberately deceiving himself and them. A veteran backbencher comments: 'I've never seen a Prime Minister lose the party like that: it was the worst performance in a PLP I've ever seen from a leader.'[240] The mood among MPs changed dramatically: some described it as 'very torrid' and 'sulphurous'.[241] Brown was heckled, which disturbed him deeply: he found the whole experience 'very difficult' and 'shocking'.[242] *The Guardian*'s Martin Kettle wrote that the meeting was 'a tipping point among the previously undecided ... old hands say they have never seen a party leader lose it the way Brown did last week'.[243] Worse news came the following week, when the Treasury Select Committee estimated that some 5.3m people would be worse off as a result of the change. Brown came under mounting pressure to abandon the policy, or to tell his Chancellor to do so.

After a brighter start to the year, the atmosphere in Number 10 deteriorated to the lowest point since Christmas, with blame and mutual recrimination prevalent. The Prime Minister fumed. Why had they not been told how the party would react? How had such disastrous consequences not been predicted? Officials in Downing Street passed the buck. 'We had no warning that this was going to be a major issue from the backbenchers,' says one.[244] Carter, who had expressly been brought in as the 'political' figure, was blamed by some for having 'no antennae into the PLP'. Others pointed out that he had not been party to the initial decision or bewailed the lack of an Alastair Campbell figure who would have spotted the problem.[245] The Whips Office was also slammed for not acting as an effective conduit of information into Downing Street. Chief Whip Geoff Hoon's response was that he found it difficult to secure impromptu meetings with Brown and it was claimed that Nye would not timetable these, knowing her boss's lack of enthusiasm for them.[246] Deputy Chief Whip Nick Brown, still smarting from being passed over in 2007, protested that it was not his job to go direct to Number 10, over the head of Hoon.[247]

Just as Brown was struggling to cope with the growing crisis over the 10p rate he became embroiled in yet another farce, which this time centred on the arrival of the Olympic torch in the UK en route to Beijing. On 10 March, large-scale protests against Chinese rule had begun in Tibet, and the authorities had responded with violence. Not wishing to be seen to condone the regime's actions, Brown decided that the torch could be photographed on 6 April outside Number 10, but he would not handle it. This approach was greeted with contempt, reviving criticisms that the Prime Minister was indecisive and preferred to 'fudge' difficult decisions.[248] On 9 April, it was announced Brown would not be attending the Olympics' opening ceremony in August and the BBC turned this into a big story. Number 10 responded furiously that this had been planned long before the outbreak of violence in Tibet, and pointed out that Brown would be going to the closing ceremony, where the Olympic torch would be handed over. He could hardly, Downing Street argued, go twice.[249]

Meanwhile, unrest was spreading in the PLP and support was growing for a Frank Field initiative to vote down the Budget. On 18 April, Angela Smith, Yvette Cooper's parliamentary private secretary, contacted Brown in the US to deny media reports that she was on the verge of resigning.[250] On 20 April, Darling was forced to say in public that it would be 'irresponsible to rewrite' the Budget, although he hinted at compensation for those affected later in the year.[251] On 21 April, reports appeared that some seventy 'concerned' Labour backbenchers might follow Field.[252] Still Brown refused to budge. The message given out was: 'Downing Street and the Treasury insist that no rethink is on the cards.'[253] Behind closed doors, however, an 'excruciating' debate was going on. Should money be found to mitigate the impact of the measure, and if so, would it make the difference between 'winning or losing' the forthcoming by-election in Crewe and Nantwich? Why did Darling not 'seem to notice the political seriousness of the issue'?[254] Field was pressing for all he was worth, and had a meeting with Darling in which he warned the Chancellor: 'The Budget will fail, with all the consequences.'[255] On the evening of 21 April, Brown, freshly back from Boston, tried to persuade MPs at a PLP meeting that he was serious about compensating those who would lose out from the abolition of the 10p rate. But MPs were no longer listening to what he had to say. The following day, forty MPs signed Field's amendment – sufficient for Labour to lose its majority. Field held a fraught meeting with Brown that day, but the offer of tax credits as a sweetener was insufficient to make him call off his revolt. Unrest spread up to Cabinet, many of whom were as disturbed at Brown's intransigence as they were by his failure to have thought through the impact of the tax change. David Miliband was forced to 'issue a humiliating plea for unity', warning that defeat would be certain if the party 'continued to argue among ourselves'.[256]

At this point, Brown suddenly changed tack. What made him change his mind? On 22 April, it was made blindingly clear to him that the party would suffer very badly at the forthcoming local elections if he did not alter course. Very unhappily, he caved in. On the morning of 23 April, he agreed to say at PMQs that a compensation package would be offered by Darling. In response, Field withdrew his amendment, now with forty-five signatories. Brown was hammered in the media for his volte face, as he knew he would be. 'The humbling of the Prime Minister,' was *The Times*'s verdict,[257] while Clegg and Cameron reacted with scorn. Field was still incensed, and described Brown in a BBC interview as 'unhappy, and prone to rage',[258] but later apologised for this personal attack. Darling announced the package in a special mini-Budget on 13 May, to the cheers of Labour MPs, a remedy costing £2.7bn. Brown's advisers argued that, as the economy needed a bit of stimulus by this time, this was not such a disaster,[259] but no one was listening.

The episode further strained relations between the Chancellor and Prime Minister. Brown had forced Darling to rewrite his first Pre-Budget Report the previous autumn with the last-minute inheritance-tax reform, now he had to rewrite his first Budget. 'As a consequence of Brown's last Budget, we had to throw an awful lot of money and resources at it, which made it difficult for [Darling],' says one Treasury official.[260] From this point, a divide opened up between Number 10 and the Treasury, which, conscious of a steady deterioration in the public finances, was wary of 'chucking money around the place to save the 10p decision'.[261] Officials subsequently looked back on the crisis in early 2008 as a time that the Treasury began to reconnect 'with its roots – sound money and scepticism about the ability of government to manage demand and the economy'.[262] These differences were to become much more pronounced during debates in 2009 over the response to the recession.

The Northern Rock and 10p débâcles had a peculiarly personal sting for Brown. He had always taken great pride in his proficiency in economic matters: if undermined on this bulwark, his confidence was prone to collapse. Fundamental questions were being increasingly asked about his performance as Chancellor, his spending decisions, and his priorities. Number 10's confidence also collapsed – there was a constant sense of 'what on earth is going to happen next?'[263]

Brown's response to the crises was characteristic – to work harder. He rose earlier and went to bed later. Aides became worried by this 'displacement activity' and his occasionally going into 'lock-down mode'. They felt that he needed a holiday badly.[264] The Prime Minister brooded, and when he eventually apologised for 'mistakes', it was too little too late and too grudging.[265] On 28 June, the Treasury Select Committee harshly criticised the mini-Budget and compensation package. It was a bitter pill for Brown to swallow. He had begun the New Year with such optimism and energy but, six months later, his self-confidence had been shattered and his leadership was on the rocks.

4

Summer of Peril

(May–August 2008)

Brown's relaunch in January, initially promising, had stalled badly. He entered this next phase in May fighting for the fortunes of his party in elections; he ended it in August fighting for his political life. During these fractious four months, he had bad luck, certainly, with MPs dying and becoming ill, necessitating unwelcome by-elections, and a deteriorating economy, which damaged Labour in the polls. But equally he had to live with the dire consequences of some of his own poor decision-making. His attempts to regain the initiative were constantly stymied by the damage to his reputation for economic competence, his weak communication skills, a still-dysfunctional Number 10, and the continuing absence of a clear philosophy to underpin his leadership.

Defeat at the Polls: May

Long before the May elections, Brown was in trouble. Parodying *The Communist Manifesto*, Martin Kettle wrote in *The Guardian*: 'A spectre is haunting the Labour Party – the spectre of Gordon Brown's failure.' Questions about him, Kettle continued, 'are being asked across the Labour Party', and the conclusion being reached was that 'the problem is Brown himself'.[1] In early May, large parts of the British public were given their first opportunity to pass judgement on their Prime Minister. Elections for English and Welsh councils fell on 1 May, as did the London mayoral and Assembly elections. At the end of the month came a by-election in Crewe and Nantwich, following the death of Labour stalwart, Gwyneth Dunwoody. These elections came against a background of fuel, energy and food prices rising significantly, with the prospect of petrol reaching £5 a gallon.[2] On the back foot, the government on 23 April announced its emergency compensation package to address disquiet over the 10p tax rate, and on 30 April, the day before the election, Brown finally admitted 'mistakes' in introducing this measure.[3] A more fulsome and genuine apology would have to wait until the autumn at the Labour Party conference.

Expectations at Labour headquarters and Downing Street were not high, but few were anticipating the loss of 334 councillors or, as some estimates suggested, the party coming third on the national equivalent share of the vote. It was Labour's worst result in forty years. A visibly dispirited Brown admitted that it had been a 'bad and disappointing' election for Labour. Its core vote plummeted in traditional heartlands such as South Wales, and it lost some key councils, including Reading. More worryingly by far, Ken Livingston's eight-year reign in London was brought to a close, with Boris Johnson, a man many in Labour thought unelectable, victorious with 53 per cent of the popular vote. The eccentric and flamboyant Johnson, who had hired a Fidel Castro suit for the campaign to mock 'Red' Ken's habit of fraternising with socialist leaders abroad, was now the most powerful Conservative in the country, and was putting the heat on Cameron. Number 10 watched the results with alarm: 'The local elections were very bad, but the worst thing for us was losing London – the citadel,' says Downing Street political strategist David Muir.[4] As luck would have it, the local elections fell on the date Labour had come to power eleven years before, and the focal point of both was the same South Bank location on the River Thames. The contrast did not escape commentators. 'On a sunny Friday in May, by the glittering water of the Thames, Tony Blair famously declared that a "new dawn" had broken. Yesterday, exactly eleven years later, Labour ushered in what will surely be its new dusk,' wrote Jonathan Freedland in *The Guardian*.[5]

The local elections were a tipping point where Brown began to lose the support of his Cabinet. Many had been in despair in private since the autumn. Now they began talking much more openly about the 'Brown problem'. Harriet Harman, one of the leading doubters, told Radio 4's *Today* programme that the results were 'very disappointing indeed'. Hoon meanwhile did nothing to reassure anyone with his words 'there's no crisis'.[6] Blame for the election results was laid firmly at Brown's door, and in particular his disastrous leadership of the 10p affair, while he pointed the finger at the economic crisis and rising fuel and food prices. Questions were increasingly asked as to who else might lead the party, with Jack Straw being viewed as a frontrunner. Patrick Hennessy speculated in his *Daily Telegraph* blog on whether the Justice Secretary was losing patience with the Prime Minister,[7] while on the *Today* programme Straw admitted that the voters had wanted to punish Brown for the 10p tax decision.[8]

Barely had the news from the local elections been digested when the eyes of the political world shifted 200 miles to the North-West, to Crewe and Nantwich, where the by-election was to be held on 22 May. The constituency was a blend of blue-collar Crewe and more affluent Nantwich, and was being viewed as a litmus test for the popularity of the major parties nationwide. The omens offered Labour no comfort. On 7 May, a Populus poll for *The Times* revealed a dramatic decline in the perception of Brown and Darling's economic competence relative to Cameron and Osborne: the proportion of the electorate that trusted the Labour team to deal with the economy well had halved to just 30 per cent (from 61 per cent in September). Worse for Brown personally, 55 per cent of Labour voters wanted him to resign.[9] Darling's mini-Budget on 13 May did nothing to boost confidence in Labour, or in the Chancellor's economic competence. 'Let no one be fooled why you are making the statement today. Not because you wanted to, but because this divided, dithering and disintegrating government are panicking in the face of the Crewe and Nantwich by-election,' jeered Osborne.[10] Number 10's retort – that the measure had nothing to do with the by-election – carried little credibility.

In the hope of capitalising upon her mother's popularity, Dunwoody's daughter, Tamsin, had been adopted as the Labour candidate. The Conservatives put up Edward Timpson, the privately educated son of a multi-millionaire family. Labour Party strategists took the decision to make his social class an issue in the election. Steve McCabe, then MP for Birmingham Hall Green, who was in charge of the local campaign, gave the go-ahead for Labour students to dress up in top hats and tails as a dig at Timpson.[11] 'It was devised to distract attention from the 10p tax and Brown's leadership,' explains one adviser.[12] The ploy subsequently backfired when it emerged that two of Labour's campaigners had themselves attended the fee-paying Manchester Grammar School.[13] A high-profile breakdown of discipline ensued when Ed Miliband and Harriet Harman publicly distanced themselves from the 'anti-toff tactics' employed in the campaign.[14] With reports of backbencher and ministerial disaffection filtering into Number 10, it decided to throw everything it could at the unsuspecting constituency. Several ministerial visits to Crewe took place in a last-minute bid to minimise the risk of a bad result.[15]

On 21 May, the day before polling, Cameron taunted Brown in the Commons for remaining in his 'bunker', rather than visiting the constituency.[16] The instant response was that Brown was merely following the convention that Prime Ministers do not campaign in by-elections; the truth was that Brown was now regarded as a liability rather than an asset. The result on 22 May was shocking for Labour, losing on a 17.6 per cent swing against the party. It was the first Conservative gain from Labour in a by-election for thirty years. Cameron proclaimed it 'the end of New Labour'.[17] Writing in the *Financial Times*, constitutional expert Vernon Bogdanor was almost alone in cautioning against reading too much into the result, pointing out that it was quite normal for incumbent governments to lose by-elections .[18] The press nevertheless made much of the fact that, if replicated nationally, the vote would give the Conservatives a landslide of a hundred seats or more.[19]

'Gordon Brown is facing the gravest crisis of his premiership ... one of the most humiliating setbacks to Labour since the era of Michael Foot [1980–83],' *The Guardian* spelt out gloomily. Pressure for a leadership challenge at the Labour Party conference in September would grow, the paper predicted, 'unless he shows that he can turn the party's fortunes around'.[20] Financial support for Labour now came under the cosh. On the day after the by-election, it was announced that individual donations to the party in the first quarter of 2008 were down 90 per cent on the same period the year before.[21] Possible successors to Brown started being more openly discussed. On 31 May, Prescott described David Miliband as 'brilliant', and tipped him as a future leader.[22] That day, Labour fared badly in a further by-election, in Henley, necessitated by Boris Johnson's election as Mayor of London. Labour came an ignominious fifth, trailing the BNP and the Greens, and its candidate lost his deposit. The skids were firmly under Brown, and there was no immediate prospect in sight for improvement. On 23 May, less than a year into Brown's premiership, former minister Graham Stringer became the first Labour MP to call for a leadership election. He told Sky News: 'The only way to deal with [the situation] is for a senior minister to stand up and challenge Gordon Brown.'[23]

Number 10's 'Unhappiest Time': January–June

Prime Ministers need Number 10 to be a place of stability and efficiency. For the six months from January to June 2008, it was anything but that. Just when Brown struggled to reassert himself following the electoral meltdown, his Downing Street operation was riven with disunity and discord, and he knew there was no one to blame but himself. His 'brainwave' solution of bringing in Stephen Carter alongside senior official Jeremy Heywood was heading for the rocks. Far from bringing unity and order, the Carter–Heywood diarchy had collapsed into a power struggle. A destructive briefing war had erupted between Carter and Brown's old guard, and morale had fallen to an all-time low. One official, who knows Downing Street intimately, calls it 'the worst time I've ever known for Number 10'. Looking back, he says: 'It became a very unhappy place.'[24]

It was the last thing Brown needed at a time of economic and political difficulty. How had he got it so wrong? Carter was an impressive figure, whose experience in strategic management should have brought a fresh perspective to the Brown Treasury clique. But he had not begun with tact. Brown made it clear to Carter he needed rapid solutions at Number 10, and the latter had started by composing a long list of Downing Street's failures in his first few days. Many of the long-standing staff were upset by the 'brusque' way in which Carter and the other new arrivals went about their work. 'Right from the start it was a total disaster. They came in like bulls in a china shop,' says one,[25] while another complains: 'They had their view about how shit everything was and how they alone would sort it out. They made us feel like a bunch of jokers.'[26] However, Carter also had his Downing Street admirers – one described his arrival as a 'symbol of the emerging professionalisation of the Brown operation'.[27]

Almost from the beginning, Carter started falling out with Brown's core team. Sue Nye, the director of government relations, whose importance in the organisation he significantly underestimated, resented the way she was treated.[28] Gavin Kelly, who had battled to keep Number 10 going after the premature departure of chief of staff Tom Scholar, felt sidelined.[29] Fiona Gordon did not feel she was rated highly.[30] Worse, she felt Brown lacked faith in her because of Carter's appointment. Communications advisers Michael Ellam and Damian McBride felt threatened and devalued after reports in the press in early February suggesting Carter wanted to bring in fresh blood to handle press relations.[31] It was believed that director of political strategy Spencer Livermore had left on account of the changes – Carter was effectively taking over his job – but he had decided to leave before the new year because he felt badly bruised by the fall-out from the autumn election débâcle.[32]

Divisions in Downing Street crystallised in mid-March, when the trade magazine *PRWeek* published an organogram of Number 10, which critics believed had been composed after discussions with Carter's team, showing Carter just below the Prime Minister at the top of the Number 10 tree and relegating others, including Ellam and McBride, to subordinate positions.[33] At the end of the month, *PRWeek* carried another article on Number 10, this time criticising Brown's speechwriting team. It said Carter had already made tentative contact with three of Blair's speechwriters, including Philip Collins, who had gone to *The Times* and was considered the archetypal Blairite.[34] Real anger was felt in the building.

More offensive to the Number 10 team, though, was Carter's inexperience of Whitehall. During his early days at Downing Street, he proposed scrapping the daily lobby briefings – a move that would have seriously damaged relations with the press, and would have been unthinkable to anyone with knowledge of Westminster. More often, though, Carter's culture came over as simply alien, and few were prepared to give him the benefit of the doubt. At a political Cabinet meeting on 18 March, he acted as moderator and asked ministers to divide up into tables of six or seven for some problem-solving role play. The move did not go down at all well as Cabinet ministers regarded themselves as being above such management games. One described the exercise as 'like something that would happen at primary school'.[35] However, had Brown's own stock been higher, perhaps ministers would have listened to his appointee with more respect.

Among Brown's political advisers, what rankled most was Carter's lack of commitment to the Labour Party.[36] He had been brought in as a special adviser – a political position – yet he was not a long-term Labour supporter, and showed little sympathy for the Labour cause. At a strategic meeting on 14 March, Number 10 aides squirmed when he referred to the Conservative leader as 'Dave'.[37] Before long, his political naiveté began to irritate Brown, too. At one point, when helping draft a speech, Carter repeatedly used the word 'choice' in reference to public services. The strong associations with Blair were lost on the newcomer, and Brown was forced to explain angrily why he was not comfortable with the word.[38] Yet when hiring Carter, the Prime Minister saw his lack of political connections as an advantage – having him on board would show the world that he could attract deep, personal commitment from a respected private-sector operator who was not a member of the Labour tribe.

Alighting on Carter as the solution to Number 10's problems need not have been the disaster it became. In the stuffy world of Whitehall, here was a direct and courageous voice, with an ability to speak 'truth to power' in a way that one member of Brown's old team wished they 'had done with Gordon – but the truth was that we didn't'.[39] His managerial insistence on correct office procedures brought order to a team that had let its modus operandi become governed by the idiosyncrasies of Brown's own working style. As one Downing Street policy adviser says: 'He was able to say things to Gordon that were blindingly obvious, like: "Why don't you have meetings with your staff?" or: "Why don't you take your jacket off when doing presentations?"'[40] Carter also helped to lift strategic communications on to a higher plane in Number 10 – a legacy that Justin Forsyth would build on later in the Brown's premiership.

But for these upsides, professional and personality clashes dominated. The tipping point was finally reached on 19 March, with a news article in *The Times* under the bold headline 'Number 10 infighting goes public'.[41] Brownite MP Tom Watson had had enough and demanded Nye give him some time with the Prime Minister. The meeting took place in the flat at the top of Downing Street. Brown was not aware of the story (he is not able to read newsprint easily and has to rely on others to keep him informed) and Watson told him that the negative press about Number 10 had to stop. Brown replied, in a 'very child-like' manner: 'But I thought Stephen was getting a very good press.'[42] He had invested great political and emotional capital in Carter's appointment, and for many weeks afterwards was in denial, refusing to accept that his big idea for solving Number 10's problems had fatal weaknesses. As with 10p, Brown struggled to acknowledge when his initiatives were failing so conspicuously.

In the absence of clear direction from Brown, briefing of the press by both camps intensified; McBride was said to be putting out 'several stories a week against' Carter.[43] Nye tried and failed to rein him in. One aide says: 'McBride treated Carter horrifically. He killed him off.'[44] Carter's team, if not the man himself, fought back, leaking stories to *PRWeek*. He was bemused by what was happening and found the anarchy of the Brown regime hard to manage. Carter believed that Brown liked to place people in boxes and that no one in Number 10 really knew what Brown felt, although Ed Balls was always a dominant figure for him.[45] On several occasions, Carter complained to Brown specifically about McBride's underhand methods, but the Prime Minister did not want to know. The view of many in Number 10 as to what went wrong with Carter and his team was simple: 'One, his arrival threatened and undermined the traditional "family business". Two, they were absolutely fucking useless: inexperienced outsiders who had zero political nous.'[46] The loathing was mutual and when a scandal forced McBride to resign the following year, Brown said to Carter: 'You're the only person who can say: "I told you so."'[47]

Carter's ultimate undoing, though, was the dissonance with Heywood. The Number 10 'permanent secretary' had an in-depth knowledge of Whitehall, understanding both the politics and the policy side of things, that left outsider Carter standing. 'From January 2008, there were two powers in Number 10. It was a case of a lion and a deer in a cage. Only one was going to emerge the winner,' says one observer.[48] According to another: 'The turf battle between Stephen and Jeremy was very bad until Jeremy established who was in charge.'[49] The tension became intense as Heywood battled to bring greater coherence to an operation that was clearly not performing satisfactorily. At one of Downing Street's daily 8am management meetings, from which Carter was absent, Heywood is reported to have said, in his authoritative and dry tone: 'Stephen has decided it is more important to play golf today than to attend the Number 10 management meeting.' The remark was quickly leaked to the press.

Carter became known as the man concerned about presentation.[50] He saw less and less of the Prime Minister, and so resorted to writing him long emails to which Brown barely responded – a sure sign that the chief of strategy was heading for the departure lounge.[51] By Easter, it had become apparent Carter no longer carried his boss's support. 'Stephen would say: "I will ensure Gordon does this by a certain date." But Gordon no longer trusted Stephen to take decisions for him,' says one senior adviser.[52] Carter found the period from May the most difficult – there was no definite word on his future, but it was clear to everyone that the game was up.

Instead of grasping the problem when it first developed, Brown had allowed Number 10 to descend into an internal briefing war. Instead of backing Carter or sacking him, he took the coward's way out and simply began to ignore him. Eventually, it fell to Carter himself to tell Brown, in August, that he wanted to leave. Anxious to avoid the departure being written up negatively – like 'rats leaving the sinking ship' – the Prime Minister asked him to wait until the autumn reshuffle, when his leaving of Downing Street would be 'a footnote in history, not a divisive headline'.[53] Brown also offered to make Carter a minister, with a brief to lead a review into 'Digital Britain'. Heywood was pivotal in persuading his former rival to take up the post, telling him: 'You'd be mad not to do it. You know the subject inside out.'[54] Indeed, Carter took much more comfortably to the role, and his report was published to acclaim in June 2009.[55]

The loss of Carter marked a victory for the old guard, and yet another failure by Brown to clean up the rot at the heart of his operation. Had the Prime Minister been more considered before Christmas, he might have found a strong political adviser in the Alastair Campbell mould who would have complemented his civil service team. Could that have kept Brown's old Treasury team – 'the family' – under control? As well as Balls and McBride, deputy Chief Whip Nick Brown and the Prime Minister's parliamentary private secretary, Ian Austin, had made it clear that they had no time for Carter from the outset. 'They hated Stephen with a vengeance, and were livid with Gordon for bringing him in as his chief political adviser and strategist without telling them. None of them wanted an outsider to come in and upstage them,' says one insider.[56] Carter's departure relieved Brown of one problem, but it had failed to address another.

Terrorism and Forty-Two Days: June

Had Brown been calmer, he would have stood back in the wake of the 10p tax débâcle and May election results, and asked himself how best to utilise the vital period leading up to the summer. He could have settled on a course to heal divisions in the party, restore confidence in his leadership and advance his still inchoate agenda. Instead, he opted for – or fell into – the very opposite, becoming embroiled in a battle over extending the period of detention without trial for terrorist suspects to forty-two days. A more counterproductive strategy at this troubled time of his premiership could barely be conceived, especially as it exposed Brown's worst political traits. Why did he do it? His decision to push forty-two days was motivated primarily by a desire to outflank and split the Conservative Opposition by attempting to make them look weak.[57] As a political calculation it badly backfired. Rather than bolstering his position in his party, it undermined confidence in his leadership still further. He had hoped to win plaudits from the right-wing media, but instead he attracted their scorn and provided them with further evidence that his premiership was spinning out of control. In the country, it alienated the liberal-left constituency he had set out to woo, just as 10p had alienated Labour's working-class constituents. His decision to play politics with civil liberties appalled some of his own advisers and frustrated key lieutenants such as Balls and Ed Miliband, who felt it did nothing at all to advance his agenda or values.[58] Heywood had warned him that, even if the measure passed through the Commons, it would be defeated in the Lords, as indeed it was.[59] At a most delicate moment he hit the reverse jackpot – a policy that emboldened his enemies and antagonised his supporters.[60] It was a case study in how not to govern.

How did Brown get himself into such a mess? As Prime Minister he took the terrorist threat seriously and the attempted attacks during the first weeks of his premiership had undoubtedly made a big impression on him. When alert levels were high, he would meet on a weekly basis with the heads of the three intelligence agencies – MI5, SIS (or MI6) and GCHQ – and he probed them intensely about the risks of a terrorist strike in Britain. Once, in the Terracotta Room, on the first floor in Number 10, he heard a loud bang across Horse Guards Parade, which immediately panicked him. 'What was that?' he asked nervously, the colour draining from his face.[61] From the beginning of his time at Number 10 Brown thought deeply about how terrorism should be tackled, and came out in favour of a long-term strategy designed to 'win the battle of hearts and minds' against violent extremists.[62]

During his Camp David visit in 2007 he had written in the *Washington Post*: 'We must undercut the terrorists' so-called "single narrative" and defeat their ideas … We must back the moderate voices and reformers, emphasising the shared values that exist across faiths and communities.'[63] 'What won the Cold War was the winning of the argument, not just military superiority,' Brown would say.[64] He spoke movingly about encouraging the establishment of a European Islamic foundation to promote moderate Islam with a shared condemnation of terrorism, and to assert the values of civilised society. With Sarkozy and Merkel he discussed the plan passionately, but the official advice he received was that governmental support for such a foundation would be counterproductive.[65] According to a senior policy adviser, he was further advised 'not to be involved in any covert discussions, because it would be exposed by the media and it would backfire badly'.[66] He found himself, as a result, intensely frustrated – unable to combat terrorism openly, or behind closed doors, as had finally brought peace to Northern Ireland, with the 'back channel' to the IRA. His deeply felt idealism was also undercut by his less idealistic desire not to alienate the right-wing press, and in particular the Murdoch press, by being seen to promote a dialogue with moderate rebels in Afghanistan. Not for the last time, his heart and his head did not align. But on the forty-two days, he did not even seem to have engaged his head.

By reopening the debate on detention without trial, Brown wanted to show he was tough on terrorism, but his method of demonstrating it was inept. Measures already existed to allow the authorities to extend the period that a suspect could be detained beyond the existing twenty-eight-day limit hammered out under Blair. Had he allowed himself to be spooked by the spooks? Soon after arriving in Number 10, he received 'a very hard steer' from MI5 and Special Branch of the Metropolitan Police on some of the 'bad things' out there.[67] Given the significant and imminent threats of domestic terror in Britain, they told him, they required more time than they were allowed under the detention limits in place to allow them to decrypt complex computer files and this meant they needed to hold suspects for longer.[68] Aides in Number 10 say that 'Gordon was convinced it was true'[69] but maintain that the precise number of days was irrelevant to him – what he cared about was easing the way to allow for legitimate extensions beyond the twenty-eight days, depending upon the merits of each case.[70]

However, it is abundantly clear that Brown's primary motivation was political. The fear of being thought soft on security issues in the right-wing media continued to haunt him. Rumours circulated among senior members of the Prime Minister's camp that Blair had spoken to Rupert Murdoch in the US, telling the media mogul he thought his successor was 'soft' on terrorism.[71] Balls blames Blair for instilling this fear in Brown, such that he felt he had to run with forty-two days to prove his anti-terror credentials. 'Blair made it very clear to Gordon he had to come across as tough; the News International people would worry if he was not. That is why he did forty-two days,' says Balls.[72] The move was also popular – at the height of the debate, a poll in the *Daily Telegraph* said that 69 per cent of members of the public supported the policy,[73] at a time when Labour were trailing the Conservatives by 25 per cent in a concurrent YouGov poll.[74] Brown saw an opportunity to destabilise the Conservatives by outflanking them on an issue on which he sensed they were divided, and seized it with both hands. An added sweetener was that making a stand on forty-two days allowed him to outdo his predecessor, succeeding where Blair had failed. 'His political people thought that he should do something tough on crime that Tony Blair hadn't been able to achieve,' confirms one insider.[75] The idea of outsmarting the Blairites and the Conservatives in one fell swoop seemed irresistibly attractive. It was classic Brown. James Purnell believes that 'Brown never gave up on "triangulation" and point-scoring'.[76]

By offering strong reassurances on judicial oversight he hoped he could keep *The Guardian* and liberals onside. He had several off-the-record meetings with Shami Chakrabarti, the influential head of Liberty, whom he liked, in the hope of winning her over. She made some sympathetic noises. The liberal left had started out with high hopes for Brown. His promise of a 'new constitutional settlement' within weeks of taking office, including the possibility of a British Bill of Rights, and his powerful speech entitled 'On Liberty' in October 2007 had kept those hopes alive. He was heavily influenced by the American Conservative thinker Gertrude Himmelfarb, especially her book *The Roads to Modernity*, which argued inter alia that British Enlightenment thinkers like Adam Smith, David Hume and Edmund Burke had made a more important and humane contribution to the debate on liberty than the French *philosophes*. Brown even wrote the foreword to one of her books. His Number 10 team was delighted to have a Labour Prime Minister who read books and was moved by ideas, but not quite like this: they were disconcerted by his lending his name to an author who was opposed to state intervention and firmly on the political right.

In any case, his ploy to keep both left and right happy was doomed to fail because liberals were never convinced by his attempt to reconcile both agendas. Worse, they thought he was playing politics with the cause of civil liberties. In November 2007, Liberty had released a report saying that Britain's period of detention without trial was already the longest among comparable nations,[77] and Brown's case was further undermined when Lord Goldsmith, Attorney General under Blair, said he could see no evidence for the need to extend the limit beyond twenty-eight days, a view that was echoed by Ken Macdonald, the Director of Public Prosecutions.[78] For many on the liberal left, forty-two days was the turning point. Disillusioned by his failure by mid-2008 to advance his constitutional agenda, they now began to turn on Brown.

If the thinking on forty-two days was ill-conceived, the execution in Parliament was worse. On 6 December 2007, Jacqui Smith announced proposals to raise the limit from twenty-eight to forty-two days.[79] At the time, she hoped to achieve cross-party agreement but, after meetings with Nick Clegg and shadow Home Secretary David Davis, it became clear there was no consensus. She pressed Brown hard to talk to Cameron directly, but to no avail. 'Gordon Brown always hated doing that kind of thing, even when it was very necessary,' says Smith.[80] He believed the government could win on its own, and he made the bill's passage a personal mission. Smith was amazed at how much time he put into drafting the bill, consulting lawyers to get the details right. 'He was always agitating: "How can we get this done?"' she adds.[81] Others saw this level of involvement not as admirable attention to detail, but rather evidence of the Prime Minister's inability to delegate and let go.

The crucial vote was to take place on 11 June. It was clear long before that Labour MPs were far from happy. The Parliamentary Labour Party (PLP) was getting more and more rebellious. 'During this period, our majority was a paper majority,' says one aide.[82] Complicating matters was the dysfunction in the Whips Office, which had previously become clear during the 10p tax-rate débâcle. Brown had no confidence in Hoon, and Hoon had little confidence left in Brown. 'The PLP wanted to know: "Why is he doing forty-two days?" It was serious,' says Hoon.[83] A parallel whipping operation to Hoon's was being run by deputy Chief Whips Nick Brown and Tommy McAvoy, which did nothing to add clarity.[84] Hoon was exasperated by a meeting with Jacqui Smith and aides at Number 10 in early June that had been intended to determine the way ahead. Brown turned up forty minutes late and the meeting broke up with no resolution having been achieved.[85]

On 3 June, Smith tried to reassure MPs by pledging that the new powers would only be granted in the event of a 'grave exceptional terrorist threat' to the UK.[86] Parliament, she said, would be allowed to review the implementation of any extensions on a 'case by case' basis. This was sufficient to win over some critics, including Keith Vaz, the influential chairman of the Home Affairs Select Committee.[87] As the key vote approached, Brown was increasingly involved in phoning or meeting with MPs in his room in the House of Commons. 'It was hugely time-consuming. Not at all a good use of his time,' says defence and security adviser Matt Cavanagh.[88] As had become increasingly evident on the 10p tax issue, some Labour MPs saw this as a referendum on Brown himself. 'I don't give a stuff about forty-two days, but I'm prepared to vote against it if it will help force Gordon out,' one told the *Independent on Sunday*'s John Rentoul.[89]

The bill slipped through on the narrowest of margins: 315 to 306, with thirty-six Labour MPs voting with the Opposition.[90] The following day, David Davis, increasingly at odds with Cameron, to whom he had lost the Conservative leadership election in 2005, resigned to force a by-election on the issue. However, it was not the Conservatives but Labour that was left badly damaged by this episode. If Brown had lost the vote, it would have brought into the open the increasingly bold internal opposition to his remaining in power.[91] He won by the skin of his teeth only because nine Democratic Unionist MPs from Northern Ireland came to his rescue. Before this episode, Brown had been deeply wary of his Northern Ireland Secretary, Shaun Woodward, but the parliamentary battle was to mark the beginning of a close bond between them.[92]

When the bill went to the House of Lords in the autumn, peers duly voted 309 to 118 to retain the twenty-eight-day limit. Advised by his whips that he did not have the majority to force the measure through the Lords, Brown chose to accept the passing down of a severely watered-down counter-terrorism bill.[93] What a price to pay for so little. It had been one of the most damaging examples of muddled thinking during Brown's premiership.

Bush in London: June

A visit by the US President to London in mid-June provided one of the rare light moments that month. This was part of a farewell tour of Europe, to thank favoured 'Atlanticist' leaders Merkel, Sarkozy, Berlusconi and Brown. Elements of the US media gave the trip a jaded assessment. 'For many Europeans, no matter how hard he tries, Bush will always be considered an ignorant, incurious cowboy,' wrote Michael Elliott on the *Time* magazine website.[94] Brown wanted the London visit to be a relaxed, 'non-ideological' affair. What should they do? There was precious little business to transact. The only source of tension concerned speculation that Brown was about to announce plans to pull the remaining British forces out of Iraq. Brown's idea of a Belfast-only meeting had not appealed to Bush – the two leaders would travel to Northern Ireland, but the President also wanted a London send-off. What should they do? Brown's idea of a meeting in Belfast (Clinton and Bush had gone there for Blair) had not appealed. British ambassador to the US Nigel Sheinwald told Number 10 that Bush was an avid reader of history and biography,[95] so why not host a dinner for historians?[96] It flattered Bush and made a big impression on him: during the President's final phone conversation with Brown shortly before he left the White House, he referred back to the dinner as 'cool'.[97] Both Bush and Brown were surprised at how well they got on: they really 'clicked when they realised they shared a passion for military history', says one official.[98] Careful thought was put into the selection of guests. Eventually, Simon Schama, David Cannadine and his wife, Linda Colley, Martin Gilbert, Alistair Horne and Piers Brendon, head of the archive at Churchill College Cambridge, were selected. Rupert and Wendy Murdoch and Neil and Glenys Kinnock also made the cut – a grand intellectuals' dinner was ideal to help keep them sweet.

The fare was stolidly British–Scottish salmon, green pea soup, Gloucestershire beef and fruit trifle, together with an English Denbigh's Bacchus 2004 wine, the virtues of which escaped the teetotal Bush. Brown was an impressive stage manager, inviting the President to move from table to table over the different courses to enable him to meet all the other guests. Both leaders delivered short speeches: Brown's was strongly pro-American, discussing his holidays in Martha's Vineyard and how much the country had meant to him,[99] while Bush's was more perfunctory. Little did he realise that Sarah Brown, ever her own woman, was wearing a CND necklace.[100] Andrew Roberts, invited he said because of his relationship with Bush, was struck by Brown's demeanour. 'I suspected I'd see a man browbeaten, but he was gregarious and outgoing,' he says. Despite their strongly opposing politics, Brown took time to show Roberts and his wife the Cabinet Room, and even ventured 'a few light-hearted gags'.[101] While they ate, 2,500 anti-war protesters in Parliament Square had to be pushed back by the police as they attempted to breach the barricades that had been set up at the entrance to Whitehall.[102] Brown enjoyed the evening immensely, although some of his pleasure was spoilt when Schama later distanced himself,[103] describing the evening as 'an absolute fucking catastrophe' and Bush as 'all-time loser in presidential history'.

Bush returned to Number 10 the next morning, 16 June, for talks with Brown in the first-floor study. Unlike Bush, Brown liked to conduct these meetings without aides present. After a while, Number 10 policy adviser Tom Fletcher, who was talking to Bush's National Security Advisor, Steve Hadley, in the White Room next door, wondered whether the two leaders had had enough time and knocked on the door. Brown indicated that he wanted longer. Before he could leave, the President beckoned Fletcher over and asked if he would pass a message on to his own waiting staff, whispering into his ear: 'Can you tell them to kiss my ass!'[104] A press conference followed later that morning in the Foreign Office's Locarno Room. To distract attention from Iraq, Number 10 deliberately decided to push Brown's line harder in the direction of the US policy on sanctions in Iran. 'We deliberately stoked up the Iran stuff and made a big deal of it as we wanted to keep away from troop numbers in Iraq: the FCO was cross with us,' says a Number 10 official.[105]

Oil and Saudi: June

Foreign affairs continued to claim much of Brown's attention over the next few days. On 19 June, he was in Paris where he and President Sarkozy signed an open letter to Burmese opposition leader Aung San Suu Kyi, supporting calls for democratic reform in her country. The next day he was in Brussels and on 22 June, he flew to Saudi Arabia.

The rise in oil and food prices had continued to worry the Prime Minister and threatened to become a major political headache at home. As household energy bills rose, the public mood had begun to turn against energy companies, and pressure was mounting in the PLP for a windfall tax on the sector. Brown had asked Shriti Vadera, who had moved from International Development to the Department of Business, Enterprise and Regulatory Reform, to come up with a solution, bypassing energy minister Malcolm Wicks. 'For all intents and purposes she was the energy minister for the issue,' says Michael Jacobs, environment adviser at Number 10.[106]

Darling and Business Secretary John Hutton were strongly opposed to a windfall tax. Brown wanted a direct discount on consumers' bills, but it would have been hugely complicated and expensive to administer. Matters were not helped when the permanent secretary at the Business Department, Brian Bender, was overheard on the train discussing details of the proposed scheme with a colleague and this was gleefully picked up by the *Sunday Times*. As problems persisted through the summer, Jacobs was called back from holiday to work on a package with Vadera and Hutton, eventually working out a series of measures that required energy companies to increase their spending on household insulation, with a focus on customers in low-income areas. Public anger about energy prices was to recede later in the year, and advisers eventually felt that they had 'just about got away with it'.[107] As one of them commented: 'A lot of politics is about being able to say we're doing something. We have an answer. And it was enough of an answer.'[108]

For now, though, Brown was in Jeddah seeking a more permanent solution. As so often in his premiership, he saw the problem in global terms, and had become concerned that higher oil prices could spark the next world crisis. The solution, he believed, must rest in greater cooperation between producing and consuming countries. To address the issue, he had resolved to fly to Saudi Arabia for a one-day summit arranged by King Abdullah, the only foreign leader to attend.[109] Brown's readiness to attend the meeting helped build international partnerships that proved vital to his efforts to resolve the financial crisis the following autumn. For the time being, he had more immediate goals. 'He wanted to take the initiative on oil prices – nothing less than a new bargain with Saudi Arabia and other producers,' says Jacobs.[110] An entire team was created in the Cabinet Office specifically to develop Brown's approach on oil. His big idea was that Gulf states should invest their oil surpluses in alternative energy technologies in return for more certainty over demand in Western markets. No one can fault its imagination. 'It was typical Gordon. He wanted a grand solution. He saw a problem and wanted to tackle it,' says one of his advisers. Ultimately 'it was a bit idealistic' to imagine that the oil-producing countries would dance to a tune emanating from cramped offices in 70 Whitehall.[111]

Trouble in His Backyard

Before the month was over, fresh difficulties hit Brown from Scotland. On 28 June, Wendy Alexander, leader of the Labour group in the Scottish Parliament (and sister of International Development Secretary, Douglas Alexander), resigned over a funding scandal. 'Brown has already lost control of Holyrood. Now [he] has lost control of the Scottish Labour Party. This is further weakening of his authority,' a 'senior Scottish Labour source' told *The Times*.[112] Brown's attempts to persuade Alexander to remain were forlorn: once the Standards Committee at Holyrood ruled that she had failed to register donations she was adamant she had to go.[113] This was trouble in the Prime Minister's own backyard at a time when he needed it least.

Alexander's turbulent reign as Scottish leader had caused Brown a major headache in May, when she declared her support for a referendum on Scottish independence in a TV interview. Ever since the SNP's historic victory in the May 2007 Scottish parliamentary elections, which had allowed them to form a minority government, Labour strategists were divided over how to respond to a resurgent Alex Salmond. Alexander was in the camp that believed that Labour needed to regain the initiative on the constitutional debate north of the Border, which led her in November 2007 to push for a commission to review the powers of the Scottish Parliament, with the aim of strengthening, in particular, its weak taxation powers. Des Browne, the Scottish (and Defence) Secretary, Darling and Straw were much more sceptical, believing that the government could not keep making concessions to Scottish nationalism. After five months Brown eventually agreed to support a review of Holyrood's tax-raising powers led by Sir Kenneth Calman. Alexander, however, believed Labour needed to do more, arguing that they should 'call the SNP's bluff' by proposing a referendum on independence that, based on a reading of the polls, she believed the nationalists would lose, leaving their political strategy in tatters. The idea was discussed at various meetings in Number 10. Browne and Darling were against the idea in principle. Douglas Alexander and Number 10 advisers could see some merit in the argument, but realised that spring 2008 was not a good time to contemplate such a risky move – unlike Brown, the SNP were still enjoying a prolonged honeymoon, while rising oil prices were considered to favour the SNP's economic case for separation. Instead of shutting the issue down, Brown fumbled: in a call with his Scottish leader he did not unequivocally rule out the idea. Alexander believed she had his endorsement and so went public. A public farce ensued as their respective public positions contradicted each other. Brown was furious with Alexander and insisted she tone down her comments.[114] The episode seemed to confirm the view that the government was out of control.

Brown loved his native Scotland, though as the first Scottish Prime Minister to govern the UK since devolution, he was always wary of expressing this too enthusiastically for fear of alienating the English electorate and press. After this débâcle he now worked hard to recover lost ground by getting fully behind the Calman Commission process, which would later succeed in building consensus amongst the unionist parties in both Holyrood and Westminster for a significant overhaul of the fiscal powers of the Scottish Parliament. Even so it is puzzling that Brown, in the face of a resurgent SNP (the party would defy the political odds in May 2011 by winning an outright majority in the Scottish Parliament), did so little to articulate a positive and compelling case for the union during his premiership. 'He regularly toyed with making a big statement setting out why the union still mattered in twenty-first century Britain but he was never able to pull it off. Neither he nor the team could work out how to develop the Britishness agenda he pursued as Chancellor and turn it into something more concrete about the role of union in a devolved context' recalls an official. In this vacuum Brown and Labour instead reverted to an entirely counter-productive strategy of trying to scare Scottish voters into backing them by portraying the nationalists as the bogeymen of Scottish politics. Such negative campaigning simply underlined Labour's lack of a distinctive vision for Scotland.

The Middle East – Iraq and Israel: July

July gave Brown no respite, with overseas work continuing to press down heavily on him. From 6 to 9 July, he was in Hokkaido, Japan, for a G8 summit, and from 13 to 14 July in Paris. Then, on 19 July he left for a three-day visit to Iraq and Israel. Brown's relationship with the military had been tense since long before his surprise visit to Iraq in October 2007 and his announcement during that trip that as part of the shift to an overwatch role – that is a move away from combat operations to a focus on training and mentoring the Iraqi army – the level of British troops would be reduced from 4,500 to 2,500 in spring 2008. Brown had settled on the target in direct opposition to advice from Chief of Defence Staff, Jock Stirrup, who cautioned: 'Don't mention precise numbers. They must be deliverable.' As Stirrup later commented, 'the military is always very cautious about hard numbers because they tend to come back to bite you.'[115] Britain's senior officer was right to be cautious: by the time Brown visited Basra for his pre-Christmas visit on 9–10 December, it had become clear, as the military had predicted, that the target would not be met because of the deteriorating security situation in southern Iraq.[116] The British decision to withdraw from Basra Palace to the city's airport had sat uneasily with the White House, sensitive as it was about the actions of its last major ally in Iraq.[117] Brown's October announcement on troop reductions had thus caused further ripples. However, the Prime Minister had never advocated a hasty retreat. His senior foreign policy adviser, Simon McDonald, himself a proponent of a gradual exit, confirms this: 'I didn't have to argue strongly with him about not scuttling. Gordon got to the point quickly.'[118] But the US administration remained alert for several months to any signs of a ramping-up of rhetoric about the British withdrawal. Brown, broadly speaking, had continued Blair's policy of a measured draw-down of troops, but had succeeded in recasting the tone of the debate to one that was less gung-ho, and instead based around a more pragmatic argument about meeting Britain's responsibilities. Of the many legacies he had been bequeathed, it was perhaps in Iraq that Brown most succeeded in balancing the twin challenges of change and continuity.

While the launch by General David Petraeus, head of the occupying forces in Iraq, of the 'surge' had succeeded in stabilising the situation in and around Baghdad in 2007, all was not tell in southern Iraq.[119] Shia militias were creating a situation of lawlessness in the Basra area, and Iraqi Prime Minister Maliki had criticised British forces for failing to tackle this. The army felt this was unfair, particularly as Maliki had not confronted the militias when he first took office.[120] Nonetheless, the criticism lent credence to an argument, much-resented by the British military, that its mission in Iraq had failed, and had only been sustainable when supported by the US army.[121]

On 25 March, against the backdrop of this tense relationship, Maliki ordered the Iraqi army to act against the militias in Basra in an operation codenamed 'Charge of the Knights'. After an uncertain start, Iraqi forces quickly gained the upper hand, and the militias were stood down five days later. Maliki claimed it as a major victory. For the British, however, the offensive had come out of nowhere. Brown was at a NATO summit in the vast, Ceausescu-era Palace of the Parliament in Bucharest when he first heard about the fighting and he promptly retired into a remote corner with McDonald and Fletcher. They had been aware of some plans for an attack, but had been given no warning of the date. Brown was put through on his mobile to Maliki. In a heated conversation, he stressed to the Iraqi Prime Minister that they needed to work cooperatively, though he readily conceded that it was right for a Shia leader to be tackling Shia militia. After Brown had made his points and saved some face, the British military were able to provide logistical and occasional artillery support to the operation.[122]

By the time of Brown's visit on 19 July, calm had returned to the region. The Iraqi intervention slowed the draw-down of British troops, so a new timetable was devised. 'I think the Americans were surprised by how supportive we were in staying on,' says Cavanagh, who listened in to the calls between Brown and Bush.[123] With the Bush administration in its final year, a key concern had become preventing Iraq, specifically the continuing British commitment, becoming an issue in the US presidential elections. Brown's team took pains to talk through their thinking at every stage with the White House, and the close cooperation paid off. 'Iraq was an issue during the primaries but no longer by the actual election itself, in the second half of the year,' recalls Sheinwald.[124]

With Britain's military engagement in Iraq shortly to come to an end (Maliki would announce on 13 October that British troops were no longer needed to maintain security in the south), hard questions were asked about what it had achieved. Fairly or unfairly, the Charge of the Knights had left the military feeling slighted over its handling of Shia militias. What particularly stung was the charge that they had failed to confront the armed groups earlier when they had the chance, and were subsequently reliant on US support when the time came to disarm them. As attention shifted during 2008 to Afghanistan, the top brass were all the more anxious that they demonstrate success in that theatre. The seeds were thus sown for the unhappiest military–political clash in living memory.

On 20 July, Brown flew to Jerusalem to deliver an address to the Knesset, the Israeli Parliament, becoming the first British leader to do so. It was an honour that carried a deep personal resonance to Brown. His passion for the Jewish story, and his interest in finding a way forward on Israel and Palestine, was a lesser-known aspect of his character. The interest had originated in childhood. Brown's father, the Reverend John Brown, had chaired the Church of Scotland's Israel Committee, and had himself learned Hebrew as a young man. Twice each year, and sometimes more, he had travelled to Israel, and on each occasion he returned with a reel of film from his trip, which he showed his children on a temperamental old projector. The silent movies delighted the young Gordon, who was captivated by his stories of the struggles and triumphs of the young nation. He would later tell the Knesset: 'I will never forget those early images in my home and the stories my father would tell.'[125] An official confirms that Brown 'saw Israel through the eyes of his father's visits' and that these 'conditioned his whole outlook'.[126] As he flew from Iraq, with a deepening political crisis at home, those memories brought him great personal comfort.

Of course, the human side of Palestinian suffering from the effects of the Israeli occupation also affected Brown deeply. He favoured a 'two-state' solution based on the 1967 borders, with a joint capital in Jerusalem. In Israel, his first meeting was with President Shimon Peres, whom he pressed hard on the case for an economic roadmap to peace. Financier Ronald Cohen, who was Brown's personal friend, had strongly influenced the Prime Minister's approach to the region and helped shape his belief that economic investment and regeneration were critical to the achievement of a just settlement. He saw analogies also from within the UK, and believed that 'economic lessons could be learned from Northern Ireland', according to McDonald, who had previously served as British ambassador to Israel.[127] Brown's vision of the way forward on Israel/Palestine thus always included economic as well as purely political elements.[128] His admiration for Israel did not blind him to the Palestinians' cause and their rights to economic prosperity.

After his meeting with Peres, Brown travelled through Israel's controversial security wall to the West Bank for a meeting with Mahmoud Abbas, President of the Palestinian National Authority, in Bethlehem. While there, he pledged an additional £16m in funding for the authority. 'Palestinians need to see real change in their daily lives, and that means jobs, housing and basic services,' Brown said.[129] In defiance of the hardline views of the Israeli right he continued: 'The whole European Union is very clear on this matter: we want to see a freeze on settlements.'[130] Later, at the Yad Vashem Holocaust memorial in Jerusalem, he resisted attempts to hurry him through the exhibition, wanting 'to stop and ponder and contemplate'.[131] In the visitors' book, he wrote: 'Nothing prepares you for the story that is told here … we must always remember so that prejudice, discrimination, racism and anti-Semitism can be banished from our world.'[132]

After talking late into the night to aides at Jerusalem's King David Hotel, Brown awoke early to work alone on his address. The draft had been prepared by his senior speechwriter, Beth Russell, with significant inputs from McDonald, but he had written the heart of the speech himself,[133] determined that it should set out his very personal vision for the region.[134] He took a hard line on Iran, a crowd-pleaser that went down well with the audience, and then spent time on the theme of building stronger international institutions, including a stronger International Monetary Fund to act as an early warning system for the world economy. But then he moved on to the meat, talking in straight terms about the Arab–Israeli conflict: 'Today there is one historic challenge you still have to resolve so that your sixty-year journey into the future is complete: peace with your neighbours.' Recalling his family's history, he said: 'When in these next sixty years, my sons follow in the steps that their grandfather and their father have taken, I also hope they will be able to see neighbours, once enemies, now friends.'[135]

Brown sought deliberately to offer support to Israeli Prime Minister Ehud Olmert, and to put his firm seal of approval on the two-state solution. It was a sign of the esteem in which Brown was held, and the persuasiveness of his rhetoric, that when he criticised the Israeli West Bank settlements, only one member of the Knesset walked out.[136] His optimism about the possibilities for peace had not been bluff: he truly believed that a historic agreement was within sight. He was thus mortified when, in September 2008, Olmert, a man he saw as a 'true friend', was forced to resign following allegations of financial impropriety. Olmert would remain as Prime Minister in an interim capacity until the following year, but his authority had evaporated. It left a bitter taste. Brown believed that Olmert's enemies had deliberately stirred up trouble to discredit him and abort the peace plan.

For now, though, Brown was delighted with the trip, and was in high spirits on the flight back to London,[137] despite an ungainly run from the Knesset to his convoy so as not to miss the plane. Even the *Daily Mail* praised the visit, reporting that 'on the world stage and at financial summits, Mr Brown is perceived as a formidable figure' and that he had delivered blunt truths to Israeli MPs with 'statesmanship' and 'courage'. His experience in Israel, at a time of great turbulence at home, brought great solace to a man with deep respect for family and faith. He was immensely proud of his father, often turning to his sermons in times of personal reflection, and sometimes giving copies to close personal friends. As things grew worse at home, it was an increasingly familiar dynamic: restorative and confidence-boosting trips abroad, only to return to domestic turbulence. As the *Daily Mail* went on to ask: 'What goes wrong when he lands back on English soil?'[138] Brown was about to be reminded just how bad things could get.

The Worst By-Election and the Worst Speech: July

When David Marshall, Labour's MP for Glasgow East, first announced he was stepping down after thirty years as an MP on health grounds, no one in Number 10 was initially worried. Here was a seat in Labour's – and Brown's – own heartland, the third-safest in Scotland and the party's twenty-sixth-safest in the UK. Surely Brown could hold on here? But his aides were dramatically shaken out of their complacency when Scottish whip Frank Roy warned Joe Irvin, who had succeeded Fiona Gordon as political secretary in late June, that Labour were likely to lose. As one aide explains: 'It's a very deprived seat. We were expecting a low turnout. Labour was very unpopular and the SNP was riding high in the constituency.'[139] What turned out to be a bruising campaign then got worse for Labour when their candidate withdrew at the last minute and there was a hiatus of several days, which was exploited by the SNP, before the successor was installed. So worried was Brown that, on 16 July, he postponed the introduction of a 2p rise in petrol duty. In another panic he also decided to defer the vote on the hugely controversial embryology bill until the autumn to try and win favour with the large Catholic vote in Glasgow East. But his efforts were thwarted when on 19 July the Catholic Church in Scotland became Labour's worst nightmare when it posted information on notice boards about the candidates' stance on abortion. Only the SNP candidate opposed it – leaving Labour campaign strategists furious with the Catholic Church for such an overt politicial intervention.[140] On the evening of the election, on 24 July, the Prime Minister was watching *Dr Who* actor David Tennant star in *Hamlet* for the Royal Shakespeare Company at Stratford-upon-Avon. Although Brown was not a natural theatre-lover, the performance seemed a good opportunity for him and Carter and their wives to play host to *Daily Mail* editor-in-chief Paul Dacre. His mood when watching the tragedy in Elsinore was not improved by news from Glasgow about the expected result.[141]

Brown went to bed worried, and woke up to the news – victory for the SNP on a gigantic swing of 22.5 per cent, with the seat changing hands on a margin of just 365 votes. Labour had eventually fielded a strong candidate and had thrown in everything it had to secure victory. There was nowhere for him to hide. 'Brown had been in denial, but was now beside himself. He blamed no one else but he was wily enough to know he was in real difficulty,' says an aide.[142] The three by-elections lost in a row (Crewe, Henley, and now Glasgow) encompassed Britain's entire demographic range, from prosperous southern professionals to the impoverished Scottish working class. The result completed 'the picture of rejection', a senior Labour MP told the *Financial Times*.[143]

Number 10 was seriously alarmed. It knew that an active campaign among some backbenchers to gain signatures calling for a leadership contest had been underway since June.[144] It was also aware that members of the Cabinet were already openly discussing Brown's position, and knew that the disasterous by-election result would embolden them. 'If he couldn't even win in his own citadel, what is the use of Gordon Brown?' was the question being asked.[145] Paul Sinclair, the special adviser who was handling the media response from Number 10, held a conference call with Deputy Leader Harriet Harman to discuss how to react, and he suggested that Des Browne, Scottish Secretary, should do as much as possible to buy time and give Brown some breathing space. Harman retorted that they should openly admit failure. It led Number 10 to question her motives, as such an approach would only add to the momentum behind those suggesting the Prime Minister should step down. 'We weren't sure what Harriet was up to,' says one aide, reflecting a widespread feeling about the Deputy Leader.[146] The unrest inevitably filtered out into the press. 'Senior ministers are now quite openly – in private at least – discussing the likelihood of a putsch,' reported the *Daily Telegraph*.[147] The media were abuzz with talk of huddled conversations between ministers, former ministers and backbenchers, and reports now filtered into Downing Street that Harman had told an aide: 'This is my moment.' As Chief Whip, Hoon had listened over preceding months to 'significant' numbers of individual MPs expressing their doubts about Brown's leadership qualities, above all over his inability to take decisions.[148] But these voices now became a cacophony. The polls brought Brown no respite. On 26 July, a ComRes poll for *The Times* found only 24 per cent of voters intended to vote Labour, a full twenty-two points behind the Conservatives.[149]

Brown could not have had a worse backdrop for the major speech that he was to deliver on 25 July at Warwick University to the Labour Party's National Policy Forum, an annual event that had been created by Blair and attracted ministers, MPs and members from across the party. Reeling from the predicted by-election result, Brown had had very little sleep on Thursday night and was fragile even before he took to the stage. He decided to speak without notes, a tactic David Cameron had used to devastating effect at the 2007 Conservative Party conference. The approach did not come naturally to Brown, though, especially at a time when his confidence was so low. For two hours before delivering it, he lay on a sofa, not talking to anyone, memorising lines in his head. He was nervous, but thought he had it straight. But then, five minutes before he rose to address the audience, Harman unsettled him by making emphatic points and 'jabbing her finger at him'.[150] He now needed to give the best speech of his premiership. He gave his worst. He needed to reach out to the party and show them why he was still worthy of their backing. He did the opposite. 'It was utterly dismal,' admits one anguished Number 10 aide. 'We had lost the by-election with a very good candidate, yet, instead of connecting with the party, Gordon delivered a speech about iPods and China.'[151] Another adviser was even more outspoken: 'The speech was garbage. What interested the public was not globalisation, which he gave them, but their standard of living. It alienated everyone.'[152] To Brown, the link between globalisation and living standards was clear, but he could not find the words to lift his party, let alone the country. Even when the financial crisis erupted later in the year he would struggle to connect these strands of thinking. Then, people would want to listen to him and to understand. Now no one cared.

A worse scenario could not have been devised for Brown. His critics and other malcontents were locked up in hotels together in Warwick with little to do other than discuss their unhappiness about his performance. He had lost many of the Cabinet, some of whom were in open revolt. Later that day, Straw and Hoon asked selected ministers for their contact details so they could speak with them over the summer holidays about taking possible action to unseat Brown in the autumn. Jacqui Smith and James Purnell were among those they approached,[153] and Hoon and Straw were also seen talking about the situation with John Hutton.[154] At the bar, David Miliband was talking to Cabinet colleagues about the Prime Minister's position.[155] For Hoon, the Warwick speech was the final straw: Brown 'rambled on for what seemed like hours in front of large sections of the party. Lots of Cabinet ministers began muttering he would have to go at around that time.'[156] Even loyalist Alan Johnson was in despair. 'The party felt he had no empathy and they had been lectured to. It was a very bleak night,' he says.[157] Michael Dugher adds: 'The atmosphere was awful. It was like a wake. All that was missing was the body of the deceased.'[158]

Party managers made a desperate effort to conclude the three-day disaster at Warwick with a show of unity, including the unveiling of a policy agenda for the coming election with proposals such as a fully elected House of Lords and a reduction of the voting age to sixteen,[159] but no one took any notice. The press was not interested in Labour's policies but reported instead that GMB general secretary Paul Kenny had called for a 'put-up-or-shut-up' leadership election like the one John Major had called in 1995, so that Labour could go into the general election united.[160] *The Observer* asked rhetorically: 'If Gordon Brown was able to convince the country he is a good leader, he would surely have done it by now?'[161]

Brown had no wish to remain in Warwick and was desperate to leave at the first opportunity. He was only too pleased to be rushed back to Number 10 on the morning of 26 July, to greet Obama, by now the Democrat presidential candidate (Hillary Clinton had conceded defeat on 7 June). The youthful senator was on a high at the end of a European tour to boost his profile and contacts, and Brown had been very keen for Obama to visit the UK. 'We worked extraordinarily hard to get Obama here first,' says an official involved,[162] although he also argues: 'In truth, they needed us at that time too.'[163] The staff at Number 10 were so excited that many came into work on a Saturday especially to see him.[164] When

Obama's motorcade pulled up in Downing Street, Brown did not greet him on the doorstep, in line with the protocol for visitors who are merely members of a legislature, and there were to be no official photos of the Prime Minister with the candidate. This contrasted with the approach taken in Paris by President Sarkozy, who was never much fussed about protocol and treated Obama as if he was already in the White House.

Sheinwald, who had helped pave the way for the visit, recalls that Brown was deliberately seeking to establish an informal and relaxed kind of relationship with Obama.[165] He wanted to keep him in Number 10 for as long as possible, and was delighted he managed a full three hours. 'We did everything we could, and kept on bringing in [Brown's sons] John and Fraser to extend the length,' says one aide.[166] The two men spoke about Afghanistan, climate change, trade and US politics. A contemporary diary recorded: 'There was a lot more emotional, intelligent stuff now from Gordon. He was learning how to play it all much softer.'[167] It was a sunny day and after a while, Brown and Obama wanted some fresh air, so they walked through the garden of Downing Street and on to Horse Guards Parade, to the war memorial in St James's Park. Brown's security team tried to stop them but Obama was insistent.[168] McDonald recalls Brown being delighted and inspired by the visit: 'He thought Obama very charismatic.'[169]

As he left Number 10, reporters outside asked Obama about Brown's popularity. 'You're always more popular before you're actually in charge,' the candidate replied. Andrew Rawnsley in *The Observer* captured the mood of many: 'The actual effect of the encounter was to paint an excruciatingly painful contrast for Labour MPs between the senator's magic touch and their leader's dead hand.'[170] A YouGov poll that day drove home the point: a damningly low 14 per cent said they were satisfied with Gordon Brown as Prime Minister, and 76 per cent expressed themselves dissatisfied.[171]Another poll, conducted in thirty vital 'swing' seats across the country, put the Conservatives on 41 per cent and Labour on just 17 per cent, behind the Liberal Democrats.[172] These figures were nothing short of disastrous.

Brown was physically and mentally exhausted. The year since January had been a long gruelling slog for him. The criticism he endured in this period – much of it self-inflicted – was getting to him. Sarah Brown and his closest aides were increasingly concerned for him. One adviser remembers this as 'a very black time'.[173] Carter's verdict was that, following the Glasgow East by-election, Brown was 'catatonically tired'.[174] His Number 10 aides felt 'he'd lost his zeal'. He stopped sending emails, a sure sign that something was up.[175]

Immediately after Obama left, Sarah took Brown and their sons off for a two-week restorative holiday. She had selected the picture-postcard seaside town of Southwold, on the Suffolk coast. Three days before he left, Brown had been categorically told by Balls, Ed Miliband, Alexander, Heywood and

Muir that he was to take a break, and 'wasn't to keep popping up in front of cameras with comments'.[176]

Summer of Unrest: July–August

The media was in overdrive on Brown's teetering position that weekend, and during the days that followed.[177] Speculation regarding a successor centred on three principal figures. David Miliband was rumoured to be preparing a leadership bid, Straw was said to be collecting names to dislodge Brown[178] and Harman was known to be testing the water. On 28 July, Miliband was reported to have been trying to persuade Johnson to join him on a 'dream ticket'.[179] Neither Straw nor Harman wanted Miliband to succeed at that point, and were enlisted to slap down the speculation. 'What would be wrong would be to respond to a very big economic challenge by turning it into a political crisis,' said Harman.[180] The old warhorse Prescott came out of his recent retirement to make a call for unity, and it looked for a while as if the moment had passed.[181]

Harman was left in charge of the country while Brown was away in August. A tenacious politician of considerable talent, her period as acting Prime Minster was, however, not a happy one, not least because Number 10 was already highly wary, even dismissive of her. They did not like the way that when she called Brown 'with her latest list of demands', she put her phone on loudspeaker. 'We never knew who was listening in her room. With Harriet, there was always a sense of a wider audience,' says an official.[182] So while she was squatting in Downing Street, Brown's aides were not overly keen to give her an easy time. Petty squabbles broke out after she was photographed walking in to Number 10 – a clear breach of protocol. She liked to do her work in the Cabinet Room but on one occasion she forgot that private secretaries listen into conversations, and said to a Cabinet friend: 'I don't know how Gordon manages to make this job seem so difficult.'[183] Reports of her comment rapidly travelled around the building accompanied by the judgement: 'That woman is a disgrace.'[184] Her difficult working relationship with Heywood did not help her cause.[185] In the highly charged atmosphere of those summer weeks, there was almost nothing that she could have done that would be seen positively. On her second day, 29 July, the 'this is my moment' remark appeared in the press and she was forced to deny she was planning a leadership challenge. Referring to Brown's premiership she said, in a way that did little to quell uncertainty, that she refused to accept that it was 'over'.[186]

The same day, an episode occurred that became known as the 'Lancashire plot'. Gordon Prentice and Graham Stringer, who were both MPs from the North-West of England, called on Brown to resign.[187] Prentice spoke for many when he said: 'A Prime Minister needs a different set of skills from a Chancellor of the Exchequer. A Prime Minister must be able to persuade and enthuse.' Of potentially greater significance was the position of George Howarth, MP for Knowsley North and an ally of Straw. The spotlight now shone on him after disobliging comments he had made were reported in the *Liverpool Echo*.[188] He denied rallying support for Straw, but spoke about the 'perilous situation' in which the government found itself and reasoned that 'the PM's role has to be up for discussion'.[189] Two factors motivated Howarth. Like many others, he had not forgiven Brown and his team for the way they ousted Blair. Then there was the top fiasco. 'It was the final straw for me,' he says. 'It just showed how out of touch we were.' Howarth had discussed his decision to speak out with Straw, who tried to discourage him, fearing it would damage his own cause.[190] However, others were much more supportive. Following his intervention, Howarth was contacted by fellow MPs Siobhain McDonagh and Joan Ryan who told him of their developing plans to launch a frontal assault on Brown's premiership.

David Miliband was the first figure in the government to openly strike out against the Prime Minister, albeit using the circuitous device of an opinion piece in *The Guardian*. When it appeared on 30 July, it was widely interpreted as the Foreign Secretary setting out his credentials for the Labour leadership. The article highlighted the lack of a clear Labour agenda and called for a 'radical' new phase for the party. Significantly, Brown's name was not mentioned.[191] An immediate reaction came from former Europe Minister, Denis MacShane, who described it as being 'like a breath of fresh air after the self-indulgent solipsism from Warwick'.[192] Despite repeated invitations to do so on BBC Radio 2's *Jeremy Vine Show*, Miliband pointedly refused to endorse Brown's leadership.[193] He defended his article by insisting that it was a duty of a senior Cabinet minister to set out Labour's vision for the future. Outside the studios, with momentum growing behind him, he signed autographs for waiting members of the public, inserting the word 'not' into a *Daily Telegraph* headline that read 'Labour at War'. However, he still put his signature underneath the headline, 'immediately creating a memorable image, and disproving the truth of his amendment'.[194]

From Suffolk, Brown watched the unfolding events with dismay. 'Gordon was very unsteady,' says one aide.[195] His reaction to Miliband oscillated wildly. At one time he would say: 'David's been a bit silly and overshot himself.' However, when his anger got the better of him he changed his tune: 'I made him Foreign Secretary and this is how I'm being repaid.'[196] Sarah Brown, in particular, never forgave David Miliband for sparking this round of leadership speculation and it turned her deeply against him. In future, he was always referred to as 'that man who ruined our summer holiday'.[197]

What was Miliband's thinking? Before it was published he had shown the article to MP Barry Sheerman (who says he 'was delighted with it') and Cabinet ally James Purnell,[198] as well as consulting a limited circle of close colleagues.[199] None of them sought to dissuade him from his planned course of action. A Foreign Office official, who was with Miliband that morning in the Foreign Secretary's residence at 1 Carlton Gardens, asked him why he had written it. His answer was less than illuminating: 'There's a time in one's life when a man has to do what a man has to do.' However, as their conversation continued, it emerged that Miliband thought Brown was completely unfit for the job and would damage the Labour Party if he remained Leader.[200]

Brown phoned Sinclair in Number 10 and asked for his thoughts on how to respond. 'Act relaxed,' was the reply. 'If you respond by attacking him, you will only give the story momentum. The article was far more about boosting his own prospects than about undermining you.' Brown said this was his view as well,[201] and the matter might have rested there, but for the intervention of Brown's attack dogs, Balls, McBride, Austin and Watson, who decided this was the moment for a display of force. Briefings against Miliband duly appeared in the papers, characterising the Foreign Secretary as 'disloyal', 'self-serving' and 'lacking in judgment'. The following night, Sinclair's phone rang. 'You said you would make this go away. You said you would close it down,' Brown screamed down the line. 'It's not possible when Balls and McBride are running their own media operation. I can't put out the fires if my own Number 10 colleagues are arsonists,' Sinclair replied. 'I can't have splits in my press office. I'll sort this out,' said Brown before hanging up.[202] Steve Richards, ever an astute observer, wrote a penetrating piece in *The Independent* about the bifurcated Downing Street media operation, quoting one MP who demanded that the briefers 'be sacked'.[203]

If Miliband had pushed hard at this point, Brown's divided citadel might have fallen. But the would-be assassin was not certain he wanted to pull the trigger, or that, if he did, his bid would succeed. Displaying the same indecision he had showed when Blair called on him to challenge Brown in early 2007, he dithered over exactly what he hoped to achieve by writing the article. One close associate explains: 'He knew people were looking to him; he felt he had to test the water.'[204] But his effort was half-baked: even though his special adviser briefed the article heavily to political journalists the night before, telling one, 'You think David hasn't got balls? See tomorrow's *Guardian*,' Miliband himself, (who has always denied he was trying to launch a leadership bid), failed to give those MPs and Cabinet colleagues that were prepared to come out against Brown sufficient warning about what he was planning. Brown's relationship with Miliband had been characterised by deep distrust for some years, exacerbated by the cat-and-mouse game played by Blair in his final months. Back then, Brown's team decided to adopt a 'good cop, bad cop' approach to the younger man to deter him from standing for the leadership. Brown courted him with a charm offensive and offered him the post of Foreign Secretary and said he would back Miliband for deputy leader if he agreed to support

Brown's claim to the Labour leadership publicly. This was combined with an implicit threat that, if he mounted a rival bid, Miliband would feel the wrath of the Brown machine and risk his credibility being damaged profoundly. 'David was going to be dealt with in a brutal way, as others had been before him if he dared so much as to stand. It was intensely unpleasant,' says one member of the Brown camp.[205] Things did not improve for Miliband during Brown's premiership: a member of Miliband's team says that during his spell at the Foreign Office they had to spend up to half their time neutralising negative briefing emanating from Number 10.[206] 'There was a deep and endless suspicion from Brown and the Brownites, but one has to say that David's actions helped keep that suspicion alive,' says a Foreign Office official.[207]

Brown was in a complete funk. Who should he listen to – the calming voices or his storm troopers? He almost invariably chose the latter, believing he needed the brutal form of machine politics represented by McBride now more than ever. Brown also listened to Balls, Austin and Watson as they told him what they thought of David's brother, Ed Miliband. A Number 10 insider recalls: 'Ed Balls was whispering in Gordon's ear: "You can't trust Ed Miliband any more."'[208] Some believe that Balls and his acolytes wanted to use this opportunity to weaken the younger Miliband whom they considered a potential threat to Balls's own leadership ambitions. They told Brown that the two brothers were very close and that it would have been impossible for Ed not to have known what David was planning (in fact the elder brother had not warned his sibling about his provocative article, and Ed was said to be deeply frustrated by David's destabilising intervention). Ed Miliband's relationship with Balls had already significantly degenerated following the fall-out from the election that never was, and this incident worsened it still further, while also weakening his relationship with Brown.[209] The situation was not helped by the Prime Minister's disappointment with what he saw as Ed's lack of energy in the Cabinet Office post and failure to bring cohesion to government policy.[210]

To assert his authority, Brown fell back on one of his few remaining prime ministerial powers – the reshuffle. He knew ministers did not want to be sacked or downgraded from posts they had spent their political lives working towards. Self-preservation played its part in the thinking of a number of members of the Cabinet that month. On 2 August, it was reported that ministers had been instructed by Brown to be in the country in early September for a near-certain reshuffle. On 3 August, a memo, believed to have been written by Blair at the height of the row over the election that never was, was leaked to the *Mail on Sunday*. It accused Brown of vacuity, hubris and failing to set out his own agenda. The sentiments matched entirely Blair's increasing sense of grievance against his successor, but he had always been scrupulous about not speaking out against Brown in public or private, mindful of the example of damage inflicted on John Major by Margaret Thatcher. Number 10 thought it unlikely that Blair had initiated the leak[211] but the damage had been done.

What was the Cabinet up to that summer? Where Miliband remained uncertain about what he wanted to do, Straw was confident of his own position. He liked to see himself as a unifying figure coming to the rescue, and thus as the most suitable successor[212] – a 'chairman of the board'. 'Jack was playing a lot of games at this time,' says one Cabinet colleague.[213] A senior backbencher says of a meeting that Straw requested with him at that time: 'It was quite clear that he wanted me to support him for leader. He told me he knew where every member of the Cabinet stood apart from Alan Johnson.'[214] Stephen Byers was also sounded out by the Justice Secretary, and he too was left with the impression that Straw was planning an assault on Brown's leadership.[215] Straw spoke to Charles Clarke, whose view was that a coup was worth attempting because if 'Cabinet was strong enough and coherent enough, they could have an orderly leadership election, which would not prove disruptive for the party'.[216] Straw left for his holiday contemplating his next move.

Brown knew he was vulnerable, though he probably never realised quite how much, as the information coming into Number 10 gave his staff a far from complete picture. Below their radar, a highly focused operation to oust the Prime Minister was in train during the summer. Throughout that time a small group of disaffected MPs and select Cabinet ministers met in a London flat to discuss tactics for replacing him. Those who gathered together knew they needed a senior figure to lead a rebellion. It was hoped that John Reid might challenge Brown, but Reid had had enough of frontline politics, and was prepared neither to be openly critical, nor to offer himself up as a leadership candidate. He had never expected Brown to be a successful Prime Minister, but he thought that it was the job of Cabinet ministers to push him aside. Charles Clarke's name was also put forward, but the view was that he had sniped for too long from the backbenches to be useful. The favoured candidate was David Miliband but there was great uncertainty about the extent to which he was prepared to strike out against Brown. The group that met had few definite answers but they also had the recess to plan their next move.

'The summer of 2008 was like the summer of 1914,' says one of Number 10's historically minded, if hyperbolic, aides. 'The drums of war were beating.'[217] Brown was under real pressure and Michael Dugher believed he was a 'whisker away from being forced out'. For now, he was saved by the summer recess, which starved the anti-Brown camp of much-needed momentum, and in this respect at least, luck was on his side. Had David Miliband's article appeared when the House was sitting it might have proved far more dangerous. The Foreign Secretary had toyed with the idea of sounding out his support, but on 2 August he went on holiday. A question remained over whether Cabinet ministers and senior MPs who had expressed concerns to him about Brown would be prepared to do anything about it when they returned in the autumn.

One figure who was watching these developments intently from across the Channel was Peter Mandelson. He thought about Brown's future long and hard before concluding that Miliband had got it wrong, and that this was not his moment to make a bid for power. Always deeply tribal, he put loyalty to the party above loyalty to any individual (except perhaps himself): when the time came for it, he would back the figure he thought most likely to succeed.[218] Number 10 watched the smoke signals emanating from his Brussels office very carefully. 'Where's Peter?' Brown had asked his staff at a delicate moment earlier in the summer. 'In Brussels,' they replied. 'No, he's in London,' said Brown. 'He must be.' The Prime Minister's belief sprang from critical press stories that he thought bore his old adversary's fingerprints. 'He had almost a naive reverence for Peter's almost superhuman powers to influence the three or four key commentators,' says one official.[219] But Brown had a plan up his sleeve so secret that he had told none of them about it.

Enter Mandelson Stage Right: February–September

Sarah Brown had given very clear instructions to her husband's staff for their summer holiday: he was not to be disturbed. 'Sarah was right,' says one aide. 'We all felt exhausted and overwrought by it all. She wanted to protect him because she loved him.'[220] But the person who broke the stipulation was Brown himself. Earlier in the year, Sarah had insisted on a new regime of food and rest for the Prime Minister. She banished the bowl of KitKats from his desk and tried to ensure that he ate healthily and went to bed at a reasonable time.[221] It was an uphill struggle. For a while, little black boxes of chopped fruit appeared on Brown's desk, but it was not long before the KitKats returned. He was more successful with coffee, which he gave up in 2008. 'The no-caffeine regime made a real difference to him,' says one aide.[222] In Southwold, he had a Pilates and fitness trainer to help get him in shape.[223] The heavy police presence protected the family from the more vociferous local residents. The destination had been selected in part to contrast with the glamorous destinations chosen by the Blairs, but also in a bid to promote English tourism. The local tourism chief was quick to seize the opportunity, claiming that the seven-point boost in support Brown enjoyed following his speech at the Labour conference in the early autumn had been due to the uniquely rejuvenating powers of the resort.[224] Even though he was visibly shattered, with the strains of the job clearly affecting his physical appeerance, Brown still enjoyed his stay, and met up with celebrity couple Richard Curtis and Emma Freud who live in nearby Walberswick.[225]

The issues exercising Brown's mind that August were responding to Miliband, improving Number 10, tackling the economic crisis and thinking through his speech for the party conference, which he knew would have to be among his best. His premiership was at stake and the pressure was on. In defiance of Sarah's diktats, and Downing Street's own self-denying ordinance, Heywood came to Southwold to talk about tightening up the Number 10 operation, then Vadera visited the next day to discuss the increasingly fragile state of the banking sector, and then Muir, now appointed director of political communications, to go through ideas for the conference speech. Helping him was a new figure who was to make an increasing impact on Brown's life. Kirsty McNeill was a talented young speechwriter who had cut her teeth in the global development movement, and who had impressed Brown with her work on the Make Poverty History campaign. Brown's starting points for his speech were his response to his political critics and the social impact that the developing financial crisis was having. He needed to show he understood the anxieties that the public had about the economy. McNeill was astonished by the sharpness of his mind and the intensity of their eight-hour sessions. He would tell her: 'I want to read this when I'm eighty and still be happy with it.' She was exhausted at the end of each day, but his mind was still racing, and he would go off to watch TED talks, then much in vogue, on his computer.[226] Gavin Kelly, holding the fort back in London, noticed the tonic effect that the holiday was having on Brown, and how it was helping him rise positively to the challenge of the Labour conference.[227]

Another visitor to Southwold was Ed Balls. He advised dismissing Hoon as Chief Whip and putting Nick Brown in his place, as well as bringing back some experienced Labour figures to provide ballast: Prescott was a grudge too far, but what about Margaret Beckett, former acting party leader and Foreign Secretary? What about Alastair Campbell? Brown listened intently to his closest lieutenant, but on one piece of news, he kept his own counsel.

When Muir was there, Brown turned to him out of the blue and asked: 'What would you think about Mandelson coming back into the Cabinet?' This was so confidential that he had asked McNeill to leave the room before dropping the bombshell. 'Bloody hell,' Muir thought. The thirteen-year animosity between Brown and Mandelson was the stuff of Labour folklore. As late as March 2007, as if to show the world that the bile was still flowing, Mandelson revealed that he would not be seeking a second term as Britain's EU Commissioner, if only to deny Brown the pleasure of sacking him. Mandelson's biographer, Donald Macintyre, wrote in the *New Statesman* that he was extremely wary of what a Brown premiership would entail for him.[228] Ever the peacemaker, Sue Nye had always kept open lines of communication to Mandelson, and Brown had even toyed with the idea of appointing Mandelson to his first Cabinet in June 2007,[229] but ultimately decided he could not stomach it. The dismal autumn of 2007 changed everything. Mandelson sensed he could help and Brown needed him.

On 21 February 2008, Brown was due to travel to Brussels for a meeting with European Commission President Barroso – an encounter he was not relishing. A short time before, the UK's permanent representative to the EU, Kim Darroch, received a phone call from Simon Fraser, the head of Mandelson's office. The Trade Commissioner had got wind of Brown's visit and was keen to talk to him, given the saliency of world trade talks. Could the diplomat engineer such a meeting? Darroch was positive, thinking it could give the Prime Minister another insight into what was happening in Brussels, and into the operation of the EU, neither of which were his forte. He rang Number 10 and spoke to Fletcher, who said he would raise it but needed to wait for the right time to do so.[230]

Nothing happened for a week until a message came by text – Fletcher was much given to this method of communication – 'It's on. Can you get Peter round before the PM's meeting with Barroso?'[231] The meeting was held in Darroch's office at 9am. Originally scheduled to last half an hour (to allow Brown time to prepare for his meeting with Barroso at 10), it went on until almost 10.30, necessitating embarrassed phone calls to explain that the Prime Minister was running late.[232] Darroch recalls that the start of the meeting was 'somewhat strained', but the two emerged from his office engaged in 'jovial banter'.[233] Gavin Kelly described it as 'a fabulously good personal meeting'.[234] Trade did indeed occupy the first part of their discussion, but, according to Mandelson: 'Within barely a minute we were talking about Gordon, about his government, and about the nosedive in public support they were both suffering.'[235] Brown told Mandelson that he believed Labour had 'all the policies and all the ideas, but were struggling to communicate them to the press and public'. Mandelson's assessment was less positive; he told the Prime Minister that the policies were not sufficiently thought-through and that they needed to be 'prepared, bottomed out, agreed and owned by relevant ministers', with less attention being given to announcements.[236]

The meeting was profoundly cathartic for Brown. He had been disturbed at the deepest level by the betrayal, as he saw it, in 1994, when Mandelson supported Blair rather than him for the Labour leadership. He lost a very close personal and political friend and the experience made him more distrusting and paranoid. On a party level too, the Prime Minister immediately saw that, with Mandelson an ally, he would have access to a quality of political advice he could get from no one else. Befriending his old adversary would also help with another constant worry – the breach with the Blairites, which was threatening to sink his premiership. So delighted was Brown with the first meeting that he began to phone Mandelson regularly and ask his advice 'on all sorts of things'.[237]

During a call in May, Brown asked Mandelson to become more involved in British politics. Regarding the Prime Minister's many difficulties, Mandelson said: 'You should see the electoral losses as a test – a test set by the public. You must rise to the challenge. If you do, you will overcome the problem of your not calling the early election.' Looking to the future, he advised Brown to 'get the MPs off on their summer holidays as quickly as possible' because he did not 'want them drinking too much on the House of Commons terrace with nothing to do other than gossip about your leadership'.[238] Back in Brussels, the Commissioner was enjoying this high-profile attention, which had been missing since Blair's resignation. 'He's so weird,' he would say of Brown to his officials, adding: 'He's ringing me six times a day. What do I do with this strange man ringing me all the time?'[239]

In early June, Brown phoned Mandelson and it was agreed he should visit Number 10 during his forthcoming trip to London.[240] Until that point, only Nye and Heywood were aware of the calls, but now Kelly, Forsyth and Wood were brought into the loop.[241] Brown decided he wanted to shift the relationship into a new gear.[242] He phoned Muir one Sunday morning in June and was 'very conspiratorial', swearing his adviser to secrecy and dispatching him to Brussels to meet Mandelson.[243] A wary Muir made the journey on 16 June and it went well, starting at four in the Commissioner's office before moving to a restaurant at seven.[244] 'We discussed different ideas for the party conference campaign theme,' Muir recalls.[245]

After Southwold, Brown went to Scotland for the rest of August and began to have daily hour-long conversations with Mandelson, with trusted staff listening in. 'In August, Gordon wanted endless conversations on policy. Suddenly I was aware that there was another voice on the calls – Peter,' says Kelly. 'He was thoroughly charming and was always asking: "How can I help?"'[246] What did they discuss? Mandelson helped Brown finalise the conference document he would publish, contributed to the conference speech, and offered him general advice.[247] Others involved in the speech included American pollster and Brown ally Bob Shrum (on words and ideas), Muir (on ideas) and McNeill (pulling it together, and shaping the message). Also back on the scene was Alastair Campbell. Had Brown become Prime Minister as he had wanted in 1997, he would have been able to use Campbell and Mandelson – why should Blair be allowed to have sole use of these two supreme political operators?

Brown had wanted to make Campbell a minister in the Lords but the latter was uneasy about returning full-time to the fray from which he had spent so long extracting himself towards the end of Blair's premiership (he also had serious concerns about Brown's personal weaknesses and suitability to the job of Prime Minister). Despite his difficult history with the two men, Brown absolutely relished spending time with them. Aides saw Brown visibly lifted when he was in their company. One says Brown 'only really trusts "grown-ups" like Peter and Alastair'.[248] Both men would also stand up to him, which no one else, apart from Balls, was capable of doing. Rather than being jealous, his Number 10 team appreciated this, as they felt Mandelson would 'vocalise things we wanted to get across, but lacked the purchase to do so'.[249] Whereas Campbell's influence began to be felt mostly from the autumn of 2009, and then initially only on PMQs, the Mandelson effect was immediate. He endeared himself to others around the Prime Minister by taking an interest in his well-being, encouraging him to relax and exercise and often asking: 'But how are *you* Gordon? Tell me how you're feeling.'[250] This was in contrast to Brown's tough old guard, who tended to handle him roughly. One thing, however, irritated Mandelson about their calls – it became clear to him that after they spoke, Brown would then talk to other close advisers such as Balls and Ed Miliband, going over what had been said and listening to conflicting advice. 'It meant the conversations kept going round in circles. It was difficult to get a decision out of Gordon,' says an adviser involved in the calls.[251] Brown's peculiar way of canvassing opinion – many opinions, as it turned out – would later drive Mandelson to distraction.

Maintaining the strict secrecy, Brown and Mandelson now began to meet up at weekends. 'Gordon behaved differently with him than with any other politician I had seen,' says one observer. 'Brown was playful. He was funny. He had been like that with the two Eds, but he was always the father to them. With Peter, they were equal. They were muckers.' Mandelson was fascinated by Brown and would regularly tease him about their past difficulties. 'If you remember at the time, your people were discombobulating me,' he said when one past episode was discussed.[252] No colleague apart from Balls had been this close to Brown for thirteen years and the Prime Minister was adamant that his Children's Secretary should be kept in the dark. Balls and Mandelson had loathed each other since 1994. Surprisingly, however, once they were back in government together they would learn to tolerate and even respect each other.[253]

However, Mandelson was not the only senior Labour figure who was about to reassert himself to Balls's cost. According to one Cabinet minister, up to this point Balls had been speaking more about the economy in Cabinet than Darling did.[254] The Chancellor of the Exchequer's edginess about the younger man's influence over Brown was well-grounded and he wanted to see Balls put in his place.[255] Now it was pay-back time.

Darling Bites Back: August–September

'Name me a reshuffle that ever made a difference to government. You can't be chopping and changing people that often,' Darling said to the journalist

Decca Aitkenhead in an interview published in *The Guardian* on 29 August 2008. Darling had not been her first choice of Cabinet big-hitter, but David Miliband had already been nabbed by *The Times*. Moreover, brewing trouble in the economy had made the Chancellor seem less grey, so she made the long journey up to the Western Isles, where he was holidaying with his wife, Maggie.[256] For his part, Darling seized on this as a chance to grab a higher profile for himself. He had had a difficult first year at the Treasury, and the humiliating interventions made by Brown in the 2007 Pre-Budget Report and 2008 Budget still smarted. He had spent August in his family croft on the Isle of Lewis mulling over his worries about his political future and, more importantly, the deteriorating economic outlook. As a 'cautious man', he was 'continually concerned' about his legacy and 'the need to be a responsible Chancellor', says Nick Pearce.[257] Although the world economic situation was yet to reach its nadir, he was alarmed by many warning signs that had emerged since the nationalisation of Northern Rock, including significant debt writedowns by RBS (April), Barclays (June) and HBOS (July). At the end of July, it was announced that UK house prices had shown their biggest annual fall since Nationwide began its housing survey in 1991.[258] While Brown's Chancellorship had seen fair weather, Darling's hit gales early on, and severe storms were on the horizon.

Brown had been losing confidence in Darling's ability to take the right decisions and to think independently of the Treasury. In August, the Prime Minister began planning his own policies for economic recovery along with Balls and Vadera, which included a plan to fix the funding markets and mortgages. The Treasury was at odds with much of the thinking emerging from Number 10.[259] A story about a possible stamp-duty holiday as a way of kick-starting the depressed housing market was briefed to the press before the Chancellor was even properly informed, let alone consulted.[260] Darling feared that he was losing control of aspects of economic policy, so he used the windfall of the *Guardian* interview as a platform to reassert it. Most controversially – if almost unreflectingly, Aitkenhead believes[261] – he said that the economic outlook Britain was facing was 'arguably the worst they had seen in sixty years'.[262] In response to his article, sterling tumbled to a twelve year low against the euro and the FTSE 100 Index dropped 42.9 points.[263] David Cameron responded on the BBC *Today* programme praising Darling for telling the truth, but upbraiding him for risking 'a crisis of confidence'.[264] An editorial in *The Guardian* did not equivocate: 'Our often infantilised politics has little time for quiet, truth-talking pragmatists.'[265] Brown, by now on holiday at home in Scotland, did not share the paper's enthusiasm. 'That fucking Darling interview! It fucked up everything,' he is reported to have said.[266] He called the Chancellor on the morning of 30 August telling him he had ruined Downing

Street's own plans to launch an economic fight back and demanded he go immediately into damage limitation.[267] Darling resented Brown's manner, but was alarmed by how his words were playing in the media. Later that morning, he told Sky News that the 'fundamentals' of the UK economy remained strong, and on the BBC on 2 September, he said that the country was facing 'a unique set of circumstances' with the combination of a credit crunch and high oil and food prices, but he remained confident 'that we can get through it and we will get through it'.[268]

However, Darling's best efforts were not enough to keep Brown's attack dogs at bay. A Number 10 spokesperson taking the sleeper from Scotland to London received a call before the train set off from Catherine MacLeod, who had recently been appointed as the Chancellor's special adviser. She said there was a problem and he told her they would look at it again in the morning. When he got off the train at 7am, MacLeod called him again to say that Damian McBride was already 'trashing' her new boss. Charlie Whelan, Brown's controversial former spin doctor, who was working for the Prime Minister informally, also started laying into Darling, telling journalists that the Chancellor was well out of his depth. Darling, a kindly, civilised man, was deeply hurt by this and did not believe that he as Chancellor, or anyone else for that matter, should be treated in this way. He would later get his revenge when in February 2010 he accused Brown and his cronies of unleashing 'the forces of hell' on him for his comments about the state of the economy. 'Nobody likes the sort of briefing that goes on,' he told Sky News.

It had been a busy summer for McBride, attacking first Miliband and now Darling.[269] Balls may have been the most assertive figure in Brown's team, but the most virulent was McBride, a Treasury official who had joined the then Chancellor's political team in 2005. Like Balls, he had a profoundly intellectual and sensitive side, but he came to adopt practices in the mould of his predecessor, Charlie Whelan.[270] Fear of poison being leaked by him into the media about their private and professional lives kept Brown's rivals at bay. It explains in part why no one challenged Brown for the party leadership in the spring of 2007, and why he was able to survive as Prime Minister. But Brown was deeply misguided if he believed that threats to his position justified this toxic behaviour and it damaged him more than he ever admitted, even to himself. Whether the Prime Minister directly sanctioned it, or even knew about it is irrelevant – he still bears the ultimate responsibility for things done in his name.

The attacks on Darling showed Brown at his worst. How could he subject a long-standing and trusted colleague to such venom? The undermining briefings and the obvious way in which Darling had been told to eat his words reflected badly on Number 10. 'It starts to look as if the government is cracking up,' wrote Jackie Ashley in *The Guardian*. [271] Her fellow columnist, Polly Toynbee, wrote: 'The smell of death around this government is so overpowering it seems to have anaesthetised them all.' To many, Darling seemed to be telling the truth, so the briefings that he was no good and about to lose his job only won bouquets for him and brickbats for Brown.

It was Darling, not Brown, who had called it right on the economy. Yet, ironically, the crisis that the Chancellor foresaw was to provide the circumstances in which Brown would be able to rebuild his premiership.

5

Brown Regains Political and Economic Control

(September–October 2008)

By the summer of 2008, Brown's position was dangerously unstable. Politically, many of his senior Cabinet ministers were looking for a safe way to oust him, as were increasing numbers of the Parliamentary Labour Party (PLP). His attempt to make his citadel at Number 10 work for him had failed: it remained as dysfunctional as ever. And, in the economy, where storm clouds had been gathering for months, a crash of thunder was now heard from America: Lehman Brothers had collapsed. The following month, the global financial system would come closer to the brink than anyone had imagined possible. Yet by the end of it all, Brown would emerge more secure as Prime Minister than he had been since his first two months in office, widely credited with pulling the British banking system back from the brink, buoyed by a successful party conference, and with Number 10 at last beginning to function. This chapter tells the story of that remarkable turnaround.

The First Coup: September

Brown returned from Scotland to Number 10 in early September refreshed and revitalised. 'He had clearly had a good holiday,' says Gavin Kelly,[1] and he was determined to use the autumn political season to remould his premiership. But was he safe? BBC political editor Nick Robinson seemed to think so. On Friday 12 September he announced on Radio 4's *Today* programme that the summer of intrigue and plots may well have passed and that Brown was now in a more secure position.[2] How wrong he and most others were. Later that day, Siobhain McDonagh MP launched an attempted coup against Brown when she became the first member of the government to call openly for a leadership contest. Over that weekend, 13 to 14 September, it emerged that she was one of twelve MPs who had written to Labour Party headquarters requesting nomination papers to force a leadership election. Vice-Chairman of the party, Joan Ryan, said it would be 'irresponsible' not to speak out against Brown, while Knowsley North MP, and close friend of Jack Straw, George Howarth did exactly that when he said: 'No one can remember a time since Neville Chamberlain, after Hitler invaded Norway, that anyone was so unpopular. We can't allow it to continue.'[3]

What was going on? The summer holidays had helped Brown as his opponents were dispersed to the beaches, but questions over his leadership resurfaced when they returned to Westminster. Frustrated by the reluctance of the Cabinet to move against Brown, disenchanted members of the PLP decided to take matters into their own hands. Siobhain McDonagh and her sister Baroness (Margaret) McDonagh knew that many in the PLP were increasingly alarmed about Brown's performance and its implications for their own re-election. They sensed a more rebellious mood among Labour MPs, especially since the '10p tax' fiasco. They wanted Brown's premiership killed off as quickly as possible by creating a platform for disaffected Labour MPs to voice their concerns.

The McDonagh sisters turned to Lord Falconer, Blair's close friend and a former Lord Chancellor, for legal advice about triggering a leadership contest under Labour's constitution. Falconer offered his strictly private views but, aware it would reflect badly on Blair if his help became known, made clear: 'I am not prepared to sign any letters or come out in open support of any leadership coup.'[4] Following the internal tribulations of the 1980s, Labour rules for unseating an incumbent leader had been deliberately tightened: a challenger needed a full 20 per cent of the PLP to support them to force a contest. At this stage, the rebels had neither an alternative leader waiting in the wings nor the seventy Labour MPs lined up to cross the threshold. Number 10 knew that, even though they were always going to struggle to reach those numbers, the anti-Brown camp would nevertheless need to cause as much noise as they could to make it almost intolerable for the Prime Minister to carry on. 'They wanted to force the issue of his leadership into play,' says one aide.[5] From late August, rebel MPs started writing to Labour Party headquarters asking for nomination papers to be sent out, and they encouraged as many of their colleagues as possible to join them in their campaign. Charles Clarke was one, and in an interview for the *New Statesman* on 4 September he fired off the latest of his salvos against Brown.

Number 10 was becoming seriously alarmed and approached Labour Party General Secretary Ray Collins to discover who was involved. 'There were no real surprises,' says one aide. 'It was full of the usual suspects such as McDonagh and Howarth, but we were still very anxious where it was all heading.'[6] At the TUC conference from 8 to 11 September, Nick Brown, Tom Watson, Jonathan

Ashworth and Brown's political secretary, Joe Irvin, systematically worked through all the Labour MPs 'to find out where each stood'. Neither Number 10 nor even the plotters were exactly sure of the answer to this. A large number of MPs were highly disillusioned with Brown but most were waiting to see where the plot would lead before breaking cover and committing themselves.

Worried where things were leading, Number 10 decided to strike first. On 12 September, in an effort to destabilise the rebels, they briefed the media with the names of the MPs who had asked for nomination papers. In addition to Siobhain McDonagh, the group included Blairite ex-ministers such as Fiona Mactaggart and Barry Gardiner, vocal critics of Brown like Frank Field, and party loyalists like Joan Ryan.[7] McDonagh and Field expressed indignation at the way they were being treated, accusing those 'close to the centre of government' of leaking the story deliberately, 'in an attempt to smash the efforts to get a gauge of Parliamentary opinion'.[8] They were not the first to be so treated. 'Number 10 used regularly to flush out people it thought were against GB, and then denounce them as traitors in the media,' explains one insider.[9] McDonagh was dismissed from her government post at 7pm on 12 September, while Ryan was also sacked from the Labour vice-chairmanship with summary speed. Both responded by taking to the airwaves to try to build momentum for their cause. Nick Brown and the Number 10 political office spent the day sounding out MPs and trying to instil some calm in those who might jump ship.[10] A Number 10 aide recalls: 'The rebels never looked like having seventy MPs but a lot were on the edge.'[11] What worried Downing Street most was the uncertainty: 'We thought it would fizzle out but you could never be sure. MPs who reassured us may have been saying the opposite to the plotters.'[12]

Attention now turned to the Cabinet. Before the summer many had spoken about the need 'to do something'. Here was their opportunity. Sue Nye was nervous, aware that several disillusioned ministers were talking to each other that week. Alistair Darling, still recovering from the vicious briefing he had to endure after his *Guardian* interview, was said to be 'weighing things up'.[13] John Hutton had spoken to McDonagh and was aware of her plans. He shared many of her frustrations. An aide to one disaffected Cabinet minister says: 'They were all talking. It was in the balance.'[14] Some special advisers to Cabinet ministers were busy 'working the phones', urging other aides to discourage their ministers from going out to defend Brown, believing this might keep the pressure on Number 10.[15] The *Mail on Sunday* reported that eight Cabinet ministers had refused to say if they thought Brown should lead Labour into the next general election, despite being specifically contacted by Number 10 and told to reply 'yes'. David Miliband, James Purnell, Alan Johnson, Jacqui Smith and Hazel Blears were among those who remained silent, according to the newspaper. 'This was not just an omission – I am told that at least three consciously decided not to answer,' wrote Rachel Sylvester in *The Times*.[16] When pressed on the BBC's *Andrew Marr Programme* on Sunday 14, Business Secretary John Hutton refused to condemn the rebels. 'I'm not going to criticise any of my colleagues who want Labour to do better. For heaven's sake, we are 20 percentage points behind in the opinion polls.'[17] Hutton thought what the rebels were doing was 'brave'.[18]

Speculation mounted as to whether a party heavyweight would now come out against Brown. David Miliband ruled himself out on the Sunday and pledged his support to the Prime Minister.[19] Backbenchers kept the pressure up on Monday 15 September, when twelve Labour MPs signed a joint article in the New Labour magazine *Progress*, calling for a 'convincing new narrative'. The signatories included known critics like George Howarth, and six former ministers, including Patricia Hewitt. Brown was not yet out of the woods. A ministerial resignation eventually came on Tuesday 16 in the form of David Cairns, a respected Scotland Office minister and former priest. His hand was forced by a briefing operation from the Number 10 spin machine. His misgivings about Brown had been reported in the press: he considered resigning but had been talked out of it by Paul Sinclair at Number 10: 'You hate what Tom Watson did to Tony Blair, so don't become Gordon's Tom Watson,' Sinclair told Cairns, referring to the events of September 2006.[20] Scottish Secretary Des Browne added his weight to persuading Cairns not to go and, early the following morning, Cairns phoned Sinclair to assure him he would be staying. Within hours, he was back on the phone. 'You bastards at Number 10 have outed me,' he shouted down the line. What had happened was that Damian McBride had given Cairns's name for the usual treatment to Andrew Porter, one of his usual conduits at the *Daily Telegraph*. A livid Sinclair rounded on McBride, saying: 'He's gone now because of what you've done.' McBride retorted that Cairns had a plan to walk out of Brown's party conference speech later that month, and thus he had no option but to give up the MP's name.[21]

Two events ended this first revolt against Brown's leadership. The Labour Party National Executive Committee met on Tuesday 16 September to decide whether or not to send nomination papers as demanded by the rebels. The rebels blamed Collins who, as General Secretary, had flatly refused to send them out. 'He was the one who killed it,' says Howarth.[22] 'We'd have been toast if the papers had gone out as it would have said that the NEC, membership and trade unions had lost faith in Brown,' agrees one Downing Street aide. That Tuesday, members of the National Executive Committee stood four-square behind the decision. But this might have been insufficient to quell the rebels had it not been for an event that took place far away from the Westminster village. Not only would it finish off talks of plots against Brown, it would pave the way for his greatest triumph. It was the collapse of the investment bank Lehman Brothers, on Monday 15 September. The biggest global financial crisis in history followed. The Cabinet responded by immediately getting behind its leader. Straw's summer contemplation had passed: 'I'm absolutely clear Gordon Brown is the man with the experience and the intellect and the strategy to lead us through these current difficulties,' the Justice Secretary said, followed soon after by Harman and Darling, who offered him their unequivocal support.

How did Brown manage to survive this first assault? Timing played to his advantage. It was inconceivable that the party could remove him during a financial crisis that he understood better than anyone else in the government. Nor did it make much sense to strike out against Brown in the run-up to Labour's party conference, a time when political parties are eager to put on a display of unity. The absence of an attractive alternative the rebels could unite around was another powerful boon. David Miliband was deemed by many to be too young and inexperienced, while others questioned whether his failure to stand up and directly challenge Brown in 2007 and earlier in 2008 meant he had the steel to be an effective leader. Straw repelled support by appearing too obviously ambitious, and by lacking a clear agenda of his own. Some big beasts thought that September 2008 was not the right moment to oust a leader who had been in office for such a short time. Hoon thought long and hard about what to do, reaching the conclusion that 'Gordon needed more time'. It was to be another eighteen months before he decided that Brown's 'time was up'.[23] Other Cabinet ministers who had made threatening noises at the beginning of the summer faded away. One factor weighing on the minds of the malcontents was the fear that, if they struck out against Brown and it failed to topple him, then they would be in an even worse position, as they would be stuck with a more damaged leader. A further source of inertia was a concern that the public would not stomach the party twice changing its leader without an election in the same parliament.

By luck more than design, Brown had formed a disjointed Cabinet whose members rarely confided in each other, and were ill-equipped to coordinate action with the disaffected in the PLP. Brown himself believed that his own henchmen had played a significant part in outwitting the opposition. 'No coup would work if you were up against the Brown machine, the pre-eminent political machine going,' says one Number 10 aide.[24] Perhaps more significant was the fact that the plotters themselves lacked an equivalent 'machine'. They were poorly organised and, as one aide recalls: 'They had no offices, no phone lines, no union backers, and too few MPs to come out in support.'[25] Then there was the Labour Party constitution, which stacked the odds in favour of the leader. The backbenchers did not come out against Brown: they growled at PLP meetings but did not bite. Barry Sheerman MP was one of many who felt the PLP was totally ineffective: it had no votes and no proper constitution, and could be easily dominated by the executive. He came out into the open in June 2009, calling for a secret ballot on the leadership, to the dismay of Number 10.[26]

Brown survived his first coup more by good fortune than by judgement. Better coordination and planning might well have killed off his premiership.

The Collapse of Lehman Brothers: September

Increasingly anxious about the gathering clouds, in January Brown had moved his trusted adviser Shriti Vadera from the Department for International Development, where she had been far from happy, to John Hutton's Business Department, where she could keep a close eye on developments and pick up early tremors from the City. The first run on a British bank in 140 years had necessitated dramatic but delayed government intervention. Northern Rock had been nationalised in February, and just a month later the US investment bank Bear Stearns collapsed. Nerves were frayed. Who else could fall? By early summer, Number 10 and the Treasury were beginning to realise that the subprime mortgage problem, far from being contained within the US housing market, was spreading. Financial products, built on the value of subprime mortgages and now worthless, had been sliced and traded around the system, and no one knew where the pieces had landed. Global capital markets were now being affected. Credit markets were freezing up. 'After Northern Rock, it soon became clear that this was a systemic problem. And that it was systemic globally and not just systemic for the US,' says an official.[27]

Even so, few foresaw the intensity of the crisis that would hit the world that September. So far, the banks that had fallen had problems of their own, and in any case they had been small relative to the governments that oversaw them. 'The idea that the financial crisis was going to bring down the whole western financial system was inconceivable,' says the *Financial Times* columnist Martin Wolf, who was closely read by Brown. Sure, the subprime problem would require a solution, but there was still time. 'I thought this would be a very bad financial crisis, but I thought it would be a manageable one,' admits Wolf.[28] 'The collapse of Lehman Brothers on 15 September changed everything,' rues a discontented Cabinet minister.[29] From that moment on, the politics of rebels and coups seemed all too petty and the financial crisis all too serious. Brown turned in an instant from a Prime Minister under siege to one on a mission. On 8 September the US government had been forced to all but nationalise mortgage lenders Fannie Mae and Freddie Mac, both of which faced massive losses on subprime loans. Between them, the two organisations owned or guaranteed almost half of all US mortgages; by bringing them into 'conservatorship', the US government had taken on exposure of between $3 and $5 trillion. From a Republican administration deeply allergic to government intervention, it was an astounding admission about the pace and depth of the crisis.

Throughout 2008, the 158-year-old US investment bank Lehman Brothers had taken a substantial hit from the subprime market. In the first half of the year, its share price had fallen 73 per cent, as loss after loss had been announced. At the end of August, shares rallied briefly after it was announced that the Korea Development Bank was considering a takeover bid. Then, on 9 September, talks were put on hold. Before trading closed, shares had plunged 45 per cent. The following day, Lehman announced a loss of $3.9bn. On the next, as Lehman announced it was seeking a buyer, the stock price fell a further 40 per cent. One thing was clear: government action alone could stop the slide.

Over the frantic weekend of 13 to 14 September, the very same weekend when Number 10 was battling to shore up Brown's political position at home, frantic negotiations were taking place in New York about how to save the bank. The best option for the US government was to find a buyer. Though the Bank of America had been an early contender, the White House chose instead to let them pursue an appetising deal with Merrill Lynch, another major household name in US banking that was in serious trouble of going under. In another startling development of these few days, the Bank of America's take-over of Merrill would be announced on 15 September. Where Lehman was concerned the only guest left at the party was UK high-street bank Barclays. If such a deal were to proceed, it would require the approval of the UK Financial Services Authority (FSA), which was nervous about the huge risk it would entail. US officials had been in disjointed discussions throughout the weekend with the body, but they had broken down under the sheer weight of activity that preoccupied bankers, lawyers, regulators and Treasury officials on Wall Street. On Sunday at 4pm, Secretary of the US Treasury Hank Paulson called Darling to talk about the takeover, frantic to save Lehman before the markets opened the next morning.

Paulson felt the British government had been stalling: his call was the last in a series of increasingly desperate attempts by American officials to convince their British counterparts to waive the regulatory strictures faced by Barclays. In reality, the FSA could not have acted differently or more swiftly, though one Treasury official acknowledges: 'By not being able to give them a definite "no" as to whether they would allow the Barclays takeover on the Saturday, the FSA perhaps allowed them to think that there was a serious option for Lehman's, which there wasn't.'[30]

Brown watched the unfolding events with fascination and concern. More than any other leader, he understood the importance of international cooperation to deal with the evolving crisis. Darling, still in Edinburgh preparing for his weekly commute down to London, had spent the Sunday talking to Brown, Barclays, and officials at the FSA. Brown had told Darling that morning that, for the sake of market stability, he should be seen to be as supportive as possible to Paulson, while not exposing the UK taxpayer or the UK economy to unnecessary risk. He was personally sceptical about the takeover; as the *Sunday Telegraph* leader put it that morning: 'Free things can still make expensive purchases.'[31] Darling had no outright objection in principle to a deal, but reminded Paulson that the British authorities would be taking a huge risk, and if it was allowed to go ahead, they would require strict guarantees from the US government. He told Paulson: 'We need to be sure what it is we are taking on, and what the US government is willing to do.'[32] Darling knew that, in practice, these were guarantees the US government would be unlikely to give before trading opened the next day.[33] But he had no choice but to ask for them. In any case, the US team had failed to appreciate that the deal would require a shareholder vote. When that was pointed out to them, they had suggested that the vote be suspended. FSA officials expressed shock: not only was that out of their remit, but even the UK government, with its wide-ranging constitutional powers, would find it difficult to repeal legislation and bypass European law in such a cavalier fashion on a Sunday afternoon.

Thus Lehman Brothers was doomed. Hanging up the phone, Paulson turned to Tim Geithner, president and chief executive officer of the Federal Bank of New York: 'He's not going to do it. He said he didn't want to "import our cancer".'[34] All weekend Lehman employees had worked frantically to save the bank. When they learned of the British government's 'no', they realised it had all been in vain. The following day, one by one, and then in streams, Lehman employees carried cardboard boxes out of their New York offices. Paulson felt let down and declared that the British government had 'grin-fucked us'.[35]

Darling had no option but to resist the insistent overtures from Manhattan. In any case, had Paulson and the US government wanted to bail out its own bank, in such unprecedented circumstances, it could very well have done so itself. 'The American purse would have been big enough to do it,' said Darling, and it would certainly have been big enough to offer support for a deal with Barclays, which was not offered.[36] Many on the British side were suspicious of the Americans' lack of commitment to saving Lehman. Why had Paulson not called Darling until Sunday afternoon, to agree a deal that needed closing before Monday morning? The episode had revealed again the depth of disconnection between the political and financial solutions being considered in the US. 'It was pretty clear to me that what they wanted was for the Bank of America to take it on, and failing that, Barclays,' says one senior official. 'But they hadn't completely ruled out letting it fail. There was a degree of volition when [the US government] let it go.'[37] Another official recalls: 'Until it started looking like an unwise decision, Hank and his team saw the Lehman collapse as a badge of honour.'[38] It was an early sign of the political conditions in which the Americans were working: pulled in two directions by politics and economics, it was politics that won the day.

When British official Jon Cunliffe heard that Sunday night that the

Americans were abandoning Lehman, he was nevertheless astonished. He sent Brown an email on the following morning saying: 'If we don't do something now, the whole system is going to go down. We have to act.' Brown and Darling were equally shocked that the US Treasury had not stepped up. The US authorities seemed, in their eyes, to underestimate the consequences of inaction.[39] Brown asked Cunliffe: 'What can we do?'[40] Indeed, what could they do? That same morning, at 6.53am, Robert Peston, the BBC's business editor, posted on his BBC blog: 'There has never been a weekend like it in my twenty-five years as a financial journalist.'[41]

British Response: 15 to 19 September

The next morning, as markets prepared for the day, the world held its breath. When the Asian markets opened on Monday 15 September, for several hours they appeared paralysed, waiting to see what their European counterparts would do. Investors and lenders worried about exposing themselves any further. Shares in HBOS, Britain's biggest mortgage lender, crashed 34 per cent in the early hours of trading on the London Stock Exchange, as investors fled, spooked by doubts about its solvency. By the time the Stock Exchange closed on the Monday at 4.30pm, a 3.9 per cent drop in the FTSE 100 Index had wiped out £50bn of value.

As the shockwaves spread, Brown watched with mounting dismay. From the early days of the crisis, he saw that the disease affecting the financial system was global, and knew that only a global solution would cure it. As the infection spread, his repeated refrain to his staff was: 'Why is this financial crisis not being fixed internationally?' Of crucial importance, he had been chair of the G7 finance ministers during the Asian crisis in 1998 and had played a pivotal role in steering them towards a shared international response.[42] He now saw more clearly than any other leader that the right way to deal with a systemic world crisis was concerted action. This insight, alongside his proposals to recapitalise the banks, proved to be his seminal contribution to the whole episode. In January at Davos, he had outlined his thinking on how to revamp the International Monetary Fund and the World Bank to provide a more responsive international structure to deal with such emergencies. The speech had been applauded appreciatively, but it had fallen on deaf ears. In April, as the problems mounted, he had sent a mission to the US to explore a joint response to the crisis, but the message came back loud and clear: 'We know how to deal with our problem. We've dealt with Bear Stearns. Back off.'[43] Brown's European colleagues, meanwhile, were telling him: 'This is not our problem. It's you Anglo-Saxon capitalists who are responsible.'[44] But the rebuffs from either side of the Atlantic only made him more determined to find a way forward internationally.

In the preceding months Brown had been reading deeply, guided by his closest financial advisers, Vadera, Heywood and Cunliffe. A further figure to shape their thinking powerfully was Jonathan Portes, chief economist at the Cabinet Office. He encouraged them to explore the banking solutions that had been pursued in Sweden and the Scandinavian countries, and the experience of Japan, where a long-running failure to clean up the banks had badly damaged the economy. As the crisis gathered pace, Brown became intent on getting to its root cause and became fascinated by the question of capital. He and his team became convinced that the problem facing banks was not the lack of liquidity, as the bankers themselves liked to think, but instead that they were undercapitalised for the toxic assets they had taken on in the boom years. In short the real danger threatening the global banking system was that a vast swathe of banks simply didn't have enough capital to cover their losses: many were insolvent. Concerns about the extent of undercapitalisation explained the assault on the banks' share price and the freezing up of the interbank market. In the months leading up to September Brown had been engaged in long email exchanges and conversations exploring questions of the significance of capital and the imperative to get the banks to declare the losses they were carrying, but not admitting, so that it would be known what it would take to recapitalise them, which Brown believed was necessary to restore confidence in the economic system. These discussions led to the question: where is the capital going to come from and how much would each bank need? Brown became increasingly convinced that any solution had not only to be internationally coordinated but must also involve a substantial injection of government capital if credit markets were going to start flowing again. In other words, the solution lay in governments buying up parts of banks. From fairly early on, says one adviser, 'recapitalisation seemed to Gordon the only logical thing to do'.[45]

Building international support for such an approach was another matter altogether. If countries did not act in unison, a specifically British recapitalisation plan would be lost in the noise. The first step to an international consensus would be the hardest. Brown realised this step had to be to convince the US of its merits – after all, it was the source of the crisis, the largest financial market in the world, and home to a deeply sceptical Republican administration. Early attempts to discuss the matter with President Bush came to nothing. Brown's team had been impressed with Bush at Camp David in July 2007 and in their subsequent meetings, but he was not a details man. 'He would sometimes wink at us when Gordon had started going on about the economy, as if to say: "There he goes again,"' recalls one adviser.[46] Bush's view was 'this is finance – Hank [Paulson] handles that for me', according to another.[47] On top of that, the

Bush team felt a deep political aversion to a programme of recapitalisation. The notion of 'owning' the banks was anathema to the President and the Republican Party. Brown by now could empathise with that feeling: he had felt the same political apprehension – too strongly, perhaps – when approaching the nationalisation of Northern Rock. But as the crisis unfolded, and the Northern Rock action quickly appeared vindicated, he grew increasingly emboldened to reject political orthodoxies. He came to believe that his task as Prime Minister was to handle the politics in order to deliver the right financial solution. He alone understood the issues as clearly as Paulson, Geithner or US Federal Reserve Chairman Ben Bernanke, while also having the will to make the necessary political calls. 'Bush was not able to bridge that gap between the financial and the political,' recalls one senior official. 'That was something Gordon proved uniquely able to do.'[48]

If Brown was to succeed, Paulson would have to play a crucial role. Having previously been chief executive at Goldman Sachs, he, better than anyone, should have understood the dynamics of the unfolding crisis, much of which was centred on the large investment banks. But the Treasury Secretary's pragmatic method of dealing with problems, institution by institution, vexed Brown, who had come to believe that individual rescues were not the right approach. He was thus pleased that when the US finally announced a systemic approach, the Troubled Asset Relief Program (TARP), its intent was comprehensive. Nonetheless, the Prime Minister remained doubtful that the precise system-wide approach it adopted would work. As Northern Rock and the failed rights issues over the summer had shown, when one institution was fixed, the problem simply moved on to the next. TARP tried to deal with the problem by giving the US Treasury permission to buy $700bn of bad assets from banks: banks could thus offload their bad, mortgage-based assets, and then start trading with other banks, no longer afraid of being stuck with their worthless assets. As confidence was restored, and trading resumed, the hope was that asset prices would rise back up to the appropriate levels, and everyone would benefit. As Brown had increasingly realised, however, the deep problem was a lack of trust in the system. Trust was the necessary condition for the financial system to work again. TARP was an attempt to restore that trust, but would it be sufficient?[49]

For now, the spotlight switched back suddenly to the British banking sector. Throughout the year, Fred Goodwin, chief executive of the Royal Bank of Scotland (RBS), and other senior British bankers had been reassuring the Treasury that they could weather the storm. 'It's fine, we can handle it. If we have to sell a few things, we'll sell a few things,' was his approach.[50] But it was quickly becoming apparent that RBS was being overly optimistic, or just naive. 'They didn't know the truth!' one Treasury official puts it baldly.[51] As the crisis gathered pace, the assets that banks had traditionally considered to be entirely safe were no longer secure. RBS was not the only badly exposed British bank – HBOS had also invested unwisely. On the Monday that Lehman had fallen, Brown and Darling had planned to meet to discuss the forthcoming Pre-Budget Report, but their focus shifted to the markets and the security of the British banks.[52] HBOS they deemed the more vulnerable of the two following a failed rights issue earlier that summer. Number 10 and Treasury officials joined in the discussion, and debated the likelihood of the bank going down. What guarantees might they give? How could they prevent a failure, and restore sufficient confidence to prevent the need for further action down the line? Following the successful move to save Northern Rock earlier in the year, the conversation naturally turned to nationalisation.[53] Would that be required for HBOS? This time, Brown was clear: politics would not get in the way of nationalisation if that was the appropriate policy response. But he remained against nationalisation for different reasons, fearing a domino effect, with one bank nationalisation following another. 'If we 100 per cent nationalised HBOS, that would have called into question RBS, which would have called into question Barclays. There was no sufficient guarantee, if we did something, what the results might be,' says one official.[54]

The ideal option was to find another bank to take over HBOS: it was the course that most appealed to Brown. It was well known that Lloyds TSB had wanted to buy HBOS for some time. By 15 September, Number 10 had received confirmation that both HBOS and Lloyds TSB were in advanced stages of discussion about a takeover. The banks wanted clarification on the status of competition law, and help with it so they could move forward without delay. While the Treasury anguished over whether such a takeover could be deemed anti-competitive, Lloyds TSB was licking its lips. The opportunity to acquire HBOS on attractive terms would give it control of a third of the UK savings and mortgage market. The FSA and Bank of England were asked to weigh up the consequences, and came back with a view that the waiver should be granted.

Number 10 was on the lookout for positive stories to boost Brown at a vulnerable time, and briefed that the Prime Minister himself had clinched the takeover deal with Victor Blank, the chairman of Lloyds TSB and a Labour sympathiser, at a Citibank cocktail party that Monday evening. Brown allegedly whisked Blank into an anteroom away from the main party. Blank said his bank was keen on HBOS, suggesting that it would be able to help the government if the problems with the competition rules could be smoothed over.[55] Life is rarely that simple. 'If you're the chairman of a bank, you don't decide to take over another bank because the PM, who's a friend of yours, asks you at a party,' says one close observer.[56] From Monday evening to Wednesday morning, an intensive thirty-six hours was spent with differing government offices examining the competition framework, and with the Office of Fair Trading and the Department of Business exploring in an increasingly strained atmosphere how a Lloyds TSB–HBOS deal could be effected.[57]

Meanwhile, in the US, extraordinary events were continuing to unfold. On 16 September, the insurance giant AIG had its credit rating downgraded, and as markets opened, its share price fell 60 per cent, hitting a low of \$1.25, some 95 per cent lower than that year's high of \$70.13. AIG was the world's biggest insurer, with tentacles stretching throughout the financial system. Allowing its failure was unthinkable. Paulson ripped up his own rulebook in a U-turn at 8pm UK time that saw AIG bailed out to the tune of \$85bn.

When the London markets opened that Tuesday, shares in HBOS halved in value in an instant. Darling was warned that the position of HBOS was 'absolutely dire'.[58] Intense pressure came from Number 10 to find a way ahead on the competition law. Though the FSA was keen to do so, the Treasury remained less convinced, still concerned about the diminution of competition in the sector and anxious to avoid, if it could, government intrusion into corporate takeover and merger discussions. But these were extraordinary times, and regulators were desperate to find a solution before the markets opened on Thursday 18 September. The solution eventually found was for government to announce its intention to amend competition law to allow the possibility of a 'national interest' exemption on financial-stability grounds, enabling the deal between HBOS and Lloyds TSB to be finalised by 9.30pm on the Wednesday. The £12.2bn takeover was duly announced at 7am on the Thursday.

Brown and Darling met with Bank of England Governor Mervyn King at Downing Street that Thursday morning to take stock. The media were positive about the news, notably outlets such as *The Times* that had been briefed about the cocktail party story. The markets, however, were ambivalent and by 5pm that day, £2bn had been wiped off the value of Lloyds TSB. The announcement that several central banks, including the Bank of England and the Bank of Japan, would be injecting £98bn worth of liquidity into the system had done little to rally the markets. The government had got through the week, though it had been one of the most tumultuous in post-war economic history. 'The feeling that we had over that period was that we were walking very close to a cliff every night. Every now and again the ground crumbled away from you and someone fell over,' recalls an official.[59]

On Saturday 20 September, Brown travelled to the Labour Party conference in a slightly calmer frame of mind. For a few days after the Lloyds TSB takeover, life quietened down. 'It looked as if we were at last ahead of events, not behind them,' says a Number 10 official.[60] But the financial crisis was never far from Brown's mind. That weekend, according to David Muir, a note was brought in to Brown's suite to say there were worries that Goldman Sachs, the bluest of blue-chip banks, might be on the verge of going under. Brown continued to think about the recapitalisation discussions he had held in preceding months, and the need for coordinated international action. Alastair Campbell advised Brown at the conference, much as he had Blair after 9/11, to seize the opportunity of the kaleidoscope being shaken up, and establish a stronger framework.[61] Then, while Brown was working on his speech on the Monday, his principal private secretary, James Bowler, appeared at Manchester.[62] A civil servant would never normally be present in this way at a party conference, but Heywood decided that the financial position was so troubling that he needed Bowler by the Prime Minister's side so that he could be given regular updates, every hour or two if needed.

Brown knew that, if his speech did not restore confidence in his leadership, he was doomed. The bubbling financial crisis was acting as a major distraction to him. But it was also to provide him with a 'get out of jail free card'.

The Annual Party Conference: 20 to 24 September

'This is the strangest Labour conference for decades,' wrote *The Independent*'s Steve Richards as delegates arrived at the Manchester Central conference centre for the four-day jamboree.[63] It is not unusual for the media to hype a conference speech as being 'make or break' for leaders, but Brown was under real pressure to perform and prove his critics wrong. As one senior aide says: 'He needed to have a very good conference, and if not, it was going to be: "Good night."'[64] *The Observer* summed up the views of many: 'The only issue is the leadership: is Gordon up to it?'[65]

Despite being under immense pressure, Brown characteristically let himself get distracted by a media sideshow concerning an article that had appeared under his name in the September issue of the *Parliamentary Monitor* (an obscure Westminster magazine) which had not been properly cleared with him, and which praised Obama.[66] The article jeopardised the neutrality protocols expected during the presidential election. Normally it would have escaped notice, but its contents went viral and were widely reported in the press. First featured in the *Evening Standard*, it subsequently appeared in the *Financial Times* and on the BBC. The next day, the McCain campaign contacted the British embassy in Washington to complain. Brown was livid and demanded to know who had written the article. He never found out.[67] Having calmed down Brown's thoughts became dominated by the speech he was due to give on the Tuesday, the most important of his entire premiership so far.

Unusually, Brown was given a dry run, addressing the conference on the opening Saturday, when he spoke without notes about the profound problems in the global economy. The decision to do this was taken by his team just two or three days beforehand. It worked a treat, going down very well with the party faithful. Not only did it underline Brown's credentials as the best-positioned figure Labour had to handle the financial crisis, it was also useful in giving him more space on the Tuesday to be personal.[68] In short, Brown's success on the Saturday emboldened him for his main speech.

Brown's Saturday appearance would not be the only novelty of this party conference. Some time before the conference, Sarah Brown had asked her husband whether she should make a short introductory speech before he spoke. 'I know him better than anyone. I can explain what he's thinking about when he gets up in the morning and what he thinks about when he ends the day,' she told his aides.[69] Sarah had been inspired by the role she had seen Michelle Obama play in supporting her husband and it had got her thinking. Brown was in two minds. 'Should Sarah say something?' he asked his close team. They were in two minds too, and kept putting off their answer because the margins for error were so tight. The evening before the speech, they had still not reached a conclusion. So Stephen Carter, David Muir and Sue Nye sat down in Brown's conference suite on Monday evening to thrash it out. Nye's gut instinct was to be cautious, Carter could see both sides of the argument, while Muir was strongly in favour. On balance they decided to recommend a thumbs-up. Brown and Sarah returned to the suite at 10pm that night. They immediately asked what the decision was and Brown looked relieved at the positive response, but Sarah did not. Only then did the enormity of what she had suggested fully hit her.[70] She was not a natural public speaker and her confidence had taken a bad knock after a poor speech she had given at Davos in 2008. Muir said they should let the conference organisers know at once. 'No way!' interjected Nye. The worry was that, if the press team (especially McBride) knew, they would let it slip in Manchester that evening to the journalists. The organising team were eventually informed less than an hour before Sarah was due to speak.[71]

Thus the conference hall was caught off guard on the Tuesday when they saw the figure of Sarah Brown walking on to the stage. 'What's this, what's happening?' Nick Robinson demanded of Muir, who was sitting by his side.[72] As she stepped up on the platform, nerves fully hit her as she realised how hard it could be to carry a party conference audience. 'She had to psyche herself up to do it, especially as she is naturally a reserved person,' says an aide.[73] All ears in the hall were attuned totally as she uttered her first words, none knowing what she might say, or even what she was doing. 'I asked if I could have a chance to talk briefly about one of the privileges of my life over recent years,' she began nervously. Speaking of her husband, she continued: 'Every day I see him motivated to work for the best interests of people around the country.' She thanked delegates for the warmth of the reception they had given her after their marriage – although this had occurred seven years before, she still wanted to show her appreciation. She finished the speech, which lasted just two minutes, by introducing: 'My husband, the leader of your party, your prime minister, Gordon Brown.' It was immediately clear from the audience response that she had more than risen to the challenge. 'Sarah's appearance was touching and starry. She is truly [Brown's] greatest asset,' reported *The Guardian*.[74] 'It was a triumph with the media because it was something entirely different and they loved that,' reflects Carter.[75]

After this introduction, Brown's own speech risked being an anticlimax but proved to be anything but. Many hands had contributed to it: Gavin Kelly and Nick Pearce leading on the policy substance, Kirsty McNeill and David Muir on the words, Peter Mandelson and Bob Shrum on the big ideas. Parts of the speech were rehearsed before cameras and analysed with input from focus groups: according to Deborah Mattinson, it showed that 'he looked like a man who had the right script but was very uncomfortable in himself'.[76] With memories of the disastrous Warwick speech still fresh in delegates' minds, expectations on the conference floor that Tuesday were not high. Muir made him practise over and over again and worked on his delivery to make him sound personable. Kelly thought the fact he was rested before it, and had been made to prepare thoroughly, made all the difference.[77]

So what did he say? His personal agenda we know was still far from established, and the distractions of the spring and summer had done little to solidify it. The speech was chock-full of the usual policy announcements, some empty but others not, such as free prescriptions for cancer sufferers and similar concessions for patients with long-term illnesses, and a guaranteed right to personal catch-up tuition. The Policy Unit had worked overtime, resulting in some heated disagreements with the Treasury, who thought some measures too costly to deliver. What captured attention, however, was not any substance but the sense that here was a new, highly personal, and contrite Brown, prepared to show that he was listening and in touch with party membership and the country at large. He chose to apologise for the 10p débâcle, and personally drafted the key paragraphs.[78] 'Where I've made mistakes, I'll put my hand up and try to put them right,' he told the conference. 'So what happened with the 10p stung me because it really hurt that suddenly people felt I wasn't on the side of people on middle and modest incomes – because I'm on the side of hard-working families. It's the only place I've ever wanted to be. From now on it's the only place I ever will be.'[79]

His most telling phrase, though, was a side-swipe at both the youthful

Opposition leader David Cameron and the young pretender to the Labour leadership, David Miliband. The phrase that this was 'no time for a novice', had come from Rebekah Brooks, then editor of the *Sun*, who had said it at a party. Ed Balls heard it, and suggested the night before that they put it into his speech.[80] 'Brilliant – we'll slot it in in the morning,' was the response of McNeill and Muir. An input from Ed Miliband, drawing on Brown's keenness for vocational training, added a neat twist: he suggested they set up the punch line with the words 'I'm all in favour of apprenticeships but'. Given the all-encompassing personal challenge Brown was under, and his unique credentials for tackling the banking crisis, it was a very clever put-down, up there with Thatcher's: 'The lady's not for turning.' Too clever? The conference and the press did not think so, and responded enthusiastically. It was easily his best conference speech as Prime Minister – partly because of the effort he had put into practising the delivery of it. But it went down badly with a small number of Cabinet ministers, 'who thought that, if a Prime Minister insulted one of their number, that was one less reason to be loyal to him'.[81] With the line, however, Brown achieved something that he had not done over the previous fifteen months: he told the party why he was uniquely qualified to be Prime Minister.

Cameron, not mentioned by name in Brown's 2007 speech, came under the cosh in 2008. The Prime Minister contrasted his own earnestness – 'if people say I am too serious, quite honestly there's a lot to be serious about' – with the 'salesman' Conservative leader. He took a risk in attacking Cameron for putting his children in front of the cameras. 'My children aren't props, they're people,' he said. Again, a brilliantly scripted put-down that contrasted the style and values of both leaders. The response came from Cameron four months later, and it was done in private. His Christmas card to Brown that December, which featured a picture of himself and his family, was signed off: 'Merry Christmas from me and "the props".'[82]

Happily for Brown, David Miliband's speech, in which the Foreign Secretary had invested much thought, flopped. Miliband ranged over foreign and domestic policy, emphasising the party should be concerned with the future not the past, and asserting that the Conservatives were 'beatable', interpreted as a criticism of the party doing so badly under Brown in the polls.[83] The speech was passable, if unexceptional. To make matters worse for Miliband, for the first time there was talk on the fringes of the conference about his younger brother, Ed, who was considered to have delivered a strong speech, being the best placed Miliband to lead Labour after Brown. The surrounding noise was to further damage Miliband's cause, on which the tide was receding. A widely recycled photograph of him grinning and carrying a banana did not convey gravitas, while a report that he had told an aide he had toned down his speech to avoid it causing a 'Heseltine moment' (a reference to Michael Heseltine's attempt to destabilise Thatcher in 1986) was circulated on the BBC. It provoked Miliband into an angry response, which produced the counter-criticism that he protested too much. The almost universal sense among delegates was that Miliband had blown his chances at the conference, while Brown had capitalised on his. Gavin Kelly noticed that, after the conference was over, Brown had a twinkle in his eye. It was a touching moment: rarely did he see Brown aware that he had delivered something special.[84] 'His body language was visibly changed. He'd regained his self-confidence,' says another Number 10 aide. Adding to his upbeat mood was the conference 'bounce'. A YouGov poll for *The Sun* on 24 September placed Labour only 10 per cent behind the Tories, a massive recovery from the earlier twenty-point-plus deficit.[85]

Some of the sheen of Brown's speech was lost that evening when there was yet another briefing débâcle associated with McBride – only this time McBride was, in all likelihood, innocent. The trouble began at 9pm when *Newsnight* called one of Ruth Kelly's advisers to tell her that a 'Number 10 source' had briefed them that the Transport Secretary was intending to resign from Brown's Cabinet. Kelly, who was at the gala dinner, was immediately informed that the story was about to break and recognised at once there was a problem: it was true. Around Easter time she had told Brown that she wanted to leave the government at the next reshuffle to pursue interests outside politics. This meant that she was not prepared to deny the story to *Newsnight*. After it was broadcast, 'all hell broke loose'.[86] With journalists and politicians locked in hotel bars the rumours started flying: some saw it as evidence of the Brown machine ruthlessly undermining a Cabinet minister, others wondered if it was another attempt to destabilise Brown. The truth is that no one knew what was going on. When Kelly's advisers met with senior figures from Number 10 including Nye, McBride, Gavin Kelly and Dan Corry (Kelly and Corry had worked for Ruth Kelly when she was Education Secretary) in the Radisson Hotel that night, the Number 10 team not only denied any knowledge of the source of the *Newsnight* story, it also turned out they had no idea that Kelly had told Brown about her planned departure. The two factions knew they had to 'shut the story down' as soon as possible and so prepared a text confirming Kelly's departure, which then led to the infamous scenes of McBride briefing the press at 3am in the bar of the Midland Hotel. McBride was deliberately joined by Kelly's media adviser, to put on a united front between Number 10 and the minister. The 'Number 10 source' behind the *Newsnight* briefing remains a mystery. Few believe that McBride was behind it. One possible explanation is that someone else associated with Number 10 had briefed the story as part of a routine effort to undermine perceived critics of Brown without realising that on this occasion it was true; only when Kelly offered no denial did the story spiral out of control. Over the years Brown had licensed so many people to operate on his behalf that it was often unclear who was behind such briefings.

For the Cabinet and other senior party figures the episode was further evidence of Brown's highly chaotic and dysfunctional media operation. If his premiership was to truly recover, this would need fixing. The briefing culture at Number 10 was a source of huge tension among ministers. Earlier in September the health minister, Ivan Lewis, who had criticised Brown in the press, faced the wrath of the Number 10 machine when the *News of the World* ran a story ('Text pest shame of minister') about how Lewis had allegedly harassed a female member of his staff with text messages.[87] Ministers, who believed that McBride was behind the story, were shocked by the brutal way Lewis was treated. As one adviser notes, by the time of conference, 'there was real momentum from within the Cabinet against Damian'.[88] Harriet Harman was particularly indignant having overheard McBride briefing against her while she was relaxing on her hotel balcony.[89] She immediately demanded that Brown take action against his Number 10 team.[90] Darling was another who had been disturbed by the briefings from McBride, whom he believed to be motivated by a desire to clear the way for McBride's close ally Balls to be made Chancellor in the upcoming reshuffle. Before the party conference began, Darling and his wife Maggie had spoken to Nye about this. Douglas Alexander and Ed Miliband joined forces, complaining: 'You can't have a Prime Minister's press spokesman calling the Chancellor a "cunt" in bars.'[91] Both demanded that Brown remove him from the Number 10 team.

Brown knew McBride was a problem, and on the advice of Tom Watson brought in two new figures as political spokesmen that October: Michael Dugher and John Woodcock. Woodcock had worked for John Hutton, an arch-Blairite, so his inclusion at the heart of the Number 10 political team sent an important signal that things would change. He was immediately welcomed by Brown's inner circle.[92] McBride's friends admitted that it was the end of the road. Brown told ministers that he would have his role changed, and he was to be taken off frontline briefing duty and given a backstage role. But he refused to sack his loyal acolyte. Failure to dismiss McBride at this point was one of the worst omissions of Brown's premiership. Why did he not get rid of him altogether at that stage? The simple explanation is he did not feel secure enough to lose him. One of Brown's team is unequivocal: 'The counter-argument was always: "Damian knows where the bodies are buried." There was always a worry about what he would say if he got drunk and let things slip out.'[93] An unlikely champion for his cause, Sarah Brown valued McBride for keeping her sons out of the press, and lobbied for his continuation.[94] Yet again, Brown missed the chance to sack him. It was to be another six months before the impact of a still-greater achievement by Brown, the London G20, was to be sabotaged by the unguided missile that was Damian McBride.

Building Global Support – New York and Washington, 24–25 September

As Brown basked in the praise at Manchester, 200 miles to the south a plane was being prepared to fly him to the US. The centrepiece of his trip was to be a UN conference that Brown himself had proposed, to drive forward progress on the Millennium Development Goals. But the real crux would be a meeting, not yet arranged, with Bush. The conference over, Brown was back to his preoccupation with how to get the Americans to engage in international action to address the unfolding crisis, and the latter half of the trip would be completely restructured around that aim.

On board the chartered BA flight from London Heathrow were Simon McDonald, Jon Cunliffe, Tom Fletcher and Michael Ellam – as well as the former Duchess of York, Sarah Ferguson, and model Elle Macpherson, who were flying to New York for a charity event. When an email went around Number 10 saying that the two VIPs would be on the flight with them, staff thought that, given Brown's emphasis in his conference speech about being a straight man with no enthusiasm for celebrities, it must be a spoof.[95] The plane touched down briefly in Manchester to pick up Brown, Sarah, Shriti Vadera and Stewart Wood, and then set off, with the usual complement of journalists at the back of the cabin, for the seven-hour flight to New York. They would be staying longer than planned.

Brown's commitment to helping developing countries originated, like most of his values, in his childhood. Until the age of eighty-two, his father was still knocking on doors raising money for Christian Aid, while as children, Brown and his brothers Andrew and John produced on an old duplicating machine in the manse what they called 'Scotland's only newspaper sold in aid of African refugees'.[96] Brown believed his moral purpose in life was to help alleviate the poverty of the world's disadvantaged.[97] His commitment to international development during his time as Chancellor was without equal. It was he who had ensured that government spending on aid was increased to 0.7 per cent of GDP, establishing a cross-party consensus on that figure. Even when spending came under pressure, he remained determined to ring-fence its allocation. 'There's just no point suggesting we don't hold development at 0.7 per cent,' says one adviser of debates in Number 10 over spending cuts. 'He would just throw it straight back at you and say "we're not cutting the development budget, end of story".'[98]

One of the enduring questions of Brown's premiership is how a man with so many personal and leadership flaws could attract such deep commitment from those around him. His conviction on global poverty is one explanation. To many on the outside, it sat awkwardly. One adviser close to Brown remembers cringing at his response to one interviewer, who had asked: 'What's the first thing you think of when you wake up in the morning?' Brown's team found his response – 'child poverty in the developing world' – incredibly admirable but also politically naive. 'Politically, he should have said something about bread-and-butter issues, but it was also strangely close to the truth.'[99] Another aide who joined the Brown team at Number 10, and who had not known the Prime Minister previously, was deeply impressed by his commitment to issues 'that, frankly, other leaders didn't have much time for'. At one point, 'half of Downing Street was writing letters to free Aung San Suu Kyi'. These 'causes burned inside him, even though he never won any votes pursuing them'.[100]

After world leaders came together at the UN in New York in September 2000 to adopt the 'Millennium Declaration', committing them collectively to reduce extreme poverty and setting out a series of targets to be achieved by 2015, Brown became one of the most enthusiastic finance ministers advocating these Millennium Development Goals (MDGs). A leading figure behind Blair's Commission for Africa, Brown was principally responsible for the several development successes at the G8 Gleneagles summit in July 2005, as he had galvanised his fellow finance ministers beforehand, smoothing the way for agreements on trade, aid and debt objectives. His pedigree included dreaming up the 'vaccination bond scheme', a financing facility to generate huge investments in immunisation programmes, helping to treat more than 500 million children. He even persuaded the Pope to buy the first bond. During his premiership, Brown refined his commitment to development into a sophisticated account of the challenges of globalisation, perhaps best captured by his impassioned speech, delivered without notes, at the 'TED' conference in August 2009. For advisers working on his domestic agenda, it was a level of commitment, clarity and coherence that they would have dearly liked to see him apply to policy on the domestic front.

For many months leading up to the UN conference in September 2008, Brown had worked hard to prepare the ground. On his first visit as Prime Minister to the US the year before, he seized on the opportunity of a speech at the UN to call for a renewed international effort to achieve the MDGs. He identified nothing less than a 'development crisis', arguing for a conference specifically to discuss progress since 2000. British ambassador to the UN John Sawers describes the significance of Brown's personal impetus: 'By throwing such energy into development, he forced it back on to the global agenda at the UN at the time that it was being forced off by climate change. He succeeded in getting it on an almost equal footing.'[101] On 27 March 2008, Brown had met with French President Sarkozy at Arsenal's Emirates Stadium in north London, where they agreed jointly to finance up to 16 million school places in Africa by 2010. Justin Forsyth, who worked on development at Number 10, described both these occasions as vital 'stepping stones' to the MDG conference.[102] During his video calls with Bush, too, Brown would press a surprisingly sympathetic President on the issue of development.

Planning for the conference had taken up much of Sawers's first year in New York. Brown's speech on 25 September, which, typically, he was rewriting up to the very last minute, was one of his most powerful to an international audience, and was interrupted several times by spontaneous applause. Delivered with a passion and commitment that few other world leaders could match, his audience sensed it was coming from somewhere deep within him. Brown's best speeches were often short and were produced when he spoke from the heart, as he did on that day. 'I am humbled to stand here and speak for the thousands of our people who are dying because they are too poor to live. ... We cannot stand aside. ... Some say this time of financial turbulence is the time to put our ambitions on hold, to cut back or postpone the dream of achieving the MDGs, but this would be the worst time to turn back,' he said. Kevin Rudd described Brown as the 'conscience of the world'.[103] Forsyth wrote in his diary: 'The final day comes – a year's work. Gordon at his peak.'[104] UN Secretary-General Ban Ki-moon, by now a firm Brown fan, estimated that the conference generated $16bn to bolster food supply, improve education and combat malaria. Shadow Chancellor George Osborne picked up on one phrase Brown used, in which he said that the 'age of irresponsibility' is over. Osborne used this as the stick to beat Brown for spending too much when Chancellor. 'The age of irresponsibility has now become the age of hypocrisy,' he said.[105] Under the circumstances, it sounded petty and misjudged.

Throughout his time in New York, Brown's mind regularly returned to the need for immediate action to restore calm to the financial markets. With the US economy still reeling from the loss of Lehman, 'it became increasingly clear to everyone that the place we needed to be was not Manhattan but Washington', press secretary Ellam recalls.[106] Following the HBOS saga, the crisis had entered a new phase, and one which Brown was utterly convinced demanded coordinated action. Vadera, his trusted financial adviser, was to play a critical role in working with Brown to deliver that solution. Now in the business department, government rules meant she could not travel in the Prime Minister's party. Brown fell back on the expedient of having her travel on the trip as the guest of his wife, who had herself played an important part in the MDG process on maternal health.[107] Ironically, Vadera had come up with the idea of an MDG conference with Brown in 2007, as minister at the Department for International Development, and had worked on the initiative until her reshuffle in January. She now found herself on the plane, flying towards the conference, but for a very different reason.

While Brown was engaged at the UN, Vadera went to see investment bankers to probe them on what they thought of Paulson's and Bush's TARP scheme, which was still struggling to make headway through Congress. Cunliffe joined her for some of the sessions. Brown and Vadera had a breakfast with some of the most important investors in banks, including George Soros, and a separate meeting with Tim Geithner. The question of recapitalisation remained their focus: they wanted to know whether the US could use, and should use, TARP funds for providing the banks with capital.[108] Beforehand, back in London, the Prime Minister and his team had become convinced that only his plan for a globally coordinated recapitalisation plan would do the job, and that it had to be delivered not through a system like TARP, in which the Treasury bought up banks' bad assets, but by direct injections of capital. After the breakfast in New York, Brown was still more convinced that recapitalisation was the right answer. A member of his team recalls: 'Gordon came out of his meetings and said we should just go and talk to Bush at once because this is absolutely the right thing to do.'[109] The problem was, though, that his plan was at odds with US thinking: Paulson was sure that the TARP approach would succeed.

On Friday afternoon, Brown's team flew down to Washington to talk to Bush. Simon McDonald had phoned Nigel Sheinwald at the British embassy in Washington the day before and asked if he could fix a meeting for the following day in the Oval Office. A quick 'yes' came back.[110] What of the journalists at the back of the plane, who would have to contend with an added stopover and a longer trip than had originally been scheduled? 'Brown was at his absolute best, because he didn't give a toss what the journalists thought. They were trivia beyond belief,' says a member of the Prime Minister's party.[111] The press pack had also failed to notice a meeting that the Downing Street team had been anxious to conceal – it was with Blair earlier in the day, at the Clinton Global Initiative, to which Brown delivered a witty, off-the-cuff speech about development.[112]

Brown and his team met Bush in the Oval Office early on the Friday evening. The meeting was scheduled to last for forty minutes but it took double that time[113] and would prove one of the galvanising moments of the crisis. The first televised presidential debate was scheduled for later that evening, and would bring home Obama's dominance over McCain. Political change was much in the air. As ever, Bush was in relaxed mood and spoke frankly about the contest. 'You can only really lose the television debate,' he told them. 'What matters is whether the public feel comfortable with you in their living rooms.'[114] Sheinwald was struck by Bush's geniality towards Brown: 'He was very, very friendly to everyone and stood around chatting. It allowed a very free and easy exchange.'[115]

Brown was on a mission: he hoped to persuade Bush to both recognise that the roots of the crisis lay in undercapitalisation, not the lack of liquidity, and the need to establish a process that would deliver coordinated, international action on the economic crisis. However, the first substantive words between him and Bush touched on the collapse in July of the Doha Development

Round of the World Trade Organization, which had been aimed at lowering trade barriers. Brown had been pushing the President hard on it in their video calls, as he had in his phone conversations with premiers Singh of India and Wen of China. Brown believed that the key to unlocking the negotiations lay with getting the US, India and China into the right places. In particular Brown urged Bush to resolve US disagreements with India over agriculture duties. Bush, who had with him Susan Schwab, his trade negotiator, tried to assure Brown: 'Gordon, Singh tells me he'll sort this out when his election is over.'[116] The Doha Round touched many of Brown's key 'spots', combining international finance, development, trade and deal-making, all of which were topics he relished.[117]

Attentions then shifted to the principal issue. Steve Hadley later spoke of how seriously the President took what Brown had to say on the financial crisis.[118] His intensity stemmed in part from being out of his depth: it was quickly apparent to the British team that Bush was lost on the substance.[119] It was equally clear to them that 'Bush was pissed off with Wall Street: they'd got him into a real jam.'[120] They were struck also by the institutional impotence of the US Presidency over domestic – as opposed to foreign policy – crises. Here was his last big issue as President, yet his TARP solution was being torn apart by Congress in the full glare of the world's press, and the American political process was proving incapable of producing a coherent response to the deepening financial crisis.[121]

Brown knew that he needed to get Bush to agree to a process that would result in coordinated action. Specifically, his hope was to persuade the President to agree to an international meeting of the G20 at leader level. Sarkozy was also convinced of the need for a leaders' conference of some sort. The two European leaders had spoken in the margins of the UN in New York and agreed that Brown would raise the issue with Bush at his meeting, and then Sarkozy would follow this up. A minor difference of view emerged on the format such a meeting should take: Sarkozy preferred a 'G8 plus 5' (that is, China, India, Brazil, Mexico and South Africa), as he had earlier proposed in 2007. In his UN speech earlier in the week, Sarkozy had already suggested that the US President host the forum. Some turbulence was then caused when Brown succeeded in persuading Bush that the meeting should adopt the 'G20' format (bringing in countries such as Argentina, South Africa and South Korea), but this was mainly an issue of public profile rather than a difference with Brown on the substance of policy.

Bush was well disposed to Brown, but he nevertheless baulked at the idea of the conference. As Steve Hadley said, there was a weary belief in the White House that a stock response among Europeans to a crisis was: 'Let's have a big meeting.' Bush's team was concerned that a hastily convened international conference without a clear objective would only raise hopes that could not be fulfilled.[122] Paulson and Bernanke were also pressing Bush hard behind the scenes not to agree to a heads of government conference. So complex were the topics involved that they believed it was better handled at finance minister level, and that involving the leaders would only politicise matters.[123]

But the game was not up. In Brown's favour, Bush was slowly realising, according to a British official present at that meeting, 'that the evolving financial crisis was turning into a leader-level nightmare. He did not know where to turn.'[124] Brown's forceful advocacy helped sway the President, especially when he made it clear that, in contrast to the Sarkozy plan, the conference should be in Washington rather than New York. That made Bush prick up his ears. Brown stressed that any meeting would focus on collective action to stem the crisis rather than, as the French President sought, the establishment of a new regulatory regime to restrict what Sarkozy called 'Anglo-Saxon capitalism'. Most importantly, Brown showed he was fully sensitive to the American anxiety that a meeting without an outcome could be hugely dangerous.

Bush was reassured by Brown's words. Having witnessed him in action at international meetings, he felt growing confidence that the Prime Minister could ensure that an outcome was delivered on financial regulation that would give just the sense of coordination that the markets were looking for.[125] The meeting then turned to the question of format. Should they go for Sarkozy's preference, the accepted formula used in Gleneagles in 2005 of the 'G8 plus 5' or adopt Brown's suggestion that it be a larger G20 format? The G20 meeting had been established in 1999 in the wake of the Asian financial crisis, with Brown a major instigator, but it had previously been limited to finance ministers and central bank governors. He was adamant this was now the right vehicle. He feared endless debate delaying matters on membership and wanted to take an existing format off the peg. One aide sums up the essence of his argument thus: 'Let's not get bogged down in the detail of discussions about who's allowed to attend: let's go with an existing forum. I know it doesn't exist at the leader level, but let's just use the G20 and get on with.'[126] There was more than just a little self-interest in this too: as luck would have it, Britain was the next chair of the G20, ensuring the further boon of an early visit in the spring of 2010 by the new US President.[127] When Sarkozy met Bush a few days later, he found, to his annoyance, that the notion of the G20 format was already firmly in his mind. An initial G20 meeting was set for November in Washington, but Brown's team hoped this would act as the curtain-raiser for a second conference in London, by which time the US would have a new President-elect. Little did the Prime Minister know he was setting in train a process that would culminate in the most triumphant moment of his premiership.

It had been a long meeting, and Brown had been heartened by his success in planting the seeds of an international process. But he and his team were dismayed that the US administration continued to believe that TARP was the right answer, and that there seemed little prospect of their more radical recapitalisation plan being adopted in the US. 'When we came out, it really dawned on us: "Bush ain't gonna do this,"' recalls one person who was present. 'We realised, this is it. If we ourselves don't act, no one else is going to.' As Brown and his team left the Oval Office, in a mood of reflection at the gravity of the position, they began catching up on their BlackBerries and all of them picked up urgent messages about Bradford & Bingley. Heywood had been monitoring the situation closely and updating Brown over the previous forty-eight hours; now Darling wanted to speak to the Prime Minister urgently. The West Yorkshire bank and former building society was now in dire trouble. They needed somewhere to talk. White House staff responded quickly, ushering them into the executive boardroom opposite the Oval Office. The anxiety was heightened further by the White House's blank zones, which caused the team's mobile phones to fail, and Brown struggled to get a secure line.

Brown and Darling shared the concern not to repeat the damaging prevarication over Northern Rock, especially as it was becoming increasingly clear that if they did not act decisively, the continuing evaporation of liquidity could put an untold number of companies out of business.[128] With confidence in the banking system running out, a government bailout seemed the only potential solution. So the Prime Minister told his Chancellor to 'get on with it'.[129] He told advisers: 'Let's just focus on what's the right thing to do, and forget the political difficulties.'[130]

Before they left the White House, the team sent a message to Heywood at Number 10. The fragility of Bradford & Bingley had galvanised Brown. Not for him Bush's prevarication. The moment had come. He knew that this situation augured badly for other British banks. Without action, the stream of new casualties would just keep flowing. Looking around on the international stage, no other leader seemed poised to act. Brown requested that Heywood send over the seminal paper Number 10 had been preparing in his absence on the case for a system-wide bank recapitalisation and Treasury estimates of the losses and capital needs of British banks. Armed with Heywood's fax, which included advice from the Governor of the Bank of England, who had been reaching fundamentally similar conclusions about recapitalisation (and which led to subsequent disputes over credit for originating the plan), Brown and his team boarded their plane at Andrews Air Force base.

Gathering his team in the first-class cabin, Brown sat with Heywood's document in hand and said: 'I think we're just going to have to do this.'[131] The decision was made at 30,000 feet above the dark waters of the Atlantic Ocean. Reading the Treasury estimates about the scale of losses incurred by British banks Brown believed that 'we were only days away from a complete banking collapse.' He feared that this would leave companies unable to pay their creditors, workers not being paid wages, and ATMs ceasing to give out cash on the high-streets. Brown asked his team for a detailed and bold plan for the recapitalisation of Britain's banks. What it would mean, essentially, was the government buying shares in financial institutions: in effect, the part-nationalisation of the threatened financial institutions. Since some of the banks would resist such a course of action, his team also decided that they would have to make access to the liquidity and medium-term funding the banks required contingent on them accepting to be recapitalised. 'There were still details to be worked out – we needed to know which banks would need capital, and how much and by when. But Gordon had decided on the fundamental policy response. Never again was there a moment when I felt he was saying: "Shall we or shan't we?"' says one official. With the world's financial system wobbling at the brink, and the world's most powerful man stunned into inaction, the crisis had forced Brown to do the unthinkable.

If the nascent plan was to succeed, Brown's long-sought international consensus would be critical. With the US fixated on their TARP programme Brown decided he had to focus all his efforts on convincing the Europeans to overcome their belief that this was still an 'Anglo-Saxon' (that is, British and American) problem, and commit themselves to joint action. Gathering his team in the first-class cabin, Brown sat with Heywood. 'I think I can convince Sarkozy and Merkel,' he told his team confidently.[132] He would need to: if Britain recapitalised alone, the infection would continue to spread. Only concerted, coordinated, global action could restore confidence. As the plane flew through the night, and its passengers drifted into sleep, Brown took out his broad felt tip pen, and began to write in his illegible script.

Going It Alone: 27 September to 4 October

'It was rather like a hospital ward,' recalls soon-to-be Treasury minister Paul Myners of the scene on Brown's return. 'We had a series of patients in the beds, and some of them were really in quite an acute state, and others less so.'[133] As the team landed early on the Saturday morning, Bradford & Bingley was only the sickest patient needing their attention. Alarmed that the crisis had yet to peak, Brown headed to Downing Street to catch up with Darling on overnight developments, while Vadera was dispatched with Heywood to discuss the developing recapitalisation proposals with the Treasury.[134]

On the evening of Friday 26 September, the FSA had told Bradford & Bingley that, without support from a third party, it could not open for business on Monday morning. Darling had spoken to Brown in Washington before the plane took off, and the next morning he summoned the leaders of Britain's biggest banks into the Treasury. They were understandably wary of each other, but were united on one point, and it was not a comforting one. None was remotely interested in buying Bradford & Bingley. Over the weekend, with the full backing of Brown, the Treasury thus developed a solution in close association with the FSA, the Bank of England and investment bank Morgan Stanley. The government was to take Bradford & Bingley's toxic £50bn mortgage portfolio on to its books and would sell the deposits to Santander, the Spanish bank that already owned Abbey and Alliance & Leicester. For months, the FSA and the Treasury had looked at different options for resolving Bradford & Bingley's problems and had found none. 'Once it became clear no other institutions were interested, we executed the resolution over just the one weekend,' says an official.[135]

The Bradford & Bingley nationalisation package was announced to the markets on Monday 29 September. But if Brown had hoped for a momentary break in the clouds, he was to be disappointed. The same day, with the US financial system continuing to struggle, Paulson's $700bn TARP scheme, designed to pull it back from the brink, was finally rejected by Congress. The markets recoiled. The Dow Jones fell 777 points, its largest one-day drop in history. Frenzy gripped financial centres across the world. In the UK, the FTSE fell by more than 5 per cent. No sooner had one patient been taken out of intensive care than another entered: this time it was RBS, which now looked increasingly exposed, losing a fifth of its value that day. Intensive negotiations took place all that week at the Treasury, the Bank of England, FSA and Number 10. Yet again, desperate plans would need to be hatched to provide a solution.

In the heat of the crisis, Brown's team and their colleagues at the Treasury had forged themselves into a powerful group, working together as they would never manage to do again during the premiership. Closest to Brown himself was Vadera, who would become an increasingly decisive presence in the next two weeks, and who carried the Prime Minister's complete confidence. Historically, she had an awkward relationship with the Treasury and, indeed, with Darling himself, dating back to confrontations over spending during his time as Secretary of State for Transport, before Brown became Prime Minister. In recent months, Vadera had come to spend much of her time in Number 10 working directly with Brown, increasingly operating outside of the remit of her role as a business minister. With her keen analytical brain and breadth of contacts, she was able to provide him with a much-needed strategic overview. 'While the Treasury officials were forced to spend their limited resources focused on the latest bank in trouble, Vadera was able to step back to develop Brown's thinking about a systemic bank recapitalisation,' one official notes.[136] Like few others in Whitehall, Vadera had an ex-banker's understanding of the markets, and was more confident than many officials and politicians in taking risks and thinking outside the proverbial box. She was, though, an indomitable figure, an inveterate BlackBerry user, whose combative and staccato style built an intimidating aura – even engendering fear among some officials. With a mind of great brilliance, her hyper-quick reactions did not always make her tolerant of those who did not keep up, and she could often appear insensitive. One official recalls her arriving at a back door to Number 10, where an official was waiting for security to buzz him in. She stormed past and hammered the door with her fist until it was opened. Few were able to match up to the levels of commitment demanded by her. Nikhil Rathi and John Kingman were among the select few officials she admired, as was Tom Scholar, with whom she had the closest working relationship during the crisis. Vadera had known Scholar for ten years, dating back to when he had been Brown's Principal Private Secretary. They worked together under the radar, developing a multi-layered rescue package. It would include liquidity, medium-term credit guarantees and, as Brown had affirmed – and in contrast to the prevailing American thinking – bank recapitalisation.

The Treasury remained cautious about recapitalisation, but for its advocates it was now the only viable option: losing just three months in the existing climate through insufficient lending and liquidity could prove disastrous.[137] The Treasury, under instructions from Brown and Darling, had been working on contingency planning for a recapitalisation, and had stepped up the pace further when the crisis had emerged over HBOS. The group was now widened by Brown and Darling to involve the FSA and the Bank of England, where Brown had found an unexpected ally in Mervyn King, who was strongly in favour of recapitalisation, and who advised Brown regularly and powerfully throughout the period. 'Mervyn's thinking was in parallel with our own on recapitalisation,' says one official.[138] The members of the tripartite system for bank regulation (the FSA, Bank of England and Treasury) were asked to look at the details – how much capital did each bank need, and what were the legal implications of such an unprecedented move? One big question in particular remained unanswered: how could the banks be persuaded to accept their *need* for capital, when that would mean accepting, in public, the level of losses they faced?

In the meantime, Vadera tested evolving thinking in strictest confidence with a small group of bankers. This was entirely new territory, and crucial to understanding how banks would react. Scholar was asked if he would attend her discussions, to keep the Treasury in the loop, albeit informally. This elite coterie of bankers included Peter Sands and Richard Meddings of Standard Chartered, Robin Budenberg and David Soanes at UBS and Michael Klein of Citigroup in the US, who had been asked to fly from New York at a few hours' notice. The consultations gave the government confidence that they were on the right track, but reaffirmed their belief that all elements of the plan would have to come together to have the right impact.

The significance of a meeting on the Thursday (2 October) evening has been overstated in media accounts: it was not the occasion when the rescue plan was hatched.[139] In addition to Peter Sands, who convened it, Vadera and Scholar, most of those bankers whom Vadera had consulted that week were present.[140] They discussed the options open to the government, including capital support, funding by guaranteeing bank debt and offering liquidity support, and they immersed themselves in a technical debate about whether capital would be in the form of ordinary or preference shares. But the meeting was used principally to gauge the reaction of those present to the government's evolving plans, rather than to elicit fresh ideas. 'Some accounts have suggested that the Sands meeting on the Thursday evening was the occasion when the rescue plan was devised. That is not true. But it was a useful opportunity for some senior bankers to offer their views,' says an observer.[141] Michael Klein of Citigroup later expressed his belief that the 'powerful decision taken in the room' – the decision that was to make the British proposal 'the blueprint for other countries' – was that the government would make access to liquidity contingent upon banks raising capital.[142] But that decision had, of course, been taken by Brown on the flight back to the UK from the US. It may have appeared to the bankers that they were party to a brave new plan being conceived. In fact, these ideas were merely being 'stress-tested'.

The meeting bolstered Vadera's confidence in the structure of the recapitalisation plan. The news that day that Paulson's TARP had eventually been given the green light by a panicked US Congress, however, did little to calm nerves in Number 10 and the Treasury: for in adopting their emerging recapitalisation plan, Britain was going it alone. 'You can't imagine how lonely it felt,' one official reflects.[143] On the substance, Brown remained confident that recapitalisation was the only logical option. But the reception it would receive was another matter: if banks, and the markets, did not like the sound of the plan, and if other countries did not rally to the cause, the results could spell catastrophe.

In the reshuffle that Brown announced on Friday 3 October (discussed in more detail later in this chapter), he moved Vadera from the Business Department to the Cabinet Office, where she could play a central role in an open way.[144] Paul Myners, the experienced City figure, was also appointed to the Treasury as a

'GOAT': earlier he had been involved in discussions, but was not able to attend meetings until his ministerial appointment was announced. That evening, he was taken aside by Vadera, who told him: 'This is what we are going to be doing over the next few days. This is the plan.'[145] Myners took a deep breath. He was deeply shocked. It was not to be an easy first week on the job.

Recapitalisation Launched: 4 to 8 October

As his recapitalisation plan took shape, Brown knew the time had come to up the international momentum. The slowness of his fellow European leaders to grasp the gravity of the crisis had increasingly irritated him. On Saturday 4 October he travelled to Paris for a summit convened by Sarkozy, but his hopes were not high. He had not wanted to be away from Downing Street when so much was happening and had resisted attending. Finding meetings with fellow EU leaders uncongenial at the best of times, he now worried that this one would not deliver the right outcome, and that his plans would, therefore, be set back. He found himself caught between two irreconcilable pressures – he knew he had one chance to get his recapitalisation announcement right, but delaying until he had secured the ideal level of international backing could do irreparable damage. Time was not on his side. As a Treasury official says: 'Our intervention really became inevitable because of leaks which damaged the share prices of banks. It became self-fulfilling.'[146]

Brown and his officials had been hitting the phones hard to European leaders and their offices over the previous few weeks to force the pace. Just before the party conference, he had called Sarkozy late one evening about the pan-European short-selling ban on 17 September. Brown's belief, not fully shared by the Treasury, was that the practice was driving down share prices, which was adversely affecting bank liquidity. 'We need to look at naked short-selling,' he boomed down the line to the French President. When talking to Sarkozy, Brown always spoke through an interpreter. 'Naked short-selling' was a new expression to her, and she translated it literally. The Cabinet Office official listening in on the call speculated about the sex-attuned Sarkozy trying to understand it and thinking 'those crazy British speculators, selling bonds with no clothes'.[147] To Brown and his team, the President's lack of urgency was further proof of European leaders not understanding the unfolding emergency. 'They didn't see it coming. They didn't understand the economics. They didn't understand how collective action could work,' explains a jaded official.[148] But by early October, while Sarkozy's knowledge of finance might not have improved, he had begun to acknowledge that this was not purely a crisis of 'Anglo-Saxon capitalism' but had potentially grave consequences across continental

Europe. Hence his calling the conference. 'It was typical Sarkozy. He saw a problem and said: "Let's call a conference,"' says a Foreign Office official.[149] Merkel, Berlusconi, Barosso and Jean-Claude Trichet, President of the Central European Bank, all duly trooped to Paris that Saturday.

Brown used the opportunity to press his case hard for a coordinated EU response (while remaining quiet about Britain's own recapitalisation plans). 'It was very clear that Gordon had a complete grasp of what needed to happen. The others were not really on top of things but were at least beginning to listen,' says one member of his party.[150] The ignorance of his fellow leaders led to the meeting being called a 'shambles' by one British official, and 'surreal' by another.[151] One particularly fraught subject of debate was the topic of deposit guarantees. The Irish had just executed a blanket guarantee of all bank deposits, much to Brown's frustration and, indeed, fury. It was precisely the kind of unilateral action that he felt would cripple the world's ability to deal with the crisis: if countries did not act together, a guarantee in one would attract deposits from another, merely worsening the situation. As one official recalls: 'We were sitting on top of a developing problem, and suddenly things exploded in Ireland, and we started to see very quickly liquidity moving from UK banks to Irish banks.' Brown called the Taoiseach Brian Cowen, furious that the Irish premier had acted so irresponsibly pursuing what he felt was a 'beggar thy neighbour' approach.

Trichet had been supportive in Paris of the idea of concerted action, but Merkel was resolutely opposed. She and Sarkozy nevertheless said they would talk to their finance ministers about it.[152] Brown returned to London feeling it had been an intensive and frustrating meeting. The next day, he was to be astonished and angered to learn that Merkel had followed Ireland, acting unilaterally to guarantee all bank deposits. Treasury officials tried frantically to reach the Germans to clarify their intentions, but 'there was no one there. Germany wasn't answering the phone.'[153] One Number 10 official puts it mildly: 'Germany's action was very damaging for us as it put pressure on us to do the same.'[154] Brown convened an emergency meeting in Downing Street on Sunday 5 October to consider what Merkel was doing, and how to manage the extra pressure it would place on Britain. The danger that unilateral action would stymie the possibility of a coordinated global response was not lost on Brown. If countries continued to act alone, guaranteeing their own banking systems, the stampede of investors from one subsidised haven to another damaged any possibility of solving the underlying problem. The celebrated unity of the Eurozone – the countries using the single currency – was most conspicuous by its absence. Adding to the drama, Peter Mandelson (appointed in the Friday reshuffle) was suffering from a kidney stone. A call was placed to government minister and medic Ara Darzi for advice.[155] When taken ill, Mandelson had been staying with Lord Stevenson, chairman of HBOS. The Treasury was far from pleased at his insensitive choice of venue, given the circumstances. The atmosphere was bleak. International cooperation was not forthcoming, and it was becoming clear that the loss of confidence in RBS and HBOS was even worse than had been anticipated the week before.

The television images might not have been as striking, but this new run on the banks was far more serious than Northern Rock. 'This was not elderly folk queuing on pavements. This was major depositors, endowments, and corporations,' recalls one minister.[156] In conditions of extreme confidentiality, a proactive Mervyn King had organised emergency funding to help save the banks.[157] Demanding unprecedented amounts of collateral from the banks in return for their liquidity, and unprecedented secrecy, King had not even felt able to officially consult all the other members of the Bank of England's Monetary Policy Committee about his actions. It was an extraordinary act that revealed the levels of fear at the events now unfolding. Markets would have panicked had they heard the news. In a few short months, the Governor had transformed from the person talking about 'moral hazard' over Northern Rock, recognising the systemic liquidity and solvency problem, to become a champion of underpinning all British banks. His role was to be utterly decisive.

Brown knew that without swift and solid action, the British banks could topple in days. That Sunday, Brown, Darling, Vadera, Myners and senior Treasury and Number 10 officials met at Number 10 with the Bank and the FSA. Following the meeting, Vadera, Myners and Scholar were instructed by Brown and Darling to work up the multi-layered, but still-sketchy, recapitalisation plan into a detailed proposal, and to be ready for an announcement to the markets as soon as two days later. Vadera was commanding, imperious even. She wanted to appoint some trusted investment bankers to provide advice over the following crucial days. When it was suggested that they should be contacted the next morning, Vadera exploded. 'That is way too late,' she insisted. 'Gordon may want to announce this in two days.'[158] Interviewing advisers, she added, would in any case 'put it all over town'. She levelled up to Myners: 'Paul, you are a minister now. You pick two banks.' She told him to consider UBS, 'to save time, because they know the plan already', and suggested that he needed a second bank, 'to test that UBS got it right', appearing to favour J. P. Morgan Cazenove. Not keen to wait around, she found the numbers, dialled them, and put Myners and Scholar on speaker phone. They agreed to meet at 8am on the Monday morning to work through a proposal that she would send them on the Sunday night. City veteran David Mayhew of Cazenove, and Nigel Boardman, senior partner of law firm Slaughter and May – both hugely impressive individuals – were to join as key figures on the advisory team.

For much of the following forty-eight hours, the group, together with officials from the tripartite financial authorities, who had been working on contingency plans, ensconced themselves on the third floor of the Treasury, working up the details of an announcement. A harried Darling had convened a political group in Downing Street comprising Balls, Mandelson, Harman and David Miliband to discuss the coming week. As plans were developing, Jon Cunliffe was in regular touch with European counterparts in Paris, Berlin, Rome, Frankfurt and Brussels, stating that Britain had plans, and telling them as much as he could to keep them in the frame in a rapidly evolving situation. Having been wrong-footed by Ireland and Germany, Brown did not want himself to be accused of going it alone and adopting the unilateral strategy of Merkel and Cowen he so deplored. The Prime Minister had long since realised that pursuing British interests demanded that officials act in concert, rather than in competition, with their counterparts abroad.

How much capital did the recapitalisation plan require? When Vadera and Myners had met, the figure of £50bn had emerged, based on fairly fuzzy estimates from the Treasury, the FSA and Bank of England. This was the figure that was later adopted. 'There was no spreadsheet to produce that number and we had very, very inadequate data,' recalls Myners.[159] It was but a ball-park estimate of the amount needed to cover actual and anticipated losses as well as providing the necessary confidence for depositors and other banks.[160] It would prove to be insufficient, necessitating a second phase of interventions in the new year.

Timing now became the predominant question. Officials say with hindsight that, at this time, they had no idea if RBS could last until Wednesday 8 October. Tuesday seemed the safer option, but some in Number 10 worried the earlier date might look panicky, risking confidence further. On the Sunday morning, George Osborne had astonished Number 10 by speaking to BBC's *Andrew Marr Show* about recapitalisation. Brown's team considered this to have been an act of profound naiveté, and it was not the last time they would consider the shadow Chancellor to have made a wrong call during the crisis. One official recalls with consternation: 'The last thing we wanted was anyone talking about it.'[161] Darling believed that Osborne's knowledge had come from an informal briefing with King. With events still unfolding rapidly, and markets now hanging on every word that came out of the government, the question of timing was utterly critical. 'Deciding whether to announce the recapitalisation on the Tuesday or Wednesday was the biggest decision Gordon Brown made as Prime Minister,' says one senior official.[162] In hindsight, Treasury officials believe that the *biggest* decision of Brown's premiership was the decision to pursue a policy of recapitalisation, rather than the timing of the announcement itself.[163]

Monday 6 October became known as 'meltdown Monday', when the FTSE 100 suffered its biggest one-day points fall on record, wiping almost £100bn off the value of Britain's top 100 companies. RBS's share price fell 35 per cent in half an hour. Shudders spread through Downing Street. The balance sheet of RBS was larger than the entire British economy. While Darling told the House of Commons that he would 'do whatever was necessary' to restabilise the banking system, Number 10 was in a frenzy. 'On [that] Monday, lots of very important people were worried,' recalls an official. 'The PM's very worried, the Chancellor's very worried. The Governor of the Bank of England's very worried.'[164] Tripartite authority (HM Treasury, the FSA and the Bank of England) officials knew that both RBS and HBOS were close to having no cash left at all.

Darling knew he had to act, and summoned the chief executives of Britain's seven biggest banks, along with Nationwide Building Society, to meet him at 9pm in the Chancellor's office. Not that he needed to say it, but he did – their discussions had to be completely secret. There followed a general exchange of views about the state of the financial system, but no specific proposals were presented. The mood among the bankers was awkward, with general moaning about the Bank of England for not providing enough liquidity, and the FSA for being too tough. Darling was exasperated. He felt they were in denial.[165] But for the recapitalisation plan to work, the majority of banks would have to cooperate. Without their express agreement, they would need to be forced to accept capital by government. It was yet another unprecedented aspect of the developing crisis, which was by now unfolding at such a pace that conventional rules had lost all meaning.

As the planning had progressed, Vadera had become more and more confident of the government's ability to push the banks on this. Having worked in the banking sector herself, she knew that the government's trump card was the banks' desperation for the short-term funds they needed to run their day-to-day operations. In exchange for this liquidity, the government could insist that banks take on capital, despite wanting to avoid government ownership and admitting that they required this kind of help. She became more and more pugnacious. Dan Corry remembers the value of having someone around who, in effect, could tell the banks that, 'if you don't do what we want, we're shutting you down tomorrow'.[166] In reality, Vadera's power came from knowing that the banks would themselves collapse if they did not get the liquidity they needed. The banks knew too that she spoke with her master's voice. Brown went to bed on the Monday evening, content to leave the detail to Vadera and Myners and Treasury officials, aware that the debate had moved beyond his own area of competence and expertise. 'Though he had been in the Treasury for ten years, he had had very little involvement with bankers and had stayed well clear of their area. We were talking about things which were very new to him,' said an official present.

Tuesday 7 October opened with Robert Peston posting on his BBC blog – under the headline 'Banks ask Chancellor for capital' – what officials regard as an inaccurate account of the meeting the previous evening at the Treasury. Peston fiercely contests this. 'There is not a scintilla of doubt that RBS was well and truly bust. Officials who moan about my blog are in denial,' he says.[167] Confidence was dealt a significant blow by it, whatever he claims. Was the journalist aware of the damage he was doing? A Treasury official is philosophical: 'I am sure he didn't deliberately mislead anybody, but he had been told a story that wasn't right.'[168] The impact of the comments of a man judged to be the best-informed financial journalist in London was hugely destabilising to the markets, with inaccuracies concerning RBS's position leading to particular trouble. Accusation and counter-accusation about the leaks to Peston flew around between the bankers, the Treasury and Number 10. Some suspicion fell on Downing Street, allegedly as they wanted to up the pressure to give the recapitalisation plan more urgency.[169] Elements in the Bank of England still blame Number 10 for deliberate leaks to Peston during the crisis.[170] Number 10 said that was nonsense, and in turn blamed the bankers.[171]

With the RBS share price falling through the floor, Darling decided to rush back from an EcoFin meeting in Luxembourg. By mid-morning on Tuesday, Brown decided that, regardless of the continuing objections from bankers, the unveiling of the recapitalisation plan had to go ahead the following morning. 'We had to make sure this was properly announced before the markets opened,' recalls Myners.[172] The Cabinet met as usual that day, with Brown welcoming back old-timers Mandelson and Margaret Beckett.[173] Brown wanted to talk to Mandelson and Balls after the meeting was over – the former stayed at Number 10 until mid-afternoon.[174] All three were desperate that the announcement be made to look orderly. At 3.45pm they decided that Michael Ellam should tell the lobby that Mervyn King and Adair Turner of the FSA were coming to see the Prime Minister and Chancellor at six. Eager for information, the media leapt on the announcement. Such was the importance of stability that it was judged best to tee the press up for the following morning. After King and Turner had left at 7.30pm, Darling confirmed rumours that the government was on the eve of making a historic announcement. It was to come in two parts: a general rescue package to be announced in twelve hours' time, and, a few days later, a second statement on the sums each bank would receive.

Meetings with bankers had also taken place during the day in the Treasury. Myners told Fred Goodwin of RBS that the government would be giving his bank money to boost its capital and ease market nerves. 'No business ever dies because it's run out of capital. They die because they run out of cash,' Goodwin is alleged to have responded with fury.[175] Myners held his ground: despite its chief executive's furious protestations, RBS would be recapitalised. End of argument. After half an hour, he was shown the door, and Eric Daniels, the American chief executive of Lloyds TSB, came in. He accepted the case for recapitalising the system, but was surprised and irritated to hear that officials felt his own bank needed government investment.[176]

So for a second consecutive evening the bankers were summoned to the Treasury, meeting in the Chancellor's second-floor office, with Darling flanked by Myners, Scholar, Vadera and the department's permanent secretary, Nick Macpherson. It was clear that the banking system collectively would have no option but to take the government's money, although the banks were still protesting that they could manage on their own. Douglas Flint, finance director of HSBC, was adamant that they did not need help and his bank would not take it because 'it will damage our franchising in the rest of the world'.[177] The mood was bleak and the bankers 'ashen-faced'. Darling did not provide them with much detail, but the bankers could guess the shape of what was coming. They were not cooperative, and expressed doubt whether the proposals mooted would indeed give enough reassurance to the markets. Darling remained firm. He asked them to carry on discussions with the team while he went to work on his statement for the next day. At around midnight, the bankers took their leave from the Chancellor. Their protestations of independence had fallen on deaf ears. Discussions continued until Darling declared at around 1am that he was going to bed,[178] telling his team to finalise the details for announcement. 'I need it by 5am,' he told them, and disappeared.[179]

The lights burned all night in the Treasury. While the bankers held their own separate discussions, Vadera and Myners led a group of officials and advisers towards a final decision. The bankers had expressed doubts about the proposed plans during the meeting in Number 11; those present now worked to improve the proposals to ensure they generated the desired market response. Finally, agreement was reached on the package which Myners and Vadera would recommend to the PM and Chancellor. At around 3am, Fred Goodwin, for the second time that day, insisted to the Treasury team that RBS 'didn't have a problem – it was market panic'. Scholar, Vadera and Myners asked him about the position of RBS, and Goodwin insisted that although the bank had a problem with funding, it was not a problem with capital.[180] As late as Wednesday morning, this is what the banker was telling officials, which is remarkable given it was only a few days later when the sheer scale of RBS losses were revealed to the world.

Heywood, Macpherson and Scholar trooped over to Number 11 just before 5.30am to brief Darling, sitting on sofas in his downstairs study. Brown was also present, as well as Vadera and Cunliffe. All were exhausted, but the atmosphere was calm. The proposed package was outlined and discussed. Darling and Brown sought clarification of exactly what was being recommended, why, and how it should be presented, explained and justified publicly. The discussions turned to the handling of the announcement and to how the politicians should respond to the various questions they might be asked by the media. There was also a short debate about whether the government should announce a guarantee of deposits. All present were worried about a further shock to depositor confidence, especially given the situation developing in Iceland. They knew an estimated 300,000 British depositors with savings in the troubled bank Icesave would have to be bailed out to avoid collateral damage on the British high street. 'It was just one more uncertainty making people nervous that day,' says an observer.[181]

After finishing in Number 11, the team went on to Brown's office in the den. 'We had a feeling that it was an historic moment,' says one present.[182] At 6.30am Brown began to call fellow European leaders, explaining what Britain was about to do, and then officials broke up to phone their counterparts in Italy, Germany, France and the US. Brown would later follow up his calls with letters outlining his government's action. 'All the European officials knew something was coming because of the RBS trouble, and they were desperate not to be surprised as we had been surprised by the Irish,' reports an official present.[183] The calls were more than just a courtesy: Brown knew that, if his plan was to work, Britain would need to be joined by others. His team were encouraged by the initial response they received. One official recalls: 'Paris saw the need to act together immediately, as did Rome. Berlin took longer.'[184]

At 7.30am, Darling hit the airwaves. He announced phase one of the package – the £50bn direct capital injection to banks, and an extension of the existing special liquidity scheme allowing banks to dispose of bad mortgages by exchanging them for Bank of England bonds. The latter was doubled in size to £200bn. A further element, the most innovative, was the government guaranteeing loans that the banks made to each other in the inter-bank market. In total, it amounted to £500bn in support of Britain's financial system, the most comprehensive rescue package since the Second World War.

At 8am, the freshly created National Economic Council (NEC), containing the key government figures involved with economic policy, convened in the Cabinet Office briefing room used for meetings of COBRA to learn what had been decided. The walls were lined with charts based on computer projections of statistics about the banks, but 'the scales weren't right and they made little sense', says Dan Corry.[185] Adding to the tension, there was no mobile phone coverage deep in the Cabinet Office. 'The atmosphere was somewhat unreal,' comments an official.[186] The NEC was to become Brown's war council for tackling the subsequent recession, and would prove one of the more successful of his rare institutional innovations as Prime Minister.

At 9.30am, Brown, with Darling by his side, arrived at the formal press conference in Number 10's state dining room, where the two men filled out the details of the plan. 'A desperate, last-ditch attempt to prevent catastrophe', railed the Conservatives. Brown had been apprehensive about their reaction. Though confident about the economics, on the politics he had taken the biggest gamble of his professional life. He was nervous about the response from just about every quarter. 'We had no idea how it was going to play out ... I was so, so frightened,' says another involved intimately, echoing the Prime Minister's thoughts.[187] 'We just knew we had to do it. Gordon Brown thought it was going to be really, really difficult,' says an official. 'He wondered if it was going to be the end of him.'[188] Another recalls: 'He didn't know how the market was going to react, whether other countries would follow, whether the package was the right sum, whether the banks would accept it, whether it would be a disaster for him and Labour politically. Everything that morning was up in the air. Everything.'[189] Exaggeration after the event? This is possible to an extent, but these accounts still capture the feeling of the moment.

The almost intolerable strain notwithstanding, Brown was steely that morning. 'He rose to it in an extraordinary way. He was at his best with something like this. When he knows what he's doing, and he has purpose, he's pretty impressive,' says a Number 10 official.[190] Brown had been convinced intellectually early on that it was the right thing to do, but executing the plan still took courage and determination. When he made the final decision with Darling to go ahead, his attitude was, 'OK, let's just do it'.[191] Calm on the surface, anxious deep inside, Brown felt the situation so serious and insecure that he confided to Vadera that he feared he would have to resign by the end of the day.[192] Indeed at 5am that morning he had told Sarah to pack their things up and be ready to leave Number 10 should his plans to rescue the banks back-fire.

Brown was due in the House for PMQs, but nineteen minutes before he rose, the Bank of England, the US Federal Reserve and the European Central Bank all cut half a point off their interest rates in a coordinated move. It was precisely the lift he needed and, as most MPs had not yet heard, announcing it contributed to a strong performance at the despatch box. The contrast with his previous appearance in July could not have been starker, much to the relief – indeed, delight – of Labour MPs. The media had already absorbed the morning's announcement, and by the time of PMQs they had begun asking what was going to happen to all the bankers who were to be given all this public money. Would they be fired? Seizing on this, Cameron demanded whether the money would be spent on bankers' bonuses as 'rewards for failure'. Brown squashed him by repeating the very words the Leader of the Opposition had used on television ten days earlier: 'What you won't hear from me this week is easy, cheap lines ... bashing the financiers. I mean, it might get you some cheap headlines.'[193] He turned the questions into the opportunity to explain the measures being taken to stabilise the banking system. At last, at PMQs his great clunking fist appeared mighty rather than clumsy. Cameron appeared insignificant amid the historic events taking place. Labour was saving the day, and was judged to be coming out on top.

Brown was far from out of the woods, however. The initial market response to the bail-out and interest rate cut was positive, but by the end of the day the FTSE 100 was down 5.2 per cent, wiping some £52bn off the value of the UK's top companies. Shares in the high-street banks were particularly hard hit: HBOS and RBS had fallen 40 per cent each, Lloyds 15 per cent, and Barclays 11 per cent. Vadera had not been to bed on the Tuesday night, and went back to her department for a twenty-minute sleep on the sofa in her office. Her slumber was interrupted by a phone call from Goodwin at RBS. As the day had worn on, he had finally begun to accept the hollowness of his position, and was now just hours from being unable to open for business the following morning. Acknowledging what he had insisted the night before he said: 'I've been talking to the Treasury because I do need capital and it's going to be a large sum. You're going to be shocked.' In fact, the Treasury had already briefed the minister that RBS was looking for £5–£10bn and she is reported to have asked him if he was sure it would be enough because she thought the bank would need more.[194] That evening, Vadera went for a drink with Brown in his Downing Street flat, while many of the other figures were off at receptions. She reported her conversation with Goodwin. 'What now?' he asked. 'We have to make sure RBS gets through the weekend,' she replied. In the end, RBS took £20bn in capital the following Monday. Brown found it difficult to accept how Goodwin, whom he knew quite well, had 'completely fucked up the management of his bank'.[195]

Brown had seized on the recapitalisation option and pushed it ahead. He had made light of the tense situation when he was interrupted by a mobile phone during a speech to the Foreign Office early on the Wednesday evening. 'I don't know if another bank has fallen,' he quipped. But Brown was not resting on his laurels. Even as he addressed the dinner, he knew that the markets had not rallied sufficiently. Brown knew the British, and the world economy, needed other countries to follow his lead. Since the beginning of the crisis it had been clear to him that a solution could only be international. As one official comments: 'We had watched Hank Paulson pulling in one US institution after another to no avail.'[196] Brown knew his government's £50bn package was far too small to make a difference and that his efforts might prove pointless if other countries failed to follow suit and shore up their own banks. 'The rest of the world needs to recapitalise as well,' he argued in *The Times* on Thursday 9 October.[197] On GMTV that morning, responding to the public mood, he again took a swipe at bankers, and spoke of his 'anger at their irresponsible behaviour,' and at the big bonuses being paid in the City. By midday, the FTSE 100 had jumped sixty-one points, but the futility of Britain conducting the bailout in isolation became clear when falls on Wall Street depressed the London markets; the Dow Jones fell to a five-year low and the FTSE 100 closed at its lowest level since 2004. Once again, Icelandic banks claimed much of Brown's attention that day. The impact of that country's banking crisis, which had seen all three of its major banks collapse, had been dealt with mostly by the Treasury. On 6 October, Geir Haarde, the Icelandic Prime Minister, warned of the prospect of total national bankruptcy. Brown and Darling were of a mind that no British depositor would lose out.[198] Frustrated by the lack of cooperation from Iceland, they invoked counter-terrorist legislation to freeze the UK assets of the country's banks, as they tried to secure the deposits not only of household depositors but also those of the many local authorities that had sought to take advantage of the attractive interest rates the banks had offered.[199]

The rescue package had been announced. Brown's team had thrown everything at the problem. It had been the most dramatic week of his premiership, and one of the most dramatic of any in living memory. Yet before the week was up, there was one final chapter to unfold. On 10 October – dubbed 'Black Friday' – the global financial system teetered closer to collapse than at any other time in the crisis. The Nikkei share index in Japan fell almost 10 per cent, its biggest one-day drop for twenty years. By 8.07am the FTSE 100 had plunged more than 10 per cent, and within minutes of New York opening, the Dow Jones crashed 8 per cent. Almost £90bn had been wiped off the value of Britain's biggest companies. Downing Street became concerned that the Wednesday package had been either too small a gesture, or wrongly conceived. Dominique Strauss-Kahn, the head of the IMF, warned that the global financial system was on the brink of meltdown. Number 10 and the Treasury discussed the chance that RBS and HBOS would be unable to open for business after the weekend. Money was being withdrawn from RBS at an astonishing pace. The bailout plan Darling had unveiled had been intended to buy the government three months' breathing time, and to allow British banks to manage their recovery.[200] But even on the Bank of England's most optimistic forecasts, RBS would be dead by Tuesday.[201] RBS had a bigger loan book than any bank in the world, with assets worth more than £1 trillion. If it went down, it might well drag Barclays and Lloyds TSB down too. If that happened, few could see a way back.

As if to remind him of the strange, conflicting pressures of being Prime Minister, Brown was due to open the Cheltenham Literary Festival at the weekend, where he would talk about his book, *Wartime Courage*.[202] A heated debate took place among his political team. Should he still go? Number 10's weekly diary meetings often had to struggle with such trade-offs. This time, advisers worried that 'it would look bad if he was seen to be promoting his own book in the midst of a world financial crisis. But if he is seen cancelling events, it adds to the sense of panic.'[203] The fear was that the Tories would jump on him for speaking. By happy coincidence, however, Cameron himself had agreed to be interviewed for the Woodstock Literary Festival at Blenheim Palace that weekend.[204] 'It was all rather surreal,' says an aide.[205]

On the Friday (10 October) some light relief came in the form of an invitation from Sarkozy for Brown to attend a meeting of heads of government of Eurozone countries at the Elysée Palace that Sunday. Germany had remained the sticking point in Europe, and Cunliffe and other officials had been working with the French and Italians to persuade the Germans and the European Central Bank of the sense in Brown's blueprint solution. It was a many-fronted assault: British officials had also pushed with the Dutch and Finns who put pressure on Berlin. The French earlier that week had suggested the meeting, and now others were signed up.

It was exactly the opportunity Brown had wanted in order to encourage a coordinated response. He needed some luck, and this was it. Sarkozy justified holding a second conference in Paris on consecutive weekends on the grounds that Zapatero of Spain had been excluded the previous week. But that did not explain why Brown made the invitation list. Though it was a Eurozone meeting, Brown was the acknowledged owner of the only bank rescue plan in town. 'We pressed the need for us to be there to explain it,' says Cunliffe. It was an unusual dynamic: Brown acting as guide to a group that he had twice prevented Britain from joining. It said much about his standing in relation to the crisis that his fellow leaders would take the unprecedented step of inviting him to address them. His relationship with the French President helped ensure his presence. 'If it had been any other leader than Sarkozy, I don't think Gordon Brown would have been asked, but Sarko just said: "This is a guy who understands, this is a guy who knows, let's listen to him,"' says the British representative to the EU, Kim Darroch.[206] Sarkozy used Brown rather like 'a one-man think tank', pointedly contrasting his vision with the hitherto intransigent Merkel, according to another official.[207] On Saturday, Brown's optimism rose, as he began to sense that, despite £2.7tn being wiped off global share values the day before, the tenor of the Wednesday measures were being generally well received. He wrote an article for the *Sunday Mirror*, in similar terms to *The Times* article, and was interviewed by Gaby Hinsliff for *The Observer*: 'The next few days would prove critical,' he said, arguing that Britain's rescue plan 'obviously is going to work best if other countries are in a position to follow'.[208]

Brown and his party left for Paris by a special flight from RAF Northolt on the morning of Sunday 12 October. On the plane, he pumped Stewart Wood with questions about Franklin Roosevelt and his policy from January 1933. As his establishment of the NEC had already foreshadowed, the questions confirmed that 'he was already moving on from the financial crisis and was beginning to think about the "real" economy'[209] – meaning the world of jobs, goods and homes. Arriving in Paris, Brown found himself in a pre-meeting, held before the Eurozone heads of government got down to their formal business. The aim of this was to bring Barroso and Trichet up to speed, a crucial step: if they could be brought on board, it would smooth the way for Brown's plans. [210]

The formal proceedings began, with Brown attending for the first hour. Eurozone heads were given a passionate defence of the importance of concerted action, and the virtues of Britain's recapitalisation plan. The Prime Minister had rarely spoken with greater passion or emphasis. Sarkozy was bursting with pride at his master stroke in inviting Brown, saying: 'My friend Gordon has the right plan, we must do it in Europe.' As the end of the hour, the French President suggested Brown could stay, adding cheekily: 'You know, if you'd like to join the euro now, just say so and we'd be delighted to have you with us for the rest of the meeting.' There was much laughter from fellow leaders – but not from Brown. He looked disconcerted and unsure how to take a flippant comment at such a grave moment.[211] Nevertheless Brown sensed their mission had worked. It became apparent to the British party that the Eurozone would follow the course they had suggested. Most leaders readily accepted that they would need to inject capital into their banking systems and to guarantee lending. That evening, Sarkozy announced the agreement of a new framework, telling assembled journalists that the crisis had entered a phase which made a 'go-it-alone approach' and further procrastination, 'completely intolerable'.[212]

Officials working for eurozone leaders subsequently confided to Darroch that, 'if they hadn't themselves come up with a package to convince their own markets by the time they opened on Monday 13 October, then their own cash machines might not have opened'. That was how close to meltdown they felt they had come and they were 'unanimous in praise of Brown' for saving them.[213] Considering the contempt EU leaders had displayed for him after the cack-handed Lisbon 'non-signing' a bare ten months before, it was an extraordinary turnaround. A senior official considered the Paris meeting on 12 October 'the high point of [Brown's] premiership'.[214] Another noticed the difference in the way Brown was treated by the leaders then compared with the Paris conference the week before. 'I could see them now watching him, listening, questioning, coming back, engaging in a real discussion. You don't often get that in a big group of leaders. It was extraordinary,' says an observer.[215] Brown had never been one to want to follow European leaders on an EU agenda. Now he got them all following him on *his* agenda. The meeting saw Brown at his best: no leader present had anything approaching his authority on the subject, nor such a commanding personality. He convinced them about the interconnectedness of the European financial system, with Deutsche Bank in London, RBS in Germany, the Banque Nationale de Paris in Spain, and on and on he went. After the jokey departure, Brown returned to meet his team back at the British embassy. 'We knew by this time we had the right solution. We felt pretty chipper,' says one.[216] It was a bright early autumn day in the lush embassy gardens when he gave the press conference. He had been toying with lines on the plane on the way out, and settled on one: Britain's greatest asset had not been the value of its shares, but 'trust'. The question was how to recover it.

On Monday 13 October, Sarkozy rushed through a recapitalisation bill for French banks, and within twenty-four hours, other major European countries followed suit. Merkel had previously been the obstacle, declaring unambiguously: 'It's up to each county to clean up its own shit.'[217] Her indecision and hyper-caution had been largely responsible for the EU's immobility, according to British officials,[218] but on Sunday she had changed her position, bringing forward emergency legislation allowing for a bailout amounting to €400bn. 'It really is quite a coup for Brown, the saviour of the world,' wrote Nicholas Watt in *The Guardian*.[219] Affirmation came too from the other side of the Atlantic, with Paul Krugman, the Nobel Prize-winning economist, writing in the *New York Times* that the UK's 'combination of clarity and decisiveness hasn't been matched by any other Western government'.[220] Krugman was dazzled by Brown's grasp of economic matters: after a three-hour conversation with the Prime Minister in New York the following year Krugman turned to an official and said: 'I've never had an evening like that before. He is way more impressive than any US politician.'[221]

Closer to home, reward for Brown came that Sunday in a YouGov poll for the *Sunday Times*, which reported that his personal approval rating had improved nineteen points over the previous month (although still in negative territory at minus thirty-four) and Labour's poll rating had gone up 9 per cent to thirty-three points over the same period.[222]

Brown had achieved his goal of bouncing the EU into a concerted response: but what of the rest of the world? Darling had left for Washington on the Thursday for the G7, part of the IMF and World Bank annual meeting. He was accompanied by Treasury official Stephen Pickford, his deputy at the G7. Brown spoke to the Chancellor by phone on Friday morning about the substandard G7 communiqué, which did not go nearly far enough in the right direction. 'One thing Gordon is an acknowledged master of is communiqués, not just the language but getting everyone signed up to them,' says an official. Between them, they managed to nudge it in the direction of recapitalising banks with public money as the only viable solution.[223]

The detailed work was far from over. The Treasury had been frantically busy since the Wednesday on 'phase two' of the plan, deciding which banks would receive the money available, and how much each required. Over the weekend, Myners, Macpherson, Kingman and Scholar held a continuous round of meetings in the Treasury with the heads of Britain's main banks to discuss this. Compared to the highly stressed atmosphere on Monday and Tuesday, the tone was now different, with HBOS, RBS and Lloyds TSB all anxious to accept immediate help. By Saturday morning, Goodwin had been ousted by the RBS board but was still negotiating on behalf of the bank. At 9am on Sunday he was told that the government wanted to inject up to £20bn into the bank, giving the taxpayer a stake of about 60 per cent. Goodwin was incredulous: both the size and the terms of the recapitalisation demanded by the Treasury and FSA were more severe than he had imagined, but he knew it represented RBS's only option if it was to open for business on Monday.[224] Vadera did not attend all the weekend meetings. Throughout the crisis, she had been an unstoppable force, but one minister suggests there were now fears that she 'might go OTT'.[225] Later, in the spring, a senior Treasury official would issue a note requesting that his colleagues only take instructions from Treasury ministers, not those from other departments – 'coded language for keeping Vadera out of the building'.[226] The impatience ran both ways.

Discussions continued late into the Sunday night on further measures and concluded at 5am on the Monday in the ground-floor study at Number 11. The government would take shares in RBS, HBOS and Lloyds TSB in return for a £37bn injection of capital. Barclays was to be recapitalised from private sources. Everyone was exhausted, none more so than Vadera and Myners, who had had six hours' sleep over the previous three nights. Brown was reassured that he had done all that he could.

At 6.25am the Treasury circulated a two-page statement to the market newswires, outlining the terms of the £37bn bailout for RBS, Lloyds and HBOS. Similar announcements from other European governments followed. By the end of the day, the FTSE 100 had recovered more than 8 per cent.[227] Watching the tide turn across the Atlantic, Paulson dropped his TARP plan and secured support from Congress for a British-style rescue, eventually pumping capital into nine major US banks. It was an extraordinary turnaround. To have the US following suit, and without further pushing, was almost too good to be believed. Washington had backed a different horse in the argument over how to stop contagion and it had lost. Government recapitalisation plans, following Brown's model, now sprang up across the world. Just one month earlier, the Prime Minister's position had looked desperately unstable, his prospects for survival weak. Now, on the international stage at least, he stood like a colossus.

Family Time: 17–18 October

It had been an utterly harrowing but exhilarating month for Brown, but it was to end with some light relief. To celebrate their son John's fifth birthday on Friday 17 October, Sarah Brown had organised a special treat for which Brown travelled to Paris for his third consecutive weekend, this time with his family.

Accompanying them were the author J. K. Rowling and private secretary Tom Fletcher with their respective families. Rowling had become close to the Browns and shared a similar political outlook. The following February she was to receive the Légion d'honneur from Sarkozy: the President subsequently told British ambassador Peter Westmacott, with whom the party stayed that weekend, that he had granted her the unusual honour 'because Gordon asked me'.[228] Brown decided at the last minute to miss out on John's birthday trip on Saturday to Disneyland, the highlight of the weekend, preferring to spend the precious time working at the eighteenth-century British embassy building, bought in 1814 by the Duke of Wellington from Napoleon's favourite sister. He did, however, spend as much time as he could that weekend catching up with his boys, whom he had barely seen over the frantic past three weeks. At one point Brown knelt on the grass in the sun to play dominoes with them. 'He was the image of the very happy father,' recalls Westmacott. It was a hard-earned moment of respite.

Brown worked in the embassy's gardens on speeches with Fletcher, while being discreetly looked after by the ambassador and his wife, Susie, who respected his desire for privacy. It was one of the rare times when the pressure eased. Those who worked closely with him relished such moments – at a weekend, in a hotel suite after a good speech, or on a return flight from a successful trip – when he would chat to them while he drank three or four glasses of champagne (never more – he was a moderate drinker).[229] Fletcher found this Paris trip the closest he came to having a 'Jock Colville experience' with Brown, referring to the closeness between Churchill and his private secretary which was recorded in the latter's diary.[230]

Fletcher's was an extraordinary relationship with Brown, and aroused inevitable jealousies, not only in the Foreign Office but in Number 10, too. For a man who was extraordinarily reticent about trusting others, and who had an innate suspicion of the Foreign Office, it was remarkable that he grew so reliant on an official from that department whom he had never met before becoming Prime Minister. They had bonded quickly and on a whole range of areas – from dealing with the Kenyan emergency to outwitting the Ministry of Defence on plans to ban more types of cluster bombs (with Forsyth a key supporter), to acting as a key intermediary in the final Hillsborough talks on Northern Ireland at the end of Brown's premiership. Fletcher was a core influence, going considerably beyond the scope of a normal junior private secretary. So indispensable had he become, indeed, that David Cameron asked him to stay on in Downing Street after May 2010. Fletcher was the strongest example of the new breed of adviser whom Brown grew to trust during his premiership, who were utterly different from the tribal and suspicious clique Brown had consorted with in 2007 and before.

A Lucky Reshuffle: Mandelson Returns: 3 October

In the very midst of the banking crisis, Brown had been hard at work on his reshuffle. Oddly, in view of the pressure on him, it proved his best. He had been enjoying talking in guilty secrecy to Mandelson, who was then EU Trade Commissioner, for several months, but as early as July he had decided he would try to bring him into the government. Brown shared his thoughts only with his closest aides, Nye, Heywood and Muir, for fear of it leaking. Upsetting Balls was his prime worry: he knew the Children's Secretary would take it badly and resort to every ploy he could to talk him out of it. So he played his cards extremely close to his chest. On 28 September, back from the US, Brown phoned Mandelson and told him that he had 'exciting plans'. On 30 September, Heywood then confirmed with Mandelson that Brown was planning something bold and let him know it would affect him personally.[231] On 1 October, Mandelson agreed to meet Brown at Number 10 the following day, where Brown told him, 'I want you to join the government as Business Secretary in the House of Lords.' The recent collapse of the Doha talks provided a pretext for Brown to pluck the Trade Commissioner out of Brussels, as he would not be removing a key player at a vital stage in the negotiations.[232] Mandelson was pleased but initially cautious about Brown's request; among others he phoned Blair, who advised him to accept the job.[233]

Even Brown's close team did not know of this plan until twenty-four hours before. 'Very rarely Gordon would keep some very big things to himself. This was one such occasion,' says one.[234] Tom Watson had been working with Brown on the reshuffle and advised him to spread out the appointments rather than allowing himself to be dictated to by the demands of the six o'clock and ten o'clock news cycles in the way that Blair had been. In the days leading up to the announcement, different magnetic names had been moved around the berths on the famous white board on wheels. Suddenly Watson recalls, 'Gordon, right in front of me, removed the name in the business department slot and picked up a marker pen, wrote "PM" on a label, and stuck it on. That was the first I knew about it.'[235] It would have been – Watson was a close ally of Balls.

Mandelson was a controversial figure but his return was a great triumph for Brown. It had a great sense of theatre to it, not least because the press had been kept in the dark. But its real strength was political. At a stroke it silenced the Blairite rebels who had been plotting against Brown over the summer. Watson says the move was 'an absolute master stroke'. One adviser describes it as 'an act of genius',[236] while another recalls: 'You could see people like John Hutton were stunned. They just didn't know which way to turn.' *The Guardian* said that coupled with David Miliband's 'disastrous' performance at the party conference, Mandelson's appointment 'convinced even hardcore Blairites' that Brown would not now be challenged.[237] In truth, the Blairites broadly welcomed Mandelson's return; he was considered the consummate political strategist and communicator of the New Labour era, and since the plots had fizzled out against Brown, they now felt they needed all the help they could get to make the most of his leadership. Of course not all were pleased. Blairite ultras like Charles Clarke and Margaret McDonagh were angry, still more so when Mandelson was seen to be propping up the Brown premiership in the months to come.[238] Little did they know, as they plotted to oust the Prime Minister over the summer, that he was in daily contact with the high priest of Blairism. With the exception of the *Daily Mail*, which ran the headline 'Arise, Lord Sleaze',[239] the appointment was well received by an intrigued press. *The Guardian* saw it as 'one of the most brilliant coups of his career'.[240] *The Observer* commented: 'The odds [have] shifted narrowly but decisively in favour of Brown leading Labour through to the next election.'[241]

Most of the Number 10 team were delighted by Mandelson's return to Whitehall. When he had begun his second period in government under Blair in 1999, there was a muted response in the building, but this time he was considered to have grown in stature and there were high hopes he would steady the ship and even end overnight the debilitating war with the Blairites.[242] 'By now he was an elder statesman, a grandee, no longer the prince of darkness,' says Michael Dugher.[243] Because the appointment was very much his own decision, it gave Brown a great personal fillip. As Nye would say: 'Confidence is very important to Gordon.' Or, as Balls puts it: 'He is a complete confidence player. When his star shines, he thinks he can never fail, but when it does not, he thinks it will never light up again.'[244]

Mandelson's return rattled the Tories. They had not had a bounce following their conference, unlike in 2007, and they were disconcerted by the polls moving in Brown's favour. But, when on 13 October he was created 'Baron Mandelson of Foy in the County of Herefordshire and Hartlepool in the County of Durham', taking his seat in the House of Lords the same day, the Tories sensed that the new Business Secretary's vanity might get the better of him. George Osborne pounced, alleging that Mandelson had 'dripped pure poison in his ear' about Brown's failings earlier that summer at the Rothschild family estate on Corfu. When follow-up stories probed Mandelson's relationship with Oleg Deripaska, a Russian plutocrat, who was also a guest at the Rothschilds' retreat, it seemed for a while as if his weakness for courting the rich and powerful might again be his undoing. Nat Rothschild and Mandelson struck back with a letter to *The Times* on 21 October alleging that Osborne had tried to solicit a donation from Deripaska. It shook Osborne. Mandelson believed that on his earlier two resignations he had not fought his corner hard enough. This time he would not make the same mistake.

The drama of the Mandelson appointment obscured other facets of a reshuffle whose importance went far beyond the appointment even of the fifteen new ministers. The financial crisis had helped underpin Darling's position at the Treasury. Balls had been anxious to get his hands on the job of Chancellor, but with the financial crisis in full swing, and Darling's apparent proficiency in handling it, such a move was never going to be on the cards. Balls's response to not being moved, and to the appointment of Mandelson, was two-fold. He became 'very assertive' in demanding that his allies receive significant posts,[245] and he withdrew from Number 10, as he did periodically when he was angry with Brown.[246] 'Ed didn't go berserk, but he was very peeved and worked extremely hard to get his people into key positions,' says an observer.[247]

Nick Brown was given the Chief Whip's job he had craved fifteen months earlier. The appointment had been mooted for several months but would have been seen as very divisive. Mandelson's appointment 'gave Brown the cover to pull it off'.[248] Another factor was that Number 10 no longer trusted Geoff Hoon, as they suspected, rightly, that he had been involved in conversations about Brown's leadership over the summer. He was moved to Transport. John Hutton, who had also strongly criticised Brown over the summer, was given the job he most craved – Defence Secretary. Jim Murphy, another Brown sceptic who had impressed Number 10 in the debates on the Lisbon Treaty, was appointed Scottish Secretary. Des Browne, to his disappointment, and Brown's enduring regret, was moved on. Margaret Beckett was recalled as housing minister as it was felt the government needed 'a bit of grit, a bit of experience', and someone Brown could trust to put in a good performance on the *Today* programme.[249] Ed Miliband was given the specially created Department of Energy and Climate Change, for which he had lobbied, and where he found his stride as a minister. He was pleased to be rid of the Cabinet Office post. To replace Mandelson in Brussels, Baroness Cathy Ashton, Leader of the Lords, was selected. Vadera and Myners were given posts at the Cabinet Office and Treasury. It was Brown's most convincing reshuffle. As one insider comments: 'He had found his mojo.'[250]

In three weeks Brown had transformed the fortunes of his premiership. He had performed well at the party conference, and even better on the world stage in rescuing the banks. This was acknowledged at the first meeting of the Parliamentary Labour Party after the reshuffle on Monday 6 October when leading rebel George Howarth effectively declared a ceasefire: he told Brown that 'the unrest was off'.[251]

A Lucky Horseshoe: Order Comes to Number 10: October

For his first fifteen months, Gordon Brown's chaotic personal style, and his inability to manage policy and structures, limited his effectiveness in the job.

By the end of the summer, it was clear to all, not least to the man himself, that Carter's appointment in January had not brought order, for all the logic behind it. By the spring, a contemporary note recorded: 'Life around Gordon was constantly feverish. Meetings were always being interrupted by messages. They often ended without conclusion because he had another meeting to attend. He involved himself in details that should have been left to secretaries of state. Rather than being soothed by some of those around him, they whipped him up, and exacerbated his worst tendencies.'[252] His relationship with his Cabinet ministers remained distant and poor: many felt that he was bored by them, and they were right.[253] Balls, following the effective withdrawal of Ed Miliband and Alexander, was the only Cabinet minister whose company Brown relished, and Vadera was virtually the only minister below Cabinet rank he fully respected. Wilf Stevenson had no illusions about his close friend's working style, and suggested that the Prime Minister needed to have a Jonathan Powell figure who would act as political chief of staff, and an Alastair Campbell figure as a communications supremo to ensure there was a unified message emerging from Number 10 on his behalf. One aide says: 'He was swamped. There was no filtering system in Number 10, and no one who was distinguishing sufficiently for him the urgent and the non-urgent.'[254]

Thus the hunt was on for two big hitters to transform Number 10 into the powerhouse it was thought to have been under Blair. Michael Ellam, the Prime Minister's official spokesman since June 2007, had gone some way in restoring trust in Number 10's relations with the lobby. Neither Ellam nor Simon Lewis, his successor from July 2009, however, was a big-hitting 'political' figure. They were in the traditional mould of reserved official spokesmen, as had served most prime ministers throughout modern history: Bernard Ingham to Thatcher and Campbell to Blair were the exceptions. Sarah Brown hit on the idea of David Yelland, Rebekah Brooks's predecessor as editor of *The Sun*. On the day of the reshuffle, the BBC asked: 'Might there be another "GOAT" in the offing? David Yelland.'[255] Yelland had indeed been into Number 10 for a series of conversations with Brown, Sarah and Nye. 'I do want to help but I'm not sure what the job is and what your objectives are,' he told them. They pressed him hard to join them but to no avail: he felt he lacked the experience (and the desire) to work the lobby. He was also bringing up his son Max alone, and was recovering from alcoholism, topics on which he was shortly to publish a book.[256] 'I admire Gordon Brown and think he's a very clever and good man: but I had too many doubts,' he concluded.[257] Subsequently, Yelland was touched to receive a letter from Sarah praising him for the priority he had given to his parenting.

Brown never found his Campbell-like figure, despite making overtures to several others. Charlie Whelan continued to be someone the Prime Minister regularly consulted, but he had too much baggage to be appointable.[258]

McBride had been removed to the back room so Justin Forsyth, whom Brown had always greatly admired, performed much of the strategic communications role. Campbell was of course an increasing presence and influence, but having turned down the invitation for a full-time job, he was careful not to get too sucked in. Even without a Campbell mark two, Number 10 began to speak with a more coherent voice from that autumn.

The search for a Jonathan Powell figure was to prove equally abortive. Brown had always wanted Balls to do the job, but his close ally would not be budged. However, Balls recognised things had to change. In the absence of a powerful chief of staff, Balls and Watson persuaded Brown to bring in Liam Byrne as a successor to Ed Miliband in the Cabinet Office (with Watson acting as his deputy) to help improve the way Number 10 worked.[259] Byrne, like Carter, was a believer in management science. He started out in October interviewing everyone at Number 10 about what they thought had gone wrong and what needed to change, quickly discovering that, in some key respects, Downing Street was in poor shape. 'I just want the pain to stop,' one person told him. Trust had broken down in vital areas. Staff had felt undermined by the briefing against each other and by a lack of loyalty. In the anarchic set-up, a dysfunctional rivalry had grown up about gaining Brown's ear. 'It was a complete mess,' Byrne concluded.[260]

At first, the Number 10 team were dismayed that Brown had decided to bring in another person to try to shake up their operation and they feared this might herald a repeat of the problems of the Carter period. However, they soon came to appreciate Byrne's input.[261] In a bid to re-engage Cabinet ministers, the new minister visited Whitehall departments one by one and tried to increase the number of political cabinet meetings to give secretaries of state greater involvement in the policy and political agenda. His work achieved only a limited amount of success, not least because he had to combat Brown's continued absence of management sense and indecision, and by now, the ingrained cynicism among Cabinet ministers. By Christmas it was apparent to Byrne that he had done all he could to help improve the Number 10 operation. He decided instead to focus on coordinating domestic policy and his own mission of advancing public-service reform. He came to the view that in Brown's Number 10 there was a large number of people trying in combination to do the job that Campbell had done for Blair and there was no one performing the role of Powell.[262]

Brown's Number 10 nevertheless was to operate far more successfully in the second half of his premiership than it did in the first. The adoption of a radically new working layout was one reason. On a visit to New York the previous April, Brown had visited Mayor Michael Bloomberg and was fascinated by the way that he organised his office in a horseshoe, with his senior staff all working close to him. The Prime Minister told Heywood that he wanted to talk more to Bloomberg about it and to introduce a similar system into Number 10.[263] His staff were very far from happy when this was first mooted. They thought Brown's working methods were not at all suited to this approach and they worried they would be distracted from their own work by his mania.[264] He prevailed nonetheless. The only suitable large space in Downing Street was the ground floor of Number 12, which had been occupied by the whips since June 2007. When Brown was away in August 2008, arrangements were made to reclaim it, and a horseshoe pattern of desks was set out with Brown's place at the head of a series of desks. The composition rotated in his final twenty-one months, but the constant elements were Heywood on his left and then James Bowler, who had joined Number 10 earlier that year as Principal Private Secretary, and Joe Irvin, Fiona Gordon's successor from June 2008, as political secretary. Sitting closest to Brown on the right was Forsyth, who became head of strategic communications, then Fletcher and Kelly. Vadera had an occasional perch, as did Shaun Woodward for a while, until his one-time friend Mandelson 'saw him off'.[265] At the end of a separate table sat David Muir, and to his left at individual desks sat Nye, Mandelson, and beyond them, diary secretary Leeanne Johnston. In a media room off to the side worked Ellam (and then Lewis), Stewart Wood, Dugher, and press officer Iain Bundred. When Brown wanted to work alone, he retired to a large office just off the horseshoe, where he would read, work on speeches and have private meetings.

The horseshoe had significant benefits but also disadvantages. Having all Brown's senior people in one room close to him aided communication and ensured a rapid response – a regular problem with Number 10 up to that point. On a deeper level, he picked up their positive energy, and this helped them to avoid being dragged down by his periodic negativity and despondency. On the downside, it further institutionalised the Number 10 team's reactive mindset, and did not assist the development of the longer-term thinking that was so desperately needed. The rolling news on the TV in the horseshoe was permanently a distraction for Brown as he would always want to respond to breaking stories. Some in the Policy Unit became increasingly frustrated that the arrangement did not do more to encourage Brown to think about policy strategically.[266] Nonetheless one of those who regularly sat around the horseshoe recorded in their diary on 23 October: 'We are now in the new open plan. GB responded much better to it than we expected.'[267] Overall, then, the horseshoe arrangement helped change the atmosphere and dynamic in Number 10: Brown's aides started working much better together with far more personal warmth and trust than had existed earlier in the premiership.[268] The final photographs of Brown with his family and team on his last day at Number 10 were actually taken around the horseshoe at Number 12.

Number 12 'Horseshoe' – Autumn 2009 Onwards

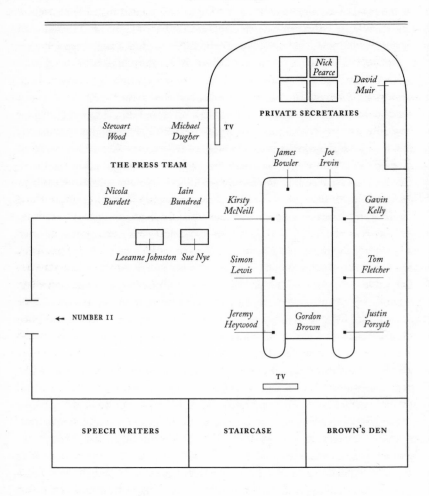

DOWNING STREET

Nick Pearce

David Muir

PRIVATE SECRETARIES

Stewart Wood

Michael Dugher

TV

THE PRESS TEAM

Nicola Burdett

Iain Bundred

Leeanne Johnston

Sue Nye

NUMBER 11

James Bowler

Joe Irvin

Kirsty McNeill

Gavin Kelly

Simon Lewis

Tom Fletcher

Jeremy Heywood

Gordon Brown

Justin Forsyth

TV

SPEECH WRITERS

STAIRCASE

BROWN'S DEN

A more important explanation for Number 10's greater effectiveness is Heywood's emergence as the pre-eminent figure there. His intelligence, work rate and understanding of policy and Whitehall put him way out ahead of any other individual. After Brown became Prime Minister, no one person had emerged as the all-powerful figure that Balls had been to him at the Treasury. The departure of Carter in the October reshuffle left the way free for Heywood to fulfil much of that role, though with his title, 'Permanent Secretary at Number 10', he was careful to stay clear of party political matters. The arrival of Bowler was also significant. Brown had badly missed Bowler, who had been his Principal Private Secretary at the Treasury. The official understood and respected Brown, and knew how to 'manage' him. His arrival helped free Heywood from some of the more routine civil service work, and enabled the latter to play the role of chief executive more effectively. Few people, however brilliant in other respects, could cope with the endless demands made by Brown, but Heywood was able to do so and keep his cool.[269] He also knew his own mind and was never again going to allow Number 10 to descend into the chaos of the preceding months. 'Jeremy regarded bringing order and coherence to Number 10 as his job: he often felt political issues let the side down, and he would tell GB to fix it,' says one close observer.[270]

The return of Mandelson brought stability not only to the government, but also helped, initially at least, the running of Number 10, as the Business Secretary's knowledge of its operation under Blair helped give a fresh perspective and optimism.[271] Stability was enhanced, too, by Balls's input. To the surprise of many, he rapidly adjusted to having a serious rival on his home patch. 'Peter was the first rival for Gordon's attention that Ed had ever had, but Gordon was very clear that he saw Ed and Peter as equals,' says Muir, who noticed how well the two collaborated. 'Ed went out of his way to make it work,' recalls one of the Business Secretary's aides. The emotional intelligence side of Mandelson's brain was so highly developed, some said, they were surprised he didn't walk around lopsided. But he showed his limitations when it came to figures. Balls excelled at anything logical or financial, but lacked Mandelson's human understanding. So they made a perfect, if distinctly odd, couple.[272] In fact, although they disagreed on a number of policy issues and on political strategy, they came to respect each other's qualities. 'Peter admires Ed as someone who can take tough decisions,' says one.[273] Mandelson had performed the same role with Blair as Balls did for Brown, and was said to sympathise with the way the younger man had become a lightning conductor for all the people with a gripe with his master.[274] Later, Mandelson would offer Balls informal advice throughout the Labour leadership contest in the summer of 2010.[275]

Sarah Brown was a final factor giving Brown, and hence Number 10, more stability. Sheinwald was one of many to notice the beneficial effect that she would have. 'I was always in favour of her coming to the Washington embassy. She had such a calming and positive influence on him,' he says.[276] She shared many of her husband's enthusiasms, not least Africa, where she had grown up, her mother running a school in Tanzania. She was fiercely protective of her children and she provided the family stability and the affirmation that Brown had lacked all his adult life.[277] She was careful not to intervene too often in his business, and was judicious when she did so. She protected him from a level of personal abuse in the media unprecedented for a Prime Minister, and helped provide a calm environment for his work. She was not without her detractors. Like Cherie Blair (though the two women were never close) she was deeply proud of the job her husband held, and was a forceful voice in encouraging him to stay on to the very end.[278] Moreover, her intense love and protection for him made her deeply angry when he was under attack, and this could heighten his paranoia about those who were seeking to do him down.[279] 'The idea that Sarah softened and humanised her husband was a deliberate image that Number 10 put out, but it didn't tell the whole truth,' says one insider.[280]

A Lucky By-Election: November

With the death on 13 August of John MacDougall, who had been MP for the Glenrothes constituency, which borders Brown's own, it looked like the Prime Minister was set for a further by-election setback. Despite a Labour majority of 10,000 votes, bookmakers were confident the seat would go to the SNP, as Glasgow East had in July, and the first opinion polls in the constituency gave Alex Salmond's party a thirteen-point lead.[281] What Brown badly needed was to show that the turnaround was real by winning a sensational victory. No one in August or September thought that remotely likely.

At its worst point that summer, the government's approval ratings had plummeted to 17 per cent, worse even than the December 1976 trough of James Callaghan.[282] Brown's approval rating sank to minus 58 per cent by mid-September, according to YouGov.[283] But then the wheel turned. His commanding performance at the Labour conference, and a lacklustre Tory conference, provided the kick-start. His handling of the financial crisis, his first acknowledged domestic success as Prime Minister, significantly boosted his ratings and those of the party, which ensured that the conference bounce endured. By early October, the Tory lead remained at 10 per cent and 59 per cent of the public approved of Brown's and Darling's handling of the crisis.[284] It had much more impact than the October reshuffle, which had left the public far from convinced about the return of Mandelson, with 50 per cent still associating him with spin and sleaze.[285]

On 6 November, polling day at Glenrothes, Number 10 was not holding its breath. Labour MPs were convinced they had lost and the SNP was buoyant. In the early evening, the expectation in Downing Street was at best a majority of 1,000.[286] Brown went to sleep that night uncertain, but was overjoyed when he woke to the news that the Labour candidate, Lindsay Roy, had romped home with 51 per cent of the vote and a majority of 6,700. It was 'not only a surprise but a stunner' in the eyes of *The Guardian*.[287] 'Gordon Brown has rewritten the textbooks for leaders in crises,' said the BBC's Nick Robinson.[288]

Brown's and Labour's popularity peaked after the by-election. In the second week of November, it stood at the highest since the honeymoon period in July 2007. For the first time, his approval ratings topped Cameron's.[289] Two days before Glenrothes, Obama had been elected US President.[290] ComRes placed the Conservatives ahead by just one point.[291] Suddenly, anything seemed possible.

6

Saving the World

(November 2008–April 2009)

The five months from November 2008 to April 2009 were gruelling for Brown. His major role in the bank rescue and the subsequent bounce in the polls were swiftly forgotten as the economic downturn threatened to engulf his premiership. Blair had presided over the politics of plenty; Brown was about to discover how much more uncomfortable it was to be Prime Minister at a time of austerity. But he drew hope and inspiration from a political figure who emerged at the beginning of this five-month period and who, at its end, helped facilitate what was arguably his greatest single achievement as Prime Minister: the London G20 summit.

News of Barack Obama's victory over John McCain came through at 4am GMT on Wednesday 5 November. Tom Fletcher could not sleep that night and went to Number 12 early to watch the events unfold on the television screen by the horseshoe. When McCain finally conceded after 5am, Fletcher sprang up the stairs to the flat to tell an excited and waking Brown. 'I want a call placed at once,' was the Prime Minister's first response. 'He becomes very frustrated when it didn't happen immediately. He goes into "overdrive", wants to write a letter to Obama and then prepare his statement,' records a contemporary diary.[1] After playing around with different words Brown decided what he would say to Obama: 'This is the moment that will live in history as long as history books are written.'

Brown and Fletcher were in the Downing Street flat wearing formal dress with white ties when later that day 'switch' told them the call from Obama was coming through. The Prime Minister fidgeted: they were running late for a formal dinner at Buckingham Palace. When Obama's voice eventually came on the line, it was warm and relaxed. His team had done their research and mentioned tennis, which, despite his restricted eyesight, Brown enjoys playing. 'We must play a game when you come over,' the President-elect said. It was all over quickly. Brown and Fletcher chatted about it on their way to the function. Brown thought Obama was 'already' presidential. His young aide told him about the line from the television serial *West Wing* when fictional President Bartlet says: 'You don't learn the presidential voice, you earn it.'[2] Number 10 staff worked hard to ensure that the call was 'briefed out positively'. At PMQs David Cameron teased Brown about it, asking him cheekily if his message to Obama had been: 'This is no time for a novice.'[3] Brown responded without humour – he had still to become comfortable in the forum – 'What I said was that serious times needed serious people.'[4]

A Tense Pre-Budget Report: November 2008

As the shockwaves of the global financial crisis transmitted into the real economy, Brown knew he did indeed face serious times. Britain was plunging into a deep recession and if he was to reassure an anxious and concerned public he would require a deftness of touch that had so far evaded him. Decisions to be taken in the imminent Pre-Budget Report, an emergency Budget in all but name, would, he knew, set the tone for the remainder of his premiership.

Alistair Darling's dire warning of the potential severity of the recession in his August *Guardian* interview appeared increasingly prophetic as the weeks went by. In October, the IMF's 'World Economic Outlook' report warned that the UK could face the worst downturn of any of the world's leading economies due to its heavy dependence on the financial and housing sectors, both of which had collapsed.[5] The British economy contracted from minus 0.3 per cent in the second quarter of 2008 to minus 0.9 per cent in the third quarter and then to minus 2.0 per cent in the final quarter of the year. Subsequent figures would show that UK output dropped 5.4 per cent between the first quarter of 2008 and the second quarter of 2009, a decline not seen since the 1930s depression.[6]

Brown and Darling saw the Pre-Budget Report as their vehicle to respond to the downturn, to stimulate the economy, and to allay public fears. Both men had cut their political teeth during the Thatcher recessions in the 1980s, when they argued that the Conservative government had done too little to protect jobs and the most vulnerable. They were not alone in their determination that they would not oversee the country entering a 'Tory-style recession'.[7] The Bank of England had been cutting interest rates aggressively throughout October and November, with base rates falling to 4.5 per cent on 8 October and to 3 per cent on 6 November. The hope that monetary policy would provide the magical tonic was being rapidly exhausted.[8] Fiscal policy, to stimulate demand in traditional Keynesian style, emerged as the big hope for Brown, the final trump card left in his hand.

It was not just the history of Thatcherism in the 1980s that was affecting Brown's thinking. He was becoming engrossed by how the world had responded to the Great Depression in the 1930s. On the flight back to London from Afghanistan in December, Number 10 aide David Muir gave the Prime Minister the book *FDR: The First Hundred Days*, by Cambridge historian Anthony J. Badger,[9] which he devoured greedily.[10] The mistake Roosevelt made, Brown came to believe, had been to cut spending too quickly following his initial stimulus. To feed his voracious appetite, Stewart Wood – who was an academic at Magdalen College, Oxford as well as a Downing Street adviser – wrote to the world's leading Roosevelt scholars and asked them about the President's response to the financial crisis and what could be learned from it today.[11] Brown turned his attention also to Roosevelt's British contemporary, John Maynard Keynes, who in the inter-war years had led a major revolution in economic thinking. Keynes's insight that governments could play an active role in stimulating demand during recessions was sweet music to Brown's ear. He had long believed in the efficacy of public spending: Keynes's contemporary relevance was that it would help bring Britain out of recession more quickly. The Prime Minister had known Robert Skidelsky for many years and was a great admirer of his three-volume biography of Keynes,[12] which he occasionally gave to friends to read. He had contacted Skidelsky in the early 1990s when the latter had written a pamphlet for the Social Market Foundation called 'Beyond Unemployment', which had intrigued the then-shadow Chancellor. When he entered government, Brown had invited the peer to a series of 'secret' seminars on Keynes. Skidelsky's publication of *Keynes: The Return of the Master*[13] in 2009 paved the way for a new phase in their relationship: he wrote to Brown, urging him to set up an economic advisory council modelled on the body Prime Minister Ramsay MacDonald set up in 1930. After he left Number 10, Brown told Skidelsky: 'I always wanted you back in the Labour Party.'[14] Brown was also a great admirer of Princeton professor Paul Krugman, especially his book *The Return of Depression Economics*,[15] which argued for an expansionary fiscal policy if the world was to avoid the problems of the 1930s.[16]

The severity of the situation demanded a dramatic response, but fiscal stimulation of the economy would inevitably mean the government would have to breach Brown's own 'golden rule', which said that borrowing should never rise above 40 per cent of GDP, and which had helped establish his reputation for prudence. To prepare the ground, Darling told the *Sunday Telegraph* in mid-October that this was not the time to take money out of the economy, and 'much of what Keynes wrote still makes a lot of sense'.[17] At the end of October at the Cass Business School, in London, he argued the case for suspending the golden rule in the light of the extreme economic conditions gripping the country. 'To apply the fiscal rules in a rigid manner today would be perverse,' he said.[18] The golden rule would not be the only New Labour shibboleth to fall by the wayside.

Dramatic events in the economy were forcing a rethink across the political spectrum. On 18 November, six days before the Pre-Budget Report was due to be delivered, the Conservatives announced a major switch in their policy, when Cameron ditched his party's commitment to match Labour's spending plans until 2010–11. This opened up a real dividing line on economic policy between the two main parties. George Osborne had made the pledge in September 2007 when he feared that Brown might call a snap election and when the policy was also part of Cameron's wider strategy to 'detoxify' his party's brand. Cameron had believed the Conservatives had been punished by the electorate because they were not trusted with public services. But he now changed tack. 'What once looked affordable in boom times is now clearly unsustainable,' Cameron told the *Daily Telegraph*. 'Unless we curb the growth of spending, taxes will need to rise in the future … the borrowing bombshell will turn into a tax bombshell.'[19] The spending pledge had never been popular with the right of the Conservative Party, and the decision to abandon it was relatively easy.[20] That it would allow the Tories to attack Brown's record as Chancellor when spending was dramatically increased also greatly appealed to Tory backbenchers. The return of the Tories to fiscal conservatism and 'sound money' played very well with the right-wing press too; the risk for Cameron, as he well understood, was that the shift would allow Labour to claim the Tory party was turning its back on vulnerable people who needed help at this time. The stage was set for a major clash of philosophies.

The Pre-Budget Report was due on Monday 24 November, but even late in the day, vital details had still not been finalised. Number 10 and the Treasury had examined different ways of fiscally stimulating the economy. 'The critical concern was that the policy chosen should make as fast an impact as possible,' says Dan Corry.[21] The Treasury and Number 10 toyed with increasing tax credits (ruled out because the computers would not be able to administer it quickly enough), giving everyone £100 (knocked out because of the lack of any mechanism to administer it) and cutting income tax (rejected because of a worry that people would merely save the extra money and it would be hard, for political reasons, to make this move only temporary). A temporary cut in VAT from 17.5 to 15 per cent emerged as the favoured choice of both Number 10 and Treasury officials, largely because of ease of administration. The cut would have the benefit of being in place in time for the Christmas shopping season, it was expected to be popular with the public, and to be seen to be fair as it applied to all, whereas a cut in income tax would benefit only those who paid it. The drop in VAT duly formed the centrepiece of the Pre-Budget Report's £20bn fiscal stimulus package, coming into effect on 1 December 2008, and scheduled to last for thirteen months. To boost the economy further, £3bn spending on capital projects (the most Treasury officials believed could be spent in practice) was brought forward from 2010–11, and further measures were introduced to protect children, pensioners and the least advantaged. This was no great Keynesian shot of adrenaline: the Pre-Budget Report's stimulus was fairly modest, representing only about 1 per cent of GDP, less than the 2 per cent recommended by the IMF. As *The Economist* pointed out, however, Britain's room for manoeuvre was more restricted than many other nations given its dependency on the financial and housing sectors.[22]

The government may have been united about the need to stimulate the economy, but it was less clear about how it should respond to the rapidly deteriorating state of the public finances. Britain's comparatively narrow tax base saw the deficit soar when revenue from the City collapsed. From at least the spring of 2008, the Treasury had become alarmed about this. 'We were continually surprised by just how big it was becoming,' says a senior official.[23] They had good grounds to be worried. In his March 2008 Budget, Darling had forecast borrowing for 2009–10 to be £38bn, but in the November Pre-Budget Report he revised that figure to a massive £118bn, and said that the Budget would not be brought back into balance until 2015. To make the giveaways look credible, Darling and the Treasury insisted that the stimulus package be balanced by pre-announced future revenue rises. The Treasury, with support from some senior officials in Number 10 and the Cabinet Office, pushed hard for raising VAT to 20 per cent after the thirteen months were up – that is, from 1 January 2010. A VAT rise appealed because it would raise a lot of money quite easily. This met fierce resistance from the political side of Number 10 who thought increasing VAT would be 'crazy politics' and 'very unfair' as it would hit the worst-off the hardest.[24]

As the delivery date for the Pre-Budget Report approached, Ed Miliband and Chief Secretary to the Treasury Yvette Cooper were two principal figures who became worried that the announcement of a future VAT rise could see a rerun of the 10p fiasco with Labour once again appearing out of touch with their traditional voters. But Darling was not listening to them, nor could they persuade a reluctant Brown to take on the Chancellor about it. They went together to see Ed Balls to share their concerns. 'You are the only person who can persuade the Prime Minister to stop this,' they told him. Balls duly saw Brown during the final weekend before the Pre-Budget Report and persuaded him to abandon the January 2010 VAT hike. Cooper was later to say that it was one of her husband's most significant interventions during Brown's premiership.[25] Was Balls's move decisive? Aides close to Brown say they never believed he would have supported the VAT hike, but as with all budgetary decisions, he was weighing up all options until the very last minute.[26]

If it was not prepared to sanction a future boost in VAT above 17.5 per cent, how else could the government demonstrate its commitment to longer-term fiscal responsibility? It had less than forty-eight hours to decide, and neither option left on the table was straightforward – raising income tax or raising national insurance. A new rift now emerged between Number 10 and the Treasury. The Chancellor was not keen on raising tax rates, but the Number 10 political team and Balls saw it as a way of championing the 'fairness' agenda. As the crisis had been caused in part by the failings of bankers, Balls argued forcefully that those who had benefited from the good times should pay more than those who had benefited less. He was irritated because he thought Darling was never really willing to put the argument on the economy in these terms, and thought this meant people ended up believing Labour were supporting bankers.[27] Brown was caught in the middle of Balls and Darling, and time was running out. He was nervous about promoting any measures that would be interpreted as increasing tax on the well-off to the benefit of the worst-off. He absolutely shrunk from the prospect of such a move being portrayed as him killing off his and Blair's 'New Labour' project.[28]

Muir had been conducting focus groups to examine the voter response to various revenue-raising measures. On the Saturday (22 November) he went with his findings to see Brown in the Number 12 study off the horseshoe. 'What are your recommendations?' Brown asked. 'All the choices we have are awful, but if we have to we can manage a rise in income tax, just, and a rise in national insurance, just,' his aide replied, also pointing out that Labour would not be thanked for any of this.[29] Brown drew a deep breath and decided to go for both: national insurance contributions were to rise by 0.5 per cent for all but low earners from April 2011, and a new top rate of income tax of 45 per cent on earnings over £150,000 would be introduced, which would again come into force from April 2011. The original plan in Number 10 was that the top-rate tax increase should be explicitly presented as a temporary five-year surcharge to finance the capital spending increase. But Darling did not believe that a 'temporary' increase would be credible, so he quietly shelved this proposition as he finalised his statement.[30] The measures were deliberately designed to come into force after the general election, which technically meant the government was not breaking its 2005 manifesto commitment not to increase the top rate of tax before the next election.

The decisions presented in the Pre-Budget Report amounted to a crossing of the Rubicon. For many around the horseshoe it was the right thing to do. 'This was a major moment for a Labour government: when the chips were down our response was to act in a fair and progressive way by looking after the most vulnerable and by asking the more affluent to bear the biggest responsibility,' was the general response from the political aides.[31] In addition to introducing the 45 per cent top rate of tax, Brown reduced tax relief for the wealthy and withdrew some tax allowances. The fiscal situation, it was asserted, had required the traditional New Labour approach to taxation to be jettisoned. 'It took a crisis to make it happen,' explains an adviser.[32] But Darling was deeply unhappy. 'I don't want to get blamed for losing the next election. I don't want a repeat of John Smith's shadow budget in 1992,' Peter Mandelson reports being told by the Chancellor.[33] Mandelson, an important voice in the debate, supported the increase to 45 per cent. He also supported the subsequent increase to 50 per cent, but felt that this change should be time limited and not billed as a permanent change to the tax system.[34] Blair, sensing the ground giving way under his New Labour edifice, privately expressed his disagreement when he got wind of the 45 per cent proposal, warning Mandelson sternly: 'Remember where we've come from, Peter.'[35]

On Sunday 23 November, the day before it was to be announced in the Pre-Budget Report, the *Sunday Telegraph* carried the headline, 'VAT cut not enough to save the High Street'.[36] The Pre-Budget Report's increase of the top rate to 45 per cent had also been leaked to the paper. Brown was livid as it took the initiative away from the government and exposed the Pre-Budget Report to criticism before it could be explained. Number 10 again suspected foul play. 'It was leaked to the Sunday papers from the Treasury mole. Someone had been feeding the Tories material over a number of years,' says one aide.[37] Investigations never found a guilty party. Should the Tories have connived in this regular breach of government secrecy? Probably not, though it is hard to believe Labour, in the Opposition's position, would have acted differently. The much-anticipated Pre-Budget Report was duly announced the following day. In his speech, Darling set out the options. There is a choice, he said: 'One can choose to walk away, let the recession take its course, adopting a sink-or-swim attitude ... or one could decide, as I have decided, and as governments of every shade around the world have decided, to support businesses and to support families by increasing borrowing, which will also reduce the impact and length of the recession.'[38]

The leak did indeed damage the Pre-Budget Report's reception. The VAT cut was met with general scepticism, with the *Financial Times* reporting that many small businesses had complained that the costs of overseeing its reduction would outweigh any potential benefit.[39] Cameron dismissed the moves, especially the VAT cut, as an outright 'failure', before the changes had had the chance to make any impact.[40] The government decision to cut VAT would ultimately be vindicated: research from both the Centre for Economics and Business Research and the Institute for Fiscal Studies later concluded that the VAT cut helped boost the economy by keeping consumer spending up.[41] The problem, however, was not the economics but the politics. Corry suggests: 'The public didn't really understand it and they slagged us off for it.'[42]

Brown's apprehensions about the political reception of the Pre-Budget Report proved well founded. 'Obituary: New Labour' said a headline in *The Sun*, declaring that 'after a fourteen-year battle with socialism ... New Labour died after a fatal dose of tax rises, plans to nationalise the entire banking system and £1tn of debt. Its heartbroken father, Tony Blair, was too upset to comment.'[43] The *Daily Mail* took a similar line, saying the Pre-Budget Report marked 'the most dramatic about-turn in government policy since the 1970s ... It is no exaggeration to say that New Labour – the enterprise-friendly party that once claimed to be "nothing less than the political arm of the British people as a whole" – is no more.'[44] In contrast *Guardian* journalist Polly Toynbee, who had been a constant thorn in Brown's side, was beside herself with delight. 'The New Labour era is over – welcome to social democracy. Following in Obama's footsteps, it is suddenly safe to tax the rich and spend to protect jobs,' she wrote.[45]

As a co-architect of the 'project' Brown was very sensitive and worried about this 'death of New Labour' analysis, and how being painted as 'Old Labour' might damage him and cohesion within the party, even with Mandelson now providing Blairite political cover. However, to his political aides in Number 10, the Pre-Budget Report signalled a turning point: it marked the 'start of Gordon becoming a much better Prime Minister', in the words of one.[46] Rising to this challenge, he began to talk much more about how the financial crisis had rewritten the rule book. 'He convinced himself the policy totems of the past had to be dispensed with,' says another Number 10 aide.[47] Brown's team advised him to relax about it. 'The modus operandi has changed: we can no longer work in the ways we did before,' they told him to say.[48] Mandelson brushed off Blair's gripes, arguing in a speech to the Institute of Directors: 'The times have changed, not New Labour.'[49]

As Christmas approached, the government continued to come under fire over the size of the deficit and how it would be repaid. The £118bn figure amounted to a budget deficit of 8 per cent of GDP, the highest since records began in 1970, and an 'astonishing' figure, according to the BBC.[50] Darling argued that 'if we did nothing, we would have a deeper and longer recession', but he and his Treasury officials were increasingly of the view that he needed to demonstrate clearly how he would bring the deficit under firm control.[51] Brown's once almost unassailable stewardship of the Treasury was also increasingly coming under the microscope, with his claim to have ended 'boom and bust' ringing hollow. If he had been a true Keynesian, his critics argued, he would have done more to protect the public finances in the good times by not spending as much as he did. Yet such criticism is often exaggerated. Britain entered the recession with its budget deficit standing at 3 per cent of GDP, which was not high by international standards. Brown's real error was that he became far too reliant on revenues generated by the City and the housing market which meant that when the financial crisis struck, Britain was left in a more precarious situation than those countries whose economies were built on broader and more sustainable foundations.

The Treasury had been very unhappy about the Pre-Budget Report's abandonment of the 'golden rule' and wanted to tie the government down to new rules to re-establish credibility. Number 10 favoured a more provisional 'operating' rule, which restored flexibility in the run-up to the election.[52] Darling announced that the golden rule would be reinstated as soon as the Budget was back in balance in 2015–16, which to many seemed impossibly far away and did little to reassure his officials. Over the months that followed, the Chancellor was to come under mounting pressure from them to cut the deficit.[53]

So Darling found himself caught between the Treasury, with its eye firmly on the currency and bond markets, anxious to return the public finances to a healthy state as soon as possible to stave off a potential sterling crisis, and the political side of Number 10, which was fixated on the electoral cycle and therefore more attuned to the problems of the real economy. One little-noticed element of the Pre-Budget Report was the decision – fully supported by Number 10 – to cut £5bn from the agreed 2010–11 Budget through 'efficiency savings' as a way of building credibility and showing a determination to cut out waste and lower-priority spending. 'This move was important as it demonstrated that we were willing to cut spending to reduce the deficit,' says Nick Pearce. Not all were pleased. Balls said it would be a mistake but was overruled. He then fought hard to save his own education budget, offsetting his losses by increasing resources for 16- to 19-year-olds to compensate for the recession.[54] This argument foreshadowed far more intense debates that were to take place on spending and deficit reduction over the following fifteen months.[55]

The Conservatives were merciless. 'Stability has gone out of the window, prudence is dead,' declared Osborne.[56] On 9 December, in a speech at the London School of Economics, Cameron accused Labour of making the recession 'longer and deeper' and having a 'spend now, forget the future' approach to the crisis.[57] The Tories deliberately targeted and politicised the deficit, believing it to be the government's Achilles heel. In January 2009, it was officially confirmed that Britain was in a full-blown recession in the 'real economy', with job losses, bankruptcy and housing repossessions becoming serious anxieties. As the months ground on, Brown became even more convinced that only a Keynesian stimulus to the economy could bring Britain most quickly out of the recession, and that worrying too much about the increase in the debt that this would involve would be a mistake. It was ironic that the financial crisis was succeeding where his aides had failed: it was providing the Prime Minister with something approaching a coherent philosophy in domestic policy.

Domestic Policy Solidifies: November 2008 to March 2009

The recapitalisation plan had brought stability to the financial system, and Brown now intended to use the full force of his fiscal powers to limit the depth and length of the resultant recession. But there was to be a further leg of his economic policy: he wanted passionately to show that a Labour recession, deep as it might be, would be different in character from the Tory recessions of the 1980s and 1990s. He was adamant that the coming downturn would not see repossessions, insolvencies and unemployment return to the nightly news. He remembered such images well from childhood. In 1964, as a 13-year-old, Brown had been deeply affected by the closure of the Barry, Ostlere and Shepherd company, whose linoleum factory stood yards from his home. He remembers watching workers stream from the factory on its last day, and the gates slamming shut behind them. Later, as a young politician in Scotland, he had watched with distress the impact of deindustrialisation on once-proud communities and their descent into idleness and dependency. Reflecting on those times, and the current recession, he would meaningfully say to his advisers in Number 10: 'I know where this ends.' The memories drove him throughout this next period of government. 'Quite simply, this explains the development of the Future Jobs Fund,' says one adviser.[58] Brown understood that losing a job meant also losing an important part of one's identity, and that each day a young person spent out of work made it harder for them to return.

In an interview with *The Guardian* on 24 October, Darling said: 'I've lived through the recessions this country saw in the 1970s, 1980s and 1990s. The difference is, this time we are determined to do everything we can and as soon as we can to help people.' As a newspaper leader put it the next day, nicely picking up the cue from Number 10: 'No one can seriously argue that there will not be a recession; the question is whether it will be a *Labour* recession.'[59] But the challenge for Brown would be not so much finding the right policy solution, as it had been for the financial crisis. Now, the issues were on a human scale. Even if he could limit the damage, could he speak to the deepening concerns of working people?

On 3 October, Brown himself built a vital new piece of machinery for tackling the recession, the establishment of the National Economic Council (NEC), described by the *Daily Telegraph* as an 'economic war cabinet'.[60] It first met on 6 October on 'meltdown Monday', when it had focused on plans for the banks. But in the coming months its focus would shift squarely to the real economy, and on limiting the fallout of the downturn. The NEC had been devised primarily by Cabinet Secretary Gus O'Donnell and Number 10 permanent secretary Jeremy Heywood, but it was originally the Prime Minister's idea. Brown's instinctive response to a complex problem was to create a mechanism in which to thrash things out; these rarely worked, not least because he soon lost interest in them. But the NEC was the one exception to the rule. Chaired by him (and Darling in his absence), it met initially once or twice a week, before switching to a fortnightly cycle. Its nineteen members included the big beasts Darling, Mandelson and Balls, as well as other ministers with economic portfolios such as Shriti Vadera and Paul Myners. To reflect the urgency of the task, meetings would take place in the Cabinet Office meeting room usually used by the government's COBRA emergency-response committee. For many of the ministers who attended NEC meetings, this was their first taste of the strange, underground briefing room and its attendant traditions. 'It was the ambience that did the thing,' says one adviser who was present. '[It] has a very different atmosphere to the rest of Whitehall.'[61] With Brown seated next to his Chancellor at the end of the small table, flanked by O'Donnell and Treasury permanent secretary Nick Macpherson, it sent a 'powerful' message across government that the committee meant business.[62]

For its critical first months, the NEC was more important than Cabinet,[63] becoming Brown's main way of driving action across Whitehall.[64] Cabinet worked no better after the October reshuffle than it had before. Brown was an adequate chairman, but its meetings were lacklustre. No one was under any illusions about where many key decisions were made. Critically, its meetings had become prone to leaks: details of discussions would routinely appear in the next day's newspapers, significantly curtailing what ministers felt they could say. Brown's was a chronically dysfunctional and mistrusting Cabinet, riven by splits between Blairites and Brown loyalists, and between those who wanted Brown to go and those who thought his departure would be too damaging. The NEC, by contrast, was to prove secure, at least in its initial and most productive months.

Below the surface, the Treasury was far from happy about the successful launch of Brown's new toy. 'It was very much about Number 10 trying to take direct control of economic policy,' recalls a senior Treasury official.[65] Number 10 worked hard to enlist its support. 'If [the Treasury] saw [the NEC] as a threat they would naturally try and undermine it,' says Corry, who worked very closely on the committee's establishment.[66] Macpherson had endorsed its creation, but even though the Treasury provided a joint secretariat with Downing Street, tensions remained.[67] It did little for the relationship between Brown and Darling. 'At this time, Gordon basically thought Alistair and the Treasury were a source of obstruction,' says an official.[68]

Treasury anxieties aside, the NEC provided the impetus as the government tried to exert control. Some in Number 10 had worried that departments had been oblivious to the seriousness of the coming crisis. Now, Whitehall was jolted into action. 'We would never have got the work done if there wasn't a meeting,' says one senior economic adviser.[69] Another says: 'It was incredibly useful to have a bit of a sense of a crisis.'[70] At each meeting, a different departmental minister would be asked to present a paper, and their officials felt the pressure to prepare them well. 'We'd say to them: "Your ministers will not want to turn up with a paper that doesn't say anything, or their colleagues will think: 'What a complete idiot.'"'[71]

Home repossessions were one of the early topics taken on by the NEC, and one of great importance to Brown. Preoccupying him throughout was his desire to prevent a repeat of the early 1990s, when 75,500 homes had been taken away from their owners. In the intervening years many more had moved into home ownership, many who were only just able to afford it, so it was likely there would be a very high number of repossessions. In January 2009 near panic was caused when the Council of Mortgage Lenders projected 75,000 repossessions for the year ahead. Lowering that figure would need fast, bold action. That would require the support of the Treasury, but housing ministers rarely had the weight to win arguments with the Chancellor. 'GB used to get very impatient on housing, so housing minister John Healey would have a go at the Treasury in the NEC, knowing GB would back him fully,' recalls one adviser.[72]

A raft of policy measures aimed at tackling repossessions spewed out of the NEC in the following weeks. The highest profile was the proposal to give struggling homeowners a mortgage 'holiday' if a member of the household lost their job. Perhaps the most effective, though, was a change to the court process for dealing with repossessions, which meant that families were given more time to repay their mortgages before their home was taken from them. Towards the end of 2008, the NEC moved on to drive a series of announcements on employment, including the expansion of apprenticeships and an enhanced system of loans to help mid-career retraining. Efforts to tackle unemployment would crystallise in the form of the Future Jobs Fund, a £1bn pot intended to create 150,000 temporary jobs for young people, and the Young Person's Guarantee, which guaranteed a job, training or work placement for 18–24 year olds who had been unemployed for twelve months. Despite being scrapped by the coalition government both initiatives were later considered to have proved successful in creating a 'significant' number of jobs by a cross-party parliamentary committee. The car scrappage scheme was to follow, paying people to trade in old cars, thus boosting vehicle sales.

With December fast approaching, Brown's thoughts turned to the Queen's Speech. It was his first – and as it turned out his last – chance to outline a full legislative programme before the general election in 2010, and a vital opportunity to sketch out dividing lines with the Tories. It was the chance for a major set-piece event, at which he could communicate to the public his efforts to protect them from the economic storm. The NEC was busy churning out policy solutions from deep underground, but Brown needed to stand on the street level and reassure people he was doing all he could to defend their interests.

In the run-up to the speech, Number 10's policy wonks became agitated that Brown had paid so little attention to public service reform in recent months, with the financial crisis and international affairs eating up his time. 'The financial crisis had usurped everything,' recalls one.[73] In the event, Brown gave them his time, and the Queen's Speech contained fourteen bills, down from the eighteen in May's draft speech. They included plans for the creation of an NHS 'constitution', setting out the rights and responsibilities of patients and staff. This marked a further step in the direction of patients' entitlements, including being able to select a doctor of their choice, and even a right of free passage to Europe for state-funded treatment if undue delays were encountered in the NHS. An equalities bill simplified anti-discrimination legislation, and introduced an obligation on public bodies to tackle disadvantage stemming from socio-economic status (later lauded by Polly Toynbee as 'socialism in one clause'). The only addition to the draft Queen's Speech was a bill enshrining into law the government's commitment to eradicate child poverty by 2020. Tellingly, the most positive reaction from the Labour benches came during the debate, when Brown announced the banks would support a two-year deferral of mortgage-interest payments for those in financial difficulties. It went to the heart of the concerns that MPs were hearing on doorsteps from voters worried about their homes and jobs. It had been a last-minute rush to have the announcement ready: as Brown spoke, officials passed a note to him saying that the banks had only agreed in principle to a deal.[74] The details would be worked out later.[75]

Elsewhere, the Queen's Speech fell flat. Political commentator John Rentoul thought it 'weak', and felt that many of the bill's stronger messages were undermined by 'having been repeated so often',[76] due in part to Brown's decision to launch the consultation on the draft legislative programme in May. The speech was deemed by Rentoul's paper, *The Independent*, to be 'the most perfunctory on record'.[77] It was certainly a far cry from the vision and drive Brown had shown in response to the financial crisis. Lack of time provides one explanation, and money another: action on the real economy was not proving cheap. But that could not explain the continuing lack of policy in key areas. On education, there was little of note. Indeed, little would happen here between the launch of the National Challenge in June 2008 and the education white paper in July 2009. And time does not explain those areas in which Brown himself had rowed back on radical action. The policing and crime bill had been intended as a vehicle for legislation on elected police authorities, but Brown soon backed off, anxious to avoid a row with the police service and Labour's local government leaders. Like Blair, Brown would fail to address the thorny issue of police accountability. The empowerment bill had been intended to give the public the right to 'recall' their MP, triggering a re-election in cases of misconduct. That too was dropped for fear of angering the Parliamentary Labour Party (PLP). New Chief Whip Nick Brown was not an advocate of a bold agenda. Even measures like the NHS constitution and the child poverty bill had hues of a government on its way out, wanting to lock its successor into progressive commitments. And, as commentators had now come to expect from a Brown speech, this was more of a shopping list than a coherent new agenda. The theme of the speech was 'fair rules', drawing from work by Justin Forsyth, who as Number 10's strategic communications director had developed a 'three-pillared' approach: 'fair say', 'fair rules', and 'fair chances' – an intriguing but overly elaborate formulation. The Prime Minister was to have better inspirations. The focus on 'fair rules' was seen in the speech's more populist measures – restricting the number of lap-dancing clubs, rolling out lie-detector tests for benefits claimants, and cracking down on first-time benefit frauds – but it did little to unite the rest.

On 31 December, in his New-Year statement, Brown would make a further attempt to carve out a unifying agenda for his policy programme. His focus here would be on the 'great global challenges' confronting the economy, the environment and security. Again, here spoke Brown the internationalist, a man who understood globalisation, but this, too, failed to achieve traction as an organising theme. Early in 2009, Brown stepped up work on the theme of social mobility, which had never been far from his mind. Advisers suggested to him that, alongside action on the economy, he needed to speak positively about the future he wanted to build in Britain. On 13 January he published the 'New Opportunities' white paper, extolling a Britain in which 'what counts is not where you come from but what you aspire to become'. In many ways it was a more impressive statement than anything he had produced in the Queen's Speech. Underpinning his thinking was the latest research from the Sutton Trust, an educational and social policy charity, which found that social mobility in Britain had fallen in recent decades. But the white paper was thin on substantive policy, in part because of a shortage of money, but mostly because the solutions were unclear, or unpalatable.[78] What it did feature was more apprenticeships and more childcare for two-year-olds, and £10,000 bonuses to retain effective teachers in high-need schools. The most discussed element of the proposals was the plan to establish a panel to identify the barriers preventing fair access to the professions.[79] To chair this new body, in an appointment that harked back to the inclusive ministerial appointments he had made when he became Prime Minister, Brown selected one-time arch foe Alan Milburn, who had stepped down as Health Secretary in 2003. Action on social mobility was exactly the initiative the left of the party had craved. 'It should have been

Labour's guiding light for the last eleven years – but better late than never,' opined Polly Toynbee.[80] When published, Milburn's review included a long list of well-intentioned but highly detailed and small-scale recommendations, though it did help to raise the salience of issues like unpaid internships that were having a damaging effect on mobility into elite professions.[81]

On 28 January, NEC deliberations bore fruit with Brown's announcement at an employers' event in London of a series of measures to tackle youth unemployment, including small businesses being given subsidies to take on unemployed young people. Enlisting businessman Alan Sugar to the cause, Brown spoke of 'a new partnership between government and employers, to create a Britain of opportunity where everyone can make the most of their talents'. The policies received a broadly positive reception, but two days earlier, a new poll had showed the Tory lead extending from five to fifteen points in the previous month. Brown had triumphed on the world stage during the financial crisis, but despite now developing a policy response that was already showing a positive effect, he was still struggling to convince voters that he had their interests at heart, and that he uniquely had the skills to bring them through the recession well.

Afghanistan Kicks Off: October 2008 to February 2009

While Brown had been so preoccupied with the economy, there was a merciful hiatus between the end of Britain's military involvement in Iraq and an intensification of the situation in Afghanistan, which would soon become a major preoccupation. Britain's armed commitments overseas, and the threat of terrorism at home, had never, however, been far from his mind. He flew to Afghanistan from a European Council meeting on 12 December, arriving on 13 December, to meet the troops in southern Helmand Province. Wearing body armour, he was then flown to the Roshan Tower post overlooking the Musa Qala district, where he was briefed about recent operations before being flown by Sea King helicopter to meet President Karzai. This was neither his best nor most eventful visit. 'Gordon Brown is a man more at home with the bleak statistics of recession than the grim toll of war,' was the BBC's take.[82] On his return to London on 15 December, after a brief trip to India and Pakistan, he spoke to the House of Commons about 'a chain of terror that links the mountains of Afghanistan and Pakistan right through to the streets of the UK and other countries around the world, and that chain of terror must be broken', phrases that he had used to the troops the day before.[83] The time had come, he said, 'not for more words but for action', and he spoke about his plans on a counter-terrorism initiative with the Pakistan government, as well as reinforcements for Afghanistan, if only 'in the low hundreds', being sent from Cyprus.

The trip came at a turning point in Britain's thinking about Afghanistan. For the first eighteen months of his premiership, Brown had been sceptical about the success and objectives of the latest phase of the military operation which had begun in May 2006 when British troops moved into Helmand. Initially, 3,300 British soldiers had been sent to Afghanistan, rising to 8100 by December 2008. The Taliban insurgency had been growing steadily from early 2007, forcing British troops into some of the fiercest fighting since the Second World War, and contributing to death tolls for British soldiers in Afghanistan of forty-two in 2007 and fifty-one in 2008. A consensus had existed among his three ministers with responsibilities for British activities in the country – Des Browne at Defence, David Miliband at the Foreign Office and Douglas Alexander at International Development. All three favoured finding a political solution and building up Afghan institutions, in particular local government, rather than laying too much weight on a military defeat of the Taliban. Miliband and Alexander were particularly worried about 'mission creep' and therefore sceptical about the case for increasing troop numbers. But in October 2008 the consensus broke down when John Hutton was appointed to Defence. Browne's relationship with the Prime Minister was at times fractious, but both were sceptical about building up military forces. Hutton, in contrast, was an advocate of troop increases and came to be seen in Number 10 as 'the voice of the military in Cabinet, rather than the voice of government in the MoD'.[84] At the same time, with the drawing down of the British military commitment to Iraq, the service chiefs were becoming newly energised about advocating greater troop numbers in Afghanistan. A sea change in thinking was occurring in the Ministry of Defence, and Number 10 was slow to spot it. In the department's new fervour, it found a ready ally in Hutton. 'The Chief of Defence Staff, Jock Stirrup, had direct right of access to the PM: why on earth did we need to have a second figure in the Defence Secretary acting as the spokesman for the military?' says one disillusioned Number 10 aide.[85]

The British military at the same time began to pick up a new mood emanating from Washington, and it was one they liked. 'I found it impossible to have a sensible conversation with anyone in Washington about Afghanistan before the beginning of 2008,' says Stirrup.[86] Prior to that, he said, Iraq was burning all the US administration's political oxygen. As the Americans began to commit more troops to Afghanistan, so they became eager for its key ally to follow suit.[87] The British military was thus more than disappointed by the small troop increase that Brown announced in December 2008: 275 troops who were based in Cyprus. 'It created quite a lot of tension,' says Hutton. 'The military found it hard to get through to him with their concerns.'[88] Hutton sent several notes to Brown recommending he followed the army's advice to boost troop numbers on the ground, but on every occasion, he said, a negative response came back, either from Number 10 or from Darling. The Chancellor was conscious that, even with a fixed number of troops, costs were escalating very rapidly and told the Ministry of Defence bluntly that, in the current financial climate, it was impossible to accede to demands for more men.[89]

Not to be deterred, in February 2009 the department put up new recommendations for more troops to be sent to Afghanistan. Pressure was coming not least from the highly persuasive and popular Chief of General Staff Richard Dannatt. A man with deeply held Christian beliefs, Dannatt's view that his troops were suffering because of inadequate numbers and equipment did not sit easily with Number 10. His outspoken public comments on Iraq and ubiquitous lobbying for greater military spending had been partly responsible for Brown blocking him from succeeding Stirrup as Chief of Defence Staff in June 2008, resulting in Stirrup's tenure being extended, unusually, for a further two years. As one foreign office official put it: 'you can't throw shit all over the Prime Minister and then expect him to make you CDS'. Dannatt was livid with Brown for not appointing him and their subsequent interactions were to become toxic, taking the relationship between the military and Number 10 to depths not seen in many years.

Over the coming months, four options were put forward for troop levels in Afghanistan: keeping the numbers at 8,100, moving them up to 8,700, or increasing them to 9,500, or even 9,800. One aide explains: 'Only the last of these four options envisaged any extra effort being devoted to training the Afghan forces, which Brown had consistently argued should be the strategic priority.'[90] Realising that the final option was not popular in Number 10, Hutton lobbied Cabinet ministers to back him on it. So, when Number 10 refused to support it, tension between them and the Ministry of Defence heightened still further. Hutton was furious that Number 10 and the Treasury were not listening to the case, and his relationship with Brown never recovered.[91] Hutton himself is very clear where the blame lay. 'Brown was never very happy with disagreement. He wanted a consensus, and when there was none, he failed to give a clear lead,' he says.[92] The generals spoke candidly to their opposite numbers in the US about their frustrations, and gave them the impression that if the Americans applied more pressure, Brown would agree to sending more troops – a ploy the Prime Minister learned about to his horror right on the eve of the G20 summit.[93]

The Chapter Closes on Iraq: December 2008 to May 2010

On 17 December, Brown went on what was to be his last trip to Iraq, a visit that was somewhat marred by a bomb attack in Baghdad that killed eighteen people.[94] On his previous trip in July, he had set out the conditions for the total British withdrawal, which included security for the region, growth of democracy, training of Iraqi troops and economic reconstruction. He was now able to say that those objectives had all seen progress. UK forces had been noisily engaged during the year in training over 20,000 Iraqi troops and an equal number of police. Provincial elections were scheduled for January 2009. Economic development, always one of his priorities, was taking off, and during the trip the Prime Minister went to see progress on the deep-water port of Umm Qasr. As he said in his statement on his return to the Commons, £9bn of new investment had been proposed recently in the Basra area.[95] The trip included his final Christmas visit to the troops, and he rounded off the visit with an unusually frank meeting with Nouri al-Maliki. Brown had not found the Iraqi Prime Minister easy to deal with and felt he had been overly critical of the British military's performance in the country, and their final meeting on Iraqi soil focused the ongoing role of the British forces in providing training. Before Brown flew home there was a final task for him to complete and it concerned the memorialisation of those British soldiers who had died fighting in Iraq since 2003. He negotiated the final details over the transfer of the 'Basra Wall', a memorial on which had been inscribed the names of all those who had died, and which was to be shipped back to Britain and placed at the National Memorial Arboretum in Staffordshire at what would be a moving ceremony in March 2010. 'We leave Iraq a better place,' Brown announced before boarding the plane.

On the flight home, Brown worked hard on the text he was to deliver the following day to the House of Commons. On his regular trips to Iraq and Afghanistan, he would typically discuss his brief for the trip during the day of the flight. Early after the return home, he would worry away at the statement he would deliver to Parliament, give his thick felt tip draft to his team, and retire if he could for a few hours' sleep. When he awoke he would fret some more. His statements were always meticulous and he laboured long to ensure that he was entirely happy with them.

This final trip was a key staging post in the ending of Britain's six-year military involvement in Iraq. The next significant step in the process was al-Maliki's visit to the UK in April 2009, which coincided with the last UK patrol and a major Iraq investment conference in London, on which Brown laid great store. The Prime Minister had presided over the withdrawal of British combat troops from Iraq, and had done well in ensuring Britain would have a continuing role in training and economic development in the country. Behind the scenes, much of the credit for the success in this area must go to Brown's senior adviser, Simon McDonald. Even as operations in Iraq were drawing to a close, the military was still preoccupied by the 'stain' on their reputation as a result of perceived British 'failures' in Basra. They were determined to prove to the Americans that they were capable of much better in Afghanistan. For Brown, this chapter would not be closed until his appearance before the Iraq Inquiry, which ended an otherwise successful aspect of his premiership on a bitter note.

Disappointment in the Middle East: January 2009 to May 2010

Brown was back in the region on 19 January 2009 to deal with a different Middle East problem. On 27 December 2008, the Israeli military had begun a major offensive in the Gaza Strip in response to rocket attacks aimed at southern Israel, deploying artillery and airstrikes to target Hamas rocket teams and alleged military facilities. On 3 January, Israeli ground forces entered Gaza.[96] The number of Palestinian casualties was estimated to be between 900 and 1,300, the majority of whom were civilians. In contrast, some twenty to thirty Israelis had been killed by Palestinian rockets. The Israeli response was viewed widely across the world as disproportionate, and in Britain widespread demonstrations took place, including one in London on 3 January that attracted 10,000 protestors.[97] Some of their anger was directed at Brown personally for his perceived lack of action in restraining or speaking out against Israel. The crisis had been preoccupying the Prime Minister over his New Year break. Paramount in his mind was avoiding the furious response his predecessor had provoked in the summer of 2006, widely condemned as a mistake, when for two weeks he had resisted calling for an Israeli ceasefire following Israel's decision to unleash its military might on Lebanon. No single event led Blair to lose so many supporters in the PLP, and it played a large part in the 'September coup' that sped him from office. Brown was instinctively more pro-Israeli than David Miliband and the Foreign Office, but less so than Blair. As the crisis developed, he engaged in regular phone conversations with the Foreign Secretary, who had flown off to New York to negotiate on United Nations Security Council Resolution (UNSCR) 1860, which demanded an immediate ceasefire. Brown was now under fierce pressure from Miliband as well as Fletcher to support it.[98] But he was deeply conflicted: he wanted to support Israeli Prime Minister Ehud Olmert, who was under his own political pressures domestically, but equally, as a compassionate and emotional man, Brown saw the injustice in the whole Palestinian story. 'The human side of the suffering in Gaza affected him deeply,' observes one aide after the Prime Minister's visit in 2008.[99]

On 4 January, after much anguish, Brown bowed to the pressure and called for an Israeli ceasefire,[100] telling Andrew Marr on the BBC the same day: 'I think the key is that the international powers are able to give guarantees.'[101] While UNSCR 1860 was being debated on the evening of 8 January in New York, Olmert tried frantically to ring Brown (in what was the middle of the night in the UK) to plead for the British to be supportive of Israel. But Fletcher refused to wake the Prime Minister up to tell him the calls were coming through (the private office always had difficulty deciding whether or not calls in the middle of the night merited interrupting Brown's sleep). When he was told in the morning about Olmert's call, he was very angry that he had not been woken.[102] UNSCR 1860 was duly approved that night by fourteen members of the Security Council, including Britain, with only the US abstaining.

France's President Sarkozy, always keen on holding international conferences, decided to convene one at the Egyptian resort of Sharm el-Sheikh, to be chaired jointly with the country's President, Hosni Mubarak. As well as Brown and Sarkozy, four other European leaders attended: Germany's Angela Merkel, Spain's José Luis Zapatero, Italy's Silvio Berlusconi, and Czech Prime Minister, and President of the European Council, Mirek Topolánek. The event proved to be a damp squib as, by the time it took place, ceasefires had been announced by both Israel and Hamas.[103] 'We were bounced into it by Sarko, who wanted to show that the European leaders were engaged. There was no point in it, frankly,' says one official dismissively.[104] Brown nevertheless took the opportunity to promise a £30m increase to the £100m of British aid for UN operations in Gaza, and as if to remind his critics of his credentials, he repeated his insistence that the peace process reach a 'two-state' solution based on the 1967 borders.[105] After what was deemed a 'scratchy conference', Brown flew up to Jerusalem by charter plane. Sarkozy was on the same route, and Brown's team put their pilot under pressure to ensure that they arrived at Tel Aviv's Ben Gurion airport ahead of the French, so they could spend more time with Olmert.[106] The pilot did as instructed and Sarkozy's plane came in second.

It was to be Brown's last visit to Israel as Prime Minister. Olmert fell shortly afterwards, and the hardliner Benjamin Netanyahu succeeded him. Brown continued to press for investment in the Palestinian territories and to urge the Israelis towards a lasting peace, but with Olmert gone, the moment had passed. Brown did not give up hope, and was encouraged by an early private meeting with Netanyahu, in which he found the Israeli leader 'incredibly open and understanding of the conflicting international dimensions'.[107] But Netanyahu's public pronouncements continued to be uncompromising and Brown learned the hard way that his private conversations 'counted for nothing'.[108] Brown had laboured hard to achieve progress with the Middle East peace process. Trying to outdo Blair on his own post-premiership path to find a settlement genuinely seems to have played no part in Brown's fervour.[109] It was a bitter pill for Brown to swallow that he had reached the end of his road. So much work and emotional energy and so little to show for it. Like John Major and Blair before him, Brown realised that, in the face of Israeli resistance, the trump card was held not in London but in Washington.

On 20 January 2009, the day after Brown's return from Jerusalem, Obama was sworn in as US President. Before Bush left the White House, Brown had a final phone call with him. 'The two of us have absolutely proved wrong those who said we could not work together,' the President told him. Brown had been handed a list of Bush's achievements as President to recite to sweeten the call. Bush was gratified, and said how touched he had been by the welcome Brown had given him at the Number 10 dinner in the spring. Officials described it as 'a lovely final call'.[110] It was indeed a touching end to a most improbable relationship.

Brown then had a debate with his staff about the language he should use to describe the Obama inauguration. He favoured 'season of hope', but his aides pooh-poohed it, worrying it sounded too much like Obama himself. 'The whole world is watching the inauguration of President Obama, witnessing a new chapter in both American history and the world's history,' was the line Brown finally settled on, and he duly delivered it to journalists in Downing Street. 'He's not only the first black American President ... he is a man of great vision ... a man of great moral purpose.'[111] US Presidents through history figured large in Brown's mental framework. He had made an improbable hit with the forty-third. How would he fare with the forty-fourth, on which so much of the success of the remainder of his premiership would hang?

The Second Bailout and Bonuses: November 2008 to March 2009

A private poll conducted by YouGov for the Labour Party on the eve of the November Pre-Budget Report was greeted with great celebration in Number 10 and at party headquarters because it put Labour and the Conservatives on thirty-nine points each.[112] But the five weeks that led up to the New Year were to be a good time neither for the economy nor for Brown personally. The October bank bailout failed to rejuvenate the lending markets, and businesses and homeowners were being starved of credit. Still petrified by their own precarious situations the banks were incredibly reluctant to let go of their capital. The bailout might have helped save the UK banking system, but it had not galvanised a recovery in the real economy. Unemployment increased dramatically, and by November it was up to 1.92m, its highest level since September 1997.[113] Voters' no doubt unrealistic and unreasonable expectations were not being met by any as yet observable effects of the Pre-Budget Report: for Number 10, it was a politically frustrating moment.

Claims – accidental or otherwise – that Brown had saved the world's banking system began to appear increasingly hubristic. In PMQs on 10 December, in response to Cameron's taunts over the failure of the October bailout to free up credit markets, Brown mistakenly responded: 'We not only saved the world ....' It was a slip of the tongue, and he quickly corrected himself. He would often be at his lowest after a poor PMQs performance and he felt especially bad after this one. 'He felt humiliated and was distraught at his gaffe,' says an aide.[114] Sue Nye stood outside his inner room in Number 12 and intercepted each person before they entered, saying to each one: 'Tell him you haven't heard anything about it. Tell him it's not been picked up by the news.'[115] The episode was a classic example of Nye taking on the role of Brown's emotional guardian, as she would at the weekly diary meetings, ensuring he had enough time to rest and sleep. 'We'll have to cancel that: his head won't be in the right place,' was a typical intervention by her.[116] But not even her fierce protectiveness could save him this time. His detractors pounced. 'Brown could not have said anything more exquisitely designed to persuade his critics that he is living in a fantasy universe while ordinary people suffer and worry back here in the real one,' said arch Brown critic, Martin Kettle.[117]

Brown knew he had lost the initiative in December and was determined to regain it. Over the Christmas holiday, he brooded on a new response and returned in early January 'very focused on the next stage of the banking agenda, full of ideas to try to get lending going in the economy'.[118] He became interested in the relationship between liquidity in the banking system and banks' lending in the real economy – he began to monitor it very closely. A problem was that some capacity had been taken out of the British market – there were fewer institutions offering less money to businesses and individuals wanting to borrow. A bigger problem still was that government policy was pulling the banks in opposite directions: on the one hand it wanted the banks to lend money, on the other it wanted them to rebuild their balance sheets so they were put on a stable footing, which was deemed necessary to boost trust in a still fragile banking system. Turning to the new administration in America, he believed Obama would be making an early announcement on a major fiscal package, and 'was eager to show global leadership by being ahead of the pack'.[119]

As so often in his premiership, the Treasury had different ideas. It was sceptical about 'rigging the market', as it put it, in an attempt to stimulate lending.[120] It thought that, after such a major package in October, the system needed time to adjust and that there was no market reason for any further initiative.[121] The earliest it favoured for any fresh plan, if there had to be one, was when banks reported in late February/early March. So it was irritated when, in early January, it came under 'immense pressure from Number 10 to get things done very quickly'.[122] Brown was irritated too, believing the Treasury was being 'unimaginative' and 'obstructive', endlessly quibbling about micro measures, and deterring him from making the kind of large-scale interventions that he wanted to make.[123] 'The Treasury was incredibly reluctant to throw its full weight behind getting the banks to lend money after the bailout,' says Corry. 'Institutionally, it would resist our calls to ramp up the pressure on the banks, not least because it thought the collapse in demand for credit was as much a problem as supply.'[124] Number 10's anger focused on Darling, who was thought to be too 'apolitical', and was not pushing his Treasury civil servants sufficiently. The problem with the Treasury, Downing Street believed, was that it saw itself as 'gatekeeper to the City'. In contrast, the Prime Minister's team liked to think that they were in touch with the 'real world', where ordinary people had concerns about things such as repossessions and redundancies.[125]

The Liberal Democrats' Vince Cable was one figure who did not agree that Number 10 inhabited the real world. He thought Vadera was 'living in a parallel universe' when she had spoken in an interview on 14 January about seeing the 'green shoots' of economic recovery.[126] It was unfortunate for her that the day she made that statement the FTSE 100 closed down almost 5 per cent and 7,200 job losses were announced. Days earlier, high-street stalwart Woolworths had closed its last branch, a victim of the reduced availability of debt-finance.[127] Vadera's words were an unhappy echo of the phrase used by John Major's Chancellor, Norman Lamont, in 1991, who was widely mocked for the remark.[128]

A head-on clash between Number 10 and the Treasury was inevitable and there would only ever emerge one winner. Downing Street's case for early action was bolstered by growing public concern over banks not lending, especially after all the money the government had offered them. Brown implored banks to lend more, and he oversaw a host of government initiatives to encourage lending and to shore up industry, all to little avail. In favour of acting was Martin Wolf, a leading light at this time for Number 10, who wrote in the *Financial Times*: 'Everything depends on avoiding a deep and prolonged recession ... letting bank lending stay frozen is not an option. The government surely knows that. Do the bankers?'[129] But when should any fresh intervention take place? With the October bailout, there had been an urgent need to act immediately, but now this was absent. The Treasury thus persisted in asserting that the market, not politics, should dictate the timetable for any government action. Heywood and Vadera felt there was a danger that the success of the October bailout might engender complacency, and were keen to act in a collaborative fashion with the Treasury in achieving a permanent solution. They were fortunate to have an ally in Paul Myners at the Treasury, who also understood that the October measures had been far from comprehensive.[130]

The scale of the lending drought shifted the argument in Number 10's favour. To restore confidence and get credit flowing again Brown and Darling discussed a number of options with their officials, and began to focus attention on the case for dealing with the toxic legacy assets that still plagued the balance sheets of the banks. The Treasury had been working with the Bank of England and the FSA to examine different ways of solving this problem. Two options that emerged were to buy the toxic assets from the banks, thereby taking them off balance sheets altogether, as the Irish had done, or employing an insurance scheme, where the government underwrote the value of the toxic assets. According to this model, the banks would retain these assets on their balance sheets, but the taxpayer would be liable for any losses made on them above a certain threshold.[131] Myners was one of those who argued strongly for the latter, believing that it would not involve putting more strain on public finances – any payment would be delayed over many years rather than coming up front as under an asset purchase.[132] The Treasury thought similarly: 'We were cautious about being lumbered with a bunch of zombie banks which had huge losses the taxpayer would have to pick up,' says an official.[133] But how would it be seen if the government was to initiate a further bailout, especially so soon after the October measures? Brown had stated unequivocally then: 'You have to get a restructuring programme right, and I think people would take exception to a situation where we announced a partial proposal then had to come back with another partial proposal.'[134] These words were remembered, and it made it harder to portray the new measures as part of a carefully conceived programme. Officials argued, however, that because the team had lacked 'enough bandwidth in October, and there was so much uncertainty in the air, it was always imagined that there would have to be a second phase'.[135]

Brown and Darling duly announced the second 'bailout' package for British banks on Monday 19 January. It did not indicate, Number 10 believed, that the first recapitalisation in October had failed, but instead it was an additional layer of support reflecting the disintegration of market conditions and the incredibly high stakes involved. It had been a hugely technical undertaking, culminating in yet another 'breathless weekend' at the Treasury. Work on this second bailout saw even more collaboration between the department and Number 10 than on the first recapitalisation package in October. The influence of the Treasury in shaping the details of the final package was accordingly greater.[136] It was so rushed that the asset protection scheme could only be completed in outline, with the detail to come later. Brown had been at the Middle East Conference in Sharm el-Sheikh and in Jerusalem during the days before the announcement, with his team frantically trying to liaise with Number 10 and the Treasury to prepare the Monday statement. The new plan consisted of three separate elements: a new asset protection scheme to deal with toxic assets, more lending to help banks, and a restructuring of the government's stake in the ailing RBS. All were designed to increase supplies of credit to the economy. On the same morning as the announcement, news came of RBS's record losses – the biggest in British corporate history. The bank's shares had immediately plummeted by 67 per cent and those in Lloyds by 34 per cent. By Wednesday, sterling was at its lowest point against the dollar for twenty-three years. 'I am angry about what happened at the Royal Bank of Scotland,' said Brown. 'I think people have a right to be angry that these write-offs are happening.'[137]

Brown was also annoyed because his rescue package had been upstaged: adverse market reaction to the revelations from RBS became entangled with the market assessment of the second bailout. This was partly why this second package went down badly, and was broadly painted by the media as a failure. 'After boasting that he had "saved" the UK's banks, Gordon Brown will hardly have relished the need for a second "comprehensive" bailout package within three months of the first ... much of yesterday's package simply unstitches bits of the October bailout that went wrong,' said the *Financial Times*.[138] 'The previous much-hailed rescue package has failed,' wrote Steve Richards in *The Independent*. 'Voters are alarmed as the government navigates in near darkness armed only with billions of pounds of their money ... the Prime Minister is the equivalent of a doctor who is asked to save the same person's life several times.'[139] More bad news followed, when on 23 January, it was confirmed that Britain was formally in recession. The public debt was confirmed as being above the 40 per cent ceiling that Brown himself had set in 1997. Public finances were 'dreadful beyond belief', wrote Hamish McRae in *The Independent*.[140] That same Friday, interviewed on the BBC's *Today* programme by Evan Davis, Brown refused to accept responsibility for the country's economic problems. Asked about 'boom and bust', he replied: 'I've got to be absolutely frank. We've been dealing with global financial failure.'[141] His own failure to admit responsibility went down badly. 'We're burning up money, which can't go on, and the frenetic activity makes us look like headless chickens,' a Downing Street adviser unhelpfully told Rachel Sylvester of *The Times*.[142] Despite the negative media response at the time it was announced, the second bailout package – which some officials in Number 10 believe was as 'important as the first in terms of stabilising the British banking system' – proved highly effective, particularly the asset protection scheme.[143] 'It's easy with hindsight to forget just how precarious the world financial system was back then: before the G20, before any sign whatsoever of recovery in the world economy. The scheme came at a critical moment, and it was a great success,' another Number 10 official claims.[144] 'If you trace back what happened subsequently, that was the low point in market confidence in relation to the banks and in relation to the UK government being infected by the banks' balance sheets.'[145]

In truth the significance of the second bailout was overshadowed by weekly revelations about the deteriorating state of the economy. In October 2008, Brown had looked to be in command while Cameron was struggling. By the time of the January announcement, their positions appeared almost reversed, and there were no signs of any famed green shoots to hearten the Prime Minister. Then the government came under fire about bank bonuses. Public fury reached a climax, exacerbated by some staff at the nationalised Northern Rock being rewarded a 10 per cent bonus in the week of the second bailout. Chief executive Adam

Applegarth received a £1.7m salary and bonus in his final year, and additionally enjoyed a £760,000 pay-off and a £2.5m pension pot. 'When millions of people are facing pay cuts or even unemployment, this is indefensible,' protested Cable. 'The government should step in to stop this now.'[146] Further anger greeted news that the Treasury itself had agreed to the Northern Rock bonuses, albeit on the condition that specified targets were met. Bankers' pay and bonuses suddenly dominated the political agenda. President Sarkozy had lit the touch-paper when he had told French bankers that they would have to lose their bonuses in return for a second round of state funding. Obama appeared to take an equally strong line on Wall Street, announcing in early February that the employees of banks that had received government aid would have their pay limited.

Then on 5 February news leaked out that Lloyds and RBS were to pay out large bonuses. The Treasury had been quietly satisfied with the work it had done on this issue, but in such a volatile atmosphere, the news was bound to receive a critical audience.[147] Much of the ire focused on RBS's Fred Goodwin personally, who had been given his knighthood in 2004 for 'services to banking'. On the BBC *Politics Show* on 8 February, Liberal Democrat leader Nick Clegg was scathing about the government's announcement that it would hold a review into the bonuses. 'We do not need an inquiry to answer the question of whether bankers should receive bonuses – the right answer is, no.'[148] When the next day Darling announced the appointment of David Walker, formerly of Morgan Stanley, to lead a government review into corporate governance, the news was greeted with 'a chorus of scepticism'.[149] Brown claimed to be 'very angry' about the bankers' bonuses, to which Cameron responded by accusing him of being 'asleep on the job'.[150] An apparently contrite Goodwin appeared before the Treasury Select Committee on 10 February, saying he 'could not be more sorry' for the events of the autumn – a sentiment that aroused little sympathy.

Brown had not anticipated finding his premiership embroiled in a major row over bankers' bonuses, and it left him skewered, unable to make up his mind. 'He never fully decided whether bankers were really bad people who we should criticise at every possible opportunity and curb their powers, or whether they were the driving force of wealth creation and a critical part of our economic success story,' observes a close colleague.[151] As Prime Minister, Brown was keen to be in regular touch with bank leaders and was always content to speak to them. After calls to Victor Blank, chairman of Lloyds TSB, or to other leading bankers, he would become more benevolent towards them.[152] There were other voices in Number 10 – not least Heywood, who had recently left Morgan Stanley, Vadera and Mervyn Davies – who argued that the City was a vital part of the British economy which could be damaged if the government appeared to be too punitive (unless the Obama administration took a similar approach to US banks, the City's main competition).[153] The Treasury took the same line. With its concerns about stability, it was very reluctant to make any moves that might further penalise the banks. Most Number 10 political staff, in contrast, wanted the bank bosses to be given a hard time. 'Vince Cable was running around saying exactly what we believed in,' says one. They had little luck with 'Treasury officials who kept telling us "you don't understand"'.[154]

The Cabinet was equally divided over its response on bonuses. One week Mandelson wagged his finger at a minister who had been critical of banks, the following week he was criticising Goodwin for failing to understand 'how people feel about this – how angry they feel and how outraged they feel'.[155] It took until 17 February for Brown to come out into the open on restricting bonuses, the day after Cameron had proposed a cap of £2,000 on bonuses in banks in which the taxpayer had a large stake.[156] 'Too little too late,' was Osborne's angry response.[157] Brown had failed to act decisively. He would later introduce a one-off 'super-tax' on bonuses in the autumn 2009 Pre-Budget Report, but this was widely seen as being motivated only by the impending general election.

Troubles in Northern Ireland: June 2007 to March 2009

On the evening of 7 March 2009, four soldiers from the Massereene Barracks, near Antrim, came out to collect a pizza delivery. As they did so, two gunmen in a nearby car opened up with semi-automatic rifles, firing sixty shots at the soldiers and the two people delivering the pizzas. Two soldiers, who had been due to fly to Afghanistan, were killed and four other people were seriously injured. They were the first British soldiers to die in Northern Ireland since 1997.[158] The 'Real IRA', the dissident Republican group responsible for the worst atrocity in Northern Ireland's history, the Omagh bombing in August 1998, later claimed responsibility. 'An act of criminal barbarism,' were the words of Northern Ireland Secretary Shaun Woodward. All eyes were on Sinn Fein to see how it would respond. 'I supported the IRA during the conflict. I myself was a member of the IRA, but that war is over. Now the people responsible for last night's incident are clearly signalling they want to resume or restart that war ... I deny them their right to do that,' said the party's chief negotiator and Northern Ireland's Deputy First Minister, Martin McGuinness. Sinn Fein President Gerry Adams described the shooting as an attack on the peace process and said it was 'counter-productive'. Number 10 felt that McGuinness's statement was spot on, Adams's 'less so'.[159]

As soon as he was told the dreadful news, Brown decided to fly to Belfast. His aides believed that something of Sarkozy's 'can-do' style had rubbed off on him.[160] The Prime Minister arrived on 9 March, visited the barracks where the soldiers had been killed, and met with representatives from across the spectrum.

The people of Northern Ireland stand united, he said, behind the peace process, which he described as 'unshakeable'.[161] Yet, at around 9.45 that evening, a police constable, Stephen Carroll, was shot dead while on duty in Craigavon, becoming the first police officer to be murdered since 1998. This time the 'Continuity IRA' claimed responsibility. 'These people are traitors to the island of Ireland,' was the McGuinness response.[162] On 11 March, vigils organised by trade unions and other groups to protest at the killings were held across the province. Many in Britain were shocked at the murders and the breakdown of law and order. Had they been following events more closely, they would not have been so surprised.

Brown's premiership began with great optimism in Northern Ireland. In Blair's final year in office, he had secured an agreement at St Andrews in Scotland designed to restore devolution. On the particularly contentious issues of policing and justice, however, the agreement produced little more than 'agreements to disagree'.[163] The devolution of these powers remained the subject of contradictory assumptions and expectations on the part of the different political parties in Northern Ireland. 'The expectation Brown inherited from Blair and his team was that this could be achieved within twelve months,' says a Northern Ireland Office official,[164] but the euphoria of Blair's final months in office obscured a grim reality. If a solution could not be found on the devolution of policing and justice powers, the political settlement in Northern Ireland might be threatened. Brown had to ensure agreement was reached on this matter.

Elections in March 2007 ended direct rule from Westminster after almost five years, and power-sharing returned to Northern Ireland. The two main parties were the DUP, headed by veteran unionist Ian Paisley, and Sinn Fein, effectively headed in the Northern Ireland Assembly by Martin McGuinness; they became First Minister and Deputy First Minister respectively. Because of the unlikely warmth and geniality they manifested early on in their partnership, they were nicknamed the 'Chuckle Brothers'. Woodward was pleased that Northern Ireland came through the first summer of the new arrangement without problems – this was always a difficult time because of the traditional 'marching season' – but he was apprehensive that Whitehall, the public and indeed the media considered the problems of Northern Ireland solved. He was equally concerned that the Irish government in Dublin had moved its attention elsewhere. Personnel and thinking had changed too. Jonathan Powell, the pivotal figure in the Northern Ireland story for ten years, left with Blair in June 2007, and Brown decreed that from now on, Northern Ireland politicians would not forever be calling and visiting Number 10 – the new locus would be the Northern Ireland Office. In Dublin, Blair's great ally, Bertie Ahern, was to be succeeded as Taoiseach in May 2008 by Brian Cowen. Whereas Blair and Ahern had an immediate rapport,

Brown and Cowen, initially at least, had absolutely none, and the strains of the financial crisis positively drove them apart.[165] The consensus among all parties in June 2007 was that the Provisional Irish Republican Army (PIRA) had disappeared as a force of violence, and that any continuing threats from dissidents were manageable.[166] The first wake-up call came when two Catholic police officers were shot in separate incidents in November 2007. Woodward became seriously alarmed. 'Every bone in my body told me there was going to be trouble,' he says.[167]

As 2008 progressed, the transfer of policing and justice powers began to dominate the Northern Irish political debate. The St Andrews agreement had set a target date of May and while Sinn Fein said it was essential that this be met, the DUP insisted the deadline had been merely 'aspirational'.[168] In response to the DUP's refusal to budge, Sinn Fein vetoed the meeting of Northern Ireland's power-sharing executive in June. It felt betrayed by the DUP and maintained that it had only persuaded its supporters to back the St Andrews agreement on the basis of the transfer of these powers to Stormont at the time agreed. The DUP continued to maintain that the St Andrews agreement had never spoken of full devolution.[169] Many in the DUP, above all the hardliners, had become angry at their leader for signing up to these provisions, and a 'Paisley must go' campaign began to spread. On 4 March, Paisley announced he would stand down from the post of First Minister and, after almost forty years, leadership of the DUP. London had not foreseen this, and it was not best pleased. Peter Robinson, who was elected to replace him on 31 May, was determined not to buckle to Sinn Fein pressure on the transfer of powers. 'It was clear to us that Peter lacked Paisley's leadership attributes, which would be vital to carry the DUP naysayers over the line,' says a Northern Ireland Office official.[170]

Woodward had kept Brown routinely in the loop on Northern Ireland for his first ten months as Prime Minister, saying he did not see any immediate prospect of political resolution as 'neither side would compromise to complete devolution'.[171] But as violence increased from the spring of 2008, the Northern Ireland Secretary began to involve him much more, telling him that the increasing political instability could, in turn, 'pose a severe challenge to the peace process itself'.[172] In June, Robinson and McGuinness travelled on a rare visit to Downing Street to see Brown, but it was clear the divisions over policing and justice powers were entrenched. Unblocking it was a major topic during President Bush's visit to Stormont on 16 June, when he held talks with Robinson, McGuinness, Brown and Cowen. Throughout the whole process, the Prime Minister felt his predecessor's legacy hanging over him and was acutely aware of the expectation that, with competent handling, completion of devolution was in the bag. 'We spent a lot of time mopping up TB's half promises, as well as benefiting from all his good bits,' says an official. 'On the downside, every time we went into a meeting with Gerry Adams, he'd brandish some promise or side deal he alleged Blair had offered him.'[173]

Little flowed from Bush's visit, however, and Brown became increasingly anxious to find a way forward before problems worsened. On 16 September he visited Northern Ireland to assess the position on the ground. 'Leaders here in Northern Ireland must reach agreement between themselves and set the date for the transfer of policing and justice,' he told the Northern Ireland Assembly. Robinson and Nigel Dodds, his deputy, conspicuously refused to applaud these remarks. Intense pressure from London on Robinson and McGuinness eventually resulted in a joint statement from them on 18 November in which they said they both supported the devolution process 'without undue delay'. For a while, a new optimism was felt. Crucially, however, no precise date for the transfer of policing and justice powers was given, though Sinn Fein believed there was a tacit agreement for it to take place in the second half of 2009.[174] This movement was nevertheless sufficient for the five-month hiatus in Northern Ireland Executive meetings to end on 20 November. The deadlock had lasted 154 days.

Stability in the province deteriorated over the next few months. In a rare public interview, the head of MI5, Jonathan Evans, said in January 2009: 'Most people think it's all over in Northern Ireland. Unfortunately it is not. If you look at the last nine months there has been a real upswing in terrorist planning and attempted attacks by dissident republican groups.'[175] Whitehall had become very alarmed about intelligence reports showing growing numbers being recruited by the dissidents. The economic downturn, which had increased unemployment and damaged confidence, played a key part in turning disaffected young people towards the terrorist organisations. On 11 February 2009, a civilian in Derry was shot dead by masked men – the first murder of its kind for over six years.[176] Brown's trip to Northern Ireland on 9 March after the two soldiers' murders marked a turning point in his commitment. He was utterly determined that terrorism would not return to the streets of the province on his watch.[177] The murders of the soldiers and the public protests were not, however, to mark an end to the violence. As Woodward says: 'For the next twelve months, there was to be a terrifying cauldron of escalating tension.'[178]

The Path to the London G20: November 2008 to March 2009

The London G20 summit held on 1 and 2 April 2009 was to be the high point of Brown's premiership. He was at the top of his game, utilising to the full his mastery of international finance and his negotiating skills to secure an agreement of real substance. Here was a Prime Minister whose domestic agenda was still inchoate, who was struggling to maintain the loyalty and respect of his own colleagues, but who was also looked up to by his fellow world leaders.

Coordinating international action to tackle the economic crisis had long been a consistent theme of Brown's. Back in September, when he had first pushed Bush on the idea of a novel 'G20' heads of state meeting, his focus had been squarely on the financial crisis. But as the New Year came around, that crisis entered a new and dangerous phase, with the spectre of global depression and a retreat into isolationism hanging over the world economy. In October, a patchwork of national bailouts had pulled the world's banks back from the brink of collapse, but major lenders remained deeply nervous. Many were now withdrawing to the relative safety of their home markets. The second half of 2008 had seen the biggest contraction in cross-border bank lending and international trade finance since records began in 1977. In the face of increasing anxiety about governments' ability to repay loans, global bond markets were drying up. In November, Pakistan, Hungary and Ukraine had been forced to turn to the IMF for funds to keep their economies turning. Whereas in the autumn policy-makers worried about the collapse of the banks, by early 2009 the withdrawal of liquidity and credit to many indebted emerging markets, particularly in Eastern Europe, meant they now grew increasingly worried about the prospect of the collapse of some national economies with all the international spill-over effects such a nightmare scenario entailed.

It was a new type of challenge and it needed a new type of response. As events gathered pace, it became clear that inaction could have a disastrous impact on the real economy, in all countries. Fears of international trade drying up were real, with world exports falling 27 per cent between February 2008 and February 2009. If governments could not borrow, spending cuts and defaults could follow rapidly. Already in March 2009, the IMF projected that the world economy would contract by between 0.5 and 1 per cent that year, the first such global contraction in sixty years. Falling demand, ceasing trade, and defaults could mean only one thing: a deeper, longer global recession. The effects back at home in Britain would be very real: repossessions, business closures and job losses across the country.

The Washington G20 on 14 and 15 November had turned out to be a modest success, despite the fact that Obama, elected just ten days before, stayed away.[179] Stock markets had already begun to fall across all sectors in the weeks leading up to the summit. As one official recalls: 'The world had just witnessed the near-meltdown of the world financial system and had decided to stop spending.'[180] It was already clear that the crisis was transferring to the real economy, so the scope of the summit had been broadened and G20 leaders had agreed not only to further measures 'to stabilise the financial system', but also that they would use fiscal policy to stimulate demand as appropriate, and ensure that poorer nations retained access to finance through the agency of the IMF and other institutions. 'More than empty rhetoric', was the verdict of *The Economist*, although the newspaper regretted that more concrete conclusions had not emerged.[181]

Washington in November had been a useful staging post for the coming London G20, not least because it had established the value of the forum for heads of government. In a novel move, the Washington meeting had also agreed forty-seven, timetabled, action-points on financial regulation, establishing a tradition of concrete commitments. 'What matters now are the follow-up actions. People are looking to leaders for a global, coordinated and fast response,' said President of the World Bank, Robert Zoellick. That said, Washington still left much to do, and Brown was anxious to build on the agreements.

The Prime Minister had pushed very strongly at Washington for London to host the next heads of government meeting. But the Japanese, as current holders of the G8 heads of government chair, were very keen that it should be in Tokyo. The decision came down to a crunch meeting between Brown and Japanese Prime Minister Taro Aso, at which Brown forcefully argued that, as the holders of the rotating G20 finance ministers' meeting in 2009, Britain should host the meeting in London.[182] It was messy international politics. Sarkozy had also wanted a slice of the action. He had been lobbying world leaders for such a summit, but Brown laid a strong claim to the idea of organising it within the G20 framework. His preference for the G20 over the traditional G8 stemmed from a belief that the larger body more accurately reflected the current state of geopolitics, with its inclusion of the new emerging powers. It also brought in leaders whom he had known well as Chancellor, including Kevin Rudd of Australia and King Abdullah of Saudi Arabia, who would otherwise be excluded. If it was to be only a G8 meeting, he would also have no claim to hold it in London, and, believing himself to be the person with the clearest vision of any world leader, he wanted to be the main man.

When Brown returned from Washington, the London meeting was not quite in the bag.[183] It had been 'effectively decided' that Britain would be the host but the Japanese, who felt sore about missing out, asked that any official announcement be postponed lest they 'lose face'.[184] Brown was thus unable to mention it to the House of Commons on 17 November in his post-G20 statement. But at PMQs on 26 November, to his delight, and Cameron's chagrin, he announced: 'We've agreed with our international partners, and particularly with Japan … that the next meeting of the G20 will be held in London … on 2 April.' He was also able to add that President Obama was planning to attend.[185]

Persuading Obama to come was the icing on a pretty impressive cake. Ever since he had emerged as the frontrunner in the US elections in the summer, the British embassy in Washington had been working hard to persuade his people that the President's first European call-over should be to Britain. 'We'd been working hard to ensure that Gordon Brown was the first European leader through the doors of the White House after the inauguration, and that London was the new President's first major visit,' says Britain's ambassador to the US, Nigel Sheinwald.[186] The difficulty was finding a precise date for the conference. Obama's aides had written in his diary that he was to visit Strasbourg on 4 April to mark the sixtieth anniversary of the founding of NATO, so Brown's team scheduled the London G20 for two days earlier to fit around this timetable.[187] What swayed it was Obama's staff recognising the importance to the US of the G20 process in strengthening financial stability across the world.[188] The added highlight for Number 10 was securing an agreement that Obama would have an exclusive bilateral with Brown before the summit: an event which Britain's increasingly frustrated generals took careful note.[189]

As the financial crisis continued to spread, Brown's ambitions for the G20 began to take shape. He wanted to secure nothing less than a comprehensive, global plan to restore confidence across national economies, and to ensure the continued functioning of trade and the global economy. Brown's aims were five-fold. First, to reassure global credit markets, additional funds would be needed for countries facing liquidity crises. Further, trade finance would need to be restored. On all this, there was broad international agreement. Brown's distinct contribution would be to continually pressurise his fellow leaders to ratchet up the amount of resources made available to stimulate growth. Second, on the real economy, Brown and Obama in particular wanted more emphasis on the coordination of different countries' plans for fiscal and monetary stimulus, to show unity to markets, and to enhance their overall impact. Brown also had one eye on domestic politics here: he needed to show there was international support for borrowing in bad times. The experience of the 1930s, when countries had pursued their own individual policies to the detriment of others, loomed large in Brown's mind. In the event, other nations (in particular Germany) were reluctant to coordinate fiscal and monetary policy (despite their own domestic stimulation policies), and so Obama and Brown drew back from pushing specific, further stimulus at the G20. Third was to act to prevent protectionism from occurring, by giving a kick-start to boosting free trade. Fourth, action was needed specifically to help the world's poor, important both as an end in itself and because of the effect that economic failures in the developing world would have on the global economy. This was to be done by using IMF gold and Special Drawing Rights (SDRs) and other resources. A final objective was improved financial regulation to prevent a recurrence of the crisis. France and Germany were keen to see action to fix the system: Sarkozy in particular rose to the idea of 'learning the lessons' of the financial crisis. What he called 'Anglo-Saxon free markets' had, he believed, brought the world's financial system close to disaster: the lessons of the episode must be understood. He had even suggested initially that the Washington summit be held at Ground Zero in New York for added symbolic importance.

The decks were now cleared, and Brown's parliamentary announcement of the London G20 gave the green light to Whitehall. Departments exploded into action, with the Foreign Office, Cabinet Office and Treasury coordinating preparations. 'The whole of Whitehall wanted a piece of it,' says one official. 'In terms of political sexiness this was the big thing in town.'[190] Some had good ideas, others less so. Harriet Harman favoured a slide show for global leaders about equality issues. The idea had merit for a centre-left government, but Downing Street erupted with disbelief. 'It showed that she simply didn't get what was going on,' recalls one Number 10 official.[191] Amid the clamour, Number 10 unequivocally asserted its pre-eminence. This was a leaders' meeting, and it was Brown's team alone that would lead. Jon Cunliffe drew personnel into his Cabinet Office team from the Foreign Office and the Bank of England, himself taking the role of head 'sherpa'. Vadera's people were to provide 'drive and imagination', while Heywood chaired cross-Whitehall meetings with his usual commanding style. 'It was Jeremy's finest hour in many ways,' recalls one colleague.[192] 'He was the key person. And kept a reasonably calm head when all about him were losing theirs,' says another. [193] Only Heywood, Vadera and Cunliffe were allowed anywhere near the big decisions.[194] Every last detail was overseen by them and Brown. One further official, Jonathan Portes, a respected Whitehall economist, who had spent much of the year discussing with Vadera the operation of the global banking system and finance, was to play a major, if largely unseen role, reaching out to academics.

The tight organisation was a striking contrast to Brown's day-to-day style. One official from outside Number 10 described it as 'unique in the Gordon Brown world, where [often] no one was told what their specific role was and everyone tried to do everything'.[195] But it was Brown himself who drove the process, pushed people to do more, and tested ideas. 'From November, he just never stopped,' recalls a senior official.[196]

Between November 2008 and February 2009, Brown capitalised on the international prestige he had won from his handling of the banking crisis to embark on a series of foreign trips and interventions, during which he forged personal relations ahead of the London G20. 'He was on fire from the autumn until April 2009,' says Gavin Kelly.[197] Among the leaders he needed on side early on were Premier Wen Jiabao and President Hu Jintao of China, Prime Minister Manmohan Singh of India and President Obama. 'He was eager to explore where he could push things forward, and he put considerable personal effort into doing just that,' says one official.[198] A festival of phone calls occurred, which climaxed in March, when he spoke to every one of the major leaders, often several times, in a friendly but 'very persuasive and serious manner'.[199] He sought to understand their positions more clearly, ascertain their concerns and political difficulties at home, and discover how he could best nudge them towards agreeing to his communiqué.[200] Not all appreciated his frenzy. 'This was the time when we had the feeling that nothing was being done except the G20: it was sucking resource out of every part of government,' complains one minister.[201]

Brown did not just stick to the telephone. Where he could, he tried to see leaders face to face. He already enjoyed a good relationship with King Abdullah of Saudi Arabia, who had impressed him during his five-day trip to the Gulf States at the beginning of November 2008, which also took in the UAE and Qatar. Brown knew the financial strengths of the Gulf Cooperation Council (GCC) states and their importance to the global economy, and hoped to persuade them to commit funds to the IMF, given the pressure it was under in this period. As always, Brown would want to talk to leaders on his own, and topics discussed with Abdullah ranged far beyond loans, oil and economics.[202] He had to work harder on his until-now uneven relationship with the UAE, and he sought to improve it. So too did they, putting him up at the impossibly lavish 'seven star' Emirates Palace Hotel in Abu Dhabi. A Western tourist approached Brown in the foyer and his aides feared a volley of criticism but the man said: 'Thank you for everything you're doing with the global economic situation.' It was a trivial incident, but it struck the aides, and the Prime Minister, as evidence of his new standing. He took with him a powerful group of British business leaders, as well as his new Business Secretary. When they touched down, his party had been told that custom demanded the most important person had to come off the plane last. Brown turned to Mandelson and said: 'That's you, Peter.'[203] The trip saw the Brown and Mandelson relationship at its early high point of trust and closeness. Officials were struck by the ease of their banter and laughter at the end of each day in Brown's hotel suite.[204]

Brown's 14 December visit to India, arranged before the London G20 had been finalised, gave him the opportunity to prepare the ground with Singh. He found it comparatively easy to convince the Indian Prime Minister of his position and to iron out some minor disputes over the World Bank. Singh had been impressed with Brown's sympathetic diplomacy in the aftermath of the terrorist attacks in Mumbai on 26 and 27 November, which made the Indian government better disposed towards Britain.[205] Brown had immersed himself in the detail of the terrorist outrage and convened a meeting of COBRA; British officials believe he played an important role in restraining India's response to Pakistan.[206] 'He hit the right note with real precision,' says British high commissioner to Delhi Dickie Stagg.[207]

On 30 January, the Prime Minister was off to Davos to argue the case again for coordinated action. His team felt the atmosphere at the World Economic Forum was 'very doom and gloom' but Brown told his audience that they need not despair: 'This crisis is not an act of God, it was caused by man, and man can solve it by working together internationally.'[208] His speech was interrupted by spontaneous rounds of applause, which is not the norm at these sober meetings.[209] Brown left reasonably content with his performance, even if it had not matched the euphoria of his first Davos trip in January 2008, and even if the star this year was not him, but Merkel.[210]

On his return to the UK, he was driven from RAF Northolt straight to Chequers, where he was dining with Chinese Premier Wen, the first foreign leader to be afforded the honour of a visit to the Prime Minister's country retreat by Brown.[211] The two men had struck up a friendship when Brown was Chancellor and they enjoyed talking economics together. Wen was an admirer of the eighteenth-century founder of classical economics, Adam Smith, as was Brown, who, like Smith, hailed from Kirkcaldy.[212] Both agreed that the real Adam Smith was to be found in *The Theory of Moral Sentiments* (1759), where he made less of the glories of capitalism than of the limits of markets in achieving social cohesion, rather than in *The Wealth of Nations* (1776).[213] Brown wanted Wen to put pressure on the IMF to increase its support for struggling countries, and to boost China's domestic stimulus package (it subsequently instituted the most significant stimulus of any major economy).[214] He was delighted that the dinner had succeeded in getting the Chinese leader on board. At breakfast the next morning, Brown was relaxed and ranged discursively about his estimation of people and institutions. 'I always value judgment above intelligence,' he said, thinking of the Foreign Office which he felt gave him ten different ways to solve a problem but without helping him see which was the right one.[215] His Cabinet continued to be a disappointment to him, but he relished the company of the world leaders, and he was in an upbeat mood that crisp, late January morning, feeling an increasing confidence that he was on the right course in his handling of the economic crisis. Brown did not have many instances as Prime Minister when he felt on top of things and relished his prospects of the job, but this was one such moment.

On 19 February, he visited Berlusconi, who treated him to a lavish lunch where all the food, including the pasta and ice cream, bore the green, white and red colours of the Italian flag.[216] Brown was growing to like Berlusconi more, and they made small talk about football, but he remained queasy with the Italian leader's vulgar flaunting of his wealth and philandering.[217] Berlusconi was all ebullience, saying naturally he was supportive of Brown's G20 goals, but the Prime Minister was never entirely certain how deep this support ran. Brown's Italian visit included a stopover at the Vatican for a 35-minute audience with the Pope, whom he invited to visit Britain (which the Catholic leader did in September 2010). That morning, *L'Osservatore Romano*, the Vatican newspaper, carried a front-page article by Brown on the financial crisis.[218] His relationship with Benedict XVI had been cemented when the pontiff had agreed to purchase the first 'vaccine bond'. 'Thanks to this bond more than $1.6bn has been subscribed, and 500 million children will have been vaccinated between 2006 and 2011,' said Brown during the visit, thanking the Pope for his endorsement.[219]

The trip to the Vatican left a deep impression on Brown. He was always intensely private about his religious faith and had no wish to have it minutely examined, and ridiculed, in the way that Blair's had been. On his trip to see King Abdullah the two had spoken about Islam, Christianity, and inter-faith dialogue. When in Scotland, he would always go to the local church at North Queensferry, where his son, Fraser, had been christened and where the two boys would attend Sunday school. The local vicar, the Reverend Sheila Munro, had married the Browns and had helped preside with great sensitivity over the funeral for their daughter, Jennifer. The influence of his father flowed very deep within him, and being brought up in that intensely Christian household shaped his whole way of thinking about himself and the world. After he went to university, religion became less important to him, but the loss of Jennifer, and Fraser's cystic fibrosis, turned him inwards. Brown began reading his father's sermons again, which had been published under the title *A Time to Serve* in 1994 to celebrate his eightieth birthday. He found much solace in them.

The US Trip: March

Just two weeks after Rome, and after a rushed and inconclusive meeting of European G20 leaders in Berlin, Brown went to see Obama. Every leader in the world wanted to be the first into Washington, hoping that some of the new President's magic would rub off on them. That honour was accorded on 24 February to Taro Aso of Japan. The race then switched to which EU leader would be the first. Sarkozy was said to have a military aircraft on 24-hour standby, waiting for the phone call to the Elysée.[220] But the British lobbying to get their man in first succeeded. Brown was not, however, the first British Prime Minister to see Obama. That honour fell to Tony Blair, who had shaken hands with him at the National Prayer Breakfast in Washington in early February.[221] As ever, Blair seemed to be one step ahead of Brown. Irwin Stelzer, a veteran US journalist and writer for *The Sunday Times*, nevertheless thought that it was a 'brilliant coup' to be the first European in, especially as Obama was 'such an anti-British President'.[222]

Obama was certainly no admirer of Britain's recent colonial history, above all in his father's native Kenya, where the Mau Mau uprising had been brutally suppressed in the 1950s. But far more significant to any change in tone towards Britain was his re-evaluation of US foreign policy. He decided not to engage in personal diplomacy, like Clinton and George W. Bush, and where he did, it would be with the leaders of China, India and Brazil. Obama believed that Britain's strategic importance to the US lay in it being at the centre of Europe.[223] Some of the key figures in the President's team like Denis McDonough and Tom Donilon were irritated by British efforts to bolster Brown's domestic reputation by basking in their man's reflected glory and they thought, as did some British diplomats, he risked demeaning himself by being so eager.[224] 'Almost everyone felt a little unloved by Obama. Not for nothing was his nickname "Spock",' says one Foreign Office official.[225] The White House team had yet to bond with their opposite numbers in London, and though the former had assented to the trip, they were not yet ready to go the extra mile for the Prime Minister.

Brown arrived on the evening of 2 March at Andrews Air Force Base on a chartered British Airways plane, accompanied by what Number 10 saw as a more than usually cynical press corps. Washington was covered in a blanket of snow when they arrived and the Prime Minister met Obama before lunch on 3 March in the Oval Office for a bilateral. This was their third meeting: their earlier encounters, in April 2008 at the British embassy in Washington, and in July in Downing Street, just before Brown left for Southwold, had gone conspicuously well. The men shared a centre-left outlook and belief in the necessity of government intervention as a force for good in the world.[226] Their hour-long conversation was followed by a formal lunch in the White House dining room with their respective teams, which overran 'in a most satisfactory way' (Foreign Office-speak for the meeting going well).[227]

Over the meal, the two leaders discussed the G20, and Brown left the White House team in no doubt of his stellar ambitions for it.[228] Brown and Obama were on the same page when it came to the need for fiscal stimulus, and the President reassured the Prime Minister that he shared his goals for the summit.[229] The encounter allowed Brown to gain a much clearer understanding of Obama's evolving thinking on foreign policy – something Number 10 and the Foreign Office were very eager to do. On Iraq, he learned more about the new administration's desire to maintain the existing strategy, though with some tonal differences. With British forces all but departed, there was little of substance to discuss here. On Afghanistan, the White House was appreciative of Britain's contribution – second only to America's – but, unhelpfully for Brown, it had yet to conclude what line it was finally going to adopt, which left the British operation in a state of limbo.[230] On Iran, the administration was still going through a similar strategic review, but was hoping to have a more constructive engagement, initially with Mahmoud Ahmadinejad, with the hope that the Iranian elections would lead to more constructive leadership – a position that was strongly supported by the British. On the Middle East, Obama had signalled his early determination to find a new way forward with his appointment of former US Senator George Mitchell as his special envoy. The President indicated he would be firm with Netanyahu about Israeli settlements on the West Bank and Brown 'egged him on' in this.[231] The Prime Minister was also delighted to hear a US president enthuse about the need to tackle climate change and move towards a low-carbon economy. Trade policy was almost the only issue on which there were significant differences between the leaders. Obama's instincts were liberal, but under union pressure he did not feel able to do more to back free trade or to try to unlock the Doha negotiations.

Brown returned to the British embassy that afternoon, content with the meeting, but deeply anxious about the following day, when he was to give the most important foreign policy speech of his premiership. He had been invited to address both Houses of Congress, only the fifth British Prime Minister to be afforded this honour (after Churchill, Attlee, Thatcher and Blair). The invitation was originally the idea of the Speaker of the House of Representatives, Nancy Pelosi, but the Foreign Office downplayed this, claiming it 'was something she said to everyone'. However, Sheinwald followed it up and, with support from Pelosi, as well as Vice-President Joe Biden and Senator John Kerry, the event was confirmed.[232]

Here was an enormous moment for Brown. 'Most of us were terrified,' says one member of his team. 'We knew it would either be a triumph or a disaster.'[233] Brown was nervous because he was so determined to get it right: there would be no second opportunity for a speech like this. He took a long walk in the garden of the ambassador's residence with Tom Fletcher to calm himself and rehearse his lines. 'He was getting in the zone for one of the biggest moments in his political life,' recalls Muir.[234] As a confidence player, raising his levels of self-belief would be critical to the success of the speech. His team worried that the text, long slaved over, was over-cooked. It was mostly his own writing, but Bob Shrum and Muir had significant input on the argument, with many of the words and phrases penned by speechwriter Kirsty McNeill.[235] As anxious as Brown was to please his audience, he was adamant he would not shy away from difficult issues. 'He wanted to be bold and to speak about issues that Congress didn't necessarily want to hear,' says McNeill.[236]

Brown's forty-minute speech on 4 March began at 11am with opening lines praising Obama and 'an America renewed under a new President' – a country whose 'faith in the future has been, is and always will be an inspiration to the whole world'. One of his seventeen standing ovations came when he spoke of his feelings for the US: 'Early in my life I came to understand that America is not just the indispensable nation, it is the irrepressible nation.' Tribute was paid to American military heroism. He then turned to the themes of the G20 and spoke passionately about the need for global action with the US at the heart. 'No matter where it starts, an economic crisis does not stop at the water's edge. It ripples across the world. Climate change does not honour passport control. Terrorism has no respect for borders. The new frontier is that there is no frontier, the new shared truth is that global problems need global solutions.'

So far, so good. He now spoke out on climate change: 'I believe that you, the nation that had the vision to put a man on the moon, are also the nation with the vision to protect and preserve our planet earth.' Some Republicans refused to applaud.[237] More audaciously still, he raised the banner of free trade, telling a sceptical audience that, 'history tells us that, in the end', protectionism 'protects no one'. Unafraid to be partisan, he announced an honorary British knighthood for his friend, the Democrat Senator Edward Kennedy. He knew his praise of Roosevelt and his New Deal, and his extolling Obama for pursuing similarly expansionary policies, would not receive universal applause. Nor did they. Nonetheless, the speech was Brown at his oratorical best, and he knew at once that he had struck the right note. The final applause was warm. 'The speech had been a very big thing for him. He loved it and it gave him great confidence, and boosted his spirits that spring as he prepared for the G20,' says Muir.[238] True, it was not an historic speech, on the level of Churchill or Thatcher, or even Blair speaking on 20 September 2001 in the wake of 9/11. But he still acquitted himself well, and spoke sense about the world and the actions political leaders needed to take urgently. In London his team in Downing Street were glued to the television screen in the horseshoe. Watching it they felt a huge sense of pride and admiration for him. It was one of his very best moments as Prime Minister. 'It made everything else worthwhile,' says one.[239]

On the flight that night back to the UK, Brown plonked himself down next to McNeill. Rather than wanting to talk to her about how well the speech had gone, his mind was already racing ahead to speeches he could make over the remaining four weeks building up to the London G20. Someone whispered in his ear that he should leave her alone as she had not slept properly for days. He muttered an apology and slunk off into the dark.[240] While the plane sped back through the night a call came through from Obama. The White House press secretary briefed out that the call had given the President a chance to congratulate Brown on his speech to Congress and to say how much he was looking forward to seeing him again at the beginning of April in London.[241] What the press spokesman did not say in public was that Obama had also shared with Brown how angry he had been by the way that his guest had been treated by the British press.

So why did one of Brown's team describe this as 'the worst overseas trip in his three years'?[242] After all, it had by any measure been a coup to have got in to see Obama so early and for him to have performed so well before Congress. Number 10 thought the British media were determined to belittle the trip and had convinced themselves that Obama was out to snub Brown, whether in irritation at British colonial history, or because he considered the Prime Minister too pushy. Negative briefing about Brown may well have come from disillusioned diplomats, of whom there were increasing numbers, or even the military.[243]

The bone of contention was a press conference, or rather, the absence of one. Brown's team had led the reporters to believe that there would be the traditional press conference with the President in the White House's Rose Garden, and they had prepared themselves accordingly. But when the British party landed, the embassy texted a message to them that Obama's team did not want to go along with the event. The most they would agree to was a 'pool spray', with two or three journalists coming in to the Oval Office at the end of the meeting. Sensing a media disaster in the making, Brown's team spent two hours on the phone to Obama's chief of staff team, eventually persuading them to agree to 'Nick Robinson, Adam Boulton and the rest of the pack' coming in. To Obama's team, 'this was their first real taster of how ridiculous the demands of our media could be', recalls one senior official who attended the trip. 'The White House were pretty scathing about all of our press guys because they asked only the usual kind of trivia, rather than about Afghanistan or the G20 – issues that Obama was focused on.'[244] The journalists, for their part, felt cheated and angry: they had come a long way for so little. Number 10 put the gaffe down to 'the Obama team being still in their early days in the White House, and frankly they hadn't checked with us'.[245] The White House tried to explain that Prime Minister Aso of Japan did not have a press conference at the end of his visit, that the weather had been too cold in Washington for them to use the Rose Garden, and that such an event had never been on the cards.[246] Obama's own efforts to be positive were disregarded. To a question from the BBC's Nick Robinson, he responded: 'This notion that somehow there is any lessening of that special relationship is misguided.' To ITV's Tom Bradby he said: 'This is my third meeting with Prime Minister Brown, and I'd like to think that our relationship is terrific.'[247] Little of this was reflected in the British media reports. 'They were determined beforehand to write the trip up as a disaster,' is the verdict of one British official.[248]

To the utter despair of Number 10, the 'snub' thesis was given a further twist with a prolonged discussion of the ritual exchange of presents, rather than over the substance of the trip and his speech to Congress. Brown gave Obama a pen-holder carved from oak timbers from the *HMS Gannet* – a ship used to suppress the slave trade. Wood from its sister ship, *HMS Resolute*, had been used to make a desk in the Oval Office.[249] He also gave the President the complete eight-volume set of the Churchill biography by Martin Gilbert (and Randolph Churchill, who wrote the first two volumes), personally inscribed by Gilbert himself.[250] The White House made a point of saying that the pen set would be displayed on the 'Resolute desk', while the books were to be placed in the President's personal study adjoining the Oval Office.[251] Obama, in contrast gave Brown (on account of his fondness for films), a collection of twenty-five classic American films on DVD. This was interpreted as another snub. 'Mr Obama's gift ... could have been bought from any high-street store [and] looked like the kind of thing the White House might hand out to the visiting head of a minor African state,' decreed the *Daily Telegraph*.[252] Not all the media condemned the trip. Oliver Burkeman in *The Guardian* commented on Brown's success in instilling a kind of 'Pavlovian reaction' from Congressmen during his speech, as they 'kept on leaping to [their] feet as internationalist left-leaning notion after internationalist left-leaning notion tumbled from the podium'.[253] Brown did not let the press reaction, which his team tried earnestly to keep from him, disturb him too much. His mind was already focused on his next task.

The World Tour: 24 to 28 March

As March progressed, searching questions began to be asked about the G20, and whether Brown's expectations were realistic. Optimism was heightened by Obama indicating he would be stimulating the US economy, and the White House economic adviser, Larry Summers, urging others to follow suit and agree to coordinated action. But then Merkel visited the UK on 14 March and poured cold water on the idea of a second fiscal stimulus in Germany.[254] It all added to a sense that Brown was being hubristic and was heading for his latest disaster. His call for the IMF and the World Bank to provide significantly more support to economically weaker countries to prevent them being ravaged by the crisis was regarded with scepticism.[255] Was this asking too much?

On 14 March, as requested by the G20 leaders when they had met in Washington in November, the G20 finance ministers convened near Horsham, West Sussex, to discuss their findings on how to deal with the economic turbulence. The main topic was financial regulation and here traditional stereotypes loomed large. 'The French and Germans worried that the villain of the piece – Anglo-Saxon market behaviour – was being let off the hook because the focus was now on the world economy,' remembers one British official.[256] The meeting ended leaving much of the final detail on regulatory reform, and the size of the IMF support, for the leaders to resolve.

With one week to go, and much still to be decided, Brown embarked on his final lobbying ahead of the London meeting by going on a mini 'world tour'. Some of his aides questioned whether this was the best use of Brown's time given the amount he had on his plate ahead of the G20.[257] First up was Strasbourg on 24 March, for an address to the European Parliament. 'One of the most eagerly awaited events of the European Union's 2009 political calendar,' wrote Tony Barber, the then Brussels bureau chief of the *Financial Times*.[258] In words that were generally positively received, Brown laid out his well-trodden agenda on international cooperation. 'We can together deliver the biggest financial stimulus the world has ever seen, the biggest cut in interest rates, the biggest reform of the international financial system, the first international principles governing banking remuneration, the first comprehensive action against tax havens and, for the first time in a world crisis, new help for the poor,' he told them.[259] Some impact was lost due to comments by Daniel Hannan, the Tory MEP, who launched a strong assault on Brown, climaxing with the words that John Smith had used to describe Major in 1992 – 'the devalued prime minister of a devalued government'.[260] More damaging still were comments made by Mervyn King just as Brown's plane was leaving for Strasbourg. Appearing before the Treasury Select Committee, the Bank of England Governor said: 'Given how big those deficits are, I think it would be sensible to be cautious about going further in using discretionary measures to expand the size of those deficits.'[261] This was a direct clash with Brown's message that day in Strasbourg that governments should do 'whatever it takes to create growth and the jobs we need'.[262] George Osborne seized on King's words, claiming they vindicated the Conservatives' position. This intervention badly damaged the Brown-King relationship; it would not recover during Brown's remaining time in Number 10.[263] With 'trade plummeting, countries facing the prospect of no funding, with the knock-on impact on the rest of the global economy catastrophic – it would be freefall', in the words of one aide; the Prime Minister's exasperation was palpable.[264]

There were other ill omens for Brown's tour. On 25 March, the day he started his travels with a flight to New York, the Treasury, for the first time since 1995, was unable to find sufficient numbers of buyers in an auction of conventional gilts.[265] The Czech Prime Minister Topolánek, whom Number 10 regarded as a loose cannon, now weighed in. He had lost a confidence motion in his country's legislature but remained EU President, and described the Anglo-American stimulus and bank bailout plans as 'the way to hell'.[266]

The prime aim of the New York leg of Brown's tour was a meeting at the UN with Secretary-General Ban Ki-moon, whom he regarded as a firm ally. At the joint press conference following their meeting, Brown promised that poorer nations would not be overlooked at the London summit. Looking after weaker economies was a vital G20 goal, and it was vital, too, for gaining broad support for the final communiqué. Before he left New York, Brown took part in a debate hosted by the *Wall Street Journal* in the grand ballroom at the Plaza Hotel, where he was questioned by the *Journal*'s managing editor Robert Thomson on deflation, reserve currencies and the G20 agenda. Again the Prime Minister stressed the importance of measures to revive world trade.[267] He also moved to play down expectations on the prospect of agreeing a co-ordinated stimulus, saying: 'Nobody is suggesting that people come to the G20 meeting and put on the table the budget that they're going to have for the next year.'[268] Henry Kissinger queried from the floor whether the brevity of the summit would preclude the realisation of its objectives. Brown gave a vigorous performance, though he repeated some of the same jokes that he had used at the Council of Foreign Relations the previous year, such as his amusement at reading a protestor's banner calling for a 'World Wide Campaign Against Globalisation', giving some who had been present at the earlier meeting a sense of déjà vu.[269] He charged on to New York University, where he took part on a panel with former US Secretary of State Madeleine Albright and former Chair of the Federal Reserve Paul Volcker. There his audience were left in no doubt about Brown's commitment to a multilateral approach in tackling the financial and economic crises.[270]

An overnight flight took his party south on 26 March to Brasilia where he met President Lula da Silva, whom Brown was 'determined to enlist as an ally'.[271] Some in Brown's team felt that the following press were now so toxic that they were positively encouraging South Americans to make statements that would embarrass him. They did not have to try hard with Lula, who said that the financial crisis had been caused by 'white people with blue eyes',[272] drowning out the Prime Minister's comments about the importance of strengthening world trade. Brown flew on to São Paulo, where he addressed Brazilian business leaders and then Santiago, where, on 27 March, he spoke to Chilean President Michelle Bachelet, and attended a meeting of the Progressive Governance Conference. The import of Brown's message was diminished here at the joint press conference where Bachelet pointed proudly to Chile's record of fiscal discipline, saying when the economy had been strong the government had built up savings in anticipation of the hard times – something the British government had failed to do. The press wrote it up as the Prime Minister being lectured by Latin Americans on how to run the British economy. *The Times* said that Bachelet's words 'could have been scripted by David Cameron',[273] while Osborne rounded on Brown, lamenting that Britain was not in a position where the government could spend money without 'recklessly adding to national debt'.[274]

One of the jokes among the press corps was that, with things going so badly for him, Brown should 'apply for asylum in Chile'. His staff worked overtime to keep the newspapers away from him, in a different part of the plane.[275] Spirits were kept up with an impromptu birthday party for Stewart Wood and Fletcher, with bounteous champagne toasts, as they were on their final leg within South America. His aides could not, however, keep from him the details of a breaking story about Home Secretary Jacqui Smith's husband claiming for the cost of a pornographic film on her parliamentary expenses. The Prime Minister was informed about the episode as he boarded the plane back to London from Chile. His initial reaction was to focus on the details of the claim itself, rather than consider the government's response to the wider issue of MPs' expenses, which was then becoming a major political story.[276] Brown was upset for her, but he did not allow himself to become unduly disturbed by it. 'The only thing that mattered to him now was how well the G20 went the following week,' says an aide.[277] The mood on the long journey back from South America was upbeat. When the cabin lights dimmed and his party were drifting off, Brown was seen concentrating furiously on his papers with his thick felt tip pen, and was constantly on the phone, as he had been all trip, ensuring his fellow leaders, including Dmitry Medvedev of Russia and India's Singh, were coming into line. There was no effort he would spare to make the G20 work. 'It felt like we'd been to the very end of the world to make it a success,' says one member of his team.[278]

Brown returned to London shattered, but even more sure that he was right to set the bar for London very high. 'His attitude was, unless we do, we're not going to achieve anything worthwhile.'[279] Irritation was caused in Number 10 by former British ambassador to Washington, Sir Christopher Meyer, suggesting that Brown was seeking the unattainable. 'The leaders gathering in London are in for an experience that ranges from the soul-crushing to the bizarre ... I pray for some as yet unseen rabbit to emerge ... Otherwise, we are left to weep for the once proud reputation of British diplomacy, after the return of our Prime Minister from a world tour of serial ambushes and crushed expectations,' he wrote in the *Daily Telegraph*.[280] His verdict, unhelpfully, was echoed in private by some of Brown's Cabinet ministers, including even his two most senior – Darling and David Miliband – who sought to dampen expectations of what the summit could achieve.[281] Brown's retort to the hubris charge was that, unless he cranked up the expectations of the London G20, and put huge pressure on leaders to agree to what some thought impossible, the conference would fall short of what the exceptional economic events demanded.[282]

The London G20: 1 to 2 April

As early as January, Brown and his close team had identified their major wish list. But right up until the final days, much remained up in the air. The final communiqué, over which he held sole possession, was taking shape, but the text had still not been agreed even when the leaders began to arrive in London in late March. One of the biggest problems was time. 'You didn't have the luxury of a year to prepare the summit,' comments one official, sardonically. 'You had to run with the ideas that cropped up, weed out those that promised little, and think up new ideas on a whim.'[283] This problem was exacerbated by the protracted US political cycle. Although Obama had been inaugurated on 20 January, his team was not fully in place until several weeks after that. British officials were exasperated to find no one in the American administration with whom the contents of the emerging communiqué could be discussed, which meant the negotiations, with the US at least, became very last-minute. 'It wasn't that they didn't want to talk, but that there wasn't anyone to talk to,' recalls one official.[284] 'We did most of the negotiation with them in the last six weeks before the summit.' Another problem was the unpredictable and changing international economic climate. 'The situation wasn't stable, so what you thought might have been the right thing to do in December looked inadequate by February,' says an official.[285] 'We knew the boxes we wanted to tick – avoiding depression and a return to protectionism, helping poorer nations, regulatory reform, and so on – even if we were not sure which proposals we would tick them with,' says another.[286]

They were determined to secure an agreement to inject funds into the global economy to avoid the development of a huge capital accounts fiasco, resembling the Asian crisis of the late 1990s. Hungary had emerged as a particular worry, 'teeter-tottering' (in the words of one official) since the last quarter of 2008, and the Polish and Czech economies had also deteriorated significantly. Securing a promise to increase IMF funds to ensure there was not a run on these emerging Eastern European markets had emerged as the preferred solution. Much progress had been made by late March on all the five objectives for the G20 Brown had outlined at the start of the year, except on the fiscal and monetary stimulus.

The Prime Minister realised he would not achieve a full second stimulus, principally due to German and French opposition, so he pulled back from this. But he did want the communiqué to reflect the general case for a stimulus, not least because it would help domestically – the Budget was imminent and he knew the borrowing figures would be terrible. Brown had succeeded in adhering to his initial decision that the summit would focus on international economics and finance alone, ignoring calls for the G20 format to discuss wider issues, such as global governance and climate change (although he was keen that development issues were not ignored). 'That's all really important, but we can deal with that after we've dealt with the crisis. [The G20] is a new piece of equipment, and we don't want to overload it,' was his view.[287]

Brown had returned from his trip with a bump. On Monday 30 March he worked from Number 10 and is described as being 'in despair' and 'very, very pessimistic'. He was in a foul mood and ranted at his officials and aides for setting the bar too low. At such times, they had learned how to bite their lips and not react or get upset. At different points during the day, he exploded, declaring: 'It is all over.'[288] The following day, however, he woke up in a better place and worked frenetically all day, endlessly on the phone to leaders, ordering his staff around, and believing that he could achieve a resolution.[289] During the day he travelled to the City of London to speak at St Paul's Cathedral – the first serving Prime Minister to do so – on the importance of the London summit. His team urged him not to make the speech as they were concerned it would eat into crucial preparation time. Brown, however, was determined to use the opportunity to make what he now considers to be his most important political statement as Prime Minister[290] in which he claimed that the root cause of the financial crisis was moral in nature. The irresponsibility and greed that underpinned the behaviour of the banks, he argued, revealed the moral limits of markets: 'The virtues that make society flourish – hard work, taking responsibility, being honest, being enterprising, being fair – are not the values that spring from the market but the values we bring to the market. Markets depend upon what they cannot create.' Brown now believes the speech had the potential to be as significant as Blair's 1999 Chicago lecture, which made the case for humanitarian intervention, but thinks its impact was drowned out by the number of speeches he was making in this period. In fact there was a more profound problem confronting the credibility of Brown's thesis: for many his sermons about the irresponsibility of the bankers was seriously undermined by his time as Chancellor when he had openly championed the 'genius' of the City and when he once told an audience that those who worked in the Square Mile extolled 'the best qualities of our country'. This inconsistency was ignored by his friend, Australian Prime Minister, Kevin Rudd, who warmly praised Brown's speech and who also spoke at the event. Later that evening, Obama and his officials arrived in town. Brown's aides were shocked to hear them say: 'Your generals tell us you're up for troop reinforcements in Afghanistan.' No such undertaking had been made by Number 10. When Obama and Brown learned that the British military had been going behind their backs, they were furious.[291]

Early on Wednesday 1 April, Obama arrived at Number 10 for a breakfast bilateral. It was his first visit to Downing Street as President, and the staff, many of whom had seen him in the building when he was still a candidate in July, lined the corridors to clap him in. He and his wife, Michelle, shook all their hands, before ascending the staircase lined with the portraits of Prime Ministers, and followed Brown into the smaller of the two wood-panelled dining rooms. Neither ate any breakfast, to the chagrin of those who had spent hours on its preparation. Fletcher and Obama aide Reggie Love hovered outside while their masters talked.[292] Their principal topic of conversation, apart from Afghanistan, was the conference the next day. They went through the leaders one by one, dividing up those who would need lobbying. Brown was impressive with Obama, knowing exactly how to handle him in order to get what he wanted to achieve from the meeting.[293] After breakfast they went over together to the Locarno Room in the Foreign Office for a joint press conference. It became clear immediately to all present that Obama was 'determined to be very supportive' to Brown,[294] and the President praised his 'extraordinary energy and leadership and initiative in laying the groundwork for this summit', for which the whole world owed him an 'extraordinary debt of gratitude'.[295] Although he was visibly nervous at the outset, journalists noticed how much more at ease Brown had become with Obama, who as usual was relaxed and witty, and some banter between the two leaders helped dispel the media's speculation in March that they did not work well together. The press conference proved significant in creating a sense of momentum and a belief that a deal could be achieved, which are often pivotal to successful summits.[296]

Not wanting to be upstaged, Merkel and Sarkozy later held their own joint press conferences detailing what they wanted the summit to achieve, which produced unsettling talk about a split between continental Europe and the 'Anglo-Saxons'. For the rest of the Wednesday, Brown held meticulously choreographed bilateral meetings at Number 10 with the principal G20 leaders, pushing them along in the right direction, while Obama's private meetings included Medvedev and China's Hu Jintao. In the early evening, the Queen hosted a reception at Buckingham Palace for the G20 leaders and their spouses. Berlusconi disconcerted the Queen by making loud remarks to Obama after the official photograph was taken. 'Why does that man have to shout?' Her Majesty is reported to have asked.[297] The real action was, however, elsewhere. While Obama busied himself squaring those who still needed it, Brown lobbied the hardest nuts of all – Merkel and Sarkozy.[298] Both the German and French leaders admired Brown's grasp of economic affairs – Merkel would regularly call Brown for advice during the financial crisis – but as with all international summits, the leaders had to keep one eye firmly on their domestic audience.

The G20 leaders returned to Number 10 for an official dinner, prepared by celebrity chef Jamie Oliver. Brown was always keen to appear statesmanlike around fellow heads of government, but he was not naturally comfortable in this hosting role. He left Buckingham Palace early to ensure he would be back in good time to greet the guests one by one according to a strict rota. The usual debate ensued behind the Number 10 door on which lady he should kiss, and which not, and how many times. His concern to get it right had been heightened by an embarrassing moment when, at the meeting of European leaders in Berlin on 22 February, his greeting of Merkel had been fumbled and photographs appeared of Brown kissing her nose.[299] It was one of those occasions when he was let down by his restricted eyesight, which added to his social awkwardness. Once, the previous year, he had demanded to know in the lobby of Number 10 how often he should kiss Sarkozy's wife, Carla Bruni. 'As many times as you can get away with,' was the advice he received.[300]

Despite Oliver's gourmet menu of farmed salmon with 'foraged samphire and sea kale', followed by shoulder of lamb 'from the Elwy Valley' and a dessert of Bakewell tart with fresh custard made with 'Duchy of Cornwall eggs', the atmosphere around the long table was flat. Obama and Rudd did their best to lift it, while Berlusconi fell asleep.[301] Brown tried to motivate his guests by delivering a warning from history: he reminded them that the failure of the 1933 London Conference to resolve trade pressures and to prevent protectionism had 'foreshadowed all the other terrible events of that decade and the one to follow'. That evening a number of World Cup qualification matches were being played, including several by the nations whose leaders were attending the dinner. Lula and Zapatero were two of those anxious to know how their teams were faring. Brown made a point of refusing to tell anyone the news until significant progress had been made towards resolution of the next day's communiqué, particularly about the language for the fiscal stimulus.[302] Sarah Brown, meanwhile, was entertaining the G20 partners at a separate dinner at Number 11, accompanied by celebrity guests and friends, including author J. K. Rowling, athlete Dame Kelly Holmes, entrepreneur Martha Lane-Fox and supermodel Naomi Campbell. After all the guests had left, Brown stayed up with Vadera and Heywood until 1am, his mind minutely engaged with the communiqué.

By 5.30am on Thursday 2 April, Brown was up and working on it again with his team. He was furious with his aides, criticising them for being too slow. 'At times like this, he thought that unless he made us feel it was a matter of life and death, things wouldn't work out properly,' says one.[303] He was particularly nervous that the headline figure to be committed by G20 nations – an exceptional $1tn – which had not been pre-briefed and which would constitute his 'shock and awe' moment, would leak to the press. 'This was typical Brown – more than one eye on a headline,' comments one in Number 10.[304] He was 'very, very apprehensive and tense with everybody', remembers another.[305] Having been briefed one final time – on overnight news – he left Number 10 at 7am in convoy for the heavily guarded London Docklands area for the meeting at the ExCeL conference centre, continuing to worry about the communiqué endlessly en route. The venue had been selected because it was practical and not flashy. 'The optics of a lavish G8 summit would have been completely wrong for this. We wanted somewhere functional,' says an official.[306]

Even before he had entered the ExCeL centre, Brown had secured his first major victory of the day. As he made his way inside he bumped into Merkel. The Germans had continued to block many of Brown's moves to have some words on fiscal stimulus inserted into the final draft. Despite twice using fiscal policy domestically to stimulate demand, Merkel remained adamant that she could not agree to the communiqué stressing as its top priority the imperative that global growth be maintained. 'It's deep in the German political psyche and history that inflation and fiscal profligacy must be avoided. Merkel couldn't agree to a communiqué that put her out of step with German public opinion,' says an official.[307] The difference was thus mainly about the detailed language. But this was at last resolved outside the centre on the morning of the meeting, announced to the other leaders by Brown at their joint breakfast and deftly slotted into the text.

On their way into the venue, Obama had seen Brown walking down the corridor towards him but, because of his eyesight, Brown had not noticed the President. Instead, Obama witnessed him going 'volcanic' with his staff. 'Tell your guy to cool it,' he said to one of them, only half joking.[308] Brown was extremely tense, and his fellow leaders saw a side of him that Number 10 knew all too well, but which they had rarely, if ever, come across before. He was like a man possessed that morning, rushing everywhere, barking out instructions, then retiring periodically to a meeting room on the third floor for updates on the latest thinking on where the other delegations stood.

Just before 11am, half an hour later than expected, the first scheduled plenary session of the conference opened, with finance ministers present. Besides the leaders of the other nineteen member states of the G20, also in attendance were EU President Topolánek, President of the European Commission Barroso, the Prime Ministers of Spain and the Netherlands, included at the invitation of the French, and representatives from the major international economic institutions, the IMF, the World Bank, the UN and the WTO. During this session the details of the financial reform agenda were finalised. This was comparatively straightforward. The leaders agreed to controls on financial-sector pay and bonuses, a financial stability board to work with the IMF, and tougher regulation of hedge funds.

After the plenary session, the leaders returned to their private dining room for lunch. Brown refused to allow the leaders to have their 'sherpas' in the room. 'I don't want those fucking people anywhere near us,' he said.[309] He wanted an opportunity to address the leaders alone and hoped to create a sense of community and camaraderie among them. However, the absence of aides created mayhem in the dining room, as several of the national leaders lacked the English to understand the conversations. Brown's worry at this fraught stage was that, if the officials were present, they would try to take control, and he would lose it.

Heywood, Cunliffe and Fletcher were in the room, because Brown, as chair, was allowed three support staff; Vadera was also there throughout. Even knowing him as they did, they were struck by the sheer brute force of Brown's personality that day. His strategy with the leaders was: 'You will not leave this room until we have it sorted, and if we fail, the eyes of the world will be upon us.'[310] Stewart Wood says: 'His strong instinct was that the only way to get a deal that will stand up, is when you get out the people who actually have objections galore and you bang their heads together. He was an incredibly tough chairman.'[311] The Prime Minister's grasp of the leaders' psychology and their need to return home with a successful deal was masterly. This was payback time for his cranking up expectations so deliberately over the preceding weeks: he knew his counterparts would not want to end the conference with their media saying little of significance had been achieved. He bruised egos and affronted people, without blushing. Many did not like the hectoring way that he conducted the meeting, but accepted, some more grudgingly than others, that he alone was capable of bringing them all together and battering out a common communiqué. Simon McDonald believes Brown pulled it off ultimately because the foreign leaders trusted his expertise, gained during his ten years as Chancellor, and believed that he had an authority they did not possess. 'He confronted everyone with the severity of the crisis and had the credibility to get away with it. Sparks were coming off him,' McDonald says.[312] Vadera believes that the leaders were forced to abandon 'their set speeches with their pre-prepared positions', adding: 'They really did change their positions and do something that they may not have come prepared to do.'[313]

Once the discussions moved on to topics that were very technical in nature, the leaders told 'Gordon' – they all addressed each other by their first names – that they really did need their advisers and translators present. Brown was forced to concede and allow the sherpas into the dining room. Once additional chairs had been brought into the room, the aides arrived for the latter part of the lunch, during which the final details of the communiqué were finalised. International meetings vary from those at which leaders are given a prepared text, which they meekly accept, to ones where leaders themselves shape the content. One sherpa says: 'The London G20 was quite a long way at the end of the spectrum where the leaders do the drafting.'[314]

One of the key debates at this stage among the leaders was whether the communiqué referred to the precise number of jobs to be saved or not. It was important to the leaders because it concerned the messages that their domestic audiences would receive. Another contentious issue was over the amount of IMF gold to be used for the poorest nations, which ran into a blockage from the Turks and the Argentineans. It had been agreed with the Americans that the IMF could sell gold to create a fund, but the Argentineans and the Turks would have been adversely affected and so they dug in. In the end, the leaders agreed that the IMF could raise up to $6bn by selling gold, something that the IMF itself had originally resisted.[315]

Brown was beginning to believe that all outstanding issues had been resolved when, at the eleventh hour, the issue of tax havens threatened to sink the summit. Sarkozy, wanting to be seen as acting tough on his domestic concerns, had publicly stated before the G20 that, unless there was action on this issue, he would walk out. The Chinese, with their own tax havens in Hong Kong and Macau, and feeling general antipathy towards the OECD, which had compiled a blacklist of the least cooperative jurisdictions, took a diametrically opposite view. Before the financial crisis, Brown, acting on civil service advice, had been careful to be protective of British Crown dependencies and thus had not spoken out against tax havens for most of his premiership, for all the personal distaste he felt. But on his March visit to the US he changed tack, telling Congress he supported tighter regulation. 'GB is very good at adapting to circumstances,' says one of his aides.[316] But doing so had put him even further from the Chinese position, and, with less than half an hour to go before the summit's scheduled end, agreement was as far away as ever. Only weeks before, the tax havens issue had been dismissed as a 'third- or fourth-order issue' by Brown and his team.[317] Now disagreement in this area threatened seriously to undermine the entire G20.

Sarkozy and Chinese President Hu were locked in a seemingly irreconcilable conflict. Minutes ticked away. Leaders were looking at their watches. The energy was draining out of the room. With twenty minutes left, Sarkozy still said again he would refuse to sign the communiqué unless tax havens were outlawed. There appeared no more that an exhausted Brown could do from the chair. At that point, Obama, acting on his own account, or under request from Brown – accounts vary – took the two leaders to one side, first separately and then together, and secured agreement that the G20 communiqué should 'note' the OECD blacklist, but not formally endorse it.[318] Suddenly, a solution had been found (though there was to be a later drama that evening when the OECD, possibly as a result of Chinese pressure, refused to publish the list).[319] All outstanding issues were now resolved, and leaders were able to give their final endorsement to the nine-page communiqué. British officials, who had been frantically tracking all the changes that had been made to the text, rushed away to type up the final document, even as the leaders were rising from the table, eager to get off to their press conferences, embassies or the airport. 'There was no time to bring the leaders back together to check: "Are you sure this is what you agreed?" We just prayed that we had captured it accurately,' recalls an official.[320]

The communiqué bound the G20 states into a series of significant pledges, with the jewel in the crown being the announcement of over $1tn to 'support to restore credit, growth and jobs in the world economy'. The resources available to the IMF were to be tripled to some $750bn – a figure that had been agreed before the summit began. An extra $250bn was to be allocated for a special IMF overdraft facility on which members could call – a figure finalised after meetings between the G20 finance deputies on the Monday and the sherpas on the Tuesday. A further $250bn was committed to supporting trade finance, and $100bn was promised in aid to developing countries via the agency of multilateral development banks. '[Brown] was adamant the whole way through that he needed to persuade the leaders that they must not forget the world's poorest. His desire to improve their lives was shared by none of the other leaders,' says Number 10's Forsyth.[321] The communiqué also contained a promise to refrain from protectionism, to help in particular those developing countries with export-driven economies.

While the leaders were locked in, thousands of the world's media were camped at the ExCeL centre. Mandelson and Treasury minister Stephen Timms spent almost the whole day speaking to them, talking up Brown's efforts. As soon as the formal meeting was over, Sarkozy rushed off to the media, eager to be the first to announce the results from the summit to the world. Brown, too, was rushed to the waiting cameras. Other leaders were more respectful, allowing Brown as their host to make his own statement before they made theirs. Foreign leaders were almost uniformly positive about him. Obama described the summit as 'a turning point in our pursuit of global economic recovery',[322] Sarkozy said it went 'beyond what we could have imagined ... all of us are delighted with this result',[323] while Lula said that the outcome was good 'for the hopes and the future of humanity'.[324] Both *The Guardian* and the *Daily Mail* ran with the headline 'Brown's New World Order',[325] while *The Sun*, as if mouthing Mandelson's words, talked about how Brown 'strong-armed America, China, Japan, the EU and nations from across the planet into historic action at a gruelling G20 summit'.[326] The *Daily Mail* admitted, 'this has been an impressive week for Brown'.[327]

However, there were some criticisms. *The Economist* disparaged Brown's 'well-known creative accounting',[328] and the 'trillion' figure was often dealt with sceptically by the serious end of the media. Most of the increased funds for the IMF had indeed been promised before the summit began. That said, the funds had been tripled, as the communiqué said, and Brown and his team had played a big role in the months leading up to the summit in making sure they were secured in the first place. Suggestions that this figure had been agreed to at the summit were fair, nonetheless (interestingly, the full sum was in fact delivered after the summit – every dollar). The Delphic vagueness of some of the aspirations expressed in the communiqué was also attacked for ultimately meaning little or nothing[329] – for example, the commitment of leaders to anti-protectionism and to be more fiscally prudent during subsequent booms.[330] Vince Cable asked how, in the light of the communiqué's intent to have 'tough new principles on paying compensation', senior RBS bosses could be remunerated so lavishly.[331]

However, for all such doubts, it must be remembered that international conferences often deliver empty platitudes. So was the G20 a damp squib? Brown had set out to achieve five objectives. Knowing that \$1tn was available helped boost confidence at a time of fear about the drying up of liquidity: an upward trend in capital and debt markets was seen as a result. The desire to boost demand via fiscal and monetary policy was only partially achieved because of resistance principally from continental Europe. But the wording in the communiqué, agreed before breakfast with Merkel, nevertheless reinforced confidence that governments would act to boost demand in their economies if the conditions were shown fully to merit it. The commitment to international free trade and the eschewing of protectionism was enshrined in the text of the communiqué, and was accompanied by the \$250bn to lubricate and reinvigorate international trade. Brown achieved most of what he wanted for poorer nations, with the agreements on SDRs and on IMF gold stocks boosting the ability of the IMF to help nations in need. Finally, the communiqué laid out a new framework on financial regulation, despite the row over tax havens. The impact of all these measures helped to rekindle optimism, building confidence that the world would not descend into a 1930s depression and that emerging economies in Eastern Europe and elsewhere would not fail, as well as helping to draw a line, for the time being at least, under the panic of the preceding six months. 'It was global coordination at its best ... The commonality of focus and purpose was obvious to the markets,' reflected respected economist Mohamed Abdulla El-Erian, the chief executive of investment firm PIMCO, in October 2010.[332]

When Brown and his team returned from Docklands to Number 10, staff gathered to offer congratulations and clapped them back into the office in Number 12. Gus O'Donnell had organised some champagne in the horseshoe and said a few words congratulating Brown on his achievement. Even James Bowler, Brown's reserved Principal Private Secretary, said: 'It doesn't get any better than this for a Prime Minister.'[333] When, the next morning, Fletcher walked to Hither Green railway station in south London and saw the ranked front pages on the newsstand speaking of the triumph, he was overcome with emotion. He realised how utterly exhausted he was, as were all Brown's staff. Was the premiership now on an upward trajectory? He was about to find out.

7

Premiership Unravels

(April–August 2009)

At the start of April, Brown stood at the highest point of his premiership. He had been commanding on the world stage. Its most powerful leaders had followed his lead. What he needed to do now was to reproduce some of the same dignity, the same clarity of purpose and strength of leadership, domestically, and many of the past vacillations and errors of his premiership would be forgiven and forgotten. Instead, in the space of just days, triumph descended into farce, and farce into tragedy. The four months from April to July were to see a string of bad decisions. On the world stage, he had provided moral leadership. That is exactly the leadership he failed to provide at home, literally in the case of some personnel practices at Number 10, and more broadly in the case of Parliament's most serious crisis in modern times. His lack of grip precipitated a Cabinet resignation that, had others followed, would have ended his premiership. Only at the very end of this period did resolve, clarity and optimism return.

The Number 10 Problem Climaxes: April 2009

Number 10's relationship with Brown had been going through its best period since the previous October, but from the New Year concerns began to be raised that the Prime Minister was harking back to his old ways. His principal domestic advice came from Jeremy Heywood, David Muir, Justin Forsyth, Gavin Kelly and Nick Pearce, but it became increasingly apparent that Brown was also talking to a parallel channel which cut across their attempts to bring order. All of them knew this twin track was a crazy way to run a Prime Minister's office, but none was prepared to confront him over it.[1] The 'back channel' consisted principally of Ed Balls, Tom Watson, Charlie Whelan and Damian McBride, and its impact was to render Number 10 dysfunctional.

Peter Mandelson decided he needed to confront the issue and took the opportunity of flying with Brown in February while he was preparing for the G20. 'Sit down with me and write down all the people you listen to for advice,' he said to Brown. When the PM had finished writing a long screed, Mandelson was taken aback, saying, 'How on earth can you ever take any decision?'[2] Brown saw the point, and assured his colleague he would address this.

These two separate groups usefully highlight the two strands in Brown's character. At his best, Brown is a very serious-minded politician who craved to be working with highly proficient, intellectually capable aides who shared his high-minded passions for international development, fairness and the rest. Those in the first group, to which can be added several others including Stewart Wood and James Bowler, brought out the best in him. But Brown's Achilles heel was always his insecurity, mainly emotional but also intellectual. The second group, to which can be added Nick Brown and Ian Austin, were political to their finger tips, appealing to and exacerbating this insecurity. This group were less interested in nurturing Brown's high-minded ideals: they played rather to his tribal and partisan side, and promoted populist images of him that they thought would give him wider appeal, such as Brown the football-lover, an image that McBride cultivated.[3] This group contained many of Brown's oldest political allies, and he felt a deep affinity with them, so much so that he blinded himself to some of their unacceptable 'machine politics' ways. Though he would often try to deny any knowledge of their activities the simple truth is that a bruised and often paranoid Brown had come to believe that success in politics required a level of toughness that his henchmen provided. After all, it was this style of politics that not only ousted his great rival Blair and secured for him the crown he had craved for so long, but which would also help him survive in office for his three years in the face of endless plotting by his enemies.

Every organisation contains toxic individuals and practices: the job of an effective leader is either to contain or banish them. Brown was caught in a terrible dilemma. He could understand why many of those close to him rebelled at Whelan and McBride et al. and their antics. But he admired McBride's and Whelan's loyalty, and believed their tactics were necessary to protect him against what he considered were equally unscrupulous opponents. 'Gordon saw conspiracies everywhere and was convinced that he needed a heavy hitter who could plant stories in the press for him,' says an official;[4] those he feared most were 'almost always fellow members of the Cabinet' recalls another.[5] The threats were real in a premiership where the Prime Minister was under almost constant challenge. Misreading Blair's premiership, Brown thought that Alastair Campbell played a similarly brutal protection role, which he appended to McBride and Whelan. Perceived danger did not, anyway, justify his henchmen's methods, which included storing up unpleasant information on people, and threatening them with it, or leaking it to 'friends' in the media in ways that made it difficult to trace. Though rumoured, it was never proved that Balls, Brown's *consiglierie*, played any part in the negative briefing. Brown could equally claim himself to be innocent of knowledge of any wrong-doing. The regime around him created an atmosphere of fear, from which those in Number 10 suffered, as did Cabinet and junior ministers and also the Parliamentary Labour Party (PLP). One of Brown's coterie says, 'If you were in the room you were briefed against, and if you were not in the room you'd be briefed against for not being important enough to be in the room.'[6] It did not make for a harmonious team or much sense of *esprit de corps*.

McBride came to personify Brown's henchmen at their worst. Highly intelligent and a gifted communicator, he had read history at Peterhouse, Cambridge, and was supervised for his dissertation by Tony Badger, author of the book on F D Roosevelt that Brown had read with fascination a few months before. After university, McBride had joined HM Customs & Excise until he caught Brown's eye and in September 2003 was appointed head of communications at the Treasury. After Treasury officials complained about his modus operandi and sought his dismissal, Brown brought him into his own team in May 2005 as a special adviser. McBride was only in his early thirties when he moved across to Number 10 with Brown, although many thought he looked much older. In many ways he was excellent at his job, contributing political edge to Michael Ellam's almost 'other-worldliness'. 'Ellam liked working with him,' recalls one official.[7] McBride had, like Alastair Campbell, a gift for language: he coined the phrase '*entente formidable*' after the Sarkozy summit at the Emirates Stadium in March 2008. In the building McBride was considered a 'genius' by many given his ability to get on top of an issue quickly and with ease. The unattractive side of his activities first came to unfavourable public attention when he briefed against Spencer Livermore and Douglas Alexander after the non-election drama in October 2007. He was in regular contact with certain journalists who took his material, including Simon Walters from the *Mail on Sunday* and Andrew Porter at the *Daily Telegraph*, McBride's favourite newspaper. Others in his circle included Patrick Hennessy of the *Sunday Telegraph*, George Pascoe-Watson of *The Sun* and Benedict Brogan of the *Daily Telegraph*. Balls himself was close to Philip Webster of *The Times*. It is striking that many of the journalists whom McBride and Balls fed most were from Tory papers, especially those elements that hated Blair, so they shared a common interest.[8] Some of the journalists thrived on the same culture of beer, sport and macho male company as McBride, and they prized him highly as some of their best inside material was supplied from sources close to him.[9]

Disquiet about McBride's methods had come to a head in the summer of 2008 with his briefing against David Miliband and Alistair Darling. He acquired the nicknames 'McPoison' and 'Mad Dog'.[10] The Conference was the final straw, and Brown decided that he would have to move him away from frontline briefing to a backseat role. He told Cabinet, who were pleased, though they would have preferred him to have gone altogether. Officials, including Gus O'Donnell and Jeremy Heywood, also wanted McBride removed from his post. 'Stephen Carter thought, very early on, that we had to get rid of Damian … with hindsight, we should have been much tougher in demanding that he left the building,' says one.[11] Instead, McBride continued briefing his network of journalists, and became even more of a liability because 'he was no longer busy enough and had too much time on his hands',[12] and 'now had more time to focus on scheming and dirty tricks'.[13] When they saw what he was still doing, Cabinet ministers were angry that Brown had not done as he said he would; they felt the Prime Minister had lied to them. McBride limped on for a few months more, but was finally brought down by an alleged smear campaign against the Tories via a proposed website, 'RedRag'.[14] Leaked emails about it began with a BlackBerry message from McBride on 13 January[15] addressed to Derek Draper, Peter Mandelson's disgraced former spin doctor who had left under a cloud in 1999, with Whelan copied in,[16] beginning, 'Gents, a few ideas I've been working on for RedRag.' These ideas included stories about a gay Tory MP, rumours that David Cameron was suffering from a sexually transmitted disease, and another attributing mental problems to George Osborne's wife.[17] Twenty minutes after receiving the email, Draper responded, 'Absolutely totally brilliant, Damian. I'll think about timing and sort out the technology this week so that we can go as soon as possible.'[18]

The emails were leaked to the media by right wing Westminster blogger 'Guido Fawkes' (aka Paul Staines) who released them early on Saturday 11 April, refusing to say how he had obtained them.[19] When the story broke, McBride and his correspondents claimed that the emails had merely been 'banter between blokes'.[20] Brown's initial response was to try to tough it out, as with earlier McBride episodes: a spokesman said, 'Neither the Prime Minister nor anybody else in Number 10, except the author, knew anything about any of these private emails.' The statement concluded, 'The author of these emails has apologised for their juvenile inappropriate nature and for the embarrassment caused.'[21] Cabinet Office minister Liam Byrne was drafted in to trot this line out. He argued that the proposed smears were never published and that the website mentioned was dormant.[22] Draper admitted that Saturday that the emails were 'a bit juvenile,' though some were also 'brilliant and rather funny'.[23]

Brown was in Scotland for the Easter Bank Holiday weekend, relaxing after the G20. It was becoming apparent, certainly to Heywood and Ellam, by early afternoon on the Saturday, that this was an issue that was not going away, and that McBride would have to go. 'To be fair to him, he knew he had to go: he did not argue,' says an insider.[24] The Prime Minister spoke to McBride on the phone from Scotland. McBride claimed that Brown was 'so angry and mortified he couldn't really speak'.[25] Knowing there was no way out, McBride duly resigned. The issue, however, did not fade, and the integrity of the government machine was now called into question. On Sunday 12 April, the Conservatives made an official complaint to Gus O'Donnell in his capacity as head of the civil service, raising 'serious concerns' over Downing Street operations and the involvement of officials in the emails. O'Donnell spoke to Brown and Sue Nye and, shortly after, Sue Gray, head of propriety and ethics at the Cabinet Office, became involved. ('You always knew that something serious was up when Sue Gray started to appear,' says an aide.[26]) Cameron leapt on the airwaves to blame Brown for allowing a culture to develop in Number 10 in which some of his political staff felt comfortable plotting to smear opposition politicians. Fraught phone calls took place between Brown, Mandelson and Balls. It was deemed too dangerous for Brown himself to admit any personal knowledge or blame. That Sunday, Number 10 thus roundly condemned the emails but re-emphasised Brown's own ignorance. Alan Johnson was one of many in the Cabinet furious that the issue had come up, and toured the broadcasting studios proclaiming the emails 'disgusting', saying they had shamed Labour.[27] Brown, still in Scotland, wrote handwritten letters to all those whose names had been mentioned in the emails, not mentioning the word 'sorry' but expressing his 'great regret', indicating that he was not personally responsible.[28] He wrote too to O'Donnell to emphasise 'no minister and no political adviser' other than McBride had knowledge of the emails.[29] When it was pointed out that Tom Watson, a Cabinet Office minister, was named in one email, Watson explained he knew nothing about it.[30] Frank Field added to the pressure, suggesting that Labour MPs were 'staring into the abyss' and articulated the feelings of many when he said, 'Harold Wilson asserted that the Labour Party was a moral crusade or it was nothing. The McBride affair has left Labour members looking at nothing.'[31]

In the post-Easter week, it was the media rather than the Tories who drove the story. On Monday 13 April, Jackie Ashley wrote an article in *The Guardian* under the title 'Gordon Brown's vicious side is now clear to the whole country'.[32] Trevor Kavanagh wrote a piece the same day in *The Sun*, '"Mad dog" was trained to maul', in which he said of Brown, 'He hand-picks smiling assassins such as Charlie Whelan and Damian McBride as hired guns, digging dirt and squirrelling it away for later deployment ...'[33] The next day Andy McSmith wrote of McBride in *The Independent*, 'His attack-dog style, blunt language and fondness for drinking and talking late into the night were signs of a man who lacked the caution of a career civil servant.'[34] That day, Muir was in Nottinghamshire and Derbyshire testing the ground and saw the full extent of the public's disgust. The local and European elections were just six weeks away. They had been disastrous for Labour in 2008 when Brown was blamed for his role in the 10p fiasco, and Muir said he was heading for a similarly bad result if he continued to deny responsibility for McBride. Brown worried that by apologising he would implicate himself in the scandal, but at some point on the Wednesday, in the face of the looming electoral backlash, he relented, very grumpily.

So, on Thursday 16 April, on a trip to Govan shipyard in Glasgow, using a carefully prepared script, the Prime Minister said, 'I am sorry about what happened.' When he first heard about the emails, he told his audience, he was 'horrified, shocked and very angry indeed', and he said he was now going to ensure that everything would be done to 'clean up politics'.[35] In response to a question, he replied, 'I take full responsibility for what happened: that is why the person who was responsible went immediately,' an explanation that begged as many questions as it answered. The contorted logic became a YouTube classic, and spoke to many of a moral weakness at his very heart.

The Cabinet met in Glasgow that same Thursday. Brown was distinctly uncomfortable in front of his ministers, knowing he had told them in the autumn that he had removed McBride from briefing.[36] They were fuming at the damage the episode was doing to the party's electoral prospects. One present recorded that the Prime Minister was 'in full apology mode but it all felt very rehearsed'.[37] To James Purnell the whole McBride issue was a final turning point: it was 'morally wrong. It made me think I can't defend this any more.'[38] Some ministers believed Brown himself was responsible for McBride's actions and had been aware what was going on but had acted in a 'mafia boss' manner, pretending to have no knowledge of the unsavoury acts done in his name. McBride himself has no doubts about the truth. 'You prove your loyalty to GB by your brutality,' he believes.[39]

Why had Brown not acted earlier to remove McBride and the worst excesses of the whole approach from Number 10? Once the emails came to light, why did he not say immediately on the Saturday, 'I was the leader, and he was on my books?'[40] He took a full five days to apologise, and when he did so it struck many as insincere, even risible. McBride had powerful defenders – above all, Balls. The description of McBride as a 'wholly owned subsidiary' of Balls's struck many as apt, and the two men worked together extraordinarily closely.

For Brown to have dismissed McBride would have been to take on Balls, and that was something the Prime Minister lacked the will to do.[41] Balls's former friends Ed Miliband and Alexander repeatedly warned Brown that McBride was damaging him, driving a further wedge between them and Balls.[42] Sarah Brown was another supporter of McBride because she felt he protected their family: she was adamant that he should not resign over the emails and argued with her husband for him to stay.[43] Mandelson, who wrote in his memoirs that he had insisted that Brown move McBride when he returned in October 2008,[44] was now in a terrible dilemma. Draper, his own protégé, was deeply involved in the McBride operation, and thus, 'he felt he couldn't be too outspoken against McBride because Draper had goaded him to some of his worst excesses'.[45] Fear, too, played its part in McBride's remaining as long as he did. 'There was a worry he might go public about the September 2006 plot to oust Blair,' says one Number 10 aide.[46] McBride did indeed inspire fear, not only in those he briefed against, but also among his allies.

The impact of the McBride episode was profoundly negative in a wide variety of ways. Cabinet's trust in Brown took a serious dent, and he lost further respect among the PLP and the public. Chris Mullin captures the mood in his diary: 'The problem is that, for all his high-minded posturing, everyone knows that this is Gordon's modus operandi.'[47] Much of the goodwill and stature he accumulated during the G20 was smashed to smithereens. The party's popularity suffered. Shortly before the affair blew up, Number 10 had hired the Benenson Strategy Group, who had done work for Obama, and they put Labour only three points behind the Conservatives. These figures suggested that a general election victory was a real possibility. Within a week of Easter Sunday, following the McBride episode, everything had changed. Cameron moved out ahead of Brown on virtually every poll, and the Conservatives' lead over Labour trebled to nineteen points.[48] It pushed Number 10 back into a state of deep despondency. 'The outside world treated us as if we were all complicit in what Damian had been doing,' complains one insider, bitterly.[49] Brown's good humour evaporated: he became down and prone to bad temper outbursts.

The affair, however, was to have a silver lining. A chief irritant between Number 10 and the media was removed, and it opened up the way for a more strategic and fresh approach. It was needed. Brown would regularly say, to the dismay of his aides, 'Why am I not on the *Today* programme? I'm the PM, I should be on it,' or, looking at the flat screen in Number 12 permanently showing the news channel, 'Why am I not on Sky?'[50] For a poor communicator, he was extraordinarily keen to be on the television and radio, and for someone who understood the media little, despite having worked in it, he was often loath to take advice. The culture of briefing, counter-briefing and rebuttal did not wholly disappear after McBride departed, (not least because Whelan was still active) but was sidelined, and a new emphasis was placed on alternative ways for Brown to reach the public. A new opportunity opened to enhance relations with the press. McBride's closeness to *The Telegraph* and *Mail* newspapers had often been to the detriment of Number 10's relationship with *The Guardian*, *Observer* and *Independent*. 'An aggressive outreach programme with the centre-left press was embarked upon' says Michael Dugher.[51] McBride, fairly or not, had become the scapegoat for all that was thought to be wrong. Others clearly had a hand in the damaging briefing operation, some of whom did not even work in Number 10 but spoke as 'sources close to the Prime Minister'. 'McBride was the most distrusted person in Number 10 and the source of most tension. In a single day, the boil was lanced. The class bully had gone,' says one insider.[52] But McBride can be blamed too much. As with Balls, Whelan and the rest, his behaviour reflected and modelled that of his master. They were all talented individuals who were 'spoilt' by the pursuit and retention of power. Those who thought McBride's departure meant all communication problems were over were about to be rudely disabused, beginning shortly with the row over expenses.

Budget Battles: April 2009

The London G20 had pushed the Budget back from its normal slot in early March. The new date was now 22 April, giving Brown just three weeks to prepare for it, at a time when he was heavily distracted and depressed by the McBride fallout. Number 10 knew that Darling's second Budget, and the first since Britain had gone into recession, 'was always going to be very difficult'.[53] That is an understatement. In the first quarter of 2009, the economy contracted by 1.9 per cent, the worst performance for thirty years,[54] and considerably worse than Darling's forecast of between minus 0.75 per cent and minus 1.25 per cent. Unemployment had risen to 7.1 per cent[55] and repossessions were widely 'predicted to soar'.[56] The Bank of England responded by reducing interest rates to a new record low of 0.5 per cent in an attempt to boost consumption.[57] In another arm of monetary policy, and with the full support and encouragement of Brown and his team, the Bank embarked on a programme of 'quantitative easing', more simply known as 'printing money', announcing on 5 March a creation of some £75bn over the following three months.[58] 'It was like bang, bang, bang. We went from the Bank recap into the fiscal stimulus, into asset protection and then quantitative easing. It was just like a series of horrific events,' says one senior official.[59]

But the depth of the recession was just one of several worries. The size of the deficit was a horrific anxiety for those planning the Budget, and how to respond to it produced bitter divisions. The longer the recession continued, the more the deficit grew, as tax revenues fell and welfare payments and other expenditure rose. In late March, the IMF released a forecast suggesting that Britain would have the worst fiscal deficit of any G7 nation.[60] Darling's Pre-Budget Report forecast for the fiscal year beginning in April 2009 was £118bn, but the IMF predicted that it would be £165bn.[61] When announced in the Budget on 22 April, it was even worse at £175bn.[62]

From the start of the year, the media increasingly locked on to the size of both the Budget deficit (the gap between government expenditure and tax revenue in a given year) and the overall level of public debt (which represents the accumulated sum of previous borrowing minus repayments). In February, *The Guardian* warned that 'debt hits record' 47.8 per cent of GDP,[63] while *The Times* stated that public debt 'could exceed 65 per cent of GDP in 2010–11'.[64] The *Financial Times* attributed the unsuccessful gilt auction in March to 'alarm over rising UK debt levels'.[65] 'The public narrative of debt had become the defining issue. It freaked everyone out,' says a Number 10 aide.[66] Concerns grew about how long market confidence would tolerate these levels of borrowing – and what might happen if it was ever to be lost.

The government seemed increasingly vulnerable to the attack heard in Cameron's speech to the London School of Economics, on 'reckless borrowing and spending'.[67] The Conservative charge that Brown was being fiscally irresponsible acquired new weight after the second bank bail out failed to produce an early lift. In mid-March, Cameron embarked on a series of speeches, the first of which, in Birmingham, outlined the problems lying ahead for British governments: 'In the years to come, we will have to make extremely difficult decisions on spending, borrowing and taxation.'[68] Tough decisions were necessary, he argued, to tackle the 'foundation of debt' that had built up on Brown's watch. This was the most effective attack that the Conservatives had launched so far against the government, and Brown had no satisfactory response.

Divisions at the very heart of government reflected and deepened these underlying concerns. The fresh breach which had opened up between Number 10 and the Treasury in late 2008 deepened month by month. Although Brown remained supportive of Darling personally, and they had been brought closer during the financial crisis, their relationship came under rising strain, which was reflected in tensions between the political advisers and officials, with ex-Treasury people now at Number 10 despairing of their former department.[69] The newly created National Economic Council (NEC) became the battleground on which some of these tensions were played out. Brown thought the Treasury was lacking in imagination and was trying to block him. Treasury mandarins thought that Brown was living in 'la-la land', apparently able to recognise neither the gravity of the debt figures, nor his responsibility when Chancellor for the structural deficit, and believing he was wedded to out-of-date economic orthodoxy which said salvation would come from still further stimulus. The Treasury had supported Brown when he had been the prudent Chancellor, as when he said in his March 1999 Budget speech, 'I'm determined to continue locking in this fiscal tightening for the years to come so that we continue to meet our fiscal rules and so deliver sound public finances.'[70] Now those very same officials, including Nick Macpherson, who had been briefly his first Principal Private Secretary, and Tom Scholar who succeeded him (and who had the spell at Number 10 as chief of staff) were losing their confidence in Brown's economic judgement. They worried that he was dangerously influenced by a misguided reading of Keynes.[71] Much of their suspicion focused on Balls, who they thought was recklessly in favour of expansion. 'Only people who subscribed to the view that Brown could save the world were welcomed at Number 10,' says a Treasury mandarin. And Balls was certainly one of those people.[72] However, Number 10 aides believe that Brown was being caricatured by the Treasury and had a more profound and subtler understanding of the economic realities.[73]

As Budget day on 22 April approached, Darling felt under pressure to massage the figures. Brown had lost confidence in the Treasury's estimates of growth, which were far more pessimistic than he and Balls felt reasonable,[74] nor did they believe that its 'orthodox methods could be applied to measuring the structural deficit' (an elusive concept which refers to share of the budget deficit that would remain if the economy recovered to normal levels of output).[75] Darling felt caught in the headlights between the Treasury and Number 10, with the latter pressuring him to hold expenditure at higher levels than he and his officials thought wise. Brown had been careful to draw a distinction between the Treasury, of which he was highly critical, and his Chancellor, whom he continued to defend, though he was unhappy with his presentational skills. Inevitably, Darling felt under the cosh. 'I know Gordon doesn't have confidence in me,' said a demoralised Chancellor. 'He might as well do as he wishes and put Ed in Number 11 to do his bidding.'[76] Balls certainly had pronounced views on what was needed. 'I'd been in the Treasury for a long time and knew how it actually worked. I took a different view on the credibility of the markets,' he says. 'What the markets want to know is whether you will deliver. The pace of deficit reduction was less important than their belief that you were serious.'[77] Balls argued strongly against Darling, saying that the national insurance rise in 2008, which Balls had pushed, had given the markets a clear indication of the government's credibility. For the Budget he again argued that tax should be raised and that they should not worry unduly about cutting spending. 'Raising tax a bit would be what would buy you the credibility you needed,' he says.[78] The Treasury countered by pushing for spending cuts, to little avail: 'We made progress in setting out a plan to close the deficit [halving it over four years],' says a mandarin, but 'we didn't succeed in getting Number 10 really focused on the spending side.' It nevertheless did thwart Brown's demand for additional spending, and it committed him to a deficit-reduction plan – what would come to be known as the 'Darling plan' – to halve the deficit in four years. 'Gordon understood that there were only so many arguments you can have with your Chancellor,' says one senior minister.[79] Nevertheless, Treasury mandarins felt that they had failed to achieve all their objectives in the Budget. 'It was very much a tax-raising Budget, which we at the Treasury saw as second best to making progress on spending.'[80]

Before Darling rose on the afternoon of 22 April to deliver the Budget, Cameron and Brown clashed at PMQs. Cameron goaded Brown by asking him provocatively whether the Prime Minister intended to abolish 'boom and bust' but Brown yet again refused to acknowledge the argument in those terms. Responsibility for Britain's economic plight lay at the door of global factors and the world economy, and expressly not his own handling of the public finances during his ten year reign as Chancellor, he insisted.[81] On the morning of Budget day, a leader in *The Times* was headed 'The election starts today',[82] a view echoed on the BBC by Nick Robinson, who said that Darling would 'define the choice for the next election' between both main parties.[83] Protecting investment in schools, hospitals and other key services Darling said was essential, and the core principles guiding the Budget were to be 'fairness and opportunity'. Brown himself saw the logic of raising the top rate of income tax on earnings of over £150,000 to 50p from the 45p introduced in the Pre-Budget Report in 2008, and also accepted the need to bring forward the year the tax-hike would kick in to April 2010, which meant that the government would now renege on their 2005 manifesto commitment not to increase the top rate of tax. Significant change also came on pension tax relief for those at the top, which had been long discussed in tax reform circles but never implemented, and restriction of income tax personal allowance for the best-off.

These moves were supported enthusiastically by many in Number 10, who believed it was morally as well as politically right that the better-off should be paying to ensure the squeeze on public spending would be fair.[84] The 50p tax rate was estimated to be likely to raise an extra £6bn by 2012, a smaller sum than was to be raised by Darling's increased taxes on fuel, alcohol and tobacco. Borrowing was to be £175bn in 2009–10, amounting to 12 per cent of GDP, and the net public sector debt was to rise to 59 per cent of GDP in 2009–10, peaking at 79 per cent in 2012–13 before falling in 2016. Darling predicted the measures he outlined would permit the economy to start growing again 'towards the end of the year': it would, he claimed, contract by around 3.5 per cent in 2009 but rise to 1.25 per cent for 2010. Additionally, measures were introduced to help those hit hardest by the recession. There was to be investment in the 'green' economy, help for mortgage payers, and the car scrappage scheme, to be overseen by Mandelson, which had been outlined in February. At the instigation of Brown, as well as Darling and Yvette Cooper, an important programme to create jobs mainly for 18- to 21-year-olds was introduced, and further measures were brought in to help those facing long-term unemployment. It addressed Brown's underlying concerns about the impact of the recession on the real economy, and the measures helped account for why joblessness in the UK remained below European levels. Most labour market economists welcomed it because, as well as being considered humane, it helped allay the culture of joblessness from taking hold in communities.[85]

'Today everyone can see what an utter mess this Labour government and this Labour Prime Minister have made of the British economy,' responded Cameron. 'The fastest rise in unemployment in our history, the worst recession since World War II and the worst peacetime public finances ever known.'[86] Darling's forecast for growth was attacked for being 'massaged' and for being likely to result in 'not a U-shaped recovery' but a 'trampoline recovery'.[87] The Chancellor's figures were treated with scepticism beyond Parliament too, and his cause was not helped by the IMF delivering its most gloomy prognosis for the world economy to date, claiming the recession would last well into 2010, exposing Darling's forecast of growth as wildly optimistic.[88]

The right-wing press predictably rounded on the increase in income tax. 'A savage and pointless attack on middle England,' wrote Simon Heffer in the *Daily Telegraph*,[89] (a ridiculous but revealing headline which suggested that the *Telegraph* believed middle England included people who earned over £150,000 a year) while *The Times* ran the headline, 'Red all over: Chancellor reads last rites over New Labour.'[90] The criticism of Brown for reneging on his 2005 election promise not to increase income tax was harsher than it had been for the rise to 45p in the Pre-Budget Report. Measures to reduce the deficit in general were deemed to be insufficient. 'The Budget was too much about political point-scoring and not enough about sorting out the public finances,' said *The Economist*,[91] while the Institute for Fiscal Studies warned that it would take 'two parliaments of pain' to restore the public finances.[92] Brown was 'apoplectic' at the negative response. 'He saw Alistair's announcement of the borrowing figure as part of a Treasury campaign to build up pressure for spending cuts,' says Mandelson.[93] The Prime Minister's response to the criticism of the Budget was in part to blame the messenger – Darling. Brown believed the way that his Chancellor had presented the case 'scared people and made the government look ineffective' and that it had 'racked up a significant amount of hostility', according to one Number 10 adviser.[94]

The Budget and its delivery confirmed Brown in his opinion that Balls should take over as Chancellor at the next opportunity, which would come in

the reshuffle he was already planning in his head for mid-summer. The Treasury
and many in Number 10 were about to be even more alarmed. Ignoring
Darling's own plan for deficit reduction, over the following weeks, Brown and
Balls fixed on the dividing line for the coming general election being their
own plans for spending or 'investment', as opposed to the Tories' plans for cuts,
which they believed would cause widespread suffering and hamper Britain's
recovery. Brown therefore positively leapt on a slip on 10 June by shadow
Health Secretary Andrew Lansley on BBC Radio 4's *Today* programme, when
he suggested that the Conservatives would cut 10 per cent in departmental
expenditure for every department bar health, international development and
schools. 'That's it! We can beat them on this,' a jubilant Brown yelled out when
he heard Lansley.[95] Brown believed he finally had a clear Labour agenda for
the future. It was a 'Eureka' moment for him. Not, however, for his team, who
saw events unfold in slow motion. Brown charged down to the chamber for
PMQs, thundered across the despatch box: 'This is the day when they showed
that the choice is between investment under Labour and massive cuts under
the Conservative Party.'[96] 'My heart sank,' says one aide. 'Gordon was insistent
he wanted campaign leaflets printed that day. He thought he'd at last found
the chink in their armour.'[97] Later that day, Labour launched their 'Mr 10 per
cent' campaign. In an article on 14 June in the *Sunday Mirror*, Brown claimed
that 'wide, deep and immediate' Tory cuts of 10 per cent would be introduced,
'in order to fund a £200,000 tax cut for the 3,000 richest families' (a reference
to the inheritance tax reform Osborne unveiled at his party conference in
2007). Conservative policy, he said, 'would actually make the recession worse,
by slowing public expenditure at exactly the time we need it most'. The damage
that would follow would be devastating. 'Cuts of 10 per cent would mean
44,000 fewer teachers, 15,000 fewer police, 10,000 fewer soldiers, and, each
year, 32,000 fewer university places. These aren't just numbers on the page, but
real jobs hanging in the balance.'[98]

Brown's team not only believed that the 'Tory cuts versus Labour investment'
strategy was misguided – as one says, 'we had nothing to invest'[99] – but they
also knew that their own figures committed the government to spending cuts.
Brown's claim at PMQs on the day of the Lansley intervention that 'the only
party proposing a cut in public spending is the Conservative Party' was simply
not true. 'My jaw dropped open when I heard him say that. He knew this was
misleading. It was clearly going to lead to trouble,' says an aide.[100] Inevitably,
Brown was accused of being dishonest about his own spending plans. The
Financial Times, which had supported Labour in the previous three elections,
was losing its patience. It thought the narrative of 'investment under Labour
and massive cuts under the Conservative Party' was dishonest, because once
factors such as inflation were stripped out, it showed that Brown intended 'a 7

per cent fall in real spending'.[101] The Institute for Fiscal Studies went further and suggested that the fall in investment under Labour would be even higher.[102]

The Conservatives saw their opportunity, and decided that rather than using the language of 'austerity' as they had in the past, they would come out into the open and say that their own plans were for 'cuts'. In an article in *The Times* Osborne argued that 'The real dividing line between the Conservatives and Labour is not about investment, but about honesty versus dishonesty.'[103] Brown continued to refuse to use the word 'cuts' and became angry when Blairite Cabinet ministers urged him to do so: 'They're on a revenge mission,' he fumed, seeing evidence of a new plot against him.[104] But it wasn't only Blairites: Chief Secretary Yvette Cooper wanted to discuss cuts in Cabinet, but got nowhere.[105] One Cabinet minister, Purnell, became so exasperated at Brown's refusal to talk about cuts that he raised the subject at a political Cabinet meeting. Brown was furious and hauled him into his study afterwards, shouting at him for 'doing the Tories' work'. But it was Purnell who would have the last laugh. He had for some time tried to raise the issue with Brown but found him deeply unreceptive. He now decided on a course of action that was to up-end Brown's best-laid plans.[106]

U-Turn on the Gurkhas: April to May 2009

After the débâcle of the 10p issue in the spring of 2008, Brown determined that he would listen far more carefully to the PLP. One year on, he failed to do so when he should have done over the Gurkhas, and did so when he should not have done on MPs' expenses. He failed roundly at both tests, the second far more seriously. PLP discipline had been a constant source of worry for Brown as Prime Minister. The 10p issue had badly damaged his support in the PLP, while the forty-two-day detention débâcle had undermined his moral authority, leaving many Labour MPs sceptical about his judgement. His authority over the PLP suffered more blows throughout the winter of 2008/09, when he faced a stormy battle with his MPs, first over the decision to press ahead with a third runway for Heathrow Airport. This was won with heavy lobbying by Brown himself, at the expense of damaging relations with the PLP – and his Climate Change Secretary, Ed Miliband – who found it hard to understand why Brown was 'making us vote for it'.[107] The second difference came over the proposal to part-privatise the Royal Mail, Mandelson's first parliamentary test since his return: in the face of a major backbench rebellion, he dropped the plan in July, arguing that 'market conditions' no longer favoured the sale. The government's critics saw this as further evidence of Brown's inability to impose his authority. If his own MPs transparently did not have confidence in him, why should the public?

The 2005 Parliament, during which Brown was Prime Minister for 60 per cent of the time, proved to be the most rebellious in the post-war era.[108] The longer a party is in power, the more truculent become the backbenchers – the syndrome is long-established. But Brown's often graceless management of Labour MPs – which contrasted markedly with Blair's natural politeness – exacerbated an already difficult position, and it was worsened considerably by his failure to provide a clear lead for the government to inspire confidence among the electorate. Rebel MPs were always finding diverse ways to be awkward. One was their increasing willingness to rebel by voting for 'opposition day motions' deliberately designed to inflict political damage on the government, on issues such as holding a full inquiry into the Iraq War and the Heathrow runway; the latter attracted twenty-eight Labour rebels, the highest number to rebel on an opposition motion since Labour came to power in 1997.[109] Another perennial problem was MPs abstaining from votes, a sign of how disillusioned his backbenchers had become. 'MPs often wouldn't bother to turn up. They'd give up,' complains an aide.[110] It was to be a rebellion on an opposition day motion, combined with a large Labour abstention that delivered Brown's first and highest-profile defeat.

The Nepalese Gurkhas had served in the British Army since 1857. Until 2004 no retired Gurkha was eligible to settle in the UK, but in that year Blair said that those who had served after 1997, when the regiment's headquarters moved from Hong Kong to Kent, could become British citizens.[111] In March 2008, Nick Clegg said the government had made a 'spectacular misjudgment' in that the 1997 cut-off date was arbitrary and unjust.[112] The Gurkha cause hit the front pages when it acquired as its champion actress Joanna Lumley, whose father had served as a Major in the 6th Gurkha Rifles during the Second World World, his life being saved by Gurkha Tul Bahadur Pun. Awarded the Victoria Cross for his bravery, Tul Bahadur Pun eventually won his battle to settle in Britain in 2007. In November 2008, Lumley and others from the Gurkha Justice Campaign presented a petition with 250,000 signatures calling on the government to permit all retired Gurkhas to settle in the UK, so that the rules governing Gurkhas mirrored those for Commonwealth soldiers. In January 2009 the High Court ordered the government to revise immigration rules pertaining to the British armed forces by 24 April.[113] On that day, it duly announced that Gurkhas who had retired before 1997 could settle in the UK if they met five quite strict criteria, the government estimating that this would increase the numbers of Gurkhas eligible to come to Britain by some 4,000. 'The Gurkhas cannot meet these new criteria,' Lumley complained, adding that she was 'ashamed' of the government.[114] The *Daily Mail* took up the cause with ardour, and *The Times* estimated that 'Joanna Lumley is probably equivalent to half a dozen by-election defeats on her own'.[115]

Brown, not for the first time, was in two minds. His instinct was to support the Gurkha cause. 'He knew he should do a deal,' says one observer.[116] But Darling and the Treasury told him that to do so would cost £1.4bn, while John Hutton and the Ministry of Defence lobbied hard against yielding because the money would come from their own budget. Labour's ministers, who had enjoyed the years of plenty, were finding it much harder having to work within a tough new financial reality. Number 10 left it to the relevant Cabinet committee, Domestic Affairs, chaired by Jack Straw, to find a compromise. When that committee recommended a very tough settlement, Number 10 – under Brown's instructions – overruled Defence and Treasury objections and insisted on concessions, but initially did not push the matter further. Number 10 was already locked into a serious dispute with the Treasury over economic policy. 'Our view was you pick your battles and we chose not to pick a row over this one. It was clearly a big mistake,' says a Number 10 aide.[117] The Gurkha Justice Campaign responded that government figures were distorted, and that even if all were entitled to British citizenship, only some 8,000 out of a total of 36,000 retired Gurkhas would want to settle in Britain.[118]

Number 10 knew it had a problem with the PLP, if not the scale of its grievances. It decided to offer concessions to discontented Labour MPs rather than concede to their demands, but it was not enough. In the opposition day debate on 29 April, Brown announced, 'We have to balance our responsibilities to those who have served the country with the finance that we need to be able to meet those obligations, and therefore not base our offer on money that we cannot afford.'[119] Number 10 knew the vote would be tight but thought it would carry it.[120] Thus it was shocked when the government suffered its first defeat in the House of Commons, by 267 votes to 246, with twenty-seven Labour MPs voting against the government and seventy-seven abstaining. Stephen Pound, a Parliamentary Private Secretary, resigned from the government to vote with the rebels.[121] 'When we lost the vote, you could hear the cheer go up around the House of Commons,' says Muir.[122] 'A stench of death' now hung around the government, wrote Peter Riddell in *The Times*,[123] while Polly Toynbee, writing in *The Guardian*, asked, 'What made Gordon Brown hurl himself on that row of Gurkha kukri knives?'[124] The press were unanimous that, although the vote was purely symbolic and in itself did not force immediate changes in government policy, it had been 'humiliating' and a 'bruising day' for Brown.[125]

Brown was distraught, and felt very let down by the system – the Treasury and Ministry of Defence in particular. 'We were stitched up by the civil servants. It turned out that it would not have been nearly as expensive as the MoD told us it would have been,' says one aide.[126] Brown himself decided on the U-turn after the defeat, and was in full agreement with one of his aides, who told him: 'You don't fight two much-loved British institutions – the brave, jolly Gurkhas and Joanna Lumley – at the same time.'[127]

On 6 May, Lumley saw Brown in Downing Street and received the answer she wanted, emerging convinced that he would institute the hoped-for changes. 'I trust him ... and I know he has now taken this matter into his own hands and so today is a very good day,' she said after their meeting.[128] The pressure was now intense. A YouGov poll conducted on 7 and 8 May revealed that only 4 per cent approved the current rules, while 74 per cent thought that Gurkhas and their families should all be able to settle in Britain.[129] An announcement was inevitable, and the delivery was left to Home Secretary Jacqui Smith, who felt the episode was 'a perfect example of what happens when you're in government for too long: people get captured by their departments'.[130] On 21 May, she duly announced to the House of Commons that 'All former Gurkhas who retired before 1997 and who have served more than four years will now be eligible to apply for settlement in the UK.'[131] Lumley responded immediately that it was 'a brave decision'.[132] Clegg was less generous. 'Gordon Brown's claim of a "moral compass" rings hollow when ... he has to be dragged every inch of the way towards doing the right thing,' he said.[133]

Brown was damaged by the Gurkhas episode, and once again appeared to be very out of touch with the public mood. But it is easy to condemn him when in fact the case was not clear-cut, especially given the context of severe economic downturn. There was an air of both populism and punishment about the campaign, with the Cabinet and PLP, neither of whom were well disposed to Brown at the time, not exactly falling over themselves to be helpful. Number 10 was ruefully dismissive of what it regarded as the blatant hypocrisy and opportunism of the Tories and right-wing media, given their views on immigration and deficit reduction. Brown was not best served by his new Chief Whip, Nick Brown, whose reach did not extend to all sections of the party, nor by his political team at Number 10; both misjudged the scale of the revolt. The worst lessons that Brown could have drawn would have been to appease the PLP regardless of the issue, and to trust his instincts less, which had been right on the Gurkhas. Both these elements were about to be tested on a much bigger canvas.

Expensive Mistake: March to June 2009

For a long period in the spring and summer of 2009, MPs' attention and public opinion were absorbed by just one issue, MPs' expenses. Number 10 was reeling. 'For over a month there was a Robespierre-like terror, with the *Daily Telegraph* as the committee of public safety,' describes one insider.[134] 'Effectively, we were not in government for six weeks. The *Daily Telegraph* ran the country,' says another, who served in Number 10 during that fraught period.[135] This was the biggest parliamentary crisis in modern British history, when public anger with politicians reached unprecedented heights and public trust in the political system all but collapsed. MPs recoiled in a state of shock: 'Some of our MPs were even put on suicide watch.'[136] Number 10 was incandescent: '*The Telegraph* was appalling and very political. If you think about their own journalists' expenses claims . . .' says one insider.[137] Michael Dugher, who was at the heart of Number 10's fightback, felt, '*The Telegraph* was neither fair nor proportional in its coverage.'[138] Another Number 10 aide says, 'They hit us much harder than the Tories and they hit us first. They also went for Gordon himself in a way that was unfair and the broadcasters followed them slavishly.'[139] The general feeling in Downing Street was that, for all the culpability of some MPs including some ministers, the whole episode reeked of hypocrisy. The saga sold a lot of extra newspapers but at the cost of damaging trust in the political system.

Expenses is a subject on which Brown could speak with unique moral authority, as his own record is as close to being financially impeccable as that of any politician, and he had no embarrassing 'Bullingdon Club'-type associations as did Cameron and Osborne, nor did he have Mandelson-style relationships with the rich that might have led to accusations of hypocrisy. The work he has been engaged in since leaving office further suggests that Brown is not motivated by personal gain. He had an unparalleled opportunity for moral leadership, to steer the country, as he had at the G20, and produce a settlement for Parliament that would have won widespread applause, not least among his own supporters as it would have addressed the constitutional agenda he had opened so promisingly. He needed to distinguish genuine abuses by MPs from inoffensive errors (the public remained confused on this, there being little clarity), and to put on the agenda a revivification of Parliament to match his grand vision for the restructuring of the institutional machinery on the world stage. But where he had stuck tenaciously to his agenda in the run-up to the London G20, he could not find, until too late, a consistent voice of his own on how to handle the expenses crisis, so the much-needed sanity and national leadership was either absent or fell to others like Cameron and Clegg to articulate.

The details of the expenses débâcle are well known. Of prime interest to us here is why Brown failed to provide the leadership that would have guided the country, Parliament and his party and thereby bolstered rather than diminished his own standing. It was not that Brown lacked ideas on the problem. His instincts were right. He saw that abuses were taking place, was repelled by them, and believed that the public had a right to expect its elected politicians to behave better than some of them did. So why did he not provide a strong lead? We set out six factors below, but first, a brief background to the saga.

In May 2008 the House of Commons lost its high court battle against

disclosure of MPs' expenses. The parliamentary authorities would thus publish
details of some 1.3 million receipts of expenses, all of which would have to
be scanned and put on an electronic disc, always to be a hazardous exercise
from the point of view of security. Under pressure from MPs on both Labour
and Conservative backbenches, Harriet Harman in her role as Leader of the
House made a last-ditch effort to block full disclosure of MPs' expenses in
January 2009 but had to U-turn at the last minute when it became clear that
the Conservatives would not support the move. On 7 February 2009, the
first indications came that this expenses material had indeed leaked when it
was revealed that Jacqui Smith had claimed £116,000 when designating her
sister's house as her own main home. On 21 March it further emerged that
Employment Minister Tony McNulty had claimed £60,000 for the house in
which his parents lived, which was only eight miles from his own home. Brown
foresaw how big an issue expenses could become: 'It will be the next big thing,'
he said while on a G20 trip in the spring.[140] He held discussions with Leader
of the House Harman and Chief Whip Nick Brown, as well as his political
office and senior civil servants, from which he concluded that he should set up
a wide-ranging review.[141] Accordingly, on 23 March, he wrote to the chairman
of the Committee on Standards in Public Life, Sir Christopher Kelly, asking
him to conduct a comprehensive review of MPs' pay and allowances, as well as
of wider issues, such as MPs' outside interests and second jobs. On 29 March,
while Brown was in Chile on the last leg of his G20 world tour, news broke
of Jacqui Smith's expenses claim for a pornographic film. Responding to this
on 30 March, and anxious to be ahead of the issue, Brown suggested that
Kelly's standards committee consider replacing the controversial 'second home
allowance system' with a simpler 'overnight allowance' for MPs, and also to
begin his review at the earliest possible opportunity.[142] On 31 March, Kelly
announced that he would bring forward his enquiry to report in late 2009. But
that was still many months off, and the public interest in the issue was far too
great to allow it to go into abeyance until then.

The 'overnight allowance' proposal would see MPs claiming expenses
where costs were incurred for staying over in London while on Parliamentary
business. A similar system operated for peers in the House of Lords. But not
all of the PLP or Cabinet liked the idea as they thought it was not fair on
MPs who lived in London. Hilary Benn spoke to Brown about their concerns,
which were shared by Hutton among others. Brown was finally persuaded
hours away from the key Cabinet meeting on 21 April to change the 'overnight'
allowance to a daily or *per diem* allowance,[143] which Cabinet endorsed, though
without giving the proposal full time for consideration. At the end of Cabinet,
Communities Secretary Hazel Blears was photographed leaving Downing
Street: the cameras clearly picked up a document outlining proposals to

replace the second home allowance with the daily rate proposal, taking away the element of surprise.[144]

Tuesday 21 April was a busy day all round at Number 10. Sarah Brown was keenly promoting the idea of her husband using new media in the wake of McBride's departure, and had convinced him to make a YouTube film to promote his ideas for fixing the expenses system, which was recorded that morning before Cabinet.[145] It was part of a new wave of thinking pioneered by Forsyth and Sarah. 'We knew that the mainstream media hated Gordon and so we deliberately sought out new forms to bypass it and talk direct to the public. Traditional media didn't like us doing this, which is why they were so damning,' Forsyth says.[146] Brown was a strong supporter of the initiative and hoped his YouTube recordings might prove as successful as Roosevelt's 'fireside chats', a series of highly effective evening radio addresses given by the President between 1933 and 1944. Some four hundred films were recorded during Brown's premiership and on the whole his team felt they were 'a great vehicle for him'. However, Forsyth realised almost immediately that expenses was the wrong topic for Brown to launch on, and that he was not in a good frame of mind to give a strong performance.[147] The original plan had been for Brown to set out his proposals for a flat-rate daily attendance allowance to MPs by letter, according to Number 10 sources, until persuaded of the merits of putting it over on YouTube.[148] Brown sensed that he had not come across well and was conscious that he had smiled unnaturally, and was about to ask for the film of his mawkish interview to be played back to him when one of his private secretaries came in to tell him that James Purnell urgently needed to see him before Cabinet started. 'So off he went without seeing the clip' explains one of those present. Brown hadn't helped matters by turning up twenty minutes late to record the film, his late arrival explained partly because of vacillations in his message and partly because Number 10 was in overdrive with Darling's Budget due the next day.[149] The message bombed. In the post-McBride climate, no one was going to give the Prime Minister the benefit of the doubt. It frustrated him greatly that he was being judged not on his important message, but on the quality of his performance. 'He considered it trivial: his policies and substance are what he cared about,' says Number 10's Theo Bertram.[150] Brown's first difficulty in handling the expenses crisis was thus finding sufficient time to think clearly. Rushing into an announcement on the hop was to lead him down a blind alley.

Brown worked hard to get his new '*per diem*' scheme through the House of Commons, and he was persuaded by his Number 10 staff to hold a meeting with Cameron and Clegg and to obtain cross-party support. It was duly fixed for the evening of the Budget, 22 April, taking place in his office in the House of Commons. The forty-minute meeting went badly. Brown was not in a good mood from the outset and came over to them poorly. Cameron and Clegg felt patronised. It was obvious to Cameron that Brown had not read his own proposals: when they walked out of the meeting, the Conservative leader turned to Clegg and said he thought that Brown was 'dysfunctional'.[151] Cameron did not like the idea of the hastily conceived daily allowance, which was always open to the charge it was merely 'clocking-on' money, while Clegg told Brown he favoured a much larger-scale solution. Brown concluded that they were just playing politics, and that they did not want to back a plan that he himself had produced. With hindsight, his officials in Number 10 wished they had persuaded him to have a second session with Cameron and Clegg when he was in a more agreeable and less suspicious frame of mind.[152]

Brown's daily allowance proposal proved no more popular with MPs than the overnight allowance. On 27 April, recognising that he was not going to achieve sufficient parliamentary support, and that he could not even rely on his own PLP, he dropped his proposals. This left the impression that Cameron was driving the agenda. Brown was intensely frustrated and angry, at both the PLP and at Cameron, who he considered was being 'hypocritical' over an issue of national concern.[153] April, which began so promisingly with the G20, had collapsed into the very worst month of Brown's premiership, with the McBride scandal dominating the first couple of weeks, the widespread and personal abuse after the YouTube clip appeared on 21 April, alarm at the size of the deficit in the Budget on 22 April, the climb-down over expenses reform on 27 April, and his first defeat in the Commons over the Gurkhas on 29 April. In this fraught atmosphere Brown was about to make his second error in his handling of the crisis, which was taking matters personally.

Geoff Hoon had earlier raised in Cabinet concerns he had heard that someone was trying to sell to the press information on MPs' expenses.[154] So it was not a total surprise when Robert Winnett from the *Daily Telegraph* called Ellam at lunchtime on Thursday 7 May, saying he had some urgent questions about the Prime Minister's expenses claims. Should he send them on a secure line? 'I'd hope all the email addresses in Downing Street are secure. Send them to me,' Ellam replied tartly, and hung up. Ellam called Dugher at once: 'You need to get back to the office as soon as possible and help deal with this.'[155] An email shortly came through from Winnett to Number 10 with a list of questions about Brown's and other Cabinet ministers' personal expense claims. It did not take long for Brown's team to realise that this was serious, with detailed questions about an episode that purported to show Brown behaving dishonestly.[156] Winnett gave Number 10 until six that evening to respond.[157] *The Telegraph* had fired its shots and prepared an explosive front-page story for the following day. Number 10 knew it would have no option but to involve Brown himself, and reluctantly agreed for him to clear his diary that afternoon so he could go through the expense claims with them in forensic detail.[158] He did not take it well, and it was rapidly clear to all that he was traumatised by the questions he was being asked, which were about the period between 2004 and 2006 when he paid cheques to his brother, Andrew Brown, from money he had claimed through expenses. As it turned out there was nothing untoward with these arrangements: the money was expressly sent to his brother to reimburse him for the cost of a cleaner he had organised for Brown's Westminster flat. Brown was accused of much as Prime Minister, but this allegation of impropriety was manifestly unjust. Aides described him that afternoon as being 'fixated with anger and frustration' as they pieced together the details of what had happened. He found it, 'intolerable, very distracting and deeply destabilising that he was being accused of dishonesty for personal gain', says a Number 10 official.[159]

By the 6pm deadline Number 10 was able to produce enough material for the newspaper to show that Brown's actions had been wholly above board.[160] The *Daily Telegraph* on 8 May nevertheless splashed on its front page the story about the cleaning arrangements, with the implication that Brown had not been fully straight. That morning, Brown, who had had a bad night, was deeply disturbed when he listened to the *Today* programme to find the story being given widespread airing. When he learned that an *Evening Standard* reporter had gone to his brother's block of flats, and shouted questions about cleaning arrangements through his front door, he was simply beside himself with anger. That Friday he was on a regional tour in East Anglia. Unable to control himself, he demanded he speak by phone to the *Daily Telegraph*'s editor Will Lewis. The long conversation, described diplomatically by the official listening in as 'very difficult', went round in circles. Brown's main point was that any politician or any individual had a right to expect honest reporting, rather than innuendo, and he had provided a straightforward explanation which the paper had not reflected in its coverage. Lewis's response was, in sum, 'We are just reporting the facts: there is a cleaning bill invoiced to your brother that you claimed for.'[161] The language was intemperate: it was one of those occasions when Brown simply 'lost it'. He concluded the newspaper was acting insincerely and was merely looking for a big front-page story to launch its scoop. The trauma affected him for several days afterwards. 'Gordon was like a wounded animal. He was deeply hurt by the accusations, and especially by his brother being dragged into the mire with him,' says one observer.[162] 'Why are they saying these things about me?' Brown would ask regularly.[163] 'He felt victimised and it lost him sight of the big picture,' says an adviser.[164] On 9 May, a *Telegraph* leader absolved Brown of personal wrong-doing: 'There has never been any suggestion of any impropriety on the part of the Prime Minister or his brother.' But the harm was done by then, and the paper knew it.[165] Brown's reacting so personally, while understandable, clouded his judgement at a critical time. He became intensely self-centred, impervious to outsiders. He showed none of the *sang froid* he displayed during the financial crisis. To be effective in crises, leaders need to be calm and objective to take the right decisions. In this instance, he was neither of these.

With Brown at bay, Mandelson fatally stepped into the breach and decreed Number 10's line, that Brown was the victim of a 'political plot, that the story was being aired in a Conservative newspaper to damage the Labour Party'. 'Bollocks to *The Telegraph*: let's front this thing out,' was his approach.[166] Mandelson was highly popular at Number 10 but on this issue many thought he made a misjudgement. 'Peter is crap at this stuff because of his feelings about his second resignation when he felt he should have faced out criticism from the press,' says one of his supporters in Number 10.[167] In public, Mandelson now rounded on the 'Tory-supporting *Daily Telegraph*' for using 'classic smear tactics' to create the appearance of wrong-doing without proof.[168] This line had some support from Brown's aides. Political secretary Joe Irvin cautioned Brown against making a general apology, which he believed would implicate him in any wrong-doing that had been committed.[169] Nick Brown was not in favour of him wearing his heart on his sleeve either. But other members of the Prime Minister's circle and his wider associates such as Michael Wills, sensing the public anger and dismay, told him straight that he needed to apologise without delay and take tough action against wrong-doers. As ever Brown was taking advice from multiple and conflicting sources. In his gut he knew that some MPs being accused were guilty of wrong-doing and he sensed the growing public anger. But in the highly charged atmosphere his third misjudgement was listening to the wrong people instead of having the confidence to trust his own instincts.[170]

When he did offer an apology, on 11 May at the Royal College of Nursing, four days after the story broke, it was paper-thin and did not resonate with the public. 'I want to apologise on behalf of politicians, on behalf of all parties, for what has happened in the events of the last few days,' some force being taken out of this statement by an official spokesman at the same time saying that he would not be taking action against ministers embroiled in the scandal where they had not themselves strictly broken the rules.[171] But while Brown was prepared to draw his line on what the rules did or did not permit MPs to claim, Cameron sensed that the public had no respect for the existing rules and he should distance himself from supporting them.

The *Daily Telegraph* turned its coverage that Monday to the Conservative frontbench, and the following day to Tory grandees before putting the heat on backbenchers. Brown felt in his bones that Cameron and Osborne, who had both claimed much larger sums than him through the housing allowance, had much more to answer for than senior Labour figures.[172] That may well have been true. But Cameron knew exactly what to say to the cameras. Unlike Brown's, his apology connected with the public. 'I want to start by saying sorry ... People are right to be angry that some MPs have taken public money to pay for things few could afford. You've been let down,' he said. 'Politicians have done things which are ... wrong. I don't care if they are within the rules – the rules are wrong.'[173] In contrast to Brown, Cameron went further by announcing that he was directing his shadow Cabinet colleagues to repay a number of claims, naming and shaming them in his press conference, including his close colleague Michael Gove, who would be repaying £7,000 for furniture.[174] Cameron rounded on Brown in the House of Commons and accused him of lacking leadership: 'I sometimes wonder whether he needs an independent commission to decide whether he has tea or coffee in the morning.'[175] Contrasting his own decisiveness with Brown's 'fudge', Clegg told his sixty-three Liberal Democrat MPs that any profits financed by the taxpayer that they made from their second homes would go straight back to the public purse.[176]

Another difficulty for Brown – his fourth – was the PLP, many of whose MPs thought they had done nothing wrong and demanded that Brown stand up for them. This had added force when combined with difficulty number five, his greatly diminished political authority following the McBride episode and his indecisive handling of the Gurkhas and much else. Even before *The Telegraph* had got hold of the expenses files, the PLP was furious with Brown given his support for full disclosure. He had been persuaded to support Harman's last-minute attempt to exempt MPs in January 2009 only because he was led to believe it would attract cross-party support. When it became clear that the Conservatives would not condone the move, Brown overruled Harman and told her to proceed with publication in full.[177] The PLP therefore blamed Brown 'for getting us into this mess'.[178] It wanted Brown to protect its members against the baying press and public, not hang them out to dry. Most of them continued to argue that they had acted within the rules, and endorsed the Mandelson line that it was all a political plot against Labour by the right-wing press. Brown was caught between a rock and a hard place, and ended up failing to be tough enough to placate public anger, but too tough for the PLP.

A sixth and final difficulty stymieing Brown in the whole saga was that many in his Cabinet, including Balls and Darling, were accused of wrong-doing. If he made statements that were too condemnatory, might it put his two most vital ministers in a difficult position? Number 10 increasingly fell out with Nick Brown, who it felt was championing the PLP view too strongly, and with Harman for becoming, as it saw it, 'a shop steward' for the PLP. 'For Gordon's deputy to take their side so strongly was the very worst thing,' says one aide, who holds Harman personally responsible for ensuring that the Executive ending up being blamed for the faults of the Legislature.[179] Within Number 10, while political advisers like Gavin Kelly and David Muir were arguing that Brown should speak directly to the public about his concerns at the abuses, others like Irvin maintained that 'A general apology would damage relations with the PLP who feel they are being fed to the wolves.'[180] The longer the dispute dragged on, the more Number 10 became divided. Cameron knew it and the longer he could prolong it, the more havoc it created for Labour.

Number 10 was divided further about the fate of the Speaker, Michael Martin, whose conduct and indifferent performance had become a subject of national debate. The hawks argued that he represented all that was worst about the ancien régime and had 'sold us down the river'.[181] Opposing pressure on Brown came from trade unionists and traditional Labour MPs who saw Martin as one of their own and demanded that under no circumstances should he be sacrificed: 'It was all about Labour Party solidarity with a working-class speaker,' says Ben Bradshaw.[182] Brown, who had known Martin for years, agonised over what to do. On 14 May, Bradshaw told Number 10 of his intention to demand in public for Martin to go. Brown saw grave danger and phoned the Culture Secretary about what he planned to do, saying, 'At least you owe me a conversation.' When they met, Brown said his concern about Martin being forced out was in part who would replace him, to which Bradshaw responded, 'It doesn't matter. MPs will vote for the reformist candidate.'[183] Very clearly to all, Brown was not in control of events. On Sunday 17 May he reassured Martin in private that he would not allow a vote of no confidence in him to be debated. The next day, Martin was savaged by MPs, who demanded that he 'give indication of [his] intent to retire' so that the Commons could have a 'new Speaker with the moral authority [to] lift this House out of the mire'.[184] Brown told Martin later that day that he had changed his view and that the Speaker's future was for Parliament to decide. Following another meeting with Brown on 19 May, Martin resigned, becoming the first Speaker to be forced from office in more than 300 years.

Would Brown ever show any grip on the issue? Well, yes, eventually he would and did. The day before the end of the sad Speaker spectacle, on 18 May, Brown at last produced a plan to resolve the expenses crisis. Throughout May he had been hunting for an alternative policy to his 'per diem' allowance to put forward. He looked with Nick Pearce and Stewart Wood at a variety of models for expenses in legislatures abroad, and out of this he now decided that the best solution was to take MPs' expenses out of the realm of politics altogether – just as he had with interest rates a decade earlier – by creating an independent regulator, based loosely on the German model.[185]

Brown's officials strongly liked the idea and pleaded with him to obtain cross-party support for it. But Brown failed to rise to the occasion and flatly refused to see Cameron a second time, so outraged was he by his behaviour during the episode. His aides were disappointed by his stubbornness, but suggested that the Cabinet Secretary meet with Cameron in his place in an attempt to depoliticise the proposal. O'Donnell duly met Cameron and Clegg, and managed to secure their backing, vital to the proposal's success.[186] Before launching the new plan, Brown did consent to talk to Cameron, albeit by phone over the weekend. It went better than the appalling meeting in his room four weeks earlier, but it was still far from satisfactory.

At his press conference at Number 10 on 19 May, Brown duly announced, 'The keystone of any reform must be to switch from self-regulation to independent, external regulation.' He stated, 'Westminster cannot operate some gentlemen's club where the members make up the rules and operate them among themselves.'[187] At the same time, he announced further tightening of expenses rules and tough action against Labour MPs with dubious expenses claims and that MPs' allowances would be scrutinised by an independent panel (to be headed by Sir Thomas Legg, whose report in the autumn would reignite the expenses furore when more than 300 MPs would be told to repay some of their claims). He further announced that Labour's NEC had given unanimous support for his proposal that Labour MPs who had broken the rules should not stand at the next general election and would have to go before a 'star chamber'. In his diary Chris Mullin recorded of the PLP meeting on 18 May: 'For the first time since the crisis began, he appears to have a plan ... At last some leadership.'[188] But the independent regulator proposal was far from popular with many in Cabinet and party, who felt these new ideas went too far. Sympathy came to focus on Ian Gibson, MP for Norwich North, who many felt was to be treated as a scapegoat by the 'kangaroo court' star chamber, 'to save Brown's own skin', and on Hazel Blears, for being singled out for public humiliation at the press conference principally because of her disloyalty to Brown.[189] MPs vented their frustration in the press, saying, 'It's all about Gordon'; that the appointment of the Legg inquiry was just to strengthen his own precarious position and that he was happy to 'throw people out of the plane' when MPs had angered Number 10 but not when they were supporters.[190] Gibson, who was deselected as a Labour candidate, immediately resigned in protest, forcing the first post-expenses by-election, in Norwich North. It took place in July, when Brown would be humiliated by a 16.5 per cent swing to the Tories.

Could Brown yet save anything from the wreckage? Seizing on the opportunity to introduce constitutional reform to make the political system more accountable was favoured by many of his ministers, including Andrew Adonis, Bradshaw, David Miliband and Wills. But Straw, Darling and Balls believed that time spent on constitutional reform would be a distraction, and that the government needed to return as quickly as possible to its strongest card – managing the economy and tackling the financial crisis.[191] Had Brown made good on his 2007 constitutional resolve, then he would have entered the expenses crisis as a proven political reformer rather than being painted as a laggard. In the two years that had passed since he announced his ambition to enact a 'new constitutional settlement' he had delivered nothing noteworthy. He would say he was distracted by the economic concerns and blocked by a divided Cabinet and sceptical PLP. But he himself was not immune to the constitutional conservatism that plagued the Labour Party, and his reforming zeal soon ebbed away as he encountered the real difficulties of putting reform into action. He had shrunk from reforming the role of the Attorney General and refused to push proposals for a British Bill of Rights. Early on in his premiership he toyed with banning MPs from holding second jobs but he did not think MPs would wear it.[192] His cautious side also got the better of him in 2008 when he asked for a 'recall' mechanism for MPs be taken out of the 'communities in control' white paper because he worried that it would be used to attack ministers unfairly.[193] A senior adviser sums up Brown's attitude: 'Gordon's heart was convinced on the need for constitutional reform, but his political head was never really persuaded.'[194]

Brown, nevertheless, attempted to use the expenses crisis as a catalyst for reviving his defunct constitutional programme when he made a major statement on the subject to the House of Commons on 10 June. He rightly argued that, 'Democratic reform ... must principally be led by our engagement with the public. It cannot be top-down.' But this was also an argument of convenience for someone who could not make up his own mind about where he stood on large swathes of constitutional policy. He declared that the government over the following weeks would be setting out proposals for reform in a number of areas: the House of Lords, individual rights, on a written constitution (which he said he personally favoured), further devolution from London, review of the voting age, and, finally, on electoral reform, which led on to a debate on the Alternative Vote over the following months.[195] But little solid came of the proposals. Constitutional reform was to remain one of the Brown government's lacunae.

Brown had not come out of the expenses crisis at all well. He was constantly behind the curve. The polling evidence pointed to the country believing Cameron handled it much better, the Tory leader coming across as more decisive and agile and communicating much more clearly with the public. In the financial crisis Brown knew what to do, which levers to pull, and which people to phone. But in the expenses crisis he struggled to know how to respond or how to cope with the visceral public anger it generated; it cruelly exposed his limitations as a leader. Successful leaders transcend the difficulties they face. Brown succumbed to his six areas of difficulty. The picture, though, is not wholly bleak. The independent regulator, though highly controversial with MPs, was the right solution that addressed the fundamental problem

– self-regulation. Abolishing the fees office, which had condoned malpractice for years, was also the right solution.

Number 10's 'Darkest Night': 2 to 4 June 2009

Brown was under enormous pressure. McBride, the Gurkhas, expenses, terrible polls, the deficit – the roll call of political disasters ran on and on. Labour MPs had had enough. By early summer, many concluded that, with Brown at the helm, electoral annihilation awaited. A terrible three days for Brown, culminating in his worst night as Prime Minister, started on Tuesday 2 June. It began innocuously when Jacqui Smith announced her intention to resign as Home Secretary. Brown had urged her to hang on for longer, but so traumatised had she been by the onslaught on her and her family over expenses that she decided she simply wanted out.[196] To lose a Home Secretary at a volatile time was worrying because of the questions that would be bound to be asked about whether she had a secret agenda – which, for all her doubts about Brown, she did not. On the same day, Beverley Hughes, the Blairite family minister, and Tom Watson, the Brownite Cabinet Office minister, announced they were standing down from the government. *The Guardian* reported that the resignations meant that Brown was 'losing control' of his reshuffle, which everyone had expected to follow the election results on 4 June.[197]

On Wednesday 3 June, *The Guardian* carried a devastating editorial that shook Brown to the core. It opened, 'Labour needs to find someone who is able to set out a case for progressive government.' The newspaper, which Alastair Campbell used to refer to as the 'Gordian', had finally lost patience. The keenest cheerleaders of Brown on the paper had been Polly Toynbee and Jackie Ashley, but both became rapidly disillusioned with him after he became Prime Minister, as to a lesser extent did his other early *Guardian* supporter, Jonathan Freedland. Two other key figures there, Martin Kettle and Patrick Wintour, had never been particular fans, but the author of the deadly editorial was none of these but Alan Rusbridger, the paper's cerebral and usually hands-off editor. Having listened to disillusioned Labour MPs drone on and on about Brown's failings for many months, he at last felt he needed to do something decisive.[198]

The Guardian had fallen out of love with New Labour over the Iraq War, but Brown's view of Blair's invasion was the hatred that dare not speak its name, so an opportunity for affinity was lost. After he moved into Number 10, his failure to pursue constitutional reform, or to define a progressive agenda on education, health or crime, all antagonised the paper's leading journalists. In July 2008, it had carried the David Miliband article,[199] which it had deliberately placed on the front page, to the author's apparent surprise.[200] The following month it had published the Aitkenhead interview with Darling, which it knew would not cause rejoicing in Number 10. As with *The Observer*, it had not been courted under the McBride regime, and Cameron and his press secretary Andy Coulson saw an opening. 'Cameron had been making a lot of overtures to us, for self-serving reasons, which we weren't naive about,'[201] says a *Guardian* insider, but the paper carried a steady flow of articles about Cameron and the Tories' progressive agenda on child poverty and the environment, which irritated Number 10 considerably.[202]

Brown knew there was no love lost between *The Guardian* and Number 10, but was still stung that he had effectively no warning of the 3 June editorial appearing. Rusbridger had consulted his senior staff about it, but decided he did not want to have a long conversation with Brown and Number 10 trying to talk him out of it. Brown had had his chance, Rusbridger concluded, and the time for further dialogue had passed.[203] For him, Brown's inept handling of expenses had been the final straw and, with expected poor results in the local and European elections the following day, he thought there was a serious opportunity for unseating the Prime Minister and having a new leader in place by September. 'The tragedy for Mr Brown and his party is that his chance to change [Parliament] has gone,' the editorial stated. 'There is no vision from him, no plan, no argument for the future and no support.' There were harsh words about Brown personally: 'Flaws in his character that drove his party close to revolt last summer now dominate again. He is not obviously able to lead. He blames others for failures and allows them insufficient credit for successes.' He was out of tune, said the editorial, with the sensibilities of Labour voters: 'The McBride affair was poisonous to his reputation but he did not seem to understand why.' On expenses: 'His timidity ... has been painful ... the Prime Minister was absent from the start of the debate and cautious now he has joined it. His instinct is usually to hesitate.' It concluded with two devastating pronouncements: 'Labour has a year left before an election; its current leader would waste it. It is time to cut him loose.'[204]

Brown was busy preparing for PMQs on the morning of 3 June and trying to shut out thoughts about the editorial when the private secretaries knocked on the door. 'Hazel Blears wants to come in,' one said. 'I'm busy,' Brown snapped. 'She says you will want to hear this,' came the reply. Nervous as to what was coming, he agreed to see her – and was presented with her resignation.[205] When he emerged from meeting with Blears in the den, he looked 'pretty wounded'.[206] His relations with her had been difficult from almost the moment she joined his Cabinet as Communities Secretary in June 2007. They deteriorated sharply during the expenses crisis, during which she felt unsupported by Number 10, notably over Brown's description at his May press conference of her 'unacceptable behaviour'. Number 10, on its side, had not forgiven her for writing a provocative article entitled 'YouTube is no substitute for knocking on doors', in *The Observer* on 2 May, which criticised the government for a 'lamentable failure to get our message across'.[207] 'She was in deep water on expenses and she jumped before she was pushed,' was the uncompromising verdict of a Number 10 aide on her departure. It regarded her as a 'serial leaker' and aides pressed Brown to get rid of her.[208] She was heavily briefed against, leading to the *Daily Telegraph* describing her as 'out of control'.[209] Reports had filtered back into Number 10 over several months of the 'women against Gordon' (alternative 'WAGs'), Brown's female ministers Smith, Ruth Kelly, Caroline Flint and Blears, who met occasionally in each other's flats 'for a gossip over a bottle of wine'.[210] Brown had not done well with his female ministers, whereas Blair had been charming to them. Women were disproportionately high in number among the Brown-haters in the PLP. There was no love lost in return.

Blears's resignation was nevertheless deeply damaging, particularly its timing: she was the Cabinet minister responsible for local government, resigning the day before local elections. There was to be one final sting. When she came in to see Brown in Downing Street, she wore a brooch which bore the words 'Rocking the boat' in small letters. The press cameras zoomed in on it and had a field day with the images. When Brown was told about the pictures he responded, 'I didn't see it. Why would anyone want to do that? ... What an awful thing that is to do.' He became 'absolutely low' about it.[211] His aides were even more disconcerted. 'This was really bad,' one of them says.[212] Blears's staff maintained that she regretted the timing of her resignation, and had not realised the 'damage it would do on the eve of the local elections'.[213] As for the brooch, it had been, they said, a present from her husband, and her staff again maintain that she had not intended the cameras to pick it up: 'It was a little bit of feistiness, a private joke between her and the team,' says one.[214] She later apologised for both the timing of her resignation and for wearing the brooch. Her reputation was badly damaged by the episode.

Number 10 was reeling. Mandelson loved such occasions, when he could be the instigator of calm and wisdom. He was the person who rallied everyone, leading the discussion and arguing that Brown needed to heap thanks and praise at PMQs on both Smith and Blears. Brown heeded the advice. 'I think the first thing the whole House would want to do is acknowledge the great work that has been done by both the Home Secretary and the Communities Secretary in the Cabinet,' he began.[215] Brown had his blood up and was on his very best form against Cameron, neatly deflecting questions about whether Darling would still be in a job by the end of the week. Mandelson's strategy then dictated he and the camera-friendly Alan Johnson 'smother the airwaves' talking up Brown.[216] Johnson was sitting on the front bench during PMQs. Before Brown began speaking, he thought to himself, 'I might be taking Prime Minister's questions next week,'[217] as he was the current front-runner to succeed Brown. The idea was not unappealing to him as an ambitious man who enjoyed the limelight. He thought very seriously about throwing his hat into the ring. Aspects of the job of prime minister appealed greatly to him. So why did he pull back? His own explanation is that he was so impressed by Brown's bravura performance that day at PMQs that he was left wondering whether he could match that level. To clear his mind, he wandered up and down Victoria Street, thrashing out his options. His conclusion was that he did not believe he could do it, so decided he would continue to support Brown's premiership.[218] On the airwaves, he duly praised Brown's 'tenacity' and 'courage', saying, 'There is absolutely no one who could do the job better.'[219] 'I remember thinking about Gordon in action during the financial crisis and thinking, "Could I really do that?"'[220]

While Brown was busy handling PMQs, *The Guardian* announced a scoop: it had uncovered a plot by backbench Labour MPs to rally disaffected voices to provoke a leadership contest. Dubbed the 'hotmail plot' after the email address that malcontents were urged to contact, 'signonnow@hotmail.co.uk', it piled still more pressure on the Number 10 team, who no longer knew what to believe.[221] The plan was for the rebels to publish a letter calling for a leadership election once they had obtained fifty signatures. By the Wednesday evening thousands of emails had arrived at the address, but only the odd one apparently from genuinely sympathetic MPs. One was reportedly from 'brownn@parliament.uk', the email address of the Chief Whip, Nick Brown, who himself was in overdrive, working up his whips to acts that some Labour MPs found intimidating and offensive.[222] Long-time Brown critics Graham Stringer, Graham Allen and Paul Farrelly were among those accused of disloyalty.[223] On the BBC's *Newsnight* programme that Wednesday evening, it was reported that Alan Milburn and Stephen Byers were behind the agitation.[224] As this was not true, Milburn was understandably furious and Nick Brown, who had given that story to the press, later had to recant his accusation.[225]

Thursday 4 June, the day of the local and European elections, was edgy in Number 10. Muir went around the horseshoe playing Jeremiah, predicting, 'This will be total meltdown. We will be destroyed.'[226] In the days leading up to election day, Nye, Gavin Kelly and Irvin had individually sensed that 'something was up' with the PLP, but they did not know precisely what. They also picked up a festering smell around Cabinet. Relations with Cabinet ministers had still not recovered from the McBride affair of six weeks earlier.[227] In the morning, journalists began calling Number 10 for a response to rumours that a new minister was about to resign. Inside the building speculation was rife. 'We all thought that it was going to be Caroline Flint,' says one aide.[228] From lunchtime, Nye began to get very nervous about Flint and what she might do, but when Number

10 contacted the minister, she agreed to make a supportive statement.[229] If the mystery minister was not Flint, then who might it be? No one knew. But from about 4pm Number 10 was unable to reach James Purnell, the Blairite Work and Pensions Secretary. 'We thought it was ominous: he always returned our calls.'[230] Number 10 spoke to Mandelson, who was close to Purnell. What did he think? 'No worries, he's absolutely fine,' he positively oozed.[231] For a while, temporary calm was restored. But when Brown's team could not subsequently get hold of Purnell's special adviser, Iain Bundred, it began to get seriously worried. When they did eventually get through to Bundred, he told them: 'Something is up.'[232]

Ambivalent from the start about Brown, Purnell travelled on a long journey over the premiership. He had agreed to serve in Brown's Cabinet in June 2007, hopeful that Brown would defy his expectations. What had happened in two years to so alienate him? Purnell spoke regularly about his qualms to his close friend Philip Collins, who had been an aide in Blair's Number 10 and was now working at *The Times*. In June 2008, Collins had co-authored an article in *Prospect* magazine entitled 'Liberalise or Die' in which he argued that Labour needed to turn its back on its centralising past – considered a personal dig at Brown because of his heavy association with governing through a high-spending strong central state – and embrace a more localist and liberal politics.[233] When told about it, Brown was furious and advised Purnell to sack him as his speechwriter, which both found odd as Collins was not actually employed by the Work and Pensions Secretary.[234] Brown was certain that Purnell must have had a hand in the article: this is not true, both say.[235] It was typical of Brown to agonise over something so trivial. 'He would read obscure blogs to see who was attacking him: it was very pathetic,' admits one of his team.[236] Number 10 remained deeply wary of Collins (whom initially it had tried to hire), particularly when editorials in *The Times* began to talk up the merits of Purnell.[237] He was indeed becoming increasingly alienated and disenchanted, not least by the bullying side of Brown's operation and the sense of drift, especially in his own departmental area. Brown had backed his welfare reform bill but he subsequently blocked all additional moves towards further reform – such as merging the basic state pension and the state second pension – because he would not stand up to the PLP, which opposed further reform. By 2008 Purnell thus felt, 'We'd left the playing field on welfare reform.'[238]

The crucial point came over the Budget in 2009, when Purnell threatened to resign over proposed delays to one of his proposals, for personal accounts (a low cost and portable occupational pension scheme for low earners), though Darling managed to 'talk him off the ledge'.[239] Purnell then wrote to Brown setting out his ideas for the next steps on welfare reform, but Brown 'never replied'. Purnell was angry. 'Why should I write to him when he's being so disloyal to me?' was Brown's response.[240] Brown's harpies further whipped him up about Purnell and made him paranoid. 'He saw plots where there were no plots,' says an observer.[241] Many in Number 10 were in despair about Brown's failure to work productively with such an obviously popular and talented Cabinet minister (when many ministers were neither). By the early summer, Purnell had decided on his course of action. If he could not make arguments in Cabinet such as for the need for cuts without being dressed down, or make any difference on welfare policy, there really was no point in being in government. Brown's machine politics, he said, had been the final catalyst, after he was asked to mouth words in support of the Prime Minister after the grisly McBride affair. He says: 'The elastic snapped', and he thought, 'I can't go on like this. I'm living a lie.'[242]

Purnell was very conflicted about the form of his exit. 'I never wanted to be one of those plotters. I hated the way they'd plotted against Tony. I developed an allergic reaction to it all,' he says.[243] Nevertheless, as the date of the reshuffle approached, he singled out selected Cabinet ministers for private conversations, asking what they thought should happen. One after another, they made it clear to him that they did not want to resign themselves. They told him their fear was that, if they failed to topple Brown, the party would be in a weaker position with a still more damaged Prime Minister.[244] John Denham, who shared his frustrations with Brown, was one of those to whom Purnell spoke early on in election week. 'I can understand part A of your plan – to resign – but what's part B? What happens next?' he asked Purnell, reporting that no answer was forthcoming.[245] Many Cabinet ministers, speculate that Purnell resigned to force David Miliband's hand as the two were very good friends. They know Purnell did not want the crown himself, so assume he wanted to be the catalyst. But this was not to be.[246] Purnell spoke to Miliband, who told him outright he did not agree with what he was doing and would not support him.[247]

On Thursday 4 June at midday David Miliband spoke again to Purnell and tried to talk him out of resigning.[248] But Purnell could not be dissuaded (Miliband would later say he regretted not fighting harder to stop Purnell from resigning that day). Who else might be the champion against Brown? Might Alan Johnson stand? Purnell did not speak to Johnson about his resignation plans that week but nevertheless knew about Johnson's reservations over Brown. However, he also knew that Johnson had 'fundamental doubts' about whether he wanted to be Prime Minister.[249] This was a blow as Johnson would have been the ideal challenger – able, and popular across the party. Purnell found himself in a desperate dilemma, with no obvious candidate to step up to the mark to pull off *The Guardian*'s dream of a 'bloodless coup' and having a new leader in place by September. Purnell's choice was whether to go quietly and keep his thoughts entirely to himself, or to use his resignation to air the whole question of the party's leadership. 'I came to the view that the latter was what needed to happen,' Purnell says.[250]

Just as the polls were about to close at 9.50 that evening, Purnell put in the call to Brown that Number 10 was dreading. The team knew that the loss of the popular Blairite Cabinet minister could be lethal at such a troubled time. Brown anxiously tried to talk him out of going, but it was too late – Purnell had already told the press of his intention and his resignation letter was in circulation. It opened, 'Dear Gordon, we both love the Labour Party. I've worked for it for twenty years and you for far longer ... I am therefore calling on you to stand aside to give our party a fighting chance of winning. As such I am resigning from government ... I am not seeking the leadership, nor acting with anyone else.'[251]

The call went out for everybody to return immediately to Number 10. When Michael Dugher returned shortly after 10pm it reminded him of the scene from *The Godfather*, 'when Michael Corleone comes back from the hospital and the place is full of people armed to the teeth – it's just this time they were all armed with their mobiles frantically speaking to everyone'.[252] When Mandelson entered the open-plan office in Number 12, he is described as being 'absolutely shell-shocked'.[253] He had not seen this coming – and could not believe that his political antennae had let him down so badly. Mandelson had spoken to Purnell about the reshuffle shortly before, and had told him Brown was considering giving him either health or education. He had picked up no indication at all about his plans.[254] Mandelson resolved now to do everything he could to protect Brown.

What to say on *Newsnight*, the first chance for a public response and beginning in just minutes, was the most pressing concern. It fell to Liam Byrne to be the mouthpiece, as he was due to appear already, to talk about the election results. At 10.28pm he and Mandelson had a frantic phone conversation working out the line. They came up with, 'James is a friend but he's got this one wrong,' which then became the official government line.[255] At 10.30pm when *Newsnight* came on air, Number 10 was in a total panic. It had no idea if it was facing a coordinated coup, linked to the departures of Blears and even Smith, or if Purnell was acting alone. 'Names were flying around. Some of our more paranoid people think Tony is behind it.'[256] Was Charlie Falconer involved? Or Charles Clarke, deemed to be very well plugged into disillusionment in the Cabinet?[257] Clarke had indeed been speaking to *The Guardian* for several days, telling the paper that there was about to be a move against Brown. 'We were sort of aware there was going to be a putsch. We weren't happy, though, not to have the inside track on it,' says *The Guardian*'s Patrick Wintour.[258] The paper's journalists, like everyone else, could only watch open-mouthed as events unfolded.

Brown himself was described by several sources as being 'calm' that evening. Towards midnight he sent his international development aide an email about policy: 'When things get tough, he would often turn to development issues:

it's his hinterland,' says one of his advisers.[259] It was reminiscent of the way he chose to focus on Burma at the height of the election crisis in the autumn of 2007. Some of his team admired the way he would never lose sight of such issues. Others, however, believed it highlighted a leadership weakness. 'He had a tendency, when things got tough, to deliberately distract himself with less pressing matters,' says one official.[260] 'It was a classic case of Gordon Brown displacement activity,' says another.[261]

Brown's team were anything but calm – Stewart Wood felt bitterly let down because he had always defended Purnell within Number 10. Kirsty McNeill says: 'Emotionally, we found it harder to deal with than the Prime Minister. We saw it as an act of immense betrayal.'[262] Another insider is even franker: '[Purnell] betrayed us, and to a Murdoch paper.'[263] Brown was always deeply suspicious of the Murdoch press but Purnell's decision to give the story to *The Sun* and *The Times* (in addition to *The Guardian*) was not part of some News International conspiracy. There was a more straightforward explanation: he played golf with George Pascoe-Watson and Philip Webster, then respectively political editors of the two Murdoch papers.[264]

In Number 10, frantic effort continued late into the night to call ministers, MPs, senior party figures, constituency parties and trade unionists to ascertain their stance and to get them out in support. Brown himself was periodically seen manning the phones calling Cabinet colleagues. 'Can I rely on your support?' he asked, baldly.[265] He decided with his team whom each should call to work out how far the poison had spread.[266] The four figures they most worried about, any of whom could have brought Brown down, were all phoned early on. Mandelson called David Miliband, the biggest concern, who reassured him that he would not have to worry about him.[267] Johnson was their next fear, but he too gave Number 10 a reassuring message. Straw was third on the list. Always watched nervously by Number 10, he had already gone to bed. The team phoned his special adviser Mark Davies, who told them he would put out a statement of support from Straw.[268] The Justice Secretary's main beef at the time was Balls, and he was adamant he should not replace Darling.[269] The fourth worry was Harman, another whom Number 10 always fretted about, but she too said she was supportive. Most ministers told Number 10 that their views echoed those of Jim Murphy, that, 'James is a very good friend, but this is not something you do on election night.'[270] Tessa Jowell had a long-standing dinner arranged that evening with her old friend and fellow Blairite Lord Falconer at his home. When her time came to be phoned and she was told, 'You've got to do an interview about Gordon,' her hackles were raised and she felt she was not going to be bullied into it. So she replied, 'I'm not sure.' Shortly afterwards she took a call on her mobile from Mandelson, whom she dispatched with equal ease. Both her and Falconer's phones went off at regular intervals, called by Brown's supporters, without anyone in Number 10 realising that they were sitting on opposite sides of the same dining table.[271]

The work began to pay dividends. From about midnight, according to one senior policy adviser, 'We began to think that Gordon might be fine.'[272] To some, the key moment came when Jowell was eventually persuaded, after 1am, to say something on television. Then they knew Brown would be safe.[273] Some, like Muir, left Number 10 in the early hours still unsure: 'As I walked down Downing Street, I wondered if it was the last time I'd walk down that road,' Muir admits.[274] An official who served in Number 10 for all three Brown years described it as 'the darkest night of any at Number 10'.[275]

A Dangerous Reshuffle: 5 June 2009

Brown had to move very quickly on the reshuffle after Purnell resigned: 'It was critical to have speed,' says one aide.[276] The date for the reshuffle had originally been pencilled in for the following Monday, to provide momentum after the election results which Number 10 was anticipating to be very poor.[277] The resignation forced it to bring the date forward to Friday 5 June. As this was being set in action, it was becoming clear that Labour had been devastated in the local elections: it lost its four remaining shire councils and 291 councillors, giving the party its worst county council elections since the 1970s.[278] Psephologists calculated that on the basis of its performance in these elections the party would poll just 22 per cent in a general election, reducing its support to its core vote.

Brown had been thinking about the reshuffle for several days. He had been 'absolutely clear' that he would use it to draw a line under the expenses saga, and he hoped it would give Labour a bounce.[279] But what about the PLP, which was tarnished over expenses? With a close team of senior advisers, he drew up a 'green', 'amber' and 'red' list of his ministers and potential appointees according to whether they were totally clear on expenses, had question marks, or were deemed high-risk. He was determined to go forward with a team of ministers with absolutely 'no expenses issues and no question marks', says an aide.[280]

Those who were tainted, fairly or unfairly, left the government, though some, including Blears and Hoon, were to leave believing they had done nothing wrong.[281] The reshuffle succeeded in this quest, but what of Darling, who had claimed for a second home while in Number 11? Brown, and indeed the press, had concluded that the Chancellor's errors, such as they were, were not hanging offences.[282] On 1 June, Darling quietly paid back the £600 in contention.[283] Like Brown, Darling's Scottish puritanism meant he had felt deeply affronted by the suggestion that he had behaved in an improper way, and, again like Brown, he was not a person remotely avaricious financially.

After Purnell, Darling's future was the biggest story by far about the reshuffle. It had been heavily briefed by sources 'close to Number 10' that the Chancellor was on his way out. The expenses cloud hanging over him had prompted questions about his future in Downing Street and beyond, aside from Brown's concerns about Darling's performance at the Treasury. The Prime Minister had become increasingly rude to the Chancellor in meetings in front of officials, cutting him off in a way that was thought undermining and unprofessional. 'I've done the Chancellor's job for ten years and I can tell you the Treasury doesn't always tell you the truth,' he would say when irritated with Darling for failing to question the Treasury's assumptions. After their spats, Darling would often go to Number 10 in the evening to talk it over with Brown, where their underlying loyalty and warmth would bring them back together again.[284] But during that spring, a Rubicon had been crossed. Brown thought Darling had become too much of a spokesman for Treasury officials from permanent secretary Macpherson downwards, few of whom he had a high opinion of.[285] Darling's unhappiness with Brown had reached new heights, too. As one official notes, he was 'exasperated with Gordon shouting at him and micromanaging his agenda'.[286] The Chancellor had become turned off by Brown's aggression and style, and was sickened by Balls and McBride: 'My God, have you learned nothing in twenty years? Why do you trust these people?' he would ask his old friend.[287] It was clear the status quo could not continue. After the 2009 Budget, Brown concluded, 'Alistair was not credible, not presenting the right image, not dynamic enough, not imaginative enough, too hesitant and too cautious.'[288]

He became convinced he needed a change of Chancellor. 'There was only ever one serious candidate for his successor, Ed Balls, who he thought would have the fight, and a much more political approach and leadership in economic policy which would positively take on the Treasury officials,' says one insider.[289] Brown hugely admired Balls's fighting qualities, his political approach and his grasp of economics from their ten years together in the Treasury.[290] Balls himself says he was far from sold on the plan. 'I never at any point was pushing Gordon to be his Chancellor,' he says. 'I was very happy for Alistair to be Chancellor,' adding revealingly, 'The issue was the nature of the judgments, not the man.' Balls had grave concerns about whether the appointment would have ever worked. 'It would have been very complicated for me to be Gordon's Chancellor. I always knew that. I knew that more than him.'[291] Even so, Balls certainly expected to be made Chancellor that week, and Darling was convinced he himself was leaving the Treasury. Late into the evening before the reshuffle, Treasury advisers shredded sensitive documents in anticipation of Darling's replacement the next day. Balls, meanwhile, had pencilled in a leaving party.[292]

Brown did a lot of 'heavy duty' talking about the reshuffle over the weekend of 31 May/1 June, before any of the resignations had occurred. He spoke to Mandelson about moving Balls to the Treasury and to his intense relief, given fourteen years of bitter animosity between the two men, Mandelson supported him. 'One good thing about [the possibility of] Ed being Chancellor was getting him out of education,' Mandelson says; he felt education reform had stalled under Balls and it needed someone else to present a stronger story in this key department in the run-up to the general election.[293] In his memoirs, Mandelson maintains that he thought the move would have been 'unfair to Alistair', a view he planned to 'bring home to Gordon', but 'things moved faster than I anticipated'.[294] The initial Brown plan was to make Purnell or Adonis Balls's successor[295] and Darling Foreign or Home Secretary, positions he himself resisted taking when Chancellor. When Darling made it clear to Brown that he would not be happy with either post, it freed up the Prime Minister's options. If Darling had gone to the backbenches, Brown would have given Mandelson his dream of becoming Foreign Secretary, and moved David Miliband across to the Home Office.

Balls was not a popular figure in Cabinet, and many of the 'big beasts' were very unhappy about Brown's hopes to put him into the Treasury. Neither did Ed Miliband nor Alexander want this to happen to their erstwhile close colleague. Darling, in contrast, was a widely liked colleague in Cabinet, and ministers viewed any attempt to move him as madness, especially in the continuing economic crisis and with the risk of destabilisation of the markets. None felt this more keenly than Straw, who came to see Brown before the reshuffle and 'read him the riot act' about not replacing Darling, least of all with Balls.[296] These concerns weighed on Brown's mind: in principle he still wanted to go ahead with the change, but as was so often the case, indecision set in as he contemplated the politics of such a move.

It will never be known whether Brown would have been able to execute the manoeuvre, and whether he would have survived the chorus of criticism from Cabinet colleagues. Right until the last moment he had his secret 'reshuffle plan' ready to go, alongside his more cautious model.[297] It is often claimed that Purnell's resignation instantly ended any hopes Brown had of executing it but in fact he began to cool on the idea of moving Darling earlier in the day as he worried about the consequences of changing his Chancellor and questioned whether he had the political strength to carry it off. Purnell's resignation confirmed that he did not.[298] Balls was stunned when he was told he was not going to the Treasury. 'I saw his face and it looked as if he had been told of a death,' says a Number 10 aide.[299] Balls and Mandelson were seen huddled together in intense discussion: Mandelson too had lost dreams of his ideal job that evening. Joined together in bereavement, Balls and Mandelson were as unlikely a couple as the great 'Chuckle Brothers' themselves, Ian Paisley and Martin McGuinness. How mortified was Brown at having to abandon his secret plan? His distress was balanced by recognising some gains in retaining the status quo. Keeping Darling on as Chancellor considerably simplified his reshuffle, and would make his relationship with the Cabinet much easier. But he also knew that Darling was now safe and unmovable all the way to the general election. Darling knew it too.

On the Friday came the announcement that Hutton and Hoon would be standing down from the government. This again aroused suspicion as to whether it was linked to Purnell's departure. It wasn't. Both shared Purnell's frustrations but they had come to the view that they would go quietly. Hutton had decided he had had enough at the Ministry of Defence. His resignation was an unwelcome bolt. Number 10 had been expecting him to quit in October, and his bringing it forward to June was described as 'unfortunate' by Brown's team.[300] It also created dismay at the Ministry of Defence that they were losing the Defence Secretary in the middle of a war, says then Chief of General Staff Richard Dannatt.[301] Hutton himself would have preferred to have remained until October, but 'Brown was determined to have a reshuffle in June' and it made no sense to him to leave three months after it.[302] Hutton was meticulous to dispel in his resignation letter any notions that he had left in protest at Brown's conduct of defence policy or of his leadership. Hoon's departure from Transport was equally without embarrassment to Brown. Expenses had put his exit on the cards. Another factor was that Number 10 were also frustrated by his performance at Transport. Hutton went on to a peerage; Hoon was heading, he believed, to an EU commissioner's job. When that failed to transpire, he would strike back against Brown early in the New Year.[303]

There would be one more resignation on that Friday, Caroline Flint as Europe minister. She says she had not planned to resign that week but that she was taken aback by the calls made from Number 10 during the day time on Thursday, in response to the apprehensions, questioning whether or not she was loyal. She had been content to defend government policy on air that evening. But she says she snapped when, after news of Purnell's resignation, she received a phone call from Brown personally. He mentioned Hazel Blears's departure to her and she thought that he was testing her loyalty, 'which really annoyed me: I thought that no matter what I did, nor how hard I worked, there were always question marks over my loyalty'. So she decided to rebuff him, declining his offer that in future she could attend all Cabinet meetings as Europe minister. 'At least think about it,' he asked her. 'There is nothing to think about,' she replied. Would she be willing to take a call from Peter, he pleaded, which she did, but rejected Mandelson's requests to change her mind. 'The lack of trust in me is why I resigned,' she says.[304] Her letter of resignation, released to the press on 5 June, was angry. 'I am extremely disappointed at your failure to have an inclusive government ... You have a two-tier government,' she wrote. 'Several of the women attending Cabinet – myself included – have been treated by you as little more than female window dressing.' She had been angered by not being invited to the political Cabinet just before the European elections, as she had been on reading in newspapers 'sources' saying she was involved in plots. 'I am a natural party loyalist. Yet you have strained every sinew of that loyalty,' she wrote.[305] Flint's outburst caused limited damage, however, because commentators suspected she had resigned because she had not been offered a Cabinet job. But still, she was the ninth senior minister to quit that week and there was some worry that it might provide the catalyst for other malcontents to follow suit. Friday 5 June was a day described in a *Guardian* editorial as 'a black Friday that left Labour at war with itself'.[306] Whether the civil war would end in regicide, *The Guardian*'s express wish, was yet to be seen.

Cabinet Secretary O'Donnell had earlier discussed with Brown ideas for creating more cohesion at the heart of government. Creating a formal post of 'Deputy Prime Minister' was one solution. Brown's lack of strength at welding Cabinet ministers together into a cohesive unit, working closely with them and monitoring their progress, was long established. The two figures he had brought into the Cabinet Office as 'enforcers', first Ed Miliband and then Liam Byrne, lacked the seniority to bang together the heads of Whitehall ministers as the post required. A bigger beast was needed. Straw made clear to Number 10 he was very keen to be given such a job[307] and claims that both Brown and Sue Nye had personally promised to make him Deputy Prime Minister back in 2007. Brown's failure to deliver on his promise greatly frustrated Straw, and had he known that during Brown's premiership 'his name was never really discussed' he might have become even more disheartened.[308] The two names that were considered at various points were Mandelson and Harman. Brown himself was never really convinced of the case of having a designated Deputy Prime Minister but, when the issue was discussed, it was clear that he had a strong preference for Mandelson over Harman.[309] However, he was concerned about the sensitivities of Harman who had claims as Deputy Leader of the Labour Party.[310]

In the June 2009 reshuffle Mandelson became 'Deputy Prime Minister in all but name'[311] by being appointed 'First Secretary of State' and Lord President of the Council. To make it still sweeter for him, his business department empire was beefed up with universities, which was taken away from the defunct department run up to that point by Denham, who succeeded Blears at

Communities and Local Government. As if to underline Mandelson's increased importance it was revealed that no fewer than ten ministers had been appointed to serve under him, twice as many as Darling had at the Treasury, while he himself was made a member of 80 per cent of all Cabinet committees, which meant he sat on more than either the Prime Minister or Chancellor did. The accumulation pleased Mandelson, though some in Number 10 worried about Harman's response and once again debated whether or not to giver her the title of 'Deputy Prime Minister' as a 'consolation prize'.[312] Brown was not, however, persuaded. 'Gordon thought that it would be difficult for it not to be Harriet, but he didn't want it to be Harriet either,' reflects one official.[313] The absence of a formal Deputy Prime Minister frustrated Brown's civil servants, who had to work hard to ensure that Brown never missed Cabinet to avoid tension over who should chair the meeting in his place.[314] It also meant it was not clear who should take charge when Brown was away from Downing Street over the summer holidays: hence the series of caretakers in the summer of 2009.

Mandelson's intervention helped prop up Jowell, who Brown felt was one Blairite too many. She was duly placed in Cabinet on full pay, to oversee the Olympics and London, which contented her.[315] Bob Ainsworth's elevation within the Ministry of Defence to full Defence Secretary was criticised in the press, though his appointment was supported by the military chiefs and strongly pushed by Hutton.[316] Ainsworth's would be a baptism of fire as the situation in Afghanistan's Helmand Province deteriorated rapidly, almost at the same rate as his own troubled relationship did with Number 10. Alan Johnson was rewarded for his time at Health, and more particularly his loyalty, with promotion to Home Secretary in succession to Smith. Johnson, the smiling survivor, was very pleased with his promotion. 'When I arrived, everything seemed to have been covered already,' he says. 'While Gordon did not have the same clarity on home affairs as he did on health, I had no problems with him.'[317] Brownite John Healey became the Housing Minister, replacing Margaret Beckett, who proved a disappointment in the role, while Jim Knight, at the behest of Balls, became Employment Minister.[318]

The reshuffle was heavily criticised in the media: Anne McElvoy described it in the *Daily Telegraph* as a 'shot-gun' reshuffle in an article entitled 'Gordon Brown, the flawed colossus'.[319] Brown was generally viewed to be executing the reshuffle from a position of great weakness following the spate of resignations and awful local election results. The media contrasted it starkly with his 2008 reshuffle, widely considered an exemplar. Brown's 'progressive' credentials took a bashing given that his reshuffle brought the number of women in Cabinet down to four and increased the number of unelected peers attending to seven. The Kinnocks were popular figures in the party, but the message Labour's MPs received with Glenys's appointment as Europe minister in succession to Flint was that they were not good enough themselves to be placed above a veteran.[320] The reduction in the number of women went down particularly badly with Labour's female MPs, especially allied to the misogyny some suspected of Brown. They harked back to Blair, who appointed women to almost a third of Cabinet posts, and abroad to Zapatero in Spain, to Sarkozy in France or to Obama, all of whom promoted female appointments. Patricia Hewitt thought it was a terribly reactionary move.[321] When Dugher looked at the reshuffle, he says, 'I thought, "that's it, we're fucking finished now".'[322] Ever-loyal Nye, who for many years had been the sole female in Brown's team, defended him, arguing that it was a 'reshuffle for desperate times'.[323]

For all the criticisms, the reshuffle strengthened the government in many respects. Heywood felt that it achieved what it set out to do, which was to produce a Cabinet untainted by questions and problems about expenses.[324] Brown regularly complained that his departmental ministers had become 'too governmental' and were not bold enough. He tried to address this via the reshuffle by appointing a new cadre of ministers.[325] Several of the new appointees were to prove successes in their new posts. Adonis, promoted to Transport Secretary from being junior minister in the department, gave the job stability after two short-serving secretaries of state, Kelly and Hoon. He forged ahead on high-speed rail, which became a flagship policy for the government, and he was surprised to find Brown to be highly supportive on it, as he was to be on a string of crises including the strike in British Airways, the Icelandic ash cloud and severe snow and ice problems over the winter.[326]

What were Brown's other successful appointments? Andy Burnham proved tenacious at Health, driving forward the social care agenda which was to give Labour a distinctive policy over the coming months. Ben Bradshaw in his short time was an activist Secretary of State at the Department of Culture, Media and Sport, and with Number 10's support managed to save various prestige projects from cuts, including the Tate Modern extension in London.[327] Liam Byrne as Chief Secretary helped improve the government's public position on deficit reduction. He was 'completely horrified and shocked' by what he found when he arrived at the Treasury.[328] The scale of the deficit was much worse than he had been led to expect even from his privileged berth at the Cabinet Office: it was 'an indication of the state of the relationship between Number 10 and [the Treasury]. It was a really scary moment,' an insider reveals.[329] Darling, Byrne thought, looked as if he had 'survived a serious car crash': it took Byrne and Tony Danker, his special adviser, three weeks to realise why – the Chancellor had fully expected to be sacked.[330] Not all the young bloods delighted Number 10. One falling into this category was Yvette Cooper, who moved to Work and Pensions: 'We did nothing on welfare after James Purnell left. Yvette wasn't prepared to confront the department,' a Number 10 aide reports.[331]

Calm Returns: 5 to 8 June 2009

With Westminster still highly volatile, Brown needed to act quickly to regain the initiative that the rushed reshuffle had conspicuously failed to achieve. He used a press conference on the Friday as his platform, working hard on it in the Cabinet Office with close aides, debating the line he would take, and tapping out final changes himself on his computer.[332] He delivered an unswerving message about his intention to stay. 'If I didn't think I was the right person leading the right team I wouldn't be standing here,' he said. 'I have the determination to continue. I will not waver. I will not walk away. I will finish the work.'[333] Three priorities for the remaining months before the general election would be, he said, economic reform and political reform, to respond to the twin crises, and renewed public service reform. He came over as upbeat and in control, and he was pleased and relieved by the way the press conference went. 'We clap Gordon back when he comes into the horseshoe,' records a contemporary diary.[334] The rest of the day was calmer, but news was coming in from the Huddersfield constituency of Barry Sheerman that he had requested a secret ballot of the party leadership. 'I did a pre-record deliberately for Sunday night, after all the election results were in, but they leaked it on Friday,' Sheerman says.[335] The Number 10 machine responded with fury, and briefed that it was part of a 'Milibandite attempt' to destabilise the government.[336] (Sheerman's daughter, Madeleine Sadler, worked for David Miliband.)

On Saturday 6 June, Brown had some respite from domestic tensions with a trip to Normandy for the sixty-fifth anniversary of the D-Day landings. He had been keen to go though it broke a tradition of British leaders not usually attending 'five-year' anniversaries. Behind the scenes, a major disagreement had been taking place between the British and French. Sarkozy wanted to claim D-Day as a major French–American occasion, to be his big Obama moment.[337] At times, the diplomatic fighting threatened to rival the intensity of the military fighting of sixty-five years before. Number 10 was 'paranoid' about the media writing it up as 'a snub'[338] so it made clear that it would not be a proper anniversary if the British were not afforded equal status. 'We expended a lot of energy ensuring that the Prime Minister was part of the Sarkozy and Obama party, not on the sidelines,' recalls a Foreign Office official.[339] News of the inter-governmental battles inevitably leaked, resulting in the press writing it up negatively. Thus recorded *The Independent*, '[Brown] tried to tag on to the Obama–Sarkozy event at Omaha with calamitous PR consequences.'[340] The media further tried to whip up a fuss about the Queen not attending; but she never had any intention of attending a 'fifth anniversary' largely stoked up 'to pander to the ego of French politicians'.[341] Sarkozy, Obama, Brown, Prince Charles and Canadian Prime

Minister Stephen Harper (who himself had a 'massive fight' for squatter rights with Sarkozy[342]) attended a ceremony at the American cemetery at Omaha beach, with Dannatt representing British forces.[343] Brown, Prince Charles and French Prime Minister François Fillon then went on to a special Anglo-French ceremony and laid wreaths in Bayeux Cathedral during a service organised by the Royal British Legion.[344]

Brown's enthusiasm to attend was partly down to a desire to be seen supporting British military landmarks. But he wanted to go also because of his affiliation with the contribution of British soldiers, sailors and airmen, honed when writing his book *Wartime Courage*,[345] first published in 2008. 'It meant a lot to him, he understood it deeply, it wasn't just a ra-ra-ra celebration,' says one of those who travelled with him.[346] Brown had worked hard on his speech with McNeill and it was one of the most lyrical he would deliver as Prime Minister. 'Sixty-five years ago in the thin light of grey dawn more than a thousand small craft took to a rough sea on a day that will be forever a day of bravery ... on that June morning the young of our nations stepped out on those beaches below and into history. As long as freedom lives, their deeds will never die.'[347] His speech was well received, even by the *Daily Mail*, which recorded, 'Both Sarkozy's effusive speech and Obama's oration were outshone by the Prime Minister's.'[348]

Brown's spirits sank as he flew back over the English coastline, knowing that the results of the European elections, delayed so they could be announced in concert with the rest of Europe, would be bad. On the Sunday morning, Brown worked downstairs in Number 12 at the horseshoe until Sarah came to collect him for lunch. The next day, as he watched the results come in, Brown said: 'You're right again,' to Muir, who had led him to expect the worst.[349] With just 15.7 per cent of the vote, it was even worse than expected: Labour was completely humiliated earning their worst election result in the post-war period. Labour was beaten not only by the Conservatives but, embarrassingly, by UKIP, too. In the South-West, Labour came fifth behind even the Green Party, and in Wales it failed to finish as the largest party for the first time since 1918. In Scotland the position was equally bleak with Labour losing out to the SNP for the first time in European elections. To really add to the misery, the British National Party secured two seats, one in Yorkshire and Humber and one in the North-West, the first win by the far-right party in national elections in the UK. The election had been fought against a backdrop of a severe recession and the fall-out from the expenses crisis. With non-major parties receiving a staggering 42 per cent of the vote, it suggested a backlash against the political class as a whole. Nevertheless, it was Brown who suffered the most.[350] The public had given up on him.

Monday 8 June was another difficult day, made more so by the anger and dismay at the European election results. News seeped into Number 10 of further plotter activity, with talk of the agitators still working to achieve the crucial seventy-one Labour MPs needed to trigger a leadership election. Indications were that they had secured the names of fifty-four.[351] Everyone at Westminster knew the showdown would come at the weekly PLP meeting that evening, which would decide Brown's fate. Very careful preparations had been made on both sides. Nick Brown and his team ensured the meeting was packed out with loyalists. The atmosphere in the hour-and-a-half meeting was tense throughout. It opened with PLP chairman Tony Lloyd insisting on a few 'ground rules', including members listening to each other without heckling. Brown spoke first with a fifteen-minute address, arguing if the party changed leader it would still face the recession and the fall-out from the expenses scandal. 'I have my strengths and I have my weaknesses. I know I need to improve. There are some things I do well and some things I do not do so well,' he said. There was 'no huge ideological difference' within Labour, he asserted, and 'not a resignation letter that I have seen that mentions differences over policy'.[352] He did well, but his fate still hung in the balance.

Lloyd then opened up the meeting for questions and called loyalist Stephen Ladyman first, prompting angry mutters that the meeting was being stage-managed. When it was discovered he was not present, the critic Tom Harris was called. 'The [European] results from last night confirmed in my mind that the electorate aren't yet sold on Cameron, but they have made their minds up about you, Gordon, and it's not going to change,' a comment that received more murmurs of support. Charles Clarke then spoke 'in stony silence', reiterating his anti-Brown argument, 'It's time to go.' Siobhain McDonagh followed, saying that policy was not the problem; 'We've got the right policies, it's the leadership not the policy that needs to change.'[353] Paul Flynn, on the left of the party, defended Ian Gibson, who many felt had been treated badly over the still raw nerve of expenses. The anti-Brown sentiment in the meeting appeared to be gaining the upper hand. Not all known critics were called, and not Stephen Byers, who left to attend a Progress rally where he launched a 'stinging attack' on Brown.

In the final phase, the loyalist old guard was called on, and they did not disappoint. David Blunkett was applauded when he declared, 'This blood-letting has to stop – critics should put up or shut up and they have twenty-four hours to do so.' Beckett, who was dismissed in the reshuffle after her nine months' tenure, said, 'If anyone in this room has a unique reason to say he didn't get it right, it's me ... but it would be madness to get rid of this man.' Finally, a specially drafted-in Neil Kinnock gave a five-minute upbeat speech calling for unity and quoting Nye Bevan's call for 'common endeavour'.[354] The balance had shifted back. Brown wrapped up the meeting with a promise to take criticism on board. He left to the sound of cheers, applause and banging of desks with the clear sense all round that the danger was past. Sheerman was one of the many critics who were not happy at the stage management, and who resented that the custom of not letting peers speak had been broken for Kinnock. The moment, nevertheless, had passed. 'Gordon gives the speech of his life. Opposition fades away – this is a turning point,' Forsyth recorded in his diary.[355]

A further blow for Brown came the following weekend in the *Sunday Times*, in an article on 14 June alleging that 'Gordon Brown is being abandoned by the multi-million businessmen who bankrolled Labour's last election campaign, endangering the party's effort to fight off David Cameron at the next election.'[356] 'It fascinates me, you have a man with eight crutches, and one by one they are being kicked away,' said one of Brown's friends on hearing the news.[357] The lack of money in the coffers was a major worry for Number 10 and Labour Party headquarters over the coming months, and it was to change the whole way that Labour planned to conduct the campaign.

But Brown had survived the terrible early days of June. Charles Clarke is one of many to believe that it was Brown's most vulnerable moment to date.[358] Had just a handful of the several senior ministers who resigned that week decided to coordinate their resignations they may well have toppled Brown. He was fortunate that Harman, Straw and Johnson had all concluded that the time was not right to move against him. Fear that if they failed to bring him down they would be left in an even worse position deterred many from more open defiance, as did the fear that a change of leader might have precipitated a general election at a time when Labour's poll showing was on the floor. That was certainly the view expressed by Brown's guarantor-in-chief that summer, Mandelson. Weeks later, Purnell spoke about it to former Conservative leader Michael Howard, who told him how Geoffrey Howe in 1990 had had no precise plan when he spoke out against Margaret Thatcher. The difference, he said, was that in 1990, there was a 'prince over the water' – Michael Heseltine. With no clear prince in waiting in 2009, and with the 'big beasts' of the Cabinet either bought off or convinced that an attempt on Brown's life would create only further disruption, the Prime Minister was safe. His absolute determination to stay, the lack of coordination of his opponents and having Mandelson as enforcer were the three main factors that combined to enable him to weather such a potentially destabilising coup. Brown would be safe until the general election, as long as all these factors remained in place. The one that Brown least expected to change was his 'to the death' pledge from Mandelson.[359]

Brown's Policy Agenda Takes Shape: June to July 2009

As the summer approached, Brown was running out of time to establish his domestic policy agenda. He knew it was the gap at the heart of his premiership, but his attempts to fill it had failed repeatedly.[360] Just as in 2007, his Queens's Speech in 2008 had been rushed, and direction again had been lost, first due to the G20, and then to the string of fresh crises. Mandelson believed strongly that, if Brown was to fight his way back from the brink again, this time he would need to have a 'policy-led renewal'[361] based on a clear, distinctive, domestic policy agenda. This would be the platform on which, in less than a year's time, Brown would fight the general election.

Throughout the first half of the year, Brown had discussed the subject regularly with advisers in and outside the Policy Unit. In late spring he was resolved on a way forward: he would publish a major new document, *The National Plan*, the centrepiece of his new push on domestic policy. Not until work was well underway did the document's name change to *Building Britain's Future* with Nick Robinson one of those to point out the unfortunate Stalinist overtones of the original title, to say nothing of a reference to Harold Wilson's ill-fated 'national plan' of 1965.[362]

Building Britain's Future was built on three policy pillars. The first set out an agenda on constitutional and political reform to help rebuild trust in the political system in the wake of the expenses crisis. It included ambitious proposals for reforming the House of Lords, which if implemented would have been groundbreaking. Further to his June announcement, in which he said he would legislate to remove the remaining ninety-two hereditary peers, he now committed his government to publishing a draft bill for a democratically elected second chamber. The second focused on the real economy: making the case for an activist role for government in the downturn, arguing that growth was the most effective way to address the hole in the public finances. The third area concerned public service reform, for which Brown had little instinctive feel: the complaint remained constant that while it was clear what he was against – a full-blown Blairite choice agenda – it was never clear what his alternative was. On the political reform and real economy strands the government had already announced a number of policy interventions, including recession-fighting measures like the Future Jobs Fund, and the guarantee of work or training for everyone under the age of twenty-five out of work for a year, while Brown had tried to reinvigorate the constitutional agenda in his speech on 10 June. The real novelty of *Building Britain's Future* came thus in the realm of public services.

Leading on the document would be Nick Pearce, who headed the Policy Unit from October 2008, working alongside Gavin Kelly, Patrick Diamond and David Muir, who were working to give Brown's policy agenda a new level of strategic and political focus. Other critical players in this process included Peter Mandelson and Andrew Adonis. They were all by now well accustomed to his tendency to try to solve problems by publishing a new document, and by the way he allowed himself to get distracted with making small policy announcements instead of working on the 'bigger picture'. They were determined to use this occasion, perhaps the last, to their advantage, hoping that hooking him on a single defining theme would give some shape to his domestic programme. 'His predilection for detail over argument was a major problem. He always gave us lists, not arguments,' complains one senior aide.[363] Many had come to the view that this was because he lacked any strategic vision for domestic policy.

As their work progressed that spring, Brown became 'engaged in endless conference calls to discuss his thinking with others'.[364] Balls was not very involved in these discussions, not wanting, in the eyes of one insider, 'an all-encompassing policy agenda to be outlined ahead of him becoming Chancellor'.[365] Indeed Balls had argued that the plan should be published in two parts: an interim in the summer followed by a full report in the autumn at the time of the Pre-Budget Report, in other words after a reshuffle in which he believed he might be moved to the Treasury. In the background, staff worked frantically with the Cabinet Office on the document itself, coordinating key policy announcements across Whitehall. For those in Number 10, the early signs from departments were worrying. At the start of the process, Heywood had taken the relatively rare step of writing to each department to set out the importance of the document. Yet in Number 10's conversations with departments, little or nothing was coming back. 'There was a total lack of ambition from departments,' says one adviser. For the first time it was becoming apparent to Number 10 advisers just how hard the next year's manifesto-writing process would be. 'It dawned on us then, this is going to be a hell of a slog,' says one.[366] Worse, although officials had long been aware of the dire financial situation, only now did it seem that Whitehall was confronting the issue head on: suddenly it was apparent that for any major announcement in *Building Britain's Future*, there would have to be corresponding cuts elsewhere. It was the first time that Brown himself had to confront the logic of the fiscal situation. 'We hoped it would improve Brown's increasingly discredited position on the deficit,' says an aide. 'But we didn't succeed.'[367]

As the document took shape, Pearce and Kelly held a series of meetings with Brown. The big new idea they had been working on concerned replacing the 'top-down' central government targets much loved by Blair and Michael Barber with a set of individual 'rights and entitlements' that would guarantee a certain level of service that citizens could expect from their hospitals, schools and police. The thinking had been in gestation since it had been 'hot-housed' before the aborted election of 2007, and had helped inform the 2008 policing pledge and the NHS constitution, both of which set out a series of citizen rights and responsibilities. They were frustrated that, despite pushing the idea with Brown on several occasions, he had never fully 'bitten'. In truth, Brown had yet seriously to engage in public service reform and, if he did, it was to promote what his Number 10 advisers considered his hopelessly 'flawed' talent agenda: 'Whatever you put to him at that time, he would ask, "How does this help me on talent?"' [368]

The Number 10 team persisted, believing that if they could develop the entitlements agenda into a set of tangible policies that the public could understand, then they might at last get Brown more engaged. Greg Beales, Brown's health adviser, understood this well and developed a plan to give patients the right to see a specialist within two weeks of a cancer diagnosis. In education, children who had fallen behind would be given the right to one-to-one tuition to catch up. And to make them feel real, the new rights would be backed by hard redress mechanisms. In the NHS, for example, patients might have the right to free private treatment if a local hospital left them waiting too long.

As the ideas took shape in the early summer, Brown at last became increasingly excited. 'Suddenly the lights went on,' says one adviser. 'The penny dropped in his mind: he saw that this could be an agenda that would run across education, health and policing.' [369] Could this be the broad, Brownite reform agenda that had so long eluded him? He relished the idea of coming up with something that went beyond Blairism, indeed *improved* on it. Politically it would provide a response to the well-established critique of New Labour's obsession with central prescription, offering a way of devolving power while also ensuring fair provision, a trade-off the left had long struggled with. [370] How would it work? Rather than central government holding a school or hospital to account through a regime of stifling targets, these bodies would be empowered to provide a service tailored to local needs, and would in turn be held to account by citizens themselves.

Delighted by their breakthrough with Brown, his advisers continued to work with colleagues in the Cabinet Office to sign up departments to major new policy commitments. Work on the document continued through the height of the expenses crisis. Over the weekend of 2 and 3 May, Brown worked intensively with Number 10 staff. 'I remember sitting with GB and others as he scribbled all over a draft and held it up, saying, "I'll present this to Cabinet." We all laughed as it was incomprehensible to anyone. No one could read his writing,' records a contemporary diary. [371] On the morning of Tuesday 5 May, Mandelson and Byrne presented the plan to Cabinet. 'It was an important moment and the first time the Cabinet had properly discussed this emerging domestic agenda,' records a diary. 'It showed that GB was developing and articulating a clear political narrative for government, linked to a concrete delivery plan.' [372]

Cabinet response was mixed. John Denham was a strong advocate of the entitlements agenda, recognising its importance for shifting power from central to local communities. But Straw was wary, reflecting Ministry of Justice concern about the language of rights; while Darling expressed the Treasury's concern about how to fund entitlements. Concerns were expressed too about tone: was the draft of *Building Britain's Future* not written in a bland, 'official' style that would fail to captivate the media and wider public? Several thought that for such a major statement of government policy, it was not 'political' enough. Jim Murphy favoured a franker, more honest tone that recognised public disquiet about the expenses crisis. The conclusion was they wanted it to be redrafted. The Number 10 team duly obliged. It was a painful process as they had to go through the rewrite line by line with Cabinet Office officials to ensure it did not begin to represent a party political manifesto. The following week, on Tuesday 12 May, a three-hour Cabinet was held to finalise agreement on *Building Britain's Future* as the platform on which the next election would be fought.

Brown eventually introduced the final document to the Commons on Monday 29 June. Power would be devolved to public service users through new, enforceable rights. Patients would be given new rights not just to rapid cancer referral, but also to hospital treatment within eighteen weeks, and free health-checks for those aged forty to seventy-four. Parents would be entitled to catch-up tuition for any child that needed it. New commitments to bolster the economy through a jobs fund and innovation fund were announced, alongside new funding for affordable housing. Brown was particularly bold on housing. At the outset of his premiership he had announced a highly ambitious target of building three million new homes by 2020. But progress against the target had stalled badly. The collapse of the construction industry during the recession had seriously hampered progress. However, the government had also taken its eye off the ball, particularly during Margaret Beckett's time at housing – described by Number 10 as a 'do-nothing' minister.[373] Nor did it help that Brown slashed capital spending in the 2009 Budget. The hiatus was broken by Brown in January 2009 with a major speech to the Local Government Association in which he effectively said that, 'local authorities can build again', which was 'a big moment' as hitherto New Labour's position on social housing had been to discourage councils from building, resulting in a massively over-subscribed social housing sector. 'We hadn't built enough houses since 1997; social housing was a big New Labour failure,' concedes one Number 10 adviser.[374] Brown now decided he wanted to steam ahead on building social housing, to help drive the economy out of recession, and settled on a two-year target of 20,000 homes. In this quest he was helped by his new Housing Minister from June 2009, John Healey. Brown sent Heywood off to do the 'heavy lifting around Whitehall' to find the resources needed to pay for the 20,000 new homes, which Brown announced in *Building Britain's Future*, before the funding had all been finalised. As was so often the case with Brown he did not begin to focus on this aspect of his domestic agenda until it was too late to effect real change: house building fell to their lowest levels on his watch. Nevertheless, whatever the merits of the policy, this was evidence that Brown was finally beginning to find his stride; he 'dithered less', says one policy adviser, and was more prepared to take risks.[375]

Cameron attacked the document for its failing to be clear about the cost of the proposals, while Clegg chose to belittle it: 'We were promised a vision of the future from the government based on decentralisation and personal entitlement ... yet many of the so-called personal entitlements are, on closer inspection, just a recycled version of the old targets.'[376] *The Guardian* gave it a mixed reception, with Simon Jenkins condemning it as 'John Major-ish, a mish-mash of ... cobbled together statistics as if [Brown] were manager of a Stalinist collective', and Polly Toynbee praising it: 'This takes Labour's best successes and sets them in legal concrete ... a politically deft manoeuvre, it throws down a difficult challenge to Cameron.'[377]

Did *Building Britain's Future* amount to anything? A Number 10 official believes it was 'the closest thing Gordon ever got to a philosophy'.[378] In its political pillar it encapsulated Brown's thinking about loss of trust. The first crisis was over bankers and banks, and the second over inappropriate behaviour by MPs and expenses. Both issues he felt were the result of a lack of strong institutional accountability. He wanted, therefore, for *Building Britain's Future* to institute plans to reform the system. But most of these measures were not implemented. The nascent entitlements agenda had great potential, particularly in providing a framework within which to unravel excessive levels of centralism in England. With entitlements Brown finally managed to produce what his premiership had so far lacked: a policy narrative that built on New Labour, without rejecting it, but which was also distinctively his own. Delivering this vision, however, required a fourth term for Labour and thus came to nothing. Nothing concrete was in fact to emerge from this work. The Health Bill was amended to include the health entitlements, easily the most advanced aspect of the entitlements policy, but it never made it on to the statute book. Brown's team hoped that after *Building Britain's Future* commentators would no longer 'write about a government that had run out of ideas'.[379] But that is precisely what they continued to do. The pity for Brown was that *Building Britain's Future* was produced in his third year in power, when time was running out, rather than at the start of his first. By the time it appeared, many had stopped listening, and the money was running out.

Within Whitehall for a year and more another problem had become clear. Brown's poor connection with his Cabinet ministers had been a growing concern, and, many believed, was significantly undermining his ability to deliver key priorities. Heywood discussed the problem with O'Donnell, who was also concerned by poor coordination in Whitehall. Ideas for a 'Deputy Prime Minister', as previously discussed, were one response. But the problem ran deep. The dysfunctional Number 10 was at last beginning to be addressed. But Brown's lack of regular policy stock takes with Cabinet ministers or even monitoring of them contributed to the entire administration being dysfunctional. Cabinet itself barely functioned as an effective policy coordinating body, and Cabinet committees less so. The National Economic Council, in contrast, had by now proved its worth: Brown's chairmanship had forced departments to get a grip on the major economic challenges during the recession, from repossessions to youth unemployment. But elsewhere there was little coordination and no such drive. In response, in June, Heywood devised a plan for the creation of two new 'councils' (in effect Cabinet committees) to replicate the NEC. A Democratic Renewal Council would look at reform of the House of Lords and the voting system, as well as the consideration of a written constitution. To drive the pledges outlined in *Building Britain's Future* there would be a Domestic Policy Council. Brown was happy with the proposals and announced them at a press conference on Friday 5 June, just after the reshuffle. Like the NEC, the two new councils would meet weekly in COBRA, conveying a sense of urgency felt to have been lacking in Cabinet committees. Initially, Brown gave the councils his commitment and time, but in the autumn, as the general election approached, the energy withered. Neither of the two new councils ever came close to the effectiveness of the NEC, and even that began to fade.

In the aftermath of *Building Britain's Future*, the Department for Children, Schools and Families published on 30 June the education white paper *Twenty-First Century Schools*. Its preparation had been fraught. Though hidden from public view, Number 10 had become exasperated by the lack of progress from Balls. With Balls so close to Brown, relations with the department were strained. Since the announcement of the 'national challenge' and the 'children's plan' in the autumn of 2007, Brown's team felt that there had been no movement. To inject some momentum, Number 10 had steadily embedded its own team within the department, knowing that Balls would resist policy initiatives if they had 'made in Number 10' written on them.[380] The initiative was to produce fruit later: for the present, though, the department produced a long list of pupil and parental guarantees, which alienated schools and was felt by Number 10 to have taken the edge off the policy.[381] More positively, the white paper stressed the importance of teacher quality in education reform, and began to flesh out a reform agenda for high-performing schools to take over the least effective ones.

July also saw the publication of the review that Brown had established under Alan Milburn into social mobility. It was a theme that lay at the heart of Brown's philosophy, but the report made uncomfortable reading, reminding the public about stalling progress under Labour, and recommending some solutions to enhance opportunities through widening participation in the education system. One adviser described it as 'respectable but not revolutionary'.[382] The report nevertheless secured substantial media coverage, a rare feat for the government's domestic policy, and earned plaudits for Brown's open-mindedness in setting Milburn on the task. Overall, June turned out, even after the dreadful start, to be a good month, and advisers felt lifted. One contemporary diary from Number 10 captures the feeling about the new agenda: 'With the launch of *BBF*, it feels more sustainable and policy-rich. It feels like we're going into the summer fighting.'[383]

Afghanistan Explodes: April to August 2009

While Brown was dealing with the early summer's domestic crises, he was having his mind yanked increasingly to Afghanistan, which by high summer had 'virtually taken over the whole of Number 10'.[384] Afghanistan was now to constitute the 'perfect storm' for Brown: a serious and deteriorating foreign war with significant British casualties, a very negative media campaign against his conduct of it, rapidly evaporating public support for a dangerous war few thought could be 'won', dissonance with Washington, and deep divisions within Whitehall. This time Whitehall's wars were not between the Treasury and Number 10, nor the Foreign Office and Number 10, but the Ministry of Defence, specifically the generals, and Number 10. Hitherto, these tensions had been mostly contained below the surface. So why did they break out suddenly in the summer?

The United States, having largely neglected Afghanistan in favour of Iraq since 2002/03, began calling the shots on Afghanistan from early 2009. After his inauguration in January, Obama had immediately ordered a strategic review under CIA's Bruce Riedel, and appointed Richard Holbrooke as his special envoy for the Afghanistan and Pakistan ('AfPak') region. Obama did not wait for Riedel to complete his task before committing 17,000 further troops to Afghanistan in February. Riedel reported in late March that the situation was very bad, and that the International Security Assistance Force (ISAF) faced defeat through lack of resources. Obama immediately sent in a further 4,000 US troops and replaced the ISAF commander, General McKiernan, with Iraq veteran Stanley McChrystal. A further strategic review of the region was to report in late 2009.

On 31 March Obama's staff arrived with the President in London for the G20 en route to the NATO summit in Strasbourg. Contrary to the indications that Number 10 and the Foreign Office had been receiving from the Americans in previous weeks, Brown's team now learned that at the breakfast meeting the following morning Obama was going to ask Brown for more troops ahead of the Afghan elections due in August. Tom Fletcher fired off an email that night to colleagues in Number 10, saying he had received an email from the National Security Council that day which gave a 'heads up that BO [Barack Obama] would very much hope that GB could commit to two additional battle groups'.[385] At 11.59 on the Tuesday evening a further email from Fletcher was sent around senior staff in Number 10, 'Oh dear, have gone to head it off.'[386] The President was quietly counselled to tone down his expectations of Brown at breakfast the following morning. Brown was angry that the British military had acted unilaterally and raised expectations with American colleagues. Suspicion grew in Number 10 that the pressure from the generals to increase British troop numbers had less to do with the real needs on the ground than with their own standing in the eyes of their American compatriots after Iraq. Reports came into Downing Street of a senior American officer saying in confidence that the specific number of troops the British put in was irrelevant to the Pentagon, as long as the British were seen to be doing something.[387]

Brown was still angry with the military when he boarded a plane on Saturday 4 April for a NATO summit,[388] the grand sixtieth anniversary jamboree. The British military were particularly keen to show that it could hold its head high there. NATO had been founded in 1949 significantly because of the work of British Foreign Secretary Ernest Bevin, and Britain had been a mainstay of NATO ever since. This was a time for Britain to show that its armed forces were still without equal. British troop levels in Afghanistan were currently 8,300 and the military wanted them to increase to the top level of 9,800. Brown had not had time to give this proper consideration because of the G20, and neither had the matter been settled in a meeting of the NSID Committee (National Security, International Relations and Development), the senior Whitehall body overseeing such matters, which contained all key people from the foreign policy, defence and international development departments. In the weeks building up to the NATO summit, the Cabinet Office had been conducting a major exercise looking at requirements and whether the troop numbers that the Ministry of Defence was seeking were indeed justified.

Twenty-four hours before he departed, Brown agreed that he should accede to the request for an extra 200 troops who would be focused on tackling improvised explosive devices (IEDs) – the devastating roadside bombs that became the main killer of British soldiers in Helmand – but he had still not made up his mind about additional troop numbers when he boarded the plane. It had thus to be thrashed out on board, when Brown and his staff Simon McDonald and Matt Cavanagh sat opposite Defence Secretary Hutton and Chief of Defence Staff Stirrup. 'I've been through all the papers and I can't do a permanent rise to 9,000,' Brown told them flatly.[389] Instead he proposed that troop levels rise *temporarily* to 9,000 until after the Afghan elections in August, and then they would have to come back down to 8,300. 'Well, Prime Minister, if that is the political decision so be it. I must tell you that, if we have to do that, then we will have to, but it will mean we will have to get out of some of the areas we are currently holding,' Stirrup replied.[390] Brown's staff maintain that on the flight Hutton and Stirrup did not object to the proposal, though Jon Day, a Defence official, probed whether such a temporary increase in troop numbers would be genuinely workable.[391] The increase in troop numbers was duly announced at the NATO conference.

The British military was, however, very far from happy, and subsequently returned to the cause. 'We hadn't given up the fight,' says Stirrup. 'We had just made a tactical withdrawal, but were determined to come back again.'[392] When Parliament returned after the Easter recess, Brown duly told MPs on 29 April that the troop levels would rise temporarily by 700 to 9,000.[393] He was concerned that the military was driving Britain towards becoming an army of occupation, whereas he wanted British soldiers to be far more involved in the training and mentoring of native Afghan soldiers. He had been tired and frustrated with hearing from the military that 'we have to clear out this hornets' nest' in order to inflict the decisive blow against the Taliban. He thought the military were always finding new 'hornets' nests'. [394] Muir believes that growing up during the Vietnam War, in which he had taken considerable interest, conditioned Brown to be very wary of the self-perpetuating momentum that can build up behind a military mission.[395] Darling was always sceptical about whether the funds could be found, and David Miliband had his own doubts about troop increases, as to an even a greater extent did Douglas Alexander.[396] All three wanted assurances that the temporary troop increase would not become permanent. So too did Brown who envisaged persuading European and other allies to provide at least 400 troops, which would allow him to bring British numbers back down below 9,000 after the Afghan elections in August. McDonald was duly sent off on a trip around European capitals trying to persuade them to send troops to join in with the British effort, with the sweetener that they were being asked to perform mainly support rather than frontline duties.

Brown sought to make his own contribution to finding the extra troops with a trip to Poland, a country he believed might be receptive. He preceded that trip with an Afghan visit on 26 April, where he visited Camp Bastion and saw Karzai in Kabul before meeting local people in Lashkar Gah. Brown flew on later that day to Pakistan. He had very high hopes for the visit, with his staff in Number 10 working up a plan for a joint counter-terrorist initiative, which he hoped to announce on his return and secure some badly needed favourable headlines in the wake of the McBride affair. Brown, like Obama, wanted to view policy towards Afghanistan and Pakistan jointly, hence his appointment that spring of Sherard Cowper-Coles as special representative to the two countries. The Foreign Office warned that Number 10's proposals for a more unified response were too ambitious and would not fly, but Fletcher, who was driving them forward, ignored it.[397] On Brown's arrival, the Pakistanis, as the Foreign Office had indicated, made it very clear that they had little interest in Number 10's plans for them to become more engaged in a strategic council combating insurgency in Afghanistan. Then, whether out of annoyance at Brown's comments earlier that day about terrorism in Pakistan, or at the arrest two weeks before of eleven Pakistani students in Britain suspected of terrorist plots,[398] President Zardari refused a joint press conference with Brown. Pakistani officials insisted that it take place instead with Brown's opposite number, Prime Minister Yusuf Gilani. The press conference itself proved a shambles, and the talk was of Brown being snubbed.[399]

Brown was in a very angry mood when he boarded the plane for Poland. 'He needed a big story out of Pakistan. He didn't get it.'[400] When the press was bad, his aides would ensure that papers were not laid out on the plane for him to pick up during the flight. 'On this occasion we didn't take them away, so all the papers were there, and he picked them up, and that got him thinking about all the bad stuff and hits back at home, and how we hadn't been able to deliver for him in Pakistan.'[401] Aides described his mood as 'the angriest he ever got with his staff', with Tom Fletcher, Stewart Wood and Simon McDonald bearing the brunt. 'He became very down on Simon [McDonald] from then on: he had done excellent work on Iraq and Afghanistan up till then, but their relationship never fully recovered,' says an insider.[402] Another aide says, 'There were bigger rages, but they were always directed at other people. This time, it was aimed at us.'[403]

Brown arrived in Warsaw late at night on 27 April. He was met by the British ambassador Ric Todd, who had worked well with him in his Treasury days. It was obvious to Todd on the journey from the airport to the hotel that 'he was clearly tired and Pakistan had not gone that well'.[404] The next morning Brown went to see Prime Minister Donald Tusk, but was disconcerted to hear him say that, although Poland would indeed be sending more troops to Afghanistan, it would not be as part of the British mission. He then went on to what an insider describes as a 'truly dreadful' meeting with President Kaczynski, who was rambling and unfocused – contrary to the official record, which describes a meeting that was both incisive and purposeful.[405] The Poles were nevertheless pleased to see him, and he gave a good television interview with Poland's answer to Jeremy Paxman (one Tomasz Lis). Todd was struck that Brown was courteous and professional throughout his time in Poland and 'went out of his way to be friendly to me and my team'.[406] Sarah had arrived in Warsaw that morning from London and flew with her husband on the short journey to Krakow.

Brown had long been interested in visiting the concentration camps at Auschwitz which lie some way outside the city. As Chancellor he had backed the Holocaust Educational Trust, which facilitates British children's visits to Auschwitz, and in his book *Wartime Courage* he wrote about Charles Coward who had saved Jews in Auschwitz III. The press behaved with dignity and were allowed just two photo opportunities, one at the 'wall of death' in Auschwitz-Birkenau and the other by the famous railway platform in Auschwitz II-Birkenau. As at Yad Vashem, the Holocaust museum in Jerusalem, which he had visited in 2008, he was deeply moved, as was Sarah, in particular by the exhibits showing the piled-up hair, the suitcases and the children's shoes.[407] The experience helped to place his own problems at home in perspective.

On his return to London, he tried to paint his whole trip in a positive light, unveiling to the House of Commons on 29 April his broader strategy of treating the entire 'AfPak' region, not just Afghanistan, as the focus of British effort. But nothing could disguise the fact that the Pakistan visit had been a humiliation for him, while the Poles had failed to come up with the troops, as indeed had McDonald on his own 'Cook's tour'. Brown would have to find other solutions to meeting the troop requirements he had promised.

The ramshackle decision-making on the plane to the NATO summit had caused ripples across Whitehall. From that point on, Brown resolved emphatically that troop levels and other core military matters would be discussed properly in the NSID Committee. But, as with many of Brown's best intentions, little changed. To the anguish of Hutton, David Miliband and Alexander, he continued to take key decisions about Afghanistan not in NSID, but often just bilaterally with Stirrup. Dannatt was one of those disconcerted by Brown's working so exclusively through Stirrup. 'It was a little counterintuitive not to tell the head of the service that is doing the heavy lifting,' says Dannatt. 'But that is the nature of Jock Stirrup, a fast jet pilot, used to making decisions at 600 knots without consultation.'[408] Stirrup, who was no fan of Dannatt by this point, concedes that Brown's shambolic practices often meant that key figures 'felt excluded from the decision making process'. Hutton, meanwhile, was barely on speaking terms with Brown when he departed in the June reshuffle. Brown rapidly lost confidence in his successor, Ainsworth, blaming him for being unable sufficiently to 'grip' the department and the chiefs of staff during the summer crisis. Ainsworth himself was frustrated at his lack of access to Brown and what he felt was an absence of respect. He only had one 'decent' conversation with Brown during his whole time at the Ministry of Defence, which came in the run-up to the 2010 Budget.[409] He felt their relationship went wrong at the outset. At a dinner given for new ministers shortly after the reshuffle, an enthusiastic Ainsworth outlined his three priorities to Brown: reinforcing the troops, publishing a green paper as precursor to a full strategic defence review, and protecting the defence budget. Brown turned on his eager new Defence Secretary and said, gracelessly, 'You realise this is costing us £3billion a year.'[410]

Brown's distant personal relationships with Hutton and Ainsworth was one reason why the NSID Committee was not a success. Members complained that he often turned up to meetings late, created an atmosphere of hostility and was distracted by scribbling notes to himself or receiving notes passed to him from his private secretaries, which attendees found degrading.[411] Officials were constantly frustrated by the absence of properly managed and well-ordered discussion on policy towards Afghanistan. 'NSID meetings were a charade. We never had proper discussions. They became more and more detached from reality,' one says.[412] Some of Brown's staff said the problems stemmed from the three departments (Foreign and Commonwealth, Defence, International Development) being in radical disagreement at official as well as political level, and from the Cabinet Office being unable to knock heads together and synthesise a proper set of options, let alone an agreed view.[413] Overall clarity on Afghanistan was the victim. Policy under Brown was often reactive and driven by the military with its own agenda, rather than a clear-sighted view from Number 10 of British national interest.

The response to Operation 'Panther's Claw', which lasted five weeks between 19 June and the end of July, was an example of this lack of clarity. The plan was conceived within the Ministry of Defence in London and Permanent Joint Headquarters (PJHQ) in Northwood, in discussion with the military in Kabul, Kandahar and Helmand. The aim was to drive out the Taliban and produce a safe zone in an area between the Helmand River and the Nahr-e-Burgha canal, north of the town of Lashkar Gah. It was not an easy campaign. Soldiers had to fight their way through fields, compounds and waterways in temperatures that one American Marine commander described as 'hot as fire'.[414] Casualties proved to be heavy, with four British soldiers killed in June and twenty-six in July, ten directly as a result of Panther's Claw.[415] July went on to prove the worst month for British soldiers since the Falklands War, climaxing with eight soldiers killed in twenty-four hours on 9 to 10 July.[416] Dannatt says that, in order to carry out their attacks for Panther's Claw, the British had to thin out troops in other areas. Places that had been held by 200 troops before were now held by thirty. The Taliban observed the thinning, particularly around Sangin, and acted accordingly, hence the higher casualties.[417]

Over the summer the British public became increasingly alarmed at the almost daily news of casualties, and public support which had been high in the aftermath of 9/11 when Britain first entered Afghanistan, quickly began to drain away. The stream of coffins that passed through Wootton Bassett, the small market town in Wiltshire close to RAF Lyneham, became a focal point for a nation that no longer understood what these brave men and women were dying for. The news on 1 July, the anniversary of the first day of the battle of the Somme, that Lt Col. Rupert Thorneloe had been killed, proved especially shocking, and particularly in Downing Street because many staff knew him from his time when he had been a military assistant to Des Browne. The Prime Minister's party was at the G8 conference in L'Aquila in Italy when the news came through. Cavanagh in London called Brown's team and was frustrated to find them in a 'trip bubble', the term given when staff are so wrapped up in a conference they are attending that they find it difficult to comprehend another reality. 'You have to understand there is wall-to-wall coverage here,' Cavanagh explained.[418] When Brown did engage with it, it hit him 'extremely hard'. Thorneloe was the highest-ranking British officer to be killed in action since Lt Col. 'H' Jones during the Falklands War in 1982. Troop casualties were beginning to worry him greatly. He felt instinctively he needed to be more hands on. Rather than return to Downing Street, he decided he should go straight to Northwood as soon as he reached London on 10 July.

Stuart Peach, chief of joint operations at PJHQ, gave the Prime Minister's party a full briefing on the operation's progress. 'How many casualties did you expect on Panther's Claw? Are they much higher than you expected?' McDonald asked. The response was that they were 'well within the range of what we expected'. Brown and his aides were forcefully struck by the thought that, if the military had expected it to be so bad, why had they not prepared the public and media much better beforehand?[419] Brown was privately shocked, failing to see why, if the operation was going as well as they were being told it was, there were so many casualties.[420] The military, it transpired, had not alerted ministers to the probability of heavier casualties even though estimates existed. Later the military would privately admit that omitting to prepare not only the government but also public opinion had been a mistake.[421] The military continued to maintain that Panther's Claw was a great success, with 200 of the Taliban apparently killed. But the figure was not proven and some in the media questioned its accuracy.[422]

Panther's Claw did not see the military being brought under the microscope on the plan's effectiveness and conduct; rather it was Brown himself who became the target of media and public blame. On 11 July, shadow Defence Secretary Liam Fox launched a savage attack on him, accusing him of the 'ultimate dereliction of duty' and 'catastrophically' under-equipping the armed forces. He had been 'resorting to spin rather than confronting the life-threatening reality' that the troops faced.[423] Fox's comments focused on IEDs, which had killed twelve of fifteen British soldiers who had died in Afghanistan so far that month. At this point, the media revealed that Dannatt had asked for an extra 2,000 troops for Helmand but had been turned down by Downing Street.[424] But Downing Street was never convinced by the military argument that troop numbers were to blame for the casualties.

Anger was stoked still further in Number 10 when Dannatt was interviewed on 15 July by Radio 4 on a trip to Afghanistan, with gunfire in the distance. To a question about why he was travelling in an American helicopter, he replied, 'Self-evidently, if I moved in an American helicopter, it's because we haven't got a British helicopter,' going on to say that the commanders out in the field needed more mobility.[425] Dannatt subsequently maintained that it had been chance that had decreed his choice of transport. 'I was assuming we'd fly in an RAF Chinook. Suddenly, two American Black Hawks landed at Camp Bastion. I saw Sarah Montague [the *Today* interviewer] look at me and she thought "ah ha" and I thought "oh dear".'[426] Number 10 was already angry with Dannatt for all the public pressure he had been putting on increases in troop numbers, and was suspected to be behind some of the negative briefing. An exasperated official claims, 'It was Dannatt who really ramped it up. When I heard him speaking on Radio 4's *Today* I was livid. Why on earth shouldn't he be on a US helicopter? We're part of the coalition and coalitions help each other out.'[427] Dannatt's landmark interview helped contribute to the story that 'Number 10 was letting the boys down'. Relations between Brown and Dannatt, which had never been good, now became deeply embittered. It turned to contempt when the news broke in October that he was to take an advisory role for the Conservative defence team, seeming to confirm suspicions that he, a supposedly impartial military officer, had been going behind the government's back in talking to the opposition.

Later on that day, 15 July, Cameron showed no mercy to Brown in the House of Commons, dismissing his efforts to boost numbers of helicopters. 'The public will find it hard to understand why as a country we have 500 helicopters, yet fewer than thirty of them are in Afghanistan.'[428] Brown had in fact written to the Ministry of Defence in 2008 and asked if more helicopters were needed, and it had responded, on advice signed off by Dannatt and the chiefs, that they were not. Officials debated the merits of revealing this information but, rightly or not, chose not to do so. The following day, the cross-party defence committee concluded that 'the lack of helicopters is having adverse consequences for operations today'.[429] Public confidence in the government's conduct of the war fell by the day. A YouGov poll for the *Daily Telegraph* at the end of July found 71 per cent of people agreeing with Dannatt that more helicopters were required and only 11 per cent thought that the Prime Minister was right,[430] while a YouGov survey for Sky News found that 82 per cent of people thought the government should be doing more to support the troops.[431] Former Chief of Defence Staff Guthrie, well known as a Brown-hater, told *The Times*, 'You can't go to war in a penny-pinching way … we need more soldiers … ideally about 25,000 more.'[432]

Number 10 found itself under fire on two fronts: from the media for failing to provide adequate equipment, and internally in Whitehall on troop numbers.

On 17 July, Dannatt warned of 'failure' in Afghanistan unless he was granted 'a shopping list' of requirements, principally concerned with counter-IED equipment.[433] That same day, Stirrup went in to see Brown in Downing Street. 'It was complete nonsense that I was delivering a shopping list,' said Stirrup later. He reports telling Brown, 'Prime Minister, we've got to make the increase of troops to 9,000 enduring and not see numbers fall again after the Afghan election.' Brown responded that he had made a statement in the House to say that he would not be doing that, and would find it hard to secure backing in Cabinet for it. 'That may be the case, and of course we will do whatever you tell us to do,' said the Chief of Defence Staff. 'But I must tell you that I think we will lose control because we will have to give up ground.'[434] At the end of a dogged conversation, Brown relented and said he would agree to 9,000 troops being the new baseline for the autumn review of troop numbers, as long as clear arguments were presented by the military, and as long as it was in line with the McChrystal review being conducted by the US.[435] 'You know it's going to be very difficult, but if it's the right thing to do, then I'll do it,' Brown conceded. Why did he change his mind? The answer would appear to be that he had simply been ground down by the media and public storm. Number 10 needed the military itself to be defending the strategy in Afghanistan, not attacking the Prime Minister in public and private briefings. When challenged on the briefing, the military's response was that it would not be appropriate for it to defend what was happening while it was so unhappy about troop levels.[436] Brown was thus being told, 'If you give us more troops, we will defend the policy.' Stirrup duly went out after his meeting with Brown and met the media. If not positively supportive, he says – 'there is no such thing as enough helicopters in an operational campaign' – he at least avoided being openly critical of the government.[437]

The negative briefings from the Ministry of Defence eased after the meeting, and Brown slowly began to get on top of the issue. For the rest of July and all of August Heywood and Cavanagh focused hard on practical ways of getting the equipment already in the pipeline delivered to Afghanistan more quickly. 'It was inevitable that when something becomes *the* dominant issue for the Prime Minister, that Jeremy Heywood gets involved,' says one aide.[438] Number 10 rapidly concluded that the Ministry of Defence and the armed forces were being too rigid in their thinking and too cautious about timescales. Given the difference some of the new equipment could make to increasing the safety of troops, it thought the Ministry of Defence was digging in its heels and coming up with inadequate excuses. Robust conversations took place. By mid-August, Number 10 and the Ministry of Defence felt they had done what they could to speed up the supply of helicopters, armoured vehicles, surveillance, counter-IED and other equipment, and the task was progressively handed over to the highly proficient Vice Chief of Defence Staff, Nick Houghton. Recovery of stability was helped further by Brown's visit to Afghanistan on 29 August, when he announced that an extra 270 armoured vehicles would be delivered by Christmas.

The visit came nine days after the Afghan elections, during which Karzai prematurely claimed victory in a contest marred by allegations of wide-spread electoral fraud. Brown was the only British figure who Karzai by now fully trusted, and he had the best relationship with him of any foreign leader, 'so much so that the White House would come to us when they wanted to say something to Karzai', says a Number 10 aide.[439] Brown and he both having children of the same age provided another connection between them: 'When Karzai visited Number 10, the boys would be paraded before him.'[440] On Sunday 23 August, Brown made a critical phone call in which he urged Karzai to 'be a statesman'. If he could act as one, the international community would support him, Brown said, but he would have to respect the judgement of the international monitors who had discovered a number of irregularities with the election. 'Brown told him very clearly that if the review recommended a second run-off election then he must accept it. He convinced him he would be a much stronger figure for doing so,' says an aide.[441] After his trip at the end of the month, Brown felt that a corner had been turned, equipment was beginning to flow in, the permanent increase in troop numbers was in train, and, with the ending of Panther's Claw, some calm was returning to Helmand – and on Fleet Street.

Summer Recovery and Fight-Back: August 2009

After a bruising few months – McBride, Gurkhas, expenses, resignations, and most recently Afghanistan – Brown was tired and in desperate need of a holiday. He left with the family for Scotland at the end of July, going to their comfortable Victorian villa in North Queensferry, near Edinburgh. The hilltop house provides views over the Firth of Forth and across its historic islands to East Lothian and the North Sea. It was here in August 2000 that the Browns were married, in one of the most successfully kept political secrets of recent times. The Fife house lies just twenty miles along the Forth estuary from Kirkcaldy, where Brown was brought up, and he now represents Kirkcaldy and Cowdenbeath, a seat created in 2005. He is a popular figure in the constituency, with his personal vote increasing from 58.1 per cent in 2005 to 64.5 per cent in 2010, and he and his family feel at home in a community that is intensely protective of them and their privacy. He is said to be a changed man when in Scotland, and it meant much to him that the Scottish press did not engage in the personal attacks that its English counterparts did. 'He is evangelical about Fife. He knows so many people there who were his friends from school and he is incredibly proud of it,' says McNeill.[442] 'He is very happy to be in Scotland at his house. Scotland's a different place, it's a different culture and it suits him,' adds a close friend.[443]

For all Brown's joy at being at home, the family decided that they wanted to spend part of August away and, as with the previous two summers, they decided to holiday within the UK. This decision meant Brown could support the British tourism industry, but 'the main motivation is they genuinely like Scotland, Wales and England', says a friend.[444] The original August 2009 plan was to spend one week in Wales and a second in the Lake District. In the preceding months, security teams worked on scouting out suitable locations in Wales. Two destinations were found but turned down, one for communications reasons and the other for security reasons. Time eventually ran out on Wales and the family was left with just the Lake District, where they went for a secluded break albeit accompanied with their constant travelling retinue of security officers, two rotating 'Garden Room Girls' (Number 10 secretaries) and a convoy of police and others.[445] The location was the Armathwaite Hall Country House hotel on Bassenthwaite lake, where they stayed for four days from Monday 10 August. The family relished the time together and Brown described it later as 'a fantastic few days relaxing in such a beautiful and inspiring place and [enjoying] walks around Buttermere and Bassenthwaite lakes and an excellent boat trip on Derwent Water'.[446] It was a quieter and shorter holiday than the year before in Suffolk, but as a result he had more time to read and think.

Before every holiday a note would go round staff at Number 10 saying, 'It's holiday time, can we have your suggestions of books that Gordon might like to read over the break?'[447] So he left for Scotland and the Lakes armed with a small library of books, which he devoured at the rate of about one a day. Few modern Prime Ministers have matched the enormous range of serious books Brown read while at Number 10, and none since Churchill probably wrote as much, though many of his most creative moments as Prime Minister went into his speeches, which were his way of thinking through the big issues and developing policy. A few of these speeches, selected and introduced by Wilf Stevenson, were published in April 2010 in a volume entitled *The Change We Choose: Speeches 2007–2009*.[448] The argument made in the book is that Brown's speeches, although ignored by many of the political commentariat when they were delivered, are based on the values and beliefs that have defined his political career. Brown's shambolic approach to speech-writing, and his poor oratory, often let him down but the fact remains that few Prime Ministers can match the range or depth of his thinking on world and domestic issues.

Brown had enjoyed writing his *Maxton: A Biography* (1986),[449] but his political career placed a major bar on book-writing, and he needed a fresh impetus if he was to return to it. The turning point for his writing was a bitter one: the death of daughter Jennifer in 2002. Losing their first child hit Sarah and him very badly, and the loss still affects them profoundly. He became absorbed in the idea of how human beings deal with adversity and emerge the stronger for it. Out of it came writing that led on to his books on 'courage'.[450] The core question he sets out to answer is: what makes ordinary men and women take difficult decisions and do the right things against the odds when there are easier and less dangerous alternatives? During 2003/04 he wrote furiously, but was not certain what to do with the output. When looking at the sheer volume of his writing, it became obvious that he had material for more than one book, and in the end three separate volumes on this topic emerged over the next few years, each dealing with the different takes on courage: 'sustained altruists' who devote their entire lives to principled causes; 'career' heroes such as those in the armed forces; 'situational' heroes such as the passengers on United 93 at the time of 9/11, and ordinary people who put community before self. All profits from these books go to the 'Jennifer Brown research laboratory' at the University of Edinburgh.

The first book, *Courage: Eight Portraits*,[451] was published three weeks before he moved into Number 10 in 2007, and was written 'in memory of Jennifer'. As he said, it 'came from his heart'.[452] The best of his books, it received generally good notices, few more so than Jonathan Freedland's writing in the *New York Review of Books*: 'No Prime Minister since Churchill has written anything quite as good, at least not while in active politics.'[453]

A second volume, *Britain's Everyday Heroes: The Making of the Good Society*,[454] also published in 2007, tells the story of thirty-three ordinary people who were inspired to make a significant difference to their local communities. It was produced in conjunction with Community Links, an East London charity, and tuned with his thinking that 'local heroes' were the 'true celebrities and the most worthy of celebration'. *Wartime Courage*[455] was the third and final volume in the series, published in November 2008. It tells the stories of ten ordinary men and women in the Second World War (eleven in the paperback edition published in September 2009), including Sergeant Hannah VC, an airman who single-handedly fought a fire in a bomber returning from a raid on Antwerp in 1940, and John Bridge, a physics teacher turned mine and bomb disposal officer who worked throughout 1940–45. Brown took great pride in his writing, and was pleased to reveal a side to him and vulnerability in his books he rarely let the world see in the flesh. He was thus doubly pained when reviews were critical. While he was in the Lakes, a row broke out over a review Boyd Tonkin had written in *The Independent*. The paperback of *Wartime Courage*, to be published the following month, had Tonkin's words added by the publishers on the front cover: 'Carefully chronicled and swiftly told'. But the review itself, which had caused Brown anguish when it had appeared the previous November, had said that the book was 'an engine-drone monotone', adding that his 'mealy-mouthed avoidance of controversial issues' actually 'downgraded' the achievements of the men and women whose heroism in the Second World War he had sought to celebrate.[456]

In charge in his absence in Downing Street was a weekly rota of Darling, Harman, Straw and, from 7–14 August, a newly bronzed Mandelson. This week constituted the high point of Mandelson's political career and ambition. Just two years before, he had been alienated from Westminster politics, a marginal figure of the past; now he was its fulcrum. He outshone the other three caretaker Prime Ministers by a distance, and by landing some major blows on Cameron's Tory Party damaged the image of near impregnability it had amassed since early in the year. In an article in *The Guardian*, Mandelson launched a stinging attack on Osborne's claims that the Conservative Party was now 'the dominant progressive force in British politics',[457] accusing the shadow Chancellor of hypocrisy in claiming to be progressive while failing to reveal in any meaningful detail Tory policies on education, health care, minority rights, workplace rights or Britain's position in Europe. More damagingly, he launched into the Tories on the NHS after Daniel Hannan, the Tory MEP, had said on American television 'he wouldn't wish it on anybody' and that it was a 'sixty-year mistake'. Sarah Brown, an enthusiastic user of micro-blogging site Twitter, persuaded her husband that they should both 'tweet' a response that the NHS 'often makes the difference' and they included the words, 'Thanks for always being there.'[458] This was part of a mass, supportive response on Twitter, piling pressure on the Conservatives. The celebrated scientist and cosmologist Stephen Hawking, an apolitical figure, was one who shared his positive experiences: 'I wouldn't be here today if it were not for the NHS.'[459]

Mandelson's attack deployed the 'two faces' argument: 'What we see is the two faces of the Conservative Party – the one David Cameron wants everyone to see and believe, and the other one presented by the Conservative parliamentarian.'[460] Brown's team always felt that Cameron was vulnerable on the difference between his beliefs and the branding. 'We instinctively felt he looked slippery and we were able to beat him up. Peter scared the pants off the Tories,' says Muir.[461] Cameron, forced on to the back foot, was left to dismiss Hannan's views as 'eccentric' while insisting the Conservatives were 'four square behind the NHS'.[462] Number 10 was ecstatic about Mandelson's performance. 'Peter comes back from Corfu and hits the ground running. This week is becoming Cameron's worst nightmare as the press finally turn on the Tories,' wrote Forsyth in his diary.[463]

The summer was also the time when Brown's team began to develop their plans for the general election in 2010. In mid July, in the week before the recess, a long strategy meeting took place at Number 10 with Mandelson and Balls, preparing for Brown's return in September.[464] 'We are feeling much more settled and confident,' says Forsyth's diary.[465] At that meeting, they decided Brown would agree to television debates during the election campaign, on the grounds Labour had no money and very little chance of getting any and thus could never match the Conservative spending on advertising. But they concluded they would not announce it at that stage. 'We decided to let Cameron carry on and talk about it over and over again,' says Muir, adding, 'He fundamentally underestimated Gordon Brown.'[466] Their strategy for the election was heavily influenced by an article written by Malcolm Gladwell in May 2009 in the *New Yorker*, entitled 'How David beats Goliath. When underdogs break the rules'.[467] What captivated them was how Gladwell described apparent underdogs turning the tables on vastly superior competition. 'From this emerged our "underdog strategy", which served us very well until latter 2009. We were liberated by the prospect of defeat,' says Muir.[468] Gladwell argued that underdogs had to acknowledge their weakness as well as choose an unconventional strategy, to enable them to fight on their own ground rather than that of their superior opponent. Within the election preparation team, a battle was taking place between Mandelson assisted by Balls, who had an optimistic vision, and Alexander, the election coordinator, whose views were much more pessimistic. What Mandelson provided to Brown's tired team was heart and a belief they could win (even if he himself had serious doubts about Brown's appeal).[469]

Mandelson also believed he had made a breakthrough in terms of improving Brown's own chaotic working methods. The Prime Minister was finally persuaded of the importance of integrating the various strands of advice he received from people inside and outside Number 10. He would now attend a single strategy meeting which included both Mandelson and Balls, as well as other senior aides like Gavin Kelly and Muir. Heywood would also attend when government business was discussed. Far from seeing this move as a threat to his influence, Balls was highly supportive of the new arrangements.[470] Indeed he was as frustrated by Brown's dysfunctional decision-making as Mandelson. In response to his Cabinet critics, a separate group was convened for the 'big beasts', including Straw, Miliband, Darling and Harman, to meet with Brown at Number 10 to 'make them feel they were more in the loop'.[471] In this period, Number 10 also managed to bring some order to his hopelessly disorganised and ill-disciplined approach to speechwriting. Brown was forever writing speeches – it was how he grappled with policy issues – but he lacked strategic focus when compiling them. 'He would cut and paste bits of speeches and send them round the office. It was utterly chaotic,' says one aide.[472] Another reflects: 'He would be running around asking: "Why the hell haven't my changes been incorporated?" Drafts would be absolutely everywhere.'[473] Early versions of speeches drafted by Brown were hacked out so quickly on his computer, and emailed without him checking the spelling, that the resulting text would be so jumbled and hard to decipher that his policy staff would refer to his offerings as being written in 'Serbo-Croat'. It fell to Kirsty McNeill to discipline Brown, a task she was emboldened to do following the success of his July TED speech, which she had drafted. After this she would say: 'I'm going to need him for three hours to work on the speech.' One official says: 'Things definitely got better.'[474]

August gave Brown a chance to reflect on the tumultuous events of the early summer. David Miliband continued to unsettle him. 'If only I could exchange all those brains for an ounce of loyalty . . .' he confided to his aides.[475] On 9 August, in expansive mood, he aired his feelings about his ministers to one or two close friends. He was disappointed by the younger members: he felt he had brought them on and given them jobs, 'but they are not decisive'. He mourned the lack of 'political' ministers and admitted that Balls was still the figure whose judgement he most valued. About Mandelson, he had no illusions. 'I knew what Peter was going to be like. He was a calculated risk. He's fighting back [David] Miliband. He keeps it together. I can live with him saying he's running the shop.'[476]

Brown felt Ed Miliband had been a 'bit of a disappointment' at the Cabinet Office; he spent his time 'fiddling around' and Brown had found him indecisive. After promotion to Environment he was better, but they fell out over his resistance to the third runway at Heathrow. Brown thought their differences had little to do with substance and were much more about his young lieutenant positioning himself politically for the post-Brown era. 'Heathrow led to the fragmentation of the Ed Miliband and Gordon Brown relationship. Ed nearly left over it and it led to the great freezing of relations between the two men,' says an aide.[477]

Brown became equally disillusioned that summer with Douglas Alexander, who like Ed Miliband was keen to distance himself politically from him. He knew what they were up to. Balls was less successful than the other two at distancing himself from Brown. But none of the three would want to spend their time defending him when it damaged their own future prospects. Sarah felt particularly strongly that they were no longer loyal to him, that all three had felt he was going to lose and they were much more concerned to position themselves in the event of that loss.[478]

It was clear to those listening to Brown that evening that he was lonely, and that he was not close to any of the 'big beasts' in the Cabinet – indeed not close to the Cabinet at all with the exception of Balls and Mandelson. These men aside, he had no remaining political friends at the top. To the end, Brown did not understand that it was not his job to wait for his Cabinet ministers to come to him, but rather for him to empower and to embolden them, as opposed to leaving them in a limbo of uncertainty and doubt. He still had a place for the mafia of Nick Brown, Tom Watson and Ian Austin, who continued regularly to phone him up and say they had heard rumours of plots, often involving David Miliband.[479] In August, he was going through a long and painful process realising that Shriti Vadera wanted to leave, as she wanted to be independent of him. She had spent too long in a high-octane environment and wanted to breathe more freely. But he interpreted it as a lack of confidence in him and as a rejection.[480] Over the summer, Brown worked with officials to devise an exit strategy for Vadera: on 24 September, it was announced that she was going to leave government to become an adviser to the next chair of the G20. That evening his mind also turned, as it always did on such occasions, to Blair. He could not understand the attitude of his predecessor to money and why he was so avaricious. But he worried about how he himself would manage financially after he left Number 10, and whether he would have enough money to support his family, pay off the significant amount of personal debt he had acquired – and sustain his voracious appetite for books.[481] That, he said, was all he needed in life.

Brown kept in touch daily with Downing Street over August, occasionally seeing figures, such as the US General David Petraeus, whom he welcomed in North Queensferry on 21 August for talks on Afghanistan. Afghanistan remained dominant in his mind throughout the month, as did his party conference speech, on which he was working constantly.[482] When he returned to Downing Street after four weeks away, 'He looked like he'd had a bit of sleep and was ready to have a serious run at it,' says an observer.[483] Kelly, Muir and Forsyth had three messages for Brown when he returned. The first was to improve his TV performance, which included directly engaging with the public (thoughts that led directly to his doing the Piers Morgan interview), second to clarify his position on the deficit, and third, to identify three or four iconic policies that defined Labour as different from the other main parties. Selected under the last were to be social care, the cancer pledge and high-speed rail, each with a trusted minister to drive them (Burnham, Ara Darzi and Adonis respectively).[484] In early September, Forsyth wrote: 'In stark contrast to the mood that had been dominant in Number 10 since January ... the team is beginning to think we can do this ... Gordon is amazingly resilient and is showing incredible inner belief ... I am not sure we can win in April/May, but we can make a fight of it. The Tories lack the killer instinct that we had in 1997.'[485]

8

Brown Finds His Stride

(September–December 2009)

Brown's fortunes had begun to turn before the summer holidays. His domestic agenda was at last beginning to take shape, the June reshuffle had seen some talented younger ministers appointed whose work would shortly bear fruit, and optimism was rising about corners being turned in both Afghanistan and the economy. Brown had major ambitions on the international stage, a place where, somewhat to his surprise, he found himself very much at home. A turning point had been his TED talk, recorded in Oxford on 21 July, where he outlined his thoughts on combining the power of modern communications with new international institutions to solve the twenty-first century's global problems. Over the summer, he resolved to press ahead on several such fronts: a new world economic infrastructure, a path to a world free of nuclear weapons, progress on maternal mortality in Africa (one of Sarah's key themes), stability in Afghanistan, reduction in the threat of terrorism, and a climate change deal in Copenhagen in December.[1] If he was to have the space to focus on all these international issues, it was essential for him to have a steady autumn, with continued pressure on the Tories, progress on economic recovery and consolidation of Labour's platform for the general election in 2010. Good fortune had not often run in Brown's favour as Prime Minister, but in the months covered by this chapter, it mostly did. Not, however, at the beginning.

'Blair's Unfinished Business' – Libya: August–September

The autumn began very badly for Brown, with his mishandling of a delicate issue; one he viewed as unfinished Blair business, and as an unwelcome intrusion on to his patch. Brown 'wasn't into Blair's deals at all ... he hadn't been engaged with it', notes a Number 10 official.[2] The issue was about the return of Abdelbaset Ali al-Megrahi. He was the sole man to be convicted for the worst terrorist attack on British soil, on 21 December 1988, when a bomb went off on a Pan American Airways flight from Heathrow to New York, above the Scottish town of Lockerbie, killing 259 people on board, and eleven people on the ground. Megrahi had been found guilty under Scottish law at a specially convened court on neutral ground in the Netherlands, and was sent to prison in Scotland for life. But, it was confirmed in October 2008 that he had advanced prostate cancer. On 20 August 2009, he was released by Scottish Justice Secretary Kenny MacAskill on compassionate grounds and flown home to Libya. It proved a highly controversial move, but the constitutional position for the decision was unequivocal: it was solely a matter for the Scottish Government. So, why did Brown get himself into such a mess?

When the issue of Megrahi's return came up, a Number 10 official went off and read all the back papers on the topic. He learned that the Blair government had been sympathetic to Megrahi's release. In response to the barrage of questions in late August, a statement was drafted for Brown, saying that 'the decision to release Megrahi was entirely a matter for Scotland', but that it was one that he respected.[3] Brown had categorically played no part in the release; indeed, had he tried to interfere, Alex Salmond, who was no friend, would certainly have protested vehemently.[4] So, why did Brown not give the statement that would have killed off the issue? Two explanations present themselves, with the truth possibly lying in a combination of both. Faced with difficult issues, Brown's tendency was not to confront them, in the hope that they would pass away, and he would avoid criticism. In this case he worried about provoking the ire of the US by being seen to support the Scottish government's right to take a decision that would prove hugely unpopular in Washington. The second explanation is that he let himself be swayed by poor political advice, from Mandelson, and from some Scottish MPs in the House of Commons, who felt that if he refrained from making any comment for a week or two, this would put pressure on Alex Salmond and the SNP, and cause them embarrassment.[5] Unusually, Mandelson's instinct let him down on this one. As often in his premiership, it was when Brown acted for short-term party advantage that he came unstuck. Whatever his motive, instead of delivering the statement his officials had handed him about the decision to release Megrahi, Brown opted to comment on the 'third-order' issue of Megrahi's reception in Tripoli, releasing a letter he had sent to Gaddafi, asking that the return to Libya be kept 'low-key'.[6]

The public was bemused by Brown's silence on the actual release and the press filled the vacuum with speculation that he had been involved in the decision to free Megrahi, and even that this had been part of a deal that Blair had agreed with the Libyans in May 2007, in the last days of his premiership, in exchange for lucrative financial contracts for British companies. Liam Fox led the charge for the Conservatives, arguing that Brown's silence was true to type: 'When the going gets tough, Gordon Brown disappears. It's the story of his political career. It's anything but leadership.'[7] Even his Number 10 team could not understand it: 'It was weird the way he handled it. He had nothing to hide, but somehow managed to convey the wrong stance,' one insider comments.[8] A Populus poll in *The Times* on 26 August reported that 56 per cent of those interviewed believed that Brown was handling the episode badly. An article in the *Sunday Times* on 30 August suggested that a deal had been done with the Libyan government, as a way of enabling BP to secure a massive contract in Libya.[9] On 1 September, Cameron accused Brown of 'double-dealing' with the British people, saying that it was shameful that he had refused to give his opinion 'on the release of this mass murderer'.[10]

Brown decided that he would have to break his silence, having been 'prevailed upon to say something to fill the vacuum',[11] and did so at a press conference in Birmingham on Wednesday 2 September, reading out the script which officials had handed him exactly two weeks earlier: 'I respect the right of Scottish Ministers to make the decision, and the decision [itself].' Brown was forced to deny that any underhand activity had taken place: 'There was no conspiracy, no cover-up, no double-dealing, no deal in oil, no attempt to instruct Scottish ministers.' He reiterated: 'We were absolutely clear throughout with Libya and everyone else that this was a decision for the Scottish government.'[12] It was the new official spokesman, Simon Lewis's first lobby and he described it as 'extremely difficult'.[13] Lewis, brother of Will Lewis, then Editor of the *Daily Telegraph*, was a senior figure in the public relations world and a former communications adviser to the Royal Family, well known to Alan Parker, Roland Rudd and others, and had been pursued for several months to take on the job.[14] Brown was desperate to bring in someone who was of impeccable repute to draw a line under McBride: 'it's the price we have to pay for Damian' he said when announcing the news of Lewis's appointment. Michael Ellam returned to the Treasury at the end of July, after his two years, having done a very difficult job well. The Megrahi affair was an appalling baptism for Lewis; it highlighted again the absence of a Jonathan Powell or Alastair Campbell figure, who would have told the Prime Minister immediately how to handle it.

The dithering, and then the pressure to make a statement under duress, made Brown look weak at home, and created a muddled start to his final parliamentary year. To the end, he found it hard to resist cheap point-scoring, and to understand that as Prime Minister he needed a loftier vision for domestic politics. Worse still, it played badly with the Obama administration.

Some 189 of the 270 victims of the Lockerbie tragedy were American citizens. The US had consistently opposed Megrahi's release and Secretary of State Clinton had phoned MacAskill on 14 August to reiterate their opposition. The Obama administration was piqued by his release on 20 August and was further antagonised, as were the American public, by the jubilant reception Megrahi received on his return to Tripoli.[15] 'The Foreign Office completely let us down in terms of not flagging up to us the depth of concern in the US on this subject,' complains one Number 10 official.[16] Perhaps. But it didn't take much to recognise that the decision would not go down well with the US. FBI director Robert Mueller launched a scathing attack on MacAskill, saying he had made a 'mockery of the rule of law' and 'reward[ed] a terrorist'.[17] In a clipped call to Brown on 10 September, a week after the release, Obama 'expressed his disappointment'.[18] Number 10 was taken aback when the White House then gave the media a 'different and less friendly angle' to the one it had put out about the call: 'It meant that, for a while, we were not on the same page as the White House.'[19] Number 10 thought, reasonably, that for a federal government of a federal country, the Obama administration seemed oddly uncomprehending of the United Kingdom's constitution. It continued to fume about the lack of any warning from the Foreign Office and about the crisis the whole affair would cause with Washington.[20] Louis Susman, the newly appointed US ambassador to Britain, tried to calm things down by saying that it was 'not going to sink the special relationship in any measure'.[21] It was the very last thing Brown needed just before an important visit to the US.

Brown in the USA: September

From Monday 21 to Friday 25 September, Brown was in the US, first attending the UN General Assembly in New York, and then the G20 Summit in Pittsburgh. In a break with tradition, Number 10 eschewed British Airways, instead chartering a Virgin Boeing 747 on grounds of cost. Brown had been keenly anticipating the trip as an opportunity to further the international goals he had delineated over the summer. On Monday evening, in New York, he was honoured as 'world statesman of the year' by the Appeal of Conscience Foundation, an inter-faith organisation campaigning for religious freedom. The award was presented by Henry Kissinger at a dinner which Brown was not able to attend, with Queen Rania of Jordan, Israeli Defence Minister Ehud Barak, and U2 musician and campaigner Bono among the audience. In his absence, Brown was praised for 'stabilising' the world economy, for showing 'compassionate' leadership, and for his 'vision and dedication' in handling the world economic crisis. The citation was barely reported in the mainstream British press, aside from a sympathetic piece in *The Guardian*.[22]

Tuesday 22 September began well for Brown, with a copy of the *New York Times* delivered to the Waldorf Hotel in Manhattan, carrying his article, 'Altogether Now', on the five global challenges (nuclear proliferation, climate change, terrorism, poverty and shared prosperity in a new economic order) which he was to outline at the UN General Assembly. On the way to the UN the next morning, his car was stuck in a complete New York gridlock, caused by all the security teams around the world's leaders travelling to the UN. 'Right, let's get out and walk,' Brown said. 'So, off we walked across Manhattan, with officials behind carrying all the papers struggling to keep up,' says one member of the entourage.[23] Impervious to hot and cold temperatures, he relished being in the fresh air. He would have liked to have jogged more, but after he was photographed running in St James's Park, his security team told him that he would have to stop and content himself with the running machines in Number 10.[24] Ever since Sarah put him on a fitness regime in 2008, Brown had tried to do what he could to keep fit. He rarely drank, except for a few glasses of champagne on the plane back from a foreign trip, and in 2009 he even gave this up as part of a health kick.[25]

On Wednesday, his speech itself was almost derailed, ironically, by Colonel Gaddafi. The Libyan leader used his first appearance at the UN to speak for ninety-six minutes, instead of the fifteen minutes he had been given. He denounced the Security Council, asked for $7.7tn in compensation for colonialism in Africa, defended landmines and demanded to know who had killed John F. Kennedy. His tragicomic performance concluded with him tearing up a copy of the UN Charter. Brown had no qualms this time in acting swiftly, rebuking Gaddafi roundly. 'I stand here to reaffirm the United Nations Charter, not to tear it up', he said.[26]

When he had first become Prime Minister, Brown had not anticipated giving much thought to nuclear weapons, which figured prominently in his speech. As Chancellor, he had supported Blair's replacement of Trident – 'In an insecure world, we must and we will always have the strength to take all necessary long-term decisions to ensure both stability and security'[27] – and he had found the £15–20bn to fund it when in March 2007 the plan was approved by the Commons, despite ninety-five Labour rebels voting against. After he moved into Number 10, the official whose job it was to talk him through his new nuclear responsibilities described him as being 'distinctly queasy' when he learned about the full damage of a nuclear war that he might unleash: 'He found it very, very bleak, not only being told about the impact of the use of British nuclear weapons, but also knowing that he would be the only person who would know the full reason why war was beginning.'[28] The use of nuclear weapons forced itself on to his consciousness increasingly, and he became absorbed in the debate that was re-emerging about them,[29] precipitated by the nuclear ambitions of North Korea and Iran, by the long-running fear of terrorist groups acquiring such weapons, and by the attractions of nuclear power for many new states faced with the decline of fossil fuels.

Brown had called for the elimination of nuclear weapons in a landmark speech at London's Lancaster House on 17 March 2009, the same day that Russian President Dmitry Medvedev ordered a major Russian rearmament in response to the risk of 'significant conflict' from NATO expansion.[30] Brown offered to reduce Britain's nuclear arsenal: 'The only way to guarantee that our children and grandchildren will be free from the threat of nuclear war is to create a world in which countries can, with confidence, refuse to take up nuclear weapons, in the knowledge that they will never be required ... Let this be a journey of hope, in which hard-headed cooperation by friends, who were once foes, defines our modern age,' he said. He laid out a 'road to 2010' plan, with proposals on civil nuclear power, disarmament, non-proliferation and fissile material security, and pledged that Britain would be at the forefront of the international campaign to accelerate nuclear disarmament.[31] The speech was praised in a *Guardian* editorial: 'It has been many years since a British Prime Minister took an initiative to reduce the UK's nuclear weapons stocks.'[32]

Brown returned to the banner at the bland G8 Summit in L'Aquila, Italy, in July 2009: 'What we need is collective action by the nuclear weapons powers to say that we are prepared to reduce our nuclear weapons.'[33] He thought deeply about the subject again over the summer and used his UN speech on 23 September to tell the Assembly that they were at a 'decisive moment', when a 'grand global bargain' was possible between nuclear weapons and non-nuclear weapons states. He advocated further sanctions on Iran and North Korea, offered British support for civil nuclear power (as long as the states concerned could prove they were not developing nuclear weapons), and called on all nuclear weapons states to reduce their own stockpiles in exchange for an agreement by non-nuclear states to renounce attempts to acquire them. To show Britain's serious intent, he said he had instructed Britain's (still embryonic) National Security Council to report on ways to reduce Britain's nuclear weapons submarines from four to three.[34] The news did not go down uniformly well, and Number 10 had to calm down the Admiralty, who immediately went into overdrive.[35]

Brown's initiative was inevitably overshadowed by Obama's own drive in the same direction. Under Obama's chairmanship, the UN passed a unanimous resolution, committing members to work towards a nuclear-free world, to comply with the nuclear non-proliferation treaty, and to ratify the comprehensive test ban treaty and ensure safeguards to prevent trafficking in nuclear material.[36] Britain played little part in the signing by Obama and

Medvedev of a new strategic arms treaty in April 2010 to reduce the number of nuclear warheads. Though little immediate action flowed from all Brown's efforts, he deserves praise for being a Prime Minister prepared to stand out against the status quo on nuclear weapons. Baroness Shirley Williams, who had been appointed by Brown as his adviser on nuclear issues, commented: 'He was held in high esteem [by international politicians] for encouraging nuclear disarmament, specifically on verification problems.'[37] She signed off, 'a prophet may be without honour in his own country, but his [international] achievements should be recognised.' Again, we see the striking disparity between Brown's standing abroad and at home.

After Brown had delivered his speech, he left the UN building and almost collided with Robert Mugabe on the pavement outside. Only the quick-footed intervention of an official stopped the sight-impaired Brown from making contact with the Zimbabwe leader, and Brown found himself shoulder-barged back inside the UN building and behind a curtain. Brown could ill afford an encounter with Mugabe's entourage. 'The UK media would have made three days out of that,' comments one official who was present.[38] Brown detested Mugabe. He had refused to attend the EU Africa summit in December 2007 because Mugabe was due to be there, sending Baroness Amos in his place.[39] Disturbing reports from the British ambassador in Harare would arrive at Number 10, including a photograph of a Movement for Democratic Change campaigner who had been horrifically beaten up and murdered in mid-2008. Brown recoiled in horror.[40] During Zimbabwe's fraudulent elections that year, he castigated Mugabe at the UN in April 2008, just yards away from Thabo Mbeki, South Africa's president, and one of Mugabe's defenders: 'No one thinks, having seen the results of the polling stations, that President Mugabe has won this election. A stolen election would not be a democratic election at all.'[41] A source of constant frustration to Brown, as it had been to Blair, was that he could take no stronger action than denouncing Mugabe, who had such powerful friends in black Africa.

If 23 September proved a good day for Brown at the UN, it was a very bad day for him with the media back home. The *Evening Standard* ran a story under the headline 'Gordon Brown dismisses "step down" health slurs',[42] in which Brown's most vociferous PLP critic, Charles Clarke, said that, if Brown remained as leader, Labour would suffer badly at the coming general election and be out of power for ten to fifteen years. 'Are we just going to stand by and watch the whole Labour ship crash on to the rocks of May 2010?' he asked. Clarke also commented on unfounded rumours that Brown might quit because of poor health: 'I think his own dignity ought to look to that kind of solution.' The Prime Minister was now forced for the first time to respond to questions about his health. 'My sight is not at all deteriorating,' he told the US broadcaster NBC, and spent an hour on a Radio 5 Live phone-in on the line to the BBC from a hot studio in New York. 'I am healthy and I'm very fit. I keep going. I have got a job to do,' he said.[43] Difficult questions also had to be fended off when Wirral West MP, Stephen Hesford, resigned as a parliamentary aide over Brown's refusal to sack Attorney General Lady Scotland, after she was fined £5,000 for employing an illegal immigrant. In his resignation letter, Hesford said he was going on a point of principle: 'Particularly at a time when the public's trust of Whitehall is uncertain ... we have to be seen to be accountable.'[44]

Worse by far was news leaking out during the Wednesday about no fewer than five attempts by Brown's staff to take advantage of the UN event to arrange an official meeting with Obama in New York. A joint press appearance by both leaders to advance their shared global ambitions would have been Brown's ideal choice. Before the Prime Minister's party left for the US, Simon Lewis had been asked by the press for a list of Brown's bilateral meetings in New York, and journalists noticed that Obama was not on it. Brown reacted strongly to the suggestion that he had been snubbed, but turned down he certainly had been. To curry favour with the White House, his staff had ordered a change of policy on the supply of swine flu vaccines to Africa, to align British with US policy. The Department for International Development was annoyed by this and was believed to have been responsible for the leak about the rebuffed overtures. *The Guardian* ran the story under the headline: 'Barack Obama snubs Gordon Brown over private talks,'[45] while the *Daily Telegraph* gave it front-page prominence with the headline: 'Barack Obama rebuffs Gordon Brown as special relationship sinks to a new low.' The state of Anglo-American relations, the paper claimed, had reached its lowest point since John Major's relationship with Clinton in the mid-1990s.[46] Rubbing salt in the wound, it said: 'Mr Brown's increasingly poor relationship with the White House contrasts sharply with that of his predecessor, Tony Blair.'[47]

'Did we ask five times for a bilateral? Yes, we did. Bilaterals take time to organise and can frequently involve more calls,' says one Number 10 official. 'The folly on our part was for our spokesperson to give this level of granularity to a press pack that had come to expect a snub story.'[48] Brown's team was so angry about it, and so worried about how their boss would react, that they phoned the West Wing and asked them to call Adam Boulton and Nick Robinson.[49] 'I received a call from the White House for the first and only time in my life', recalled Robinson, 'I was with the White House producer for the BBC and I mouthed the name of my interlocutor.' The producer pointed upwards, indicating it was someone big. 'Mr Robinson, I want you to know that the President thinks very highly of Mr Brown,' said the White House aide. 'Yes, but did he ask for a meeting that he didn't get?' pressed Robinson. The source refused to deny it and both the BBC and Sky News duly led on the snub story. The travelling Number 10 machine went into overdrive to counter it and briefed the media that Brown and Obama had had a fifteen-minute conversation in the kitchen of the UN headquarters in Manhattan as they were both leaving. This itself was written up disparagingly, portraying Brown having 'to settle ... for a snatched conversation with the President in a New York kitchen'.[50] 'Junk journalists at it again,' was Chris Mullin's comment.[51]

The Obama White House was indeed very irritated with Brown, mostly because of Megrahi. It was unusual for it to brief out so blatantly as when it said that the President had told Brown in a bilateral phone conversation that he disapproved of the outcome. Feelings in America were running very high. Kathy Tedeschi and Sue Kosmowski, Americans who had lost husbands in the Lockerbie bombing, had travelled to New York and were protesting outside the UN headquarters. The White House felt that Number 10 was being overly demanding in wanting a bilateral with the President in New York. It had had to contend with the 'nonsense' over the 'pool spray' in March. Had they not done enough for this British Prime Minister? As Obama himself said in his speech to the UN: 'The time has come for the world to move in a new direction.' That new direction meant closer relations with the emerging powers. Accordingly, the White House had earmarked his bilateral time in New York for meetings with Chinese President Hu Jintao, the new Japanese Prime Minister Yukio Hatoyama, and Russia's Medvedev.[52] Number 10 was in turn narked: 'The White House should have wised-up, it had been there for nine months and should have agreed to a short meeting in New York between Gordon and the President.'[53]

Brown hated the bad press. Worse still, on a personal level, was the news breaking on the *Financial Times* website under the heading: 'Is Shriti Vadera about to quit the government?'[54] Brown knew the press would try to insinuate that she was leaving a sinking ship. The official who went in to tell Brown about the snub headlines, and the breaking story about his favoured minister, describes it as 'a very bad moment'. When Brown and his party flew down to Pittsburgh for the G20 later that day, he says it was 'the lowest ebb of any trip'.[55] That evening, Brown and Obama chaired a meeting together on Pakistan and the fight against terrorism, at a time when the White House was still in the middle of a deep rethink over Afghanistan. Obama's team were staying in the same hotel in Pittsburgh as Brown's, which gave them the chance to mend fences and get back on the same side. Brown's aides were surprised to discover how divided the White House was on Afghanistan, with Chief of Staff Rahm Emmanuel, in particular, described in a Number 10 diary as being 'in a very bad place' over Afghanistan. He was openly advising Brown's advisers to read Gordon Goldstein's 2008 book, *Lessons in Disaster: McGeorge Bundy and the Path to War in Vietnam*.[56] Number 10 aides learned how far the often almighty

National Security Council had been marginalised under Obama, and how, on Afghanistan, Emmanuel, and Vice President Joe Biden were both doves: 'They'd be the people whispering in Obama's ears after the generals walked out of the Oval Office, saying: "Are you sure? What's the exit strategy?"'[57]

Nigel Sheinwald, the British ambassador to Washington, came in for some flak from Brown's team, perhaps as a scapegoat for the damaged relations. Although bad blood from the leaked 2008 Sheinwald memo about Obama had been forgotten, he was still associated in the minds of Obama's team with being particularly close to Bush and his entourage. 'They were not naturally well disposed to those who had been part of [Bush's] circle,' says one Number 10 aide.[58] Realising they may have gone too far, Obama's team became anxious in Pittsburgh to build bridges, and expressed sympathy about the British media's treatment of Brown. On Friday, Emmanuel turned to Brown's team: 'Your press are fucking criminals. What do we have to convince them about our special relationship? Do they want to have pictures of Gordon getting it on with Michelle in the Oval Office?'[59]

Ultimately, however, the Obama and Brown relationship suffered because of a lack of personal chemistry. 'Brown never got Obama right' recalls one official. 'He would want to push Obama on the fine detail of policy which is not how the President likes to work'. Another who saw them at close quarters explains that Obama often found Brown 'frenzied'. It was 'a relationship that never really got going', with an eye on the polls Obama's team concluded that the future lay not with Brown but with David Cameron.

The opening of the G20 Summit that Friday was effectively hijacked by the announcement of Iran's secret nuclear uranium enrichment plant at Qom, south of Tehran. Once the Iranians had discovered that western satellites had detected the plant, they sent a letter to Mohamed El Baradei, head of the UN's International Atomic Energy Agency (IAEA).[60] Britain, the US and France had discussed whether they should reveal the news during the United Nations meeting, but decided that it was too sensitive to announce it in New York, with Obama worried that it might adversely affect the debate on nuclear proliferation, so it was held over to Pittsburgh.[61] At the press conference on Friday morning, Brown, Obama and Sarkozy called for tougher sanctions if Iran refused to comply with international undertakings. 'The level of deception by the Iranian government ... will shock and anger the whole of the international community and it will harden our resolve,' said Brown.[62] The announcement, while serious in itself, was deliberately 'stoked up' to secure maximum publicity: 'It was easy to dramatise Iran when we wanted to create a diversion,' says one official.[63] Nick Robinson and the BBC crew failed to turn up to the press conference on Iran, but this was a deliberate ploy by Number 10 to extract revenge. 'We were completely fed up with Nick,' says the official.[64]

When he phoned up to ask what was going on, he was apparently told: 'It's all pretty quiet ... He thus missed the press conference, a deliberate effort to make it a bit harder for him that day, which was slightly vindictive.'[65] A major row followed with the BBC, after which peace broke out, and for a while relations between Number 10 and the broadcaster improved.[66]

Brown had consistently taken a harder line on Iran than other western leaders. He realised that, if that country did acquire nuclear weapons, it would shift the whole balance of power in the Middle East, with serious adverse consequences for Britain's strategic interests.[67] He was happy to let the Iranians engage in a civil nuclear programme, but only if they gave requisite international understandings.[68] He had been the first international leader to press for sanctions against Iran's oil and gas industry, in his Lord Mayor's Banquet speech in November 2007, but his argument lost force internationally in the face of opposition from the Chinese and Russians, who were anxious to protect their own commercial interests and hence were reluctant to criticise Iran in public (though in private they did).[69] The White House, too, was cautious about making damning public statements on Iran, because it did not want to alienate the Chinese and Russians.[70] Cynics would say that Brown's unequivocal line was aided by Britain having no serious trade links with the country, but his views were nevertheless deeply felt.[71]

The Pittsburgh G20 may have lacked the scope and drama of the London G20, but it achieved more than commentators wrote at the time. Leaders pledged not to withdraw domestic stimulus measures until a durable recovery was in place, and they agreed to try to harmonise economic policy, to minimise imbalances highlighted by the USA's deficits and Asia's savings glut. On climate change, they undertook to eliminate subsidies for fossil fuels, but only in the vague 'medium term'. On trade, the leaders managed only a weak commitment to ensuring that the Doha round would be back on track for 2010. Bankers' pay was always going to be one of the more contentious issues, with France and Germany wanting the G20 to endorse strict limits on bonuses; the outcome was a fudge in the direction of the US laissez-faire position. While many of the policy statements were bland, the Pittsburgh Summit was significant for the decision to institutionalise the G20 as the prime global economic forum, replacing the western-dominated G8. India, China and Brazil were thus given a permanent seat at the top table, a transition for which Brown deserves immense credit. The IMF was rejuvenated, with developing countries securing better representation and voting rights from 2011, while the Financial Stability Board (FSB) was broadened to include the major developing countries, and its monitoring role confirmed with tougher financial regulations, providing an enhanced early-warning system for risks. US Treasury Secretary Tim Geithner told reporters that he now saw the FSB as the 'fourth pillar' of the modern global economy, alongside the IMF, the World Bank and the World Trade Organisation.[72] That neither Pittsburgh nor its successor summit in Toronto in June 2010 lived up to the achievement of the London G20 owed much to the urgency of the 2008/09 financial crisis, but another reason they fell short is there was no equivalent Gordon Brown figure to drive and cajole world leaders into action. At the closing press conference in Pittsburgh, Brown said that the G20 was to become the 'premier' body for monitoring international economic problems: 'The old systems of economic cooperation are over ... New systems of economic cooperation from today, have begun.'[73]

Brown had his long-awaited bilateral with Obama on the Friday, after the formal G20 sessions concluded. They discussed nuclear matters and Pakistan and, even if their meeting was not exactly the agenda-setting meeting of minds that Brown had originally hoped for, to give muscle to his ambitious international agenda, he was pleased enough that it had taken place.[74] Brown was much more positive when he boarded the flight home on Friday evening, his mind already turning to the party conference, less than forty-eight hours away. McNeill and Muir worked on his speech throughout the flight. They worked in the cars that met them at Heathrow, and they continued all through Saturday at Number 10. Brown sensed that this might be his last conference speech as Prime Minister, and he hoped it would be his best.[75] Nick Robinson's blog on 26 September concluded: 'No ordinary week for the PM ... The special relationship was, once again, put back on track. The same certainly cannot be said of the relationship between Gordon Brown and the media.'[76] It was a prescient observation. It had indeed been no ordinary week for Brown, highlighting a contrast that was becoming increasingly apparent. As *The Guardian* noted: 'At home [Brown] is reviled, distrusted ... abroad, or in the US at least, it is different; night and day different.'[77]

Party Conference

'The Labour Party faces Herculean challenges if it is to recover any momentum,' said an editorial in *The Independent* on Monday 28 September, as the Labour Party conference was getting under way. 'The Prime Minister must try to make sense of his leadership, which the polls suggest is deeply unpopular, and try to convince doubters that he is the right figure, with the appropriate policies to guide Britain through the recession and beyond.'[78] The polls did indeed look bleak for Brown. Labour had not picked up since its disastrous pre-summer by-election defeat on 23 July in the safe seat of Norwich North, which saw its 11 per cent lead over the Tories in 2005 overturned. On the eve of the party conference, analysis in the *Financial Times* showed that support for Labour was lagging behind the Tories, even in its traditional heartland of northern England. In 2005, Labour had led the Tories by nineteen points in the region; now they trailed them by four points.[79] An eve of conference Ipsos MORI poll even had Labour slipping into third place behind Nick Clegg's Liberal Democrats.[80] 'It was a pretty bleak atmosphere as we went into the conference,' recalls the Policy Unit's Patrick Diamond. 'There was the kind of hope that something would turn up.'[81] Everything was going to hinge on the conference. 'We don't look as if we've got fire in our bellies. We've got to come out fighting,' admitted Darling in an interview in *The Observer* as the conference began,[82] in which he likened the party to 'a football team that had lost the will to live'. To Chris Mullin, it was: 'Doom and gloom everywhere. Everyone knows this is the end.'[83]

Brown's personal position was vulnerable. Fears of an immediate coup may have been at bay since the PLP meeting on 8 June, following the Purnell resignation and reshuffle. But Cabinet remained far from happy with him, and the polls suggested that they had every reason. A ComRes poll for *The Independent* on 25–27 September suggested Brown's leadership was an electoral liability. With him at the helm, Labour was lagging fifteen points behind the Conservatives, levels of support that would translate into a majority of almost fifty seats for the Tories. The party would fare better, it suggested, if any one of eight potential successors were to replace him as party leader. Moreover, were David Miliband or Straw to take over, the polls suggested that Labour would return as the largest party in a hung parliament.[84] The Cabinet was not actively plotting in September to depose him, but swathes of ministers and ex-ministers, including David Miliband, Alistair Darling, Tessa Jowell and Geoff Hoon, were sceptical about whether he would last until the general election, and remained unimpressed by his leadership ability. Brown knew that he would have to perform. He had to 'bark back and bark loudly', as Mandelson said in an interview in the *Daily Mail*.[85] The First Secretary also suggested that Brown would benefit from letting the electorate see his more light-hearted side, which rarely came across in public.

Brown's first test came in an interview with Andrew Marr on Sunday morning. Marr gave him a hard time, quizzing him on his attitudes to the deficit and demanding to know where exactly the axe would fall, on his vacillation during the Megrahi affair, on his support for Baroness Scotland, and on his response to the question of bankers' bonuses. 'It's not working. I mean, that's the brutal truth, but it is the truth,' Marr told him about his performance as Prime Minister. His interrogator kept landing punch after punch. 'Looking at this party, it has lost the fight, it's "lost the will to live",' he said, quoting Darling. Turning on Brown himself, he asked: 'Are there any circumstances in which you would stand aside, because you know, as things stand at the moment, [Labour] is going to be slaughtered?' Brown was visibly under pressure, but retained his self-possession. The question however, that caught all the attention, was whether Brown had been taking 'prescription painkillers and pills' to help him get through. A question which Marr said 'everybody has been talking about out there in the Westminster village'. Brown had not expected this, and the camera showed that he was taken aback. He responded by talking about the injury to his eye, and the restricted vision this had left him with, but he did not respond to the question about drugs. Even though Clarke had raised the issue of his health in the *Evening Standard*, the previous week, as a legitimate excuse for stepping down, no one in Brown's team had prepared him.[86]

'I took the view that medical questions affecting very senior politicians' ability to do the job were fair game. The Americans wouldn't have understood the controversy that followed,' says Marr.[87] In the previous six months, Marr had held a number of private discussions with senior politicians and officials, including those close to Brown, about his 'rages, the smashing of stuff, the language he used, and his losing control completely'. The question being asked, he said, was: 'Is he on something? Should he be on something? And if he isn't, why not?' More recently, Marr had picked up the rumours on the internet about the Prime Minister taking pills. These received wider attention when repeated in *The Independent* in an article by Matthew Norman, which appeared on 10 September.[88] Norman was discussing a story that had appeared on a blog by a John Ward about Brown apparently dropping Chianti and cheese from his diet, which patients on a certain group of strong anti-depressants are advised not to consume. The article concluded: 'The only worthwhile question left for him to answer is whether he's stockpiled enough [pills] to spare a few for the rest of us.'[89] The story had been categorically denied by Number 10, which it believed should have been sufficient to kill it.[90]

The interview finished amicably enough and Brown's staff told the BBC crew that they were quite happy with it. Marr himself was pleased by the main story that he thought would come out of the interview, namely, Brown admitting that he had failed to foresee the banking crisis, or to regulate the banks better when he was Chancellor. When Brown returned to his suite at Brighton's Metropole hotel, his team, who had all been watching it intently, gave him a round of applause. 'That's the best thing he's ever done,' texted Campbell. 'What did they put in your coffee?' asked an excited Mandelson. Brown stood rigid and said: 'I can't believe he asked me about the pills.'[91] When his team mulled it over, their views hardened, and before long they were calling Marr's questions 'a disgrace' and wholly unacceptable.[92] Even Caroline Flint, no friend of Brown's, said on GMTV that morning that the innuendo behind the question on pills was 'despicable'.[93] By noon, Brown's team had gone into overdrive: complaints were put to the BBC, and the message sent out to the media that: 'Marr is disgraceful. The BBC is disgraceful. This isn't acceptable journalism.' The programme's editor, Barney Jones, told Brown's team that he had no idea that Marr was going to be asking the question. Director of BBC News, Helen Boaden, made a formal apology on behalf of the BBC. Marr believes that Number 10's indignation had an ulterior motive: 'I still wonder if it wasn't a deflecting operation from his admission to me about the financial crisis.' He reflected subsequently on his question about the pills: 'I didn't like myself any better for asking it. It's hard to look someone in the eye and say that. I didn't enjoy doing it.'[94]

Assaults like this one almost always rebounded in Brown's favour. His position was further strengthened by conference speeches from his three most senior Cabinet ministers, bolstering his own position and the sense of a united party. Darling was the first big hitter up to the podium on 28 September. In an uncharacteristically hard-hitting speech, Darling declared that the government should wage a 'legislative war' against the greed and recklessness that had contributed to the financial collapse, and outlined the 'financial responsibility bill', which would enshrine in statute the government's commitment to reducing the deficit in four years, a proposal that the *Financial Times* described as 'newspeak straight from the Ministry of Truth'.[95] It was easy to ridicule, but it was designed to show a sceptical City that Labour were serious about deficit-reduction. 'Darling's most authoritative performance as Chancellor', was, however, the verdict of Martin Kettle in *The Guardian*.[96]

Mandelson was also to give the conference performance of his lifetime. Not renowned for his oratory, he delivered a rousing speech, threaded together by the underdog leitmotif. 'He was extremely nervous before he gave it,' says Patrick Loughran. 'It was a very big and emotional moment for him.'[97] Expectations were high. Appointed 'First Secretary' in June, and having put in a dazzling performance as acting Prime Minister in August, Mandelson was at the peak of his powers. 'If I can come back, we can come back,' he said, to laughter from the audience. At last he felt confident enough to recall to the conference Blair's words, which had long resonated in his ears: 'I know that Tony said our project would only be complete when the Labour Party learned to love Peter Mandelson. I think perhaps he set the bar a little high.' He pitched and timed the comment like a master. Then, in a significant display of public loyalty, he turned to Brown and said: 'Gordon, I'm proud to serve in your government ... you will have my full, undivided attention and my full undivided loyalty until we win that next election, and beyond.' However, these were words that within weeks he was to confound. 'A barnstorming speech that delighted delegates and transformed the former Prince of Darkness into the Lord of Light,' declared the *Daily Mirror*. The reception, generally, was very positive. 'A demoralised Labour conference sprang into life,' said *The Guardian*'s political editor, Patrick Wintour,[98] although his colleague, Nicholas Watt, more soberly suggested: 'Peter's panto act will be lost outside the conference bubble.'[99]

At the end of the three days came David Miliband's most powerful conference speech of his three as Foreign Secretary. Any hopes from discontented MPs, backbenchers and ministers, that he was going to lay down a final challenge to Brown were dispelled in his tub-thumping attack on the Tories, without a hint of any reservation about Brown's leadership. The links of the Conservatives with the far-right parties in the European Parliament, he said, made him feel 'sick'. Brown was relieved and his team were delighted by what he said. 'David's speech lifted us,' says one.[100]

Brown's own speech came on Tuesday 29 September. Muir and McNeill had a difficult journey in the back of the car down to Brighton on Saturday: both were sick from the exhaustion, and then they thought they had lost the entire speech on the computer. Both knew how much work still had to be done. 'There was less build-up to this speech than in 2008 because of how busy we had been,' recalls McNeill.[101] Having spent two nights without sleep, Muir declared at 11pm on Saturday evening that he had to go to bed. He passed a bodyguard outside Brown's suite, who had been with them on the US tour, who was half asleep against the door post and trying to stay awake. They marvelled together at Brown's physical stamina – having had little or no sleep, he was still working flat out – and wondered: 'How on earth does he do it?'[102]

It was to be the most last-minute of his three party conference speeches as Prime Minister, with the content not finalised until minutes before he was due to leave to deliver it. His mood pacing around in his suite at the Metropole Hotel was described as: 'stoical, angry, defiant and tired'.[103] A group of people were working around him during the final hours. They all knew how much was at stake. They were all exhausted. In the corner of the room stood a lectern, where he practised sections of his speech; David Yelland, who was called in for advice, thought his delivery on the conference floor was far better than anything they had heard in rehearsal.[104] McNeill was shouted at regularly, but never answered back, tapping away at her computer as she revised draft upon draft. Lucy Parker was working on Brown's presentation before the cameras, and he listened carefully to her.[105] Muir, Pearce and Kelly were worrying away at the content until the final minute, along with Dan Corry, who was leading the Policy Unit in a brave resistance against Brown's attempt to cram the speech full of expensive policy recommendations (his endeavour would only partly succeed).

Two items were dropped at the final hurdle. Brown had been toying with announcing details of a 'Tobin tax',[106] which he had discussed with Treasury officials over the preceding months. This was a tax on financial transactions, designed to discourage speculative and risky trading, but it was workable only as an international measure. Achieving the necessary levels of compliance would have been a hurdle for Brown, even at the height of his international prowess

at the start of the year. Vadera, whose advice he would always heed, arrived in
his suite to announce that neither the US State Department nor the EU was
ready to support the measure. His political staff wanted him to be bold, but
all were concerned about the potential fallout with allies if Britain went ahead
unilaterally – Brown could ill afford another publicly damaging fracas with the
US. Prudence decreed that he should talk more to fellow international leaders
before announcing the measure, as well as prepare the domestic audience for
it, as it was expected to be received negatively.[107] The second announcement,
dropped at the last minute, was a purely internal affair, and concerned Brown's
participation in the televised leaders' debates during the election. His team
argued strongly that he should include it in the speech. 'If I do, everything
in the speech will be forgotten, and all the media will report [will be] about
the TV debates,' he insisted. Mandelson's advice was to be cautious, and the
argument in favour of delay carried the day.[108]

On the flight back from the US on Friday evening, Sarah Brown had asked
her husband: 'Should we think about me introducing you again?'[109] It was her
decision to describe him as her 'hero'. 'Everybody loves her,' says Mullin.[110]
She again worked her magic and after she spoke a film called *Fighters and
Believers* was shown to the delegates. Consistent with the underdog theme, its
message was of Labour achieving great success against the odds, overcoming
challenges and triumphing. 'The history of Britain is the history of fighting for
what is right against the odds. Now we fight again,' said the voiceover.

Brown then began his speech with a long recital of everything that Labour
had achieved since 1997. McNeill said: 'It was designed to challenge the idea
that Gordon was not proud of all Labour's achievements since 1997. It was a
very public coming together of the work of Tony and Gordon.'[111] Building
bridges with the Blairites ahead of the election was a core purpose of the
speech. Antisocial behaviour had been quietly dropped from Brown's agenda
after 2007, but he now very deliberately picked up from where Blair had left off,
speaking about 'action squads' to 'crack down in problem estates [and] protect
the public spaces', and promising to get tough on teenage parents with his
support for placing 16- and 17-year-old parents in a 'network of supervised
homes'. In a reprise of his neglected socially conservative agenda, he said that
24-hour drinking should be banned when it damaged communities. Brown
also announced that he was extending 'family intervention projects' – an early
intervention scheme involving social work teams providing intense support
to dysfunctional families – to the 50,000 most disruptive households in the
country. Number 10's private focus groups showed that this part of the speech
went down very well with the public. Brown's Policy Unit also encouraged
him to champion academies – another Blairite favourite – but this was
blocked by Balls.[112] Indeed, education did not feature much in this, Brown's

most policy-rich speech, because Number 10 and Balls could not agree a way forward.[113]

The speech contained a number of important ideas and would have made an ideal speech for the 2007 party conference, as he was embarking on his premiership. Pearce had submitted a paper to Brown at the beginning of the summer recess containing a number of ideas for the speech. One of these only made it in at the very last moment. It proposed free social care at home for all elderly people judged to have 'high needs', and entailed abolishing means testing for some 350,000 people. In the fraught financial climate, discussions had taken place all Tuesday morning between ministers and advisers in Pearce's hotel room to finalise the funding for it. 'When we finally agreed it, we ran into Brown's room with only minutes to spare. "The deal is done," we told him.'[114] More ambitiously, Brown also gave his backing for the creation of a 'national care service', which he believed was the long-term solution to the pressures of an ageing society. The speech saw movement on constitutional reform, with the significant announcement that Labour would include a commitment in its manifesto to hold a referendum on the Alternative Vote: 'There is now a stronger case than ever that MPs should be elected with the support of more than half the voters – as they would be under the alternative voting system,' he declared. 'We really didn't know whether he would make the announcement in the speech. He took it at the very last minute.'[115] It was a personal triumph for Gavin Kelly and the Number 10 Policy Unit, who did much to push Brown on AV over the summer. On Lords reform, Brown reaffirmed his intention 'to make the House of Lords an accountable and democratic chamber for the very first time'. AV and an elected second chamber, Brown argued, would make the political system more accountable to the people, which he believed was crucial for rebuilding trust after the expenses crisis. He also came out in favour of a recall mechanism, which would enable constituents to trigger an election for MPs guilty of financial corruption. All of this was strong stuff; the question was, would he be able to deliver on it?

The speech touched on a topic that resonated strongly with Brown. In his 2008 conference speech, he had spoken about finding a cure for cancer. It was an *idée fixe* with him, and he was obsessed in particular with improving research as well as treatment. He had held a series of meetings about it in 2009 and put in work on a possible timetable for the cure for cancer. His staff became nervous that he would suddenly make an announcement that he wanted to see cancer cured outright. 'He was always edging towards it,' says Greg Beales, who told him about the episode in *West Wing* where the fictional President Bartlet announces that he wants to cure cancer.[116] Alastair Campbell, who was increasingly present around Brown from the autumn, strongly supported his ambitions and encouraged him to persist with them. In his speech, he said that patients suspected of cancer would be tested and receive their results 'within a week' of being referred, a move to be funded by savings in the hospital buildings programme. This was Brown's 'diagnosis guarantee', which, aligned with a right to see a cancer specialist within two weeks, formed an important part of his entitlements agenda, as set out in *Building Britain's Future*. He was pleased to have found the money to do this, but when Obama later announced that he wanted to see cancer eradicated 'within a generation', he joked: 'Why did Obama get to this first? You spent the last six months telling me it can't be done, and he's gone and done it!'[117]

Childcare was another issue close to Brown's heart, but his announcement to expand free childcare for some 250,000 2-year-olds would come back to bite him. The policy was popular, but the decision to fund it by reforming a universal scheme of childcare vouchers provoked a major backlash among Blairite ex-ministers, who believed it was political folly to withdraw the popular vouchers for 'middle England' families in the run-up to the election. As with the Gurkhas and 10p, his critics believed it was further evidence of Brown's weak political antennae. In December, Brown was forced into a humiliating U-turn, which meant he was no longer able to pursue his proposals for expanding childcare.

Fighting to establish that Labour was still fresh, and had a programme for government in a harsh funding climate, posed its own difficulties. Few believed Brown's claim that the money was available to fund all the new commitments he had announced. For many it was proof that Labour couldn't be trusted to manage the nation's finances. 'We were proposing a new entitlement to free social care at the time of a ballooning budget deficit. It all sounded a bit ridiculous'. 'It would have been a lot more expensive still, had Liam Byrne, as Chief Secretary, and treasury special advisers not intervened,' says an aide.[118] Resolutely, Brown refused to discuss 'cuts' in any detail, 'which leaves us just a teeny bit vulnerable.'[119] The omission deeply frustrated his Cabinet who felt it gave the impression that Brown only knew how to *spend* money. Nor did the speech provide an animating message about the meaning and purpose of Brownism – like all his speeches, there was a stark imbalance between the scattergun list of policy announcements and a coherent argument.

Brown was nevertheless happy with his performance. He made a particular point this year of thanking everyone who had helped him write his speech, and was generous with his praise. His staff, if not everyone in the PLP, left thinking: 'We can still do this.'[120] The media were mostly measured, with typical responses like the one by Philip Stephens in the *Financial Times*: 'Unlike Mrs Brown, the Labour conference does not adore the Prime Minister. But yesterday, Mr Brown did enough to reassure the party that his heart was in the right place and that he was ready for the electoral fight ahead.'[121] It was 'not a speech to save a premiership', though Brown 'won respectful, occasionally warm applause'.[122] In *The Economist*'s view: 'There wasn't quite the urgency and boldness that you might expect from a leader in Mr Brown's position.'[123] The consensus was that he had done enough, just, to underpin his position, and that the party appeared to be united behind him.

The whole impression of the conference was then upended, however, as the perpetrators intended, by *The Sun*'s switch in allegiance. After twelve years of supporting Labour, it had had enough, and produced the headline: 'Labour's lost it.'[124] Brown had spoken to Dominic Mohan, Rebekah Brooks's successor as Editor, earlier in the day after his speech, but Mohan had not mentioned the switch to him. 'Gordon was angry that the Editor did not have the guts to tell him; he thought that was disrespectful.'[125] In her new capacity as chief executive of News International, Brooks had tried to call him to tell him what *The Sun* was doing. He 'decided not to take the call',[126] as he knew what she wanted and had no wish to give her the satisfaction of breaking the news to him. Brown's team feared a switch was on the cards, but did not know exactly when. On Friday 11 September, Simon Lewis had travelled to News International in Wapping, London, and had a fish-and-chips lunch with Brooks. 'We'll probably go for the Conservatives, but not with a big bang,' she told the dismayed, newly appointed official spokesman. Other News International titles, apart from *The Sun*, would, she said, 'come to their own decisions' on which party they would support. Lewis duly reported back to Brown that it looked as if *The Sun* would be abandoning Labour, 'so there was no surprise'.[127] Brown's aides suspected that the announcement would be timed to inflict the maximum hurt and damage on Brown personally, and on the party.

Denied access to Brown himself, Brooks phoned Mandelson. There are two distinct versions of their conversation. According to Mandelson, Brooks was in a panic when she spoke to him. 'What's wrong, Rebekah?' he asked with mock solicitude. 'We're coming out for the Tories tomorrow and I wanted to let you know.' 'And?' Mandelson asked innocently. 'I thought you'd want to know.' 'Well, it's not exactly unexpected, is it? I know you're worried about falling circulation.' 'This is nothing to do with falling circulation,' Brooks snapped back. 'But you'd expect sales to rise tomorrow?' Mandelson asked. 'Yes.' 'I thought you said it's got nothing to do with circulation'. The call ended abruptly shortly afterwards. Mandelson recycled his version of their conversation all evening to lighten the mood in Brown's camp, amid much guffawing.[128] According to Brooks, however, the conversation was much angrier. 'Peter has been very rude to me,' she complained when she called Lewis early on Tuesday evening. She had spoken to him earlier that day to say: 'This is a courtesy call to you as the Prime Minister's official spokesman. We've been in conference all day and we've come to the conclusion that *The Sun* is going to come out for the Conservatives.'[129] She was calm and businesslike. When she called the second time, she was much more agitated.[130] News International had hosted a party that evening in Brighton, and Brooks went around telling everyone that Mandelson had called her a 'cunt'.[131] Mandelson denied this and said he had called her a 'chump', which many found unconvincing. Mandelson made light of what she claimed. 'It's not a word I use,' he said.[132]

Later that evening, Brown retired to his room with Mandelson, Nye, Kelly and Forsyth. He was angry that the timing of *The Sun*'s announcement would wipe out reports of his speech in the morning papers, as the paper intended. His colleagues commiserated with him, but they had begun to think News International might have made a tactical error with its timing. 'The instant reaction from some was to get very down about it but very quickly we began to feel *The Sun* had come out too early and that it would liberate us from the kind of expectation [that] being endorsed by *The Sun* implied,' says Gavin Kelly.[133] McNeill, who joined the discussion, chipped in that she thought it would have been more damaging had the paper declared its switch during the Conservatives' conference.[134] The team was also united in their belief that *The Sun*'s hostility to Labour and Brown was being personally driven by Brooks: 'they took their political line direct from Rebekah' says one. Mandelson ruled that they should not go on the attack against *The Sun*, but use its decision to support the 'underdog thesis', which was already playing strongly at the conference.[135] By late evening, 'Gordon is calm, but we all know this will be a blow. We agree some lines. Gordon goes to bed,' reads the entry in a contemporary diary.[136]

The next morning Brown managed to stick to the script of being philosophical rather than angry on the BBC's *Today* programme. But then, angered by the BBC making too much of *The Sun* story, instead of concentrating on his own speech, he completely flipped.[137] 'He became like a bear with a sore head, and did a number of television interviews, all of them dreadful,' remembers one adviser.[138] The worst was his interview on BBC's *Breakfast* with Sian Williams, when he found it hard to conceal his contempt and rounded patronisingly on her. His staff watching it on the television screens up in his suite winced and watched on with mounting horror. 'It looked like this big Scottish bloke having a go at this short woman. It was a real shocker.'[139] Brown's interview with Adam Boulton on Sky was similarly painful. Boulton was surprised that Brown's team had agreed to do his 'pooled' live interviews, with the major broadcasters on the floor of the conference hall, and without closing it off as a sterile area. This meant anyone with a conference floor pass, including most journalists, could overhear everything that went on.[140] Boulton was also irritated by the assumption he was picking up from the conference, that Sky was linked with *The Sun* as part of a News International 'anti-Brown' conspiracy. He singled out Mandelson, in particular, for promoting this story. So, tempers were frayed on both sides before they went on air. What Boulton wanted was for Brown to talk about the television debates – galling for Brown, as he had rejected the advice to mention in his speech that he would be taking part. Brown wanted to talk about the substance of the speech he had given the day before, because he felt it was not getting the attention it deserved in the media, and said: 'You haven't given me the chance to talk about our political reforms, which you praised yesterday, and you haven't given me the chance to talk about our economic ...'. But Boulton didn't want to know and cut him clean off, asking: 'So, you will, hand on heart, in all circumstances, lead Labour into the next election?' Both men were frustrated and the interview, which became a classic on YouTube, finished with Brown storming off angrily, unfortunately still attached to a microphone. 'I pressed him about the TV debates and he accused me of campaigning,' was Boulton's subsequent comment on their contretemps.[141] When Brown came back up to his suite, his staff decided the time had come to give him 'a proper bollocking' for losing his temper. His performances were reported negatively in the media for containing 'angry exchanges'.[142] Mandelson was cross that he had not adhered to his handling advice, but when he saw him so downcast, he pulled back, and decided to lift his spirits by building him up instead.[143] Brown was angry for letting himself down, and angry with *The Sun* for their meanness.

By the time he returned to London by train later that Wednesday, travelling in second class because of sensitivities over expenses, and with his security team blocking access at either end of their carriage, Brown had pulled himself together. Travelling with him in the compartment were his wife and Mandelson and, unusually, David Miliband. It was a rare occasion when Brown was pleased with his arch rival, and he believed his speech had gone a long way towards rehabilitating him with those elements of the party still angered by his 'disloyalty' in his *Guardian* article. To the Foreign Secretary's surprise, Brown repeatedly told him that he thought his speech was 'very good indeed'.[144] What Brown's team did not tell him was that the indications from their private polls were showing that the expected (and badly needed) bounce had not materialised. It was looking to be only three points, in stark contrast with the nine-point bounce just after the 2008 conference. Forsyth and Muir realised they would have to find the right moment to break this to him.[145] 'It was a very low point, that day. I felt that if we don't get momentum soon we would all be fucked,' reads an entry in a contemporary diary.[146]

The next day, Forsyth and Muir sat Brown down in the first-floor study at Number 10, which had been used by Mrs Thatcher. It was obvious to Brown from their faces how down they both were.[147] 'We've got to regain the

initiative,' they said to him, and 'the only way we can do that now is to make
the announcement about the TV debates'. Brown paused. 'Okay, we'll do it,'
he said. 'When?' 'This weekend,' they chimed in unison. He sighed: 'Let's get
everyone together on the phone.' Several conference calls later, it was agreed
that making the announcement immediately would unsettle the Conservatives
ahead of their conference.[148] No one seriously objected. That evening, Muir
walked all the way from Downing Street to his home in East London because
he felt so miserable. They had all worked so hard, and had made so many
sacrifices over the summer, and it all appeared to have been for nothing. But
when the announcement was made on Saturday 3 October that the Prime
Minister would 'in principle' be willing to participate in the debates, his staff's
spirits began to rise. They had at least the prospect of success.

Afghanistan – Brown Regains Control: September–December

Brown decided over August that establishing a personal grip over policy on
Afghanistan was to be one of his core objectives. The summer had been bloody,
and he was very angry, with the military for what he believed were its underhand
methods of pursuing greater troop numbers, and with the media for consistently
misrepresenting his case. His new strategy included a series of speeches, and
visits to Afghanistan at the end of August and again in December. Brown also
decided that his team should brief Fleet Street editors and broadcasting chiefs
directly, as he no longer trusted the message coming from the military itself. He
wanted further to respond to the personal criticism directed at him, and to shore
up public support for the campaign; something he thought the military were
failing to do.[149] It began taking over his life. 'True to form, he became obsessed
with details, and was forever calling in military officers and Ministry of Defence
officials, overseeing the minutiae of policy,' says one official.[150] Officials were
amazed by his capacity to 'absorb an incredible amount of detail', so that he
could master his brief. He would personally order large quantities of books from
Amazon, not only on the current situation in Afghanistan, but also histories of
past military failures in the region.[151]

For all the best-laid plans, the period opened badly with the resignation
on 3 September of Eric Joyce, Parliamentary Private Secretary to Bob
Ainsworth.[152] The government's problems with the defence community, Joyce
complained, required 'fixing with greatest urgency'. Brown delivered a major
speech on Afghanistan the following day, which he had been thinking about
over the summer. It was designed to be a considered response to the public's
and the military's concerns about the conduct of the war. British aims, he said,
were 'realistic and achievable', but they were also 'radically different' from those

of other participating nations, like Russia, who 'stayed in the cities and ignored the country, and did not seek to empower Afghans themselves'. British forces, by contrast, were taking the fight to the Taliban, and having to adapt to the different tactics needed for guerrilla fighting. 'We will adapt and improve our counterinsurgency strategy for central Helmand,' he said. 'Afghanisation' was a central aim of British policy. 'The more Afghans can take responsibility in the short term, the less our coalition forces will be needed in the longer term.'[153] To his disappointment, the speech received little coverage, while on Sky News it was reported on a split screen, with coffins being driven through Wootton Bassett. What press comment it did receive was generally sceptical. Gaby Hinsliff criticised it in *The Guardian* for being leaden, and for failing to make a 'passionate case for this war from first principles'.[154] Martin Kettle said it was: 'A speech which needed to be made ... a good speech too.' But he also criticised it for not coming down firmly on either the escalation of troops or retreat.[155] Had the speech promised extra troops, it would have received considerable coverage, but even though it represented the best way forward, no one wanted to hear the Prime Minister philosophise about Afghans taking over.

Brown was unsure what more he could say about Afghanistan in his conference speech. 'He felt very passionately that he should support the troops, and felt personally desperate that he was accused of selling them short,' says a close friend.[156] Brown asked his Afghan adviser, Matt Cavanagh, to work up a possible speech announcement about increasing troop numbers. Although he remained highly sceptical about the military case, he foresaw that the risks of a public rift between the government and the military might become so great as to leave him no choice. In the build-up to the Brighton conference, it was decided, however, to delay any firm decision on troop numbers until after both the Afghan election (a second round run-off presidential election was scheduled for November) and the publication of the second Obama review, especially in the light of that administration's ambivalence on Afghanistan.[157] 'A problem for us was we had little visibility on their long, ponderous review: we just didn't know where the Americans were going to come out,' says a Number 10 official.[158]

The military was angry that his conference speech did not make a commitment to boost numbers. In a separate briefing, Brown did announce the conditions that would need to be met for further troop increases, including the Afghan government's serious commitment to training their own troops alongside British troops, and every British soldier being fully equipped. But this did not placate the military. At the Conservative Party conference the following week, Cameron announced that Richard Dannatt, who had retired as Chief of the General Staff (CGS) in August, would become a member of the House of Lords and advise a future Conservative government. Within hours, Dannatt was to embarrass the Conservative front bench by saying that it 'lacked expert understanding on military matters'.[159] Cameron's announcement went down exceptionally badly in Number 10, and it confirmed their suspicions that Dannatt had been talking to News International chief executive Rebekah Brooks, and to Cameron's media chief, Andy Coulson, while still running the army – a clear breach of military protocol, as well as giving the Murdoch press privileged information that other newspapers did not have.[160] Reflecting on the relationship between News International and Dannatt, one very senior military figure recalls a conversation with Brooks in which she said of Dannatt 'We regard him as one of ours'. However unconvincing, Dannatt himself flatly denies the charge that he leaked information to the press, though he concedes that others in the army 'may have done the deed'. Certainly he was prepared to make his views public: 'Once I knew I was retiring I had nothing more to lose, so on the issue of troop numbers ... I was always going to be vocal and agitating because it was the right thing to do.'[161] Dannatt was not alone. Many current and retired senior officers believed that Britain needed to have a larger presence in Afghanistan, to regain credibility with the Americans and erase the 'stain of Basra', as well as to ensure that the army's morale and capability were properly maintained.[162] Many military figures were speaking to the media, but Number 10's ire focused primarily on Dannatt. It came to believe that his emergence as an overly political figure damaged his credibility and standing, and that, ironically, played its part in 'turning it around for Gordon'.[163] Some felt Dannatt had been naive, and had let Andy Coulson exploit him on behalf of the Conservatives, who wanted to milk Brown's vulnerability on Afghanistan.[164] 'Brown felt that Dannatt persistently undermined him, and that Jock Stirrup had no control over Dannatt,' claims one Number 10 official.[165]

Dannatt's departure in August and the succession of David Richards as CGS did not dampen the military's enthusiasm for an increase in troop numbers. They invited Brown and Number 10 staff to the MoD shortly afterwards, for what they termed a 'briefing'. An embarrassed Ainsworth and armed services minister Bill Rammell suggested that the Number 10 team join them in the Defence Secretary's office for a quiet word before the briefing. A clearly uncomfortable Ainsworth began by apologising for the lack of warning, but explained that the military had only told him days before that troop numbers needed to be increased if they were to maintain all their current operations, and that Afghan forces had not proved to be sufficiently reliable to compensate. 'We're being told either give us the 9,500 troops now or give up some of our roles,' said Rammell bluntly.[166] He and his team thought this was a visit aimed at repairing relations with the MoD on their home turf, while Brown was expecting an update on efforts to counter IEDs (improvised explosive devices).[167] Brown felt he had been ambushed by the military, and that he had been lured over to the Ministry of Defence on false pretences. He was visibly angry at the lack of notice and sudden change of direction, and the meeting with the military went very badly indeed. 'It was all madness: madness to put in troops before the Obama review, madness to do so before the Afghan elections, madness to do it before we had an international plan and strategy agreed, and madness without a guarantee from the chiefs that the troops would be properly equipped,' says one of his team.[168] 'We felt we had already gone out in the lead in Afghanistan with troops, compared to other nations, and risked being left carrying the baby,' says another, expressing Number 10's anxiety that Britain could find itself overly committed if not in step with the US.[169]

What were the military up to? Intensely frustrated by the lack of progress on troop numbers, they were using the brigade roulemont (changeover) in September and October as an attempt to bounce Brown into action. On Stirrup's instructions, Ministry of Defence officials told Brown and his team that since 13 per cent of troops were on R&R at any one time, the overall number could be increased within existing policy to 9,500, as it would mean the real number in the field would never exceed the 9,000 figure that had already been agreed. This struck Brown's team as risky – and vulnerable to accusations of 'secret' troop increases – and the response was a categorical 'forget it'. The military told Brown: 'We will ask again, and if you turn us down again and we are not given the extra 500 troops, we will immediately withdraw from the reserve battle group.'[170] Brown's team responded that if they persisted now, the answer would still be a flat 'no', but if they asked in some three weeks' time, when the US position was clearer, they might get a different answer.[171]

Meanwhile, the bad news continued, with seven soldiers being killed on 1 November, five of them shot dead and eight wounded by a single traitorous Afghan policeman.[172] That week saw the UN withdraw half its staff from Afghanistan after a vicious attack on a compound, and Kai Eide, head of the UN mission, declared ominously that the war was now 'at a critical juncture'.[173] On 6 November, Brown faced a difficult audience of senior military personnel, when he gave a speech at the Royal College of Defence Studies. 'There is no strategy that is without danger and risk,' Brown said. 'We cannot, must not and will not walk away.'[174] It was a reasoned analysis of the problems the coalition faced, and the failure of the Afghan government to stand up to corruption. But the media response remained hostile. 'Another mishmash of the wooden phrases and meaningless platitudes,' was the response from Benedict Brogan in the *Daily Telegraph*.[175] The new strategy was still failing to shift public perceptions of the war. A YouGov survey for Sky News, conducted between 5 and 6 November, found that only 21 per cent of those interviewed thought that British troops should be fighting in Afghanistan, only 40 per cent thought the reasons for the war were clear, and 81 per cent thought the government should be doing still more to support British troops.[176]

Obama was not without pressure from his own military, with Stanley McChrystal's interim report in September concluding that the war 'will likely result in failure' unless more troops are committed.[177] After weeks of waiting, the second review reported in November, and Obama outlined his response in a speech at West Point on 1 December. Thirty thousand new US troops would be going to Afghanistan, he said, though they would begin to return home after eighteen months. He presented European allies, including France and Germany, with a request for extra support in Afghanistan, from which he expressly excluded Britain. At Brown's behest, McDonald had travelled to Washington the previous week, to ensure that Obama's administration did not apply public pressure on the UK for more troops. A demand to which National Security Advisor General James Jones had 'grudgingly' acquiesced, recognising that the UK was already the second largest NATO contributor.[178]

With the US review finalised, NSID (the ministerial committee on National Security, International Relations and Development) discussed it on 30 November and decided to accede to the army chiefs' request for the extra 500 troops, with the key proviso that they were fully equipped for the tasks they were asked to undertake.[179] It did not go all the military's way; Brown managed to extract a rare agreement for a military task to be dropped, specifically in Kandahar. Brown duly announced the increase to the House of Commons later that day, saying that with the 'special forces' (notably the SAS) the total would rise to over 10,000.[180] He was emphatic that he had received express assurances from chiefs of staff and commanders on the ground that they endorsed the combination of force and equipment levels, in an effort to obviate any future squabbles over troops not being sufficiently supported. 'The military thus achieved by the end of the year what we had hoped to achieve at the beginning,' Stirrup reflects wryly. 'And thus the extra 500 were in place for Operation Moshtarek when it started in the New Year.'[181] The military had won the battle, by fair means and foul, against the politicians. 'It didn't feel like we'd lost in Number 10,' says an aide, though.[182] Brown had punched back hard, not only by securing the military's agreement to drop a task, but by 'ending their endless cycle of asking for more troops while giving nothing up', and putting the onus squarely on the Ministry of Defence 'to sort out the equipment problem', a problem Brown in any case believed had been the fault initially of the generals.[183]

Brown was still angry about the way the war and his role had been portrayed, and he was determined to end the year on top. On 12–13 December, Brown visited the country for the third time that year, staying overnight at Kandahar airfield, before going on to Kabul to meet President Karzai (who remained in office after his rival Abdullah Abdullah pulled out of the run-off election citing concerns about continued electoral fraud). The visit was briefed out as: 'The first Prime Minister since Churchill during the Second World War to spend a night in the war zone.'[184] The accomplishment was upstaged by Cameron, who had spent three days in Afghanistan the week before, but it was all the time that Brown's timetable, and his security advisers, would permit him. On his return to the House of Commons, he gave a no-nonsense statement, emphasising the improvements, since the summer, in numbers of helicopters, Mastiff patrol and Ridgeback mine-protected vehicles, and aerial surveillance.[185] By Christmas, the corner had mostly been turned on Afghanistan, in domestic political terms at least, even if enduring progress on the ground remained elusive.

However, Brown's struggle was still far from over in Afghanistan. The spike in casualties at the start of November showed that public concern remained every bit as high, and public opinion, despite all his efforts, remained far from supportive of his position. It was a moot point whether Brown was shaping British policy or merely managing pressure from the services, and public opinion whipped up by the media. The Afghan election result, the crumbling of governmental authority in Pakistan, and slow progress to Afghanisation all remained deeply troubling. A key factor, meanwhile, in Brown's regaining some credibility as a leader, came from a most unlikely quarter: a routine letter he wrote to a grieving mother, over which *The Sun* newspaper so overplayed its hand that it helped turn the tide of public opinion in his favour.

The Jacqui Janes Letter: November

The Sun's fury over Afghanistan, full of crusading zeal at what it saw as brave British soldiers being forced to die because of an incompetent and half-hearted Prime Minister, climaxed in the summer of 2009. On 5 August, a *Sun* 'exclusive' highlighted the deaths since 19 July of eight soldiers in 'equipment blunders', calling them 'inexcusable'.[186] Brown was deeply antagonised, and believed that the newspaper was cynically using Afghanistan as a way of discrediting the government. He thought their attacks were 'completely wrong, almost immoral, and damaging the cause of Afghanistan in the public's mind'.[187] Even some in the News International circle were distressed by the line *The Sun* was taking, believing that it was damaging the image of the war in Britain. 'Brown believed that the stories News International ran about him not caring did the country real harm in its fighting in Afghanistan,' says David Yelland, Brooks's predecessor as editor of *The Sun*.[188] Others, including the security services, were becoming increasingly concerned at the damage *The Sun* campaign was doing in turning public opinion against the war. One casualty of the discrediting of intelligence reports during Iraq was that Brown had to contend with an additional burden: the media disputing his public statements about the links between Afghanistan and Pakistan, and security threats to the UK, which formed the central basis of his case for Britain's continued presence in Afghanistan. These were always based on the intelligence assessments he received: 'After Iraq, we were pretty scrupulous to base such comments on the reports that Gordon had received. We would clear the statements, word for word, with the intelligence agencies. We'd just ask: "Can we say this?" Gordon would then say to the editors: "This is straight from the intelligence we're getting."'[189] But he failed to persuade a sceptical media. The situation became so serious that on at least one occasion Brown asked the heads of the intelligence agencies to speak directly to the media, who were told in no uncertain terms: 'When the government says there are links between Afghanistan and Pakistan conflicts and British security threats, that is true.'[190] It is difficult to assess precisely what difference these security briefings, which took place in October 2009, made to the media's coverage of the war. Their fury against Brown did begin to fade in the late autumn of 2009, so they may have played a part, but there were other important factors at work, too, such as the improved situation on the ground in Helmand itself, and, importantly, the way *The Sun's* most vicious attack on Brown backfired.

'Don't you know there's a bloody war on!' was the latest line in *The Sun* on 28 August, an aggressive attack on Brown and the government, accused of not appreciating the magnitude of the Afghan conflict. The issue contained a number of articles by well-known military figures, including former SAS soldier Andy McNab, as well as one by Janette Binnie, whose son, Corporal Sean Binnie, had been killed in the war, criticising government policy.[191] Brown was incandescent with rage that morning, and again deeply distressed, feeling humiliated and betrayed. He held a long conversation with Heywood that morning, about how to deal with what he thought had become a personal vendetta.[192] When Lewis joined Number 10 at the beginning of September, he recalls how all-encompassing the issue had become: 'Afghanistan was exercising the Prime Minister the most. Certain papers, notably *The Sun*, were actively trying, he felt, to undermine him.'[193]

After *The Sun's* switch of allegiance in late September, the paper became more, not less, aggressive. Its campaign climaxed on 9 November with a two-pronged attack. First, it charged that Brown had 'failed to bow at the cenotaph' the previous day at the Armistice Sunday service in Whitehall, under the headline 'Bloody shameful' – a terrible caricature of a Prime Minister whose sentiment on such commemorations was beyond reproach. The second prong was a story that, when writing to a grieving mother of a twenty-year-old guardsman killed near Helmand on 5 October, he had carelessly misspelled her surname, writing 'Jacqui James' rather than 'Janes'. Her son's name was

Jamie. 'His gaffes come despite *The Sun*'s campaign to remind him there is "a bloody war on",' said *The Sun*. Journalist Tom Newton-Dunn, who wrote the story, had phoned Lewis at home on the Sunday evening to alert him that the paper was running the story about the double blunder. His team promptly called Brown in a now familiar routine to let him know that bad headlines were coming. It was obvious to his aides from his change of voice that he was very deeply upset, as well as hurt that the paper was suggesting that he had not shown proper respect.[194] After he put the phone down, he immediately phoned the duty clerk downstairs at Number 10 and asked him to bring up to the flat the photocopy of the letter that he had written. 'There's nothing wrong with it,' he said, bringing it close to his eyes and turning it over and over in his hands.[195]

Brown's instinctive reaction, when he thought he had upset someone was to want to speak to them personally. 'I'm going to phone her,' he announced promptly. But the incomparable 'switch' at Number 10 had difficulty tracking down her phone number, and the call could only be placed late that Sunday evening. By the time Brown spoke to Jacqui Janes at 10pm, for thirteen minutes that evening, she had spoken to *The Sun* and they had advised her, unbeknown to Brown, to record the conversation. 'He had no idea; she didn't sound like someone recording a call, but rather like a grieving mother,' says the official from Number 10 who listened in to the conversation.[196] In what read like a rehearsed script, she opened the conversation by saying: 'I have the deepest respect for the fact that you are Prime Minister, but I am the mother of a soldier who, really, you know, his death could have been prevented in several ways, lack of helicopters being the main one.' The transcript was reprinted verbatim in *The Sun* two days later. Number 10, which was itself recording the interview, confirmed its accuracy.[197] Jacqui Janes continued: 'I don't need anyone to tell me how brave my son was. My son paid the ultimate sacrifice.' Brown replied: 'Okay, Mrs Janes, I'm sorry that I can't, I can't, er, satisfy you, but I tried my best.' The conversation makes painful reading. To her comment that him referring to her as 'Mrs James' was 'disgraceful', he responded: 'I think I was trying to say Janes, as your right name. Maybe, maybe my writing looks bad, but I was trying to say your right name. And I think I spelt Jamie right, I understand.' The revelation that Brown had in fact earlier mispronounced her surname (though it is hard to tell precisely from the audio record) in an oral answer to questions about the most recent losses in the House of Commons on 14 October compounded the embarrassment. Whether his eyesight failed him as he detailed the names of those killed in action to the House, or his brief was miswritten, is unclear.[198]

On Monday 9 November, Brown flew to a grey Berlin, for the twentieth anniversary of the fall of the Wall. He delivered his speech by the Brandenburg

Gate in the pouring rain to a large crowd of Berliners, in the presence of Angela Merkel, Nicolas Sarkozy and other dignitaries. It revealed how far his speechwriting had improved, with deft contributions from McNeill, among others: 'You dared to dream in the darkness ... What has happened here in Berlin tells the world that the tides of history may ebb and flow, but across the ages history is moving towards our best hope, not our worst fears; towards light not darkness; and towards the fulfilment of our humanity, not its denial.'[199]

In his absence that Monday, the lobby meeting at Number 10 was described as 'very unpleasant, nasty and hostile'.[200] Even the normally understated *Financial Times* described it as a 'strong meeting'.[201] The repeated criticism of Brown focused on his failure to apologise, picking up again on the theme from the Megrahi episode. Elements of the media spun the Janes episode as yet another instance of Brownite obstinacy. Lewis responded on Brown's behalf by talking about the thought and emotion that Brown put into his letters of condolence, but to little effect.[202] According to one official present, Brown was visibly anguished on the plane home. 'He buried his head in his hands', before brandishing his thick black pen, this time writing out the name 'Janes' over and over again as if to try to convince himself as much as anybody else that "it was just my writing", and that he hadn't really made the mistake'.[203]

Every time a soldier was killed, doubts crept into his mind, but he always came round to the same view, which was that British troops were needed in Afghanistan, and that the soldiers had not died in vain. Each death made him redouble his determination to ensure that Afghanistan stopped being a safe haven for terrorists who might bring harm to the UK, and to press forward with getting the Afghans running security in their own country as soon as possible. 'He never thought we should quit as soon as we could,' says McDonald.[204] 'It was the hardest aspect of the job for him,' says McNeill. 'For the press to claim he did not care about people who had lost their children hurt him more than anything else in his premiership.'[205] 'There's nothing I do that they won't attack me for,' he remarked to his aides.[206] 'He despaired that people could have such a low opinion of him, and found it incomprehensible that people could believe he lacked integrity and decency.'[207] The loss of his daughter Jennifer gave him a fellow feeling with families who had lost sons and daughters, recalling the still raw emotional experience. 'When news of casualties came in to Number 10, everyone felt a heavy weight of responsibility, the door-keepers, the receptionists, the officials, the policy people – everyone.'[208]

When Brown heard about his taped phone call, he was not angry with the mother, but he was very angry with *The Sun*. Rupert Murdoch personally intervened to try and repair relations between the government and News International and told Brown in a phone call on 22 November that he thought the paper was 'wrong to publish the Janes story'. The tone of the conversation between the two was described as 'warm'. Brown said: 'Rupert you know I respect you and hold you in the highest regard. You know that I have never criticised you personally, and I have never let my people criticise you personally, but your people in London are making a great mistake. You've got to sort them out'. 'I hear you' replied the media mogul 'and I want to apologise.' Those who observed the two men together were often struck by their similarities: 'they were both outsiders, both from a long line of Scottish Presbyterian stock, they valued hard work, they both operated on the basis of knowing more than others, and they both had a phenomenal drive to win' says one. On the call they disagreed only on Brown's claim that *The Sun*'s campaign was 'undermining our mission in Afghanistan'. The atmosphere of the conversation then began to deteriorate when Murdoch pleaded with the Prime Minister three times to speak to Rebekah Brooks, who was also on the line. 'I have no interest in speaking to the woman who is persecuting me' said Brown stubbornly. After more pressure from Murdoch he finally conceded. During a very tense conversation Brown raged: 'How dare you do this to me!' A breathless Brooks tried to deny she had anything 'to do with the headline' and claimed that she had been on holiday when the decision to run the story was taken. 'I know you're lying to me' Brown yelled and slammed the phone down. It would be the last time the two spoke.[209]

The Janes episode led to a great outpouring of support for Brown himself, contrary to the expectations of *The Sun*, with 'hundreds' of letters arriving at Number 10. One that struck him in particular was from a man who was badly dyslexic, who wrote that he had never admitted his dyslexia to anyone, and that when leaving cards went round the office to be signed, he would have to go to the toilet to excuse himself from signing them. Hearing about Brown's own difficulties with his writing had encouraged him to talk about his dyslexia for the first time.[210] *The Sun*'s publicity for the story provoked a backlash in the country. Polls showed that a majority of the public sympathised with Brown's reading problems and thought that *The Sun* had cynically exploited a grieving mother. The *New Statesman* described it as a 'vulgar campaign against Brown',[211] while on 11 November the *Daily Mirror* reported that its rival had indulged in 'a mean-spirited political vendetta [that] has revolted the nation'.[212] Brown was never particularly popular with the British public and of course there were some who would never be reconciled to him, but the Janes incident was one of the few times, perhaps the only time of note, when Brown attracted public sympathy.

'After you've been working with someone for a while, you can distinguish between bullshit and reality,' says Stirrup, talking of Brown's reaction on hearing of British casualties. 'Gordon Brown may have faults, but one of them is not a failure to be a human being.'[213] Until the autumn of 2008, when a parent wrote in to complain, Brown would sign letters of condolence that had been prepared for him by the Ministry of Defence. One bereaved parent complained at what looked to be a standard, typed letter with Brown's unreadable felt tip scrawl at the bottom. He wrote a long letter of apology to the parent concerned, and from then onwards, wrote personal handwritten letters to the bereaved, who included not just the parents, but also the wives, and the parents separately if they lived apart, setting a time aside each week to do this.[214] Number 10 knew how bad his handwriting was, and debated whether to let neatly typed letters be sent or allow him to proceed with his handwritten letters. They let him have his way. He would thus receive information about the fallen soldier from officials, which he would then absorb before composing his letters, ensuring that each was personal and appropriate. Not uncommonly, he was asked to rewrite a letter, because it was either smudged or illegible.[215]

Brown was meticulous about meeting families of bereaved soldiers when they asked to see him. He would greet them with his wife in the entrance hall of Downing Street and take them up to the White Room, and though the families were often angry and the meetings could be difficult and emotional, he was felt to handle them with sensitivity.[216] He would make a point of visiting military hospitals in the UK – Selly Oak and Headley Court – as well as hospitals in theatres of conflict, where he would talk to wounded soldiers in private. He was much more at ease talking to soldiers individually, or in small groups, than in set pieces, when his wooden comments would be much mimicked.[217] His personal experience of loss and illness, as well as his writing on courage in war, gave him a particular interest in befriending wounded soldiers and hearing their stories.

The national interest in the Jacqui Janes story prompted a bereaved relative to say that they had not received a letter after their son had died. Number 10 promptly carried out a major review of all its correspondence. It transpired that it was not one, but three, relatives that he had not written to, so he promptly wrote a handwritten letter to each of the families, with a covering letter from Heywood in his capacity as permanent secretary at Number 10, apologising for the error. The father of one of the soldiers, Jack Sadler, killed in December 2007 in Helmand, went to the press to voice his discontent. 'It goes to show what this present administration thinks of our soldiers,' he wrote, dismissing Brown's late gesture as 'hollow'. 'I would rather have Jack back and the proper equipment given to him,' he added.[218] Sarah Brown, who became very involved in the quality control of the letters from that point onwards, suggested Brown send a Christmas card to the families of all the bereaved. Her proposal was looked into thoroughly, but Number 10 decided that it could not be certain that all the addresses and details for the families were current, and in the light of the furore at previous slips, Stirrup advised on balance against pursuing the idea, which was quietly dropped.[219]

The Janes letter episode put Brown at the lowest ebb of his premiership. He used the occasion of his monthly press conference on 10 November to draw a line under it. 'I know what I'll say,' he said brusquely when his team asked him if he wanted their help.[220] On this issue, there was only one person whose advice he wanted, and that was Sarah; together they decided that he should take it in a very personal way, talking about the pain that parents feel when they lose a child. 'I was sorry if any offence had been caused,' he told journalists about his conversation with Jacqui Janes. 'I understand very well the sadness that she feels ... That loss can never be replaced ... Comfort comes from understanding that your son has played an important role in the security of our country and died in such a courageous and brave way that nobody will ever forget him.'[221] 'He speaks without notes. He looks and sounds very sympathetic ... He looks strong and in charge. It was all down to him in the end,' records a contemporary diary. [222] The author continues: 'I felt very drained by all of it. It felt like the Jacqui Janes week had been a very tough week. The toll on Gordon is quite high, but he comes out of it stronger.' After the press conference, Brown returned to Number 12 and went straight through into his study, closing the door firmly. He then asked Sue Nye, his longest-standing personal adviser, to see him. He was still visibly very distressed. There were not many occasions when he would ask Nye to see him alone. His team looked at the closing door and fell very silent.[223]

Europe's Top Jobs: November

The EU had been a regular feature of Blair's premiership; in Brown's, it had but a walk-on part, although, when fleetingly on stage, it made quite an impression. By mid-2008, Brown had become an unlikely hero to many Europhiles across the EU. He did not, as many feared, block the passage of the bill approving the Lisbon Treaty, as he might have done after the Irish rejected it in a referendum on 13 June. Instead, he pushed through parliamentary ratification, and did so in the face of strong opposition from the right-wing media, and large parts of the eurosceptic British public, who demanded a referendum on the Treaty (Blair had said there would be a referendum on the original EU constitution). The bill had passed through the House of Commons on 11 March, but the critical battleground was the House of Lords, where Labour lacked a majority. It was piloted through personally by the Leader of the Lords, Baroness (Cathy) Ashton. The passage was on edge until the final moment. 'We are so nervous here at Number 10. I must admit, I'm starting to have a drink,' texted Stewart Wood, Brown's point person on the EU, to Ashton.[224] She found Brown supportive throughout, though Cunliffe, the Cabinet Office official working on it, had made the team regularly nervous by his hyper-caution.[225] On the day of the vote (18 June) Brown's staff were anxiously glued to the television screens. When the bill passed, her final text from Wood said: 'Gordon has just punched the air. He's really happy.'[226] Across Brussels, dinner parties reverberated with the words: 'The Brits have saved the Treaty.' When he came to the European Council the following day, on 19 June, Brown found himself feted. To his surprise, he found he 'really quite liked it'.[227]

On 3 October 2009, the Irish eventually approved the Treaty at a second referendum, and on 3 November, the Czech Republic became the last of the twenty-seven member states to ratify it. 'Today is a day when Europe looks forward,' Brown said, welcoming the news.[228] But his euphoria would not last. Just eight days later, the Swedish Prime Minister Fredrik Reinfeldt, the final rotating president of the European Council, announced that the two newly created posts, President of the Council of EU Leaders and the High Representative (in effect, the EU's Foreign Secretary) would be filled at a special summit of EU leaders on 19 November. The new President would replace the six-month rotating president, and be in post for two and a half years, renewable once, while the High Representative of the Union for Foreign Affairs and Security Policy, to give it its formal title, would be appointed for five years. José Manuel Barroso, in his capacity as President of the Commission, would himself then nominate the remaining twenty-six positions on the Commission, at least one of which – the internal market services portfolio, effectively the EU's economic and financial minister – was deemed of particular prestige and significance to Britain. What unfolded was to be one of the biggest dramas, or tragicomedies, of Brown's three years at Number 10, and the only time before the 2010 election that Brown, Blair and Mandelson were all brought together in a single endeavour.

Following Britain's assent, the race was on for the twenty-seven EU member nations to try to secure one of their own nominees for the prestigious jobs of either President or High Representative, or obtain one of the more important posts on the commission. Knowing that the remaining countries which had opted to hold a referendum would be likely to vote in favour of Lisbon, Whitehall tried to encourage Brown to focus his attention on which posts he hoped to get, and to think strategically about which candidate to field. From Paris, British ambassador Peter Westmacott was repeatedly saying to Brown from late 2008: 'Are you ready to discuss this, because Sarkozy wants to talk to you about it?' But Brown, typically, had yet to make up his mind or work out his strategy, and in any case was too distracted with the financial crisis to turn his mind seriously to it.[229] At stake was the opportunity to secure for Britain positions of major influence over EU policy, and the chance to build on Brown's new-found reputation within the EU, to shape it powerfully and achieve major credit for himself. Indeed, the very high value of the prize was one reason why he made the fatal mistake of dithering. It proved a costly mistake.

The early front-runner for the post of President was Blair, who was coy in public about whether he wanted the job, repeatedly insisting that he could not stand as candidate until the Treaty had been formally ratified and there was officially a job for him. Brown had a long conversation about Blair's candidature for President at Chequers on 31 January, and whether it would be 'politically neutral' to have him. A question in Brown's mind was whether he would be more or less likely to win the general election if Blair was European President; if he was a major success in the post, it could be difficult for him, as unfavourable comparisons were bound to be made. Mandelson's advice was duly sought. A text was sent to his BlackBerry saying: 'We need urgent talk about EU ... [the] most important thing is that TB/GB agree publicly and privately what is in their collective interest, and don't dance around it.' Mandelson's reply was that Merkel's reservations about Blair were no longer as strong, and that 'TB would like early discussion with us'. Brown's team came back to him to say: 'I think you need to engineer a political discussion about whether TB running helps or hinders GB at next election, and do so in way that doesn't make GB/TB feel uncomfortable or cornered ... If TB runs, has to be with unqualified GB backing. If not, it must not appear that GB blocked.' Mandelson responded positively, saying: 'I see no political disadvantage for GB in TB getting job.'[230]

Brown debated Mandelson's advice with his team, but discounted it as being too partisan. Brown's dilemma, even as early as January, was that he could not afford to be seen to be doing anything that was not fully supportive of Blair's cause.[231] Behind the scenes, Blair's team was lobbying hard for him to try to make it happen. Since standing down from Number 10, he had been repeatedly frustrated in achieving his ambitions on Africa, climate change and progress in the Middle East, in part because he lacked an official job as well as a large office behind him. The EU was an institution which he had done much to shape, being such a powerful backer of enlargement, and the President's job held obvious attractions for him. But he was loath to ask Brown to back him.[232] Britain's representative to the EU, Kim Darroch, had breakfast once a month in London with Blair's former chief of staff, Jonathan Powell.[233] Darroch urged him to talk to Blair about getting Brown on side before it was too late. After much dancing around between the two proud men, Brown publicly backed Blair's candidature for the presidency on 15 July, a fateful day.

Brown remained ambivalent about Blair. As the year ground on, he became more anxious about the implications of a Blair presidency. He had spent thirteen years waiting to move into a more senior job than Blair, and the

job of EU President in the right hands could out-trump any of the national
leaders within the EU. Brown knew that Sarkozy's support for Blair would
make or break it, and Sarkozy had been an admirer of Blair's in the short
period they overlapped as national leaders. As early as October 2007, Sarkozy
said Blair's appointment as President 'would be quite a smart move'.[234] But, if
Sarkozy was to back Blair, he wanted to secure his own nominee as the internal
market commissioner. The problem was that that was exactly the portfolio that
Brown wanted for Britain; he wanted to boast of obtaining something positive
from the appointments, and Blair as President wasn't what he'd had in mind.
Within Whitehall, a debate had raged on whether Britain should aim for the
internal market or the High Representative job. Cunliffe and his Treasury
team convinced him it should be the former. So, when Brown met Sarkozy at
the Elysée that summer, it went very badly. The conversation never progressed
past the initial stages. 'Let's both support Blair, certainly, but actually what I
really want is the internal market commission post,' Brown opened. Sarkozy
was struck dumb. 'Well, in fact I wanted that for France,' he said. 'No, no,
it's got to be a Brit. I can never persuade the City to accept reform unless it
goes to a Brit,' Brown responded.[235] The conversation broke up inconclusively.
Sarkozy decided from that point on: 'Fuck the Brits. They want everything.
They want Blair for top job. They want the internal market commissioner, and
they won't have it.'[236] Sarkozy stopped returning Brown's calls and on 15 July
made it known that he had withdrawn his backing for Blair's candidacy, and
that Merkel, too, was opposed to Blair getting the post.[237]

On the same day, shadow Foreign Secretary Hague came out extremely
hard against Blair. Number 10 believed he had acted without Cameron's
foreknowledge. 'Any holder is likely to try to centralise power for themselves in
Brussels and dominate national foreign policy. In the hands of an operator as
ambitious as Tony Blair, that is a near certainty. He should not be let anywhere
near the job.'[238] Hague proceeded to lobby the centre-right European People's
Party (EPP), the dominant group in the European Parliament, to refuse
Blair,[239] who was further tarnished by the news of the Iraq Inquiry, which
rekindled hatred across Europe of a war, and a leader, that many Europeans
had strongly disliked.

Brown continued with the twin-track strategy – presidency plus internal
market commissioner – throughout the summer, while the bureaucracy in
Whitehall and at the permanent representative's office in Brussels worked
overtime lobbying for it to happen. 'We knew we were aiming high in trying to
get our own people appointed to both, but we pushed hard, nevertheless,' says
a senior British EU official.[240] Intense pressure came from the City of London
to ensure that Britain secured the internal market post, fearful about new
regulations on hedge funds, especially if Sarkozy and the French obtained the

post. The City was an enemy Brown least needed at this moment, so he became even more obsessed by the need to obtain the post for Britain, while avoiding the very worst scenario of all, which was to see it go to the French. Yet, he was also committed to supporting Blair, and it was to be the riding of both horses that was to be his downfall. 'There is no doubt that if we had produced an acceptable name for the internal market commissioner, whom Barroso liked, ideally a woman, because he wanted more women, the UK would have got the post,' says a senior British official.[241] In the face of Sarkozy's continuing objections, Blair began to distance himself from the post. Brown now adopted a new strategy, fatally flawed, which was to keep Blair's hat in the ring, and then to try to extract maximum support for agreeing to drop it: 'Gordon was very keen on that strategy of maximum concessions for our gracious agreement to drop him.'[242] Against all advice, Brown still failed in the summer of 2009 to concentrate fully, or to decide who the British nominee for the internal market commissioner might be. Shriti Vadera was mentioned at one time, but she would have been too junior and too little known in the EU, despite her gender and obvious expertise, to have been acceptable.[243] Besides, Brown did not want to lose her. Director General of the CBI Richard Lambert was another figure he actively considered, as too was Alistair Darling, but the signals emanating from his camp were not positive.[244] It was too late in any case. The door had closed to Britain on the economic post, resulting in 'much grumpiness' from Cunliffe and the Treasury.[245]

Brown had dithered for too long. A fatal blow to his aspirations was dealt in October 2009, when he learned at the European Council on 29–30 October, from the European Parliament's centre-left group, the Party of European Socialists (PES), that they wanted to secure one of their own nominees for the High Representative position, in a deal which left the presidency to the centre-right EPP group. The significance was immediately obvious to him: 'At a stroke, Blair was cut out completely.'[246] Blair knew it, too. 'TB called up, but we didn't want to let people know [he had conceded] because we still wanted to extract maximum concessions,' reads a contemporary diary.[247] Brown was aghast. With Blair now dead in the water, there was no likelihood that Brown could extract any concessions on the internal market post by agreeing to abandon his own support for him. The prospect of a British President had one final flare before all hope was finally extinguished: Brown himself. 'Stand yourself,' Sarkozy said to a surprised Prime Minister in Berlin on 9 November. Brown grunted. He had no interest. He was not a Europhile, and he had no intention of quitting Downing Street.[248] Might Brown come to regret this decision? Ironically, despite his defiant opposition to Britain joining the euro, he would have been uniquely well qualified to help lead Europe out the debt-crisis it became engulfed in after he left office.

Brown arrived at the special meeting of EU leaders on 19 November with no clear way forward. He had lost out on securing both his prizes, the presidency and the internal market post, and his only hope now was to secure for Britain the High Representative job. In a desperate mood, he attended a pre-Council meeting of the PES group, convening in the dusty Austrian delegation building. The door closed on the smoke-filled room containing the comparatively few European leaders from the left, including José Luis Zapatero, leader of the PES Martin Schultz, and the Danish PES President Poul Nyrup Rasmussen. Brown's pitch to them reportedly was as follows: 'Look, I'm one of you. You know I am. Tony Blair never was, but I am. Now I need your help. I can't walk away from this Council with nothing. I've got to walk away with the High Rep job. If you back me, you can choose which Briton you want.'[249] It was unconventional, certainly, but it worked. They backed him, and he then presented them with a list of three names: Peter Mandelson, whom he did not want them to choose; Geoff Hoon, a former MEP; and Cathy Ashton, who had gone on from leader of the Lords to succeed Mandelson as trade commissioner in autumn 2008 and who had impressed colleagues on both the left and right in the EU machine.

Not on the list was the figure Brown would dearly have loved to nominate: David Miliband. This would have secured a palpably well-qualified figure for the post, as well as removing from the UK his principal challenger.[250] Miliband's tub-thumping speech on Europe to the party conference on 1 October was followed up by a speech on 26 October to the International Institute for Strategic Studies, in which he stressed the value to Britain of a strong EU foreign policy. The Lisbon Treaty, he argued, gave the EU the opportunity to develop clear strategic priorities for its role in the world, and they were opportunities that Britain and its European allies should embrace.[251] It was as if he was writing a job application. But then he cooled, and nothing came of it, because the high points of his enthusiasm and Brown's enthusiasm never coincided. Brown did offer Miliband the post. 'But he didn't push me,' says Miliband. 'He left me to make up my mind.'[252] And he said no, eventually deciding that his hopes for the future, with a likely Labour defeat at the general election and change of leadership coming up, for which he was in pole position, lay in Westminster politics rather than in Brussels.

Brown was strongly torn about another option in place of Miliband: Mandelson. According to Mandelson's account in his memoirs, Blair called him, having just spoken to Brown, to tell him that there were only two British candidates for High Representative, Miliband and himself, and as Miliband had ruled himself out, that left just him. 'Gordon phoned shortly afterwards and asked if I was interested.'[253] However, Mandelson's own account fails to mention that he was himself canvassing European leaders strongly for the job, which when he found out left Brown feeling very let down.[254] Having rehabilitated him by bringing him back in October 2008, and making him First Secretary in June 2009, Brown was puzzled and hurt to find that Mandelson within three months had been operating behind his back.[255] Others were angered and disillusioned too, including at least one of Mandelson's Cabinet colleagues: 'Having grabbed all the jobs and all the titles, he was prepared to bugger off and go to Europe. It would have left us in a terrible position if he had gone.'[256] Initially, and before he was aware of Mandelson's scheming, Brown appeared quite supportive. He never really understood why Mandelson wanted the job – and worried about how his First Secretary might react if he thwarted him. Brown's team in Number 10 were shocked. 'What are you doing? We can't lose Peter. Peter's far too important,' they told him. Brown looked at them 'as if they were all daft', and said: 'I've got to ask him whether he wants to do it.'[257] Nye, who had known Mandelson from the days before 1994, when he and Brown were still close friends, then went to see him and burst into tears. 'You can't leave us, you can't leave us,' she said.[258]

Brown need not have worried. As soon as he put up Mandelson's name to the EU, word came back immediately that he would not be acceptable to the PES group. 'They couldn't stand Peter because of his close association with Blair, and because, when he had been trade commissioner, he had treated them with contempt,' says one senior EU insider.[259] For example, he spurned their regular socialist dinners in Brussels and made them feel that he did not have time for them. So strong was the animosity towards Mandelson that Martin Schultz later revelled in revealing to the media his role in opposing Mandelson's candidature.[260] By the arrangement struck with the EPP, the candidate whom the PES selected for High Representative would have had to be acceptable to the EPP, and influential leaders on the European centre-right also disliked Mandelson.[261] Neither Sarkozy nor Merkel would have ever tolerated him.[262]

With Mandelson binned, the options cleared. Assuming that the PES group was going to grant Brown his wishes, it left them with a straight choice of Hoon or Ashton. Of the two, Brown lent towards Hoon, but only just. Hoon had the recommendation of being an MEP from 1984 to 1994, but that was fifteen years before, and few in the PES now knew him. He had some support, but in the end his involvement in the Iraq War as Blair's Defence Secretary, and relative obscurity, counted against him.[263] Brown would later joke: 'There was no real support for Geoff because no one knew him; there was even less support for Peter, and they all know him very well.'[264]

That left Ashton, who, for the PES, had precisely the virtues that Mandelson lacked: 'She inspired trust across the political spectrum, and had good relations with senior figures in the PES. She was good friends with Schultz, treated Rasmussen like a serious statesman, and had been a regular attendee at their socialist dinners. Critically, Barroso was also very happy to have her.'[265] To Brown's surprise, Ashton was the one they said they wanted.[266] When Brown rang Ashton to inform her of the news she made it very clear to him that she would stand aside if he was unhappy with their decision. Brown, however, raised no objections and her name thus went forward as the nominee for High Representative, while Belgium Prime Minister, Herman van Rompuy, a comparative unknown, was nominated as President. In January, the European Parliament approved both appointments. Brown tried to paint it as a victory. 'It's a sign of the regard that people have for both Britain and for Cathy Ashton that we've secured this important position for our country,' he said at the concluding press conference.[267] But, privately, he knew the whole saga would reflect badly on him. He knew Ashton's appointment would be slammed by the media.

'A pitiful lack of global ambition,' was the verdict of *The Economist*, on the selection of the 'two mediocre mice', adding: 'It is hard to see the political leaders of America, China and India, or even their foreign ministers, ever taking Mr van Rompuy and Lady Ashton entirely seriously.'[268] Both were seen as a far cry from the ambitions of those who had envisaged the roles in the new constitution for the EU. Had Blair been given the job of President, it would have been afforded a far higher authority on the world stage; and in his own way, Mandelson, too, would have made a powerful international figure representing the EU's interests. Both fell because they did not inspire sufficient trust across Europe. Some saw Mandelson's work behind the negative and personal press coverage.[269] The *Financial Times*'s Westminster blog said of Ashton: 'Even friends are stunned that someone so low key could have been elevated to such a high-profile job.'[270] The response in the US was equally dismissive. Europe was 'living down to expectations', said the *New York Times*. 'The selection of such low-profile figures seemed to highlight Europe's problems instead of its readiness to take on a more united and forceful place in world affairs.'[271]

Domestically, the fallout caused Brown significant problems: Mandelson and Hoon were both angry with him, and both blamed him personally for their not being made High Representative. Even without Blair as President, which meant he could not work in tandem with him, Mandelson had badly wanted the High Representative post, sharpened by the prospect of Labour's defeat and the end to the swish of ministerial life just months away. He blamed Brown for not pushing his name and using his authority hard enough in Brussels.[272] 'Gordon knew on the day Ashton got the job that he'd be in real trouble from Peter,' says an official.[273] Mandelson appeared blind to his own reputation in Brussels, and preferred to blame others; he is said to have believed that Ashton was manoeuvred into her position by Barroso, as he wanted someone compliant, and that she advanced her suit by undoing some of his work as Commissioner to curry favour with Barroso.[274] Hoon was equally furious with Brown and planned over Christmas what his next step would be, with potentially disastrous consequences for Brown.[275] 'I was indeed very frustrated by the way Brown handled the Europe job,' admits Hoon.[276]

Worse was to come for Brown. A few days after the two main appointments, Barroso put together the members of his commission. The focus for Britain was who would get the internal market portfolio. Officials believe Brown could still have obtained the finance commissioner post for Britain. His best moment would have been when Barroso told him he wanted Ashton as High Representative, but he did not seize that moment to bargain. The day after her appointment, he called Ashton, asking: 'Can you sort this out with Barroso?' She phoned Barroso at once and he said that, if Brown and Sarkozy agreed that Britain should have it, he would support it. But Brown refused to call Sarkozy. In the meantime, Mandelson was pouring poison into the ears of the media about what a disaster it would be if the French had the job. 'If Gordon can't stop Peter briefing the press here that the French will be a disaster, you will lose it,' Barroso said to Ashton.[277] Eventually, says an official, the French snapped: 'To have a British Cabinet minister feeding poison to the press about the French made them very angry. It became a matter of honour.'[278] Sarkozy's blood was now fully up, and, in the face of Brown's express wishes, he nominated Michel Barnier, the former French Foreign Minister. This was Brown's worst nightmare. Sarkozy immediately declared his appointment a 'victory' and it led to immediate fear in the City of London that Barnier would use his post to push French-inspired restrictive regulation against it, fears that were only marginally allayed by the appointment, at the instigation of Ashton, of a British figure, Jonathan Faull, as the senior official working with the Commissioner.

Brown felt betrayed by Barroso and believed that, in return for supporting his re-election as President of the European Commission in September 2009, Barroso would reward him, if not by giving the financial portfolio to Britain, then at the very least by ensuring that the French did not have it.[279] It was one of the moments when Brown became so angry he lost all self-possession. He phoned Ashton and demanded that she intervene personally to change Barroso's mind. 'I cannot do that,' she said. 'The decision's already been made. It's a done deal, he promised it to Sarkozy.' When he heard this, Brown started ranting at Ashton for twenty minutes, with a stream of abuse and profanities before he ended the phone call.[280] Compounding matters, Brown then phoned Barroso to remonstrate with him over his decision. Officials believe that it was the most offensive exchange he had with a foreign leader in his three years as premier.[281] Again, he swore repeatedly down the telephone and shouted at Barroso, accusing him of betrayal.[282]

Three weeks after the call, a still-shaken Barroso summoned Darroch to complain about his treatment by Brown. Brown's relationship with Barroso had never been good, but after the phone call, they barely spoke again.[283] In a move deliberately designed to provoke Brown, Sarkozy said of Barnier's nomination at the end of November: 'The English are the big losers in this business.'[284] In fact, Barnier did not prove to be such an ogre to the City, while a strange boon of Mandelson's petulance was that it brought Brown and Blair back together again. 'In that weird love triangle, discussing how to handle Peter made them closer,' says an official.[285] In his late premiership, Brown was generally a much steadier figure. The saga of the appointments of leaders of the new European Union, in contrast, showed him at his most indecisive and volatile. And the enemies that he made were to come back to bite him.

Climate Change and Copenhagen: December

If the kerfuffle over the appointments of the President and High Representative to the EU in November constituted the low point of Brown's leadership in his final months, the UN climate conference at Copenhagen in December showed him at his best. Though the outcome was widely regarded as a failure, Brown's interventions, not just at the summit itself, but also in the six months of intense diplomatic activity before, were instrumental in preventing the conference from collapsing altogether. The highest praise for his role came from former Vice President Al Gore, who said that Brown had done 'more than any other world leader to bring momentum to this process'.[286] Copenhagen was the culmination of support for the green cause that largely escaped public attention when he was at Number 10.

Brown's close interest in the issue of global warming was given real impetus when, in 2005, he commissioned his chief economist at the Treasury, Nick Stern, to conduct a review of the economics of climate change. Published in 2006, the Stern Report provided a powerful economic rationale for urgent action to reduce greenhouse gas emissions. It gave Brown a distinctive approach to the issue, combining an economic narrative on the benefits of building a 'low carbon economy' with a moral claim to justice: climate change was caused by the richest countries in the world, but hurt the poorest the most.

Brown articulated these themes in his first 'green' speech as Prime Minister, made to the Worldwide Fund for Nature on 19 November 2007, when he announced that a major aim for Britain would be to achieve 15 per cent of its energy supply from renewable sources by 2020. Brown had taken this decision the previous month (accepting an EU plan agreed the previous March by Blair), but in the face of resistance from Business Secretary John Hutton, saying it was not practically achievable and would be economically costly.[287] This was the first in a series of Brown initiatives over the coming two and a half years, shaped by his astute Policy Unit adviser, Michael Jacobs, which made a significant mark on the UK's energy and climate change policy. In January 2008, a white paper giving the green light to a new generation of nuclear power stations was published, and that spring, the government pushed both an energy and a planning bill through the House of Commons, facilitating their construction.

In the October 2008 reshuffle came Brown's biggest institutional initiative on green policy, when he established a new ministry, the Department of Energy and Climate Change, to bring climate and energy policy together, appointing Ed Miliband as Secretary of State. The following month, the Climate Change Act, originally drafted by David Miliband when he was Environment Secretary, received Royal Assent, creating legally binding targets to cut the UK's CO_2 omissions by at least 26 per cent on 1990 levels by 2020, and by at least 60 per cent by 2050. Over the following year, Ed Miliband took the agenda forward, putting in place a series of policies designed to achieve the targets, while at the same time raising them to at least 34 per cent by 2020, and at least 80 per cent by 2050. Collected together in a comprehensive plan in June 2009, to unusual praise from both the CBI and environmental campaign groups, these constituted Labour's most significant policies to date on Britain's transition to a low carbon economy.[288]

In the summer of 2009, Brown settled on climate change as one of the major international issues he wanted to drive forward over the following six months. He focused on the financial assistance which rich nations would give to developing countries, to help them cut their emissions and adapt to the impact of climate change, believing this to be the key to unlocking stalled international negotiations. In a speech on 26 June at London Zoo, he argued that the developed world should provide $100bn a year by 2020. This was properly a matter for the EU as a whole, and Brown knew that he would arouse hostility by announcing a figure. The speech went against the express wishes of Barroso's office, which said that it would be a 'terrible mistake'. Brown, who never had much time for the EU deliberative process, was convinced that the EU had to be bounced into taking a position.[289] His intervention, recognised by *The Guardian* as a bold attempt to 'seize the political initiative on climate change',[290] had significant influence in boosting international momentum.

Yet, as Copenhagen approached, huge fault lines remained between the positions of the major countries. Brown believed that the UN conference, the culmination of two years of negotiations, could not be allowed to fail; if it did, another chance might not come around again during the Obama presidency. On 20 September, just before the UN General Assembly in New York, he announced that he would be attending Copenhagen himself.[291] It was a huge risk: UN climate conferences had never been 'summits' for national leaders – they were meetings of officials and environment ministers. In arguing that the issue was so important it should be for heads of government, Brown was raising the stakes of the conference, and exposing himself to looking foolish if fellow leaders did not follow suit. He knew he could not fail, and over the following three months engaged heavily, persuading them to attend and urging them towards negotiating compromises. In the ensuing weeks, some of Brown's more cautious aides advised him to pull out, fearing that Copenhagen would be a damp squib: 'Number 10 was very sensitive about positioning him in anything that might not be perceived to be successful; but he was very clear that he had taken a lead on it, and it would be very inappropriate if he didn't attend.'[292] His response to the slow take-up was to raise the temperature. 'There are now fewer than fifty days to set the course of the next fifty years and more ... the world is watching,'[293] he said in a speech on 19 October to ministers from the world's major economies, gathered for climate talks in London. Drawing on the Stern Report, he argued that failure to act now on climate change would have a greater economic impact on the world in the twenty-first century than both World Wars and the Great Depression combined had had in the twentieth century.

Brown's single-minded focus on Copenhagen helped turn the biannual meeting of the Commonwealth heads of government in Trinidad and Tobago from 27 to 29 October into a climate change negotiation. To the hosts' 'considerable annoyance', Brown asked Sarkozy to attend the conference.[294] Brown was at his best, flattering, cajoling and persuading his fellow leaders,[295] and managing to secure backing for a $10bn per annum 'Copenhagen launch fund' to help poorer nations adapt to climate change and to cut their emissions.[296]

Next up for Brown was to ensure Obama's presence in Copenhagen and, most specifically, a US commitment to sufficient action on emissions, and finance, to pave the way to an international deal. Passing an energy and climate change bill was one of the President's principal objectives, but as Copenhagen approached it was clear that a majority could not be achieved in the Senate in time, and Obama's concern was that attending Copenhagen and agreeing to a deal there might jeopardise it. Obama was very clear: he told Brown in a video teleconference conversation that a deal at Copenhagen was not worth it for him if it meant sacrificing his bill.[297] If the US did not legislate to cut its emissions, he warned, it didn't matter what was agreed at Copenhagen, it wouldn't be implemented. Finance for developing countries was the most sensitive issue of all. Brown's $100bn proposal by 2020 was out of the question, Obama said, and agreeing to it would simply mean 'losing the bill'.[298] Brown would not be put off. 'Gordon just worked at him and worked at him, eventually persuading him not only to come but to become actively involved,' says an adviser.[299] In early December, Obama announced he would attend the Copenhagen conference. It 'dramatically raised the prospect of a global deal on climate change', said the *Financial Times*.[300]

'Copenhagen must be a turning point. Our children won't forgive us if we fail,' Brown wrote in *The Guardian* the day the conference opened on 7 December. 'We need to build a low carbon economy across the world, with a deal that helps developing nations and ensures trust.'[301] It was a two-week meeting, so, while officials met in Copenhagen for the first week, European leaders gathered in Brussels on 10–11 December for the EU Council. At Brown's urging, Swedish President Fredrik Reinfeldt, who was in the chair, went around the table and asked each head of government how much they were prepared to commit towards the $10bn per annum climate fund. After they had all put in their offers, Brown disconcerted the meeting by saying that the total was insufficient to pay Europe's fair share of the global total. 'We need to do more than this,' he told them bluntly.[302] Berlusconi complained that his finance minister Giulio Tremonti would not let him give any more. 'Do you want me to ring him?' asked Brown, who knew Tremonti well from their days as fellow finance ministers. Berlusconi shrugged. A few minutes later, Brown came back from the phone call to tell Berlusconi that his finance minister had agreed with him a higher Italian contribution.[303] When the Council reconvened, Reinfeldt announced that the total EU commitment was now considerably larger. The conference concluded on 11 December optimistically, with Brown and Sarkozy announcing plans to finance the amelioration of climate change by a global transactions tax.[304]

But to the north, in Copenhagen, all was not going nearly as well. Formal negotiations were in crisis. The texts produced by officials in the first week remained overly long and with almost no significant issues resolved. The leak of an apparently secret 'alternative text' prepared by the Danish government was greeted with outrage by developing countries and media. Then attempts by the Danish presidency to convene a smaller group of countries to streamline negotiations were consistently blocked by developing countries, led by China. On 14 December, the 'G77' group, led by African countries, staged a walkout, concerned that the 1997 Kyoto protocol, which committed industrial states to reduce greenhouse gases, with financial penalties for failure, would be abandoned.[305] Brown, against advice from his officials, was determined to intervene himself, to salvage what looked like a conference falling apart. He flew into Copenhagen on 15 December, two days ahead of the scheduled leaders' meeting, to seek agreement with other heads of government.[306] In a series of private meetings, with Chinese Premier Wen Jiabao and others, Brown urged compromise. When the formal negotiations broke down altogether on 17 December, UK officials, led by Ed Miliband, helped organise an impromptu negotiation among a 'coalition of the willing', which led eventually to Brown chairing a meeting of around twenty-five leaders committed to achieving a deal. Then, in a development which vindicated the pressure he had put on Obama, Hillary Clinton announced that the US would, after all, support the proposal for $100bn for developing countries by 2020, and $10bn by 2012.

By 17 December, with just a day left, there was still stalemate. The Danish hosts openly admitted that a deal was remote, and that the talks were on the 'brink of collapse'.[307] That evening, after the ceremonial dinner for heads of government, hosted by the Queen of Denmark, Danish Prime Minister Rasmussen made a final plea to find a way forward. His proposal was that a representative group of some thirty heads of government, including all the major developed and developing economies, meet to try to hammer out an agreement. The meeting lasted around two hours, from 11pm to 1am. Before retiring to their beds, the leaders gave instructions for their 'sherpas' to negotiate the text of an outline political agreement for the leaders to consider the following morning. Ed Miliband led the British team, while Brown went back to his hotel. The sherpas met from 3am to 6am, working on a short Danish draft.[308] But by dawn they had barely started on the key paragraphs and the gulf between the developing and developed countries round the table remained gaping. As day was breaking, in a short debrief, the European officials agreed that the conference was effectively over.

Few leaders would be sadder about this than Brown, and his staff knew it. Jacobs and Cunliffe, the Prime Minister's principal advisers, rushed to his hotel at around 7am. 'I think it's finished,' Jacobs told him. 'We're still way off an agreement.' Brown would have none of it. 'Give me the amendments! Give me the amendments!' he shouted, determined that the text could still be rescued.[309] Jacobs quickly sat at a computer in Brown's hotel room and wrote out a series of fifteen possible amendments to the text. Brown was already in the lift to go down to the conference centre when Jacobs handed him the typed-up draft. The thirty heads of government reconvened at 8.30am – though Wen of China and India's Manmohan Singh sent ministers in their place. Seated around a table in a hopelessly small conference room, with Rasmussen in the chair, flanked by the UN Secretary-General Ban Ki-moon, and with around a hundred officials and advisers packed behind them, the leaders pondered the stalemate. Brown took the floor. He pleaded with his fellow leaders to find a way through. 'We are trying to cut emissions by 2020 and 2050,' he said. 'That is the only way we can justify being here, and justify the public money that is being spent to do so. It is the only way we can justify the search for a treaty.'[310]

As with the London G20, he knew that his fellow leaders would not want to return to their countries empty-handed, for their media to say that they had failed. 'This is a crisis,' he said. 'And I have a series of amendments here.' He shuffled around for the document and proceeded to read out the amendments to the text he had been handed just before the meeting. Rasmussen proposed that they consider these in turn.

'It was a surreal meeting, and an extraordinary drama,' Jacobs recalls,[311] as the world leaders went through the text line by line, proposing and painfully agreeing amendments, including those proposed by Brown. It was highly unusual for leaders to negotiate an agreement themselves in this way, without prior agreement by their officials. At around 10am, President Obama made a dramatic entry, straight off his plane from Washington. Replacing Hillary Clinton in the US seat, next to Brown, he calmly joined in the negotiation. Facing him, extraordinarily, was Chinese Foreign Vice-Minister He Yafei, a mere deputy.[312] 'It would be nice to negotiate with somebody who could make political decisions,' Obama said, regarding this as a serious insult.[313]

As the negotiation proceeded, it was clear that the larger developing countries, notably China, India and Brazil, were deeply uncomfortable with the pressure they were being placed under to agree a deal. The Chinese insisted that the key targets for emissions cuts in 2050 should be removed, including those applying to developed countries alone. They were simply unwilling to be bound in a way they believed would hinder their development. In the afternoon, Obama left the conference to see Wen in his hotel, where he was met by not just Wen but also Singh, and Presidents Lula of Brazil and Zuma of South Africa. They told him that they would accept the text as it was now drafted, but, critically, that they would not agree that it should become the basis for a legally binding UN treaty. China conceded some weak language agreeing to international monitoring of emissions. Obama returned to the conference centre to report back to the principal European leaders. Sarkozy reacted angrily, and it was left to Brown and Merkel to argue that, though extremely disappointing, the agreement was clearly better than nothing, and they had little choice but to accept. By mid-evening, amid some exhaustion, the leaders had concluded the text of an outline agreement, which they called the 'Copenhagen Accord'. Obama, keen to catch his flight home to avoid snow preventing his landing in Washington, held a press conference to announce it. Pointedly, he thanked China, India, South Africa and Brazil, but not the Europeans or others. After making a short statement of his own, Brown flew back to London.

The drama was still not over. The twenty-nine countries represented in the small-room negotiations might have reached an agreement, but this had still to be confirmed by the 192 countries of the United Nations as a whole. In the reconvened plenary, agreement could not be achieved. A number of countries objected both to the manner of the 'closed-door' negotiations between a small number of leaders and to the watered-down content of the Copenhagen Accord itself. After a further night of emotional speeches, a compromise was reached in which the Accord was neither agreed nor voted down, but was 'taken note of' by the conference as a whole.

'It is progress, but it is not enough,' admitted Brown that day.[314] Global media reaction was scathing, both about the chaotic negotiations and the weakness of the settlement. No legally binding treaty had been agreed, nor were there emissions reductions commitments in the Accord itself, which was merely a place marker for countries to enter their targets and actions later. And with the conference as a whole refusing to endorse the text agreed by the leaders, it was not clear what status the document had at all.

Why was more not achieved? The blame bandwagon began to roll before the tyres of the leaders' planes had left the tarmac at Copenhagen's Kastrup airport. Brown said that the full and binding treaty that he had sought had been 'held to ransom' by a small number of countries, while Ed Miliband named China's disruptive tactics during the formal negotiations as the principal cause of the disarray. Sarkozy agreed, describing Chinese behaviour as 'utterly unacceptable', and accusing it of 'hypocrisy'. This absolved the developed countries – particularly the US – of their responsibility for failing to agree stronger emissions cuts. Prime responsibility for causing climate change lay with the developed countries, and for Copenhagen to have worked, they needed a step change in their commitment to cut emissions, a change for which they were not yet ready.

Did Brown overreach himself in hyping up Copenhagen? The failure of the conference was principally due to forces beyond his grasp – a geopolitical clash between the US, China and other newly emerging powers over a far-reaching economic problem requiring more political will to solve than was available at that point. If the strategy was overambitious, Brown also made tactical errors along the way. He could be naive, and be carried away by adrenalin. As an official notes: '[Brown] worked on an assumption that if he got leaders where he wanted them to be, and got an understanding with his counterpart, then all would work out with the country.'[315] It meant he could be cavalier in assuming the leader could carry their country, and he did not always use his own Foreign Office properly or listen to it. Brown had arrived at Number 10 suspicious of diplomats, and he never changed. 'Like every Number 10, we always assumed that the FCO would tell us what other countries wanted us to hear,' says an official. Hence, by the time Brown got to Copenhagen, 'he was pretty much discounting FCO advice'.[316] William Ehrman, British ambassador in China, had been saying for some time that the Chinese were not in the right place, and could not be pushed beyond their announced positions. On India, too, Brown needed to spend time with leaders other than Singh, notably the leader of the Congress Party, Sonia Gandhi. His swashbuckling style worked for the financial crisis, but leaders did not believe that this was a crisis, or, at least, not one that demanded an immediate concerted response.

In hindsight, the Copenhagen Accord looks better than it did at the time. By mid-2010, over 130 countries had endorsed the agreement, and over eighty, including almost all the world's major economies, covering 80 per cent of global emissions, had entered into it their emissions reductions commitments. For the developing countries this was a first. The Accord endorsed, again for the first time in an international agreement, the goal of limiting global warming to two degrees Celsius above pre-industrial levels. It provided for approaching $30bn in assistance for developing countries from 2010 to 2012 (as Brown had proposed to the Commonwealth conference and got agreed in the EU), and set a goal of reaching $100bn in annual flows by 2020 – the figure Brown first put forward the previous June. The absence of formal UN agreement gave all this uncertain international status, but there is no doubt that both Brown's tireless efforts to pursue a climate finance package and his initiative in turning Copenhagen into a leaders' summit generated much of the momentum for an agreement. 'Gordon played his hand at Copenhagen as well as anyone could have expected,' says Gavin Kelly.[317]

Brown was disappointed by the outcome of Copenhagen, but although he may not have made the progress on climate change that he had on development and international finance, or achieved the same status, he was happy with his own performance. Before his Christmas rest, he had still to attend to the fall-out from the Pre-Budget Report, which he had spent six months building up.

The Politics of the Deficit and the Pre-Budget Report: June–December

The defining domestic issue of the Brown premiership was the debate over the response to the economic downturn. In 2008, the financial crisis had demanded an immediate, comprehensive and bold response, which came in the form of the 2008 Pre-Budget Report fiscal stimulus, and included a cut in the rate of VAT to 15 per cent. But the April Budget, which exposed the scale of the damage the recession had inflicted on the public finances, brought to the fore issues about how to balance economic recovery with a credible response to the ballooning government deficit. In his Budget Darling announced the government's intention to halve the deficit in four years. Come the December Pre-Budget Report, he would need to take another step, setting out in more detail his plans to return the public finances to balance. This time, the key battle would be in an area that Brown found deeply uncomfortable: public spending cuts.

We pick up the story where we left it, in June 2009. Mandelson and Darling were becoming increasingly exasperated with Brown's reluctance to neither discuss cuts or publicly associate himself with his Chancellor's own deficit reduction plan. It 'created the impression we would simply keep on spending, borrowing and taking on debt', says Mandelson.[318] Brown's dour persistency and refusal to admit to cuts – let alone to countenance using their vocabulary – played into the hands of the Tories, who had taken the decision to politicise the issue of the deficit, arguing that spending needed to be cut as a priority in order to safeguard Britain's credibility with the markets. Brown was coming under constant pressure from the Tories and the media to spell out how he would tackle Britain's deficit.

But it would not be easy for Brown to shift his position. He felt powerfully bound to the economic arguments that had defined his years as Chancellor. The strategy of 'Labour investment versus Tory cuts', whose roots ran deep in his own political and economic philosophy, was one he had been instrumental in developing, and their hold was firm. Brown's reluctance to focus on the deficit was also explained by his deep belief that government policy should prioritise economic growth and he was therefore desperate to shift public debate away from cuts and on to the broader terrain of how to kick-start Britain's flagging economy. His mistake was that he failed to realise that until he sounded credible on the deficit he would not get a hearing for his growth agenda. More prosaically, Brown felt strongly that New Labour owed much of its political success to the 'cuts versus spending' argument. 'There is something in Gordon that equates success with growth in public spending,' observes one Number 10 aide astutely.[319] Now struggling in the polls, and with an election round the corner, why would he ditch the very strategy that had brought such success? Yet, Brown faced an increasingly stark reality. Pressure from the opposition, media and markets had already forced him into a commitment to halve the deficit. That was not a target he could fluff: it was set down, in public, in hard numbers, and had hard implications. Whichever way one looked at it, a plan for reducing the deficit could not be credible without some clear language on spending cuts. That meant resisting the pull of his political and philosophical loyalties, and engaging with a more nuanced argument with the Tories about the speed and nature of cuts.

Privately, Brown accepted that there would have to be constraints on spending, whoever won the election. But he consistently rejected the argument put forward by many in his Cabinet that a more credible narrative – and dividing line – would be: 'Nice Labour cuts versus nasty Tory cuts'.[320] Brown feared that if Labour came out for cuts then it would legitimise a race-to-the-bottom contest with the Tories, which Labour could only lose. Following shadow Health Secretary Andrew Lansley's '10 per cent' public spending cuts admission in June, Brown went on a summer offensive, lambasting the Tories' spending plans. On Wednesday 17 June, Brown taunted Cameron at PMQs: 'His is the party of cuts; we're the party for investment.' A week later, on 24 June, Cameron rounded on Brown, accusing him of being caught 'red-handed' giving wrong figures. Treasury numbers, he said, confirmed that Brown, too, would have to cut some departments by 10 per cent. For Cameron, the media, and most at Number 10, Brown was living in denial. Brown lashed back: 'We have brought forward public expenditure ... they would cut by 10 per cent, savagely.'[321]

The 'Mr 10 per cent' strategy, as it became known, spread despair in Number 10. The Treasury numbers were clear: under sensible assumptions about the amount that could be delivered through tax rises, cuts of 10 per cent or more were a simple, mathematical implication of halving the deficit while protecting key public spending departments. Here, if ever, was a train wreck waiting to happen. And Brown was driving his government full steam towards it. For many in the Cabinet, too, it marked a tipping point in their confidence in Brown's economic strategy. As the days moved into July, ministers began to drift behind Darling, sharing his growing concerns about the economic strategy.[322] For Brown's own advisers, the PMQs sessions had revealed quite how far they still needed to move Brown before the PBR. Bank of England Governor Mervyn King also joined the fray, appearing before the Treasury Select Committee on the afternoon of the PMQs on 24 June, to warn: 'The scale of the deficit is truly extraordinary.' King told the committee that a plan was badly needed for the next Parliament to 'show how these deficits will be brought down'. Though refusing to be pressed on figures, he said: 'I do not think the Chancellor is remotely relaxed about the fiscal position.'[323] Brown was furious at what he felt to be a political intervention by the Governor, and his relationship with King 'collapsed completely'. 'They didn't say a single word to each other in Brown's remaining months in office,' says a senior Number 10 official.[324]

On Tuesday 30 June, ministers gathered for a political Cabinet. The mood was glum. Shortly before, an Ipsos MORI poll had put the Conservatives at 38 per cent, with Labour trailing at 21 per cent.[325] Increasingly seen as being out of touch with reality, Brown's ratings were slipping to new lows. The June PMQs had galvanised Heywood, Kelly and Pearce to push Brown harder to move away from a purely anti-cuts message, towards one that focused on *how* a deficit reduction should be achieved, and how fast it should be done.[326] The 'Tory cuts' message could have no traction while the public believed that cuts were inevitable.[327] Eventually, it was Mandelson who secured the breakthrough. In July, Mandelson worked backwards from the Pre-Budget

Report – due in the late autumn – and won Brown's agreement to a series of interventions by senior ministers that would set out the government's revised policy position. According to Mandelson's special adviser, Patrick Loughran: 'Peter was determined to get the government off the hook it had impaled itself on.'[328] In this period, says Patrick Diamond, Mandelson became 'critical in shoring up support for Gordon'.

On 11 July, Darling made the first of the planned interventions, arguing in an interview with the *Daily Telegraph* that it was important to 'try to level with people'[329] on the question of public spending. On 15 July, Mandelson himself followed up, in a speech at the press gallery lunch, saying that 'less spending [would be needed] in some programmes'.[330] It was 'the first step towards repositioning ourselves', says Mandelson. 'The argument was finally out there.' It was a bold but carefully crafted strategy, designed by Mandelson to shift the ground beneath Brown's feet. The statements would help to frame the debate around how cuts should be made. It seemed to be working, until 16 July, when a clearly uncomfortable Brown appeared before the Liaison Committee in the House of Commons. The committee questioned him repeatedly about Mandelson's comments the previous day, but Brown assiduously avoided any mention of the word 'cuts' in his response. Polly Toynbee summed up the view of many in *The Guardian* after the recess on 21 July: 'Brown has been left floundering ... he sounds as if he knows there must be deep cuts, but won't admit it – ending up in the worst of all worlds, his perennial resting place.'[331] For the BBC's Nick Robinson, Brown was stuck in a 'hopeless disregard for reality'.

Robinson himself had long conversations on the subject with Mandelson and Forsyth, and was so struck by the former's candour at a private dinner in late July that he invited him on to *Newsnight*, which he was presenting that week.[332] On 28 July, Mandelson spoke on the programme about the need for a fiscal adjustment to rebuild the public finances, although he, too, scrupulously avoided the word 'cuts'.[333] Brown himself may not have been moving, but Mandelson's strategy was proceeding apace, and in the next of the planned interventions, in Cardiff on 8 September, Darling used the opportunity of the 'Callaghan lecture' to emphasise the 'hard choices' that needed to be made. In a speech at the London School of Economics on 14 September, Mandelson went further, talking about a 'responsible approach' to reducing the fiscal deficit 'that will not eat into the fabric of people's lives'. He attempted to define the new dividing line between Labour and the Conservatives as 'progressive state reformers versus ideological state retrenchers'.[334]

By late August, the constant pressure was again starting to show. At lunch at Darling's Edinburgh home, Brown agreed to use his speech to the TUC conference on 15 September publicly to acknowledge the case for 'cuts'. Two days before the speech, a poll for *The Times* showed that 60 per cent of the public preferred cuts in spending to higher taxes. Come the day of the TUC speech, Brown finally used the word his colleagues had waited so long to hear: 'Labour will cut costs, cut inefficiencies, cut unnecessary programmes and cut lower-priority budgets.' It was a vital breakthrough, even though he went on to emphasise that these would be 'Labour' cuts, not cuts to 'vital frontline services' or cuts that would put 'the recovery at risk'. The Number 10 team regarded it as a 'significant moment',[335] and there was 'relief around the Cabinet table' that he had spoken the word. 'We have finally cleared away the undergrowth,' said one minister.[336] Meanwhile, George Osborne described Brown's statements to an audience at *The Spectator* magazine as: 'a complete capitulation'.[337]

However, any celebrations were premature. Far from feeling liberated, Brown was furious; furious that he had delivered the speech, and furious with those who had pushed him in that direction. 'Well, are you satisfied all of you?' he asked, rounding on Mandelson. 'We should not be in this place! We have got to move to growth. Don't give me all this about spending cuts.'[338] The outburst said much about the depth of his emotional commitment to the 'investment versus cuts' line, and the strength with which he associated that position with Labour's glory years. 'It was incredibly hard for Gordon to be asked to unravel all of that,' reflects one adviser.[339] That stubbornness was now creating profound tension within the government – particularly between Brown and Darling – and it was cooling relations between Brown and Mandelson. But even the damage maintaining his position was doing to these important relationships did not persuade Brown to change his mind. 'Gordon had spent months at the despatch box attacking the Tories on cuts, and he found it incredibly difficult to retreat. He's a very proud man,' says one adviser. 'The "cuts versus investment" line was just part of his make-up,' says another. Politically, Brown could not see the damage he was doing.

Brown's intransigence stemmed not only from an emotional commitment; it also had intellectual foundations. Over the autumn, as the Pre-Budget Report approached, Brown, ever the historian, had turned again to accounts of the failures of the 1930s and 1980s to deal with the fallout of recession. He was particularly attracted to the work of Robert Skidelsky, and to the accounts of Philip Snowden, Labour Chancellor in 1924 and from 1929 to 1931. Snowden's resistance to radical Keynesian measures to combat the recession had long appealed to Brown as a cautionary tale. 'I want a Labour budget. I don't want to have a Snowden budget,' he would sometimes say to advisers. Once, as a contemporary diary records, Brown said to Heywood: 'You are not going to turn me into Snowden.'[340] In rare moments of calm, he revelled in long discussions on Snowden, Keynes and the inter-war Treasury with his team, and loved reciting the story of how a Treasury official scrawled the words 'extravagance', 'inflation' and 'bankruptcy' on the cover of Keynes's co-authored pamphlet *We Can Conquer Unemployment*. One adviser recalls Brown saying to him: 'When the crisis of capitalism they had predicted came, they ran away. As Oswald Mosley put it: "It was like the Salvation Army turning on its heels on the Day of Judgment."'[341] For Brown, then, a reluctance to talk about cuts, and turn away from a single-minded focus on growth 'was simply consistent with his Keynesian beliefs'.[342]

Brown's reading of history did little to make his position more palatable to senior Treasury officials. As one of them says: 'Brown was beholden to an ersatz-Keynesianism, and a belief in the efficacy of micro-measures.' Nor indeed did the Treasury accept Brown's reading of history. 'To suggest that Keynes would be saying today, "spend more" is laughable,' says one Treasury official.[343] Another reflects: 'I actually think Snowden was a pretty good Chancellor. In fact, I'm thinking about writing a biography of him when I retire.'[344] More importantly, though, the growing divisions between the Treasury and Brown simply reflected their different concerns. While Brown remained transfixed by the political cycle, Treasury officials were genuinely, and increasingly, concerned about the size of the UK debt, and reactions from the bond markets. Nick Macpherson, permanent secretary at the Treasury, despaired, often saying to colleagues of Brown: 'He just doesn't get it.' Macpherson 'was desperate not to be the one who [would have] to go to the IMF', recalls one Number 10 official.[345] The permanent secretary had been close to Brown during his Treasury days but their relationship deteriorated badly in this period.[346] Darling, too, having survived what he knew would be Brown's last reshuffle, was increasingly concerned about his legacy as Chancellor. To be clear, Darling was no hawk on cuts – he would, for instance, strongly support Brown's decision not to hold a spending review – but he felt that the government's credibility would be damaged if Brown persisted in ducking the issue of cuts. As one senior Number 10 official recalls: 'It's easy to get hot under the collar about their differences, but the only fundamental difference was over the degree of openness about the cuts side of things.'[347] But that remained a significant difference, and Darling was adamant that, for the markets, a medium-term plan was needed for getting spending and debt under control. Both the OECD and IMF warned of the need for a credible plan to bring the budget into balance, and Standard and Poor's ratings agency said it was putting Britain's 'AAA' credit rating on review. 'Making those in-roads was a higher priority for him and the Treasury than exactly how you did it. You can't afford to be too fussy,' says one Treasury official.[348]

Brown's relations with the Treasury had been strong throughout the financial crisis and G20, but now they soured. A senior official says that, while 'no personal rivalries' remained, a gap now opened on questions of policy.[349] Brown became critical of Darling for being too accepting of Treasury advice.

'We were being scaremongered about debt,' says one Number 10 official. 'Gordon felt Alistair was unduly worried about the fiscal position, and that it would be madness to dilute the political message by announcing that there would be cuts,' says another.[350] Brown's distrust of Treasury officials went back a long way. 'In his early years as Chancellor, Brown and Balls set up a series of structures designed to neutralise the Treasury,' says a senior mandarin from the department.[351] Underpinning that was the classic Labour view of the world – that the Treasury would be 'out to get' a Labour government. By 2009, Brown's sights had narrowed and 'towards the end, Brown was seeing the Treasury as an institution which was out to get him personally'.[352] One official in Number 10 believed that the Treasury 'would goad Alistair to stand up to him and show "who was the man"'.[353] Brown felt the Treasury had let itself become 'petrified' of the rating agencies, and the risk of a sovereign debt crisis. Again, he drew historic parallels, believing that the Treasury in 2010, like the Treasury in the 1930s, was a 'prisoner of economic orthodoxy'.[354] 'Officials from the top down were not measured in their concerns about those agencies,' says a Number 10 aide.[355] Ed Balls believed that the Treasury was in a state of deep shock from the tumultuous events of the previous year which had happened on its watch. 'The Treasury reacted to the financial crisis by retreating into a traditional and defensive posture about public spending which Gordon found very frustrating. He was especially irritated by the pressure Treasury officials put on Darling,' comments one close to these things.[356] Both Brown and Balls felt that former Treasury mandarins such as Terry Burns and Andrew Turnbull, both ex-permanent secretaries who were unhappy with the way Brown ran the deparment, were encouraging serving officials to use the debate on the deficit to 'take back control'.[357] For his part, in the words of officials: 'Alistair took a more proper view, based on Treasury advice, that the fiscal position did need to be sorted out, and that, politically, it was more sensible to be transparent about that.'[358] Increasingly, Darling's Treasury officials could point to unfolding events in the euro area to justify their concerns about the rising cost of financing government debt, and King shared their concerns. But, for Brown, the Bank of England Governor was doing little more than 'tweaking George Osborne by driving into him the fear that we would have a crisis with sterling'.[359]

It was in that environment of growing distrust that Mandelson and others had pushed Brown to give his TUC speech. Now, he feared that having shown them an inch, the Treasury would take a mile. And so, too, would the Tories, who, he felt certain, would exploit the volte face and push for ever greater cuts. As October approached, and with it the Pre-Budget Report, tensions rose. Deadened by anxiety, Labour's conference was a lacklustre affair and failed to deliver the usual bounce in the polls. With Darling's statement looming large on the horizon, some worried that Labour would sink so low that it would never recover. 'We worried that Alistair would make things appear, with his Scottish accent, a lot worse than they actually were. Each time we had a Budget or PBR, it put us five to ten points behind. We knew that if he did that with the PBR this time around, we wouldn't have any time for a recovery,' says one senior aide.[360]

Mandelson's repositioning strategy had all but run its course and now began the period for negotiations over the substance of the Pre-Budget Report. Brown, though, was still playing his cards close to his chest. 'Throughout September, October and November, there was not a huge engagement from Brown at all on the PBR,' says a Number 10 official. 'Gordon didn't want to commit himself until the way the economy was going became far clearer. His refusal to commit heightened the difficulty in managing relationships.'[361] Communication between Number 10 and the Treasury ground to a halt, as all the big decisions for the Pre-Budget Report had to wait for Darling and Brown to decide. 'The problem was that their meetings failed to resolve matters, or they would be cancelled at the last minute.'[362]

When meetings did take place, little progress was being made and, increasingly, Brown's isolation was coming out into the open. At one of the irregular meetings to discuss the Pre-Budget Report, in early October, Darling walked across to the Cabinet Room at Number 10, accompanied by his junior minister Paul Myners. Darling and Brown tried to address their differences, but it soon became evident that they were getting nowhere. Brown turned to Myners for support, but the latter indicated that he backed Darling's judgement. He could tell from the look on Brown's face that he was deeply disappointed. From that moment on, Myners felt he was 'dead' in Brown's eyes.[363]

There was one figure, though, whom Brown was not prepared to lose. Balls's relationship with Brown had chilled a little after the reshuffle, in which Balls, once again, had been denied the chancellorship he so craved. Balls himself was deeply resistant to the idea of spending cuts, especially if they were on education. 'I don't see how, as the Labour Party, we can go into an election campaign cutting. If the Labour Party exists for anything, it's for the protection and improvement of the NHS, and to provide a decent level of education for our children,' he said.[364] At a meeting in early November in the Cabinet Room, Brown tried to lighten the tone during one of Balls's passionate pleas for education spending. Balls argued passionately that the Conservatives had promised to increase spending on the NHS in real terms, but had made no similar pledge about education. 'You're only speaking from your brief,' Brown joked. Balls saw red: 'I know that's what you think. I know that's what Peter Mandelson thinks. I know that's what all the staff here think. And to be frank, if that's what you're going to accuse me of, you can forget me ever coming to one of those meetings again. You're on your own.' Brown's staff were stunned. Most had never seen Balls go for Brown like that in public. They were even more amazed by Brown's tame reaction. 'Don't be like that,' he said.[365]

It was hardly the ideal context for Pre-Budget Report negotiations. Over the next three weeks, major decisions would come to define the dividing lines for the general election. First, there would need to be detail on efficiencies, to show that the government was serious about controlling spending, and in ways that would not damage the quality of services. Second, there would need to be words on tax, including specific measures to increase revenue. And third, and most difficult of all, more would need to be said on the question of cuts. In that area, perhaps the most critical decision had already been made: in June, Brown and Darling announced that they would not be publishing a three-year spending review, which would have meant setting out departmental spending totals for the next three years, including precise details on where any cuts would fall. 'Why on earth would we choose to prescribe what exactly we would be doing from April 2011 from the uncertainty of late 2009? We deliberately decided that we would not go into detail,' says a Number 10 official.[366] Brown's argument was that, at a time of such economic uncertainty, such projections were impossible. In the run-up to an election, that was an all too convenient truth. When eventually announced, their decision aroused the following inevitable and contemptuous response from Osborne: 'The Chancellor is prepared to tell us what he will spend money on, but he stays almost totally silent on where the real axe will fall. He is achieving the previously impossible trick of ring-fencing a black hole.'[367]

As negotiations progressed, officials noticed a change in Darling. Reinvigorated and empowered by the June reshuffle débâcle, he now seemed to care much less about placating Number 10. With a likely election defeat approaching, he had one eye on the long term, and the way his chancellorship would be judged in history. His attitude reminded one Treasury official of Ken Clarke, when he was Chancellor from 1993 to 1997, during the dying days of the Major premiership, and whose predominant concern was 'How do we get things back on track?' rather than party politics.[368] According to one adviser, Darling's mindset became: 'We're going to lose, but I may as well do the right thing.'[369] Observers noticed that his body language and tone changed when he resolved that, if Brown was not going to listen to him, then he would resign – which he knew would inflict great damage.[370] A fellow minister notes: 'Alistair increasingly becomes his own Chancellor, and that's at its most evident in the run-up to the PBR, where there was huge tension.'[371]

The Chancellor's newfound confidence emboldened those below him, and raised the tensions in relations between the Treasury and Number 10 to new heights, though it was nothing compared to the distrust that existed during the Blair–Brown years. Never would the relationship approach the animosity of that period, but at official level, previously smooth interactions now became less easy, and information flows began to dry up, especially when Number 10 asked for data on the state of the public finances. Technically, of course, Brown could overrule his Chancellor, so at the highest level, major disputes could be resolved. As Heywood once put it in an email exchange with Number 10 colleagues, after an overzealous Treasury adviser had rejected a Number 10 request: 'Perhaps someone should remind him that GB is First Lord of the Treasury.'[372] But, in the reality of day-to-day interactions, Treasury officials held great power in their control over information. In the run-up to the Pre-Budget Report, and the Budget the following March, Number 10 was so routinely denied key information that advisers were forced to rely on their own internal model of public spending figures, allowing them to play with spending scenarios, and guess at the numbers Treasury colleagues would not give them. Their strength was greatly boosted by Josh Goodman, working at Number 10's Policy Unit, and himself a former Treasury official. Highly rated by colleagues, Goodman's work enabled advisers to weigh up spending options, and estimate Treasury figures, such as the levels of unemployment assumed in forecasts.

The area of least difficulty in negotiations was 'efficiencies'. Working closely with Heywood, Liam Byrne, Chief Secretary, masterminded a white paper, launched two days before the Pre-Budget Report, and called the 'Smarter Government Initiative'. At Brown's request, Byrne had put together a dedicated team of officials in the Cabinet Office for the task. Agreement between Darling and Brown came easily. Brown himself had long been excited by the idea that new technologies could transform the quality and efficiency of public services. At the start of the year, he had encountered Tim Berners-Lee, the man credited with inventing the World Wide Web, at a party. He had gone on to host a meeting for Berners-Lee and others at Number 10, which he dominated with an enthusiasm that bemused his colleagues. Now, in negotiations over the Pre-Budget Report, one Number 10 aide recalls Brown 'becoming obsessed with using IT to save money; he drove the paper through by chairing lots of meetings in a very short space of time'.[373] Innovations in the NHS IT programme, and a new online system for citizens' advice fed through directly into Darling's Pre-Budget Report, forming part of the £16bn efficiency savings that the Chancellor announced he would achieve by 2012–13. '[Brown's] grasp of how technology was transforming the world was actually quite impressive when you consider that he was born in the 1950s in Fife,' says one close adviser.[374]

Efficiencies, though, would never be enough to convince the markets and the media that Labour had a credible plan. Tax increases would also be needed. Raising VAT seemed an obvious option. It was favoured by the Treasury, as it had been in the previous Pre-Budget Report, as an efficient, non-distorting way of raising large sums. The Number 10 Policy Unit, however, had deep concerns about the regressive nature of VAT, and put up a paper to Brown arguing that a VAT rise would hit the least well-off and, politically, would risk splitting the PLP just before the election. If tax rises were to be saleable to the party, the claim of 'fairness' needed to ring true. Within Number 10, that put an increase in national insurance at the top of the list. It was a tax that had more positive associations for some in the building, having been used to fund increases in NHS investment. As Muir explains: 'Our belief was that the British public associates national insurance with raising money for schools and the NHS. If there's one tax they are prepared to pay it's national insurance.' Brown saw the logic of his political team's case. Darling did not, and remained resolutely in favour of raising VAT (as did his officials, and some Number 10 officials). The Chancellor was particularly concerned that an increase in national insurance would be painted by the Conservatives as a 'tax on jobs'. On that, he would be proved right. Darling was supported by Mandelson, but in the end Brown went for the national insurance move, especially after Balls, who was strongly opposed to raising VAT, intervened.

Brown's political team would have liked to have gone further and lobbied him to rule out further VAT rises before the election campaign. It would, they felt, provide a stick with which to beat the Conservatives: strategic planners in Number 10 believed that the Tories could be attacked for planning a VAT hike, if Darling could be persuaded to rule out any increase himself. As one Number 10 insider puts it: 'Our view was: "Since it's off the table, why can't we make political capital out of it?"' Darling vetoed this outright.

Darling would later announce in the Pre-Budget Report on 9 December that VAT would return to 17.5 per cent from 1 January 2010, and that national insurance contributions would rise for those earning over £20,000 by 0.5 per cent in 2011. The move was mocked by Osborne: 'That is his answer to Britain's unemployment problem – higher costs for struggling businesses, and more money taken from families.'[375] This aspect of the Pre-Budget Report touched squarely on the fairness agenda, newly dramatised by the banking crisis. Labour's own analysis claimed that 50 per cent of all the tax revenues raised since the 2008 Pre-Budget Report came from the top 2 per cent of earners – a figure Number 10 felt gave a clear indication of the government's commitment to fairness.[376]

The move on high earners had been made easier by the public outcry on bankers' pay and bonuses, following the financial crisis. Bonuses in particular had come under fire, and were the focus of another significant part of the negotiations. In his party conference speech in September, Darling had pointed to new laws governing bonuses. Officials beneath him were reluctant to sanction any move that would be interpreted as damaging or penalising bankers: 'It took a lot of political pressure to move the Treasury on bankers' bonuses.'[377] But public opinion carried the day, and Darling, with strong support from Brown, announced a one-off tax on bankers' bonuses, specifically to fund training schemes for the long-term youth unemployed – a 50 per cent levy on any individual discretionary bonus above £25,000. 'The government arguably did sail very close to the wind, and gave off too much of [an] anti-aspiration signal in the PBR,' reflects a Number 10 official afterwards. Nevertheless the tax proved a success, raising £3.5bn, four times more than the Treasury originally forecast.

The most difficult discussions, though, as Number 10 and the Treasury had expected, came over spending. Darling and Brown agreed on the need to shield front line services from cuts. The real tension came over Darling's desire to balance the protection for front line services with a number of bold and illustrative cuts which he believed, rightly, were needed to rescue Labour's crumbling credibility on the deficit. Brown, egged on by Balls, tried to block his Chancellor at each turn. One particular challenge came over welfare spending. Byrne had wanted to make a significant move on welfare reform, something explored at length by both Number 10 and the Treasury. According to one Number 10 source: '[Work and Pensions Secretary] Yvette Cooper fought a tough fight to protect her budget, and the integrity of pensions reforms against a Treasury raid. It went on until the early hours of 9 December, the day the PBR was announced.'[378] When Darling presented the Pre-Budget Report to Cabinet that morning, Cooper reportedly claimed that the style of the Treasury's departmental negotiation was: 'Macho and wrong, and that there were fairer ways of raising resources than delaying pensions reform for low earners.'[379] According to another present, 'the Cabinet were stunned and transfixed' by her outburst, though she was quickly consoled by Harman and others.[380] In the event, Cooper held out against cuts to welfare spending.

With welfare spending all but saved, the big question that remained was how much detail to give of other departmental spending decisions. Fundamental differences persisted from the summer, with Brown and Balls generally on one side of the debate, and Mandelson and Darling on the other. That division explains why so many key decisions on the Pre-Budget Report were resolved so late in the day – indeed, many details were finalised only in the final twenty-four hours. It also explained why the report was so light on detail. Settlements for many departments had been strongly contested right up until the eleventh hour – and past it in some cases. Particularly tenacious were Balls and Cooper, who were said to have 'harangued Darling and his civil servants continually'.[381] Balls accepts that his officials were haggling with Treasury over funding for 16- to 18-year-olds until the early hours but strongly denies the accusation that he personally rang Darling in the middle of the night.[382]

Chief Secretary Byrne was the principal enforcer on departmental settlements and oversaw the negotiations with spending ministers about where the cuts would fall on areas not deemed 'frontline services': the protected list included health, schools, police numbers and development. These areas were chosen by Brown's team to reflect the values they wanted to champion ahead of, and during, the election. One consequence of having so many protected areas was that Byrne was forced to get very tough with Cabinet colleagues in non-frontline demands.

After Darling had delivered his speech, the media response was almost uniformly negative. 'This partisan political Pre-Budget Report ill-serves the British public,' said William Buiter in the *Financial Times*.[383] Number 10 had expected, and largely discounted, such comments in advance. But it was pleased by the market reaction,[384] as well as by the public reaction monitored through its own focus groups. The political team at Number 10 were united. '[It was] what we had been arguing for,' says one senior aide.[385] 'It was not obvious to me that we could have done better,' says Pearce, while Muir describes it as a 'real success considering the circumstances'.[386]

How had the central disputes of the summer and autumn played out? Animosities between the Treasury and Number 10, both real and imagined, certainly played through into December. According to Number 10 political advisers, at a drinks party following the Pre-Budget Report in the Treasury, senior Treasury officials were openly critical of Brown and expressed their frustration that they had not achieved more public spending cuts. 'Alistair's own officials were criticising his own PBR: he was completely blameless himself, but why was he unable to control his people?' asks a Number 10 official. 'At this point, relationships really took a nosedive.'[387] The ire of the Treasury was directed at Balls, as reported by the BBC's Nick Robinson on 10 December. It all left a rather messy impression.

Insiders, though, felt relatively satisfied with where things had landed. A Treasury source calls the disputes between the Treasury and Number 10 'a score draw': 'Number 10 got their narrative and a national insurance increase, while Number 11 got more fiscal tightening and, more importantly, some spending reductions.'[388] One Number 10 insider reflects: 'Overall we got our message across about investment and unlocking the economy for the future. It was a pity though that it was blurred by those unguarded comments at a party by some Treasury officials.' High spirits at the Treasury aside, Number 10 felt it important that at last it had a clear narrative of the recession: the government was serious about halving the deficit within four years, made binding by its promise of a Fiscal Responsibility Bill; and health, schools and most of policing would not lose out.[389] Number 10 dates the improvement in the poll position, up to the mid-twenties by Christmas and 30 per cent subsequently, back to the Pre-Budget Report. 'After the PBR, people began to look more seriously at what we were saying, and increasingly began to question the Conservatives,' says Muir.[390] Number 10 had carried Darling to more or less where it wanted him to be, without his resigning, and with minimal leakage to the media this time of divisions. 'One sees a clarity in the message and a confidence which had hitherto been absent for much of Brown's premiership,' wrote one insider.[391] The day of the Pre-Budget Report, Nick Pearce sent a note to stakeholders which stated that the commitment to maintaining a strong welfare state, support for businesses and homeowners, and fairness in tax had meant that the social dislocation and injustice of previous recessions 'has not been experienced this time around'. 'In the New Year, we will set out further plans for our country's future,' the note continued.[392] In Number 10, with Christmas coming up, there was a definite sense of 'game on'.

On 1 December, rejoicing in Number 10 came with the publication of a ComRes poll in *The Independent*, indicating that Britain was 'heading for a hung parliament'. Although it put Labour on only 27 per cent, 10 per cent behind the Conservatives, the skewing of the national vote in favour of Labour meant the Conservatives would have been six short of an overall majority. A 'trend of slipping Conservative support that was apparent in many polls throughout last month … Cameron really does have reason to worry', was how John Curtice, a leading psephologist, described it in *The Independent*.[393]

Yet for all the successful compromises on the substance of policy, politically, the Pre-Budget Report remained something of an unhappy compromise. Though it had proved enough to calm the markets, and to minimise the effects on public services and the poorest, a political strategy required greater self-assurance. Byrne himself outlined the concern, saying: 'If we do not show that we are a party for all seasons, then quite simply, we won't be hired to work in all seasons.'[394] Mandelson, Darling and even Number 10 advisers themselves had done their best to respond to that concern, pushing Brown away from an anti-cuts message, to one about how fast and where to cut, a position more in keeping with the economic realities of the time. In truth, Brown's reticence had limited his government's ability to portray Labour as the party of progressive cuts as well as the party of investment. The great danger was that the public would feel that at a time of cuts they should hire the experts – and that would not be Brown.

9

Safe at Last

(January–April 2010)

Brown's three-year premiership saw almost constant threats to his survival as Prime Minister; only in his initial and final months was he totally secure. Ironically, it took a third and final attempted coup to make him safe at last from challenges. The arrival on his team in October 2008 of Blair's closest lieutenant, Peter Mandelson, had helped Brown to stabilise his position and to see off the second attempt to unseat him in June 2009. But being safe in Number 10 until the general election was one matter; surviving there beyond it, and offering the electorate a clear policy platform, was quite another. In these four months, from January to April, Brown knew that he had to build an overwhelming case for why Labour should be re-elected, and why he was uniquely qualified to lead it into the future.

Tory Wobble: December–January

How can Labour's recovery in the polls in the run-up to Christmas be explained? Brown himself was in good form, and was displaying a confidence and sureness of touch at PMQs, which suffused the PLP with confidence. On 2 December, he had put in what *The Times* thought was his 'most combative Commons performance for many months'.[1] He had dispatched Cameron dismissively: 'The voice may be that of a modern public relations man. But the mindset is that of the 1930s.' To roars of approval from his own benches, he had rounded on the Conservatives' controversial plans to raise the inheritance-tax threshold to £1m; this was the policy Osborne had pulled out of his hat in autumn 2007, and which was credited widely with precipitating Brown's catastrophic decision not to call an early election. However, this was now considered to be something of an Achilles heel for the Tories. Zac Goldsmith, the Conservative environment adviser and parliamentary candidate, who, like Cameron, had been a pupil at Eton College, was attacked for his 'non-dom' status. 'I have to say that with him [Cameron] and Mr Goldsmith, their inheritance tax policy seems to have been dreamt up on the playing fields of Eton,' said Brown.[2] Right-wing blogger Iain Dale wrote: 'Gordon Brown won the exchanges at PMQs today. It wasn't so much for what he said ... but the way he said it. For the first time he seemed comfortable without a script, and for once he was able to think on his feet. For the first time in his premiership, Brown got genuine, rather than orchestrated, cheers.'[3] Steve Richards of *The Independent* noticed a change of style, with Brown making a direct attack on his opponent and 'deploying humour in doing so'.[4] Simon Lewis told the lobby that Brown's newfound confidence was down to 'a very hearty breakfast. He is a full English kind of breakfast guy.'[5] Perhaps more important than the large breakfast he demolished each morning was the input since the autumn by Alastair Campbell into Brown's PMQs preparation.

Blair had mastered this forum; his performances inspired confidence, and he often enjoyed the occasion. Brown had found it a trial from day one. In his first year, PMQs preparation dominated his working week: he would spend much of Monday and Tuesday on it, and all of Wednesday morning. In his defence, he would say he needed to spend all this time mastering government-wide policy – it was his crash course in areas on which, despite being Chancellor for ten years, he had no background. But in his second year, he still set aside an incredible amount of time to get ready for PMQs: four hours on Monday, four on Tuesday, and, again, all of Wednesday morning. By his final year, he was spending roughly the same time as Blair had done: two hours on Tuesday, and some time on Wednesday morning. His core PMQs team – his Principal Private Secretary James Bowler, Theo Bertram and Nicholas Howard – found that the less time Brown spent, and the less he agonised about it, the better he became.[6] Campbell was only the last and most successful of the series of individuals – Geoff Hoon, Lucy Parker, Michael Wills and Shaun Woodward – on whom Brown would alight and draft in to help him prepare, only to drop them a while later. His parliamentary aides, like Ian Austin, would chip in with comments from the day's press. It could often be shambolic, especially early on.[7]

Blair trusted the material his team gave him, but Brown did not, and would interrogate the briefs he was handed, making notes on the back with his pen. His eyesight was often a real difficulty for him. As he found it so difficult to read his briefs quickly, he would try to memorise as much as he could, with the result that he placed the stress in the wrong places, made points in the wrong order and overlooked key messages – all of which was compounded by his poor sense of timing and flat tone. As a result, while he might win the argument, he'd often lose the debate. His team, listening to him in despair, would feel: 'We could always predict what DC [David Cameron] would say at PMQs. We never could with what GB would say.'[8] Getting the measure of Cameron was something he found very hard to do. 'He treats PMQs like a game,' Brown complained. 'But it is a game,' his team would say back to him.[9] 'Lighten up and make a joke,' Hoon would advise. 'I can't do that,' was the reply, which the Chief Whip found very revealing.[10] 'Why doesn't he ask me about the big issues of the day,' the Prime Minister regularly lamented at Number 10. 'He's only interested in gossip and innuendo.' Brown would often become intensely angry that he was unable to command PMQs as he wanted. He liked Parliament and was pleased when Number 10 told him his attendance in the chamber was much higher than Thatcher's or Blair's.[11] It took him the best part of two years to understand that PMQs were not the forum for him to announce new policy and that Cameron was playing on his weaknesses to embarrass and annoy him. '[Cameron] will ask you about the most embarrassing issue of the day, not the most important,' he would be told, yet it seemed continually to surprise him.[12]

'Gordon loved having Alastair around. I think he had got quite lonely at Number 10. He was visibly lifted whenever Alastair came into Number 10, and would relax immediately,' says Theo Bertram.[13] An official compared Campbell in action to 'watching the over-thirty-fives play at Wimbledon: full of lots of neat shots, but not exerting themselves fully'.[14] Campbell helped Brown to be more honest with himself and lifted not only the Prime Minister's spirits, but those of everyone else in Number 10. Like Mandelson, he was treated in Downing Street as a giant.

Campbell's advice prompted Brown into his attacks on the Tories' social class, a taboo area when Blair had been leader. The ground had been prepared by poll research for the party in September, by the Benenson Strategy Group, which showed that the electorate feared that, despite Cameron's 'marketing gloss', the party underneath had not changed. Brown's aides searched for ways to exploit that perception, and social class was one of them. 'Cameron went to a school that is a symbol of class and privilege, and a fairly big barrier to [his] efforts to present himself as someone who gets the life of most people,' Campbell wrote in his blog in early December.[15] Brown maintained this attack throughout December. 'I sometimes think the Conservatives do not understand that people on middle and low incomes cannot rely on private health, cannot rely on private education, cannot rely on private security,' he said in the *Daily Mirror*, under Campbell's prompting, just before Christmas.[16] Did the ploy work? The *Financial Times* thought so. Brown's attacks on the Tories as the party of privilege were responsible, it believed, for Labour's improved polls in December, by drawing median-income voters back to the party.[17]

Early signs of economic recovery were also assisting Labour; by Christmas, Number 10 noticed key indicators in the real economy all becoming more positive since the autumn. It had feared unemployment would increase up to the general election and beyond, but some indicators had it falling, and Number 10 began to look forward with some optimism to 'Q4', i.e. fourth quarter figures (from October to December), which were due in late January.[18] Repossessions had been another major worry, with the possibility of their rising to 100,000 that year, which would have disastrous consequences for middle-class confidence. The government's swiftly enacted housing measures helped ensure that repossessions did not become the major problem that they had been in the 1990–92 recession. Insolvencies were a final worry, yet these, too, did not prove the problem that Number 10 had feared, and they reached only half the rate they had during the early 1990s downturn. Business and consumer surveys started showing increased confidence in the weeks leading up to Christmas, and small business looked buoyant. In contrast to the distressing news the year before of the closing of Woolworths, John Lewis reported a 15 per cent boost in pre-Christmas sales.[19]

A new strategy was crystallising in Number 10. 'The decision was to be optimistic and to show that the Tories had made an enormous error in emphasising the need for austerity and big cuts,' says Justin Forsyth.[20] The Pre-Budget Report, Brown felt, imparted a great sense of clarity to the Labour cause. It promised to protect frontline services – particularly health and education – and the most vulnerable in society, while avoiding the negative aura of cuts. Brown was feeling vindicated in his argument against the Treasury. Labour ministers sensed that the pessimistic note that the Conservatives had sounded at their Manchester conference in October had been too funereal, and they accused the Tories of feeling 'glee' at the prospect of making cuts.[21] While Labour was emerging in good shape from the recession, the Conservatives, having been forced off the 'detoxification' agenda devised by their strategist Steve Hilton, seemed to be knocked off course. They appeared to have lost their self-confidence, and to have retreated into a gloomy place where they were intent on looking after their own.[22]

Anxious to maintain momentum, Number 10 devised a 'military operation' for January, entailing 'a fresh story every day', with a different minister attacking the Tories. 'The preparation for Christmas through to the New Year period was better than last year,' records a contemporary diary.[23] Over the holiday, Number 10 deliberately set out to repair its fractured relations with the Treasury and closely worked with it and with the policy team at the Labour Party's Victoria Street headquarters to produce a 148-page document exposing a 'credibility gap' in the Conservatives' fiscal policies. Since the summer, Number 10 had been anxious to get at their spending proposals. However, it was only when the Treasury team – now free of the Pre-Budget Report – joined them that the vital detail and rigour was provided.[24] 'We worked like dogs on this document with Darling's team of Sam White, Catherine McLeod and Torsten Henricson-Bell. There was a fantastic esprit de corps. It felt like we were the Labour Party again getting ready for an election campaign,' says Muir.[25] So, when Cameron launched his election campaign with a speech at the Oxford School of Drama on 2 January, promising that tackling the deficit would be a future Tory government's top priority, Labour was ready to strike.

'One of us is going to have an interesting day,' said Muir to Cameron's chief of staff Ed Llewellyn when he bumped into him on the morning of 4 January, the launch day for Labour's counter-attack. 'They had their big poster launch, and we decided we were going to bugger it up for them. We made their spectacle a disaster,' says Muir.[26] Number 10 had drawn on the experience of the Conservative Chancellor Norman Lamont (1990–93), who had attacked Labour's spending plans to devastating effect in the run-up to the 1992 election.[27] Dan Corry, who had worked for Labour during that period, remembered its effectiveness all too clearly, and was delighted that the Conservatives were now receiving the same treatment. Labour accused the Conservatives of a £34bn 'credibility gap' in their fiscal policies; the Opposition's tax policies, Labour argued, would cost some £45bn, compared to only £11bn in savings so far identified. 'Complete junk,' was Cameron's immediate response to the Labour document.[28] So, who was right? The authoritiative Channel 4 News 'FactCheck' blog concluded that Labour's figures were exaggerated but that nevertheless the 'credibility gap' highlighted in its document was real.

Cameron was forced on to the back foot. Questioned by the BBC later on 4 January about tax breaks for married couples, he said that, because of the 'vast' deficit, he was not certain that he would be able to introduce the measure during the first parliament of a Tory government. Realising at once that he had made a slip under pressure on a key Tory commitment, he released a statement before the end of the day pulling back. 'Recognising marriage in the tax system is something I feel very strongly about and something that we will definitely do in the next parliament,' he said. 'We will set out exactly how in due course.'[29] Labour's attack had unnerved the Conservatives and had damaged their plan to launch their manifesto incrementally in the lead-up to the general election.

Worse still was in store for the Tories at PMQs on 6 January. In the first session of the New Year, Brown reprised the confidence he had displayed in December. With Cameron in trouble, the Prime Minister quipped: 'He is the person who cannot give a straight answer on the married couple's allowance – he cannot say "I do" or "I don't".'[30] Brown then stuck the knife in further. 'He cannot go round the country promising everything to everyone,' he said when attacking Cameron for the '£34bn gap in his proposals'. The Tory leader's clumsiness was exploited ruthlessly. Long attacked himself for lacking a coherent agenda, Brown now shifted the criticism on to his opponent: 'He said one thing on Monday morning, something different on Monday afternoon, and something different on Monday evening.'[31] Brown then pounced on inheritance tax policy, delighting Labour's benches with an assault on the Conservatives for offering huge tax breaks to the wealthiest, while arguing that their policies on the deficit would punish the most vulnerable.

But even while Brown was landing some of his most effective blows on the Conservatives of his entire premiership, his personal position again came into question. Despite the greater optimism in the polls and in the economy, many in Cabinet and the Parliamentary Labour Party were concerned that they would suffer badly at the fast-approaching general election if Brown remained at the helm. The Prime Minister's own standing had barely improved from the November poll that had shown that 59 per cent of the electorate were dissatisfied with his leadership, compared to only 34 per cent who were happy.[32] The talk in Cabinet was that a hung parliament was the likely outcome. Many believed that a fresh leader, even this late in the day, might just tip Labour into the lead. Number 10 despaired at 'the sense of deep pessimism' that infected some ministers.[33] It was a sign that all was not well. But no one gave serious thought to the stony faces of Harriet Harman sitting on his right, and Jack Straw next to her on the government benches, as Brown rose to give a commanding performance at PMQs on 6 January. Little did he know what was going through their minds.

Brown and Mandelson Fall Out: December–January

From the moment he arrived in his Cabinet in October 2008, Brown was dependent upon Mandelson as his ultimate guarantor. The high point of his value to Brown came during the James Purnell resignation crisis in June 2009. His cutting adrift of Brown in January 2010 now paved the way and encouraged a further coup, which might even have unseated the Prime Minister. How did their relationship, so close from late 2008 to early to mid-2009, unravel so quickly? Mandelson had paid a high price for his support for Brown, from Blair himself, and in the cold hostility from the Blairite ultras, when they saw him prolong the Brown premiership. He was never wholly at ease with his new role as Brown's friend, especially not when the criticisms mounted.

Brown's refusal to accept the need for cuts in public spending marked the earliest major policy rift between him and Mandelson. Having expended great efforts to manoeuvre Brown into talking about cuts in his TUC conference speech in September, the Prime Minister's subsequent distancing of himself from this position irritated the Business Secretary intensely. Number 10 attributed Brown's nervousness about the subject to 'Peter spending a lot of time talking to journalists, many of them right-wing, who were rattling his cage on cuts rather than talking to ordinary voters'.[34] Mandelson's anger flared up again during the December Pre-Budget Report, when he supported Darling's call for a rise in VAT, and when he thought Brown had lost the opportunity to seize the initiative by framing the 'economic debate ahead of the election'.[35] 'Peter wanted to shift the cuts argument on to new territory,' says former Mandelson adviser Patrick Diamond.[36] Instead, he saw his old nemesis, Ed Balls, whom he had worked with closely for much of the previous year, replacing him again as the Prime Minister's key adviser and using this position to secure big increases in spending for schools, which made the Business Secretary 'really furious'.[37] 'Peter thought the [Pre-Budget Report] was our last opportunity to present a clear political message about what we stood for,' recalls Michael Dugher. 'He was worried we were running out of time to set out our stall.'[38] He showed his anger by keeping away from Brown and not attending the Monday-afternoon strategy sessions at Number 10. In his first months back, Mandelson had been a very regular presence at Number 10, forever plonking himself down on the seat in Brown's study in Number 12, or chatting to everyone round the horseshoe. But after the Pre-Budget Report, 'he was hardly seen at all', and, in the words of one senior Number 10 official, he had become 'semi-detached'.[39] For Brown and Balls, normal service continued. 'They had a telepathic relationship to the end,' says Andrew Adonis.[40]

Mandelson's disillusion with Brown's handling of the Pre-Budget Report came on top of a growing frustration with the Prime Minister's modus operandi. Mandelson was infuriated by Brown's dysfunctional working practices, his failure to guide his Cabinet colleagues better, and by the lack of definition in his agenda.[41] 'The endless conversations that produced no decisions at the end of them really began to irritate Peter,' says his special adviser, Patrick Loughran.[42] On top of this came Mandelson's anger that Brown had not secured his candidacy for the position of the EU High Representative. 'Gordon knew that Peter would not forgive him,' says one close observer.[43] Mandelson became 'very annoyed that [Brown] hadn't pushed his candidacy more'.[44] He preferred to blame the Prime Minister rather than accept his own shortcomings. Number 10 took some time to work out that 'EU leaders were telling Mandelson to his face that he would be great as High Representative, but at the same time telling us in colourful terms that they would never have him'.[45]

With no exit strategy back to Brussels, Mandelson's fortunes were pinned inexorably to the mast of the Labour Party. This created serious problems for him, because, as he joked in October, he feared the government was 'finished'.[46] Others in Cabinet shared this conviction. From the end of the party conference season, an understanding had sprung up among ministers: 'We searched desperately for a winning formula, accepting that we had Gordon at our head, and that he was one of our biggest electoral challenges, but with Peter the pivotal figure telling Gordon when he had to take decisions and advising him what they should be,' recalls an insider.[47]

Worse still for Mandelson, Brown was not engaging properly, as he saw it, with the need to formulate a coherent election strategy. The previous months had seen a struggle between Mandelson and Douglas Alexander over control of the election strategy. In April 2009, the latter had worked up a presentation with Philip Gould of fifteen to twenty slides, outlining Labour's strategy for electoral recovery, and presented it to Mandelson. There had been no follow-up, and when Alexander spoke to Brown over the summer, it was clear to Alexander that Mandelson had not told Brown anything about the presentation. So, he duly sent it to him at Number 10 himself. When again nothing transpired, Alexander, of his own accord, set up a group involving Gould and Loughran, and bringing back Spencer Livermore. Other ministers, too, were becoming agitated by the lack of election preparation; Harman told Brown in November: 'We have got to have structures. We've got to have organisation. We've got to work out our strategy.'[48] The group set up by Alexander to produce a strategy for four weeks from mid-November, presented an election 'war book' to Brown on the last day of the parliament before Christmas, emailing another copy to him in North Queensferry on 23 December.[49] The document advocated what they termed a 'look again' strategy, as explained by Loughran: 'It asked the electorate to look "more closely" at Cameron and Brown and to assess them accordingly.'[50]

Mandelson had been on a ministerial trip to India before Christmas, and he was only briefly back in London before leaving for a holiday in Marrakesh. While in town, he wrote Brown a long email, summarising the main points in the war book. He was infuriated that 'Gordon refused to engage properly' with him on it.[51] 'Peter was very, very down in the run-up to Christmas,' recalls a Number 10 aide.[52] Sensing Mandelson's rejectionist mood, some Cabinet colleagues – who had never been totally sure of him before – became more and more open about their own reservations about Brown's leadership. This was of great concern to Brown's staff, who were aware of what Mandelson had done for Brown following James Purnell's resignation. 'The defeatists really put Peter's wind up over the Christmas period. We began to worry about him and the Peter–Gordon relationship,' says Muir. When Brown's calls to Mandelson were not returned, he became increasingly alarmed by his silence.[53]

The press picked up on this disharmony, as it usually did if Mandelson was involved. 'Over the Christmas holiday, we started to read a lot of stuff about Cabinet dissatisfaction in the press,' says a Number 10 insider.[54] 'Labour MPs hatching a new plot to oust Gordon Brown' was a headline in the *Daily Mail* on Boxing Day.[55] Brown began thinking: 'I wonder if Tony's winding Peter up.' 'That's ridiculous. Don't be paranoid,' his political aides told him, although, as events unfolded, they wondered whether they had been naive.[56] Nevertheless, Muir, Forsyth and Nye were all increasingly anxious for Brown's position. Political secretary Joe Irvin, whose job it was to keep on top of the mood in the PLP, thought Brown's backbenchers were in a much better place than they had been, buoyed by Labour's boost in the polls. 'It's all okay, there's nothing to worry about,' he said.[57] Brown made a point of phoning Harman and Straw from Scotland over the Christmas holidays, to check that they were in the right place, but picked up no signals from them to cause undue alarm.[58] He had a calmer Christmas than usual. 'He is not calling us every ten minutes, he is much steadier and much more reflective. When he calls it is to say what is the plan and we tell him, and he accepts what we say,' reads the entry in a contemporary diary.[59] When he came back down from Scotland, he gave a fighting performance on the *Andrew Marr Show* on Sunday 3 January, repeatedly deflecting his interviewer when he tried to draw him out on the date of the general election.

The fast-approaching general election was exactly what was troubling Cabinet that Christmas and New Year. With the exception of Balls, Ed Miliband and Chief Whip Nick Brown, Brown had no staunch allies left there. The big beasts had all lost faith in him: Harman, Straw, Darling, David Miliband, Alan Johnson, Tessa Jowell and Alexander. The inclusion in the list of that last name, a man who owed his political career to Brown's patronage, was particularly significant.[60] None was, however, prepared to move against Brown as long as Mandelson was standing guard at his door. But when they became aware that the Business Secretary shared their own doubts, the geological strata began to shift. 'Almost everywhere I looked, and for everyone I talked to, the question was whether Gordon would – and perhaps should – throw in the towel,' Mandelson writes.[61] He kept his views to himself during the late autumn, although he did admit to David Miliband in a conversation on Remembrance Sunday that he 'did not think we could win with Gordon, as things stood'. He even admitted that he feared the scale of defeat could be colossal.[62] Brown's Cabinet had long been frustrated that their leader wasn't a team player. They felt he had not developed any sense of collective endeavour, and had grown tired of his attitude of: 'You're either with me or against me.'[63] Brown in turn had no higher opinion of them and remained deeply reluctant to delegate to those he did not fully trust. 'He ran a closed shop,' says David Miliband.[64] Shortly before the Christmas break, Darling phoned Mandelson to say: 'We're going to lose ... We all know what the real problem is. It's not because of what the government is doing. It's who's leading it.'[65]

Mandelson knew in his bones that Darling was right, and had done for some months. He changed subtly from seeing Brown as a liability to be managed, to a liability that could be dispensed with. The Purnell coup in June, he thought, was too early, and the economic outlook was too uncertain, for a change. Give it time. See if he improved, if the polls picked up. But neither happened.[66] Charles Clarke was the figure who had agitated most continuously against Brown's leadership since 2007. In November, he went to see Mandelson in his rooms in the Cabinet Office. What he told Clarke was explosive: 'Gordon will lose the election. I will not do anything to precipitate his departure, but, if others do, I will not intervene to defend him as I did in June.'[67]

In his memoirs, Mandelson claims he had 'known nothing about [the] plan' for unseating Brown that was about to unfold.[68] Clarke's claim to have spoken to Mandelson before Christmas suggests otherwise. Clarke relayed his conversation to Patricia Hewitt, adding that Mandelson had said he thought it inappropriate for him to lead the coup himself 'as a member of the House of Lords'. She, Geoff Hoon and Clarke all saw that as 'a very significant shift in Peter Mandelson's position since the summer' and 'it certainly encouraged [them] to go ahead'.[69] Mandelson later admitted privately that he regretted, with hindsight, his intervention to save Brown during the Purnell coup.[70] His memoirs do not mention the claims that he tacitly encouraged the plotters and considerably boosted their chances of success.

The Harman Coup: January

'Harriet was behind it', a senior figure told us a couple of days after the coup. For the first edition, however, it was hard to find irrefutable evidence to stand up that claim. But now a succession of former Cabinet ministers have verified to us that Harriet Harman was indeed the instigator of the January 2010 coup. From the summer of 2009 onwards, many in the Cabinet and on the backbenches were despairing of Brown and there was widespread agreement that there should be one final attempt to oust him. Harman progressively lined up the big Cabinet ministers including Straw, Darling, Jowell and Alexander. She spoke to David Miliband in October to gauge his support, telling him she already had big players behind her. She cornered Bob Ainsworth on a flight back from Belfast in early December. The message to all of them was the same. Brown's performance and lack of direction would spell disaster in the coming general election and they had to act now. Miliband told her it would only work if there was 'overwhelming support' from the Cabinet. 'We have it,' she told her colleagues and fellow conspirators. Her list contained some surprising names. Alexander had been one of Brown's closest confidants when Chancellor but he had lost faith in him. As for Darling, he was sick to death of fighting Brown on economic policy and was disgusted by Balls's *modus operandi*. Straw was cautious as ever but he was prepared to act if he was sure the heavyweights were on board. Alan Johnson was in the minority in not wanting to go along with the plot; he told Ainsworth he had been burnt once and did not want to push his luck again.

On the backbenches, former Cabinet ministers Clarke, Hoon and Hewitt were all working in a similar direction, but initially independently of Harman. They were aware that significant Cabinet support must be secured if any potential coup were to succeed. Hoon and Hewitt told Clarke that they were reasonably confident of support from Harman and David Miliband – the latter had hinted via intermediaries that he thought it should come at the very beginning of the New Year.[71] 'For that reason, we held off doing it in November or December because we thought that support at that level would make a major difference to the whole success,' says Clarke.[72] Clarke set about preparing a plan for triggering a leadership election and, more importantly, completing the contest quickly, so that the party had a new leader in time for the election. He gave a copy of the plan to Harman before Christmas, who was 'very interested' in what he proposed.[73] He also spoke at length to David Miliband, who repeated what he had said to Harman, telling Clarke that 'it needed overwhelming force from Cabinet to be successful'.[74]

The plans began to come together in discussions before Christmas, when discontent about Brown was expressed, but it was decided to delay more detailed conversation until a New Year's Eve get-together at Harman's home near Woodbridge in Suffolk.[75] Complaint followed complaint about Brown's leadership there. 'The consensus was that, for the sake of our party, we needed to change the leader, and this was our last chance of doing it,' recalls one of those present.[76] Everyone, including Harman, was absolutely insistent that 'we have to make a go and get rid of him', recalls another attendee.[77]

What should they do? Harman, as Deputy Leader, was in a very delicate position. However convinced she might be that she was acting in the party's interests, moving against a sitting Prime Minister, and risking disruption so close to an election that could rebound very negatively, was a huge move for one so senior. She made it clear that 'something had to be done' and said she was 'willing to confront Brown herself', but the ground had to be firmed up before taking such a giant step.[78] How might the move be instigated? Mention was made of a rallying article criticising Brown's leadership that Hoon was known to be considering. Hoon, as Darling's closest ally, was a senior figure, but no longer the big player he had once been. Hewitt, with much less to lose than Harman, both because she was a backbencher and because of her public plans to step down at the election, said she would talk to Hoon as soon she was back in London, to test out the ground. She was anxious to provide cover for Harman, who had been a long-established friend since their time together at the National Council for Civil Liberties (the forerunner of Liberty) in the 1970s, and was willing to risk the limelight herself to set a rebellion in train, if that was what was needed.[79]

Number 10 had no inkling of what was happening in Suffolk but was alarmed enough by a 'splutter of musketry' in and around Westminster.[80] On 30 December, Clarke, testing the water rather than firing a starting gun, posted a blog saying: 'All the evidence suggests that Brown's leadership reduces Labour's support'.[81] On New Year's Eve, the MP Barry Sheerman released a statement calling on Brown to resign, saying: 'We need new leadership and new thinking'.[82] The same day, dissident MP Greg Pope released a statement saying that Brown was disastrously unpopular.[83]

These were mere sideshows, however, to the real battleground, which was being marshalled by Hewitt and Hoon. By late 2009, Hoon's never very strong relationship with Brown had broken down completely. He had been demoted from Cabinet in the June 2009 reshuffle and was very disappointed to have been overlooked for the EU High Representative position in November, admitting later it 'was certainly a factor with me'.[84] In his view, Brown was leading Labour towards an electoral disaster that might be avoided if a new leader were installed. 'I came back from the Christmas recess even more disillusioned with Gordon,' he says.[85] A series of conversations with family and friends, and listening to people saying 'they voted Labour in the past but would not do so again as long as Brown remained its leader', had hardened him. A final catalyst was a conversation over Christmas lunch with his family about the state of the party and the Prime Minister. Hewitt was not a close colleague, personally or politically, but when she spoke to him on 1 January, he was struck that his former Cabinet colleague had reached the same conclusions as himself. 'I didn't want, on the day after the general election, to be looking around the battlefield seeing so many good colleagues who had lost their seats. I wanted to see if I could do something about it. That was the spur for me,' says Hewitt.[86] Her disappointment at having been one of the few prominent Blairites to be demoted from Cabinet when Brown entered office had seen her relationship with Brown deteriorate markedly and was doubtless also a factor.[87] Hoon and Hewitt thus believed they were acting in the interests of the party. But both were also motivated by personal grudges with Brown.

Hoon had been mulling over his planned article explaining why Brown should no longer be Prime Minister. He told Clarke about this just before the weekend and Clarke relayed the information to Hewitt. She said to Clarke that they had to stop him, because if the plot failed to topple Brown it would mean the Tories plastering their billboards up and down the country with quotes from the article saying that Brown was unfit to be Prime Minister.[88] The three of them talked together over the weekend of 2–3 January and came up with a plan to ditch the article and instead release a joint letter from Hewitt and Hoon on Tuesday evening. The letter would avoid any personal attack on Brown, demand a vote of the PLP to 'settle the issue once and for all', and be designed to create a 'media firestorm', to give disillusioned members of Cabinet the platform to come out against Brown.[89] 'The aim was to provide room for Cabinet to go in and say: "You can see you've lost support; you have to go for the sake of the party."'[90]

The three former Cabinet ministers knew they would have to speak directly to Cabinet themselves, but were nervous about doing so because they were not certain whom they could trust and 'whether it would get back to Number 10'.[91] Over the New Year dinner, names had been mentioned of ministers on whom they felt they could count – Ainsworth, Alexander, Jim Murphy and David Miliband.[92] Hewitt thought about speaking to Straw, always the mystery man when it came to the crunch, but decided that she did not know enough about where he stood, and worried that he might feel he had to inform Number 10.[93] They also wanted to ensure that ministers could say 'hand on heart' that they had not spoken to either Hewitt or Hoon themselves and were thus not part of any 'plot'. The atmosphere among Cabinet ministers on the Monday and Tuesday was 'extremely tense'.[94] Based on their soundings, Hoon and Hewitt decided to delay their letter from Tuesday evening until Wednesday afternoon, keen to avoid the accusation that they had sabotaged PMQs by handing Cameron ammunition to use against Brown. On the Tuesday evening, Harman told one Cabinet minister that 'something was about to happen', and 'not to come out and support Brown' when it did.[95] Hoon and Hewitt remembered all too well how Number 10 had been able to muster support during the evening when Purnell resigned by picking off people individually, and they wanted to give Cabinet ministers the maximum opportunity in the afternoon 'to talk quietly to each other to decide what to do'.[96]

Totally unknown to Hoon, Hewitt and Clarke, in the atmosphere of high anxiety and fear about what might leak out, another critical initiative was being hatched. Jowell and Straw, who was felt still to be smarting at not having been made Deputy Prime Minister in the June reshuffle,[97] were holding their own conversations about the 'Brown problem'. They, too, had spoken to each other just after the New Year and had agreed to see Brown and tell him that he would have to 'think very hard about remaining as leader'.[98] Jowell saw him at 6pm on Monday 4 January and her understanding was that Straw would see him at 7pm. Jowell called Stewart Wood in Number 10 to arrange an immediate meeting with Brown. In she marched and reportedly told him: 'I want to see you because this is a conversation only you and I can have.' He replied: 'Let's be clear, I have asked to see you.' They bickered over who had requested the meeting before Jowell moved on to her purpose. 'It's not fair, but you're costing the Labour Party a considerable degree of support,' she is said to have told him. 'Tony told me that if ever he was an encumbrance to the Labour Party, I must tell him. I feel I owe it to you Gordon, to tell you directly that this is now the case. I will never talk to the press about it, but you should still know what I think.' Piling on the agony, she continued: 'Even at the end, Tony still had six people in Cabinet who would die for him; you have only one, Ed Balls … It's not fair, but people don't like you. They don't understand you. But fifty MPs are going to lose their seats because of you. If you decide to carry on, I'll continue to support you, but you owe it to the Labour Party to think again.' At that point, Brown's morale apparently collapsed and he asked: 'Are you telling me I have to go?' She replied: 'No. You have to think very hard whether or not it's right for the Labour Party for you to stand down.'[99]

He rallied and came back with the argument that the Labour Party would fragment in six directions and that his unique ability was to hold it together. No one could be certain that any successor would be able to achieve that, he said. At that point, their meeting was interrupted by a call from UN Secretary-General Ban Ki-moon. Jowell said that they needed to continue their conversation urgently and talk a second time, and he agreed. Before they could meet again, leaks spread from Number 10 that she was about to resign. She was livid, but Michael Dugher and Sue Nye hotly denied to her that they had been responsible for the briefing.[100] The stories were circulated round the press. 'Jowell denies resignation rumours' was the headline in the *Daily Mirror* above a story about rumours spreading around Westminster tea rooms of a possible plot to remove Brown as Labour leader ahead of the general election.[101] Mandelson was Jowell's protector, and when he heard that Number 10 had briefed this against her, he went 'ballistic', shouting down the line to Number 10: 'How dare you bully her.' They had never heard him more angry.[102] But what of Straw? Jowell called him on the Monday evening to see how his own meeting had gone: 'I ran out of time,' he told her, and was thus unable to raise the question of Brown's future with him.[103]

The Jowell foray was inconsequential. The action now shifted back to the main drama: the Hoon/Hewitt letter, postponed from Tuesday evening to arrive in Labour MPs' email inboxes just as PMQs was ending. Earlier that morning, a number of ministers and MPs had received a text message from Clarke telling them to 'stand by for a significant development straight after PMQs'.[104] At 10.59am on Wednesday, MPs received a blank email sent by Hoon. If MPs saw it before they went into the chamber, they clearly thought nothing of it. Hoon had sent the empty email unintentionally.[105] Then, at 12.26pm, he sent round the real email, signed off: 'Yours fraternally, Geoff Hoon and Patricia Hewitt'. It opened: 'Dear Colleague, As we move towards a general election, it remains the case that the Parliamentary Labour Party is deeply divided over the question of the leadership … We have … come to the conclusion that the only way to resolve this issue would be to allow every member to express their view in a secret ballot … This is a clear opportunity to finally lay this matter to rest.'[106] Contrary to what they were later to say in public, Hoon and Hewitt were clear that 'laying the matter to rest' meant 'it being settled against GB'.[107]

PMQs began at 12 noon and soon Brown was trouncing Cameron over the married couple's allowance. Labour MPs were enjoying the spectacle, but towards the session's end, the atmosphere began to change. Tory MPs started picking up news on their BlackBerrys about the Hoon/Hewitt letter. Cameron's Parliamentary Private Secretary, Desmond Swayne, passed his BlackBerry to the Tory Leader, and some Opposition MPs began waving 'bye-bye' to Brown, who was completely unaware of what was going on. Bertram, who was watching PMQs, sent someone out to check Sky News. Outside the Chamber, the news of the Hoon/Hewitt letter was everywhere. Would the Conservatives be able to capitalise on it and humiliate Brown during the PMQs? Sensing their last chance, the BlackBerry was passed to Conservative backbencher Ann Winterton, and she was told what was going on outside. 'If she had asked a question about the coup, it would have been a total disaster for GB, but mercifully she didn't change course and asked about wind farms. Tory ineptitude saved us from disaster,' says Bertram.[108] Winterton had asked a question at Blair's last PMQs and, for a few nervous minutes, Brown's team feared history might repeat itself, this time with Brown at the despatch box.

Without telling Brown, so as not to unnerve him, Number 10 had picked up on the coup that morning. Michael Dugher had been special adviser to Hoon, and they had remained close. 'In the morning, we began hearing really bad things via Michael, who thought Geoff was being mad. We knew that something was going to happen that day,' says a Number 10 official.[109] Just after 11pm, Nye called Mandelson for advice and told him they had decided 'not to tell Gordon about it before his despatch box bout with Cameron'. 'Don't overreact,' he said. 'You've got to be relaxed today. You don't need the same kind of operation we had when James Purnell left.' Reacting strongly, he told her, would only give the coup credence, and putting up anyone in front of the cameras to speak in support of Brown would be an error.[110] 'Peter took the decision that Cabinet ministers should not go out and make a speech and that it should be treated as an episode of no import,' says an aide. Number 10, for all their regard for Mandelson, now debated whether he was playing games with them. The conclusion is telling. A senior aide reveals: 'We decided that we would not take any notice of the advice he gave us.'[111]

Since the autumn, Blair had been following intently the various discussions about the Brown question. Blair had despaired of him, but was fierce that no one could say he had been a party to, or had foreknowledge of, any plot. He spoke to Peter Mandelson on the morning of the Hoon/Hewitt coup, and they agreed that Mandelson should not positively encourage it, but that neither should he 'go into overdrive' as he had done when Purnell resigned.[112] Jowell, one of his closest confidantes, is adamant that she did not discuss her planned visit to Brown with Blair.[113] As always, Blair was resolute that he would not do to Brown what

Thatcher had done to Major. On Wednesday morning, an angry Mandelson had spoken to Brown himself on the phone, and, according to Loughran, 'they had their worst row' since Mandelson's return in October 2008.[114] The proximate cause was disagreement over a speech Mandelson was to give, over which he was furious at what he regarded as unacceptable intervention in his affairs from Number 10. Then, just after the news of the coup had broken, he told Nye, when she asked if he would take a call from Brown: 'I'm in such a bad mood with him I'm not sure what I would say.'[115] Mandelson went to lunch with the French economist Alain Minc, during which he claimed to have been out of any kind of touch. When he returned to life in the early afternoon, he spoke to Miliband, who told him about planned visits to Number 10 by Darling, Harman and Straw. What was Mandelson's thinking? Loughran admits: 'From 'Number 10's point of view, Peter's silence would have looked very threatening, especially given their row earlier in the day.'[116] Number 10 saw nothing to alter its belief that he was deliberately standing aside and 'letting events happen'.[117] It was as if he was saying to Brown, as one Number 10 aide put it: 'If you get a grip on the election and do what I want, I'll be there for you.'[118]

Simon Lewis saw Brown before he went into PMQs. He had just presided over the briefing to the lobby, where no journalist had given any hint of any move about to happen, although there was some 'turbulence' around Jowell's denials the night before about whether she would resign. Minutes later, when Lewis learned about the letter, his first thought was: 'How can this man who clearly commands such authority on the world's stage be under such attack by his party here?'[119] Events began to unfold very speedily. Just after 1pm, Hoon told BBC Radio 4 that Labour was failing to get its message across, and he restated his call for the leadership issue to be resolved one way or the other, repeating that he had not himself spoken to any members of Cabinet (a claim Hewitt could not make).[120] In Number 10, it was all hands on deck. Once again, the team were working the phones to rally support behind Brown. At 1.26pm, PLP chairman Tony Lloyd gave a clear indication to the media that the calls for a leadership ballot had no support whatever among backbenchers, who had cheered Brown on against Cameron in the Commons that lunchtime. 'This represents a pinprick, fundamental miscalculation and a side-show,' concluded Lloyd.[121] Number 10 later described his intervention as 'useful but not decisive'.[122] Many in the PLP were angry at this move, made by two MPs who would not themselves have to face the electorate at the election. Even some of the backbenchers who were not huge fans of Brown criticised Hoon and Hewitt. John Mann, one of only a few Labour MPs not to nominate Brown for the leadership, very significantly and prominently dismissed the affair as 'sour grapes'.[123] This strong show of support for Brown by the PLP was to be critical. Although the coup intended to achieve its objectives by encouraging an uprising against Brown by members of a disillusioned Cabinet, the fact that the PLP came out so vociferously in opposition would have done little to encourage Cabinet sceptics to act.

Shortly after PMQs, Lloyd had spoken to Alan Johnson, viewed by some as a potential successor. 'It's daft,' Johnson had told him. 'That's what I am going to say.'[124] At 2.15pm the PLP issued a statement saying that a secret ballot would be 'unconstitutional', while Tony Woodley, the influential joint General Secretary of the UNITE trade union, said a secret ballot call was unwelcome and divisive. Once again, the unions had remained loyal to Brown; they never moved against him during his premiership.[125]

To journalists, it was clear by early afternoon that the coup was not going to succeed. Their puzzle was not the noise from the PLP, but the silence from Cabinet, which was slow to declare its loyalty. The first Cabinet minister to emerge to defend Brown was Andy Burnham, who said, at 1.32pm: 'The whole thing is puzzling just after Gordon demolished David Cameron at Prime Minister's Questions.' Then Shaun Woodward appeared at 1.56pm, following Mandelson, who, at 2.07pm had put out a written message via an aide that 'no one should overreact to this initiative', words that could mean anything to anyone.[126] Ed Balls then emerged on the street outside Downing Street to give a thumping rallying statement: 'This afternoon is a diversion, but I think it is a damp squib. We will move beyond it very quickly. The country will think we've lost our marbles.'[127] Balls's appearance seemed only to highlight the absence of the Cabinet big beasts. What were they doing?

The express idea behind the email of creating a media 'firestorm', so that Harman and other Cabinet ministers could confront Brown and tell him a ballot must be called, was not running according to plan.[128] The core message spread by Harman and the other leading critics was that ministers should keep away from the cameras. 'The silence from Cabinet was very deliberate and very planned. Cabinet was told: "For goodness' sake don't say anything." Those who remained silent had all agreed to do so,' says one insider.[129] Harman and Straw met in the former's office room in the House from 1.30pm to 2.30pm to discuss what they would do, with Alan Johnson present for some of the discussion. Iain Bundred came over from Number 10 and asked Straw and Harman in the ministerial corridor as they disappeared into her room: 'When are you going to come out and speak for Gordon?' They told him: 'We've just got to have a meeting.'[130] Jowell was also called by Brown's team but, still seething from the briefing operation launched against her, replied bluntly that she would not make the public declaration of loyalty to the Prime Minister sought by Downing Street.[131] Alan Johnson was spoken to by Number 10 but, regardless of what he told Tony Lloyd, he flatly refused to support Brown in public then and there. 'I'm not going to be boxed in,' he told Brown's team.[132] When phoned by Number 10, Straw said he would put out a supportive statement but then 'disappeared for hours'.[133] Jowell, Hoon, Hewitt and Clarke had always been nervous over whether he would have the stomach to join them, and induced his friends, including George Howarth and Janet Anderson, to lobby him in the days before the coup attempt, to stiffen his resolve.[134]

As Number 10 desperately tried to persuade the Cabinet to come out in public opposition to the plot, in Harman's Commons office, one of the most important meetings of Brown's premiership – and one of the most shrouded in mystery – was continuing. When Harman suggested to Johnson that a leadership ballot might be 'what the PLP and party wants', he believed he was being sounded out by them to see if he wanted to become leader. Before Christmas, Straw had said to him that, when things start to happen: 'It has to be you.'[135] But Johnson did not want to be leader, and he told Harman and Straw the plan was crazy; it was too late, and he did not support any move against Brown.[136] With Johnson so opposed, with the PLP so publicly dismissive, and with other Cabinet ministers so evasive, Harman came to the inevitable conclusion that the game was up.

Darling, who was not involved in the planning of the plot, but who had been kept informed of developments through his Parliamentary Private Secretary, Ann Coffey MP, and Hoon himself, recognised that Brown's position that afternoon was weak. Key Cabinet ministers were invisible and mute; now was the time to extract the concessions from Brown on economic policy he had sought for so long. At about 3pm, the Chancellor went to see Brown. Sensing the strength of his position, he demanded that Brown be far stronger in future about tackling the deficit and speaking about cuts. Darling's views about Brown were complex: for all his profound reservations and anger at how Brown had behaved, he still questioned whether this was the right time to push him out. He also felt that the plot was very poorly organised and worried that it would backfire on the party. What of David Miliband? He was not visible in Westminster, but was aware of what was going on, and knew of the movements of most of the key players.[137] With leadership ambitions of his own, he was desperate not to be the only one to wield the knife. Throughout that chaotic afternoon he and his special adviser Madeleine Sadler tried to keep the pressure on Harman and Straw, urging them not to back out of bringing Brown down. Miliband left a pleading message on Straw's mobile: 'It's time we sorted this out once and for all. We've got to tell him to go.'[138] His call wasn't returned. As the afternoon proceeded a disappointed Miliband came to the view that the plot would not work as the Cabinet was not prepared to move against Brown in sufficient numbers. His hopes of leadership, he now realised, would have to wait until after the election.

With Harman and Straw finally convinced by mid-afternoon that there was insufficient stomach in the Cabinet and party for a palace coup, they called

Nye at Number 10 and asked to see Brown together. Nye tried to insist that they see him separately, and that, as Deputy Leader of the party, Harman should see him first. Harman flatly refused and demanded that they both come together.[139] Number 10 was 'extremely apprehensive' they would tell him that his time was up and that he should resign. 'We were all anxious; no one in the building knew what they were going to tell him,' says an official.[140] The sense of foreboding was heightened when Straw arrived at Number 10 in dark hat and coat, earning him the description 'grim reaper' as he walked up to the door. Like Darling, however, they came not to bury Brown but to extract concessions. Harman demanded that she be given a more clearly defined and high-profile role in the campaign, while Straw emphasised the need to abandon the 'core vote' strategy, to do more to reach out to marginal seats, and be more consultative.[141] Brown could not believe his luck. When the doors to the Number 10 den were opened after their half-hour meeting, Brown emerged slapping Straw on his back, while Harman was smiling. Brown himself was described as being 'remarkably cheerful'.[142] Number 10's view was that both of them had 'bottled it' and were trying to extract something from Brown as a way of saving their faces. As one Number 10 aide puts it: 'They knew they'd fucked it up and were looking for a way out.'[143] When his political team nervously asked Brown what he had conceded, he shrugged his shoulders to indicate: 'No big deal'.[144]

At 5.01pm and 5.06pm, respectively, Johnson and Darling made supportive statements. At 5.28pm, five hours after the Hoon/Hewitt email, Straw eventually took to the airwaves to defend Brown and to predict that there would be no change of leadership before the election.[145] At 6.25pm, six hours after the email, Harman issued a terse statement saying that ministers were 'united in our determination to do what's best for the country, which is for Labour, led by Gordon Brown, to win the general election'.[146] The only one of the discontented heavyweights yet to speak up was David Miliband. Just before 7pm, he was caught by the media on the steps of his Primrose Hill home in north London, where he said he 'supported the re-election of the government [Gordon Brown] leads'. The following day, Miliband was to give an unequivocal statement of support to Brown's leadership.[147] But what of Hoon and Hewitt? They had been completely abandoned by Harman and were left beached, carrying the blame for destabilising the party at a critical point. That evening, they met in Hoon's House of Commons office, along with Clarke, Margaret McDonagh, Malcolm Wicks, Nick Raynsford and Charlie Falconer, to see if their endeavour was still alive.[148] But in their hearts, they had known from early afternoon that it was finished.

The panic over, Number 10 turned its mind to asking themselves what had happened, and why had they failed to pick it up? Within twenty-four hours, it was sure that Harman had been the principal ringleader, mainly because of her close relationship with Hewitt (though in public Clarke received the blame).[149] It was felt she was obsessed by her position, and by the way she had been treated, and that she had never come to terms with Mandelson's role, especially after his promotion to First Secretary. A final straw had been the expenses row: 'In her biggest test as Leader of the House she acted like a shop steward for the PLP on expenses,' says one of Brown's aides.[150] Number 10 didn't take her seriously after it, and she felt it. Aware that Number 10 would suspect that Harman had something to do with the plot, Hewitt and Harman 'constructed a fire wall' between themselves, to ensure they didn't discuss the plot directly.[151] On Harman's side, she believed that Brown had belittled her, and that he had consistently failed to give her the trust and respect that she deserved in her position.[152] She was not the only frontline Cabinet minister from whom he failed to bring out the best; her failure to perform better, with the Equalities Act a notable exception, was his fault as much as hers. Her performance as interim leader from May to September 2010 showed what she could achieve.

Number 10 thought Straw was another leading agitator among the Cabinet. He was respected and liked by Number 10, but was never a reliable ally on whom it could count, always ready to support a different cause. His biggest frustration with Brown was the sidelining of his own advice, and that of fellow Cabinet big beasts, above all in favour of Balls and other 'minions'.[153] 'The one person he would go out of his way to cause bodily harm to was Ed Balls,' says an aide.[154] Straw was furious with how he saw Balls prevailing over Darling during the Pre-Budget Report in 2009.[155] The influence that Balls was having over the election strategy was another source of deep disquiet to him (even though Balls was at most marginal on it).[156] Balls himself believes that, though Harman and Straw singled him out as a destabilising influence in government they were really frustrated with Mandelson, because it was he who had prevented one of them becoming Deputy Prime Minister.[157] Straw and Harman were united, as were Darling and David Miliband, that the regular meetings between Brown, Balls and Mandelson had to cease and that the regular government strategy group, which met every Monday, be restored to its proper, central place. So, Number 10 put it out that Brown would behave in a more collegial way in the future, but it caused anguish among the big beasts by then announcing that Mandelson was to be given overall responsibility for running the election campaign. Ainsworth was another Cabinet minister who felt deeply bruised and antagonised by the way he had been undermined since he took over in June. His turn to see Brown came on Friday 8 January, when he was promised that he would be able to draw up a green paper as a forerunner to a defence review.[158]

One week later, Number 10 ranked the Hoon/Hewitt coup as a 'six' on the Richter scale, compared to '9.5' when Purnell resigned.[159] In the light of subsequent revelations, the threat would appear to have been much higher than a six, and more serious than Purnell. Had Harman and other big beasts acted as expected, Brown would have fallen. So, why did it fail? 'In fairness to Harriet, there were droves of MPs telling her they would support her, and endless rumours of letters and emails doing the rounds, but the support never materialised,' says one Number 10 adviser.[160] The early show of unequivocal backing for Brown by the PLP was a fatal blow. The Cabinet malcontents waited to see how the PLP would respond, and the PLP came out in support of Brown. Both Hoon and Hewitt had lost influence among the PLP since they had ceased to be ministers, and both were believed to have had their own agendas. They needed the big beasts to speak in public. The PLP were concerned about the damage that might be inflicted on their electoral prospects by a divisive leadership election and by the Conservative argument that Labour had had 'three leaders within the life of one Parliament'. The plotters had very bad luck with the timing. The movement of the polls towards Labour before Christmas came just at the right time, as did the trenchant fight back after the New Year on the £34bn 'black hole' in Tory spending plans, coupled with Brown's pugnacious performance at PMQs on the very day of the coup. Contemporary reports suggested that: 'While many backbenchers longed to see Brown gone, few were prepared to give that sign.'[161]

The plot's failure can also be pinned on the continuing reluctance of the Cabinet malcontents to be no more decisive against Brown than they had been in 2008 or 2009. David Miliband was conflicted by his own leadership ambitions. The plotters were not confident of Darling either, for all his disillusion. 'He and Gordon went back too far, but we didn't need Alistair,' says one.[162] The plotters were also never convinced that Johnson would come out in public in favour of holding the ballot, but equally they did not think he was indispensible.[163] So that put the emphasis on Harman and Straw stepping up to the mark. Others would follow. Hewitt had made it clear to the Cabinet ministers she spoke to beforehand that there wouldn't be a vast number of backbenchers coming out to endorse the plans, although 'we had a few organised to keep the story going'.[164] But they had deliberately avoided giving MPs prior notice of the coup, barring a very select group, expressly because of the fear that it would leak, as it most certainly would have done. The plot was thus critically dependent on Cabinet 'doing the business'.[165]

Both Hewitt and Hoon were disillusioned when they manifestly did not do the business. Said the latter: 'Frankly, it did not succeed because the various people who had told us they were willing to speak to Gordon to ask him to stand aside did not do it. If they had told me in the days before that they were not going to do it, then the coup would have been aborted.'[166] Hoon refused to blame MPs for the plot's failure: 'It was absolutely focused on a handful of people who said that they were willing to tell Gordon it was time for him to go, and they didn't.' Its instigators had thought the chances of the coup succeeding were high. If they had not, they wouldn't have put their heads on the line in the way they did.[167]

Why then did the malcontents pull back? Hoon blamed himself for not doing more to talk to Cabinet ministers, to build a campaign beforehand. The widespread fear of leaks prevented that: 'There were too many bilateral conversations, and not enough group conversation. I didn't do as much as I should have to tie up these people.'[168] Equally, there was very little conversation between the dissenters in the Cabinet. Cabinet members themselves had no idea what their colleagues were thinking or felt should happen. In the eyes of Hewitt: 'The atmosphere made it impossible to have the kind of conversations that we needed to have. People were afraid who might tell other people.'[169] Harman herself, who had the most at stake, never felt able to convene a meeting so that they could thrash out a collective course of action.[170] Another involved suggested the 'climate of fear around Brown' was the key factor in killing the plot, because it dissuaded Cabinet colleagues from discussing moves against him with one another.[171] Clarke agrees: 'There was a deep fear among the key Cabinet members that it was too dangerous to seek to overthrow Gordon because of his absolute determination to stay in all circumstances, regardless of the impact on the party.'[172] 'When Mrs Thatcher was removed, Cabinet spoke to each other about her and shared views. There was a great fear of the brutality about some of the people around Gordon which prevented that happening,' says one.[173] Frank Field believes the plot failed because 'Gordon was ruthless' and Cabinet ministers were scared to make a stand against him.[174] 'Ridiculous,' says a Number 10 source,[175] with justice – the Cabinet malcontents were treated no differently after the coup.

Brown's enemies worried further, they say, about Brown's 'irrationality' and the 'technicalities of his going to the Palace'.[176] Fear for their jobs, and loss of income or titles, weighed in the balance. For some, as previously in 2008 and 2009, there was a worry he might say: 'I've lost my Deputy Leader and my Foreign Secretary, but the country needs me and I am not going.'[177] He might have stayed on, more damaged than before, leaving Labour's prospects at the election in an even more perilous situation. Disagreement over who would succeed Brown – David Miliband was not universally popular – again was a factor, as in 2008 and in 2009, in hampering the development of the united purpose and direction required for the coup to be a success. So Brown survived, ultimately, because the forces of inertia were far stronger than the forces of revolution and because the Labour Party is traditionally much less ruthless to its leaders than the Conservative Party. Hoon compares Brown's three years to those of Michael Foot: 'Both leaders survived in the face of massive criticism. I think ultimately because the Labour Party is a sentimental party.'[178]

Brown was keen to move speedily on from the coup, partly because the media enabled him to do so by not taking it very seriously, but also because he did not allow himself to be disconcerted by it. On Thursday 7 January, he dismissed it as a 'storm in a teacup'.[179] At Cabinet the next day, he said: 'What's done is done,' before going on to discuss the government's response to the severe ice and snow that had gripped the country.[180] He made a point of going round the table inviting ministers to give their opinions, taken as a signal that he had heeded the concerns about his lack of collegiality. Over the next few days, Number 10 saw the prodigal son parable repeat itself several times over. And like the biblical father, Brown showed no bitterness. He may not have succeeded in establishing himself as 'father of the nation', but here, at the end of his premiership, he was making a bid at being father to his Cabinet reprobates. Over the weekend of 9 and 10 January, he spent a long time talking to Mandelson about the election strategy. The coup had cleared the air between them, and for the first time for several weeks they were back together, working as a united pair.[181] As a concession to Straw, he was shown the election war book, though Brown's staff were surprised, or perhaps not, that, barring a few comments, such as using the word 'contrast' rather than 'dividing line', he had little of substance to offer.[182] Darling, too, returned to the fold and that weekend joined Brown, Mandelson and Balls in talking about how to refine policy. His concerns – how best to stimulate growth and to communicate about the cuts they agreed to make, while protecting frontline services – remained.[183]

On Monday 11 January, the weekly PLP meeting finally put leadership speculation to bed. Hoon and Hewitt did not attend. Clarke did, but did not speak. Brown was not angry; others were there to express this. 'This evening's jam-packed party was seething with anger towards the plotters,' records Mullin in his diary. Tony Lloyd from the chair declared: 'No personal attacks,' and was greeted by cries of 'Why not?'[184] 'I am not a team of one. I am one of a team,' the newly emollient Brown told MPs, a phrase he would later repeat in his speech announcing the general election. Flanked by Mandelson and Harman, he told MPs: 'You are all leaders of this campaign.'[185] Determined to show that he was listening, Brown told the PLP that he had been reflecting about the conduct of the election campaign and confirmed that Alexander would be election coordinator, Mandelson the head of strategy, and that Harman would have a 'key role' as Deputy Leader. A leadership ballot had been called for the meeting, but it did not happen. The moment had passed long before. 'A ballot was never the way to do it,' says Alan Johnson. 'Ironically, the plot cleared the air and allowed us to move forward, thus meeting its stated objective.'[186] Not that anyone was on hand to thank Hewitt and Hoon for it.

On 12 January, Brown chaired a three-hour political Cabinet. 'Everyone is up for the election. Things are much better now,' was the contemporary comment of an official.[187] 'Gordon Brown is relaxed,' records a Number 10 diary. 'Alistair

Darling says: "The Tories crumble under pressure," while Peter congratulates Gordon for his leadership. The talk is about the many not the few. Hilary Benn rallies everyone with a call for unity.'[188] Ministers were clear that the election should not be made into a class war debate. No one mentioned the plot throughout the meeting, until Benn praised the element that killed it: 'The PLP have shown iron determination,' reads the diary.[189] 'Regardless of what anyone thought about Gordon, the plot was complete madness,' Benn later reflects. 'I thought someone had to mention it. It had been the elephant in the room.'[190]

Irony was in the air. Brown had been rejuvenated by the whole coup experience. He was also philosophical. 'GB learned to accept it as a fact of life. He learned to live with the fact that Jack was a schemer. That Harriet couldn't be trusted. That David Miliband wanted his job,' says one of his aides, adding ruefully: 'But it was profoundly unhelpful to have had the constant speculation about leadership running through the life of his government.'[191] History may judge that the plotters needed either to kill him off quickly or get squarely behind him. Instead the Cabinet fudged it, leaving the party in the worst of all positions: they failed to remove Brown but made it abundantly clear to the outside world that they had little faith in his leadership. Brown's optimism and confidence were buoyed still further when a Populus poll for *The Times*, taken the weekend after the plot, showed improved personal ratings for himself, especially among Labour's core support of unskilled manual workers. The party, in contrast, had lost two points since December, falling to 28 per cent, while the Tories had gained three points, up to 41 per cent. No party had ever made up such a gap so close to a general election.[192] The fight was on.

Domestic Success: January

Heavy January snowfalls still covered Britain in a thick white blanket of snow. Britain was running out of the salt required to keep its roads safe and, indeed, open. The Transport Department panicked and proposed closing down a section of motorway. When Brown heard about it, he immediately intervened and phoned Prime Minister Zapatero to help hasten a delivery of salt from Spain. Somewhat antithetically, just as the heavy snowfall was rendering many roads impassable, the January coup had performed the job of clearing the pathways for Brown, and, within days, the coup had acquired an almost surreal quality. The Conservatives were quickly back on the back foot. Brown's first post-coup opportunity to outline his thinking came at the Fabian Society's New Year Conference on Saturday 16 January. On one level, it was a response to those like Straw who had cautioned strongly against a 'core vote' electoral strategy. But it was deeper than that. His team were struck by Obama's promise to protect 'middle America' and believed Brown should attempt a similar pitch in Britain. 'Don't use the term middle class in a *Daily Telegraph* kind of way,' they advised him; the middle classes are not those on £90,000 or above: 'They are those straight down the middle of the country.'[193] This was something that Brown and his team had always recognised, and with the election approaching, they needed to show this demographic why Labour was the party that best represented their interests. There was no time to waste. So he seized the opportunity to exploit concerns about the Conservatives' inheritance tax plans for protecting the wealthiest, while offering a vision of a Labour alternative as the protector of the middle class. A Conservative government, he told the Fabian conference, would mean fewer jobs for the middle classes, less money invested in schools and downgrading of the public services much used by the middle classes, such as child benefits and the 'Sure Start' programme.[194] The Tories, he said, would cut services and diminish middle-class 'quality of life'. In an article the day before in *The Guardian*, he had argued: 'I want to see an expanded middle class, not a squeezed middle class.'[195] To the Fabians he said: '[Tory cuts would affect] not a wealthy few, but teachers, taxi drivers, plumbers – you.'

Before the speech, Brown's team had been worried that illness might hinder him from delivering the speech well, and reduce the efficacy and force of its message. He had been vomiting throughout the night before he gave the speech. 'Gordon never gets ill. He was very nervous and very unsure about it,' says one adviser.[196] They need not have worried. 'We laughed because people were saying that he was newly energised and reinvigorated, whereas in fact he was very unwell. He went straight back to bed when he got back to Downing Street.'[197] His delivery was strong, and he even told a joke well about him being Mandelson's 'warm-up act'.[198] The media response to the speech was generally positive, with admiration for its 'sheer cheek'. 'What could be more counter-intuitive than to present the Tories as the enemies of the middle class?' asked Matthew d'Ancona in the *Sunday Telegraph*.[199] Brown later built on the speech in a Fabian Society pamphlet, *Why the Right is Wrong*, which ventured to provide an intellectual grounding for Labour's position. The Conservatives, he argued, had been wrong on the recession and were now wrong on the recovery, because they were committed to an ideology of 'dogmatic hostility to government action, no matter what the circumstances'.[200]

On 26 January, the Office of National Statistics produced its long-awaited results on the performance of the British economy in 2009 'Q4', i.e. the last three months of the year. Brown had had regular bad news during his premiership, but the information that growth in the quarter had been 0.1 per cent, despite being lower than he and his team had hoped, was as sweet to him as any news he received as Prime Minister. With the election looming, it could not possibly have come at better time. Darling promptly declared the figures showed the country was on 'the path to recovery',[201] and that they vindicated the government's strategy in tackling the downturn. 'The figures showed the recession was behind us,' says Gavin Kelly. 'They wrong-footed the Conservatives, and showed that at last our policy and our communications were both working in step.'[202] The heat was on the Conservatives even more now. Since September, Osborne had been promising an 'emergency Budget' within weeks of entering office; the Tory leadership now became worried that they would be seen to be over-reacting with overly stringent cut proposals. On 31 January, Cameron responded on the BBC *Politics Show* by saying that cuts in the first year of a Conservative government would be limited. 'We're not talking about swingeing cuts. We're talking about making a start in reducing our deficit,' he said.[203] Nick Robinson pounced on him: 'By seeking to reassure the public that there will not be "swingeing cuts", David Cameron has acknowledged Labour's arguments that the wrong approach to public spending could pull the rug from under the recovery.'[204] Labour made much of Cameron's 'U-turn'. The Tories had it 'too easy for too long', wrote Steve Richards in *The Independent*.[205] Brown had had Cameron on the run at the start of January on married couples' tax breaks, and he had him back on the run at the end of the month on spending. The atmosphere in Number 10 was upbeat: 'There was a clear sense that we were not yet out of the mire. There was a sense that here was something on which we could build.'[206]

Northern Ireland: September 2009–April 2010

Gordon Brown was not dealt an easy hand on Northern Ireland, the scene of his predecessor's most widely applauded achievement. If violence escalated and progress on constitutional reform was seen to stall, he would be blamed for squandering Blair's legacy, an ever-present nightmare for him. If he managed to guide the province to significant and urgently needed resolution of outstanding differences, he would receive little or no credit for a topic most in Westminster and Fleet Street considered a 'done deal' by Blair after the Good Friday agreement and the 2006 St Andrews agreement. There was, however, one very significant and pressing issue left over from St Andrews – the devolution of justice and policing powers. Brown inherited an unhelpful expectation from the Blair team that resolution of this issue 'could be achieved within twelve months'.[207] Disagreement over it had already led to the six-month hiatus in 2008, when Northern Ireland's power-sharing executive was suspended, a dangerous precedent. The issue was becoming so serious that fears were emerging that it could threaten the survival of the political institutions in Northern Ireland.

With the general election looming in spring 2010, Brown knew that his window of opportunity for securing a breakthrough was narrow, and closing.

Before the summer of 2009, Northern Ireland Secretary Shaun Woodward and the Northern Ireland Office (NIO) had been 'moderately optimistic that things would move ahead in the autumn on devolution of policing and justice'.[208] However, the European election campaign, culminating in the June poll, had marked a hardening of tone and attitude. By early September, Woodward, his NIO officials, permanent secretary Jonathan Phillips and his deputy Hilary Jackson, were becoming increasingly concerned by the statements from the Democratic Unionist Party (DUP) and its head, Peter Robinson, who was now Northern Ireland's First Minister. Robinson was judged by London to be the best hope of sustaining devolution, though the question was whether he had the same authority as his long-standing predecessor, Ian Paisley, to rein in his reactionary DUP members.[209] Intelligence reports of increasing terrorist threats were a further cause of alarm.

On 8 September, Robinson had been invited to give a speech at Ulster Hall in Belfast. His convoluted words appeared to be saying that the transfer of policing and justice powers remained contingent upon more fundamental reform in the Assembly. Envisaged was the government moving from the *enforced* coalition arrangements established by the Good Friday agreement (under which the parties holding the most unionist and nationalist votes have an effective veto over government decisions) towards a *voluntary* coalition agreement (with community confidence being maintained by the imposition of a 65 per cent majority rule in the Assembly). Deputy First Minister Martin McGuinness was incensed, declaring of his colleague: 'He's obviously come home with sunstroke or been too long in Disneyland.' The Sinn Fein MLA accused Robinson of trying to unpick the St Andrews agreement.[210] Woodward was alarmed and told Brown that Northern Ireland's devolved government was in jeopardy, with Robinson in intransigent mood, and Sinn Fein – despite its resolute commitment to pursuing a path of peace and politics – now losing control of some of its supporters, who were looking increasingly to violence.[211]

Brown's involvement as Prime Minister in Northern Ireland intensified significantly after the three murders in the spring of 2009. In the early summer, he had become involved in the detailed discussions of a financial settlement for the transfer of policing and justice powers in a series of meetings at Downing Street. He saw Robinson and McGuinness again in New York during his G20 visit, keen to try to crunch the financial settlement. In each of these meetings he became increasingly aware of the intricacies of the balance of power both between and within the parties, particularly within the DUP. Robinson's succession had occurred in June 2008, but London became increasingly concerned by his apparent unwillingness to bang together the heads of the DUP hardliners, some of whom, like Nigel Dodds and Gregory Campbell, regarded the devolution process with deep suspicion, and Sinn Fein with even deeper suspicion. Brown decided that he had no option but to visit the province himself. Monday 5 October, just after the Labour Party conference, was the earliest date that could be put in the diary. When there, Brown held detailed discussions with Robinson and met Dodds, Campbell and other hardliners. The money available from Whitehall to pay for the devolution of policing and justice was raised as an immediate block to progress. Pressure on this score from the DUP was partly genuine and partly spurious – some were raising money merely as a way of slowing down the process. 'Very well,' said Brown. 'We need to sort this out.' His response was to blast a way through this roadblock by offering to fund devolution costs fully, resulting in a financial package of over £600 million being placed on the table within a week of his visit.[212] Throughout October, long meetings on finance, chaired by Heywood, took place between Sinn Fein, the DUP and the Treasury, to finalise the details. The DUP was eventually satisfied by the financial deal, but they were still raising objections to the whole transfer of power.

On 30 November, the Northern Ireland Assembly passed the Department of Justice bill, which was required to facilitate a transfer of powers, by setting up a department to which the powers could be devolved. But this served only to intensify disagreement between Sinn Fein and the DUP over its timing. Brown found himself pedalling back from his very deliberate decision when he became Prime Minister that he wouldn't have Adams, Paisley et al. endlessly phoning Number 10, as had happened to Blair and Jonathan Powell.[213] In November, he found himself increasingly drawn in. 'It was becoming clear to him that it was going to be very difficult to get all the necessary legislation through Westminster before a widely expected general election on 6 May, unless agreement was reached over the following few weeks,' says Phillips.[214] A series of further private meetings between Brown, Robinson and McGuinness, including one in the Commons on 7 November, failed to resolve differences between the parties. To add to the difficulty, a new issue now emerged, taking the place of finance as the main obstacle to agreement: the role of the Parades Commission. The DUP began demanding that the Parades Commission be abolished as a precondition for the devolution of police and justice powers. Unionists regarded the Commission, which adjudicated over the controversial Orange parades, as inherently biased in favour of the Catholic community. Disputes over parades, memorably the standoff at Drumcree in the 1990s, had come close to destroying the peace process and led to widespread outbreaks of violence.[215] The DUP favoured instead the recommendations produced by former Liberal Democrat leader Lord Ashdown, who had been appointed to chair a Strategic Review of Parading in Northern Ireland in 2007. Ashdown had recommended that the Parades Commission be abolished and replaced by a panel of mediators and a greater role for local politicians, with the First Minister and Deputy First Minister being the final arbiters.

On 14 December, a crisis point was reached when McGuinness and Robinson clashed during a visit by Irish Taoiseach, Brian Cowen. McGuinness accused Robinson of reneging on an agreement with him and 'raising roadblocks' to a deal.[216] McGuinness publicly demanded a resolution by Christmas, while Robinson flatly refused to be held to any deadline. The NIO, watching all this being played out, formed two distinct interpretations of the game Robinson was playing: either he was trying to push devolution forward as quickly as his critics would allow him, or he was doing the bare minimum to ensure that he kept McGuinness and Adams on board, but with no intention of seeking a deal. The latter view saw Robinson just stringing all parties along until after the general election. 'I'm not sure I'd put my name confidently to either option,' says a senior official.[217] By Christmas, the NIO feared the worst: 'Short of a miracle, it was apparent by December that this could go over the cliff.'[218] An additional imperative for a solution was that the intelligence services were reporting that the number of dissidents was still rising, with former members of the Provisional IRA (PIRA) being recruited back to the armed struggle. The atmosphere in the NIO at Christmas was 'pretty gloomy' and the possibility of violence exploding again in the New Year was real.

During the autumn, Brown and Cowen had been toying with the idea of holding another 'country house meeting' as a way of unblocking the impasse. They had precious few options left to them. Woodward had become convinced that the British government could not stand by and see blatant procrastination by both Northern Irish parties continue any longer and strongly encouraged Brown to seize the moment and intervene. He found Brown to be very receptive: 'If the politics fails, we will have to reimpose direct rule. There will come a moment when I ask you to back me totally,' he told Brown. 'You have that support,' was the reply.[219] A complicating factor all along was that Brown's relationship with his Irish opposite number, Cowen, was not on the intimate and trusting level of the Blair relationship with the previous Taoiseach, Bertie Ahern. Brown and Cowen were very different people, and their relationship had not been helped by differences during the financial crisis. However, since the summer of 2009, they had begun to understand each other's perspectives and personalities better,[220] and had begun to carve out a good working relationship. Both governments argued that any conference should not be an event like St Andrews, held outside Northern Ireland, but rather it should take place in the very heart of the province itself. Early on, it was decided to hold it at Hillsborough Castle, the eighteenth-century mansion, which, from 1922–72, had been the residence of the Governor of Northern Ireland, and then became the residence of the Northern Ireland Secretary, as well as the official residence in Northern Ireland of the Queen. The NIO was adamant that, if a way forward was to be found, it must be 'made in Belfast' and, even more critically, that it must be an agreement between the

Northern Ireland parties themselves, merely watched over and facilitated by the British and Irish and US governments.[221]

At this delicate stage, the Northern Ireland political world was rocked by two scandals. On 29 December, Iris Robinson, wife to Peter, announced her intention to stand down as an MP on account of mental illness. The following week, news broke of her affair with a 19-year-old and stories emerged about the £50,000 investment she had secured as start-up capital for a cafe business her young flame was looking to start. Robinson decided on 11 January 2010 to step aside as First Minister until the matter was resolved, designating his colleague Arlene Foster as a stand-in First Minister, though he was to remain leader of the DUP and integral to the talks on devolution. Brown was 'very sympathetic' towards Robinson and the predicament he found himself in.[222] News also broke that the late father of Gerry Adams had abused children, and that Adams's own brother had abused Adams's niece. The latter scandal appeared on the surface to have had little effect on the pace of progress, while the Robinson scandal did. In fact both created separate momentums in their respective camps, and the British government seized on what it adjudged an opportunity to force the hands of the Northern Irish politicians, helped by pressure from a willing Hillary Clinton and assurances from Cameron that the Conservative Party would not play fast and loose with the DUP.[223] The principal block to successful resolution remained Robinson's hardliners and his own reluctance to take them on. Almost unaccountably, his personal scandal seemed to stiffen his resolve to find a way forward. 'It left him nowhere else to go,' says one insider.[224] Both parties thus went into the talks at Hillsborough Castle, which opened on Monday 25 January, with a greater sense of optimism than for several weeks. Brown and Cowen arrived that day hoping that a speedy resolution might be possible. Officials involved were less optimistic: 'We told Number 10 that the chances of fixing it in twenty-four hours were very slim,' said one.[225]

The pattern of the negotiations was similar to that followed by the talks for the Good Friday agreement and St Andrews, with Prime Minister and Taoiseach speaking individually to both parties to find mutual ground for progress and negotiation. No one expected a repeat of the Blair–Ahern double act, and eyes watched carefully to see how Brown and Cowen would work together. They need not have worried. 'Being parked in a sitting room in Hillsborough and seeing all these recalcitrant politicians brought them much closer together,' says one official.[226] Cowen and Sinn Fein also viewed Stewart Wood and Tom Fletcher, Brown's influential advisers on Northern Ireland, as more 'green' (i.e. pro-Irish) than other British figures. Mindful of Brown's desire to maintain a distance, at least for the first two years, they would be the figures who would talk to the Taoiseach's office and the White House about Northern Ireland. Brown trusted both implicitly, while feeling in his bones that no one, in the NIO or Number 10, could handle Northern Ireland as well as he.[227]

The principal objectives for Hillsborough were: gaining the DUP's support for devolution, and settling the dispute over parading, which remained at the top of the agenda. Beginning at 5pm on the Monday, Brown continued until 4.45am on Tuesday morning. He then announced that there would be a brief break for rest before discussions would resume at 7am. With progress from the DUP on devolution, the parading issue became the prime obstacle on the Tuesday, with strong feelings on both sides. The conversations continued all morning, afternoon and evening, until 5am on the Wednesday. Brown 'ruthlessly and doggedly drove the meetings forward'.[228] At last there was a small glimmer of hope, when McGuinness asked: 'Is there anywhere I can stay at Hillsborough tonight?' All parties took that as a symbolically significant sign, because he was prepared to sleep somewhere so inexorably connected with the British state.

Brown and Cowen had made it clear that neither of them could remain at Hillsborough beyond that Wednesday morning. Before he left, Brown produced a draft script of a final agreement, covering, among other things, parades, which both leaders now recognised as the deal-breaker issue. Discussion on this script seemed the most promising way forward, but they would not force the DUP and Sinn Fein to accept it. Both leaders were determined that the Northern Ireland parties should themselves be responsible for reaching agreement, but announced that, if none had been reached by Friday 29 January, they would set out their own proposals based on the draft. 'Take some time and talk about it and see if you can reach agreement. If you can't agree, though, it is our last offer,' they said. Brown confided in Woodward: 'I know you can do this. I have to return to London. Don't let it go.'[229] In his heart, says one official, Brown felt that Wednesday morning that 'a deal was almost done'.[230]

Before Brown boarded his plane, he held a press conference, where he was felt to be exceptionally impressive. His sleep deprivation notwithstanding, he was almost word perfect, and his responses won him fresh support in both communities in Northern Ireland, helping to dispel their beliefs that he was not as committed to Northern Ireland as Blair, nor as capable of understanding its problems. But the fate of a settlement still hung in the air. 'We have not concluded a deal today and I am deeply disappointed,' said McGuinness. Sinn Fein, he said, could not accept 'citizens' rights' being subject to a 'Unionist veto'. Robinson retorted that the DUP were not prepared to accept a 'second-rate deal' to suit 'someone else's time-limit'.[231]

When Brown left for London with Stewart Wood and Tom Fletcher at lunchtime on Wednesday, to see President Karzai of Afghanistan that afternoon, there was still much to be done, and Woodward and Irish Foreign Affairs

Minister Michael Martin were left with the difficult task of holding the reins. 'The departure of the two Prime Ministers inevitably reduces the momentum of the talks,' said Mark Simpson, the BBC's Irish correspondent. 'In the words of one source, the air has gone out of the balloon.'[232] Thursday 28 January was a particularly bleak day. With the parties saying they wanted to decamp from Hillsborough to Stormont, Adams temporarily took over negotiations from McGuinness. There was widespread conjecture, after McGuinness took the break, whether he and Adams were on the same page. 'They probably were, and this was likely yet another in the long line of Sinn Fein negotiating tactics,' says one official with hindsight.[233] Brown monitored developments minutely from Number 10. He was desperate to see a resolution. 'Follow your instincts. Go for it. I trust you to do it,' Brown said down the line to his team in Belfast.[234]

The Obama administration was also watching developments with keen interest. Unlike Bill Clinton, Obama did not become personally involved, but Secretary of State Hillary Clinton did, and she had come to Belfast in October 2008 to try to help push the political process forward. During those critical days, she personally made direct phone calls to numerous Northern Ireland politicians, including calls to Robinson's own mobile. She was always careful to stress that this was a decision for them, but she worked hard to win their confidence with promises of further investment, if the DUP would agree to a resolution.[235] Her involvement aroused mixed emotions among the unionists. According to one official: 'Robinson was irritated by the American pressure to reach a settlement, but was very sensitive to the promise of American investment.'[236] The Irish and British governments intervened directly on Thursday when they produced a joint document on parades, which put an unequivocal proposal on the table for both sides to chew over. While this irritated the Sinn Fein negotiators, the fact that London and Dublin had both now signalled clearly that parades had to be dealt with was hugely important in enabling progress to be made.[237] As had been the case from the 1990s onwards, a common position between both governments meant that the Northern Irish parties were left with considerably less wriggle room. Cowen's throwing his full weight behind the proposals allowed Robinson to say to his supporters that it was probably the best deal they would ever get, that they had secured a very good financial package, and that the whole devolution programme would be at risk if they did not sign up.[238]

Despite Brown and Cowen having set a deadline for agreement on Friday 29 January, the talks proceeded beyond this date, over the weekend and into the next week. Robinson had been called away over the weekend, to deal with both a family crisis and, it was to emerge later, negotiations between the DUP, the UUP and the Conservative Party. Sunday was a day off from discussions and from the moment they returned to Hillsborough on Monday a more optimistic mood prevailed. Sinn Fein raised a number of demands, including government funding to promote the Irish language in Northern Ireland. In the end, such a clause was inserted into the final agreement and £20m of government money promised, but this was always insignificant compared to their primary objective since 1998: final devolution of powers. After several hours of heated debate within the DUP, Robinson put the proposals to his party. Although the secret ballot of DUP members of the Legislative Assembly resulted in a 60:40 split in favour of the deal, the number of opponents was higher than the leadership had anticipated and left them reeling. Robinson needed much more than this slim majority. The whole political process was now in meltdown.

Back in London, with mounting excitement at the regular updates he was receiving, Brown was itching to return to Belfast to sign a deal, and had a plane on stand-by, manned with security staff, by the runway at RAF Northolt. All Monday, he and his team waited in Downing Street until they received the bad news about Robinson and his party being in crisis following the rebellion in the secret ballot, and the talks breaking down. Both Westminster and Dublin believed they were fighting to save not just the talks, but the political process itself. Both sides were ready to walk out. Brown was on the phone constantly for the next thirty-six hours, trying to find a way through, which would enable Robinson to win the confidence of his party.

On the morning of Wednesday 3 February, Woodward flew back to London. Even though he was preparing for PMQs, Brown wanted to talk to him face to face, and they spent much of the morning talking about how to unblock the process. Nerves were fraying as those involved in the negotiations waited to see if the DUP would back the agreement. Finally, the breakthrough came on Thursday 4 February, with the thirty-five DUP Assembly members deciding unanimously to back the devolution proposals. Robinson announced the result just before midnight. Brown and Cowen flew to Belfast on the morning of Friday 5 February for the announcement of the resolution. On the flight over, Brown and Fletcher pondered what they might say, with Blair's famous words at the time of the Good Friday agreement about feeling 'the hand of history upon our shoulders' in their minds. They joked about Brown saying: 'I feel the hand of Peter Robinson in my pocket and the hands of Gerry Adams on my balls.'[239] Caution prevailed, and Brown adopted the safer strategy of describing it as: 'The day we have secured the future.'

Hillsborough had been the longest, unbroken negotiating exercise in the entire Northern Ireland peace process. With great relief and some emotion, Brown announced: 'We are closing the last chapter of a long and troubled story, and we are opening a new chapter for Northern Ireland.'[240] McGuinness said that the devolution deal 'could turn out to be the most important of all'.[241] A date was set of 12 April 2010 for policing and justice powers to be devolved, a decision informed by the likely date of the general election on 6 May. Seventeen days after the deal was reached, on 23 February, a car bomb went off outside Newry courthouse, miraculously leaving no one killed or injured.[242] Dissidents were determined to show that, the agreement notwithstanding, they could still pack a punch. On 22 March, MPs in Westminster approved the Parliamentary Orders necessary to transfer policing and justice powers to the Stormont Assembly on 12 April, a measure fully supported by both Labour and Conservative MPs. Parliament was adjourned on 8 April. Brown had achieved the deal just in time.

'A walk-on part' was how the *Belfast Telegraph* described Brown's role. '[He] helped create a sense of crisis' by his decision to attend Hillsborough, but wasn't crucial to finding the deal.[243] That diminishes hugely Brown's achievement. He may have come late to Northern Ireland, but once he was engaged on it, from the summer of 2009, he gave it top priority and, in the two weeks of the Hillsborough talks, his constant attention. Unlike Blair, Brown deliberately did not create an all-commanding figure in Number 10, like Jonathan Powell, who guided and shaped the evolution of policy, and who had an intimate knowledge of all the issues and people involved. Instead, Brown chose to empower Woodward. Brown's fierce, not to say hectoring, negotiating skills helped line up the parties; what he lacked in tact he made up for in his command of detail. His motives in finding a settlement had been mixed – 'the nightmare that Northern Ireland would explode on his watch' was constantly in his mind, and he wanted to notch up a deal to match Blair's. But he had loftier ideals, too, and genuinely wanted to entrench peace and stop Northern Ireland from descending into terrorism.[244] His relationships with McGuinness and Robinson, and with Cowen, showed he had a subtler understanding of character and motivation than many allowed. The negotiations had shown Brown at his best: goal-driven, tenacious, full of stamina and, though lacking Blair's easy charm with people, someone whom all parties came to respect, if not always to like. Economic factors and Hillary Clinton's interventions both facilitated the resolution on the devolution of policing and justice powers. As long expected, Brown received little credit for his contribution to the final settlement, but that does not mean that praise is not merited. Hillsborough was never going to be as important historically as Good Friday or even St Andrews, but it ensured that the work of Major and Blair endured. By a strange quirk of history, whether its hand was on their shoulders or balls, Northern Ireland proved the arena which saw the very best of all three prime ministers.

Afghanistan – The Reckoning: January–May

After all the turbulence in the summer and autumn of 2009, government policy on Afghanistan became more settled by Christmas: US and UK strategies became better aligned; equipment arguments were largely in the past, with helicopters arriving in force from December; the military were happier now they had more troops; and *The Sun* was more muted since the Jacqui Janes backlash. Press criticism continued, but at a much lower level than in 2009.[245] To Douglas Alexander, Obama's decision in late 2009 to make Afghanistan a multi-national force commitment was a major factor in winning back public confidence.[246] Having the military hell bent on increasing forces and provision had distracted Brown, who, except for a couple of periods in autumn 2007 and winter 2008/9, had not given a high priority to strategic thinking. However, the situation in Afghanistan and Pakistan was among his five international objectives in autumn 2009, and although it was crowded out in the short term that autumn, in January he was able to think more seriously about it. Four main options, not all exclusive, were on the table. This is a summary of how they were presented to him. First, an all-out military solution. But that was never going to succeed as the allies lacked the resources for a full-scale counter-insurgency campaign. Second, a strategy aiming to win over the population while at the same time resisting the attacks of the insurgency, across the whole of Afghanistan. Money and equipment were not the only hurdles in achieving this: the coalition forces lacked the language and cultural resources, including an intricate knowledge of inter-tribal dynamics, required to execute such a counter-insurgency approach with maximum efficacy. Third was a political solution, which entailed talking to the Taliban and finding common ground. Miliband and Alexander were always very keen; Brown, though, was more cautious, questioning whether enduring deals with the Taliban would ever be attainable. He himself favoured the fourth route: a long-term economic solution which included building up local government and other Afghan institutions. Like most parties to the process, he was also a strong advocate of 'Afghanisation', i.e. building up the Afghan security forces and empowering the Afghans themselves. Brown believed this was essential if Britain and others were to be seen as partners in the region, not occupiers.

Brown decided that his personal contribution to making progress would come in the form of convening a major international conference on Afghanistan, to help him recover the initiative, and to drive the international community, as well as the Afghans themselves, to flesh out a strategy and a timeline for handing over responsibility to domestic forces. After much groundwork, and lobbying of the White House, he announced the conference in mid-November. It would be held at Lancaster House in London on 28 January,[247] would bring together representatives from seventy countries, and participants would include Ban Ki-moon and Hillary Clinton. Many, both in Britain and elsewhere in NATO (including the US), were sceptical – what could be achieved? Was this Brown indulging in a Sarkozy-style penchant for convening conferences? However, by the time the conference came round, it was seen as a real opportunity to reset the international strategy after a difficult year. After so long in reactive mode, Brown surprised many by playing a significant role at the conference in making 'the coalition focus on the whole issue of transition'.[248] The government briefed beforehand that its aim was: 'Giving western public opinion the confidence that there is a strategy not only for fighting the war but also for getting out of it.'[249] Did it achieve its goals? Yes, to a limited extent. It helped put McChrystal's counterinsurgency strategy for fighting the war in the context of a broader strategy, including work towards a political solution. It established a date for handing over Afghan security to Afghanistan's own forces, subject to conditions being met. It agreed figures for an increase in the size of the Afghan army to 171,000 by October 2011, and on a 'civilian surge' to intensify civil programmes promoting good governance and economic development. As the day approached, Number 10 had feared that Miliband 'might try to dominate the conference' and upset the balance between the political and military aspects, and was relieved that he did not.[250] Brown opened and closed proceedings, and did so with some aplomb. The conference attracted predictably little attention in the British media.

While Brown was at work on the London conference, the military had been planning Operation Moshtarak, a combined British and American operation with the objective of seizing Marja, a town with a population of 60,000, ringed by poppy fields and irrigation canals and a densely populated area between Marja and existing British-controlled zones called Nad-e Ali. These areas, Marja in particular, were thought to be the last major Taliban strongholds in Helmand. The plan had been signed off in November, but its launch was held up as the British awaited extra troops and the newly arrived American Marines took longer than expected to prepare and 'shape' the operation. On the British side, a smarting lesson had been learned from Panther's Claw about the importance of alerting the public and media in advance to the likelihood of significant casualties. 'The military feared that if the public was given this information they would panic, but in fact it made them more assured,' says Brown's aide, Matt Cavanagh.[251] On 7 February, Ainsworth duly warned: 'Casualties are something that we have come to expect when we are involved in these operations.'[252] The media picked up the hint. 'The bloodiest fighting in the eight-year war in Afghanistan is expected to break out this week,' said *The Independent*.[253] On 13 February, British forces, under the command of Brigadier James Cowan, launched what was billed as the biggest helicopter assault in British history, with thirty-seven choppers airlifting 1,200 British and Afghan soldiers into sixteen locations.[254] In the early days of the fighting, Brown spoke frequently to Sir Jock Stirrup and asked for written updates every day. But the calls became more irregular as the campaign ran on. British intelligence told Brown that Marja would be much the hardest nut to crack, and he had doubts about whether it was worth it at this stage in the war. A particular concern was for the safety of the American forces, which were about to enter the area identified by intelligence as 'particularly dangerous and difficult'. 'Are you really sure you want to be taking this on?' he asked Obama and, when the Americans met severe problems, his fears were vindicated.[255]

Shortly after the successful first phase of Operation Moshtarak, on 6 March, Brown made his final visit to Afghanistan as Prime Minister, visiting bases that had only just been captured from the Taliban. The operation, he claimed, had 'brought results which are better than anticipated'.[256] Two hundred new armoured vehicles, officials travelling with the Prime Minister said, would be ordered to replace the controversial 'Snatch' Land Rovers, to give soldiers better protection. The visit was not free of the controversy that surrounded his earlier seven to Afghanistan. The Conservatives said, as they had with justice of his October 2007 Iraq visit during the aborted election period, that he was using it for political purposes. His attire – a shirt, slacks and new walking shoes – came under attack, too, with Britain's special envoy, Sherard Cowper-Coles, saying he thought Brown turned up looking 'as though he had just been spun out of a washing machine'.[257] On his return to the House on 8 March, Brown gave a detailed statement about troop numbers and equipment – enduring problems throughout his premiership, which were only resolved at the very end of it.[258]

The Brown years mark the lowest point in trust between Number 10 and the Ministry of Defence in modern times. Superficially, the generals never rated Brown because he never cut it as a military figure. But deeper than that, the root cause was that they never forgave him for his time as Chancellor when, rightly or wrongly, they believed he had behaved neither honourably nor fairly towards the Armed Forces, an accusation levelled at him in public with the publication of Richard Dannatt's memoirs, *Leading from the Front* (2010). 'Quite clearly Brown had little interest in defence,' Dannatt says. 'As Prime Minister, the military retained an underlying attitude that he short-changed defence.'[259] Concerns on this score flared up again when he announced in October 2009 that the Territorial Army would halt all training for six months as an economy measure. Brown's antennae told him this would be bound to lead to trouble, another Gurkhas in the making, but the Ministry of Defence prevailed against Number 10, and the announcement went ahead.[260] Brown eventually intervened personally and cancelled the proposal to head off the threat of a Commons revolt. *The Sun* nevertheless slammed the decision and again castigated him for not listening to them more: 'The government's humiliating U-turn on Territorial Army training expenses exposes once again its scandalously half-hearted approach to the war in Afghanistan.'[261]

Brown was equally castigated by others for listening too much to the press. Contemporaries believed he was fearful that middle England, as represented by the *Mail* and *Telegraph* groups, would say he was soft on terrorism and charge him with 'appeasement', and that he accepted largely uncritically their credo that terrorism was being exported from Afghanistan, without looking sufficiently at whether his own actions were exacerbating terrorist activity.[262] Members of Brown's team vociferously dispute this analysis.[263] 'He kept questioning and looking at the advice he was getting,' says one insider.[264] The regular intelligence reports Brown received throughout his premiership, while pointing to the increasing importance of areas such as the Horn of Africa in eradicating the terrorist threat to Britain, were clear that the border regions between Pakistan and Afghanistan remained the most important target in the fight against terrorism. His intelligence consistently confirmed that action in these regions was helping to degrade and suppress the capabilities of the 'core' of al Qaida and other terrorist groups in the area.[265] That may be so, but Brown still struggled to convince the British public that action in Afghanistan would make them safer at home.

Brown was never able to break the ice with the senior commanders. On very rare occasions he broke through the almost impenetrable barrier between himself and senior officers, as in a question and answer session in September 2009 at the Royal United Services Institute, but only after the television cameras had been switched off following a talk.[266] 'He's not so bad after all,' was a typical comment, as they realised he was perhaps not the ignoramus on military matters they had assumed. But occasions when he allowed himself to be human in front of officers were extremely rare. He tried hard to be seen as a worthy national leader, by making his regular visits to Iraq and Afghanistan, and the esteem in which he held soldiers of the armed forces was clear from his personal letters and private hospital visits. Pointedly, he referred to the military in his final words as Prime Minister in the street outside Number 10. Nothing he did or said made any difference with the senior officers, who had never wanted him and mostly treated him with contempt to the end.

The implacable animosity of the senior military commanders was only one reason why Brown never formulated a consistent long-term strategy for Afghanistan until it was too late. Whereas his leadership of the end game in Iraq can be considered a success, the same cannot be said of his leadership of the British cause in Afghanistan. Leading the nation during the Afghan war posed a much harder challenge for Brown. He did not have the requisite communication skills needed to comfort and reassure a country shocked by the escalation in troop casualties. The conflict exposed his weaknesses as a leader in a modern media age. The change of administration in the US half-way through his premiership did not help, leaving him dangerously exposed for much of 2009, taking an active role, but without clarity or cover from the US. When the US came off the fence in late 2009, it was much easier for Britain to follow suit, and commit itself to additional troops. Brown's poor relationship with Miliband, made worse after the latter's *Guardian* article, did not help either. It deepened Brown's suspicion of the Miliband-Alexander argument that Britain should be talking to the Taliban. Hampered by his frustration with Miliband, and by his December 2007 statement that Britain would 'never' talk to the Taliban, Brown ended up distancing himself from a political resolution. Thus, neither MI6, nor indeed the CIA, was ever formally authorised to talk to the Taliban, in contrast to Northern Ireland, where there had been a secret channel in existence for twenty years before Major started talking to the IRA. 'The truth is we can't communicate with the Taliban. We don't even really know who they are. Gordon Brown repeatedly refused to authorise anything in that area,' says a senior official.[267] Without a background in defence, and in the face of such difficulties, Brown badly needed one Defence Secretary to be there throughout his premiership; instead, he had three in rapid succession, the first of whom, Des Browne, to the irritation of the military, combined his job with the additional responsibilities of his appointment as Secretary of State for Scotland. All three had their virtues, but none stayed long enough to make a decisive mark. The military compared the political roundabout to the US, where Defense Secretary Robert Gates remained in post across the Bush–Obama transition, in recognition of the need for political continuity.[268]

The military chiefs cannot themselves be absolved from blame for Britain's failure to produce a coherent policy, or for the deeply damaging breakdown of trust. Nor can they escape their own responsibility for ensuring the troops had the right equipment for combat, when they were active players in the planning and procurement process. Dannatt was an indefatigable supporter of the soldiers under his care, but he lost his sense of perspective and was fatally undermined in the eyes of politicians when he was openly critical of the government in his 2006 BBC interview. Even fellow officers now believe that he became 'quite irrational and emotional', and 'did not cover himself with glory' during his time as CGS.[269] 'The problem with Richard,' says another senior military figure, 'is that he thinks he is on a mission from God. He never understood that he was doing more harm than good. A number of very senior people in the army believe that he made a big mistake in the way he stoked things up with the politicians'. Allowing himself to be used by Cameron's press chief Andy Coulson in the autumn of 2009 was an inglorious end to his career. Condoning and not doing more to prevent anti-government leaks to the press damaged the British case, clarity of thinking about the war, and the integrity of the army. Brown's team came to believe the military was pressing for escalation in Afghanistan, for reasons that were not wholly based on an objective evaluation of needs on the ground: erasing the 'stain of Basra' on

Britain's military reputation, restoring credibility with their opposite numbers in the United States, and maintaining troop numbers to ward off a hostile defence review, were all factors that weighed in the equation.[270] Professor of Government at Oxford University, Vernon Bogdanor, in an article for *The Times* in March 2010, warned military leaders that by continually criticising government policy in public they risked the politicisation of the armed services where ministers would be encouraged to appoint 'yes men'.[271] The military's actions during 2009 saw this anxiety reach a high-water mark. Muir describes the impact of Afghanistan throughout Brown's premiership: 'It was like an abscess that would flare up; ultimately it was a battle we had to fight.' In the end, the Afghanistan problem was impervious to any easy solution and, although Britain was the second power in the region, all the key decisions effectively were taken in Washington. That said, a great Prime Minister would have taken stock and devised a policy from the *outset* of their premiership that was clearly driven by objectives in Britain's national interest; as it was, the drivers of the policy were not the politicians, not even Miliband and Alexander who remained in their posts throughout the three years, but too often the unelected military.

Iraq: The Reckoning: January–May

Iraq was the war that would not leave New Labour. It dogged Blair's premiership and it came to dog Brown's, too. Despite two inquiries in 2003 – by the Foreign Affairs Select Committee into the decision to go to war and by the Intelligence and Security Committee assessing the intelligence on weapons of mass destruction (WMD) – and a further two in 2004 – the Hutton Inquiry into the death of David Kelly and the Butler Review into the intelligence on WMD – public disquiet continued. On 17 March 2008, in response to a letter from the General Secretary of the Fabian Society, Sunder Katwala, Brown promised a full public inquiry. Two days later, he told the Commons, however, that an inquiry 'would not be right when we have troops in danger and at risk'.[272] Pressure mounted as soon as the last British troops left Iraq and on 16 March 2009 a ComRes poll for the BBC found that 72 per cent of those asked favoured an inquiry into the conflict.[273] On 25 March, David Miliband told MPs that one would be approved 'as soon as possible', hinting it would be conducted mostly in private, the model being the Franks Inquiry into the Falklands War of 1982.[274]

The Blairites were furious with Brown, believing he had conceded the case too easily. 'There'd been four inquiries, for goodness' sake; how many more were needed?' says one senior official.[275] Blair himself feared a 'show trial' if the new inquiry were conducted in public. Aware of the depth of public anger at the conduct of the Iraq War, Blair thought that, if there were to be a further investigation, the panel itself, and still more those giving evidence, would feel under intolerable pressure and the truth would be obscured.[276] Brown came under intensive lobbying, above all from Mandelson. 'Peter put in a big claim to ensure that it was made a private inquiry, because it was about defending Tony,' says a senior figure.[277] Blair's view, which Mandelson forcefully expressed, was that if the inquiry was to happen, it should be on Privy Council terms, which, in effect, meant proceedings would be conducted in private.[278] Clarification of what was intended was supplied when, on 15 June, Brown told MPs that an inquiry would be set up to 'learn the lessons of the war'. He said that it would be 'fully independent of government … It covers an eight-year period, including the run-up to the conflict and the full period of conflict and reconstruction … No British document and no British witness will be beyond the scope of the inquiry.'[279] The controversial, if not unsurprising, aspect of Brown's announcement was that the inquiry should be mostly conducted in private; Brown announced that he had accepted the advice of Gus O'Donnell, head of the civil service, that the confidential model used by Franks did indeed offer the most suitable precedent.[280] 'Much more would be learned behind closed doors than if it was done in public,' says one official.[281] Brown had been led to believe further that the Tories would support proceedings being held in private. 'We sounded out the Tories at the time and they said "fine",' recalls one official.[282] So Brown went into the announcement believing that the only opposition in the House would come from the Liberal Democrats.[283]

At the last minute before his statement to the House, Brown removed a phrase to the effect that 'as much as was possible' would be heard in public.[284] He was far from convinced himself. 'I'm not sure it's right to do it this way,' he said to his aides on the morning of his announcement. He was shocked when Cameron responded: 'Given that this inquiry is of interest not only to us politicians but to the public and the families of servicemen and women who gave their lives, should there not be some proper public sessions? Is that not what many will want and many will expect?'[285] Brown felt betrayed by the Tories, not for the first time. But 'what really upset him' was that the Blairites, who had put him under so much pressure, 'didn't even turn up for the debate to support him'.[286] He was incandescent. After he left the chamber, he went back to his office in the House of Commons, where he was in one of his blackest moods. He slammed the door of his office. James Bowler went in to see him. He emerged minutes later shaken and 'white-faced'. Bowler was normally, along with Sue Nye and Sarah, the best at calming the Prime Minister down at these times. One who had been with him for his last two years described it as his 'worst rage' in that entire period.[287]

Brown found himself placed in the ironic position of having to defend the establishment, consisting of Blair, the military and Whitehall, and the Iraq War, while taking the flak on all their behalf.[288] When the public outcry at his announcement started, with accusations that it would be a cover-up, 'the Cabinet Office, the Foreign Office and the MoD all started saying that they felt all along the inquiry should be in public', says one Number 10 source with bitterness. 'But their advice beforehand was exactly the opposite.'[289] In desperation, Brown called Ainsworth: 'Find me a general who will come out and support this decision.' The Defence Secretary replied: 'There is no general alive who will back you on this.'[290] Brown yet again found himself in a place where he had been all too often: unsustainable remaining where he was, but facing the certainty of abuse as a 'bottler' and a 'U-turner' if he changed his mind. Heywood ultimately took the decision what to do. 'Time and again it was Jeremy who took the key decisions on difficult matters at Number 10,' says a senior adviser.[291]

On 17 June, Brown duly wrote to John Chilcot, the retired official appointed to head the inquiry, to say that its manner of conduct should be a matter for his personal discretion. On 21 June, Chilcot was in no doubt, and responded: 'I believe it will be essential to hold as much of the proceedings of the inquiry as possible in public, consistent with the need to protect national security.'[292] Brown, as predicted, was attacked, not least by *The Sun*, for betrayal and vacillation. On 24 June, he won a difficult Commons vote on the inquiry, facing down an alliance of Conservatives and Liberal Democrats who wanted the composition of the inquiry changed to include those with military and ministerial experience.[293] Brown was blamed, although it was not he who had decided on the membership, but O'Donnell and Fletcher. Chilcot, a former permanent secretary at the Northern Ireland Office, had been selected for his considerable experience in intelligence. The four other members were: one former diplomat, Rod Lyne, who had been Major's foreign affairs private secretary in Number 10 and subsequently ambassador in Moscow; two academics: Lawrence Freedman of Kings College London, and Churchill's official biographer, Martin Gilbert; and the then chair of the Judicial Appointments Commission, Baroness Prashar.[294] The list had been cleared with Hague.

The Blair and Brown teams had consulted closely, with palpable continuing irritation among Blair's advisers that the inquiry was to be held. The original understanding was that interviews with key witnesses, including Blair and Brown, would not take place before a general election. Brown was not unduly concerned about appearing himself in public. His advisers thought: 'It would not be a problem for Gordon; there was no smoking gun. We were clear that it was something that he should do.'[295] On 23 December, a statement on the Chilcot Inquiry's website announced that Brown would appear, but only after the general election; it quoted Chilcot as saying the delay was to avoid the occasion 'being used for political advantage'.[296] This news did nothing to quell agitation for an early appearance. At PMQs on 13 January, Clegg asked: 'Will the Prime Minister now do the decent thing and volunteer to give evidence to the inquiry before people decide how to vote on his record in government?' Brown responded that he had 'nothing to hide' and was happy to give evidence.[297] In the light of this line of attack, Chilcot decided it would be unfair if Brown was not given the chance to respond before polling day, and on 22 February it was duly announced that he would give evidence on Friday 5 March.[298]

As Blair was to be playing no instrumental role in the general election, there was no solid reason for his own attendance at the inquiry to be delayed, and he appeared on 29 January. The former Prime Minister appeared tired and drawn, and found the questioning an ordeal.[299] He had the opportunity to be candid: to speak about his multifaceted reasoning for supporting the invasion of Iraq, to confess he should have done more to prepare for the post-war invasion, and to explain why he had extracted so little from President Bush as the price of British support.[300] Instead, he gave a dogged reiteration of positions he had stated before: 'If we had left Saddam in power, we would still have had to deal with him, possibly in circumstances where the threat was worse … The decision I took – and frankly would take again – was if there was any possibility that he could develop WMDs we should stop him.'[301] The performance lost him widespread support from those who were looking for more honesty and humility, now that Britain's military was no longer in Iraq.[302]

Five weeks later, it was Brown's turn. Mandelson was ostentatiously absent during Brown's meticulous preparations. Brown knew all too well that Mandelson's advice would be 'you must protect Tony', so he was relieved that Mandelson chose to distance himself on this. Aides described it as 'pretty difficult' for their relationship.[303] In the end, Brown spent twelve hours preparing for it and had special 'Post-it' notes stuck on his brief with the key messages and phrases that his team wanted to appear on Sky News as he spoke. A fraught debate took place within the political team in Number 10 between those who wanted him to distance himself from the war and others who said that that would come across looking weak, and that he should say instead that he had been fully party to Cabinet decisions. The arguments went back and forth, with the actual truth of what had happened and what he thought at the time being secondary to calculations of where his best advantage was thought to lie. His team kept probing him, asking what he had done wrong or what he would have done differently. He hated having to answer such questions and always found a way round them, says one official.[304] The truth was that Brown had never been keen on the whole Iraq War. He regarded it as 'Blair's adventure', but he judged at the time, that if he were to express a scintilla of doubt about it, it would damage his credibility as Blair's successor. Nevertheless, it was eventually resolved that he would come across to Chilcot as a war supporter.[305]

Once his line had been resolved, his team relaxed and joked about whether he should announce an end to the 'sofa government' style so criticised in the Butler inquiry. They speculated whether he should say that in future he would have no more cosy chats on the sofa with his Foreign Secretary, deliberately poking fun at his troubled relationship with Miliband.[306]

'It was the right decision and it was for the right reasons ... Everything Mr Blair did in this period ... he did properly,' Brown brazenly told the inquiry, before going on to 'pay his respects' pointedly to all who had been injured and died fighting, including the many Iraqi civilians.[307] While he spoke to the inquiry, his team, watching his performance nervously on on Sky News, thought he did well in the first session.[308] In the break, they rushed in to see him in his room and 'built him up'.[309] During the lunch session he had a difficult meeting with a bereaved family, but his team judged that he sprang back well and 'was very good in the afternoon'.[310] Much of Brown's performance was planned to be in deliberate contrast to Blair's. While the latter had entered the building via the underground car park and left at speed, for example, 'we had GB walking in looking relaxed'.[311] Nick Robinson was one of many to pick up the contrast: 'Mr Brown expressed his sadness at the loss of life, while Mr Blair angered many by refusing to do that. The Prime Minister smiled at the waiting audience where his predecessor had avoided eye contact with them.'[312]

Brown himself was pleased with his four-hour appearance. He created exactly the impression he wanted, of being loyal to Blair and Cabinet collective responsibility, while coming across as more sympathetic to the suffering the war had caused, and avoiding opening up any new and potentially unsettling lines of inquiry ahead of the general election. The major question that he did not answer, as an editorial in *The Guardian* was to remark the following day, was why he did not 'take a stand against the war', especially when 'everyone in British politics in 2003 knew that, if Mr Brown had opposed the Iraq war, it would not have happened'.[313] The answer to that question was explosive, which is why he studiously smothered any information hinting at his scepticism in 2002/03. The main media attack came in *The Sun*, which ran the headline, 'Brown: it wasn't me', above an article that claimed that he had 'repeatedly denied ANY blame for the Iraq war and the failings that cost British lives'. Former Chief of the Defence Staff Lord Guthrie was invited to write an article to the edition and used the platform to bash Brown again, accusing him of being 'economical with the truth' and 'disingenuous' about the problems of poor equipment, which began when he was Chancellor, when he had been 'unsympathetic to the MoD'. Susan Smith, the mother of a soldier killed in Afghanistan, wrote a further article, saying of his expressions of regret: 'To be honest I just get a feeling that some of it is spin.'[314]

Did Brown deserve blame for Iraq? Although he held an effective veto, the decisions over the Iraq war were made ultimately by Blair and his team in the den in Number 10. The inquiry failed to tackle him properly on why he, along with others in the Cabinet, did not do more to assert their fundamental concerns about the war, which might have resulted either in Britain not participating, or doing so with much more leverage on Washington and in a way that was far more cognisant of the needs of post-war Iraq. The Brown they interviewed was not the de facto Deputy Prime Minister he saw himself to be, but the man responsible for the purse strings. The important questions he was asked at the inquiry thus related to funding, especially as he was accused by Guthrie of squandering soldiers' lives as a result of inadequate spending. Brown strongly asserted that he had funded every single request the military had made, and he told the inquiry he had no regrets about his financing of the war and its aftermath.[315] One particular point he made had to be retracted later: his claim that the spending that he had sanctioned for the military had risen above the rate of inflation each year of the ten that he was Chancellor. Twelve days after he spoke to the inquiry, on 17 March, he told the House of Commons: 'I do accept, in one or two years, defence expenditure did not rise in real terms.'[316] The military continued to dispute his figures, and his comments before the inquiry did nothing to dispel the belief of many in the services that he had deliberately stinted on military spending because of a lack of empathy as Chancellor with the fighting both in Iraq and Afghanistan.[317] Brown's sins of omission in 2002/03, and his lack of candour about them in 2010, are stains on his political career.

The inquiry at the end of his premiership muddied the earlier impression that Brown had handled the end game in Iraq well. It left him morose, feeling that he would never free himself from 'TB legacy issues', such as Megrahi and Iraq.[318] He found it all very distasteful, and it ensured that his final months saw no unfreezing of relations with his predecessor. Some officials in Number 10 that spring took to writing long records of everything they themselves were doing, fearing a time when their future careers would be subject to a chain of official inquiries in which they had to explain themselves.[319] Brown himself was angry that the noise around the Iraq Inquiry had sullied much that he had tried to achieve since 2007. He had been more intelligently sympathetic to the lives of ordinary soldiers than many Prime Ministers, and his urgency on economic reconstruction was improving lives in Iraq, as it was in Afghanistan. But the acrid resentment that his ten years as Chancellor had caused among the military had created a legacy of mistrust from which he never succeeded in freeing himself.

Finding His Agenda

A great paradox of Brown's premiership is that a politician grounded exclusively in domestic policy should have given more of his time to foreign policy and an international agenda, and often been clearer about his objectives in it, while leaving impetus in his domestic policy, even more so than Blair, until late in his premiership. After two years of distraction, clarity eventually came with *Building Britain's Future* in the summer of 2009, his policy-rich conference speech that year, and in the November 2009 Queen's Speech. However, it still fell short of anything that could be called a coherent 'Brownite' domestic policy agenda. That is partly because he had ceased, in the wake of the financial crisis, to be Brownite, in the sense of wanting more direct state control in public services and less market-based diversity. By the summer of 2009, Brown was recognising that Labour had to offer voters greater value for money in public services, and promote greater choice for users. However, much of the agenda appeared far too late to be enacted and several of his most important policies fell at the last hurdle as the general election approached. Had he won another term, it is at least arguable that he could have fashioned these into a more enduring political project.

Brown's team had discussed the Alternative Vote (AV) model of electoral reform before he became Prime Minister, but it went the same way as the other constitutional reforms that Brown had proposed in his first flush of enthusiasm when he entered Number 10. The expenses crisis proved a major spur, and he returned to the subject of constitutional reform in his 2009 conference speech, announcing that Labour would make a manifesto commitment to holding a national referendum on AV. However, as so often with constitutional progress, other more immediate priorities intervened that autumn. 'A fallow period followed the conference speech when nothing happened,' reports one insider at Number 10.[320] Brown came under pressure again from aides and ministers, including Michael Wills and Alan Johnson, to seize the initiative. The latter pushed the idea of holding a referendum on AV on the same day as the general election. Cabinet Office advice was unequivocal: there was insufficient time to pass the legislation that would make that possible. In addition, Number 10 worried it would lose a referendum, with 'no' votes taking support away from Labour.[321] Wills and Number 10 aides instead urged Brown to introduce a referendum bill for AV *before* the election, by amending the Constitutional Reform and Governance (CRAG) bill then going through Parliament. Mandelson and Balls strongly advised against making political reform a priority in the election, while Brown's own attention was distracted in the run up to Christmas by Copenhagen and the Pre-Budget Report. Straw said he would take soundings in the PLP to ascertain the degree of support for AV. His unsurprising conclusion was that the party was split, with all the Scottish MPs totally against, believing that electoral reform would damage Labour north of the Border. Within the Cabinet, Scottish Secretary Murphy and Burnham were against, while both Milibands, Johnson, Hain, Adonis and Ben Bradshaw were in favour.[322]

In the New Year, Brown discovered a fresh zeal for constitutional reform, spurred by polls predicting a hung parliament, with Labour's attraction to the Liberal Democrats much strengthened if it showed a strong commitment on AV. He spoke passionately about electoral reform to the Institute for Public Policy Research (IPPR) in February, announcing his intention to pass a referendum bill before the election. But was there time to get the legislation through? Brown's old guard was divided: Tom Watson told him it could be done, while another member of his cabal, Chief Whip Nick Brown, was heavily sceptical. Brown was tenacious: he called Nick Brown and the whole of the Whips Office into Downing Street and told him: 'You will deliver this for me. Go and fix it.'[323] A reluctant Chief Whip steered it through the Commons, with only three Labour MPs voting against, but he was telling sceptics not to worry because it would never be enacted before the general election was called. 'Nick Brown never believed it nor wanted to get it through,' believed Number 10.[324]

It fell to the Chief Whip to negotiate bills during the 'wash-up' phase (the short time after an election has been called, but before Parliament has been formally adjourned), when he happily sacrificed the CRAG bill. The push for AV was not, however, entirely futile. In the talks with the Liberal Democrats after the general election, Labour's commitment to a referendum on AV helped force the hand of the Tories into offering the Liberal Democrats a chance of electoral reform. On the day that Brown delivered his IPPR lecture, Number 10 phoned Clegg's office and pleaded with them not to attack his initiative; the Liberal Democrats subsequently gave it lukewarm support rather than ridiculing it altogether.[325] It was indicative, nevertheless, that Brown's most decisive move on constitutional reform, his support for a referendum on AV, was made as much for party political reasons and a desire to optimise Labour's position as from genuine political conviction. What of his summer promise to drive Lords reform? Straw did draft a bill for an elected second chamber, which Brown personally favoured, but it never saw the light of day because the Prime Minister was intensely nervous about offending the Church of England, given that a democratic upper house would see the bishops thrown out. These concerns meant he was not prepared to overturn Cabinet opposition from Mandelson, Murphy and Nick Brown. Nor did he achieve his goal of removing the remaining hereditary peers – this proposal fell with the CRAG bill too. Blair had shown little personal enthusiasm for leadership on constitutional activity in his first term, which had owed much to the legacy of John Smith, so the area was wide open for Brown to introduce much-needed reform. He saw the case intellectually, but his premiership will be known more for constitutional innovations pledged, as on AV, than implemented.

Education was the one area of domestic policy where many expected Brown to make the most decisive impact, not the least after he put his principal lieutenant, Balls, in charge of running the newly created Department for Children, Schools and Families. The National Challenge programme, launched in 2007, to turn around the poorest schools across the country, had been seen very much as the product of Brown's encouragement. The programme had got off to a positive start, with the number of failing schools dropping from over 600 in 2007 to 237 in 2009, and was a significant success for Balls who drove it forward, as was his handling of the 'Baby P' affair. But he was not a creative force in the way Number 10 wanted him to be, and it became worried when education under his aegis slipped down the agenda, 'which is never a good place for Labour to be', says a Brown aide.[326] Brown would regularly ask his officials in Number 10, 'What's our radical education policy?' and they would reply: 'You haven't got one.' 'Why not?' he would bark back, and they would say: 'You know why not.' They did not need to say any more. They were embarrassed to tell him. They did not need to. He knew that the reason was Balls, with whom he became increasingly frustrated.[327] Brown once turned to an adviser after putting the phone down from Balls and said in dismay: 'I guess that's another "fuck off" from Ed then.'[328] Number 10, both officials and political advisers, found Balls exasperating on education matters. 'Normally the Number 10 policy person would have a direct and close relationship with the Secretary of State. It was impossible with Balls. He largely did what he wanted, and Brown was very rarely prepared to overrule him.'[329] Balls's team in the Children's Department became as frustrated with Number 10: the feeling was mutual.[330]

During the course of 2009, the Policy and Strategy Units had developed a new ploy – embedding their own policy team within Balls's department. Had the ideas emanated from Number 10, Balls would have rejected them out of hand.[331] 'It had been like trench warfare, a daily grind. But with people inside the department, it gave the impression that he had dreamt up the policies himself,' says an aide.[332] Intellectually the most brilliant minister in Brown's Cabinet, Balls had a deep commitment to improving the education system. So why did he not prove more innovative? A late arrival in a department which he had not shadowed, he did not come to schools with a clear agenda, or with a detailed understanding of his own. More fundamentally Balls was at all costs determined 'not to be a Blairite in the way he ran the department'.[333] So choice, diversity, academies and empowering parents were all downplayed or mothballed. Significantly, it also meant watering down the Blairite drive on school standards. 'Politically this was a disaster for us. Ed never gave the impression that he cared about improving school standards. He even banned the use of the term "failing schools"'. So, as the election approached, he began carving out dividing lines between himself and Michael Gove, which meant opposing the idea of parents having a stronger voice in the running of schools

– one of Gove's core aims. Number 10 was also frustrated by Balls's reluctance to embrace their entitlements agenda and his abiding preference for 'micro-managing everything from the centre through targets'. One official says: 'We could never move Ed away from this.'[334] Some suspect his heart was never in schools, that he saw the job as a launch pad for his ambition to become Labour leader after Brown's departure, and that meant avoiding taking on any interest groups, including unions and local government, which could damage his upward trajectory. 'He was only interested in reform in so far as it would boost his standing in the party,' says one fellow minister.[335]

With the election approaching, the drive was on to produce a coherent education platform. 'We were heading for polling day, and no one knew what our education policy was,' says one Number 10 aide.[336] In the lead up to Christmas, Brown was scheduled to have made a number of key policy speeches, but they slipped.[337] Knowing that no further delay was possible, the date 23 February was written firmly in the diary for a speech at Woodberry Down Community Primary School in Hackney, an event shared with the charity promoting graduates becoming teachers, Teach First. But what would Brown say in Hackney? Number 10's policy team had for some time been working away in Balls's department on an approach to poorly performing schools being taken over by better state schools, academy schools or even accredited private schools. The major disagreement was over the trigger to enable failing schools to be taken over by these accredited school providers. Number 10 had for some time been pushing for measures which gave parents more power and favoured an automatic trigger, so that a consistently poorly performing school would have been taken over if specified targets were not met. Balls resisted the idea, and a fight looked likely. With only days before the speech, Brown and Balls spoke on the telephone. 'Suddenly, Ed put up the idea of *parents* being able to trigger takeovers,' and Brown readily assented to the idea. His officials were flummoxed, because Balls had 'had a blind spot on parent power' for the previous two years.[338] Balls had belatedly concluded that, with Gove receiving such a positive press about his plans to empower parents, he needed to seize back politically important territory that he had ceded. On Monday, with hours to go before the speech, Tim Kiddell, Brown's civil service speechwriter, weaved the new language into the text.

Brown arrived in Hackney with a stressed-looking Sarah and delivered a speech with the ink on it still wet. He announced that parents dissatisfied with the local school would now 'have a new right to initiate change in the leadership of that school' and announced the first six organisations to be recognised as 'accredited school groups'. Balls was happy with the policy and was ready to front it in the media. The *Daily Telegraph* was signed up to make a major splash, but it was bumped at the last minute, though it was well reported on television and radio. Brown's relatively bare cupboard of achievement on schools and universities is striking, especially given his consistent commitment to enhancing social mobility, and his readiness to intervene himself from early on, notably over the Laura Spence affair in 2000. Instead, he allowed Balls to put up a roadblock to what Number 10 regarded as significant reform, without ever clearly defining a path of his own.

Social care was another area where great progress was expected, given, again, Brown's deep personal commitment to it. 'We need to carry out a major reform in social care,' he told a policy adviser in the first few weeks of his premiership.[339] Labour had danced around the issue since 1997, and, with an ageing population, it was becoming an urgent issue. Brown was determined to tackle it. But for two years he stalled because of concerns over how to fund reform, which put several Cabinet ministers off, not least his then Health Secretary Alan Johnson.[340] Nonetheless Brown initiated much exploratory work to scope the options, resulting in a Department of Health green paper in July 2009. The green paper was light on details and deliberately did not commit the government to a specific package, though it did advance the case for eventually moving towards a 'national care service'. A real turning point came when Andy Burnham became Health Secretary in June 2009. Burnham was determined to push reform and Brown had great respect for his boldness on the issue. At one point, he said: 'Andy, do you realise that this could be the breaking of us?' Burnham shot back: 'Gordon, you are right, but it could also be the making of us.'[341] Burnham and Number 10 pressed Brown to build on the green paper and this led to his conference announcement that he would provide free social care at home to the most needy. 'We warned Gordon that the government would be chastised if the green paper led nowhere – Labour was already vulnerable that it had wasted more than a decade on the issue.'[342] Brown thus favoured a staggered approach – legislation before the election to provide free care for those with 'highest needs', followed by more detailed proposals setting out his vision for future fundamental reform. As with education, Number 10 sent a team from the Strategy Unit into the Department of Health to help work up policy, a tactic favoured by Pearce as head of the Policy Unit to tackle what he saw as Whitehall conservatism. But social care was another policy dog that did not bark, though his aides believe 'it would have become a centrepiece of the Brown government had he won the election'.[343] With the Prime Minister and Secretary of State determined to see reform, why did he not achieve more?

Time was a clear factor: the impetus needed to have come in June 2007, not November 2009, when Brown introduced his free personal care bill. It met fierce opposition in the Lords, particularly from Labour peer, Lord Lipsey, who believed the policy to be both misguided and, given the state of the public finances, unaffordable. Brown pressed his Chief Whip to get the bill through the wash-up negotiations but Nick Brown, who was personally sceptical, barely put up a fight and the legislation was torpedoed.[344] Brown's Cabinet was then split over whether the government should announce its plans for more radical long-term reform ahead of the election. Brown was convinced it was the right thing to do and was backed by Burnham and Ed Miliband (who wanted to include the plans in the manifesto). Opponents included Peter Hain and Yvette Cooper, both of whom worried about the implications for changes to the attendance allowance – a benefit paid to the elderly to fund support in the home. Ministers' main concern, however, centred on the thorny issue of how to fund an expanded care service. They were particularly worried about the idea of a 'death tax' – a proposal considered in the green paper for a compulsory levy to be paid on death. On 9 February 2010, the Conservatives opened an advertising campaign attacking Labour for it with the line 'Now Gordon wants £20,000 when you die'. Burnham accused his opposite number Andrew Lansley of 'shafting him' on an understanding that he thought they had reached, and the 'death tax' proposal was therefore dropped by Darling on 29 March. The Tory campaign proved how toxic the politics of reform could be. On 30 March, the government published the social care white paper that restated its commitment to a national care service. But good intentions were a far cry from the hard policy that Brown had wanted to deliver, although he deserves some credit for putting the topic, consistently overlooked by Blair, on the map. That said, social care reform was one of the major items of unfinished business for New Labour.

Instinctive hostility to Blair's policies was not to blame for the lack of progress on social care, but it certainly was in the field of law and order. Brown had a barely concealed contempt for Blair's emphasis on this, which originated from the latter's stint as shadow Home Secretary from 1992 to 1994, and which was also influenced by his experience as a barrister. When Brown made Jacqui Smith his Home Secretary in 2007 he failed to outline a clear agenda for her other than 'ensuring that she did not do anything that smacked of Blairism'.[345] 'Certain topics, like knife crime, captured his interest, but most of the time, I was left to get on with my own thing, undisturbed, and without any instructions,' she says.[346] Against her express wishes, he moved Louise Casey, Blair's feisty head of the 'respect taskforce', into the Cabinet Office, where he placed her under the jurisdiction of an unsympathetic Balls at the Children's Department, who was no believer in the antisocial behaviour agenda. Balls felt Blair's obsession with antisocial behaviour meant there was too much focus on punitive action and too little on prevention. He did not believe the success of a society should be judged by the number of Asbos it handed out.[347] Politically, however, his prevention agenda, which included a stronger emphasis on youth services, failed to resonate with the public. 'Respect was Tony's big thing' says Jacqui Smith, which meant that Balls wanted nothing to do with it. 'It was a prime example of how Brown's government dropped something because they wanted to be different from Blair but failed to put anything concrete in its place. It caused real problems for us.'[348] As with education Balls's desire to distance himself from Blair meant that Labour gave up important political territory to the Conservatives.

Brown's first speech on crime did not come until his party conference speech in September 2009, when his premiership was three-quarters over. What accounted for the late change of heart? As often in the law and order field, a high-profile case produced a rethink of policy, not always wisely. In September 2009, the inquest into Fiona Pilkington, who had killed herself along with her disabled daughter two years before, received widespread publicity when it became known that no action had been taken against a gang of youths who had repeatedly terrorised her neighbourhood. At the party conference, the new Home Secretary, Alan Johnson, declared that there should be 'no excuses' for cases such as hers, and that government needed to do 'much, much more' to tackle antisocial behaviour.[349] Johnson succeeding Smith at the Home Office in June 2009 gave a fresh impetus to the agenda, but far more energy came from Brown's realisation that embracing it would be a popular rallying cry with the right-wing press as the election approached, and, most important of all, that it would appeal to the manual working class, whose communities were blighted by this behaviour. Only late in the day did Brown understand what Blair had understood fifteen years before – that the working classes are the main sufferers from lawlessness.

On 1 March 2010 in Reading, he gave a powerful speech on antisocial behaviour, in which he unveiled a series of policies, exceeding anything in scope that his government had proposed before. Eye-catching measures included a new lease of life for the '101' non-emergency number (a telephone number for citizens to report episodes of antisocial behaviour to which Brown had cut the funding in 2007), the promise that police would spend more time on the streets, and stricter punishments for those on Asbos. Brown's reluctance to do more earlier had angered Smith. 'When he came to the agenda in late 2009, it failed to resonate with the electorate because it was only half-heartedly pursued,' she says.[350] Number 10, too, was in despair at his reluctance to take the agenda forward, especially when they had been pointing out that it was Labour voters who were so often the victims of crime. Forsyth acknowledges it was 'an obvious example of a gap in Brown's policy programme'.[351] The one exception concerned neighbourhood policing, which was successfully rolled out across the country on his watch. The whole area was one where he would have benefited from sitting down calmly before June 2007 and thinking without prejudice about what was required. In three years, though not for want of trying in his final year, he failed to produce a coherent agenda on how to tackle antisocial behaviour and crime.

The pattern on immigration was very similar: initial caution and then only when it was too late the emergence of a stronger position, set out in a speech in November 2009 and then a final one in March 2010. Brown's basic analysis was initially similar to Blair's. He shared the view that immigration was good for Britain, but that the public had legitimate concerns. He also shared with Blair the tactic of dancing around the central issue of tackling immigration numbers by focusing instead on a related issue to demonstrate action was being taken – for Blair this meant asylum seekers and for Brown it was a bigger argument about Britishness and national identity. Policies like 'earned citizenship' set out in his March 2008 speech were pushed hard by Brown and his team. But these initiatives failed to make the break-through he hoped for. Two factors explain this. Firstly, Brown's credibility on immigration never really recovered from his populist 'British jobs for British workers' speech in September 2007, which in the words of one Number 10 insider 'gave us one day's good coverage followed by three years in which it became, rightly, a rod for our back.' More fundamentally, while the Tories were making hay with their policy of an immigration cap, Labour was still failing to directly address the issue most voters had now latched onto – the overall level of immigration. It was not until 2009 that Brown decided to change tack. In a split decision at Cabinet, Brown, supporting Jacqui Smith and Liam Byrne, overruled a group that included Mandelson, Darling and both Milibands in arguing that Labour needed to speak directly to the public's concerns about immigration numbers. Balls was again on the losing side of the argument. His claims in the Labour leadership election to have spent the last eighteen months of Brown's premiership saying that immigration could not be swept under the carpet were, in the words of one former colleague, 'diametrically opposed to the truth'. In his March 2010 speech, entitled 'Controlling Immigration', Brown told an audience in Shoreditch, east London, that numbers mattered and that his points-based system would see them fall over time. The speech was undermined firstly because his claim that immigration numbers were falling was immediately challenged by the UK Statistics Authority, and secondly because as with much else on the domestic front, his intervention had come too late: 'we had lost the argument by then, and more seriously we had lost the public's trust on the issue' says an adviser. Brown would make one final intervention on immigration as Prime Minister, and it would prove very costly indeed.

Realising that he had an achievement-light domestic record with the election looming, his staff had secured his agreement over the summer of 2009 to identify three or four iconic policies, which included the cancer pledge and high-speed rail. The latter was the last of Brown's policies to be advanced late in his premiership. Transport for Brown, as for Blair, had been a 'Cinderella' area. Neither of his first two Transport Secretaries, Ruth Kelly and Geoff Hoon, made any substantial impact. Energy, however, was to be injected by the appointment as junior minister in October 2008 of Andrew Adonis, who had a real passion for a high-speed rail line from London to the Midlands and the North. It had been mentioned in a report by Blair's 'blue skies' thinker, John Birt, but had not been enacted before Blair left Number 10. The 2007 Eddington report had been sceptical about its economics, while Transport Department officials were unconvinced by its environmental credentials. Adonis, who had been Blair's head of policy, had been captivated by the promise. He was concerned that other European countries had developed high-speed tracks, and that the Conservatives had latched on to it, while Labour had remained uncommitted to this substantial piece of public investment.[352]

He discussed it with Brown in the summer of 2008 and took to it in earnest when he was promoted as Transport Secretary after Hoon's departure in June 2009. Within a fortnight of taking up his role, Adonis had come to Number 10 to present his ideas to Brown's team, which, to their delight, included plans for reprioritising capital spend in his department, to fund high-speed rail and the electrification of two major railway lines, at no extra cost. Brown was deeply impressed. 'You could see in Gordon's eyes how excited he was by what Andrew was talking about,' says Gavin Kelly.[353] Conservative opposition this close to the election could scupper the plan. So Adonis spoke to Osborne. 'We agreed to have a "non-aggression" pact to stop any brickbats being hurled at the government over the level of spending,' he says.[354] In the House of Lords on 11 March 2010, Adonis unveiled his plans for an initial link between London and Birmingham, including a blueprint for how the line would be extended to Manchester and Liverpool in the North-West and to Leeds and Sheffield in the North-East.

High-speed rail was indeed a signature policy and helped sum up long-termism, investment and modernisation, themes that were clearly important to Brown. It was conspicuous for being a rare example under Brown of a Cabinet minister driving forward a policy on their own. Number 10 was frequently irritated by what it saw as the lack of innovative thinking from Cabinet ministers, only too happy to have their feet under the famous coffin-shaped table in Number 10, but reluctant to make the weather once back in their departments. 'We had a real problem with ministers throughout his premiership. They became boxed in by their civil servants, and became far too cautious and governmental,' says one Number 10 aide.[355] 'At Cabinet, ministers were forever saying they wanted the government to be "bolder" and "more radical", but they would then back away.'[356] Creative Cabinet ministers, like Adonis, Liam Byrne, Burnham and Purnell, were in the minority. Sometimes they were fortunate in their junior ministers, as Johnson was at Health with Ara Darzi, who oversaw successful policy change. But too many ministers impeded progress.

Brown frequently became exasperated by the lack of proactiveness from his Cabinet, which was reciprocated in their own irritation and increasing desperation at his inability to define his own clear agenda, or to share his thinking with them. Blair did not define his personal agenda until 2002–03 – his sixth year in office – so one should not be too harsh on Brown. The start of a long period of government, as in 1997, is also a more propitious time for innovation than its latter years. The phase of the governmental cycle, the lack of money, the depletion of ministerial stock, and the seismic impact of the economic crisis in 2008 and the expenses crisis in 2009, all go some way to explaining why Brown's domestic policy agenda was not fuller. But Brown cannot be absolved of responsibility himself. 'Everything in his premiership comes back to his lack of definition about what he wanted to achieve,' said a senior official in 2009.[357] When he became Prime Minister he had worked out what he was against – Blair – but not what he was for. To make matters worse he had used up many of his best ideas during his early phase as Chancellor. His failure to arrive with a clear programme for government badly weakened him from the outset and meant he had to invent one in office – a tough ask for any Prime Minister, but something Brown, as an instinctively cautious and indecisive politician, found difficult to pull off. He worked best when he was forced to react to events, like the financial crisis, but, when there was less immediate pressure to act, paralysis would often set in. This helps explains why public service reform stalled on his watch. Balls's intransigence was another factor. While Brown himself finally came to appreciate the strategic importance of having a clear 'reform story' for the country along Blairite lines, he never felt sufficiently strong enough to take on his protégé.

Brown, who was not lacking in capable policy advisers at Downing Street, failed to provide them with the clear sense of policy direction they needed to structure their work, and then compounded it by a distant and wary relationship with almost all of his Cabinet ministers, which fell short of providing an encouraging environment for them to devise initiatives of their own. In contrast to Blair, Brown was never interested in policy implementation and there were no monthly stocktakes with his ministers, which further impeded progress. The deficit in domestic policy achievement was to be of no help to the government as it came to face its next challenge: winning the general election. But would Brown himself be the liability many in the party feared?

The Real Gordon Brown

Throughout the pages of this book, the real character of Gordon Brown has been a constant issue: was he a good man who could be occasionally bad, or the opposite? These two very different interpretations of him were brought into relief in the media in February 2010: an engaging and personable side on *Piers Morgan's Life Stories* on television; and an aggressive and bullying side in

Andrew Rawnsley's book, *The End of the Party*. Rawnsley's portrait appeared in the pages of *The Observer*, which began to serialise the book, a sequel to his earlier *Servants of the People* (2001), towards the end of February.

Brown's advisers had long been saying he needed to engage more directly with the public, and come across in the media as a more human figure.[358] They despaired that so many who met him in the flesh departed saying things like 'he was totally different to what I expected', evidence of a wider failure to communicate effectively to the electorate the best parts of Brown's character, the humane, compassionate and caring side those close to him saw so often.[359] In late 2009, Piers Morgan had interviewed him for *GQ* magazine under the title 'Being Prime Minister is much harder than I thought'. Morgan had known Brown well from the days when he had been editor of the *Daily Mirror* (1995–2004) and had been keen to interview him as Prime Minister. His arrival at Number 10 for the *GQ* interview had caused quite a stir before Christmas: 'It was the poshest-looking car that I'd seen outside Number 10, apart from Alan Sugar's, and people were stunned at his chutzpah at persuading the police to let him park outside the black door,' says an official.[360] Morgan was so pleased with the interview that he suggested to Sarah that he should build on it by interviewing him on television. 'Sarah was a good soldier. She never ran a parallel operation. She would check in,' says one of Brown's team.[361] So she put the proposal to Muir, who decided to talk it over with Forsyth and Nye. Together, they trooped over to the Foreign Office canteen (the 'food there is much better') and took the decision that Brown should go for it. 'We put it to Gordon. He took our advice,' recalls Muir.[362]

Agreeing to it was one thing, preparing for it quite another. 'There's no doubt that Gordon isn't the most telegenic politician,' says Ben Bradshaw, highlighting one of the key problems.[363] Brown was conflicted about it himself and became surly. 'Why do I have to do all this? Why do I have to bare my soul?' he wondered aloud to his advisers. 'Because people deserve to know who their Prime Minister is,' was their reply.[364] Brown had enjoyed having Campbell around since the autumn, and his team knew that if anyone could bring out the best in him it would be him. 'Alastair knew he would have to perform. He knew he'd have to behave. He knew he'd have to do his very best.'[365] So, Campbell was drafted in to play the role of Morgan in a series of practice sessions in early February, described as being 'like a joint therapy session between the pair of them'. There was some unfinished business there. Campbell confronted Brown about his behaviour with Blair and pushed him relentlessly to explain himself. The team began to worry that too much rehearsal time was 'being spent on the Blair stuff', but reasoned that it was 'forcing Gordon to realise that he couldn't fudge this one and [that] he would have to be honest'.[366] Campbell manoeuvred Brown into admitting that his behaviour had often been quite poor towards Blair, climaxing in the terrible rows over the timing of the latter's departure.

At the final rehearsal in the morning, his team eventually became happy: just in time, 'we felt we had got him into the zone'.[367] Brown began what became a three-and-a-half-hour interview apprehensively; he was defensive about his moods, and sound on policy. But he was at his most arresting when talking about the death of his daughter, Jennifer Jane: 'I turned to the doctor and I said: "She's not going to live, is she?" And he said: "No, I don't think so. She's not going to live." So we had a weekend where we just knew that she was not going to survive, and she was baptised, and we were with her, and I held her as she died. [Pictures of Brown and Sarah shedding a few tears were played while he was talking.] Sarah and I [found] that very difficult, because it was our first child, and she was such a beautiful baby.'

The interview attracted 4.2 million viewers and was described by *The Spectator* as 'the best television the Prime Minister will get this year, and probably ever'.[368] Fraser Nelson praised it: 'He kept smiling in a credible way – telling anecdotes in exactly the way he does in private … he spoke and behaved utterly differently to how he does normally. That was as good as it gets from him.'[369] The media reaction was overwhelmingly positive, but not unanimous. An editorial in *The Times* suggested that the interview had eroded the dignity of the office of Prime Minister: 'A private man, Mr Brown finds it hard to conjure the words to evoke our imaginative sympathy. There is something not quite right – like a man who learned to dance from a series of still pictures.'[370]

Brown had found the interview 'emotionally gruelling', but was walking on air when he arrived back in Downing Street. 'Gordon knew he had done bloody well. He's very funny when he knows he's done a good job. He acts humbly and has a big smile on his face.'[371] Even though only a quarter of the interview appeared in the fifty-minute broadcast programme, his staff immediately sensed it had gone well: 'We were off to the races with it. People would see a completely different side to him.'[372] What impact did it have? The BBC's 'poll-of-polls' on 18 February suggested that the interview had made little impact on Labour, which dropped one point to 30 per cent, with the Conservative rating 39 per cent, the same as ten days previously.[373] But Brown enjoyed the biggest one-month jump in his leadership ratings. 'I should have done this a lot earlier,' he reflected and began to see that he was stronger when he told the truth and was straightforward.[374] It made him realise he could display his vulnerable and personal side, and people liked him more for it. He didn't need 'bully boys' around to protect him. This mindset fed through to his touchingly personal final exit from Number 10. The interview helped prepare him for the television debates. It bolstered his team: 'It reminded us of why we worked for him.'[375] It was ironic that the Morgan interview, designed to boost Labour's ratings, made little difference, while the Rawnsley book, which it was feared would leave a very negative impression, seemed to have the opposite effect.

Rawnsley's *The End of the Party* made a number of allegations against Brown personally, including taking the place of a secretary because he thought she was typing too slowly, grabbing Gavin Kelly by the lapels and shouting: 'They're out to get me!' at the time of the lost computer discs in the autumn of 2007, and shoving Stewart Wood in the arm at the top of the stairs in Downing Street. In addition, the book mentioned a series of angry outbursts he allegedly made when travelling in his official car, and it claimed that O'Donnell had been so shocked by the Prime Minister's behaviour towards Number 10 staff that he had spoken to him about it.[376] Rawnsley had 'lunched or dined' people over the years he had been working on the book, and many expressed surprise to find themselves quoted in it, when their agreement had not been sought.[377] He spoke disproportionately to those who had fallen out with Brown, such as Spencer Livermore on the aborted election, but included among his sources, to their discomfort, two of the most senior officials – O'Donnell and Heywood.[378] Brown and Sarah were most livid with O'Donnell, because they believed that he had been one of the sources behind Rawnsley's bullying claims. Brown's relationship with his Cabinet Secretary rapidly deteriorated at this point, while Sarah would later say that she didn't feel able to trust O'Donnell by the end of her time in Number 10. The allegations and the book became a leading news story for several days, and appeared to gain weight when cofounder of the National Bullying Helpline Christine Pratt announced that three or four calls had been made to her charity by Downing Street staff. For two or three days, Brown looked very vulnerable, as his behaviour and the book's sources came under the media microscope. But after three of the Helpline's patrons, including former Tory minister Ann Widdecombe, quit as a result of Pratt's perceived lack of professionalism in going public, and with questions asked about whether the charity was too close to the Conservatives, the sting was drawn.

An article for the *Mail on Sunday* by journalist Suzie Mackenzie, whom Brown had asked to write his biography in April 2007, kept the story alive, however.[379] In the article she described how much she had once admired him, but over the three years during which she had been given 'privileged access' to his family and friends, and spent time with him and Sarah in Scotland, she had become suspicious. She said this was because the people she was seeing, like Sue Nye, Tom Fletcher and Justin Forsyth, seemed to be holding something back. She described how she had spent 'hours' listening to people denigrate Damian McBride and his 'treachery', but when she herself listened to him talk for 'seven hours', she formed the impression of 'a kind and fundamentally decent man'. What finally made her break was watching an interview on *Channel 4 News* on 20 February. 'Brown told [Krishnan] Guru-Murthy he could ask him anything and he would tell the truth,' she says. 'When asked if he had ever pushed anyone, he promptly lied and said he had not. Had Brown lied in the House of Commons he would have had to resign. My feeling was that lying to the public, his electorate, was just as serious.'[380]

To the horror of those who had granted her interviews, she decided to print the transcript of one she had recorded with Stewart Wood on 14 January in the Cinnamon Club, a Westminster restaurant. Wood was quoted saying: 'I was standing at the top of the stairs at Number 10. There was a reception for EU ambassadors and I was waiting ... he was in a really bad mood. He walked up the stairs and I leant forward and he went "Outta my way!" and did that [Dr Wood makes a sweeping gesture with his arm]. "Get outta my way!" then he walked off ... I was slightly shocked. I stood there and went something like: "Bloody hell!"' Mackenzie felt that her decision to make the tape public was in the public interest, particularly in the run-up to the general election. Her article was explosive. Some praised her for giving hard evidence of a man who had, on occasion, treated people badly. Critics said she had betrayed the trust that had been placed in her and written the article for money because her access to Brown and her book had stalled.[381] Mackenzie fiercely denies this: 'Access had not stalled. It was as it had always been – good.'[382] Indeed, Mackenzie had interviewed Shriti Vadera the Tuesday before her article was published. She believed that Brown's team were 'having kittens about Rawnsley's revelations' and were trying to keep her onside.[383] Many feared further revelation so Sue Nye phoned her to ask for an undertaking that she would release no further tapes, at least not before the election, to which Mackenzie happily assented.[384] Wood, who had been her 'minder' in Number 10, now went on the front foot, writing: 'Allegations that Gordon struck or punched me are totally wrong. As I recall, he was in a hurry that day, and barged past me ... but he didn't shove me. It did annoy me at the time, but it was an isolated incident.'[385]

Cameron and Clegg called for an inquiry into the allegations. A spotlight fell on O'Donnell and the allegations that he had reprimanded Brown. The Cabinet Office promptly released a statement saying: 'The Cabinet Secretary would like to make clear that he has never raised concerns with the Prime Minister about him acting in a bullying or intimidating manner in relation to Number 10 staff, let alone giving him any sort of verbal warning.' On 24 February, O'Donnell had to backtrack and admit that he had held a discussion with Brown about how to achieve the 'best' from his staff.[386] Inside Number 10, Brown's close staff attempted to make light of it with the man himself, teasing him that 'no one wants to brush past you any more in case you push us'.[387] Some of the wider staff at Number 10 were nevertheless unhappy and, indeed, there had been concerns about Brown's hectoring, which had leaked to the press as early as autumn 2007.[388] Top-level discussions took place about whether anything should be said to reassure them. Doing nothing risked further stories that it was being 'swept under the carpet', but acknowledging it could be construed as a confession that the accusations had weight. Heywood decided to write to the staff to let them know that the concerns were being taken seriously. 'Within twelve minutes of it going out by email, it had reached Adam Boulton at Sky News.'[389] 'It was incredibly disappointing,' laments one official.[390]

Brown was also forthright in his own defence. 'It is simply a lie to say that I've ever hit anybody in my life,' he told the *Independent on Sunday*.[391] To *The Guardian*, he said: 'The Cabinet Secretary has made it clear that he's had no inquiries, there's been no reprimand, there's been no private message to me … [the] story is completely wrong.'[392] To *Channel 4 News*, he admitted that 'in the heat of the moment', he might 'throw newspapers on the floor or something', but went on to say: 'Of course, you do get angry, mostly with yourself. But I'm very strong-willed, I'm very determined.'[393] In private, Brown became very despondent about the allegations. Whenever accused of wrongdoing, 'he would come back to his parents', and in particular his father, and sense 'how disappointed he would be in him for letting himself down'.[394] The Rawnsley book and the media scrutiny 'led to a difficult few days in Number 10, particularly over the first weekend, but we had been through so much, we had become inured to it'.[395]

So, was Brown a bully? The time has come to get to the heart of this matter. Brown is a highly emotional man, capable of many acts of exceptional kindness and human sympathy. He would often respond with alacrity when he saw others distressed, in a way that could be precipitous and even embarrassing. He cared deeply for the staff that worked with him. He may not have been a pre-meditated bully, but his actions and manner often intimidated others. At times he failed to control his temper. 'He could get very angry, aggressive, and shout a lot,' says one Number 10 official,[396] and this was often driven by frustration if Brown thought that something was not as he wanted it to be, or if he thought that some of his staff were not doing as well as he wanted them to. More often his anger expressed his deep frustration with his own shortcomings as a leader. Those people in his tighter circle around the horseshoe had grown to accept, manage and forgive it, but those outside the coterie could be deeply offended by his personal abuse, and by his shouting in person or on the phone, often with liberal use of the word 'fuck'. One figure who served with him throughout Brown's time in Number 10 says: 'He would phone you very early on, often to yell at you. Switch got used to him screaming at people. They would call and say, considerately: "Have you just woken up? Would you like a moment before we put him through?"'[397] The least attractive facet of his personality was his blind ambition. He felt justified by his mission to do good in the world (though his intentions were not always clear or, indeed, altruistic), to ride roughshod over people, trampling them out of his way if he thought they were obstructing him. This aspect of his character was seen most before he went to Number 10. His thwarted ambition when Blair beat him for the leadership in July 1994 drove him into dark moods of despair and desperation. He sanctioned and committed acts that he knew were unworthy of him. When he moved into Number 10, he tried to put that way of life behind him, but his own emotional insecurity, and the reality of being under constant threat from his Cabinet colleagues, meant he continued to condone practices that were unbecoming to a Prime Minister and failed to meet his own high standards. He would have been a better and more effective leader if he had disposed of the people on whom he had relied during his ascent, such as Whelan, McBride, Austin, Nick Brown and Watson. They could all bring out the worst in him and exacerbate his tendency to paranoia. He pushed himself far too hard and when exhausted he had even less self-control. His tantrums were like a small child's; indeed, they were the actions of a small child who had never learned as an adult to moderate their behaviour. During his three years at Number 10, the public at large had little appreciation of how unbalanced he could be. He had the unfortunate trait of not being honest with himself about elements of his character and behaviour, as they embarrassed him, and sat uneasily with his self-image as his father's son. His lieutenants would thus engage in briefing and intimidating activities that he did not want to know about; but when he denied all knowledge, his lack of candour caused deep suspicion and mistrust.

Brown's manner could thus be hectoring and rude, especially when stressed, and, unforgivably, he could be dismissive with junior staff. So caught up was he in his own concerns that he was usually blind to his effect on others. When he calmed down, and he could see what he had done, he would be contrite. Bullies only bully down, and cause intentional hurt. He did not set out to cause pain. He would rant equally at peers – as he did to a welfare minister in early 2007, snatching papers out of his hands and shouting: 'Who the fuck gave you this data?'[398] – and at those senior to him, notably Blair, to whom he regularly said before June 2007: 'When the fuck are you going to quit?' Even European Commission President Barroso was at the receiving end of many profanities in November 2009, after the Finance Commissioner post went to France. His lack of self-possession led to periodic violent acts, but these were directed at objects. Odd pushes aside, maybe, he was never physical with people. At the height of the lost tax discs saga he became so infuriated that he threw the phone at the wall in the middle of a meeting with aides.

Brown's saving grace with his team, whom he pushed beyond reasonable limits, was his inner kindness and the high ideals he often articulated. 'We didn't suffer from "Stockholm syndrome" because he would lift us with his vision of a better world,' says an official.[399] 'He would often become very angry indeed: on small issues, on big issues, and behind small doors with a number of us. He would then apologise and say: "I'm angry with myself," and turn it on himself,' says another.[400]

Brown's demeanour and performance were critically affected by four key women while he was in Number 10. While not good with a whole stream of women in Cabinet – including Harman, Jowell, Smith, Caroline Flint and Hazel Blears – he was heavily reliant on women in his inner court. Nye knew him the longest and was a powerful presence throughout his premiership. She was an extraordinary public servant, but she did not do much to moderate Brown's excesses, skilful though she was at handling him when he lost control. Ultimately, she knew her place. If she had challenged him more in his febrile court, and delivered home truths, she would have lost influence. In this sense she did not have the influence on Brown that Anji Hunter or Sally Morgan had on Blair. Kirsty McNeill, who became an increasingly important figure in Brown's life after she joined his speechwriting team in 2008, and where she contributed many of his best lines, became one of his staunchest defenders and confidantes. Conscious of the negative impact people like Whelan, Balls and McBride had on him, she encouraged Brown to see them less.[401] She continued to work with him after he left office. Shriti Vadera had a prodigious influence on policy, especially economic and financial, and was a powerful intellectual and emotional prop, although viewed by some in Number 10 as divisive. She had had enough of it by mid-2009 and progressively removed herself from Brown's team. He pined after her, especially with Balls fading from his life, missing her intellectual certainty and loyalty. She was like a female equivalent of Balls – fiercely bright and self-confident, and equally impatient of those who did not share their quickness or raw intelligence. However, Sarah Brown was the most significant influence on him, providing emotional stability during moments of high pressure, giving him with the boys a sense of perspective in his hectic life, and providing decisive advice on his presentation to the public. She was often a voice of sanity in the court but, when her husband came under pressure and attack, she would, naturally, become very defensive of him, and would often reinforce rather than soothe his suspicion and resentment of others.

At heart, Brown was a good man, but his good nature could be very deeply concealed by his overweening ambition and insecurities. As Prime Minister, he became a better man, who wanted to do the best for the least privileged and was devoid of personal financial ambition. When told that Cameron had said he wanted to be in Number 10 because he thought he would 'be good at it', Brown exploded. He didn't think that you should be in politics for instrumental reasons, but to do good in the world.

Ironically, it was only to be in his final weeks in office that he truly found his voice, just as Cameron was managing to remove him from his office.

The General Election

(April–May 2010)

In his final hours in Number 10, when Brown believed that he might be able to form a coalition with the Liberal Democrats and stay on as Prime Minister, he turned to Tom Fletcher and said: 'If I am allowed to form a new administration, I'm going to be like President Bartlet.' The official looked at him oddly. He was not aware that Brown was a devotee of the American television serial *West Wing*, about life in the White House under a fictional liberal US President. He puzzled over exactly what was in the Prime Minister's mind and never got the chance to ask him, but it is likely that Brown was thinking that he would return as a more high-minded figure, less prone to losing his self-control, and able to enact the agenda at home and abroad he knew was largely unfinished.[1]

Brown's behaviour, which he knew had often let him down, had certainly been much in his mind in the preceding weeks. On 6 April, the day he called the general election, the Prime Minister had come close to apologising for how he had often acted towards his staff over the previous three years.[2] He knew he had not done either himself or the country justice during his time at Number 10 – he had not been the Prime Minister that he wanted to be. Only in the last few months had he become much clearer about what he wanted to achieve as head of government. He was passionately keen to be given a second chance, as Bartlet had been in the drama, and this time he wanted to get it right.

On the evening of 11 May, the real US President called Brown as David Cameron was crossing the threshold of Number 10. Obama was 'very pally and supportive', offering his commiserations and saying: 'I'm watching it on the screen as we talk.'[3] During the general election campaign, Number 10 felt they had received 'strong messages' from the White House that, for all the periodic differences between the President and Prime Minister, they wanted Brown to win, 'primarily because they thought we were on the right side on financial consolidation'.[4] However, the Americans could not say or do anything publicly that might prejudice their relations with a future government led by Cameron. Obama had hoped that Brown would be able to participate in the nuclear summit he was organising in Washington in April, but since this would clash with his preparation for the all-important first TV debate, the Prime Minister declined, against official advice. Obama was understanding when Brown told him he could not make it. The President's parting words were: 'Go kick their ass.'[5] How Brown might have fared if he had gone to the summit, and had his mind and spirit raised onto international matters, where, throughout his premiership, he performed more strongly than on the domestic political stage, is now only a matter for conjecture. In an election campaign described as 'the most unpredictable contest in a generation' by the *Financial Times*, anything could have happened.[6]

20 February–6 April

Brown was relieved as the general election at last heaved into view. He enjoyed elections and was energised by them. Throughout early 2010, his conviction grew that he could win or, more realistically, deny Cameron a majority, and thus still realise his dream of securing his own mandate. The thinking was 'to get up to 30 per cent of the vote by the time the campaign started, and rein in the Tories from that point'.[7] He had kicked off Labour's campaign unofficially at Warwick University on 20 February, launching what would effectively become the party's campaign slogan – 'A Future Fair for All'. On 27 February, he went to Swansea to speak at the Welsh Labour Party Conference, taking sons John and Fraser with him on the train. He was in fighting form. 'Gordon gave a great speech. He felt really lifted by that,' Justin Forsyth recorded in his diary.[8] Sunday 28 February was a still better day for him, with the *Sunday Times* running the headline 'Brown on course to win election', and a YouGov poll showed Labour within two points of the Tories – a level of support that could allow it to win the biggest share of seats.[9] On the same day, a poll of polls put the Conservatives only six points ahead.[10] That same day, a strategy meeting was held at Philip Gould's north London home. The mood was upbeat but no one had any illusions about the mountain they had to climb, and the work it would take to deliver their man on the top.

The election team had firmed up during the course of the New Year and had been formally announced by Brown at the Parliamentary Labour Party meeting following the failed January coup. Mandelson, as head of election strategy, was to be the dominant voice, alongside Douglas Alexander, the general election co-ordinator, with Philip Gould, David Muir, Justin Forsyth, Gavin Kelly and Sue Nye as core members. Throughout January and February, the group met regularly, and gradually increased its grip on the campaign as the election approached. The broad direction they followed from this point had been laid out in the 'war book' presented to Brown in December. In these meetings, this basic approach was developed and its execution refined: 'The feel, the tone, the messaging of the campaign came from these meetings,' said one.[11] The team had been very anxious to engage Alastair Campbell, who was an influential, if irregular, attendee. 'Everyone wanted Alastair to come back, but he was determined that he wasn't going to be sucked in and be with us day to day,' says Forsyth.[12] Despite his best efforts, however, the former spin doctor's presence became more and more frequent. With Mandelson, Gould, Brown and now Campbell on board, they had reassembled the 'dream team' that had overseen the three previous general election victories. Even without Blair, who had played such a crucial role in these campaigns, they were streets ahead of the Conservatives in terms of experience. But would they be able to re-create some of the old magic?

Things were not going well for Cameron. Pressure mounted on him that spring over Lord Ashcroft, the millionaire donor to the Conservative Party, who featured regularly on the front pages in February and March. Ashcroft, a demon figure in the eyes of Labour, eventually admitted that he was still a 'non-dom', which allowed the government to say that the Tories were being bankrolled by someone who only paid taxes on part of their income to the British Exchequer.[13] Mandelson was relentless in applying pressure on Cameron, who claimed not to have known about the tax status of his party's former treasurer. 'If he knew the truth, he should have fired Ashcroft. If not, why was he too afraid to ask Ashcroft the awkward direct question?' the Business Secretary probed.[14] The *Daily Telegraph* was becoming edgy. 'One more wobble and the game's over,' it said on 6 March,[15] while the *Sunday Times* criticised Cameron for a 'lack of grip'.[16] By early March, the Conservative lead had fallen to four points. Criticism focused on Cameron. 'He is trying both to float like Tony Blair in 1997 and sting like Margaret Thatcher in 1979,' said *The Economist*.[17]

The optimism in the polls emboldened Brown's team to consider bringing the election forward. Though a June date was technically possible, most had assumed that 6 May was already written in stone. In late February and early March, though, Brown's team debated an April poll. 'We looked seriously at going earlier at that time, with discussion lasting for ten days,' says Muir.[18] 'When Labour did something unexpected, the Tories always stumbled,' maintain the advocates of an early poll. 'When you've got an opponent who's very clever and has lots of resources, the only way you can fight is by disrupting the rules of the game.'[19] Another argument for this timing was the economy: the election team was worried about the publication of the first-quarter figures for 2010 in late April, which they feared might well not be as promising as the fourth-quarter figures for 2009. 'The Q1 figures were a very big deal in terms of timing,' recalls one team member.[20] In campaign strategy meetings, much energy was consumed speculating about what information they might contain and how Labour should respond.[21] April 1 and 15 were the two dates the team focussed on. The first was dismissed as being too early, the second was ruled out only in early March, though they 'deliberately held back' from announcing the decision to go for a 6 May poll.[22] The date confirmed, the team focused on the key messages, which were unveiled at a rally of Labour activists in Nottingham on 27 March. In an echo of 1997, Brown announced five simple 'pledges' that he would enact if elected: securing the economic recovery, including halving the budget deficit; raising family living standards; building a high-tech economy; protecting frontline investment in schools, the NHS and police; and strengthening 'fairness' in communities. The team had encountered immense difficulties trying to produce a document on which all the politicians involved could agree – a 'terrible omen', according to one[23] – so, though they were disappointed by the muted response from the media, they were also pleased simply to have the core messages 'out there'.

To help him look presidential, Brown's team was anxious to exploit all opportunities to parade his status as a world leader. President Sarkozy came to Downing Street on 12 March and was on 'great form'. In the privacy of Number 10, he 'was as critical of Merkel and Obama, as he always was', while at the press conference he lavished praise on Brown, saying: 'We have always worked in a spirit of partnership and trust.' The team felt these comments were 'very helpful'.[24] It was a fitting final meeting for two men from opposing sides of the political spectrum, who had begun their relationship on such an unpromising basis, given Brown's lack of personal engagement with the EU. But he and Sarkozy were alike – both, in some senses, outsiders, both in a hurry and both unwilling to accept the world as they found it. Over his three years as Prime Minister, they developed what officials described as 'the closest relationship Brown had with any world leader'.[25] If Sarkozy was the accelerator in their tripartite relations, Merkel was the brake. Number 10 had also been keen to get her over to the UK during the election period. The meeting was eventually fixed at Chequers on 1 April, with the economy, Afghanistan and nuclear proliferation the main topics for discussion.[26] But the real motive was to upstage Cameron, whom Merkel did not have time to meet on her visit. As Brown was driving to Chequers for what was to be his last visit, he was lost in thought. An official turned to him to ask how it felt to be going back there. 'I don't need big houses,' the Prime Minister responded curtly.[27] After the expenses crisis, Brown deemed it 'inappropriate' to be seen spending time at Chequers and his visits became much less frequent.[28]

Three days before, on Wednesday 24 March, Darling had unveiled his final Budget. The main debate beforehand was over whether the Chancellor should go further than he had in the 2009 Pre-Budget Report in detailing Labour's plans for tackling the deficit and, in particular, where the cuts to public expenditure might fall.[29] Within Cabinet, Andrew Adonis, Ben Bradshaw and Tessa Jowell joined Mandelson in arguing that the time had come to be much more candid, that the public spending position was unsustainable and that the party would gain credit for being specific about its intentions.[30] They believed it would further have forced the Conservatives to be more explicit about their own position. But in the end, the voices of caution won the day. Darling himself was 'pretty circumspect about how much we could lay out before the election about the pain that was to come'.[31] Unusually, Brown was quite distant from the Budget process – he had made his views clear on the Pre-Budget Report in 2009, and the Budget was essentially a consolidation of those plans. Civil servants in the Treasury and in Number 10 were relieved that he did not try to yank the process still further in the direction of evasion over the state of the public finances. Balls's advice carried most weight with Brown in his final six months in Downing Street. 'Both were in total denial about the need to signal a tough approach,' complains a Number 10 official, concerned that, to the end, 'the Prime Minister didn't really believe the Treasury numbers'.[32] Brown's obstinacy on the figures had come to create difficulties for his officials, with some feeling that they had been left with a difficult conflict of duties, trying to support the Prime Minister while ensuring that they did the right thing by the economy.[33] On this final Budget, however, the Number 10 and Treasury political teams worked together harmoniously. Past tensions evaporated as they came together to focus on the common Tory enemy and they were determined to ensure that it dovetailed with the Labour election platform.[34] Ed Miliband, who was responsible for drafting the manifesto, met with Darling to go through the party's promises in relation to taxation and public spending. This led to the inclusion in the Budget of a number of measures that Brown planned to campaign on, including scrapping stamp duty for first-time home buyers (on houses worth up to £250,000) for two years, funded by raising duty on homes worth over £1m, increasing child tax credits for families with toddlers and the winter fuel allowance for pensioners, and extending the employment and training guarantees for under-twenty-fours until 2012.

In the Budget, Darling argued that the global recession had hit the UK hard, but that Labour's interventionist response had been vindicated. 'The choice before the country now is, whether to support those whose policies will suffocate our recovery and put our future at risk, or support a government which has been right about the recession, right about the recovery, and is right about supporting the people and the business of the country to build a prosperous future,' he declared.[35] 'Cutting support now would take demand out of the economy, pull the rug from under the recovery, and delay our return to sustained growth,' he continued. 'We have worked too hard as a country to come through this recession to throw it away now.'[36] With tax receipts better than expected, Darling revised borrowing figures downwards by £11bn from the £178bn forecast in the December Pre-Budget Report. He reiterated the government's intention to halve the deficit by 2013/14 but argued against cutting spending until after 2010/11, after which he warned of the need for the 'toughest' spending review in decades. He refused to be drawn on the detail of what would have to be cut; and, because the economy was performing better than expected, he was able to set out £11bn in efficiency savings, on top of £4bn of cuts in public sector pay and a reduction of £5bn in departmental budgets.[37]

The Conservatives responded that 'the only things Labour are bringing are debt, waste and taxes', accusing the government of dropping 'tax bombshells' timed to go off after the election. Cameron was in full flow: 'It is like the captain of the *Titanic* saying: "Let me command the lifeboats." It is like Robert Maxwell saying: "Let me reinvest your pension." It is like Richard Nixon saying: "I'm the man to clean up politics." Does the Prime Minister really expect the British people to turn round and say: "Thank you for nearly bankrupting the economy?"'[38] But the reception was not all bad. 'A workmanlike affair adorned with an array of smallish giveaways,' wrote Philip Stephens in the *Financial Times*.[39] *The Guardian*'s Larry Elliott thought it 'cautious, sensible and unflashy',[40] while Steve Richards wrote in *The Independent* that it was the 'most politically astute Budget of [Darling's] stormy reign at the Treasury'.[41] Mandelson worked hard with the business community to ensure a positive reception, with some success. CBI Director General Richard Lambert said it was a 'clever, political budget'.[42] Doubts remained, however, in the private sector and beyond, about how realistic Labour's deficit reduction plans were, and whether the growth forecasts for 2011 and beyond were still overly optimistic.

On 30 March, Brown's election team benefited from a fleeting appearance on the campaign trail by the fifth and final member of the dream team – Tony Blair. Speaking to the Trimdon Labour Club in the Sedgefield constituency, where he had announced his resignation in 2007, he urged Labour and the electorate to look to Britain's future. But Blair's intervention was a mixed blessing for Brown. To some, it brought a Clintonesque glamour and continuity to the party's cause: to others; it was a reminder of what a true master of political communication sounded and looked like. There were to be two Blairs during the general election. He encouraged his own press officer, Matthew Doyle – who was to do what was considered to be an 'excellent job' handling the media for the three televised leaders' debates[43] – to work with Brown's team, and he did nothing to suggest any differences with the Brown message, or with how the election was being fought. To the end, he remained true to his word, spoken on his final day as Prime Minister, that he would not intrude on his successor's premiership. However, in private, his frustration was mounting. A meeting between both men before the election had not gone well. 'Tony felt that Gordon simply didn't "get" the electorate, and that he had a "tin ear" and wouldn't listen,' recalls Jonathan Powell.[44] Blair not only despaired at Brown's failure to connect with the electorate, he also thought he was living in denial believing he could win.[45]

Whether Blair was right about Brown was about to be put to the test. On Sunday 4 April, Blair joined a strategy meeting of senior advisers, including Mandelson, Balls and Alexander. '[Brown] was more upbeat than he had been. We felt that he was finally in a good place,' says Forsyth. His advisers thought: 'What a shame it's taken so long for him to get there.'[46] The team debated a final time whether the focus during the campaign should be on Labour's record in office, the economy or the future promises. Brown was clear: he wanted to fight on the economy. 'He was adamant that the Tories' proposals were completely wrong and they were cutting too early,' says Forsyth.[47] The following evening – Monday 5 April – Brown stood in the Pillared Room of Number 10 and rehearsed words that he would say the following morning to call the general election. David Muir was watching him and felt that he was calm and focused. On Tuesday 6 April, the Prime Minister came down from his flat to the horseshoe room in Number 12 at 7.30am and ate his breakfast at his desk before going to his study to rehearse his statement yet again. He had forgotten to put on a tie so an official slipped him his. They practised his entry to make certain he looked presidential. 'He was leaving nothing to chance,' says one of his private secretaries.[48]

It was decided that Brown should announce the election outside Number 10, with his full Cabinet standing behind him. The setup was the brainchild of Nye, who also took on the difficult task of getting ministers in the right place.[49] Referring to the intricate choreography, Mandelson quipped: 'If we can pull this off, we can win the bloody election!'[50] As an excited if uneventful Cabinet meeting finished, the Queen's private secretary Christopher Geidt called Heywood to tell him she was ready for her audience with the Prime Minister. Brown walked out of the room to supportive noises from his Cabinet, he walked down Number 10's long corridor and, accompanied by Heywood, got into his waiting car outside. Brown took his regular meetings with the Queen very seriously and had always prepared for them meticulously. His attitude to the monarchy was described as 'extremely proper, courteous and dutiful'.[51] The Queen liked him, and was once heard to say: 'He's such a charmer.'[52] When he returned from the Palace, he went back to his room to continue rehearsing his lines. Cameron was first in

front of the cameras. 'It's about the future of our economy, it's about the future of
our society, it's about the future of our country. It's the most important general
election for a generation,' he said.[53] Around the horseshoe, a debate had taken
place about whether Brown should now go out earlier than intended. The advice
was to hold back. His team then clapped him out through the door, where, with
Harman and Johnson looking on supportively over his left shoulder, he said: 'The
future is within our grasp. It is a future fair for all. Now all of us, let's go to it.'
By 11.00am he was back indoors. It was when speaking to his staff that he came
close to 'apologising for his behaviour over the last three years'.[54] At 11.45, he left
Downing Street to begin campaigning.

Labour launched its manifesto on 12 April. It was done in a rush because
the publication had to be brought forward so as to take place before the first
televised election debate, on 15 April. Ed Miliband had been charged with
writing a manifesto in 2007, and had drafted a 25,000-word document with
Nick Pearce, Gavin Kelly and Dan Corry for the aborted election in the autumn
of that year. The early work had to be substantially rewritten in the light of the
global economic crisis in late 2008 and early 2009.[55] Patrick Diamond, who
joined the manifesto team in March 2009, says: 'When I arrived we were trying
to define a post-crisis agenda both in politics and economics.'[56] Miliband and
the Number 10 team circulated requests to ministers for proposed policies but
to their surprise – or not – they found they 'were not besieged with ideas –
a sign that we were ending a long period in government', according to one
adviser.[57] More material came from drawing on Labour's core statements:
'Building Britain's Future' in July 2009, Brown's party conference speech that
September and the Pre-Budget Report in December. These contained the
key tenets of Labour's platform for the election: halving the budget deficit
in four years, increasing national insurance rather than VAT, and protecting
frontline spending in health, schooling, childcare and the police. The team drew
further on policy announcements from earlier in 2010, in particular on social
care, the constitution, and high-speed rail, as well as on the thinking behind
Brown's Fabian speech in January with its 'squeezed middle' argument.[58] Brown
personally favoured the manifesto showing a demonstrable commitment to
growth – avoiding the doom and gloom that he saw being peddled by the Tories,
and showing that only an activist government would help restore growth.[59] This
thinking explains why he was keen to include investment commitments in the
manifesto (in the rail network, broadband and the digital economy, and work on
low-carbon technology), as well as endorsing Mandelson's industrial strategy.[60]

The decision not to conduct a Comprehensive Spending Review meant it
was difficult to cost policies fully; commitments therefore had to be 'finance-
light'. In education, one thousand secondary schools were to become part
of a chain to be run by 'executive' head teachers, a policy which Brown was

particularly keen.[61] He was equally enthusiastic about the commitment to one-to-one tuition, 'to be rolled out' to every primary school child who needed it. He failed to have his way, though, on a promise for free school meals to all children in England, which was rejected on the grounds that it would not be affordable and could therefore damage the document's credibility.[62] The manifesto pushed hard on tackling poor performance in the education, health and police services, where the government said that good schools, hospitals and police forces would be allowed to take over failing ones. The idea, though controversial, elicited a positive response from the media, reflecting a boldness on public services reform that was reminiscent of the Blair era. Indeed by 2010 Brown had come to embrace and build on the Blairite 'choice' agenda that he had rejected so emphatically while Chancellor and early on in his premiership. His 'entitlements' agenda was seen in the legally binding guarantees for patients, including the pledge that patients with suspected cancer would be able to see a specialist within two weeks. There was also a new emphasis on prevention, and on all hospitals becoming foundation trusts. Balls, however, was far from happy with the way that Mandelson spun the manifesto as 'Blair plus'. He believed that it was 'bad politics' to place such an emphasis on the past in the branding of a document that looked to the future.[63] 'Even after three years, it showed Balls was still locked into looking at everything through the Blair–Brown prism,' complains one of the manifesto authors.[64]

Tension arose over VAT, with Ed Miliband, backed by some political advisers in Number 10, pressing hard for the manifesto to rule out a rise throughout the next parliament. 'If we can rule out raising the top rate of income tax, why not VAT,' they argued. But Darling was utterly opposed and won the battle, a sign of his political strength late in his chancellorship.[65] Northern Rock was the topic of another battle between Number 10 and the Treasury. The former wanted to make it into a mutual society but the latter was against, and wanted it to be sold off to the biggest bidder, hence the compromise in the manifesto.[66] There was also considerable angst over constitutional changes. The proposal to hold referenda both on introducing the Alternative Vote (AV) system for electing MPs and on House of Lords reform was included in the face of opposition from Mandelson, Chief Whip Nick Brown and Scottish Secretary Jim Murphy. Brown's caution was once again driven by concerns about how the Church of England would react given that a fully elected upper chamber would exclude the bishops.[67] Jack Straw was deputised to speak to Buckingham Palace about it, while Brown spoke to Archbishop of Canterbury Rowan Williams.[68]

The clarity and conviction of some these proposals highlighted Brown's lack of both, on the domestic stage at least, since 2007. It begged the question how much more coherent and successful his government would have been if he had reached these conclusions three years earlier. For all that, the manifesto's successful launch propelled the party into the election battle, securing 'the best day's coverage for Labour in its entire campaign'.[69] Not everyone was convinced, however. To veteran political commentator Peter Riddell: 'The manifesto was not that clear and read like an accumulation of separate departmental self-justifications and wish lists, with little overall theme.'[70] True, the manifesto, like so many of Brown's speeches and statements as Prime Minister, lacked an overarching narrative. It struggled to provide voters with a compelling story about what a fourth term Labour government would do. But any verdict on the quality of the manifesto needs to take account of the adverse conditions in which it was crafted. The dire state of the public finances provided a significant constraint, as did Brown's demoralised Cabinet, who by this stage had ceased to be a source of bold and imaginative policy ideas.

The Campaign: 6 April to Election Day, 6 May

As the announcement of the election on 6 April approached, Gavin Kelly and Nick Pearce had lunch with Bernard Donoughue, who had been head of the Policy Unit under the previous Labour government (1974–79), so had been in Downing Street the last time the party was ejected from office. What did he think now? He was relatively upbeat; 2010 offered a more optimistic scenario than in 1979, when 'the tide of history was turning against Labour'.[71] They left buoyed by his assessment. However, elsewhere serious problems were brewing.

Cameron and Osborne played their trump card in late March with their announcement that they would not introduce Darling's 0.5 per cent rise in national insurance for anybody earning less than £45,000. The move would be funded by cutting £6bn of waste from the public sector, and would form part of an emergency post-election Budget. 'Not a single penny will come from the frontline services that people depend on,' Osborne told a press conference in Westminster. The Tory leadership then launched a devastatingly effective campaign against the 'tax on jobs' that would dominate the campaign agenda until the TV debates. Osborne's policy drew solid support from a number of business leaders, lending it weight and credibility. When MPs gathered on 7 April for the last PMQs before the dissolution of Parliament, Cameron attacked Brown for failing to secure the support of the business community for the national insurance changes: 'Does the Prime Minister know more about job creation than business leaders?'[72] Brown fumed, considering the Conservatives' attack opportunistic, but Labour's response was 'hopeless', according to a senior member of the election team.[73] 'We didn't manage to get a single business leader to come out and support our policy,' complains another.[74]

The Labour campaign had descended into disorder. In the run-up to the election, the strategy meetings had functioned well, but as soon as the election was called that structure broke down. 'There was no grid – no strategy. We didn't know what we were doing from one day to the next.'[75] The dream team of Mandelson, Gould and Campbell simply created confusion. 'The old guard were always second-guessing each other and changing their minds. They thought it was their campaign, but they gave it little grip, coherence or energy,' says an aide.[76] With no overall commander, messages were confused. A senior strategist said: 'It was most definitely a case of too many chiefs. We needed one or two of them to provide leadership and to develop a coherent election strategy but instead they were all jostling for control.'[77] Mandelson said himself: 'The 1997 campaign had been a Rolls Royce; 1987 was a Ford Cortina. This one was even poorer.'[78] One senior adviser, with long experience of elections, is unambiguous in his condemnation: 'Without a doubt it was the worst campaign I've ever been involved in. It was a complete disaster.'[79] There was a lack of coordination between Labour's head office and the mobile operation in the country. 'Gordon would turn up at a school and party HQ would be putting out campaign messages about health.'[80] Brown himself was having to get used to being the 'candidate', rather than masterminding the strategy. Alastair Campbell offered this verdict: 'There are two things missing in this election – Gordon's strategic brain at HQ, and Tony's razzle-dazzle on the campaign trail.'[81]

Labour's chaotic and cash-strapped campaign was, however, partly concealed from public view by the TV debates which, once they got underway, came to dominate the rest of the election. 'No one fully understood how transformative the debates were going to be. They changed the whole rhythm of the campaign,' says one.[82] Mandelson complained, 'It's as if the media didn't have any interest in anything else.'[83]

Given his lack of natural skills as a television communicator, the debates represented a significant risk for Brown. Labour's strategy was 'to put [Cameron] under real pressure and to show that, while [Brown] had substance, he was thin'.[84] The Prime Minister may have appeared wooden on all three occasions, and failed to convey either the passion he was occasionally capable of in set-piece speeches, or the winning vulnerability he revealed in the Morgan interview, but if anyone failed to meet expectations, it was Cameron. Indeed Tory donor Lord Ashcroft has since argued that the TV debates allowed the Liberal Democrats to seize the mantle of 'change', which undermined the Tory campaign and helped deny them a majority.[85] Undoubtedly, the TV debates helped Labour compensate for their lack of spending power.

Brown was nervous according to Mandelson, and 'had to learn an entirely new format and genre'.[86] Huge effort was put into coaching him and during the debate preparations Campbell played the role of Cameron, while Theo Bertram, who was so convincing in his performance as Liberal Democrat leader, thereafter became known as 'Nick Clegg' by Brown's team.[87] From the US, Joel Benenson, the pollster and strategist whom Obama had used before his television debates with John McCain, was flown over, and advice was sought from Obama's senior adviser, David Axelrod.[88] The team even brought in Michael Sheehan, the media trainer who had assisted Clinton on his presidential campaign and debates.[89] However, Brown arguably did not need the best presentation gurus in the world. He needed someone to tell him to be himself.

Following the first debate, which was hosted by ITV on 15 April in Manchester and attracted a television audience of 9.4m,[90] the main story was the rise of 'Cleggmania'. The Liberal Democrat leader had put in a very impressive performance and two days later, a YouGov poll put Labour in third place behind his party, which had jumped between ten and twelve points – the largest surge ever recorded in an election campaign.[91] The second debate, hosted by Sky a week later, focused on international affairs and again saw an uncharismatic performance from Brown. The strategy of presenting him as more substantial than Cameron and Clegg made him appear mannered and stilted. While some polls showed Brown coming second and even first, the instant polls were unanimously less positive and they are what shaped the wider media narrative. Mandelson derided 'those bloody instant polls' for distorting Labour's campaign message.[92]

Before the third debate, Brown visited Rochdale on 28 April, where he experienced, in the words of one adviser, 'definitely the worst moment of the campaign'.[93] His advisers blame themselves for the 'Mrs Duffy débâcle', when, in the apparent privacy of his car, the Prime Minister referred to the 65-year-old Labour voter to whom he had just been speaking as a 'bigot', and his comments were picked up on a Sky News microphone he was still wearing. The night before, Brown and his team were at the Radisson Hotel in Manchester. The location held fond memories, as this was where he had stayed a year and a half before, when he gave the party conference speech that had helped change the fortunes of his premiership. His team stayed up late discussing the campaign with him and they later wondered if, had he gone to bed earlier, he would have avoided the calamity the following day.[94] It was a dreadful lapse, and revealed to the public, in the most inescapable way, some of Brown's worst features, including blaming others (in this case Nye), and bad-mouthing people who annoyed him. Worse, it seemed to expose just how out of touch Labour had become on the electorally salient issue of immigration – the subject on which Duffy chose to accost Brown. After an uncomfortable interview on the *Jeremy Vine Show* on BBC Radio 2 immediately afterwards, Brown returned to the Radisson distraught. Television cameras had relayed images of the Prime Minister with his head in his hands as Vine questioned him on the incident. It looked very bad. As with Jacqui

Janes, his immediate instinct on hearing of his error was to apologise in person, so he went to Mrs Duffy's home. 'He was deeply upset and traumatised. He thought he'd let the whole team down, and feared he'd blown the whole election campaign,' says one of Brown's friends.[95] For a confidence politician, it was a fatal mistake, coming before the major hurdle of the third televised debate. Having failed to shine in the first two, he badly needed to prove himself. But the terrain of the election had shifted. Before the Duffy episode, the sense at Labour Party headquarters was: 'We can pull this off.' Afterwards, the internal discussion was more 'Can we avoid coming third?'[96]

The topic of the third debate, hosted by the BBC in Birmingham on 29 April, was Brown's home territory and the subject Number 10 had wanted to be discussed first – economic affairs. However, despite his formidable experience in this area, he was still judged to have come third. The Prime Minister looked tired, gave his answers stolidly and lacked inspiration. The election seemed to be slipping away. Despite meetings between Number 10's political advisers and the editorial teams of the major newspapers, the press continued to desert the Labour cause. On 1 May, *The Guardian* came out for the Liberal Democrats, and *The Times* for the Conservatives. Brown's only support came from *The Mirror*. While some of the excesses of the Blair years had been avoided, he never learned to handle the media well and had alienated the chief political correspondents from the major networks – Nick Robinson (BBC), Adam Boulton (Sky), Tom Bradby (ITN) and Gary Gibbon (Channel 4). In private, none of them had much of a good word to say for him. On 2 May, polls showed the Conservatives increasing their lead, climbing to 33 per cent, with Liberal Democrats and Labour on 28 per cent each.[97] Drawing on their considerably greater financial means, the Conservatives were able to send personalised copies of their manifesto to the 3m voters in key seats who would decide the outcome of the election.[98]

At this bleak moment, Brown finally found his voice. Some in his team were hopeful that a psychological corner had been turned following his strong performance on 2 May during a tour of ten key marginal constituencies across London, including a passionate speech in Streatham. The next day their hopes were confirmed. Shaun Woodward thinks the Mrs Duffy episode had been responsible for Brown deciding to 'become his own man', and compares it to the moment John Major 'got on his soapbox' in Luton in the 1992 general election.[99] He had spent the greatest part of the campaign up to this point on the road with Forsyth and Kirsty McNeill, believing that, if only he could get his arguments across to the 'real electorate', he would win. But coordination with Victoria Street was often poor and his audiences were small, creating scepticism in the media about this approach.

But it all came good on 3 May in Brown's speech to an assembly held by community organising alliance Citizens UK at Methodist Central Hall,

Westminster – an invitation he had accepted only days before. McNeill helped write the speech and travelled with him to the event, but the words he spoke were his own. 'Everything Gordon had ever believed in came together in this one setting,' says McNeill, who noticed the Prime Minister coming 'utterly alive' the moment he arrived. 'I'm home now. I know these people,' he said. 'He could smell it, he could tell it was family, being with hundreds of people in that room who voluntarily gave up their time for others,' McNeill adds.[100] His upbeat speech questioned the strategy of building the election around the debates, and surrounding him with media minders. Tellingly, he asked to be left alone for ten minutes before he spoke – 'the surest sign he is in the right zone'.[101] 'As you fight for fairness, you will always find in me a friend, a partner and a brother,' he said, using language that verged on the religious. He praised 'the people in the crowd, the people whose names are not recorded in the books of history … the people who make history by being there and demanding change'[102] – a theme he had also stressed in his book *Everyday Heroes* (2007). He spoke about his past, when he had campaigned for disinvestment in apartheid South Africa, and fought for 'decent pay' for university cleaning staff. [103] Drawing huge applause, he talked about ensuring that all government departments would in future pay a higher 'living wage', in line with Citizens UK's campaign.[104] 'That speech will live forever,' a colleague wrote to McNeill. 'I always knew you and Gordon would do the great summons to justice.'[105] To Purnell, one of Brown's most trenchant critics, it was 'an incredible speech … a rare glimpse of the old Gordon. He rediscovered the moral authority he had lost.'[106] 'It was like Gordon was breaking free of some self-imposed chains,' recalls Forsyth. Throughout the campaign, members of the Prime Minister's team had played 'Don't Stop Believing' by Journey as motivational music. 'We played this on our iPhones every day, and we played it on the loudspeakers when we landed on the one helicopter trip of the campaign', says one.[107] Now finally they felt that, after all their hard work in the face of huge financial difficulties, which had forced the team to travel in second class with the press pack, the campaign had finally hit the right note. Its impact was well caught by Jonathan Freedland in *The Guardian*: 'His language was scriptural, perfectly judged … what we saw on Monday was Brown unleashed.' But, as Freedland acknowledged, the door was closing. It may be 'the last hurrah of a candidate who knows he's going down. But it is also a tantalising glimpse of what might have been'.[108]

By the end, Brown himself knew that he had lost, but fought on doggedly. On Wednesday 5 May, he gave another strong speech in Dumfries, in which he promised that Labour would 'never walk away'.[109] On the way home, he phoned Douglas Alexander and acknowledged his expectation of defeat the following day. He discussed the latest polling and apologised, saying: 'I'm sorry I thought I could turn it around.'[110] The Prime Minister spent the night in his North Queensferry home, and on polling day, he toured the constituency, working on the statements he would make for different election outcomes. He had a conference call with his staff during the day, discussing what the polls were saying. Inconclusive, he felt. In the event of a hung parliament he was anxious to avoid Cameron repeating what Alex Salmond had done after the 2007 Scottish elections, declaring victory as soon as the SNP emerged as the largest party but short of a majority. His media team spoke to the broadcasters to encourage them not to declare Cameron the 'winner' in the same circumstance.[111]

In the late evening, he went to the count in his Kirkcaldy and Cowdenbeath constituency and was personally lifted that his majority of 29,000 was up 5,000 on the 2005 figure. Results were still coming in as he was driven to Edinburgh airport for the flight down to London. Earlier, none of Brown's team had believed the exit polls about the Liberal Democrats doing badly: 'We never thought [their vote] would be that low.'[112] Now, the results confirmed that the centre party had not made the breakthrough once thought likely.[113] Arriving at the airport at 3.27am, he told reporters: 'It's been a very long night, but there's still a long way to go.' Every time a Labour win came in, his team let out a muted cheer that rippled around the plane. In the early hours, he was driven to Labour's Victoria Street headquarters. The news was now much less good than when he had set off from Scotland: seats thought winnable had been lost in the West Midlands. After thanking all the staff, he met in a side room at about 5.30am with Mandelson, Campbell, Nye, Forsyth and Muir. It now looked as if Britain had elected a hung parliament. They discussed the results, who should appear on the *Today* programme on Radio 4 the following morning, and what could be said.[114] David Blunkett had caused exasperation when he had said on air that Labour had lost. Pearce, who had worked for him when he was Home Secretary, was delegated to phone him, opening the 'comradely conversation' with the words: 'Please David.'[115]

The possibility of a coalition with the Liberal Democrats was discussed. Brown himself was keen, while Blair, they heard, was completely opposed. '[Brown] genuinely felt that his last great mission, the last great thing he could do for Britain was to save the country from the Conservatives,' says Mandelson.[116] Before the election, the Prime Minister had commissioned work from his advisers to explore the ramifications of a Lib–Lab coalition. He was genuinely excited by the possibility: he viewed Labour and the Liberal Democrats as natural coalition partners, with a clear overlap of policy on the economy, public service reform, and, since his late conversion, on electoral and constitutional reform. It would be a progressive government that the country needed. Brown went back for a short rest to Downing Street, his mind already abuzz. After retaining his seat at 6.50am in Sheffield, Clegg acknowledged: 'This has obviously been a disappointing night for the Liberal Democrats. We simply haven't achieved what we'd hoped.'[117]

For months, Cabinet Secretary Gus O'Donnell had been planning for an inconclusive outcome, with different civil servants role-playing the different leaders.[118] He had sought advice widely. Brown learned from him that, according to constitutional authorities such as Vernon Bogdanor, Robert Hazell and Peter Riddell, 'if there is no majority, the Prime Minister should not resign, but should stay and see if he can form a government'.[119] He was also advised that it was his constitutional duty to remain as Prime Minister until he could advise the Queen on a successor. Clegg, however, had already made clear his view that it was the party with the strongest mandate that should be given the first opportunity to form a government. On Friday morning, Kelly and Pearce sat down to work out what a coalition agreement with the Liberal Democrats might look like. They had done some initial work on this on election day and produced a note laying out Brown's options. The Policy Unit had also drawn up confidential documents based on potential points of agreement and friction between the manifestos of the two parties in the preceding weeks.

End Game: 7–11 May

It is the day after the general election. Brown soberly absorbs Labour's final tally of 258 seats. With 29 per cent of the vote, the party has put in its worst performance at a general election since Michael Foot was its leader in 1983. But deep down, the Prime Minister is happy that the result is not even worse. Labour's parliamentary representation is too small, even with fifty-seven Liberal Democrat MPs, to hold an overall majority: a Lib–Lab pact would still leave them eleven seats short. In contrast, if Clegg joins forces with Cameron's 306 Conservative MPs, they will command a working majority of seventy-eight. When Brown speaks outside Number 10 at 1.30pm on Friday, he is clear about where he stands: 'Should the discussions between Mr Cameron and Mr Clegg come to nothing, then I would of course be prepared to discuss with Mr Clegg the areas where there may be some measure of agreement between our two parties.' He also declares that Labour will legislate for a referendum on AV if they go into a coalition with the Liberal Democrats.[120] Secretly, he refuses to believe that Clegg can find enough in common with the Tories to form a workable or sensible coalition agreement. He notes ruefully that Clegg has not followed the advice of the constitutionalists when he asserts that Cameron has a right to form a government. Nonetheless, time is short and, given the parliamentary arithmetic, the Labour team know that the odds are massively stacked against them. Brown, however, is incredibly determined to put a deal together. He starts to put great pressure on his aides to come up with ways of making a Labour-headed coalition work. 'He called me all the time, asking:

"What else can we do?" He was utterly focused on doing a deal,' says one adviser.[121] Early on Friday morning Gavin Kelly starts calling up the former Policy Unit members, saying: 'Come in. You are needed.'[122] Brown's advisers, now congregated at Victoria Street, are feeling very uneasy about their absence from Number 10. Brown is still Prime Minister, and there are no clear rules on whether they are allowed to remain with him in Downing Street. Kelly phones the duty clerk at Number 10 and tells him that a number of them will be arriving shortly. Kelly, Muir, Pearce, Irvin and McNeill enter via the back door, having handed in their security passes four weeks before. Once inside, they are greeted with large jugs of coffee and told by the Prime Minister to get to work immediately on drafting policy statements and negotiating positions.[123]

One member of Brown's political team recalls the atmosphere in Number 10 at this time: 'There was a weird dynamic to the morale of us all. Each morning we would trudge in – usually by the back door or through 70 Whitehall because the broadcasters had set up camp outside the black door – convinced it would be our last day in the building. The day proceeded, usually with us having little to do but sit and talk through every permutation under the sun. Various rumours would spread, the odd meeting would happen. Then, by some strange emotional shift, we all would leave in the evening, amazed that we lived to fight another day and somehow convinced once again that GB might just be able to pull it off.'[124]

At 2.30pm, across St James's Park at St Stephen's Club, Cameron issues his first significant statement of intent since the election results were announced, saying he wants to make a 'big, open, and comprehensive' offer of a full-blown coalition with the Liberal Democrats, stressing that he is willing to 'compromise' to produce an outcome 'in the national interest'. 'It just seemed to me the right thing to do,' he says later.[125] He recognises that there are significant differences between the two parties, not the least over Europe, defence, and taxation, but he says he believes that they can be overcome.[126] Later that afternoon, Cameron and Clegg speak on the telephone, and both end the call confident that they can indeed work together.[127] Cameron then phones several members of his shadow Cabinet to ensure they are behind the principle of a formal coalition – William Hague is a particular anxiety, and needs to be kept onside.[128]

Clegg is determined to keep his options open, partly to enhance his leverage in any negotiations. At 5.35pm he calls Brown for their first conversation since the election. Brown thinks Cameron's offer is a strategic mistake that reveals the Conservative leader's weakness. Listening on the phone are Heywood, Muir and Kelly. Brown is forceful in putting across his belief that agreement can be reached between Labour and the Liberal Democrats. As Muir's contemporary notes show, he urges Clegg not to 'doubt our political will'.[129]

Brown outlines his grand vision for a political realignment of the centre-left and the prospect for a progressive coalition to transform Britain. He offers a commitment to fixed-term parliaments and tells Clegg that, in the event of an agreement, he would give Liberal Democrats a number of key Cabinet positions. Contemporary notes reveal he has pencilled in Cable as Business Secretary, David Laws as Chief Secretary to the Treasury, Chris Huhne as Environment or Local Government Secretary, and a 'constitutional position' for Clegg himself.[130] Brown reminds Clegg that Labour has a much less sceptical position on Europe than the Conservatives, which the Prime Minister knows is a key issue for the Liberal Democrats. As Muir recalls: 'He was deliberately pushing Clegg's buttons.'[131] Brown is remorseless, stressing that 'there are no big differences between us', and, where there are, over ID cards for example, 'they can easily be dealt with'.[132] He is keen to open up negotiating channels between the two parties. Given the Greek economic crisis and the need for any agreement to settle the markets, Brown is also keen that Cable speaks to Darling, saying: 'We need urgently to get them together.' Brown is thrilled when Clegg says he is 'very grateful' for his thoughts and: 'I think our two parties working together are much more likely to achieve change than with the Conservatives.'[133] However, he adds that he is 'duty bound in terms of choreography', saying: 'I did say publicly I'd go with the Conservatives first.' However, Clegg's main worry about a Lib–Lab coalition is not over policy differences, but the lack of an overall majority. 'You were second, we were third: doesn't it look ridiculous?' he asks.[134] Nor is 'parliamentary arithmetic' the only obstacle – there is also the tricky question of the Prime Minister's future role. Early on in their call, Brown addresses this head on, saying: 'There is something I need to speak to you about, but I can only do it face to face.'[135] His team listening in knows what that means: 'He was saying: "I know I might be a stumbling block towards making this deal work. I am more than prepared to fall on my sword but I don't think anyone else can get it through the Labour Party at the moment."'[136] This is the first hint that Brown is willing to remove himself from power to ensure the formation of a progressive coalition.

Brown had toyed with the idea of making a public announcement before the general election campaign that he would stay on to ensure some vital reforms were passed, and then give the public the opportunity to decide whether he serve a full term.[137] On 1 April, just before the campaign began, the Prime Minister called Muir into his study in Number 12, and asked him what he thought of an announcement that he would do 'only two more years'. It was no April Fools' joke. He had been saying to Muir for some time that the 'prospect of five more years of Gordon Brown hardly sounded that attractive to the electorate'. The plan was sketchy but the general idea was that, before the election, he would announce that, if Labour won, he would remain as Prime Minister only for as long as it took to secure the economic recovery and legislate for a referendum on electoral reform. Brown would regard the AV referendum as a confidence vote on himself. If the public voted against, he would leave office immediately. More radically, he also considered holding a 'mega-referendum' encompassing his wider political and economic agenda, giving the British public an opportunity after two years to pass judgement on his record and plans for the future.[138] The suggestion collapsed in the face of strong opposition from his most-powerful advisers: Balls, Douglas Alexander, Mandelson, Ed Miliband, Nye and Forsyth were all against it, with Muir the sole advocate. Balls reminded Brown 'this is what knackered Tony'.[139] However, this episode shows that Brown had already become philosophical about his own position, recognising the weakness caused by his lack of popularity. Typically, his thinking would vacillate – at one time he would be determined to stand down, at another he would say to himself that he was the only figure capable of leading the party.[140] At different points during the campaign, he had returned to this idea, and even drafted a speech announcing his intention to resign, until he was talked out of it by his team.[141]

The momentum is with the Conservatives. After Clegg and Brown have spoken, formal conversations take place between the Conservative and Liberal Democrat negotiating teams in the Cabinet Office. For the moment, there is little Labour can do. 'There was a lot of sitting around, especially on the Friday,' remembers one party figure.[142] Brown goes to bed early, his mind racing at the prospect of how he can build a coalition. As his thoughts turn to a 'rainbow' coalition, he begins thinking increasingly of how he can entice some or, even more audaciously, all of the eighteen Northern Ireland MPs to support a Lib–Lab government. He speaks to Shaun Woodward about bringing them on board. Over the weekend, further conversations take place, which include the possibility of joining forces with Plaid Cymru and the SNP, neither of which is anxious to see Cameron as Prime Minister. Woodward speaks to Darling to seek assurances that Northern Ireland would be 'looked after' financially (there are fears there that a Cameron government will impose harsh cuts on the Stormont budget). By the end of the weekend, Woodward is saying to Brown that he feels he can deliver the Northern Ireland MPs.[143]

These are the balls Brown has in the air on the morning of Saturday 8 May, as he attends the official ceremony at the Cenotaph to mark the sixty-fifth anniversary of VE day. Reflecting the current political position, all three main party leaders lay their wreaths in Whitehall in unison, rather than, as is customary, in order of precedence determined by their number of MPs. Brown is increasingly irritated by the claim made by *The Sun* that he is 'squatting in Number 10'[144] and his team discuss how to respond. Adonis and Kelly draft a statement setting out a timetable for the completion of coalition negotiations and the creation of a new government, believing this will strengthen Brown and show that he is not clinging on to power. Mandelson disagrees with the plan. At 3.15pm, having spoken to President Sarkozy of France and Prime Minister Zapatero of Spain, among others, Brown instead decides to take his wife and children back to their home in Scotland. This move is not just about avoiding the charges of 'squatting'; with the Conservatives being given the first chance to negotiate with the Liberal Democrats, there is little Brown can do at the moment to influence proceedings. He remains convinced that a deal can be done with Clegg and his party, but realises that Labour will have to wait for its turn. 'He knew he couldn't do anything to change things at that time and so he'd rather kick his heels in the beautiful surroundings of Fife,' says one aide. Brown's team feel the same – the real action is taking place in the talks between the Conservatives and the Liberal Democrats, not in Downing Street. Even though the Prime Minister's officials and political team remain, there is a peculiar sense in Number 10 of 'power no longer being in the building', recalls Pearce.[145]

Shortly after Brown and his family take to the air, his team, comprising Mandelson, Adonis, Ed Miliband, Balls and Kelly, sit down with the Liberal Democrat negotiating team for a round of informal talks. The meeting takes place in Portcullis House, across the road from the Palace of Westminster, and is kept secret from the Conservatives. The Labour team are immediately surprised by the Liberal Democrats' more bullish position on public spending cuts. What is going on? Having put in a great deal of work analysing the Liberal Democrat manifesto, the Labour team is surprised by how little attention their negotiating partners are paying to the positions on which they have just fought a general election. Kelly and Adonis have also prepared for the meeting by consulting a group of constitutional experts on how early it would be possible to hold a referendum on AV. The Labour team does not sense that their desire to find an agreement is shared and are curious to know why. They come to believe that the Liberal Democrats' negotiating document is the same one that has been used for discussions with the Conservatives. 'They didn't even bother writing a separate negotiating document based on our manifesto,' says one Labour representative.[146] Some conclude that they are just being strung along, and that the Liberal Democrats are not serious about doing a deal. They are surprised, too, by apparent tension between Huhne and Clegg's chief of staff, Danny Alexander, over their party's position.

At 7pm on the Saturday, Cameron and Clegg meet at Admiralty House. It looks as if the chance of a Lib–Lab deal is slipping away. 'We were getting on … it felt as if this was beginning to click into place,' Cameron says later.[147] That evening, Brown speaks to Douglas Alexander for forty minutes. The Prime Minister restates his belief that an agreement with the Liberal Democrats can still be reached and that he is willing to step aside in order to secure a coalition of what he sees as Britain's two progressive political parties. 'He was clear that the issue was not about him and his own future, but about the party. He was reconciled to anything,' Alexander says later. 'It was Gordon at his best.'[148]

On Sunday morning, Brown goes to church in Kirkcaldy. On the way, he brushes off media questions; unlike others in the Labour Party and his Cabinet, who are resigned to defeat, he remains optimistic. That morning, he puts in a call to Cable, an old friend whom he regards as a deal-maker. 'He felt that the Liberal Democrats were natural allies of his party and that we should work with him and not with the Conservatives, and he made that point very strongly to me,' Cable later recounts.[149] Brown flies back to London for his first face-to-face meeting with Clegg. Again, this needs to be kept secret, but where to hold it? The two teams look at meeting away from Downing Street, but it is decided that, if Brown is to travel anywhere with his police convoy, the media crews in their helicopters will follow him. The Foreign Office provides convenient cover. The two leaders meet in the office of permanent secretary Peter Ricketts, and the understanding that emerges becomes known as the 'Ricketts accord' by Brown's team. Beforehand, a note is sent to Clegg's team, worked up by Kelly and Pearce, laying out shared policy positions, areas of difference, and how they can be resolved. Dismissed by Mandelson in his memoirs as of little importance, the meeting is, as Muir and Forsyth confirm, the first time that Brown says explicitly that he is willing to resign in the autumn – once he has successfully steered an electoral reform bill through the Commons – if this is the price of a coalition with the Liberal Democrats.[150] Brown reasons with Clegg: 'I'm the only person who could get it through the Labour Party.' He also knows success here would provide him with the legacy he craves. His willingness to resign to secure agreement is made 'absolutely clear' to Clegg at the meeting.[151] For the first time, Clegg becomes convinced that Brown is serious about trying to make a Lib–Lab pact work. Both men get on well. Forsyth and Fletcher, standing quiet outside, hear laughter through the door.[152]

That afternoon, Brown phones key members of his Cabinet to find out where they stand. Members of the Number 10 staff have also been testing the water over the weekend. Most appear supportive, if highly sceptical about whether it will come off. Strongly against are Jack Straw and Andy Burnham.[153] Both have constituencies in the North-West of England, where there is a history of Labour viewing the Liberal Democrats as the main enemy. Straw disappoints Brown when he says that a period in opposition might not be bad for Labour: 'Jack is very: "We have to accept that we lost. We need time in opposition blah, blah, blah ..."' says a Brown adviser dismissively.[154]

The Prime Minister has a second meeting that evening with Clegg, but this time in the House of Commons, and with Mandelson present. To keep this secret, they travel to the Commons via an underground tunnel once used by Churchill. But the encounter goes less well. Brown repeats his offer to serve as an interim Prime Minister for a short time only. Clegg keeps saying: 'I don't doubt that on policy we can find accommodation.' But he is concerned about legitimacy. He tells Brown: 'If there's going to be a new government, it's got to be a new government.' The message is clear – the coalition will never be sold unless the Prime Minister moves on 'in a dignified way'.[155] Brown's pride has kicked in during the day, and he becomes anxious about the perception being formed that he is being forced out by the Liberal Democrats. At this meeting he is more equivocal about the timing of his own departure. He says he wants to stay on to lead the campaign for a yes vote in the AV referendum and also to allow time to work with Cable, whom he likes and admires, to oversee the recovery of the economy. That is too far for Clegg, and the meeting breaks up with no conclusions being reached.[156] Clegg is concerned that Brown has shifted his position from earlier in the day.

What of the Conservatives? Cameron is disconcerted when he hears that Clegg and Brown have met for a second time that day. Peter Snowdon, the historian of the Conservative Party in this period, writes that Cameron is worried that he may yet end up on the back foot.[157] Brown's own spirits sink late that evening. 'That night he feels that lots of people are writing him off,' says a close adviser.[158] Among those doing precisely that are a number of officials in the Cabinet Office and in Number 10, who are sceptical about whether a Lib–Lab coalition would be viable. Few of Whitehall's senior mandarins are picking up much enthusiasm from Clegg or his party for Brown's offer, and they ask themselves, even if this was accepted, how it would be sustainable without an overall majority.[159] Equally, they remain clear that Brown must remain where he is until there is a credible alternative to present to the Palace.

Brown begins Monday 10 May hopeful, even as many of his team fear that Cameron might be Prime Minister by the end of the day. He knows that many Liberal Democrat MPs are closer to Labour than to the Conservatives, and are urging their leader in that direction. But this is not true of Danny Alexander and David Laws, who worry that Clegg is going too far in negotiating with Labour, and that Brown will try to hang on as Prime Minister. At two o'clock that morning, Laws had phoned former Liberal Democrat Leader Paddy Ashdown, saying: 'Look, it is a bit of a disaster. Gordon has reneged from the understanding he gave earlier.'[160] Ashdown has long believed that Brown undermined Blair's big-tent vision of bringing the Liberal Democrats into government in 1997, but has begun to think that a Lib–Lab deal might now be possible. At 6am, Cable and Brown speak on the phone, with the former saying: 'The arithmetic doesn't work and it would be very difficult to work with you as party leader.'[161] Clegg meets a worried Brown later that morning. 'Policies are not the issue between us. We are agreed on most things. I am sure we can form a progressive alliance between us. I genuinely believe it can work,' the Prime Minister pleads, adding: 'If it increases the possibility of forming a progressive alliance, I'm prepared to stand aside as Labour leader.'[162]

Brown is not prepared to let his staying on in Number 10 stand in the way of a Lib–Lab coalition. The Liberal Democrat overnight wobble has convinced him he has to make his intention public.[163] He also wants closure and at 5pm, he plays his ace. He walks out into Downing Street and announces his resignation as Labour leader to the waiting media. 'The reason that we have a hung parliament is that no single party and no single leader was able to win the full support of the country. As leader of my party, I must accept that that is a judgment on me. I therefore intend to ask the Labour Party to set in train the processes needed for its own leadership election,' he says.[164] The effect is electric. The Liberal Democrats announce that they will begin formal talks with Labour. Clegg says that, although progress is being made with the Conservatives, they have not yet 'reached a comprehensive partnership agreement for a full parliament', meaning it is 'responsible to open negotiations with the Labour Party'.[165] Stewart Wood says to a colleague: 'The funny thing about Gordon is that in every crisis he has the ability to turn everything on its head by playing one strategic masterstroke.'[166] Later that day, Clegg phones Downing Street to say that he has ruled out a loose pact with the Conservatives. From now on, it will be a full coalition, or nothing. Brown has become calm. 'Being leader of Labour meant more to Gordon than being Prime Minister,' believes Muir. 'Once he walked away from it that afternoon, he was at ease with himself because he knew he was doing the right thing.'[167] His team feel a new energy and optimism. 'We were all pumped up and believed this might just work,' says one.[168]

The Cabinet meets that evening at 6pm, some of them joining by phone. Brown's mood is upbeat and expectant. Few of his colleagues share his optimism, but they accept that Clegg's remarks following Brown's announcement raise the prospect of a coalition agreement with the Liberal Democrats. The question now is whether such an agreement is desirable for Labour. Brown lays out his position at the start of the meeting, saying: 'Collectively we have to agree to negotiate with the Liberal Democrats, and what the basis of any deal is.' There is overwhelming support for starting talks. Ed Miliband is strongly supportive of a deal. Balls, David Miliband, Alan Johnson, and Tessa Jowell also speak in favour, though they express differing degrees of doubt about whether the country will regard such a government as legitimate. Hain refers to the positive experience of coalition Labour enjoys in Wales. Denham, Cooper, Benn, Ainsworth and Alexander are also in favour. Shaun Woodward tells Cabinet that all the Northern Ireland parties would either support Labour or abstain. Harman pays tribute to all Brown has done for the party, noting that her Peckham constituents would suffer if the Tories got in and these sentiments are echoed by all present. Brown is touched. She then tells colleagues: 'This is not the time for leadership campaigns.' David

Miliband looks embarrassed.[169] Jack Straw and Alistair Darling are evidently sceptical but they do not oppose formal talks. Darling says any deal must be fiscally responsible. Only one member speaks out against. Andy Burnham frets: 'When the next election comes, there will be a reckoning.' Despite doubts as to the likelihood of securing agreement, Cabinet decide to endorse Brown's strategy of trying to negotiate a deal. 'I sensed that their collective residual respect for Gordon meant they felt he deserved a shot at doing a deal,' says one individual present.[170] 'They had no choice really. This was Gordon's final request. How could they deny him?' comments another member of Brown's team.[171] Yet many in his Cabinet only agree to his last request because they believe it will lead nowhere. They are beginning to focus on life after government. That day both Miliband brothers begin to make preparations for their forthcoming battle for the leadership of the party.

That evening after Cabinet, Labour and Liberal Democrat negotiators meet formally for the first time in the House of Commons to hammer out the details of a possible deal. Brown's team consists of Mandelson, Balls, Ed Miliband, and Andrew Adonis. Brown looks to Adonis to lead the negotiations and asks Pearce to support the process as a Labour official. As a former supporter of the Liberal/SDP Alliance in the 1980s, Adonis retained many contacts in the merged party and has the confidence of senior Liberal Democrats. It says a lot about Brown that he is prepared to trust a man who was one of the chief architects of Blairism with this responsibility. Mandelson wants to take Heywood to the talks to underline the seriousness of the negotiations but the latter is uncomfortable being the only civil servant in the room. He feels that a political negotiation is not a matter for officials.[172] While O'Donnell is spending more time with the Conservatives and Liberal Democrats, Heywood has been in constant contact with Labour's high command so there is an 'institutional firewall' between them both.[173] But he, like O'Donnell, is careful to draw the line between the policy and the political, especially in such unfamiliar territory.

When formal talks open, Adonis assures Danny Alexander, a senior figure in the Liberal Democrat team, that Labour will legislate quickly for a referendum on AV, so the new system could be implemented rapidly.[174] He also makes clear that Labour will campaign for a yes vote (their policy until then was simply to hold a referendum). The Labour team also show they mean business by tabling a series of significant concessions that include 'the introduction of a bill to protect civil liberties and rights' which would mean 'the ID cards scheme and the National Identity Register will not proceed.' This is a clear departure from Labour's manifesto.[175]

During this first formal meeting the Labour team is again surprised by the gulf between the Liberal Democrats' negotiating stance and the policy positions the party had adopted during the election campaign. On 19 March

Clegg had insisted that Tory plans for swift and deep cuts were dangerous: 'Let's say a Conservative government announced, in that sort of macho way: "We're gonna slash public spending by a third, we'll slash this, we'll slash this, we'll do it tomorrow. We have to take early, tough action." ... I think if we want to go the direction of Greece, where you get real social and industrial unrest, that's the guaranteed way of doing it.'[176] Now the Liberal Democrats have changed their tune on this crucial issue. Laws, a senior member of the Liberal Democrat negotiating team, now argues that one of the key conditions of any coalition deal with Labour must be an agreement to begin public spending cuts in 2010, as a down-payment on reducing the deficit. Laws says he has seen a Treasury note setting out how £6bn can be cut in 2010/11 without harming the recovery. This is not the only surprise. 'They didn't push tuition fees, they didn't push immigration amnesties, they didn't push the pension tax relief, and the issue of the mansion tax didn't appear,' says one figure close to the Labour team.[177]

However, it is the change in the Liberal Democrats' stance on public spending cuts that most shocks the Labour camp. Some of them are convinced that this change is the result of conversations between Clegg and the Governor of the Bank of England. 'It then became pretty clear to us that Mervyn King had spoken to them and argued that the financial markets were so unsettled that immediate cuts were necessary,' says one.[178] The next day, Brown places a call to King, and asks him directly if he has been speaking to the other parties.[179] King says he has not.[180] The Bank denies that 'there was any contact with the Liberal Democrats until after the coalition was formed, when Mervyn King was asked to speak to Clegg in his new role as Deputy Prime Minister'.[181] The Labour team leave the meeting less hopeful of reaching an agreement than before, but still believe it might be possible.

Brown trusts Adonis completely, but has some doubts about the sincerity of his negotiating team. 'Gordon pulls Andrew into a room and asks: "Is Ed Balls being a ... ? Is Ed Miliband this ... ? What is Peter doing ... ?" It is clear it was Andrew he trusted the most,' says an aide. 'Gordon has total respect for Andrew, he really admires him.' Subsequently, Clegg says to Brown: 'We won't have any more Ed Balls, thank you.' However, the Labour team tells Brown that Balls is being set up as the scapegoat.[182] Balls was 'combative, as was his way, but he did not obstruct the talks', says Mandelson.[183] Indeed, a fair amount of scapegoating is going on. Messages come back to Brown that his team are more intent on looking at their BlackBerrys than taking the negotiation seriously, while counter claims fly around the Labour camp about how serious the Liberal Democrat team genuinely are.[184]

If the Liberal Democrat tactic of holding formal talks with Labour is aimed at extracting further concessions from the Conservatives, it is achieving its aim. At 7.15pm on Monday evening, Hague announces the Conservatives are prepared to offer a referendum on AV, but this is their final offer.[183] Cameron has reasoned that, if the Liberal Democrats reach an agreement with Labour, then a move on AV is inevitable; it is therefore better that the Conservatives are in government, shaping the direction of the debate, rather than sitting watching it happen from the Opposition benches. Cameron later admits that on that Monday evening he does not know whether he will end up as Prime Minister.[186]

Tuesday 11 May is the most dramatic day of Brown's premiership. That morning, from 10am until noon, the Labour and Liberal Democrat negotiating teams reconvene in Portcullis House. The Labour team meet Brown first thing in the morning at Number 10 to prepare a revised coalition agreement document, which includes further concessions. They table this at the meeting. It includes another major U-turn from their manifesto with the promise that 'no plans will be taken forward for additional runways in the South-East in this [next] Parliament'. The Labour team also sign up to the Liberal Democrat 'pupil premium' policy for disadvantaged children, with the caveat that it must be funded from *additional* resources in the education budget. But Liberal Democrat demands for ambitious targets for renewable energy are judged unrealistic.[187] Labour then raise the stakes on electoral reform saying that Brown is willing to assent to a multi-question referendum giving the voters a choice between the status quo, Labour's preferred option – AV – and the Liberal Democrat 'Holy Grail' – full proportional representation. Adonis adds that Labour would make the referendum legislation an issue of confidence to guarantee its safe passage through the Commons. But the Liberal Democrats want AV to be introduced *without* a referendum. It is rumoured that Brown offered this concession to Clegg during his meeting in Ricketts room. However, the Labour representatives say they cannot sign up to a change to the voting system without a public vote. Throughout the second meeting it is clear to the Labour team that Liberal Democrat interest in a deal is fading. At the end, Adonis suggests to Danny Alexander both sides integrate their notes into one document – the basis of a programme for government. Alexander replies: 'Let's wait and see what happens between Nick and Gordon.' Adonis and his team realise the significance of that statement; it is a clear signal that the Liberal Democrats 'don't expect talks to go any further'.[188] Nevertheless, they remain hard at work on their negotiating position. 'But I began to feel early in the meeting that the Liberal Democrats were not serious and Peter felt the same,' says Pearce. 'Afterwards the briefing started against us.'[189]

By lunchtime, the Labour team are sure that Clegg is continuing negotiations with them simply to improve his bargaining position with Cameron. 'We thought Gordon was being used,' says Balls.[190] They are also indignant about Liberal Democrat attempts to pin the blame on Labour for the failure to clinch a deal. 'None of it was true about our seriousness,' says one member of the team.[191] Brown, too, is losing his patience. 'Look, I'm going to the Palace. I've had enough. I'm not sitting here while they finalise the details of their deal,' he says.[192] His mood began to change some time shortly before noon. 'It really annoyed him that he was now only at Number 10 because Clegg kept demanding more time and because constitutionally he had to stay until there was the prospect of a new government. He was ready to go,' says one aide.[193] Brown's team recognise it is over. They turn their attention to managing his exit from Downing Street. 'We were resolved not to let the Lib Dems or etiquette leave Gordon looking weak or slow to leave,' says one aide.[194] Working away with his team at parliamentary offices in the Norman Shaw South Building, Cameron has no idea that the Lib–Lab talks are breaking down: 'He was very agitated and nervous, much more so than at any point in the campaign.'[195]

Brown is under pressure to stay on as Prime Minister from the three most powerful officials in the land. O'Donnell, Heywood and Geidt all think there is a clear constitutional imperative for him to remain in Downing Street until a clear and strong government emerges to replace the outgoing administration.[196] At 12.30pm, an increasingly impatient Brown leaves Number 10 for the House of Commons. On the phone to Clegg he asks: 'Are we meeting for more talks today Nick? I need an answer. This can't carry on.' Clegg says no but stresses: 'We need more time. In Europe, coalition negotiations take much longer.'[197]

Back in Number 10 in the early afternoon, Brown finally takes his decision and asks Heywood to tell Geidt that he wishes to tender his resignation but the Queen's private secretary refuses to accept it. Geidt notes that it is still not clear that a successor is able to assume office, and that will put the Queen in a very difficult position. Geidt's advice is clear: 'The Prime Minister has a constitutional obligation, a duty, to remain in his post until the Queen is able to ask somebody, either Gordon or an alternative, to form an administration. He'll have to wait a bit longer until things become a bit clearer.'[198] According to an adviser, 'Gordon gets really agitated by this'.[199] Then, just after 2pm, Geidt is called into Number 10 where he meets with Brown and Heywood. Brown makes it clear that, if he is being asked to remain as Prime Minister for another twenty-four or thirty-six hours, he will do so, but only at the express request of the Queen.[200] At 3pm, Geidt returns to the Palace where, as Brown anticipates, the Queen says she will accept his intention to resign.[201] At 3.45pm, former Lord Chancellor Charlie Falconer tells the BBC: 'I think that we are doing ourselves damage now in trying to do a deal and probably it's time to stop.'[202] Former Labour heavyweights, John Reid and David Blunkett both warn publicly against Labour joining a coalition, while Burnham says the party has to 'respect the result of the general election and we can't shy away from the fact that Labour didn't win'.[203]

From 3.30pm onwards, 'a surreal atmosphere' descends on Number 10, as staff begin to pack up their personal belongings and the mood becomes sombre.[204] 'There is little clearing away to be done as most staff had packed up at the beginning of the election campaign, so it was only their weekend possessions that they had brought in while we camped in Number 10 for the duration of the talks.'[205] At 5.30pm, Brown speaks to Clegg again: 'I need to tell you, I'm going.' Clegg becomes very animated and tells him that they still have a lot of work to do. 'I still think we can do this deal, I still think there's a great opportunity,' he tells Brown. Brown relents and says he is still open to talks, but only on the condition that Clegg confirms then and there, that he will break off negotiations with the Conservatives. Clegg responds that he will have to speak to his colleagues and cannot take the decision on the phone. Muir tells Brown not to give the Liberal Democrats more than an hour. It is approaching 6pm, and 'we are all keen that he leaves in daylight, not in the dark'.[206] At 6.40pm, Clegg calls back asking for more time. 'A groan goes up in the office when he says that,' says an aide.[207] By this stage, even O'Donnell thinks it is over: he has gathered that this would be absolutely the last phone call.[208] Brown tells Clegg his position is insupportable and he must go to the Palace to resign. The atmosphere lightens in the den as discussion turns to past Christmas parties, at which Brown would recite the same list of jokes he had been telling for years. Balls steps up and repeats the jokes, intentionally mixing up the punch lines.[209] When he finishes, Balls takes a big swig from a bottle of fizzy water and chokes. 'Peter's trying to kill him off again,' Brown quips.[210] At about 6.50pm, the phone goes in Brown's office one final time. 'Gordon, we need more time. The Tory position on Europe is dreadful. They can't be trusted on Europe. You must not resign,' says Clegg. 'Clegg's tone was really desperate,' remembers one adviser.[211] It is too late. 'Your time is up,' Brown tells him. 'I can't wait for you while you try and get more out of the Tories. This can't go on. I'm going to resign.' The Prime Minister has had enough. 'He tells Clegg the Liberal Democrats have missed "a major historic opportunity" to build a progressive government but adds: "I wish you the very best."'[212] Mandelson, fearing that Brown might give way to Clegg once more, places a card in front of his nose on which he has written: 'No more time!'[213] Campbell records the historic moment in his diary: 'Clegg called and asked for more time then again. But finally GB said: "Time for what? Unless you can tell me you've broken off talks with the Tories in favour of discussions with us, I'll assume you're going with the Tories. I'm now in an impossible position. I have to go to the Palace. Nick, Nick, Nick, I have to do this now, I can't stay on, it's a choice one way or the other. You've made the choice, I'm not going to hold on." Final words were: "OK, thanks Nick. Goodbye." And he turned to us and said: "OK, let's do it."'[214]

When Brown puts the phone down, the emotion breaks in the horseshoe room. His team rise to their feet, clapping him on the back. He walks to his desk and Sarah enters the room with John and Fraser.[215] One of the boys looks up at his father and says: 'Daddy, you know everything don't you?'[216] McNeill describes it as like a 'family scene, with everyone gathered around him: some who'd been with him for three years, some for ten, some from the very beginning. It is like different parts of his life are suddenly coming together at that point.'[217] She describes Brown as being 'very calm: his concern is for his boys, and for us. He feels his role as a protector at these times. He takes his responsibilities to everybody very seriously.'[218] 'He was a true leader that day: calm, focused and determined,' recalls one political aide.[219]

The room is filling up with figures from throughout Number 10 and from the Cabinet Office, including Cunliffe and McDonald. Brown's private office and political staff had developed a surprisingly warm relationship during his time in office. As tears began to fill the eyes of his closest staff, he goes around the room and thanks everybody individually for making him and his family feel so welcome.[220] The two boys stand on the table as Brown gives his farewell speech: 'I've just written a letter to my successor (I should say successors) in which I've noted that they will never work with a finer, more public-spirited group of people with such a strong sense of duty and huge talent as they will find in the civil service ... What we have achieved, we have achieved together.'[221] It is the end of a gruelling month, he says, and, for many, gruelling years. 'We're off to grandma's,' one of the boys interjects excitedly. His private office staff, including all of the men, are in floods of tears. Even Campbell is emotional: 'It was thirteen years we'd been in power and, you know, this was it.'[222] Outside, the daylight is fading. A podium has been set up in front of the door to Number 10. Brown's staff begin to trickle away and line up along the passage to the front door, joined by people across Downing Street. Back in the office, in the seconds before leaving, Brown takes a pen and writes a message to Nelson Mandela, addressing it to 'Madiba', the South African leader's tribal nickname, and to his wife Graca, in which he thanks them for inspiring him and 'a whole generation'. 'I want my last letter from Downing Street to be to the two people I admire most – for your courage, leadership and your friendship,' he writes.[223] He also pens a note to Aung San Suu Kyi, the Burmese pro-democracy leader. The letters signed, Brown walks with Nye and Mandelson from Number 12 to behind the Number 10 door.

At 7.16pm, Brown leaves Number 10 for the last time as Prime Minister, with his family. This was the boys' idea – earlier that morning they had said that they wanted to walk out with him. 'They're a very democratic family; nothing is ever done without the boys' involvement,' says one aide.[224] A draft of Brown's speech had been written the weekend before, with inputs from Bob Shrum and McNeill, though the final text is his own.[225] 'I have informed the Queen's private secretary that it is my intention to tender my resignation to the Queen. In the event that the Queen accepts, I shall advise her to invite the

Leader of the Opposition to seek to form a government. I wish the next Prime Minister well as he makes the important choices for the future. Only those who have held the office of Prime Minister can understand the full weight of its responsibilities and its great capacity for good. I have been privileged to learn much about the very best in human nature and a fair amount, too, about its frailties, including my own.'[226] He has 'loved the job, not for its prestige, its titles and its ceremony – which I do not love at all. No, I loved the job for its potential to make this country I love fairer, more tolerant, more green, more democratic, more prosperous and more just.' Notably, he praises the armed forces, which represented 'all that is best in our country'. He concludes: 'Above all, I want to thank Sarah for her unwavering support as well as her love, and for her own service to our country. I thank my sons John and Fraser for the love and joy they bring to our lives. And as I leave the second-most important job I could ever hold, I cherish even more the first – as a husband and father. Thank you and goodbye.'[227] With Sarah, John and Fraser, and the admiration of many in the country who had hitherto been cynical about him, he boards the waiting car and sets off for the Palace.

After Brown and his family leave through the front door, his team return for a final time to the horseshoe, to watch the scenes on television. After the car sweeps out through the gates of Downing Street, they say goodbye to the civil servants, 'which was difficult, really difficult. They were all quite distressed. We were all quite distressed.'[228] The team then races through St James's Park to Victoria Street for the final farewell at Labour Party headquarters.[229] Emotions run equally high in the building; although Brown had been the party leader for only three years, he had overseen the three previous general elections. Again, he has thought carefully about what to say, knowing that the words are to go out to the Labour Party across the country. The family are again applauded as they get in the car to go to the airport for a flight to Scotland. Brown's team, punch-drunk, repair to a pub with the rest of the Labour Party staff, in nearby St James's.[230] On his way to the airport that evening, he makes a point of calling all of them from Sarah's phone to thank them for what they have done.[231] He calls Fletcher at the exact moment the official is walking into Cameron's office to brief him for a call to Obama. His mind is already turning to how he wants to spend the rest of his life, advancing his ideas for progress. He knows he has not achieved what he wanted as Prime Minister. He knows he squandered opportunities. But he will not give up. Kirsty McNeill has just wrestled through the crowds of exhausted aides, and paid for a pint at the Old Star pub, when her mobile rings. It is Brown. 'Can you get a plane up to Scotland?' he asks. 'I want you to start work. Tomorrow.'[232]

Epilogue: Brown after 10

The life of a former Prime Minister – as this elite club adjusts from the frenzy of Number 10 to relative anonymity thereafter – is far from easy, though many who have never held responsibility, let alone responsibility at this level, find this hard to believe. As Simon Jenkins wrote: 'No animal in the political jungle is more awful in its misery than an ex-prime minister.' For all the inherent difficulties in adjusting to life after power, however, Brown has hardly covered himself with glory since leaving Downing Street.

Back in June 2007 there had been many who hoped that, once he finally achieved his life-long goal and entered Number 10, he would become a more grounded and positive human being. They were disappointed. Equally, those who hoped for a transformation in Brown once he left Number 10, building on the magnanimity he displayed on his final day in office, were to be frustrated. Brown's character difficulties were so deep-rooted that they were impervious even to these two major transitions in circumstance.

In his first few weeks outside Downing Street, Brown retreated with Sarah and the boys to his house in North Queensferry, Scotland. Early on, Fraser gave him a stone on which he had painted the word 'Dad'. 'I never did anything like that for my father,' Brown said, lost in sadness. He felt intensely vulnerable. What should he do? He wasn't comfortable going to the House of Commons, afraid of humiliation in public, and anxious to avoid giving the Tories a target. His defence was that he had spent the previous three years almost exclusively in Westminster and now was the time for him to concentrate on his constituency. The attractions of volunteering and community work fired him, inspired as he had been by the example of Citizens UK in the final days of the election campaign, but he found it peculiarly hard to accept that he was no longer Prime Minister. He would crave releasing statements, and in periodic speeches he found it equally hard to curb his tendency to make policy announcements. 'You're not Prime Minister anymore,' he had to be reminded regularly.

Much of those first few weeks were spent on the telephone, talking to friends across the world. Bob Geldof was one with whom he mused about a future role. Agreeing to co-convene a high level panel for the Global Campaign for Education was one of several international commitments into which he entered early on. He felt great pride when Aung San Suu Kyi was released from house arrest in November 2010, knowing how much work he had done to bring this about.

The ghost of his father remained as ubiquitous in his mind after May 2010 as it had been before. Its influence can be seen in one area where Brown's reputation since leaving Number 10 has been impeccable: he always said he would not aggrandise himself financially, and he appears to have abided by his ideals of frugality. Brown's Number 10 suits were promptly marched off to a charity shop in the constituency; the £588,000 he earned in the year after leaving, from his book and other writing, has been spent on his office or given to charity. 'I have not earned one penny for myself, and I have not received one penny,' he said – he was determined not to have profited from office. There was more than a touch of showing that he was going to be very different from Blair about all this. His defiant line on money concealed the fact that he and Sarah were struggling financially: his final months in Number 10 had been plagued by anxieties about how he would manage to look after the family if he lost the election. They had significant debts, which were exacerbated after he left Downing Street by the Cabinet Office sending him a series of bills for food and drink he had consumed in office. It made him extremely angry, and Sarah resolved to write her book in part to gain money to build up their reserves.

Brown remained as hypersensitive to criticism after Downing Street as he always was. His sense of being a victim and his self-pity were palpable in the early months. Much of his pain that first summer and autumn emanated from the fact that no one went on the airwaves to defend his character or his policies. His team, initially Kirsty McNeill and Brendan Cox, fought to steer him clear of domestic politics and deter him from defending himself. So he sought solace in talking to Charlie Whelan, who started, to the horror of his team, briefing and bullishly defending his record. The one mistake that Brown would admit to making was his disparaging comment about Mrs Duffy, though he conceded that he held on to McBride for too long and that he should have been better at leading a united team in Number 10. He also believes that he mishandled Blair and regrets expending so much energy trying to block his public service reform agenda. On all other decisions during his premiership he was in the right, and if errors had been made it was the fault of others.

Brown was at his most prickly in defence of his economic record. Despite his impressive contribution to saving the banking system in the autumn of 2008 and boosting economic confidence during the G20 in April 2009, his immediate economic legacy found few defenders. Labour's reputation on the economy has fallen to its lowest point since the 'winter of discontent' of 1978–79. His refusal, when Prime Minister, to talk about cutting the deficit did his reputation irreparable damage. At a time when the current government are scrabbling around to find ways to promote growth, he must be kicking himself for failing to appreciate that until he was considered credible on paying down Britain's debts he would not get a hearing for his own plans for reviving Britain's economy. Always more the historian than the economist, it must be bitter for him to reflect that it has been much easier in history to lose reputations for economic competence than to gain them.

Brown's first party conference for thirteen years as neither Chancellor nor Prime Minister was always going to be a big hurdle. The days leading up to it were marred by a row between him and acting leader Harriet Harman over precisely when he should give his address. She wanted him to speak after the new leader was announced; he wanted to do it before. With memories of her leadership in the coup against him earlier that year still smarting, Brown was in no mood to compromise – he felt that she was merely trying to avoid being upstaged by him. His worry was that if he spoke after the new leader was announced, no one would be interested in him, and he wanted the conference speech to be his grand farewell. In the end it was his will that prevailed.

Brown was desperately keen for Balls to win the leadership election. 'Gordon believed that only Ed had the intellectual weight and political instincts to make a success of the job,' said a confidant. His post-Number 10 team would challenge him about his fixation with his former lieutenant; he would concede Balls had a dark side, but he never relinquished his faith in him. To Brown's upset, most of his former team were backing Ed Miliband, whose campaign team, especially Stewart Wood, put Brown under considerable pressure to vote for their man. But Brown stood his ground and refused to make a public intervention. Brown's biggest hope, however, was that it would be David Miliband who would lose. He continued to believe that, throughout his premiership, the older Miliband had treated him very badly.

Brown devoted much of the remaining autumn to his book, which he wanted to be regarded as 'intellectual and serious', in stark contrast to Mandelson's *The Third Man*, published in July 2010, or Blair's *A Journey*, published in September 2010 (in which Blair in fact let Brown off remarkably lightly). Brown was 'outraged' by Mandelson's book, which he thought was 'contemptuous', castigating it for being 'mere gossip' and 'beneath him'. Mandelson invited him to his book launch party, which Brown's team thought was hilarious – the recovery of their relationship had been short lived and was by now firmly returned to the state of mutual loathing that had predominated since Blair's accession in 1994. Brown decided not to write his memoirs but to focus narrowly on the financial crisis. His book, *Beyond the Crash*, received much input from McNeill and Vadera, and was published in December 2010, though he felt, with some justice, that it failed to receive the attention it deserved. So intense was the period of writing that Sarah had to leave Scotland for London, as he was sucking the energy out of her when she was trying to concentrate on her own writing. Her own book, *Behind the Black Door*, was published in March 2011.

Sarah's book shows that she remained as staunch in defence of her husband after the premiership as she had been during it. Indeed, while in Number 10, she could be even more partisan than her husband in her judgement of others, as Cherie Blair had been before her. Gus O'Donnell was a particular focus of Sarah's ire, and at the time of the book's publication she spoke of a lack of trust in him. To her anger towards O'Donnell for allegedly telling Andrew Rawnsley that her husband was a bully was added Brown's own conviction that the Cabinet Secretary had betrayed him during the coalition talks. He believed that O'Donnell had conspired to ensure that there was only ever one serious option on the table: a Conservative-Lib Dem coalition. Historical analogies to the fore as ever, he believed, as had Labour governments of old, that he had been betrayed by the Civil Service. Clegg was another who he felt had betrayed him in the coalition talks, merely stringing him along. His bitterness erupted when Obama addressed parliamentarians in Westminster Hall in May 2011, with Brown insisting that his seat be moved away from Clegg's.

Another object of Brown's disdain was News International and the way they had treated the Prime Minister in his last months in office. He was spoiling for a fight and one fell into his lap with the furore over News International and allegations of phone hacking in the summer of 2011. During his final months at Number 10, O'Donnell had prevented him, he alleged, from holding an investigation into the whole affair. Brown was intensely frustrated that the whole saga had not come to the surface before and he released his pent up dissatisfaction in a thirty-five minute, rage-fuelled speech in the House of Commons in July 2011. His accusations against News International included accessing the medical records of his son Fraser, born in July 2006 with cystic fibrosis. Here was an unrivalled opportunity for him to deliver a statesman's speech on the unacceptable face of the media; instead, his bombastic address seemed to many to be motivated by bile and self pity, confirming their worst suspicions of a man lacking in self-knowledge and a sense of appropriate conduct. His and Sarah's overt courting of the Murdoch press after its alleged intrusion into their son Fraser's medical history in 2006 rebounded against him, smacking of hypocrisy. Brown's accusations, to his immense chagrin, were mostly rebutted. It is hard to think of any speech by a retired Prime Minister in the last fifty years that has been more damaging to their reputation.

Brown had proved again that he was still his own worst enemy, as he had been since 1994. Yet at his best he has much to offer as an ex-premier, particularly in global development and international economics. As someone who had played a dominant role in the 2008/09 crisis, in the evolution of the G20 and in the architecture of international forums, his eye was now firmly on the prize of the Presidency of the IMF. Brown's April 2011 speech at Bretton Woods in the US (the birth place of the IMF in 1944) was designed, as his book had been, to help his cause. He had lined up some formidable support in the US via his close friend and ally Larry Summers, as well as from China, India and France, fostered in personal meetings with Wen, Singh and Sarkozy. But Osborne in particular would not stand for it and actively lobbied his fellow finance ministers to block Brown's candidacy. (Brown refused to pick up the phone to speak to Cameron about the job, preferring to remain aloof. Cameron, in contrast, has spoken regularly to Blair, and it is Blair's example that Cameron's Number 10 sought regularly to follow – though Cameron was less dismissive in private of Brown than they chose to be in public). Brown could have read the runes better; instead, when Cameron spoke out on Radio 4's *Today* programme against his candidacy he was distraught. Cameron himself regretted the starkness of his pronouncement but Brown was inconsolable. He felt he had been treated 'appallingly'; it was 'unpatriotic and very undignified', he said, to treat a former Prime Minister in this way.

The financial crisis in the summer of 2011 was torture for him. Had he still been in power, he believes that he alone had the financial understanding and clout among leaders to steer the world away from economic catastrophe. He had to resort to journalism, speaking of Europe 'throwing away' the chance of a restoration of stability. His advice was sought by leaders: but he wanted to be leading from the front himself. Whatever his other shortcomings his track record as Prime Minister suggests that he would have gripped the latest financial crisis better than the current international leadership has proved capable of doing. The global economic arena is worse for Brown's absence.

So Brown simmers on, feeling betrayed and badly treated. In his worst moments, he suffers from paranoid feelings that the world was against him as Prime Minister: the Parliamentary Labour Party, the Cabinet, the service chiefs, the media and the Civil Service, all conspired to do him down and thwart his ambitions to build a better Britain and a better world. With rich irony, by the end his paranoia was no longer groundless. Many in these groups did indeed want to see him harmed and even destroyed. He talks now a great deal about his boys and has become increasingly fascinated by the world of education. His best hope for the future, if no job on the world stage falls to him, and if he is indeed unable to reconcile himself to his own demons, is that he will progressively live his life through his children and hope that, if indeed he never fully became the son that his father would have wanted him to be, then at least he could become a father who his own sons could admire.

Polling Records During Brown's Premiership

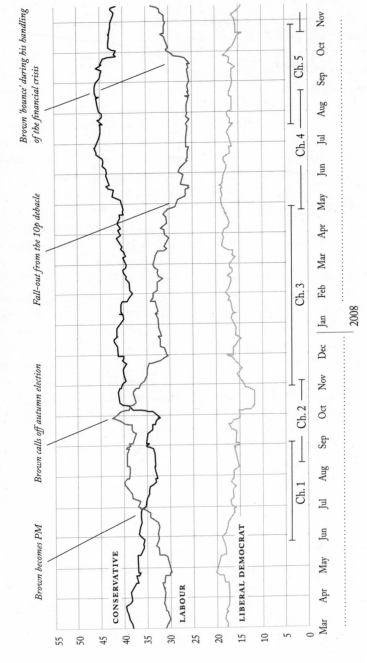

Brown becomes PM

Brown calls off autumn election

Fall-out from the 10p debacle

'Brown bounce' during his handling of the financial crisis

CONSERVATIVE

LABOUR

LIBERAL DEMOCRAT

Ch. 1   Ch. 2   Ch. 3   Ch. 4   Ch. 5

Mar Apr May Jun Jul Aug Sep Oct Nov Dec | Jan Feb Mar Apr May Jun Jul Aug Sep Oct Nov

2008

55 50 45 40 35 30 25 20 15 10 5 0

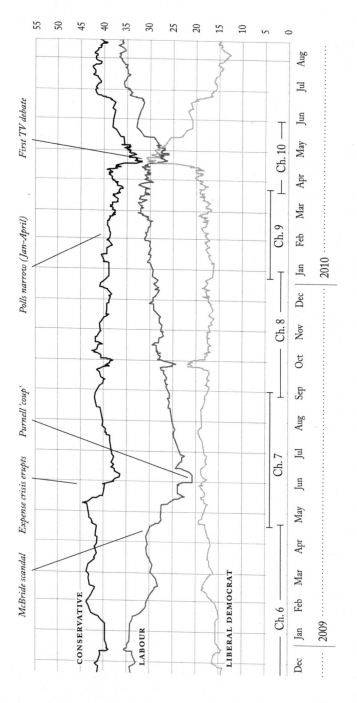

This graph shows a rolling average of polling data recorded by YouGov, ComRes, BPIX, Populus, Ipsos-MORI, Opinium, ICM, Angus-Reid, TNS BRMB, and Harris polling agencies on behalf of national newspapers. Each independent polling organisation asks voters to indicate how they would vote were the General Election to occur the next day. A comprehensive list of the aggregated source data can be examined at the UK Polling Report Website: http://ukpollingreport.co.uk/blog/voting-intention.

Endnotes

INTRODUCTION

1. Philip Ziegler, *Edward Heath*
2. Private interview
3. Private interview
4. Interview with Tessa Jowell
5. Interview with Andrew Turnbull

CHAPTER I

1. Private interview
2. Private interview
3. Private interview
4. Private interview
5. Private interview
6. BBC News, 27.07.07
7. Interview with Theo Bertram
8. Interview with Spencer Livermore
9. Private interview
10. Private interview
11. Private interview
12. Private interview
13. Private interview
14. *Guardian*, 01.07.07
15. Private interview
16. Private interview
17. Interview with Dan Corry
18. Private interview
19. Private interview
20. Private interview
21. Interview with Ed Balls
22. Interview with Ed Balls
23. Interview with Ed Balls
24. Private interview
25. BBC News, 22.12.09
26. Interview with Andrew Adonis
27. Private interview
28. Private interview
29. Interview with Fiona Gordon
30. Interview with Jacqui Smith
31. Private interview
32. Interview with Tessa Jowell
33. Private interview
34. Private interview
35. Interview with Lord Owen
36. Private interview
37. *Observer*, 01.07.07
38. Private interview
39. Private interview
40. Interview with Ara Darzi
41. *Observer*, 01.07.07
42. *Daily Telegraph*, 29.06.07
43. Private interview
44. Private interview
45. Private interview
46. Private interview
47. Private interview
48. Private interview
49. Private interview
50. Private interview
51. Interview with Ed Balls
52. Private interview
53. Private interview
54. Interview with Gavin Kelly
55. Private interview
56. Interview with Ed Balls
57. Private interview
58. Private interview
59. John Smith Memorial Lecture, April 1996
60. Interview with Ed Balls
61. Deborah Mattinson, *Talking to a Brick Wall: How New Labour Stopped Listening to the Voter and Why We Need a New Politics* (Biteback, 2010) p. 174
62. Interview with Ed Balls
63. *Independent*, 09.08.07
64. Interview with Dan Corry
65. *Guardian*, 07.07.07
66. Private interview
67. Private interview
68. Steve Richard, *Whatever it Takes*, (Fourth Estate, 2010) p.218
69. Private interview
70. Private interview
71. *Guardian*, 25.07.07
72. Interview with Jacqui Smith
73. Private interview
74. MSN News, 11.05.10
75. Private interview
76. Private interviews
77. Private interview
78. Private interview
79. Interview with Caroline Flint
80. Private interview
81. Interview with Hilary Benn
82. Private interview
83. Private interview
84. Private interview
85. Private interview
86. Private interview
87. Private interview
88. YouGov/*Sunday Times* poll conducted 8–10 August 2007
89. Private interview
90. Interview with Nigel Sheinwald
91. Private interview
92. *Daily Telegraph*, 14.07.07
93. BBC, 13.07.07
94. Private interview
95. Interview with David Manning
96. Interview with David Manning
97. Interview with John Sawers
98. Private interview
99. Private interview

100. Interview with Ed Balls
101. Private interview
102. Private interview
103. Private interview
104. Private interview
105. Interview with Simon McDonald
106. Private interview
107. Interview with Simon McDonald
108. Private interview
109. Interview with Simon McDonald
110. Private interview
111. *Glasgow Herald*, 27.07.07
112. Private interview
113. Private interview
114. Private interview
115. *Observer*, 29.07.07
116. Private interview
117. Private interview
118. Private interview
119. Private interview
120. Private interview
121. Private interview
122. Private interview
123. Private interview
124. Interview with Matt Cavanagh
125. Private interview
126. Interview with Matt Cavanagh
127. Private interview
128. Private interview
129. Private interview
130. Private interview
131. Interview with David Manning
132. *Washington Post*, 31.07.07
133. Private interview
134. Interview with Simon McDonald
135. Private interview
136. Interview with Steve Hadley
137. Private interview
138. Interview with Nigel Sheinwald
139. Private interview
140. *New Statesman*, 28.05.07
141. Private interview
142. BBC News, 31.07.07
143. Interview with xxx
144. Private interview
145. Private interview
146. Private interview
147. Private interview

148. Interview with Dan Corry
149. Private interview
150. Interview with Nick Pearce
151. Private interview
152. Private interview
153. Private interview
154. Interview with Michael Jacobs
155. Private interview
156. Private interview
157. Private interviewr
158. Private interview
159. Private interview
160. Private interview
161. Private interview
162. Private interview
163. Private interview
164. Private interview
165. Private interview
166. Private interview
167. BBC News, 11.08.07
168. Private interview

CHAPTER 2
1. Interview with Ed Balls
2. The fullest accounts are in Andrew Rawnsley, *The End of the Party*, (Penguin, 2010) pp.496;
   Deborah Mattinson, *Talking to a Brick Wall*, (Biteback, 2010) p.177
3. Interview with Douglas Alexander
4. Interview with Spencer Livermore
5. Interview with Fiona Gordon
6. Interview with Dan Corry
7. Interview with Douglas Alexander
8. Deborah Mattinson *Talking to a Brick Wall* p.177
9. Interview with Shaun Woodward
10. Andrew Rawnsley, *The End of the Party*, p. 496
11. Interview with Spencer Livermore
12. Private interview
13. Interview with Spencer Livermore
14. Interview with Stephen Carter
15. Interview with Spencer Livermore
16. Private interview

17. Interview with Douglas Alexander
18. Private interview
19. Steve Richards, *Whatever it Takes*, (Fourth Estate, 2010), p. 292
20. *Daily Telegraph*, 31.08.07
21. Interview with Jacqui Smith
22. Private interview
23. Interview with Shaun Woodward
24. Private interview
25. Private interview
26. Interview with Douglas Alexander
27. Interview with Douglas Alexander
28. Private interview
29. Private interview
30. Interview with Spencer Livermore
31. Private interview
32. Interview with Dan Corry
33. Steve Richards, *Whatever it Takes*, p. 290
34. Steve Richards, *Whatever it Takes*, p. 291
35. Private interview
36. Interview with Nick Pearce
37. Interview with Douglas Alexander
38. Interview with Ed Balls
39. Private interview
40. Private interview
41. Private interview
42. Interview with Jacqui Smith
43. Private interview
44. Douglas Alexander, *Guardian*, 22.09.07
45. *Guardian*, 23.09.07
46. Interview with Gavin Kelly
47. Steve Richards, *Whatever it Takes*, p. 292
48. *Guardian*, 24.09.07
49. Private interview
50. Steve Richards, *Whatever it Takes*, p. 294
51. Private interview
52. Interview with Stan Greenberg
53. Interview with Stan Greenberg
54. Interview with Stan Greenberg
55. *The Times*, 26.09.07
56. Interview with Justin Forsyth

57. *Guardian*, 28.09.07
58. Private interview
59. Private interview
60. *Guardian*, 28.09.07
61. Interview with Gavin Kelly
62. Private interview
63. *Daily Telegraph*, 10.09.07
64. *New Statesman*, 27.09.07
65. *Daily Mail* 27.09.07
66. *Daily Mail*, 25.09.07
67. Private interview
68. Steve Richards, *The Brown Years*, Radio 4
69. Steve Richards, *The Brown Years*, Radio 4
70. Private interview
71. Private interview
72. Interview with James Purnell
73. Private interview
74. Private interview
75. Private interview
76. Private interview
77. Toby Helm, *Daily Telegraph*, 27.09.07
78. Private interview
79. David Cracknell, *Sunday Times*, 30.09.07
80. Steve Richards, *Whatever it Takes*, p. 295
81. Peter Snowdon, *Back from the Brink*, (Harperpress, 2010) p.261
82. *Sunday Telegraph*, 22.07.07
83. Peter Snowdon, *Back from the Brink*, pp.266, 275.
84. *Sunday Telegraph*, 30.09.07
85. Peter Snowdon, *Back from the Brink*, p.276
86. Private interview
87. Private interview
88. Private interview
89. Interview with Spencer Livermore
90. Private interview
91. Steve Richards, *Whatever it Takes*, p. 297
92. Private interview
93. *Guardian*, 02.10.07
94. Peter Snowdon, *Back from the Brink*, p. 278
95. *Daily Telegraph*, 04.10.07
96. Deborah Mattinson, *Talking to a Brick Wall*, p.181
97. Interview with Spencer Livermore
98. Interview with Fiona Gordon

99. Private interview
100. Deborah Mattinson, *Talking to a Brick Wall*, p. 183
101. Private interview
102. Patrick Hennessy and Melissa Kite, 'How will history judge Gordon Brown?', *Daily Telegraph*, 07.10.07
103. Interview with Stan Greenberg
104. Private interview
105. Interview with Douglas Alexander
106. Private interview
107. Private interview
108. Interview with Douglas Alexander
109. Private interview
110. Private interview
111. Private interview
112. Private interview
113. Private interview
114. Private interview
115. Private interview
116. Private interview
117. Interview with Justin Forsyth
118. Interview with Adam Boulton
119. Interview with Adam Boulton
120. Andrew Marr, BBC News, 06.10.07
121. Andrew Marr, BBC News, 06.10.07
122. *Guardian*, 08.10.07
123. *Guardian*, 12.10.07
124. *Guardian*, 08.10.07
125. Tom Clark, *Guardian*, 08.10.07
126. Interview with Douglas Alexander
127. Private interview
128. Interview with Paul Sinclair
129. Interview with Paul Sinclair
130. Private interview
131. Private interview
132. Private interview
133. Private interview
134. Private interview
135. Private interview
136. Private interview
137. Private interview
138. Private interview
139. Interview with Paul Sinclair
140. *Daily Mail*, 08.12.07

141. Interview with Spencer Livermore
142. Private interview
143. Private interview
144. Private interview
145. Private interview
146. Interview with Ed Balls
147. House of Commons Debate, 09.10.07
148. Private interview
149. *Daily Telegraph*, 10.10.07
150. *Economist*, 11.10.07
151. Simon Jenkins, *Guardian*, 12.10.07
152. Poly Toynbee, *Guardian*, 12.10.07
153. Hamish McRae, *Independent*, 10.10.07
154. *Daily Telegraph*, 14.10.07
155. *Economist*, 13.10.07
156. House of Commons Debates, 10.10.07
157. *Sunday Telegraph*, 13.10.07
158. *The Times*, 06.11.07
159. *Independent*, 07.11.07
160. Private interview
161. Private interview
162. Interview with Dan Corry
163. Private interview
164. Private interview
165. *The Times*, 02.11.07
166. *Sunday Times*, 18.11.07
167. *Daily Telegraph*, 30.11.07
168. Private interview
169. Steve Richards, *The Brown Years*, Radio 4
170. Interview with Stephen Carter
171. Private interview
172. Private information

CHAPTER 3
1. Interview with Patrick Loughran
2. BBC News, 21.11.07
3. Interview with Alistair Darling, *Guardian*, 30.08.08
4. In March, a junior official at HMRC had contravened security procedures by sending to the NAO a very sensitive copy of HMRC's Child Benefit data. In September, the personal details of some 15,000 Standard Life customers

had been lost en route to HMRC. That same month the laptop of an HMRC employee containing around 400 personal savings details of customers had been stolen.

5. *Guardian*, 21.11.07
6. BBC News, 25.06.08
7. *Daily Mail*, 21.11.07
8. Interview with Tom Watson
9. Private information
10. Private interview
11. Private information
12. Private interview
13. *Independent*, 22.11.07
14. *Daily Mail*, 18.12.07
15. Private interview
16. Private interview
17. Private interview
18. Peter Watt, *Inside Out: My Story of betrayal and cowardice at the heart of New Labour* (Biteback, 2010), p. 179
19. Private interview
20. Private interview
21. Private interview
22. Steve Richards, *Whatever It Takes* (Fourth Estate, 2010), p. 311
23. Private interview
24. Private interview
25. Private interview
26. *Independent*, 11.11.07
27. *Sunday Telegraph*, 18.11.07
28. Richard Dannatt, *Leading from the Front* (Bantam Press, 2010) p. 316
29. *Daily Mail*, 21.07.08
30. *Reuters*, 12.10.07
31. Private interview
32. House of Commons debate, 12.12.07
33. Private interview
34. *Independent*, 12.12.10
35. Private correspondence, 28.06.10
36. Private interview
37. House of Commons debates
38. Private interview
39. Private interview
40. Private interview
41. Richard G. Whitman, Chatham House, Kafebabel. com, 25.06.07
42. BBC, 23.05.05
43. Private interview

44. Private interview
45. Private interview
46. Private interview
47. Private interview
48. Private interview
49. Private interview
50. Private interview
51. Private interview
52. Private interview
53. Private interview
54. Private interview
55. Private interview
56. Private interview
57. Private interview
58. Private interview
59. Private interview
60. Private interview
61. Private interview
62. Private interview
63. Private interview
64. Private interview
65. Private interview
66. Private interview
67. Private interview
68. Private interiew
69. Private interview
70. *Times*, 11.12.07
71. *Guardian*, 13.13.07
72. *Daily Telegraph*, 14.12.07
73. Private interview
74. Private interview
75. Private interview
76. Private interview
77. Private interview
78. Private interview
79. Private interview
80. Private interview
81. Private interview
82. Private interview
83. Private interview
84. Private interview
85. Private interview
86. Private interview
87. Steve Richards, *Whatever It Takes* (Fourth Estate, 2010), p. 277
88. Private interview
89. Private interview
90. Private interview
91. Private interview
92. Private interview
93. Private interview
94. Sue Cameron, *Financial Times*, 27.11.07
95. Steve Richards, *The Brown Years*, Radio 4

96. Private interview
97. Private interview
98. Steve Richards, *The Brown Years*, Radio 4
99. Steve Richards, *The Brown Years*, Radio 4
100. Steve Richards *Whatever It Takes* (Fourth Estate, 2010), p. 316
101. Private interview
102. Private interview
103. Private interview
104. Private interview
105. Private interview
106. Private interview
107. Private interview
108. *Daily Telegraph*, 04.04.08
109. Private interview
110. Private interview
111. Private interview
112. Private interview
113. Private interview
114. Private interview
115. Private interview
116. Private interview
117. Private interview
118. Private interview
119. Private interview
120. Private interview
121. Private interview
122. Private interview
123. Private information
124. Private interview
125. Interview with John Sawers
126. Private interview
127. PInterview with Stephen Carter
128. Private interview
129. Private interview
130. BBC News, 30.12.07
131. *Daily Mail*, 08.01.08
132. Private interview
133. *Observer*, 01.07.07
134. *The Times*, 08.01.08
135. *Guardian*, 07.01.08
136. Interview with Alan Johnson
137. Private interview
138. Private interview
139. Private interview
140. Private interview
141. Private interview
142. Private information
143. Private interview
144. Private interview
145. Private interview
146. Private interview

147. Private information
148. Private interview
149. Private interview
150. Private interview
151. Private interview
152. Private interview
153. Private interview
154. Private interview
155. Private interview
156. Interview with Michael Barber
157. Private interview
158. Private interview
159. Private interview
160. Private interview
161. Private interview
162. *Guardian*, 13.02.10
163. Private interview
164. Interview with James Purnell
165. Private interview
166. Private interview
167. *Reuters*, 19.01.08
168. *Guardian*, 18.01.08
169. Private interview
170. Private interview
171. Private interview
172. *Independent*, 21.01.08
173. BBC News, 21.01.08
174. Private interview
175. *Times*, 26.01.08
176. *Guardian*, 25.01.08
177. Interview with Stephen Carter
178. Private information
179. Gordon Brown, New Year Message, 2008
180. Nick Robinson, BBC, 17.09.07
181. Private interview
182. David Cameron, BBC News, 17.02.08
183. Private interview
184. *Times*, 22.01.08
185. Vince Cable, *Independent*, 21.01.08
186. House of Commons debates, 21.01.08
187. BBC News, 17.02.08
188. Private interview
189. Private interview
190. *The Andrew Marr Show*, BBC, 27.09.09
191. Private interview
192. Private interview
193. Interview with Ed Balls
194. Private interview
195. Private interview

196. Interview with Ed Balls
197. Private interview
198. Private interview
199. *Financial Times*, 17.02.08
200. Larry Elliot, *Guardian*, 19.02.08
201. Interview with Steve Hadley
202. Private interview
203. Private interview
204. Private interview
205. Private interview
206. Private interview; *Sunday Times* 09.03.08
207. Private interview
208. Private interview
209. Private interview
210. *Times*, 12.04.08
211. *Times*, 12.04.08
212. Interview with Steve Hadley
213. *Guardian*, 18.04.08
214. Interview with Simon McDonald
215. Private interview
216. Private interview
217. Private interview
218. Private interview
219. Private interview
220. Interview with Simon McDonald
221. Private interview
222. Private interview
223. *Guardian*, 18.04.08
224. Private interview
225. Private interview
226. *Guardian*, 18.04.08
227. Private interview
228. Private interview
229. Private interview
230. Private interview
231. Private interview
232. Interview with Frank Field
233. Private interview
234. Private interview
235. Private interview
236. *Guardian*, 13.03.08
237. BBC News, 13.03.08
238. *Guardian*, 02.04.08
239. Private interview
240. Private interview
241. *Independent*, 07.04.08
242. Private interview
243. *Guardian*, 12.04.08
244. Private interview
245. Private interview
246. Private interview
247. Private interview

248. *Daily Telegraph*, 07.04.08
249. Private interview
250. Politics.co.uk, 18.04.08
251. BBC News, 20.04.08
252. *Evening Standard*, 21.04.08
253. *Independent*, 07.04.08
254. Private interview
255. Interview with Frank Field
256. *Guardian*, 21.04.08
257. *The Times*, 28.04.08
258. BBC News, 13.05.08
259. Private interview
260. Private interview
261. Private interview
262. Private interview
263. Private interview
264. *Times*, 24.09.08
265. BBC, 28.06.08

CHAPTER 4

1. *Guardian*, 12.04.08
2. *Times online*, 16.04.08.
3. BBC, 30.4.08
4. Interview with David Muir
5. Jonathan Freedland, *Guardian*, 03.05.08
6. BBC News, 02.05.08
7. Patrick Hennessy, *Daily Telegraph*, 03.05.08
8. BBC Radio 4, *Today* programme, 03.05.08
9. *Times*, 07.05.08
10. House of Commons debates, 13.05.08
11. Private interview
12. Private interview
13. *Daily Mail*, 18.05.08
14. *Times*, 19.05.08
15. *Daily Telegraph*, 18.05.08
16. House of Commons debates, 21.05.08
17. *Guardian*, 23.05.08
18. *Financial Times*, 26.05.08
19. *Daily Telegraph*, 25.05.08
20. *Guardian* leader, 23.05.08
21. *Financial Times*, 23.05.08
22. *Times*, 31.05.08
23. Sky News, 23.05.08
24. Private interview
25. Private interview
26. Private interview
27. Private interview
28. Private interview
29. Private interview
30. Private interview
31. *Times*, 19.03.08

32. Interview with Spencer Livermore
33. *PRWeek*, 27.03.08
34. *PRWeek*, 27.03.08
35. Patrick Hennessy, *Sunday Telegraph*, 23.03.08
36. *Independent*, 20.03.08
37. Interview with Michael Jacobs
38. Steve Richards, *Whatever it Takes*, p.325
39. Private interview
40. Private interview
41. *Times*, 19.03.08
42. Private interview
43. Private interview
44. Private interview
45. Private interview
46. Private interview
47. Private interview
48. Private interview
49. Private interview
50. Private interview
51. Private interview
52. Private interview
53. Private interview
54. Private interview
55. Stephen Carter and Ben Bradshaw, *Digital Britain* (BERR, June 2009)
56. Private interview
57. Private interview
58. Private interview
59. Private interview
60. Steve Richards, *Independent*, 12.06.08
61. Private interview
62. BBC, 11.05.07
63. Gordon Brown, *Washington Post*, 30.07.07
64. Private interview
65. Private interview
66. Private interview
67. Private interview
68. Private interview
69. Private interview
70. Private interview
71. Interview with Jon Trickett
72. Interview with Ed Balls
73. *Daily Telegraph*, 10.06.08
74. YouGov, *Daily Telegraph*, 29.05.08
75. Private interview
76. Interview with James Purnell
77. Liberty: *Terrorism Pre-Charge Detention Comparative Law Study*, 12.11.07

78. *BBC News*, 21.11.07
79. *Guardian*, 07.12.07
80. Interview with Jacqui Smith
81. Interview with Jacqui Smith
82. Private interview
83. Private interview
84. Private interview
85. Private interview
86. *Guardian*, 03.06.08
87. *Guardian*, 03.06.08
88. Interview with Matt Cavanagh
89. *Independent on Sunday*, 29.06.07
90. *Times*, 12.06.08
91. Patrick Hennessy, *Daily Telegraph*, 22.06.08
92. Interview with Shaun Woodward
93. *Guardian*, 14.10.08
94. Matthew Elliott, *Time* website, 11.06.08
95. Interview with Nigel Sheinwald
96. Private interview
97. Private interview
98. Private information
99. Private interview
100. Private interview
101. Interview with Andrew Roberts
102. *Daily Telegraph*, 15.06.08
103. *Independent*, 16.06.08; *Guardian*, 03.11.08
104. Private interview
105. Private interview
106. Interview with Michael Jacobs
107. Private interview
108. Private interview
109. *Times*, 23.06.08
110. Interview with Michael Jacobs
111. Interview with Michael Jacobs
112. *Times*, 29.06.08
113. *Scotsman*, 28.06.08
114. Private interview
115. Interview with Jock Stirrup
116. Private interview
117. Private interview
118. Interview with Simon McDonald
119. Thomas E. Ricks, *The Gamble: General Petraeus and the Untold Story of the American*

Surge in Iraq 2006–2008, (Allen Lane, 2009) p. 243
120. Private interview
121. Private interview
122. Private interview
123. Interview with Matt Cavanagh
124. Interview with Nigel Sheinwald
125. Gordon Brown, Knesset speech, 21.07.08
126. Private interview
127. Interview with Simon McDonald
128. Private interview
129. *MSNBC.com.*, 20.7.08.
130. *MSNBC.com.*, 20.7.08.
131. Private interview
132. *Daily Telegraph*, 20.07.08
133. Private interview
134. Private interview
135. Gordon Brown, Knesset speech, 21.07.08
136. Private interview
137. Private interview
138. *Daily Mail*, 21.07.08
139. Private interview
140. *Scotsman*, 19.07.08
141. Private interview
142. Private interview
143. *Financial Times*, 26.07.08
144. Private interview
145. Private interview
146. Private interview
147. *Daily Telegraph*, 27.07.08
148. Private interview
149. *Times*, 26.07.08
150. Private interview
151. Private interview
152. Private interview
153. Private interview
154. Private interview
155. Private information
156. Private interview
157. Interview with Alan Johnson
158. Interview with Michael Dugher
159. *Financial Times*, 27.07.08
160. *Daily Telegraph*, 25.07.08
161. *Observer*, 27.07.08
162. Private interview
163. Private interview
164. Private interview
165. Interview with Nigel Sheinwald
166. Private interview

167. Private diaries
168. Private interview
169. Interview with Simon McDonald
170. *Observer*, 27.07.08
171. YouGov, 26.06.08.
172. CrosbyTextor poll for *The Daily Telegraph*, 26.07.08
173. Private interview
174. Private interview
175. Private interview
176. Interview with David Muir
177. *Evening Standard*, 28.07.08
178. *Sunday Times*, 27.07.08
179. *Independent*, 28.07.08
180. *Evening Standard*, 28.07.08
181. *Independent*, 05.08.08
182. Private interview
183. Private interview
184. Private interview
185. Private interview
186. *Guardian*, 29.07.08
187. *Independent*, 29.07.08
188. Private interview
189. *Independent*, 29.07.08
190. Private interview
191. David Miliband, *Guardian*, 29.7.08
192. *New Statesman*, 31.07.08
193. *Daily Telegraph*, 31.07.08
194. *Independent*, 03.08.08
195. Private interview
196. Private interview
197. Private interview
198. Private interview
199. Private interview
200. Private interview
201. Interview with Paul Sinclair
202. Private interview
203. *Independent*, 31.07.08
204. Private interview
205. Private interview
206. Private interview
207. Private interview
208. Private interview
209. Interview with David Muir
210. Private interview
211. Private interview
212. Private interview
213. Private interview
214. Private interview
215. Private interview
216. Interview with Charles Clarke
217. Private interview
218. Private interview
219. Private interview

220. Private interview
221. Private interview
222. Private interview
223. *Guardian*, 07.08.08
224. *Daily Telegraph*, 02.03.10
225. Private interview
226. Interview with Kirsty McNeill
227. Interview with Gavin Kelly
228. *New Statesman*, 18.06.09
229. Private interview
230. Private interview
231. Private interview
232. Interview with Kim Darroch
233. Interview with Kim Darroch
234. Interview with Gavin Kelly
235. Peter Mandelson, *The Third Man: Life at the Heart of New Labour* (Harper Press, 2010), p.6
236. Peter Mandelson, *The Third Man*, p.6
237. Private interview
238. Interview with Justin Forsyth
239. Private interview
240. Peter Mandelson, *The Third Man*, p. 11
241. Private interview
242. Private interview
243. Interview with David Muir
244. Interview with David Muir
245. Interview with David Muir
246. Interview with Gavin Kelly
247. Private interview
248. Private interview
249. Private interview
250. Private interview
251. Private interview
252. Interview with David Muir
253. Private interview
254. Private interview
255. Private interview
256. Email, Decca Aitkenhead to Anthony Seldon, 04.08.10
257. Interview with Nick Pearce
258. *Daily Telegraph*, 31.07.08
259. Private interview
260. Andrew Rawnsley, *The End of the Party* p. 562
261. Email, Decca Aitkenhead to Anthony Seldon, 04.08.10
262. *Guardian*, 29.08.08
263. *Guardian*, 01.09.08
264. BBC, *Today* programme, 01.09.08
265. *Guardian*, 01.09.08
266. Peter Mandelson, *The Third Man*, p. 30

267. *Times*, 01.09.08, *Daily Mail*, 31.08.08
268. *Daily Mail*, 01.09.08, BBC, 02.09.08.
269. Private interview
270. Private interview
271. *Guardian*, 30.08.08

CHAPTER 5
1. Interview with Gavin Kelly
2. BBC, *Today* rogramme, 12.09.08
3. BBC News, 16.09.08
4. Private interview
5. Private interview
6. Private interview
7. Private interview
8. *Independent*, 15.09.08
9. Interview with Paul Richards
10. Private interview
11. Private interview
12. Private interview
13. Private interview
14. Private interview
15. Private interviews
16. *Times*, 16.09.08
17. *Guardian*, 16.09.08
18. Private interview
19. *Guardian*, 15.09.08
20. Interview with Paul Sinclair
21. Interview with Paul Sinclair
22. Interview with George Howarth
23. Private interview
24. Private interview
25. Private information
26. Interview with Barry Sheerman
27. Private interview
28. Interview with Martin Wolf
29. Private interview
30. Private interview
31. Andrew Ross Sorkin, *Too Big to Fail: Inside the Battle to Save Wall Street* (Allen Lane, 2009), p. 348
32. Andrew Ross Sorkin, *Too Big To Fail* p. 348
33. Andrew Ross Sorkin, *Too Big To Fail* p. 348
34. Andrew Ross Sorkin, *Too Big To Fail*
35. Andrew Ross Sorkin, *Too Big To Fail* p. 350
36. Darling, in Rawnsley, *The End of the Party* p. 576

37. Private interview
38. Private interview
39. Private interview
40. Private interview
41. Robert Peston, BBC blog, 15.09.08
42. Private interview
43. Private interview
44. Private interview
45. Private interview
46. Private interview
47. Private interview
48. Private interview
49. Private interview
50. Private interview
51. Private interview
52. Private interview
53. Private interview
54. Private interview
55. Private interview
56. Private interview
57. Private interview
58. Andrew Rawnsley, *The End of the Party*, p. 577
59. Private interview
60. Private interview
61. Interview with David Muir
62. Interview with Gavin Kelly
63. *Independent*, 23.09.08
64. Private interview
65. *Observer*, 21.09.08
66. Private interview
67. Private interview
68. Interview with David Muir
69. Interview with Kirsty McNeill
70. Interview with David Muir
71. Private interview
72. Interview with David Muir
73. Private interview
74. *Guardian*, 24.09.08
75. Interview with Stephen Carter
76. Deborah Mattinson, Radio 4
77. Interview with Gavin Kelly
78. Interview with Kirsty McNeill
79. BBC, 23.09.08
80. Private interview
81. *Independent on Sunday*, 28.09.08
82. Private interview
83. *Times*, 23.09.08
84. Private interview
85. *Sun*, 25.09.08
86. Private interview
87. Andrew Rawnsley, *The End of the Party*, p. 565
88. Private interview
89. Private interview
90. Private interview
91. Private interview
92. Private interview
93. Private interview
94. Private interview
95. Private interview
96. Private interview
97. Private interview
98. Private interview
99. Private interview
100. Private interview
101. Interview with John Sawers
102. Private interview
103. Private interview
104. Interview with Justin Forsyth
105. *Times*, 28.09.08
106. Private interview
107. Private interview
108. Private interview
109. Private information
110. Private interview
111. Private interview
112. Private interview
113. Private interview
114. Private interview
115. Interview with Nigel Sheinwald
116. Private interview
117. Private interview
118. Interview with Steve Hadley
119. Private interview
120. Private interview
121. Private interview
122. Interview with Steve Hadley
123. Private interview
124. Private interview
125. Private interview
126. Private interview
127. Interview with Nigel Sheinwald
128. Interview with Dan Corry
129. Private interview
130. Private interview
131. Private interview
132. Private interview
133. Interview with Lord Myners
134. Private interview
135. Private interview
136. Private interview
137. Private interview
138. Private interview
139. Private interview
140. George Parker, *Financial Times*, 13.10.09
141. Private interview
142. George Parker, *Financial Times*, 14.10.09
143. Private interview
144. Private interview
145. Interview with Lord Myners
146. Private interview
147. Private interview
148. Private interview
149. Private interview
150. Private interview
151. Private information
152. Private interview
153. Andrew Rawnsley, *The End of the Party*, p. 581
154. Private interview
155. Private interview
156. Private interview
157. Private interview
158. Private interview
159. Interview with Lord Myners
160. Interview with Lord Myners
161. Private interview
162. Private interview
163. Private interview
164. Private interview
165. Private interview
166. Private interview
167. Interview with Robert Peston
168. Private interview
169. Private interview
170. Private interview
171. Private interview
172. Interview with Lord Myners
173. Private interview
174. Private interview
175. *Sunday Times*, 3.10.09
176. *Sunday Times*, 3.10.09
177. Private interview
178. Private interview
179. Private interview
180. Private interview
181. Private interview
182. Private interview
183. Private interview
184. Private interview
185. Interview with Dan Corry
186. Private interview
187. Private interview
188. Private interview
189. Private interview
190. Private interview
191. Private interview
192. Steve Richards, *Whatever it Takes*, p. 378

193. House of Commons debates, 08.10.08 and BBC *Andrew Marr Show*, 28.09.08
194. Private interview
195. Private interview
196. Private interview
197. *Times*, 09.10.08
198. Private interview
199. Private interview
200. Private interview
201. *Times*, 3.10.09
202. *Times*, 10.10.08
203. Private interview
204. *Independent*, 10.10.08
205. Private interview
206. Interview with Kim Darroch
207. Private interview
208. *Observer*, 12.10.08
209. Private interview
210. Private interview
211. Private interview
212. BBC, 12.09.08
213. Interview with Kim Darroch
214. Private interview
215. Private interview
216. Private interview
217. *Times*, 18.10.08
218. Private interview
219. *Guardian* 13.10.08
220. *New York Times*, 12.10.08
221. Private interview
222. *Sunday Times*, 12.10.08
223. Private interview
224. Private interview
225. Private interview
226. Private interview
227. *Guardian*, 13.10.08
228. Interview with Peter Westmacott
229. Private interview
230. John Colville, *The Fringes of Power: Downing Street Diaries: 1939-55*, new edition (Weidenfeld & Nicolson, 2004)
231. Peter Mandelson, *The Third Man*, p.34
232. Interview with David Muir
233. Peter Mandelson, *The Third Man*, pp. 36-7
234. Private interview
235. Private interview
236. Private interview
237. *Guardian*, 06.10.08
238. Private interview
239. *Daily Mail*, 04.10.08

240. *Guardian*, 04.10.10
241. *Observer*, 10.10.08
242. Interview with Patrick Diamond
243. Interview with Michael Dugher
244. Private interview
245. Private interview
246. Private interview
247. Private interview
248. Private interview
249. Private interview
250. Private interview
251. Private interview
252. Private interview
253. Private interview
254. Private interview
255. BBC, 03.10.08
256. David Yelland, *The Truth About Leo* (Puffin, 2010)
257. Interview with David Yelland
258. Private interview
259. Private interview
260. Private interview
261. Private interview
262. Private interview
263. Private interview
264. Private interview
265. Private interview
266. Interview with Patrick Diamond
267. Private diary, private information
268. Private interview
269. Private interview
270. Private interview
271. Private interview
272. Interview with David Muir
273. Private interview
274. Private interview
275. Private interview
276. Interview with Nigel Sheinwald
277. Private interview
278. Private interview
279. Private interview
280. Private interview
281. *Independent*, 09.11.08
282. *Independent*, 03.07.08
283. YouGov, *Daily Telegraph*, 18.09.08
284. *Sunday Times*, 12.10.08
285. *Sunday Times*, 12.10.08
286. Anthony Seldon, *Times*, 09.11.08
287. *Guardian*, 11.11.08

288. BBC, Nick Robinson's blog, 07.11.08
289. *Times*, 11.11.08
290. ICM poll, *Guardian*, 16.12.08
291. ComRes survey, 28-29.11.08

CHAPTER 6
1. Private interview
2. Private interview
3. Oral Answers, House of Commons, 05.11.08
4. Oral Answers, House of Commons, 05.11.08
5. IMF, 2008
6. Lodge, Guy & Schmuecker, Katie, *Devolution in Practice*, (IPPR, 2010)
7. Private information
8. Private interview
9. Anthony J. Badger, *FDR: The First Hundred Days* (Hill & Wang Inc., US, 2007)
10. Interview with David Muir
11. Private interview
12. Robert Skidelsky, *John Maynard Keynes: Hopes Betrayed 1883-1920* (Macmillan, 1983); *John Maynard Keynes: The Economist as Saviour 1920-1937* (Papermac, 1993); *John Maynard Keynes: Fighting for Britain 1937-1946* (Macmillan, 2000)
13. Robert Skidelsky, *Keynes: The Return of the Master* (Allen Lane, 2009)
14. Email, Skidelsky to Seldon, 17.08.10
15. Paul Krugman, *The Return of Depression Economics* (W. W. Norton and Co., 2000)
16. Private interview
17. Alistair Darling, *Sunday Telegraph*, 18.10.08
18. *Times*, 29.10.08
19. *Daily Telegraph*, 18.11.08
20. Peter Snowdon, *Back from the Brink: The Inside Story of the Tory Resurrection* (HarperPress, 2010), p. 333
21. Interview with Dan Corry
22. *Economist*, 27.11.08
23. Private interview
24. Interview with Dan Corry
25. Private interview

26. Private interview
27. Private interview
28. Private interview
29. Interview with David Muir
30. Private interview
31. Private interview
32. Private interview
33. Peter Mandelson, *The Third Man: Life at the Heart of New Labour* (HarperPress, 2010), p. 454
34. Interview with Patrick Loughran
35. Interview with Patrick Loughran
36. *Sunday Telegraph*, 23.11.08
37. Private interview
38. House of Commons debates, 24.11.08
39. *Financial Times*, 05.12.08
40. *Financial Times*, 02.01.09
41. Richard Blundell, 'Assessing the temporary VAT cut policy in the UK', Fiscal Studies, Vol. 30, No. 1, March 2009, pp. 31–8
42. Interview with Dan Corry
43. *Sun*, 26.11.08
44. *Daily Mail*, 25.11.08
45. *Guardian*, 26.11.08
46. Private interview
47. Private interview
48. Interview with David Muir
49. BBC News, 27.11.08
50. BBC News, 24.11.08
51. BBC News, 24.11.08
52. Private interview
53. Private interview
54. Private interview
55. Private interview
56. George Osborne, BBC, 24.11.08
57. London School of Economics, 09.12.08
58. Private interview
59. *Guardian*, 25.10.08
60. *Telegraph*, 03.10.08
61. Private interview
62. Private interview
63. Private interview
64. Private interview
65. Private interview
66. Interview with Dan Corry
67. Private interview
68. Private interview
69. Private interview

70. Private interview
71. Private interview
72. Private interview
73. Private interview
74. Private interview
75. Private interview
76. *Independent*, 04.12.08
77. Leader, *Independent*, 04.12.08
78. Private interview
79. New Opportunities, white paper, 13.01.09
80. *Guardian*, 13.01.09
81. *New Opportunities*, White Paper, January 2009
82. BBC News, 14.12.08
83. House of Commons debates, 15.12.08
84. Private interview
85. Private interview
86. Interview with Jock Stirrup
87. Interview with Jock Stirrup
88. Interview with John Hutton
89. Private interview
90. Private interview
91. Private interview
92. Interview with John Hutton
93. Private interview
94. *New York Times*, 17.12.08
95. House of Commons debates, 18.12.08
96. *Guardian*, 03.01.09
97. BBC News, 03.01.09
98. Private interview
99. Private interview
100. *Times*, 05.01.09
101. *Times*, 05.01.09
102. Private interview
103. *Economist*, 21.01.09
104. Private interview
105. *Guardian*, 18.01.09
106. Private interview
107. Private interview
108. Private interview
109. Private interview
110. Private interview
111. BBC, 20.01.09
112. Private interview
113. BBC, 21.01.09
114. Private interview
115. Private interview
116. Private interview
117. *Guardian*, 10.12.08
118. Private interview
119. Private interview
120. Private interview
121. Private interview

122. Private interview
123. Private interview
124. Interview with Dan Corry
125. Private interview
126. BBC News, 14.01.09
127. *Times*, 10.01.09
128. Anthony Seldon, *Major: A Political Life*, (Phoenix, 1998), p. 239
129. *Financial Times*, 27.11.08
130. Private interview
131. Private interview
132. Interview with Lord Myners
133. Private interview
134. *Times*, 09.10.08
135. Private interview
136. Private interview
137. *Times*, 19.01.09
138. *Financial Times*, 20.01.09
139. *Independent*, 20.01.09
140. *Independent*, 23.01.09
141. BBC, *Today* programme, 23.01.09
142. *Times*, 27.01.09
143. Private interview
144. Private interview
145. Private interview
146. BBC, 21.01.09
147. Private interview
148. BBC, *Politics Show*, 08.02.09
149. *Times*, 10.02.09
150. *Guardian*, 10.02.09
151. Private interview
152. Private interview
153. Private interview
154. Private interview
155. *Sun*, 27.02.09
156. *Times*, 17.02.09
157. BBC News, 17.02.09
158. BBC News, 09.03.09
159. Private interview
160. Private interview
161. BBC News, 09.03.09
162. BBC News, 10.03.09
163. Private interview
164. Private interview
165. Private interview
166. Interview with Shaun Woodward
167. Interview with Shaun Woodward
168. BBC News, 05.02.10
169. Private interview
170. Private interview
171. Interview with Shaun Woodward

172. Interview with Shaun Woodward
173. Private interview
174. Professor Rick Wilford and Robin Wilson (eds), *Northern Ireland Devolution Monitoring Report, January 2009* (UCL Constitution Unit, 2009)
175. Professor Rick Wilford and Robin Wilson (eds), *Northern Ireland Devolution Monitoring Report, January 2009*
176. *Guardian*, 11.02.09
177. Private interview
178. Private interview
179. Private interview
180. Private interview
181. *Economist*, 16.11.08
182. Private interview
183. Private interview
184. Private interview
185. House of Commons debates, 26.11.08
186. Interview with Nigel Sheinwald
187. Private interview
188. Private interview
189. Private interview
190. Private interview
191. Private interview
192. Private interview
193. Private interview
194. Private interview
195. Private interview
196. Private interview
197. Interview with Gavin Kelly
198. Private interview
199. Private interview
200. Private interview
201. Private interview
202. Private interview
203. Private interview
204. Private interview
205. Private interview
206. Interview with Simon McDonald
207. Interview with Dickie Stagg
208. Private interview
209. Private interview
210. Private interview
211. Private interview
212. Private interview
213. Private interview
214. Reuters, 31.01.09
215. Private interview
216. Private interview
217. Private interview
218. *Times*, 19.02.09
219. *Times*, 19.02.09
220. *Daily Mail*, 05.03.09
221. BBC News, 05.02.09
222. Interview with Irwin Stelzer
223. Private interview
224. Private interview
225. Private interview
226. Private interview
227. Private interview
228. Interview with Simon McDonald
229. Private interview
230. Private interview
231. Private interview
232. Private interview
233. Private interview
234. Interview with David Muir
235. Private interview
236. Interview with Kirsty McNeill
237. Private interview
238. Interview with David Muir
239. Private interview
240. Private interview
241. The White House press office, 04.03.09
242. Private interview
243. Private interview
244. Private interview
245. Private interview
246. *USA Today*, 03.03.09
247. The White House press office, 03.03.09
248. Private interview
249. *Daily Mail*, 06.03.09
250. Private interview
251. The White House press office, 04.03.09
252. *Daily Telegraph*, 07.03.09
253. *Guardian*, 05.03.09
254. *Guardian*, 14.03.09
255. Private interview
256. Private interview
257. Private interview
258. *Financial Times*, Brussels blog, 23.03.09
259. *Daily Telegraph*, 24.03.09
260. BBC News, 27.03.09
261. *Guardian*, 24.03.09
262. *Times*, 25.03.09
263. Private interview
264. Private interview
265. *Daily Telegraph*, 25.03.09
266. *Daily Telegraph*, 25.03.09
267. BBC News, 25.03.09
268. *Guardian*, 25.03.09
269. Private interview
270. BBC News, 25.03.09
271. Private interview
272. BBC News, 27.03.09
273. *Times*, 27.03 09
274. *Daily Telegraph*, 27.03.09
275. Robert Winnett, Gordon Rayner, *No Expenses Spared* (Bantam Press, 2009), p. 50
276. Robert Winnett, Gordon Rayner, *No Expenses Spared*, p. 55
277. Private interview
278. Private interview
279. Private interview
280. *Daily Telegraph*, 31.03.09
281. *Daily Telegraph*, 30.03.09
282. Private interview
283. Private interview
284. Private interview
285. Private interview
286. Private interview
287. Private interview
288. Private interview
289. Private interview
290. Private interview
291. Private interview
292. Private interview
293. Private interview
294. Private interview
295. CBS News, 01.04.09
296. Private interview
297. *Independent*, 03.04.09
298. Private interview
299. *Daily Mail*, 23.02.09
300. Private interview
301. Private interview
302. Private interview
303. Private interview
304. Private interview
305. Private interview
306. Private interview
307. Private interview
308. Private interview
309. Private interview
310. Private interview
311. Steve Richards, *The Brown Years*, Radio 4
312. Interview with Simon McDonald
313. Shriti Vadera on Radio 4 programme *The Brown Years*
314. Private interview

315. Private interview
316. Private interview
317. Private interview
318. Interview with Brendan Cox
319. Private interview
320. Private interview
321. Interview with Justin Forsyth
322. BBC News, 02.04.09
323. *Guardian*, 02.04.09
324. London Summit website
325. *Daily Mail* 03.04.09; *Guardian*, 03.04.09
326. *Sun*, 03.04.09
327. *Daily Mail*, 03.04.09
328. *Economist*, 08.04.09
329. *Guardian*, 03.04.09
330. *Economist*, 08.04.09
331. *Daily Telegraph*, 04.04.09
332. Per Jacobsson Foundation Lecture, October 2010
333. Private interview

CHAPTER 7

1. Private interview
2. Private interview
3. *Scotsman*, 25.02.06
4. Private interview
5. Private interview
6. Private interview
7. Private interview
8. Private interview
9. Private interview
10. BBC News, 14.04.09
11. Private interview
12. Private interview
13. Private interview
14. *Guardian*, 12.04.09
15. *Independent*, 12.04.09
16. *Times*, 13.04.09
17. *Sunday Times*, 12.04.09; *News of the World*, 12.04.09
18. *Guardian*, 12.04.09
19. BBC News, 13.04.09
20. *Sunday Times*, 12.04.09
21. BBC, 11.04.09
22. *Sunday Times*, 12.04.09
23. *Sunday Times*, 12.04.09
24. Private interview
25. *Scotsman*, 21.07.09
26. Private interview
27. *Times*, 13.04.09
28. *Times*, 13.04.09
29. BBC News, 14.04.09
30. *Guardian*, 14.04.09
31. *Daily Telegraph*, 14.04.09
32. *Guardian*, 13.04.09

33. *Sun*, 13.04.09
34. *Independent*, 14.04.09
35. BBC, 16.04.09
36. Private interview
37. Private interview
38. Interview with James Purnell
39. Private interview
40. Private interview
41. Private interview
42. Private interview
43. Private interview
44. Peter Mandelson, *The Third Man: Life at the Heart of New Labour* (HarperPress, 2010), p. 461
45. Private interview
46. Private interview
47. Chris Mullin, *Decline and Fall: Diaries 2005–2010*, (Profile Books, 2010) p. 319
48. *Mail on Sunday*, 19.04.09
49. Private interview
50. Private interview
51. Interview with Michael Dugher
52. Private interview
53. Private interview
54. *Daily Telegraph*, 24.04.09
55. Office for National Statistics, 12.05.09
56. *Daily Telegraph*, 20.02.09
57. Bank of England, 05.03.09
58. *Guardian*, 05.03.09
59. Private information
60. *Daily Telegraph*, 20.03.09
61. *Independent*, 20.03.09
62. BBC news, 22.04.09
63. *Guardian*, 19.02.09
64. *Times*, 27.02.09
65. *Financial Times*, 25.03.09
66. Private interview
67. David Cameron, speech to London School of Economics, 09.12.08
68. *Times*, 14.03.09
69. Private interview
70. House of Commons debates, 09.03.99
71. Private interview
72. Private interview
73. Private interview
74. Peter Mandelson, *The Third Man* (HarperPress, 2010), p. 463
75. Peter Mandelson, *The Third Man* (HarperPress, 2010), p.

463
76. Peter Mandelson, *The Third Man* (HarperPress, 2010), p.463
77. Interview with Ed Balls
78. Interview with Ed Balls
79. Private interview
80. Private interview
81. House of Commons debates, 22.04.09
82. *Times*, 22.04.09
83. BBC, 22.04.09
84. Private interview
85. Private interview
86. House of Commons debates, 22.04.09
87. House of Commons debates, 22.04.09
88. Bloomberg, 22.04.09
89. *Daily Telegraph*, 23.04.09
90. *Times*, 23.04.09
91. *Economist*, 23.04.09
92. Robert Chote, *Two Parliaments of Pain* (Institute for Fiscal Studies, 2009)
93. Peter Mandelson, *The Third Man* (HarperPress, 2010), p. 464
94. Private interview
95. Private interview
96. House of Commons debates, 10.06.09
97. Private interview
98. *Sunday Mirror*, 14.06.09
99. Private interview
100. Private interview
101. *Financial Times*, 11.06.09
102. Institute for Fiscal Studies
103. *Times*, 15.06.09
104. Peter Mandelson, *The Third Man* (HarperPress, 2010), p.466
105. Private interview
106. Private interview
107. Private interview
108. Philip Cowley and Mark Stuart, *Dissension Amongst the Parliamentary Labour Party, 2008-2009: A Data Handbook* (revolts.co.uk, 2009)
109. Philip Cowley and Mark Stuart, *Dissension Amongst the Parliamentary Labour Party*
110. Private interview
111. *Guardian*, 24.04.09
112. House of Commons debates,

19.03.08

113. *Daily Telegraph*, 24.04.09
114. *Daily Telegraph*, 24.04.09
115. *Times*, 30.04.09
116. Private interview
117. Private interview
118. *Guardian*, 24.04.09
119. House of Commons debates, 29.04.09
120. Private interview
121. BBC News, 29.04.09
122. Interview with David Muir
123. *Guardian*, 02.05.09
124. *Guardian*, 02.05.09
125. *Daily Telegraph*, 30.04.09; *Guardian*, 30.04.09
126. Private interview
127. Private interview
128. BBC News, 06.05.09
129. YouGov, 11.05.09
130. Interview with Jacqui Smith
131. House of Commons, 21.05.09
132. *Daily Telegraph*, 22.05.09
133. *Daily Telegraph*, 21.05.09
134. Private interview
135. Private interview
136. Private interview
137. Private interview
138. Interview with Michael Dugher
139. Private interview
140. Private interview
141. Private interview
142. BBC News, 30.03.09
143. Private interview
144. *Guardian*, 21.04.09
145. Private interview
146. Interview with Justin Forsyth
147. Interview with Justin Forsyth
148. Private interview
149. Interview with Theo Bertram
150. Interview with Theo Bertram
151. Private interview
152. Private interview
153. Private interview
154. Private interview
155. Private interview; Robert Winnett, Gordon Rayner, *No Expense Spared*, (Bantam Pres, 2009) p. 128
156. Private interview
157. Private interview
158. Private interview
159. Private interview
160. *Daily Telegraph*, 08.05.09
161. Private interview
162. Private interview
163. Interview with Michael Dugher
164. Private interview
165. *Daily Telegraph*, 09.05.09
166. Private interview
167. Private interview
168. *Guardian*, 09.05.09
169. Private interview
170. Private interview
171. *Daily Telegraph*, 11.05.09
172. Interview with Michael Dugher
173. *Daily Telegraph*, 13.05.09
174. BBC, 12.05.09
175. *Daily Telegraph*, 13.05.09
176. BBC News, 13.05.09
177. Private interview
178. Private interview
179. Private interview
180. Private interview
181. Private interview
182. Interview with Ben Bradshaw
183. Interview with Ben Bradshaw
184. House of Commons debates, 18.05.09
185. Private interview
186. Private interview
187. BBC News, 19.05.09
188. Chris Mullin, *Decline and Fall*, pp. 332–3
189. *Daily Telegraph*, 25.07.09
190. Private interview
191. Interview with Patrick Diamond
192. Private interview
193. Interview with Paul Richards
194. Private interview
195. BBC News, 10.06.09
196. Private interview
197. *Guardian*, 02.06.09
198. Private interview
199. *Guardian*, 29.07.08
200. Private interview
201. Private interview
202. Private interview
203. Private interview
204. *Guardian*, 03.06.09
205. Private interview
206. Private interview
207. *Observer*, 02.05.09
208. Private interview
209. *Daily Telegraph*, 17.05.09
210. Private interview
211. Private interview
212. Private interview
213. Private interview
214. Private interview
215. House of Commons debates, 03.06.09
216. Interview with Justin Forsyth
217. Interview with Alan Johnson
218. Interview with Alan Johnson
219. BBC News, 03.06.09
220. Interview with Alan Johnson
221. *Guardian*, 04.06.09
222. *Guardian*, 11.06.09
223. *Guardian*, 11.06.09; *Daily Mail*, 04.06.09
224. *Daily Mail*, 04.06.09
225. Private email
226. Interview with David Muir
227. Private interview
228. Private interview
229. Private interview
230. Private interview
231. Private interview
232. Private interview
233. Phil Collins, *Prospect*, July 2009
234. Interview with Phil Collins
235. Private interview
236. Private interview
237. Private interview
238. Interview with James Purnell
239. Private interview
240. Private interview
241. Private interview
242. Interview with James Purnell
243. Interview with James Purnell
244. Interview with James Purnell
245. Interview with John Denham
246. Private interview
247. Interview with James Purnell
248. Interview with James Purnell
249. Interview with Alan Johnson
250. Interview with James Purnell
251. BBC News, 05.06.09
252. Interview with Michael Dugher
253. Private interview
254. Private interview
255. Private interview
256. Private interview
257. Private interview
258. Interview with Patrick Wintour
259. Private interview
260. Private interview
261. Private interview

262. Interview with Kirsty McNeill
263. Private interview
264. Private interview
265. Private interview
266. Private interview
267. Private interview
268. Interview with Michael Dugher
269. Interview with Nick Pearce
270. Private interview
271. Private interview
272. Private interview
273. Private interview
274. Interview with David Muir
275. Private interview
276. Private interview
277. Peter Mandelson, *The Third Man*, p. 70
278. Tony Travers's 'Time for Change? Electoral Politics after the Local and European Elections', *Public Policy Research*, June–August 2009 (Wiley Blackwell/IPPR)
279. Private interview
280. Private interview
281. Private interview
282. Private interview
283. *Daily Mail*, 01.06.09
284. Private interview
285. Private interview
286. Private interview
287. Private interview
288. Private interview
289. Private interview
290. Private interview
291. Interview with Ed Balls
292. Private interview
293. Private interview
294. Mandelson, *The Third Man*, p. 471
295. Private interview
296. Private interview
297. Private interview
298. Private interview
299. Private interview
300. Private interview
301. Interview with Richard Dannatt
302. Email, John Hutton to Anthony Seldon, 21.08.10
303. Private interview
304. Interview with Caroline Flint
305. *Daily Telegraph*, 05.06.09
306. *Guardian*, 06.06.09
307. Private interview
308. Private interview
309. Private interiview
310. Interview with Patrick Loughran
311. *Times*, 06.06.09
312. Private interview
313. Private interview
314. Private interview
315. Private interview
316. Private interview
317. Interview with Alan Johnson
318. Private interview
319. *Daily Telegraph*, 07.06.09
320. Private interview
321. Private interview
322. Interview with Michael Dugher
323. Private interview
324. Private interview
325. Private interview
326. Interview with Andrew Adonis
327. Interview with Ben Bradshaw
328. Private interview
329. Private interview
330. Private interview
331. Private interview
332. Private interview
333. *Guardian*, 05.06.09
334. Private diary
335. Interview with Barry Sheerman
336. *Spectator* Coffee House Blog, 05.06.09
337. Private interview
338. Private interview
339. Private interview
340. *Independent*, 02.06.09
341. Private interview
342. Private interview
343. BBC News, 06.06.09
344. BBC News, 06.06.09
345. Gordon Brown, *Wartime Courage: Stories of Extraordinary Courage by Ordinary People in World War Two* (Bloomsbury Publishing, 2008)
346. Private interview
347. *Sunday Telegraph*, 07.06.9
348. *Daily Mail*, 07.06.09
349. Interview with David Muir
350. Tony Travers 'Time for change?'
351. *Guardian*, 10.06.09
352. *Evening Standard* blog, 09.06.09
353. *Evening Standard* blog, 09.06.09
354. *Evening Standard* blog, 09.06.09
355. Interview with Justin Forsyth
356. *Sunday Times*, 14.06.09
357. Private interview
358. Interview with Charles Clarke
359. Private interview
360. Private interview
361. Private interview
362. Private interview
363. Private interview
364. Private interview
365. Private interview
366. Private interview
367. Private interview
368. Private interview
369. Private interview
370. Private interview
371. Private interview
372. Private interview
373. Private interview
374. Private interview
375. Private interview
376. House of Commons debates, 29.06.09
377. *Guardian*, 29.06.09
378. Interview with David Muir
379. Private interview
380. Private interview
381. Private interview
382. Private interview
383. Private interview
384. Private interview
385. Private interview
386. Private interview
387. Private interview
388. Private interview
389. Interview with Jock Stirrup
390. Interview with Jock Stirrup
391. Private interview
392. Interview with Jock Stirrup
393. Oral Answers to Questions, Prime Minister, 29.04.09
394. Private interview
395. Interview with David Muir
396. Private interview
397. Private interview
398. *Guardian*, 27.04.09
399. *Daily Mail*, 27.04.09
400. Private interview
401. Private interview
402. Private interview

403. Private interview
404. Interview with Ric Todd
405. Private interview
406. Interview with Ric Todd
407. Private interview
408. Interview with Richard Dannatt
409. Private interview
410. Private interview
411. Private interview
412. Private interview
413. Private interview
414. CBS/AP, 08.07.09
415. BBC News, 27.07.09; *Times online*, 27.07.09
416. BBC News, 11.07.09
417. Interview with Richard Dannatt
418. Interview with Matt Cavanagh
419. Private interview
420. Private interview
421. Private interview
422. *Guardian*, 18.08.09
423. *Daily Telegraph*, 12.07.09
424. *Daily Telegraph*, 12.07.09
425. BBC Radio 4, *Today* programme, 15.07.09
426. Interview with Richard Dannatt
427. Private interview
428. House of Commons Debates, 15.07.09
429. *Guardian*, 16.07.09
430. YouGov, 31.07.09
431. YouGov, 17.08.09
432. *Times*, 25.07.09
433. *Times online*, 17.07.09
434. Interview with Jock Stirrup
435. Private interview
436. Private interview
437. *Daily Telegraph*, 18.07.09
438. Private interview
439. Private interview
440. Private interview
441. Private interview
442. Interview with Kirsty McNeill
443. Private interview
444. Private interview
445. Private interview
446. BBC News, 14.08.09
447. Private interview
448. Gordon Brown, *The Change We Choose: Speeches 2007–2009* (Mainstream Publishing,

2010)
449. Gordon Brown, *Maxton: A Biography* (Mainstream Publishing, 1986)
450. Private interview
451. Gordon Brown, *Courage: Eight Portraits* (Bloomsbury Publishing, 2007)
452. *Independent*, 23.03.09
453. *New York Review of Books*, 25.10.07
454. Gordon Brown, *Britain's Everyday Heroes: The Making of the Good Society* (Mainstream Publishing, 2007)
455. Gordon Brown, *Wartime Courage: Stories of Extraordinary Courage by Ordinary People in World War Two* (Bloomsbury Publishing, 2008)
456. *Daily Telegraph*, 19.08.09
457. *Guardian*, 12.08.09
458. BBC, 13.08.09
459. BBC, 13.08.09
460. *Independent*, 14.08.09
461. Interview with David Muir
462. BBC News, 14.08.09
463. Justin Forsyth's diary
464. Interview with Justin Forsyth
465. Justin Forsyth's diary
466. Interview with David Muir
467. *New Yorker*, 11.05.09
468. Interview with David Muir
469. Private interview
470. Private interview
471. Private interview
472. Private interview
473. Private interview
474. Private interview
475. Private interview
476. Private interview
477. Private interview
478. Private interview
479. Private interview
480. Private interview
481. Private interview
482. Private interview
483. Private interview
484. Interview with Justin Forsyth
485. Interview with Justin Forsyth

CHAPTER 8
1. *Guardian*, 23.09.09
2. Private interview

3. Private interview
4. Private interview
5. Private interview
6. *Guardian*, 23.08.09
7. BBC, 23.08.09
8. Private interview
9. *Sunday Times*, 30.08.09
10. *Independent*, 02.09.09
11. Private interview
12. *Guardian*, 02.09.09
13. Interview with Simon Lewis
14. Private interview
15. BBC News, 20.08.09
16. Private interview
17. *Times online*, 23.08.09
18. *Guardian*, 10.09.09
19. Private interview
20. Private interview
21. *New York Times*, 22.09.09
22. *Guardian*, 23.09.09
23. Private interview
24. Private interview
25. Private interview
26. *Guardian*, 23.09.09
27. BBC News, 21.06.06
28. Private interview
29. Ian Kearns, *Prospect*, December 2007
30. *Times*, 17.03.09
31. Gordon Brown ed. Wilf Stevenson, *The Change We Choose*, (Mainstream Publishing, 2010) p. 115
32. *Guardian*, 17.03.09
33. *Daily Telegraph*, 10.07.09
34. BBC, 23.09.09
35. Private interview
36. BBC News, 24.09.09
37. *Guardian*, 02.09.10
38. Private interview
39. *Times*, online, 07.12..09
40. Private interview
41. *Daily Telegraph*, 17.04.08
42. *Evening Standard*, 23.09.09
43. *Guardian*, 02.09.10
44. *Times*, 24.09.09
45. *Guardian*, 24.09.09
46. *Daily Telegraph*, 24.09.09
47. *Daily Telegraph*, 24.09.09
48. Private interview
49. Private interview
50. *Daily Telegraph*, online, 23.09.09
51. Chris Mullin, *Decline and Fall: Diaries 2005–2010*, (Profile Books, 2010), pp. 373

52. *Guardian*, 24.09.09
53. Private interview
54. *Financial Times online*, 24.09.09
55. Private interview
56. Private interview
57. Private interview
58. Private interview
59. Private interview
60. *Guardian online*, 25.09.09
61. Private interview
62. BBC News, 25.09.09
63. Private interview
64. Private interview
65. Private interview
66. Private interview
67. Private interview
68. Private interview
69. Private interview
70. Private interview
71. Private interview
72. *Economist*, 26.09.09
73. BBC News, 26.09.09
74. Private interview
75. Private interview
76. Nick Robinson BBC blog, 26.09.09
77. *Guardian*, 23.09.09
78. *Independent*, 28.09.09
79. *Financial Times*, 24.09.09
80. Ipsos MORI, 25–27.09.09
81. Interview, Patrick Diamond
82. *Observer*, 27.09.09
83. Chris Mullin, *Decline and Fall*, p 376
84. *Independent*, 28.09.09
85. *Daily Mail*, 24.09.09
86. Private interview
87. Interview with Andrew Marr
88. *Independent*, 10.09.09
89. *Independent*, 10.09.09
90. *Independent*, 10.09.09
91. Private interview
92. Private interview
93. *Guardian*, 28.09.09
94. Interview, Andrew Marr
95. *Financial Times*, 09.12.09.
96. *Guardian*, 29.09.09
97. Interview with Patrick Loughran
98. *Guardian*, 28.09.09
99. *Guardian*, 29.09.09
100. Private interview
101. Interview with Kirsty McNeill
102. Private interview
103. Private interview

104. Interview with David Yelland
105. Private interview
106. Private interview
107. Interview with David Muir
108. Private interview
109. Private interview
110. Chris Mullin, *Decline and Fall: Diaries 2005-2010*, (Profile Books, 2010) p. 377
111. Interview with Kirsty McNeill
112. Private interview
113. Private information
114. Interview with Nick Pearce
115. Private interview
116. Interview with Greg Beales
117. Private interview
118. Private interview
119. Chris Mullin, *Decline and Fall*, p. 377
120. Private interview
121. *Financial Times*, 30.09.09
122. *Financial Times*, 30.09.09
123. *Economist*, 29.09.09
124. *Sun*, 30.09.09
125. Private interview
126. Private interview
127. Interview with Simon Lewis
128. Private interview
129. Private interview
130. Private interview
131. Private interview
132. Private interview
133. Interview with Gavin Kelly
134. Private interview
135. Private interview
136. Private interview
137. Private interview
138. Private interview
139. Private interview
140. Interview with Adam Boulton
141. Interview with Adam Boulton
142. *Daily Telegraph*, 30.09.09
143. Private interview
144. Private interview
145. Interview with Justin Forsyth
146. Private interview
147. Interview with David Muir
148. Interview with David Muir
149. Private interview
150. Private interview
151. Private interview
152. Channel 4 website, 03.09.09
153. BBC News, 04.09.09
154. *Guardian*, 04.09.09
155. *Guardian*, 04.09.09
156. Private interview

157. Private interview
158. Private interview
159. *Guardian*, 09.10.09
160. Private interview
161. Interview with Richard Dannatt
162. Private interview
163. Private interview
164. Private interview
165. Private interview
166. Private interview
167. Private interview
168. Private interview
169. Private interview
170. Private interview
171. Private interview
172. BBC News, 04.11.09
173. *Guardian*, 05.11.09
174. Channel 4 News, 06.11.09
175. *Daily Telegraph*, 06.11.09
176. YouGov/Sky News, 05–06.11.09
177. *Washington Post*, 22.09.09
178. Private interview
179. Private interview
180. House of Commons Debates, 30.11.09
181. Interview with Jock Stirrup
182. Private interview
183. Private interview
184. *Daily Mail*, 14.12.09
185. House of Commons debates, 14.12.09
186. *The Sun*, 08.05.09
187. Private interview
188. Interview with David Yelland
189. Private information
190. Private information
191. *Sun*, 28.08.09
192. Private interview
193. Interview with Simon Lewis
194. Private interview
195. Private interview
196. Private interview
197. Private interview
198. House of Commons debates, 14.10.09
199. BBC News, 09.11.09
200. Private interview
201. *Financial Times*, 11.11.09
202. Private interview
203. Private interview
204. Interview, Simon McDonald
205. Interview, Kirsty McNeill
206. Private interview
207. Private interview

208. Private interview
209. Private interview
210. Private interview
211. *New Statesman*, 10.11.09
212. *Daily Mirror*, 11.11.09
213. Interview with Jock Stirrup
214. Interview with Simon McDonald
215. Private interview
216. Private interview
217. Private interview
218. *Daily Telegraph*, 03.12.09
219. Private interview
220. Private interview
221. *Guardian online*, 03.12.09
222. Private interview
223. Private interview
224. Private interview
225. Private interview
226. Private interview
227. Private interview
228. BBC News, 03.11.09
229. Private interview
230. Private interview
231. Private interview
232. Private interview
233. Interview, Kim Darroch
234. *Guardian*, 19.10.07
235. Private interview
236. Private interview
237. *Daily Mail*, 16.07.09
238. BBC News, 15.07.09
239. Private interview
240. Private interview
241. Private interview
242. Private interview
243. Private interview
244. Private interview
245. Private interview
246. Private interview
247. Private interview
248. Private interview
249. Private interview
250. Private interview
251. *Times*, 27.10.09
252. Interview, David Miliband
253. Mandelson, *The Third Man*, p. 494
254. Private interview
255. Private interview
256. Private interview
257. Private interview
258. Mandelson, *The Third Man*, p.496
259. Private interview
260. *Economist*, Charlemagne Blog, 26.11.09

261. Private interview
262. Private interview
263. Private interview
264. Private interview
265. Private interview
266. Private interview
267. ITN News, 19.11.09
268. *Economist*, 26.11.09
269. Private interview
270. *Financial Times*, Westminster blog, 19.11.09
271. *New York Times*, 19.11.09
272. Private interview
273. Private interview
274. Private interview
275. Private interview
276. Interview, Geoff Hoon
277. Private interview
278. Private interview
279. Private interview
280. Private interview
281. Private interview
282. Private interview
283. Private interview
284. Reuters, 29.11.09
285. Private interview
286. *Guardian*, 18.12.09
287. Interview with Michael Jacobs
288. Private interview
289. Interview with Michael Jacobs
290. *Guardian*, 26.06.09
291. *Guardian*, 20.09.09
292. Interview with Simon Lewis
293. Labour press release, 19.10.09
294. Private interview
295. Private interview
296. *Independent*, 27.11.09
297. Interview with Michael Jacobs
298. Private interview
299. Private interview
300. *Financial Times*, 04.12.09
301. *Guardian*, 07.12.09
302. Private interview
303. Interview with Michael Jacobs
304. *Times*, 11.12.09
305. *Daily Telegraph*, 14.12.09
306. Private interview
307. *Guardian*, 17.12.09
308. Interview, Michael Jacobs
309. Interview, Michael Jacobs
310. *Der Spiegel*, 05.05.10
311. Interview, Michael Jacobs
312. *Independent*, 19.12.09
313. *Independent*, 19.12.09
314. *Independent*, 19.12.09

315. Private interview
316. Private interview
317. Interview with Gavin Kelly
318. Mandelson, *The Third Man*, p. 477
319. Private interview
320. Private interview; Rachel Sylvester, *Times*, 07.07.09
321. House of Commons debates, 24.06.09
322. Private interview
323. Treasury Select Committee, 24.06.09
324. Private interview
325. Ipsos MORI poll, 21.06.09
326. Interview with Nick Pearce
327. Andrew Grice, *Independent*, 02.07.09
328. Interview with Patrick Loughran
329. *Daily Telegraph*, 11.07.09
330. *Times*, 16.07.09
331. *Guardian*, 24.07.09
332. Interview with Nick Robinson
333. BBC, *Newsnight*, 28.07.09
334. *Guardian*, 24.09.10
335. Interview, Nick Pearce
336. *Independent*, 16.09.09
337. *Guardian*, 15.09.09
338. Peter Mandelson, *The Third Man*, p. 484
339. Private interview
340. Private interview
341. Private interview
342. Private interview
343. Private interview
344. Private interview
345. Private interview
346. Private interview
347. Private interview
348. Private interview
349. Private interview
350. Private interview
351. Private interview
352. Private interview
353. Private interview
354. Private interview
355. Private interview
356. Private interview
357. Private interview
358. Private interview
359. Private interview
360. Private interview
361. Private interview
362. Private interview
363. Private interview

364. Private interview
365. Private interview
366. Private interview
367. House of Commons debates, 09.12.09
368. Private interview
369. Private interview
370. Private interview
371. Private interview
372. Private interview
373. Private interview
374. Private interview
375. House of Commons debates, 09.12.09
376. Memo from the Number 10 Policy Unit post-PBR
377. Private interview
378. Private interview
379. Private interview
380. Private interview
381. Private interview
382. Private interview
383. *Financial Times*, 09.12.09
384. Private interview
385. Private interview
386. Interviews with Nick Pearce; interview with David Muir
387. Private interview
388. Private interview
389. Private interview
390. Interview with David Muir
391. Private interview
392. Nick Pearce, Memo, 10.12.09
393. *Independent*, 01.12.09
394. *Guardian*, 12.11.09

CHAPTER 9

1. *Times*, 02.12.09
2. House of Commons debates, 02.12.09
3. Iain Dale, blog, Dec 2009
4. *Independent*, 04.12.09
5. *Independent*, 03.12.09
6. Private interview
7. Private interview
8. Private interview
9. Private interview
10. Private interview
11. Private interview
12. Private interview
13. Interview with Theo Bertram
14. Private interview
15. *Independent*, 04.12.09
16. *Daily Mirror*, 22.12.09
17. *Financial Times*, 29.12.09
18. Private interview

19. *Observer,*. 22.11.09
20. Interview, Justin Forsyth
21. *Observer*, 22.11.09
22. Private interview
23. Private interview,
24. Private interview,
25. Interview, David Muir
26. Interview, David Muir
27. Private interview,
28. *Guardian*, 04.01.10
29. *Guardian*, 04.01.10
30. House of Commons debates, 06.01.10
31. House of Commons debates, 06.01.10
32. *Observer*, 22.11.09
33. Private interview
34. Private interview
35. Peter Mandelson, *The Third Man*, p. 490
36. Interview, Patrick Diamond
37. Private interview
38. Interview, Michael Dugher
39. Private interview
40. Interview, Andrew Adonis
41. Private interview
42. Interview with Patrick Loughran
43. Private interview
44. Interview, Patrick Loughran
45. Private interview
46. Peter Mandelson, *The Third Man*, p. 490
47. Interview, Andrew Adonis
48. Peter Mandelson, *The Third Man*, p. 496
49. Interview, Douglas Alexander
50. Interview, Patrick Loughran
51. Interview, Patrick Loughran
52. Private interview
53. Private interview
54. Private interview
55. *Daily Mail*, 26.12.09
56. Private interview
57. Private interview
58. Private interview
59. Private interview
60. Private interview
61. Peter Mandelson, *The Third Man*, p. 489
62. Peter Mandelson, *The Third Man*, p. 491
63. Interview, David Miliband
64. Interview, David Miliband
65. Peter Mandelson, *The Third Man*, p. 503

66. Private interview
67. Interview, Charles Clarke
68. Peter Mandelson, *Third Man*, p. 507
69. Interview, Patricia Hewitt
70. *Sunday Times*, 10.01.10
71. Private interview
72. Interview, Charles Clarke
73. Interview, Charles Clarke
74. Interview, Charles Clarke
75. Private interviews
76. Private interview
77. Private interview
78. Private interview
79. Private interview
80. Private interview
81. *Guardian*, 07.01.10
82. *Daily Express*, 02.01.10
83. *Daily Mail*, 03.01.10
84. Interview, Geoff Hoon
85. Interview, Geoff Hoon
86. Interview, Patricia Hewitt
87. Private interview, Muir
88. Private interview
89. Private interview
90. Private interview
91. Private interview
92. Private interview
93. Private interview
94. Private interview
95. Private interview
96. Private interview
97. Private interview
98. Private interview
99. Private interview
100. Private interview
101. *Daily Mirror*, 05.01.10
102. Private interview
103. Private interview
104. Andrew Rawnsley, *End of the Party*, p. 688
105. *Sunday Times*, 10.01.10
106. BBC News, 06.01.10
107. Private interview
108. Interview, Theo Bertram
109. Private interview
110. Private interview
111. Private interview
112. Mandelson *The Third Man*, p. 505
113. Interview, Tessa Jowell
114. Interview, Patrick Loughran
115. Mandelson *The Third Man*, pp. 506-7
116. Interview, Patrick Loughran
117. Private interview

118. Private interview
119. Interview, Simon Lewis
120. BBC News, 06.01.10
121. *Guardian*, 06.01.10
122. Private interview
123. BBC News, 06.01.10
124. Private interview
125. Private interview
126. *Sunday Times*, 10.01.10 127. BBC News, 06.01.10
128. Private interview
129. Private interview
130. Private interview
131. Andrew Rawnsley, *End of the Party*, p. 690
132. Private interview
133. Private interview
134. Interview, Charles Clarke
135. Private interview
136. Private interview
137. Peter Mandelson, *The Third Man*, p. 507
138. Private interview
139. Private interview
140. Private interview
141. Private interview
142. Interview, Simon Lewis.
143. Private interview
144. Private interview
145. BBC News, 06.01.10
146. *Daily Telegraph*, 07.01.10
147. BBC News, 07.01.10
148. Private interview
149. *Guardian*, 07.01.10
150. Private interview
151. Private interview
152. Private interview
153. Private interview
154. Private interview
155. Private interview
156. Private interview
157. Private interview
158. Private interview
159. Private interview
160. Private interview
161. *Sunday Times*, 10.01.10
162. Private interview
163. Private interview
164. Interview, Patricia Hewitt
165. Private interview
166. Interview, Geoff Hoon
167. Private interview
168. Interview with Geoff Hoon
169. Interview, Patricia Hewitt
170. Private interview
171. Private interview

172. Private interview
173. Private interview
174. Interview with Frank Field
175. Private interview
176. Private interview
177. Private interview
178. Interview, Geoff Hoon
179. *Daily Telegraph*, 07.01.10
180. *Sunday Times*, 10.01.10
181. Private interview
182. Private interview
183. Private interview
184. Chris Mullin, *Decline and Fall*, p. 411
185. *Times*, 12.01.10
186. Interview, Alan Johnson
187. Private interview
188. Private interview
189. Diary 11.01.10, Chris Mullin
190. Interview, Hilary Benn
191. Private interview
192. *Times*, 12.01.10
193. Interview, David Muir
194. *Guardian*, 15.01.10
195. *Guardian*, 15.01.10
196. Private interview
197. Private interview
198. Private interview
199. *Sunday Telegraph*, 17.01.01
200. Gordon Brown, *Why the Right is Wrong*, (Fabian Society, 2010)
201. BBC News, 27.01.10
202. Interview with Gavin Kelly
203. BBC *Politics Show*, 31.01.10
204. BBC News, 02.02.10
205. *Independent*, 02.02.10
206. Private interview
207. Private interview
208. Interview, Jonathan Phillips
209. Private interview
210. BBC, 07.09.09
211. Interview, Shaun Woodward
212. *Financial Times*, 10.10.09
213. Private interview
214. Private interview
215. *Guardian*, 30.12.09
216. *Belfast Telegraph*, 14.12.09
217. Private interview
218. Interview, Shaun Woodward
219. Interview, Shaun Woodward
220. Private interview
221. Interview, Shaun Woodward
222. Private interview
223. Private interview
224. Private interview

225. Private interview
226. Private interview
227. Private interview
228. Interview, Shaun Woodward
229. Interview, Shaun Woodward
230. Private interview
231. BBC News, 27.01.10
232. BBC News, 27.01.10
233. Private interview
234. Interview, Shaun Woodward
235. Interview, Shaun Woodward
236. Private interview
237. Private interview
238. Private interview
239. Private interview
240. *Daily Telegraph*, 05.02.10
241. *Reuters*, 05.02.10
242. *Daily Telegraph*, 24.02.10
243. *Belfast Telegraph*, 11.05.10
244. Private interview
245. Private interview
246. Interview, Douglas Alexander
247. *Daily Telegraph*, 16.11.09
248. Interview, Simon McDonald
249. BBC News, 28.01.10
250. Private interview
251. Interview with Matt Cavanagh
252. BBC News, 07.02.10
253. *Independent*, 07.02.10
254. *Sunday Telegraaph*, 07.03.10
255. Private interview
256. *Guardian*, 06.03.10
257. Private interview
258. House of Commons debates, 08.03.10
259. Private interview
260. Private interview
261. *Sun*, 27.10.09
262. Private interview
263. Private interview
264. Private interview
265. Private interview
266. Private interview
267. Private interview
268. Private interview
269. Private interview
270. Private interview
271. *Times*, 12.03.10
272. House of Commons debates, 19.03.08
273. BBC News, 16.03.09
274. *Guardian*, 25.03.09
275. Private interview
276. Private interview
277. Private interview

278. Private interview
279. House of Commons debates, 15.06.09
280. House of Commons debates, 15.06.09
281. Private interview
282. Private interview
283. Private interview
284. Private interview
285. House of Commons debates, 15.06.09
286. Private interview
287. Private interview
288. Private interview
289. Private interview
290. Private interview
291. Private interview
292. House of Commons Written Answers and Statements, House of Commons, 13.07.09
293. House of Commons debates, 24.06.09
294. Private interview
295. Private interview
296. BBC News, 23.12.09
297. BBC News, 13.01.10
298. *Guardian*, 22.02.10
299. Private interview
300. Anthony Seldon, *Times*, 29.01.10
301. *Guardian*, 29.01.10
302. Private interview
303. Private interview
304. Private interview
305. Private interview
306. Private interview
307. BBC News, 05.03.10
308. Private interviews
309. Private interview
310. Private interview
311. Interview, Simon Lewis
312. BBC News, 05.03.10
313. *Guardian*, 06.03.10
314. *Sun*, 06.03.10
315. BBC News, 05.03.10
316. House of Commons debates, 17.03.10
317. Richard Dannatt, *Leading from the Front*, (Bantam, 2010) pp. 184, 341 and 351
318. Private interview
319. Private interview
320. Private interview
321. Private interview
322. Private interview
323. Private interview

324. Private interview
325. Private interview
326. Private interview
327. Private interview
328. Private interview
329. Private interview
330. Private interview
331. Private interview
332. Private interview
333. Private interview
334. Private interview
335. Private interview
336. Private interview
337. Private interview
338. Private interview
339. Interview, Greg Beales
340. Private interview
341. Private interview
342. Private interview
343. Private interview
344. Private interview
345. Private interview
346. Interview with Jacqui Smith
347. Private interivew
348. Interview, Jacqui Smith
349. *Daily Mail*, 29.09.09
350. Interview, Jacqui Smith
351. Interview, Justin Forsyth
352. Interview, Andrew Adonis
353. Interview, Gavin Kelly
354. Interview, Andrew Adonis
355. Private interview
356. Private interview
357. Private interview
358. Interview, Justin Forsyth
359. Private interview
360. Private interview
361. Private interview
362. Interview, David Muir
363. Interview, Ben Bradshaw
364. Private interview
365. Private interview
366. Private interview
367. Private interview
368. *Spectator*, 14.02.10
369. *Spectator*, 14.02.10
370. *Times*, 14.02.10
371. Private interview
372. Private interview
373. BBC Poll Tracker
374. Private interview
375. Private interview
376. Andrew Rawnsley, *End of the Party*, p.552
377. Private interview
378. Private interview

379. *Mail on Sunday*, 28.02.10
380. Interview, Suzie Mackenzie
381. Private interview
382. Interview, Suzie Mackenzie
383. Interview, Suzie Mackenzie
384. Interview, Suzie Mackenzie
385. *Daily Mail*, 01.03.10
386. BBC News, 24.02.10
387. Private interview
388. Private interview
389. Private interview
390. Private interview
391. *Independent on Sunday*, 21.02.10
392. *Guardian*, 22.02.10
393. BBC News, 21.02.10
394. Private interview
395. Private interview
396. Private interview
397. Private interview
398. Private interview
399. Private interview
400. Private interview
401. Private interview

CHAPTER 10

1. Private interview
2. Private interview
3. Private interview
4. Private interview
5. Private interview
6. *Financial Times*, 06.05.10
7. Private interview
8. Justin Forsyth diary
9. *Sunday Times*, 28.02.10
10. *Independent on Sunday*, 28.02.10
11. Private interview
12. Private interview
13. BBC News, 01.03.10
14. *Guardian*, 08.03.10
15. *Daily Telegraph*, 06.03.10
16. *Sunday Times*, 07.03.10
17. *Economist*, 04.03.10
18. Interview with David Muir
19. Interview with David Muir
20. Private interview
21. Private interview
22. Private interview
23. Private interview
24. *Guardian*, 13.03.10; private interview
25. Interview with Tom Fletcher
26. *Times*, 01.04.10
27. Private interview
28. Private interview

29. Private interview
30. Private interview
31. Private interview
32. Private interview
33. Private interview
34. Private interview
35. BBC News, 24.03.10
36. *Guardian*, 25.03.10
37. *Guardian*, 25.03.10
38. House of Commons debate, 24.03.10
39. *Financial Times*, 25.03.10
40. *Guardian*, 26.03.10
41. *Independent*, 25.03.10
42. BBC News, 25.03.10
43. Private interview
44. Interview with Jonathan Powell
45. Private interview
46. Private interview
47. Private interview
48. Private interview
49. Private interview
50. Private interview
51. Private interview
52. Private interview
53. *Daily Mail*, 06.04.10.
54. Private interview
55. Private interview
56. Interview with Patrick Diamond
57. Private interview
58. Private interview
59. Private interview
60. Private interview
61. Private interview
62. Private interview
63. Private interview
64. Private information
65. Private interview
66. Private interview
67. Private interview
68. Private interview
69. Private interview
70. Interview with Peter Riddell
71. Private interview
72. *Daily Telegraph*, 07.04.10
73. Private interview
74. Private interview
75. Private interview
76. Private interview
77. Private interview
78. Private interview
79. Private interview
80. Private interview
81. Private interview

82. Private interview
83. Private interview
84. Private interview
85. Michael Ashcroft, *Minority Verdict* (Biteback, 2010)
86. Private interview
87. Private interview
88. Private interview
89. Andrew Rawnsley, *The End of the Party* (Penguin, 2010), p. 719
90. BBC News, 16.04.10
91. YouGov, 17.04.10
92. Private interview
93. Private interview
94. Private interview
95. Private interview
96. Andrew Rawnsley, *The End of the Party*, p. 733
97. *Guardian* website, 02.05.10
98. Peter Snowdon, *Back from the Brink: The Extraordinary Rise and Fall of the Conservative Party* (Harper Press, 2010) p. 407
99. Private interview
100. Interview with Kirsty McNeill
101. Private interview
102. *Totalpolitics.com*, 03.05.10
103. *Totalpolitics.com*, 03.05.10
104. *Totalpolitics.com*, 03.05.10
105. Private interview
106. Interview with James Purnell
107. Private interview
108. *Guardian online*, 04.05.10
109. Sky News, 06.05.10
110. Interview with Douglas Alexander
111. Private interview
112. Private interview
113. Private interview
114. Private interview
115. Private interview
116. Nick Robinson, BBC, *Five Days that changed Britain*
117. Nick Robinson, BBC, *Five Days that changed Britain*
118. Nick Robinson, BBC, *Five Days that changed Britain*
119. Private interview
120. BBC News, 07.05.10
121. Private interview
122. Private interview
123. Private interview
124. Private interview
125. Nick Robinson, *Five Days that*

changed Britain, BBC
126. Peter Snowdon, *Back from the Brink*, p. 414
127. Peter Snowdon, *Back from the Brink*, p. 415
128. Peter Snowdon, *Back from the Brink*, p. 415
129. Private interview
130. Private interview
131. Interview with David Muir
132. Private interview
133. Private interview
134. Private interview
135. Private interview
136. Private interview
137. Private interviews
138. Private interview
139. Private interview
140. Private interview
141. Private interview
142. Private interview
143. Interview with Shaun Woodward
144. *Sun*, 08.05.10
145. Interview with Nick Pearce
146. Private interview
147. Nick Robinson, *Five Days that changed Britain*, BBC
148. Interview with Douglas Alexander
149. Nick Robinson, *Five Days that changed Britain*, BBC
150. Private interview
151. Private interview
152. Private interview
153. Private interview
154. Private interview
155. Private information
156. Andrew Rawnsley, *The End of the Party*, p. 752
157. Peter Snowdon, *Back from the Brink*, p. 416
158. Private interview
159. Private interview
160. Nick Robinson, *Five Days that Changed Britain*, BBC
161. Nick Robinson, *Five Days that Changed Britain*, BBC
162. Steve Richards, *Whatever it Takes*, (Fourth Estate, 2010), p. 28
163. Private interview
164. Nick Robinson, *Five Days that Changed Britain*, BBC
165. Peter Snowdon, *Back from the Brink*, p 417

166. Private interview
167. Interview with David Muir
168. Private interview
169. Private interview
170. Private interview
171. Private interview
172. Private interview
173. Private interview
174. Private interview
175. Labour Negotiating Document
176. *New Statesman*, 29.07.10
177. Private interview
178. Private interview
179. Private interview
180. Private interview
181. Interview with the Bank of England
182. Private interview
183. Private interview
184. Private interview
185. Andrew Rawnsley, *The End of the Party*, p. 755.
186. Nick Robinson, *Five Days that Changed Britain*, BBC
187. Private interview
188. Private interview.
189. Interview with Nick Pearce
190. Nick Robinson, *Five Days that Changed Britain*, BBC
191. Private interview
192. Private interview
193. Private interview
194. Private interview
195. Peter Snowdon, *Back from the Brink*, p. 418
196. Andrew Rawnsley, *The End of the Party*, p. 757
197. Private interview
198. Nick Robinson, *Five Days that Changed Britain*, BBC
199. Private interview
200. Private interview
201. Private interview
202. BBC News, 11.05.10
203. *Telegraph online*, 11.05.10
204. Private interview
205. Private interview
206. Private interview
207. Private interview
208. Private interview
209. Private interview
210. Private interview
211. Private interview
212. Private interview
213. Steve Richards, *Whatever it Takes*, p. 34
214. Nick Robinson, *Five Days that Changed Britain*, BBC
215. Private interview
216. Private interview
217. Interview with Kirsty McNeill
218. Private interview
219. Private interview
220. Private interview
221. Private interview
222. Nick Robinson, *Five Days that Changed Britain*, BBC
223. *Daily Mirror*, 20.06.10
224. Private interview
225. Private interview
226. BBC News, 11.05.10
227. BBC News, 11.05.10
228. Private interview
229. Private interview
230. Private interview
221. Private interview
232. Interview with Kirsty McNeill

Bibliography

Autobiographies and memoirs

Ashcroft, Michael, *Minority Verdict: The Conservative Party, the voters and the 2010 election* (London: Biteback, 2010)

Blair, Tony, *A Journey* (London: Hutchinson, 2010)

Brown, Sarah, *Behind the Black Door* (London: Ebury Press, 2011)

Campbell, Alastair, *The Blair Years* (London: Hutchinson, 2007)

Campbell, Alastair, *The Alastair Campbell Diaries Volume 1: Prelude to Power 1994-1997* (London: Hutchinson, 2010)

Campbell, Alastair, *The Alastair Campbell Diaries Volume II: Power and the People May 1997 to June 1999* (London: Hutchinson, 2011)

Campbell, Alastair, *The Alastair Campbell Diaries Volume III: Power and Responsibility 1999 to 2001* (London: Hutchinson, 2011)

Cowper-Coles, Sherard, *Cables from Kabul: The Inside Story of the West's Afghanistan Campaign* (London: Harper Press, 2011)

Dannatt, Richard, *Leading from the Front* (London: Bantam Press, 2010)

Mandelson, Peter, *The Third Man: Life at the Heart of New Labour* (London: Harper Press, 2010)

Mullin, Chris, *Decline and Fall: Diaries 2005-2010*,(London: Profile Books, 2010)

Powell, Jonathan, *The New Machiavelli: How to wield power in the modern world* (London: Bodley Head, 2010)

Watt, Peter, *Inside Out: My Story of Betrayal and Cowardice at the Heart of New Labour* (London: Biteback, 2010)

Monographs

Badger, Anthony J, *FDR: The First Hundred Days* (New York: Hill and Wang Inc., 2007)

Brown, Gordon, *Why the Right is Wrong* (London: Fabian Society, 2010)

Brown, Gordon, *Britain's Everyday Heroes: the Making of the Good Society* (London; Mainstream Publishing, 2007)

Brown, Gordon, *Wartime courage: Stories of Extraordinary Courage by Ordinary people in World War Two* (London: Bloomsbury Publishing, 2008)

Brown, Gordon, *The Change we choose: Speeches 2007-2009* (London: Mainstream Publishing, 2010)

Brown, Gordon, *Beyond the Crash: Overcoming the First Crisis of Globalisation* (London: Simon & Schuster, 2010)

Bower, Tom, *Gordon Brown Prime Minister* (London: Harper Perennial, 2007)

Campbell, John, *Pistols at Dawn: Two Hundred Years of Political Rivalry, from Pitt and Fox to Blair and Brown* (London: Jonathan Cape, 2009)

Colville, John, *The Fringes of Power: Downing Street Diaries 1939-55* (London: Weidenfeld and Nicholson, 2004)

Cowley, Phillip & Kavanagh, Dennis, *The British General Election of 2010* (London: Palgrave Macmillan, 2010)

Hasan, Mehdi and Macintyre, James, *Ed: The Milibands and the Making of a Labour Leader* (London: Biteback, 2011)

Himmelfarb, Gertrude, *Roads to Modernity: The British, French and American Enlightenments* (New York: Vintage Books, 2005)

Kavanagh, Dennis & Seldon, Anthony, *The Powers Behind the Prime Minister: the hidden influence of number ten* (London: Harper Collins, 2010)

Lodge, Guy & Schmuecker, Katie, *Devolution in Practice 2010* (London: IPPR, 2010)

Marquand, David, *Britain Since 1918: The Strange Career of British Democracy* (London: Weidenfeld and Nicholson, 2008)

Mattinson, Deborah, *Talking to a Brick Wall: How New Labour stopped listening to the voter and why we need a new politics* (London: Biteback, 2010).

Price, Lance, *Where Power Lies: Prime Ministers V The Media* (London: Simon & Schuster Ltd, 2010)

Radice, Giles, *Trio: Inside the Blair, Brown, Mandelson Project* (London: I B Tauris & Co Ltd, 2010)

Rawnsley, Andrew, *The End of the Party: Second Edition* (London: Penguin, 2010)

Richards, Steve, *Whatever it Takes: The Real Story of Gordon Brown and New Labour* (London: Fourth Estate, 2010)

Ricks, Thomas E., *The Gamble: General Petreaus and the Untold Story of the American Surge in Iraq 2006-2008* (London: Allen Lane, 2009)

Seldon, Anthony, *Blair* (London: Free Press, 2004)

Seldon, Anthony, *Blair's Britain 1997–2007* (Cambridge: Cambridge University Press, 2007)

Seldon, Anthony, *Blair Unbound* (London: Simon & Schuster Ltd, 2007)

Seldon, Anthony, *The Blair Effect* (London: Little, Brown, 2001)

Seldon, Anthony, *Major: A Political Life* (London: Weidenfeld and Nicholson, 1997)

Skidelsky, Robert, *Politicians and the slump: The Labour Government of 1929-31* (London: Pelican, 1967)

Skidelsky, Robert, *Keynes: The Return of the Master* (London: Allen Lane, 2009)

Snowdon, Peter, *Back from the Brink: The Inside Story of the Tory Resurrection* (London: Harper Press, 2010)

Sorkin, Andrew Ross, *Too Big to Fail* (London: Allen Lane, 2009)

Toynbee, Polly, & Walker, David, *The Verdict: Did Labour Change Britain* (London: Granta Books, 2010)

Winnett, Robert & Rayner, Gordon, *No Expenses Spared* (London: Bantam Press, 2009)

Wolf, Martin, *Fixing Global Finance* (Yale: Yale University Press, 2009)

Woodward, Bob, *Obama's War* (London: Simon & Schuster Ltd, 2010)

Ziegler, Philip, *Edward Heath: The Authorised Biography* (London: Harper Press, 2010)

Documentaries

Gordon Brown: Fit for Office? (Channel 4, 14 May 2007)

Gordon Brown: Where did it all go wrong? (Channel 4, 9 June 2008)

Crash Gordon (Channel 4, 8 June 2009).

On the frontline with British troops in Afghanistan (Guardian/Channel 4, 18 August 2009).

Five days that changed Britain (BBC TV, 29 July 2010).

The Brown Years (BBC Radio 4, 21 & 28 September 2010, 5 October 2010)

Index

About the Authors

Anthony Seldon is a political historian and one of the foremost commentators on contemporary Britain. The co-founder and first director of the Institute of Contemporary British History, he is also author or editor of some thirty books, including the best selling *Blair* and *Blair Unbound*. He is Master of Wellington College.

Guy Lodge is an associate director at the Institute for Public Policy Research, the UK's leading progressive think tank. He specialises in political reform and has published widely in this area. He is also a Gwilym Gibbon Fellow at Nuffield College, Oxford.

By Anthony Seldon

Churchill's Indian Summer (1981)
By Word of Mouth (with Joanna Seldon, 1983)
Contemporary History (ed. 1987)
Ruling Performance (with Peter Hennessy, 1987)
Political Parties Since 1945 (ed. 1988)
The Thatcher Effect (ed. with Dennis Kavanagh, 1989)
Politics UK (joint author, 1991)
The Conservative Century (ed. 1994)
The Major Effect (ed. with Dennis Kavanagh, 1994)
The Heath Government 1970-1974 (ed. with Stuart Ball, 1996)
The Contemporary History Handbook (ed. with Brian Brivati, 1996)
The Ideas That Shaped Post-war Britain (ed. with David Marquand, 1996)
How Tory Governments Fall (ed. 1996)
Major: A Political Life (1997)
10 Downing Street: An Illustrated History (1999)
The Powers Behind the Prime Minister (with Dennis Kavanagh, 1999)
Britain Under Thatcher (with Daniel Collings, 2000)
The Foreign Office: An Illustrated History (2000)
The Blair Effect 1997-2001 (ed. 2001)
A New Conservative Century? (with Peter Snowdon, 2001)
Public and Private Education: The Divide Must End (2001)
Partnership not Paternalism (2002)
Brave New City (2002)
New Labour, Old Labour (ed. with Kevin Hickson, 2004)
Blair (2004)
The Conservative Party: An Illustrated History (with Peter Snowdon, 2004)
The Blair Effect 2001-05 (ed. With Dennis Kavanagh, 2005)
Blair Unbound (2007)
Blair's Britain (ed. 2007)
An End to Factory Schools (2009)
Trust (2009)

Also available from Biteback

ED

MEDHI HASAN & JAMES MACINTYRE

"In this biography, based on interviews with scores of his friends, critics and colleagues, two of Britain's finest young political journalists penetrate far beyond the prevailing gossip and hearsay to provide an illuminating portrait of the youngest Labour leader in the party's history. Writing with verve and acuity, the authors provide the first authoritative account of Miliband's dramatic rise to power."
JONATHAN DIMBLEBY

Ed Miliband is perhaps the least understood political leader of modern times. This book reveals where he has come from and where he is going. It charts his unique upbringing, against the backdrop of tragedy and with a prominent Marxist thinker for a father. *ED* follows his coming of age at Oxford, his election to Parliament and asks whether the pressures of being Labour party leader are swaying him from deep personal and ideological convictions.

But Ed's story cannot be fully understood outside the context of his struggle to emerge from the shadow of his elder brother, David. Ed followed David to the same college at Oxford, into Parliament and into the Cabinet before, at the eleventh hour, snatching away David's dream of the leadership.

352pp hardback, £17.99

Available from all good bookshops or order from
www.bitebackpublishing.com

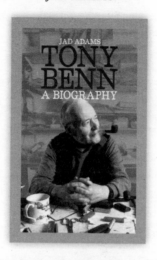